Mastering
System Center
Configuration Manager

Santos Martinez

Peter Daalmans

Brett Bennett

Senior Acquisitions Editor: Kenyon Brown

Development Editor: Kim Wimpsett

Technical Editor: Matt Hinson

Production Editor: Rebecca Anderson

Copy Editor: Elizabeth Welch

Editorial Manager: Mary Beth Wakefield

Production Manager: Kathleen Wisor

Executive Editor: Jim Minatel

Book Designers: Maureen Forys, Happenstance Type-O-Rama; Judy Fung

Proofreader: Amy Schneider

Indexer: Ted Laux

Project Coordinator, Cover: Brent Savage

Cover Designer: Wiley

Cover Image: ©Thomas Northcut/Getty Images, Inc.

Copyright © 2017 by John Wiley & Sons, Inc., Indianapolis, Indiana

Published by John Wiley & Sons, Inc. Indianapolis, Indiana
Published simultaneously in Canada

ISBN: 978-1-119-25845-2
ISBN: 978-1-119-25894-0 (ebk.)
ISBN: 978-1-119-25846-9 (ebk.)

Manufactured in the United States of America

Library of Congress Control Number: 2016960166

I want to dedicate this book to the following: my wife Karla; you are my soul mate and I want to grow old with you. To my kids Bryan and Naomy, I hope this gives you some inspiration one day of what you can achieve. And finally to all my family and friends for their support in my craziness.
—Santos Martinez

I dedicate this book to my father; since 1999 still deeply missed. To my mother, for all of your love and support in my life. To my girlfriend Samantha, our son Stef, and our upcoming newborn; thanks for putting up with me and for all of your love and support while writing this book. Love you all!
—Peter Daalmans

I dedicate this book to my family and friends, and I greatly appreciate the support you provide.
—Brett Bennett

Acknowledgments

I want to thank my colleagues across Microsoft for their support on this book, and our technical editor Matt Hinson for his commitment and great work. Thanks to the contributor authors, Nickolaj Andersen, Cliff Hobbs, and Alessandro Cesarini, for sharing some of their knowledge and experience with the readers.

To my coauthors, Brett Bennett and Peter Daalmans, thanks for staying on the project and giving the best of yourselves; I know the readers will enjoy learning from both of you.

Thanks to my friends for their support on the book and for providing a great elevator pitch to your customers.

Finally, I want to thank all the Configuration Manager and Enterprise Mobility + Security community, which has always been so passionate about the technology and willing to help us improve our writing. Let's keep the conversation going.

—*Santos Martinez*

Special thanks to my family and friends. I had to balance my time with you with my commitment to writing this book. I couldn't have done this without you guys!

I also want to thank Wiley/Sybex for giving me the opportunity to write this second book. It was again a great pleasure to work with the Wiley team; I'm looking forward to any new project! Also many thanks to the writing and editorial teams, you all rock!

Furthermore, many thanks to the Configuration Manager product team, who created this great product, and Cathy Moya especially, our great and dedicated MVP lead from within the product team. They all give us the opportunity to learn as much as we want about Configuration Manager and the Enterprise Mobility + Security products.

Also special thanks to my employer and colleagues at IT-Concern, for giving me the space to speak at conferences and to be of value for the community.

Finally, many thanks to the Configuration Manager and Enterprise Mobility communities and in particular all my fellow Enterprise Mobility MVPs; thanks for your support.

—*Peter Daalmans*

I would like to thank my wife Rosalie, and my children Brittany, Jamie, and Justin for the support they have provided me in my career. I would also like to thank Microsoft, both as my employer for the past 10 years and also for the amazing products they develop that have kept me gainfully employed for the past 30 years. I would also like to thank the coauthors Santos and Peter, the reviewers, and the entire team at Sybex/Wiley who helped put this book together.

—*Brett Bennett*

About the Authors

Santos Martinez was born in Caguas, Puerto Rico, in 1982, and grew up in Caguas. Santos has more than 16 years of experience in the IT industry. He has worked on major implementations and in support of Configuration Manager and Enterprise Mobility + Security for many customers in the United States and Puerto Rico. Santos was a Configuration Manager engineer for a Fortune 500 financial institution and an IT consultant before joining Microsoft. For the Fortune 500 companies, he helped with the implementation and support of more than 200 Configuration Manager Site Servers and support of more than 300,000 Configuration Manager and Intune device clients worldwide.

Santos was a SQL Server MVP from 2005 to 2009 and then a Configuration Manager MVP from 2009 to 2011. He is well known in the Microsoft communities as a mentor for other MVPs and Microsoft FTEs and for helping other IT community members. He has also participated in Midwest Management Summit, and Microsoft Ignite as a technical expert for Configuration Manager, SQL Server, and Microsoft Intune. Santos is also a former Puerto Rican martial arts champion and currently holds a fourth-degree black belt in TaiFu Shoi Karate Do; he earned the title of Shihan Sensei.

Santos and Karla, a pastry chef, have been married for 16 years and have two children, Bryan Emir and Naomy Arwen.

Santos currently is a senior premier field engineer for Microsoft in security infrastructure.

You can get in touch with Santos via his Twitter account @ConfigNinja or his blog at http://aka.ms/ConfigNinja.

Peter Daalmans is a senior technical consultant at IT-Concern, a Gold Certified Microsoft partner in the Netherlands. Peter has been awarded as an Enterprise Mobility MVP every year since 2012 for his work in the community. Peter worked with deployment tooling from Microsoft competitors since 1998; in 2005 Peter discovered (BDD) Business Desktop Deployment and (SMS) System Manamagent Server 2003 deployment tooling and has embraced them since then. In recent years, numerous (international) deployment projects have crossed Peter's path.

Peter is one of the founders of the Windows Management User Group Netherlands and shares his Configuration Manager and Microsoft Intune experience with the community via his blog (http://ConfigMgrBlog.com).

Besides speaking at the Windows Management User Group Netherlands, Peter speaks every year at several events like user group meetings in Europe, TechDays Netherlands, and ExpertsLive. In 2013 he had the honor to speak at TechEd Australia and TechEd New Zealand. Peter has also been a speaker at conferences like BriForum in London, Denver, and Boston; IT/Dev Connections; and the Midwest Management Summit.

Peter resides in beautiful Breda, in the south of the Netherlands, with his girlfriend Samantha and his son Stef, with a newborn due Christmas 2016. In addition to his daily work, he is the chairman of the NAC Museum Foundation, which preserves the history of the soccer club NAC Breda. Australia is also a huge passion; he travels Down Under whenever he gets the chance to sniff the outback and the Aussie lifestyle.

You can reach Peter via @pdaalmans and peter@ConfigMgrBlog.com or look at https://ref.ms/aboutme for the latest information.

Brett Bennett lives in Texas and has been with Microsoft for over 10 years, currently as a Senior Premier Field Engineer. Brett has been in the computer industry for almost 30 years and has used every version of SMS/SCCM since SMS 1.0 beta was released in 1994. He has been involved with the development of several technical books over his career and has spoken at several technical conferences.

Brett is married to Rosalie Bennett and has three children (Brittany, Jamie, and Justin), three dogs (Yogi, Boo Boo, and Reeses), and one granddog (Rue). Brittany and Jamie are both graduates of Texas A&M and are now in the workforce, and Justin is currently finishing up his degree at A&M. Brett enjoys driving his Dodge Challenger, riding bikes, playing guitar, expanding his vinyl collection, and preparing tasty food in his Weber smoker (especially Texas-style beef brisket). You can reach Brett at texasmcse@yahoo.com, @texasmcse on Twitter, or on his blog at https://blogs.technet.microsoft.com/breben.

About the Contributing Authors

Nickolaj Andersen is a senior consultant at Lumagate in Sweden and has made a name for himself for all the tools and scripts that he has shared with the community over the past years. Experience-wise, he has been in the IT industry for almost 10 years. Nickolaj is originally from Denmark but moved to Sweden with his mother when he was six years old. Today, Nickolaj lives in Stockholm with his lovely wife and daughter. In 2015, Nickolaj was awarded PowerShell Hero by the PowerShell.org community, for his extensive PowerShell contributions and scripts related to Configuration Manager.

Cliff Hobbs is the founder (in 2003) and CEO of FAQShop.com, one of the longest running websites covering System Management Server/Configuration Manager. In 2004 Microsoft awarded Cliff their MVP status in SMS; he was the first recipient from the UK and has received the award every year since. Cliff's passion is writing and sharing the knowledge he has gained working with the product since SMS 2.0 SP2 back in 1998. He has worked for some of the largest companies in the world, including Microsoft, HP, and Electronic Data Systems (EDS). Although Cliff currently lives in the UK with his wife Necy and his sons, he is looking for an opportunity that will allow him to emigrate with his family to Lisbon in Portugal, where he met his wife. Feel free to contact Cliff through FAQShop, where you can see the various ways Cliff can help you get the most from Configuration Manager.

Alessandro Cesarini is a premier field engineer at Microsoft and is based in Madrid. With more than 20 years of IT experience in multinational environments (Spain, the United Kingdom, France, Austria, Hungary, Poland, and Italy), he is helping customers with migration and deployment of Windows using Windows Assessment and Deployment Kit (ADK), Microsoft Deployment Toolkit (MDT), and System Center Configuration Manager. When he is not working or traveling, Alessandro is riding his bicycle, cooking at home, playing squash or Pádel, and spending time with his wife Eva.

Contents at a Glance

Contents

Introduction

The Enterprise Mobility + Security product group has completed one of the most successful management products of all time. These folks work very hard to ensure that the product meets the higher standards and are always looking for feedback about it.

This book is written by a group of individuals who have endured the growing pains of this product, some even from day one, and who have helped Microsoft improve Configuration Manager with countless hours of real-world use and testing.

Welcome to *Mastering System Center Configuration Manager*. You will gain the knowledge you need to unlock Configuration Manager and Enterprise Mobility + Security to its full potential.

The Mastering Series

The Mastering series from Sybex provides outstanding instruction for readers with intermediate and advanced skills in the form of top-notch training and development for those already working in their field and provides clear, serious education for those aspiring to become pros. Every Mastering book includes the following:

- Real-world scenarios, ranging from case studies to interviews that show how the tool, technique, or knowledge presented is applied in actual practice

- Skill-based instruction, with chapters organized around real tasks rather than abstract concepts or subjects

- Self-review questions, so you can be certain you're equipped to do the job right

What This Book Covers

Mastering System Center Configuration Manager covers Microsoft's System Center Configuration Manager and Enterprise Mobility + Security. We detail the changes to Configuration Manager since 2012 R2.

These new features include, but are not limited to, the following:

- A completely new mechanism for content distribution—focusing on the needs of the user while retaining the ability to distribute to systems as well

- A user self-service catalog for content deployment

- Updates to software update management and operating system deployment

♦ The ability to manage mobile devices, including Windows Phone, iPhones, iPads, Android, and more, with Windows Intune

♦ A robust alerting mechanism

♦ A redesigned infrastructure to increase scale and reduce complexity

♦ The ability to manage profiles with Compliance Settings

♦ Integration with Cloud, using Windows Azure and Intune

What You Need to Get the Most Out of This Book

To be able to follow the step-by-step instructions in this book, it is recommended that you have a minimum of Windows Server 2012 R2 or Windows Server 2016 and SQL Server 2014 with all the applicable updates installed; read more on this subject in Chapter 2. Also, make sure you have the media for Configuration Manager, because we will go through installing this software in the first few chapters. Your computer also needs an Internet connection so you can download updates in various parts of the installation process. Evaluation versions of any of this software are fine for our purposes.

How We Structured This Book

To help you understand the features of Configuration Manager, we have structured this book to match the names of features as they are listed in the Configuration Manager Administration console wherever possible, with a few exceptions.

Chapter 1, "Overview of System Center Configuration Manager and Microsoft Intune," is an introduction to Configuration Manager features and Microsoft Intune integration and features.

Chapter 2, "Planning a Configuration Manager Infrastructure," covers site roles, how they are leveraged, and their application in your enterprise.

Chapter 3, "Migrating to Configuration Manager," covers the process of moving to Configuration Manager. Discussions include planning the migration, using the new migration tool, and more.

Chapter 4, "Installation and Site Role Configuration," covers the details of site role installation, configuration, and troubleshooting.

Chapter 5, "Client Installation," covers client installation aspects in relation to Configuration Manager , such as the various installation methods found within Configuration Manager 2012.

Chapter 6, "Client Health," covers the mechanism Configuration Manager uses to help ensure clients remain healthy.

Chapter 7, "Application Deployment," provides a comprehensive look at planning, configuring, and using the application deployment model in Configuration Manager, including elements like deployments, deployment types, dependencies, rules, and relationships.

Chapter 8, "Software Updates," gives you a step-by-step guide of this completely redesigned feature that is now based on Windows Server Update Services.

Chapter 9, "Operating System Deployment," gives you an in-depth look at how Configuration Manager allows an administrator to deploy a single operating system to multiple types of machines.

Chapter 10, "Inventory and Software Metering," focuses on the heart of Configuration Management, one of the core features that most other features tie into.

Chapter 11, "Asset Intelligence," covers the mechanism Configuration Manager uses for tracking assets, including hardware, software, and licensing.

Chapter 12, "Reporting," discusses probably the most used aspect of Configuration Manager by users outside the IT department. It gives other users the ability to report on various parts of Configuration Manager.

Chapter 13, "Compliance Settings," offers an in-depth look at setting up a predefined level of standards for all your devices and how Configuration Manager will ensure your clients are maintained at that standard.

Chapter 14, "Endpoint Protection," details the use of Configuration Manager to manage malware protection throughout the computing environment.

Chapter 15, "Role-Based Administration," covers the new approach to security in Configuration Manager. Role-based security is used to assign the access needed for specific job functions.

Chapter 16, "Disaster Recovery," provides the information necessary to protect your Configuration Manager databases by backing them up properly so that you can use those backups to recover from a disaster if it strikes.

Chapter 17, "Troubleshooting," shows how to ensure your Configuration Manager environment stays healthy and gives you a baseline of where and what to look for if problems arise.

Chapter 18, "Enterprise Mobility and Configuration Manager," provides information on Enterprise Mobility + Security and its integration with Configuration Manager.

Errata

We have done our best to make sure that the content in this book is as accurate as possible at the time it was written. If you discover any mistakes that we have missed in the editing process, please let us know at http://sybex.custhelp.com so we can address them in future versions of this book.

Chapter 1

Overview of System Center Configuration Manager and Microsoft Intune

System Center Configuration Manager and Microsoft Intune focus on the management of PCs, servers, and mobile devices, all from a single management console. Microsoft Intune supports both a hybrid scenario as well as a standalone configuration, which will not be covered in this book.

As technology continues to change at an ever increasing rate and with the increased demand to support scenarios such as Bring Your Own Device (BYOD), many organizations are faced with the challenge of finding the right balance between allowing their employees to choose which devices they use versus the management of devices that will need to have access to corporate systems and potentially store corporate data as well as employee personal data.

To support scenarios like BYOD, technologies such as Configuration Manager and Intune are required to provide a comprehensive, cross-platform, and user-centric way to deploy applications and manage user devices, whether they are corporate connected or cloud based.

In this chapter you will learn about the different features of Configuration Manager and Intune, which is a key foundation given future chapters go into far greater detail on each feature available in these products.

A Brief History of Configuration Manager

Before we go much further, let's take a brief look at the history of Configuration Manager and how it has evolved over the years (see Table 1.1).

TABLE 1.1:   Configuration Manager versions and release dates

RELEASE NAME	RELEASE VERSION	RELEASE DATE
System Management Server	1.0	1994
System Management Server	1.1	1995
System Management Server	1.2	1996

TABLE 1.1: Configuration Manager versions and release dates *(continued)*

RELEASE NAME	RELEASE VERSION	RELEASE DATE
System Management Server	2.0	1999
System Management Server 2003	2003	2003
System Center Configuration Manager 2007	2007	2007
System Center Configuration Manager 2012	2012	March 2012
System Center 2012 R2 Configuration Manager	2012 R2	2013
System Center Configuration Manager (Current Branch)	1511	December 2015
System Center Configuration Manager (Current Branch)	1602	March 2016
System Center Configuration Manager (Current Branch)	1606	July 2016
System Center Configuration Manager (LTSB) Long-Term Servicing Branch	1606	October 2016

As you can see from Table 1.1, Configuration Manager has evolved over the years to the latest version, which is known as System Center Configuration Manager (Current Branch).

NOTE For now don't worry about the version numbers such as 1511, 1602, 1606, and so on. We'll discuss this topic in the "Overview of the New Servicing Model for Configuration Manager" section later in this chapter.

Configuration Manager is a very powerful product with many years of improvements, support, and commitment from Microsoft, the Microsoft Most Valuable Professionals (MVPs), and the community, all of which has resulted in the product that is available today.

Configuration Manager Features

Before you can begin planning to deploy Configuration Manager, you need a basic understanding of the features it provides. Configuration Manager has its own administrator console, as shown in Figure 1.1.

The major features of Configuration Manager Current Branch are covered next.

Application Management

The Application Management feature of Configuration Manager allows you to create, manage, and deploy applications in your environment. This feature also provides monitoring capabilities that allow you to monitor application deployments and take appropriate action in the event of any issues.

The concept of packages and programs from previous versions of Configuration Manager is still supported in Configuration Manager Current Branch, and there may be occasions where you should use these rather than applications (which are explored in Chapter 7, "Application Deployment").

FIGURE 1.1
Microsoft System
Center Configuration
Manager Console

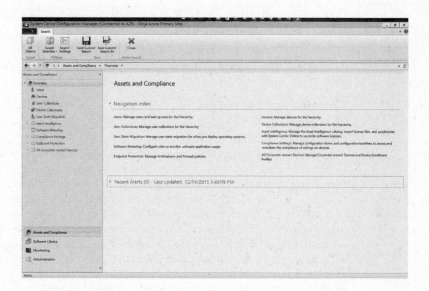

FIGURE 1.1
Microsoft System
Center Configuration
Manager Console

This is probably the most used feature of all the previous versions of Configuration Manager, and it's probably the most dangerous if not used carefully. It is likely that just about all Configuration Manager admins have accidentally deployed a piece of software that they shouldn't have (if you haven't, then keep up the great work!). This isn't a fault of this feature but something that can happen if you don't test, test, test, and then test again. Anything you plan on deploying to client computers must be carefully managed, and you must pay close attention to the details of what you are doing.

Collections

Collections are simply a way of grouping resources together that share a common criterion such as "Which resources are running Windows 8 with more than 2 GB of RAM, with more than 1 GB of free disk space, and with a certain BIOS version?" Typically collections are based on queries, allowing them to be updated dynamically based on a configurable schedule or by directly assigning resources. Collections can consist of computers, users, user groups, or any discovered resources in the Configuration Manager site database. Collections, as a fundamental feature, have not changed much since previous versions, but they are now the necessary building blocks used to enable other features such as maintenance windows and collection variables, which will be explored in later chapters.

Company Resource Access

Using the Company Resource Access feature, you can create and deploy profiles to control access to your company's resources. Profiles that you can create and deploy include

- Certificates
- Email

◆ VPN

◆ Wi-Fi

This feature is discussed in more detail in Chapter 13, "Compliance Settings."

Compliance Settings

The Compliance Settings feature is designed to address configuration drift within the enterprise. Enterprise administrators (for workstations and servers) as well as security teams need a tool that enables them to set configuration baselines (based on the Sarbanes–Oxley Act, the Health Insurance Portability and Accountability Act, the Gramm-Leach-Bliley Act, or other compliancy regulations), that contain configuration items detailing how a specific item should be configured (for example, the local guest account should be disabled, Windows Integrated Security for SQL Server should be enabled, and so on). These configuration baselines are then deployed to the appropriate resources and the results reported back to provide details of any configuration drift, thus allowing the appropriate action to be taken.

Microsoft delivers configuration packs that jump-start an organization in the compliance areas mentioned and help you set up a baseline of standards for your workstations and servers, allowing you to audit your environment against that baseline.

You can configure your baselines from scratch, or you can use best practices from Microsoft and their partners in the form of Configuration Manager Configuration Packs, which can be modified if needed. The ability to configure, monitor, and remediate the systems based on specific needs is key to IT operations management and operations on Information Technology Infrastructure Library (ITIL) and Managed Object Format (MOF), respectively. This feature will be covered in Chapter 13.

Endpoint Protection

The Endpoint Protection feature allows you to manage antimalware policies and Windows Firewall security for your Configuration Manager client computers. Endpoint Protection requires a separate license because it installs its own client that is separate from the Configuration Manager client.

Endpoint Protection is covered in Chapter 14, "System Center Endpoint Protection."

Inventory

Configuration Manager offers you the ability to inventory the hardware and software of devices in your enterprise. Hardware inventory can gather information from your systems such as processor information, the computer manufacturer, and the amount of installed memory. Software inventory can gather lists of file types and their versions installed on your computers, with EXE files as the default. Combine this with extensive information in the Asset Intelligence (AI) knowledge base, and you can use Configuration Manager to get a good handle on what hardware and software is being used in your environment.

Inventory is the backbone of Configuration Manager. Although you can install and run Configuration Manager without enabling Inventory, you wouldn't be able to do much, since so many other features, such as software updates, require Inventory. We will go into more detail about Inventory in Chapter 10, "Inventory and Software Metering."

Mobile Device Management

Configuration Manager Current Branch includes two types of mobile device management:

◆ Mobile Device Management with Windows Intune

◆ On-premises Mobile Device Management

The following sections provide an overview of these; they are discussed in greater detail in Chapter 19, "Enterprise Mobility and Security."

MOBILE DEVICE MANAGEMENT WITH WINDOWS INTUNE

Mobile Device Management (MDM) with Windows Intune allows you to use Configuration Manager to manage Windows Phone, iOS, Android (including Samsung KNOX), and even Windows devices using the Microsoft Intune service over the Internet.

However, even though Intune is used, the actual management tasks are completed by the service connection point, which is a new site system role in Configuration Manager Current Branch.

Using MDM provides the following management capabilities on devices:

◆ Retire and wipe

◆ Deployment of line of business applications to devices

◆ Collect hardware inventory

◆ Collect software inventory by using built-in reports

◆ Deploy applications to devices that connect to Windows Store, Windows Phone Store, App Store, or Google Play

◆ Configure compliance settings such as passwords, security, roaming, encryption, and wireless communication

ON-PREMISES MOBILE DEVICE MANAGEMENT

As its name suggests, this type of mobile device management allows you to enroll and manage Windows 10 Enterprise PCs and Windows 10 mobile devices using the Configuration Manager infrastructure without the need for a Windows Intune subscription.

Management of these devices is performed by the management functionality built in to supported devices and does not require the Configuration Manager client to be installed.

Operating System Deployment

Operating System Deployment (OSD), as its name suggests, is the ability to deploy an operating system to a machine. Configuration Manager Current Branch includes several improvements to OSD, especially in the distribution of Windows 10 with the inclusion of a new in-place upgrade scenario that can significantly reduce the time and complexity of deploying Windows 10.

As in previous versions, OSD allows you to create and distribute operating system images that include any required updates and applications, to computers both managed and unmanaged by Configuration Manager using PXE boot or bootable media such as USB flash drives, DVD, or CD set.

OSD is discussed in greater detail in Chapter 9, "Operating System Deployment."

Power Management

Saving energy and preserving the environment are important goals for IT professionals and organizations. The Power Management feature allows you to create different power plans that configure Windows' power management settings on your computers based on your organization's needs. These plans can then be applied to collections of computers where they will be enforced. Configuration Manager includes various reports relating to power management that allow you to ensure the power settings have been deployed correctly and are in place on the relevant computers.

Queries

Queries allow you to retrieve information from the Configuration Manager site database about the resources in your environment that meet certain criteria, such as all machines running a certain version of Windows, or all users running a certain piece of software. Queries can be used to answer questions quickly or make mini-reports that might not be used often enough to be imported into the reporting interface. Of course, queries can be used to create reports, but their primary use is as the basis for *collections*, which we looked at earlier in the "Collections" section.

Remote Connection Profile

The Remote Connection Profile feature allows you to create profiles that contain Remote Desktop Connection settings that you can deploy to users in your Configuration Manager hierarchy.

Users can then use the company portal to use Remote Desktop using the Remote Desktop Connection settings deployed to them via the remote connection profile to remotely connect from their Windows, iOS, or Android corporate device to their work computer when they are not connected over the Internet or connected to your domain.

NOTE   You only need a Microsoft Intune subscription if you want users to be able to connect to their work PC using the company portal. If you don't have Intune, users can still use a VPN connection to connect to their work PC using Remote Desktop using the settings configured in the remote connection profile.

This feature is discussed in more detail in Chapter 19.

Remote Control

The Remote Control feature allows computer support staff to remotely troubleshoot problems with users' computers just like they are sitting in front of the computer. This feature is still integrated with Remote Assistance and Remote Desktop, and it works pretty much the same as it did in previous versions of Configuration Manager.

This feature is discussed in more detail in Chapter 10.

Reporting

The Reporting feature allows you to create and run reports to show data from the Configuration Manager site database for all of the various features, whether it be client installation, inventory, software deployment/updates, or even status or alert messages.

Configuration Manager Current Branch ships with over 400 out-of-the-box reports that you can edit. You can even create your own custom reports using SQL Reporting Services to meet your specific needs.

Reporting is discussed in several chapters and is covered fully in Chapter 12, "Reporting."

Software Metering

Software metering (covered in Chapter 10) allows you to collect information on software usage to assist in managing software purchases and licensing. Using software metering, you can do the following:

♦ Report on the software that is being used in your environment and on which users are running the software

♦ Report on the number of concurrent users of a software application

♦ Report on software license requirements

♦ Find software that is installed but isn't being used

The twist to software metering is that the metering rules are automatically populated, or created, but disabled by default, based on the software inventory. This allows you to rapidly meter applications and gain insights into usage. Software metering is part of the Service Measurement process in ITIL and Change and Configuration SMF in MOF. Based on the utilization of software, you can measure when applications are properly used in the environment for better inventory of the current assets.

Software metering is discussed in more detail in Chapter 10.

Software Updates

Using this feature, you can manage the daunting task of deploying updates to Microsoft applications and operating systems. Not only does this apply to Microsoft security patches and updates, but having this flexible and extensible environment has allowed partners (such as HP, Dell, IBM, Citrix, and others) to create custom catalogs to update server and desktop BIOS, firmware, and drivers as well as to create internal catalogs. This enables customers to create their line-of-business application update catalogs and update them through the same streamlined process as Microsoft uses for patch management.

Deploying updates require a Windows Server Update Services (WSUS) server. Configuration Manager leverages WSUS with its functionality and provides a higher level of granularity than is available with WSUS alone. Software updates are an important phase in the Incident Management process and IT Operations Management function of ITIL and the Operate Phase in MOF. We will cover software updates in more detail in Chapter 8, "Software Updates."

User Data and Profiles Configuration Items

The user data and profile configuration items in Configuration Manager Current Branch allow you to manage roaming profiles, offline files, and folder redirection on computers running Windows 8.

This feature is discussed in more detail in Chapter 13.

Wake on LAN

The Wake on LAN feature, added to software distribution, was available in SMS 2003 only by purchasing third-party software. It allows you to leverage technology built into computer hardware to wake up computers that have been turned off so they can run assigned deployments. Chapter 7 shows how to enable it.

Asset Intelligence

Asset Intelligence, which was included within Configuration Manager 2007, now comes with its node within the admin console. This is not the only new aspect of Asset Intelligence; AI also became part of the Software + Services initiative within Microsoft. The services component of AI is not a fee-based feature but is just another extension of the holistic approach; it includes the following functionality:

- New catalog and license management UI in the Configuration Manager admin console

- The ability to customize the local catalog—in other words, create new categories and families

- On-demand or scheduled catalog update synchronization through the Configuration Manager console

- The ability to tap software assets unknown to the catalog and pass them up to the online service for async identification

- The ability to import licensing data from Microsoft and compare it to installed inventory

Asset Inventory is one of the reporting structures used to analyze and ensure that every asset on the system is being used properly and report this to management. We'll discuss this further in Chapter 11, "Asset Intelligence."

Application Virtualization Management

With the newest release of App-V, Configuration Manager leverages its existing infrastructure and extends its reach to deliver virtual applications:

- It integrates Microsoft App-V 5.0 with Configuration Manager.

- Application Virtualization Management (AVM) allows you to use Configuration Manager to manage and deploy virtual applications, when possible, to make managing virtual applications for the Configuration Manager administrator the same experience as managing standard or physical software.

- AVM has version checking, user-based targeting, and streaming functionality.

- This new version of Configuration Manager integrates with other presentation servers such as Remote Desktop Services' RemoteApp capability or Citrix XenApp.

Client Health and Monitoring

Configuration Manager displays client health evaluations results and client activities directly in the console, providing alerting and remediation capabilities if health statistics fall below established thresholds. In this version, you can see several improvements related to client health activities and how the client remediates each of them. Now with the in-place upgrade, you can always have the latest client running in your organization. We will discuss more on this topic in Chapter 6, "Client Health."

Microsoft Intune Features

There are many ways you can benefit from Microsoft Intune. This book will be dedicated to the Cloud Extension with Configuration Manager. However, you can use Microsoft Intune stand-alone as part of your Microsoft Office 365 subscription, or as part of the Microsoft Enterprise Mobility Suite.

The primary features the Intune provides are

◆ Mobile device management (MDM) that allows you to enroll devices so that they can be provisioned, configured, monitored, and managed

◆ Mobile application management (MAM) that allows you to publish, push, configure, secure, monitor, and update mobile applications for your users

◆ Mobile application security that helps you secure mobile data by segregating corporate data from personal data and facilitating just the corporate data to be wiped if required

Overview of the New Servicing Model for Configuration Manager

Previous versions of Configuration Manager had a version number such as 2007 or 2012 indicating that they were a major release and the year of their release. In line with Microsoft update policy at the time, service packs, cumulative updates, and "R" releases were typically released throughout the life cycle of the product.

With the advent of Windows 10, things have now changed in Microsoft. Windows 10 will be the last version of Windows with planned updates released every three months, which will be denoted in YYMM format—for example, the November 2015 release of Windows 10 is known as 1511, the February 2016 release is known as 1602, and so forth.

In addition Windows 10 has the following three servicing branches:

◆ Current Branch (CB)

◆ Current Branch for Business (CBB)

◆ Long-Term Servicing Branch (LTSB)

In a nutshell these different branches allow users to control how often they want to update their version of Windows 10 going from every three months in the case of CB through to once a year in the case of LTSB.

More information can be found here:

```
https://technet.microsoft.com/itpro/windows/plan/windows-10-servicing-options
```

Does this affect Configuration Manager? Yes and no. Configuration Manager has adopted the Windows 10 servicing model partially. For example, Configuration Manager now does not use version numbers but instead uses the YYMM format, with 1511 being the first release of the new version.

As of this writing, there is also only one servicing branch for Configuration Manager and that is Current Branch (CB), which is designed to keep pace with Windows 10 and its CB releases.

Baseline vs. Incremental Update Versions

Microsoft will periodically release what is known as a *baseline* release. In other words, for a new installation this is the minimum version you will need to start with (as of this writing, the latest baseline version for Configuration Manager CB is 1606).

Then every three to four months Microsoft will release an update known as an *incremental update version* that you install on top of the baseline version. These updates will still have the YYMM format, so in the case of Configuration Manager CB the first incremental update, known as 1602, was completed in February 2016. The next scheduled release as of this writing (known as 1610) is due for completion in December 2016.

Incremental updates have the following features:

◆ They replace service packs and cumulative updates used in previous versions.

◆ They contain both fixes and new features, giving you the flexibility to control which new features you use and when.

◆ You decide which updates you install and when.

◆ Once you decide to install an update, Configuration Manager will automatically upgrade all of the relevant components such as the site server and its components, consoles, and clients. If you are running a remote console, the next time you load it and it connects to a site running a later version, you will receive a notification that an updated console is available and you will be offered the opportunity to install it.

◆ You no longer need to download and install the updates manually. Incremental updates now appear automatically in the new "Updates and Servicing" node of the Configuration Manager console (located in the Administration workspace under Cloud Services). A key benefit of this is that you will know when an update is available rather than encountering an issue and then discovering a fix was released for it that you weren't aware of.

You will learn more about the Configuration Manager Current Branch servicing model in Chapter 18, "Hierarchy Planning."

Overview of the Servicing Model for System Center Configuration Manager

Two versions of Configuration Manager are available today: the Current Branch and the Technical Preview. Those in the Technical Preview space will receive monthly releases—for example, 1512, 1601, 1602, and 1603 (see Figure 1.2). This will give Technical Preview users the ability to test and validate new product capabilities that may be released to the Current branch.

FIGURE 1.2
Servicing model in the
Technical Preview

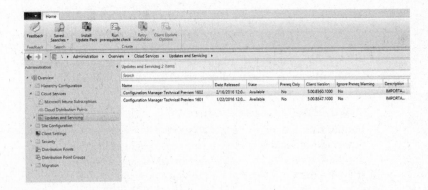

The Current Branch will receive updates that have been tested and declared ready for enterprises; this release may follow a different path than the Technical Preview. In this example, the releases may look like this: 1602, 1606, and 1610 (see Figure 1.3). These updates will be available for enterprises to upgrade to those Current Branch releases and be able to update their infrastructures to those builds.

FIGURE 1.3
Servicing model in the
Current Branch

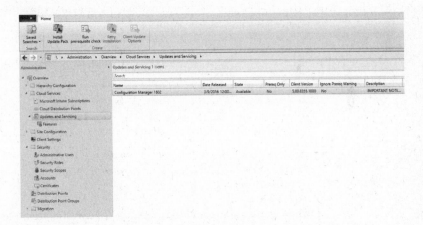

The Software as a Service (SaaS) model will give customers an edge on the latest capabilities of the product and will show what is coming next and how can they be ready for a Current Branch release. You should have both versions in your infrastructure so that you can understand what is coming next.

The Update Process

To access the latest build, you must go to Configuration Manager Console ➤ Administration Workspace ➤ Cloud Services and click on Updates and Servicing. Once there, you will be able to see the latest update of Current Branch that you can choose. From here, you can right-click or use the ribbon to run the prerequisites check, as you can see in Figure 1.4. Doing so will validate that the site meets the requirements to perform the upgrade; this is key to ensure the site will be updated to the Current Branch, as shown in Figure 1.5.

FIGURE 1.4
Servicing model in
the Technical Preview,
prerequisites check

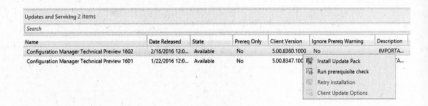

FIGURE 1.5
Servicing model in the
Current Branch, pre-
requisites check

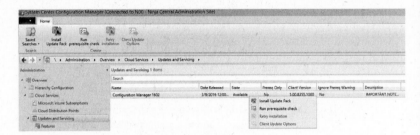

Once the tool finishes validating the requirements, you will be able to install the update.
Download the updates using the DMPDownloader and store this information in the
EasySetupPayload folder (see Figure 1.6).

FIGURE 1.6
EasySetupPayload
folder

To validate the progress of the prerequisites check from the servicing, you can choose
Monitoring Workspace ➢ Site Servicing Status and you will be able to see the status there, as in
Figure 1.7.

FIGURE 1.7
Monitoring Workspace,
Site Servicing Status

Once the prerequisites check is completed, in the console under Updates and Servicing, Yes will appear under Prereq Only, as you can see in Figure 1.8.

FIGURE 1.8
Prereq Only

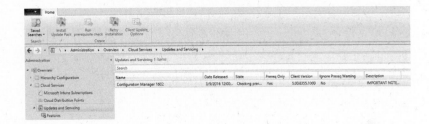

Now you are ready to install the Current Branch to your site. All you have to do is right-click on the Current Branch update and click Install Update Pack. Doing so will launch the Configuration Manager Updates Wizard, as you can see in Figure 1.9.

FIGURE 1.9
Configuration Manager Updates Wizard in the Technical Preview

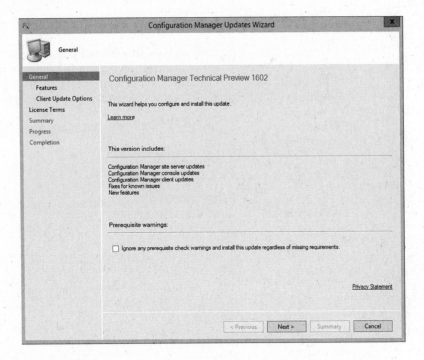

Once in this wizard, click Next once. In the Features Included In Update Pack page, you will see what is available in that pack (Figure 1.10); then click Next.

FIGURE 1.10
Features in Update
Pack

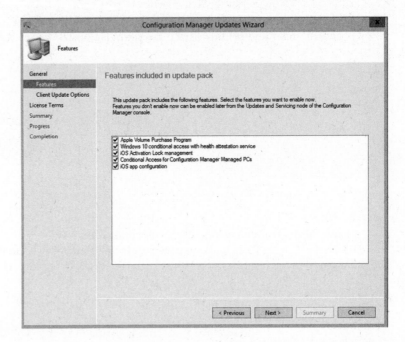

You will then see the Options For Client Update page (Figure 1.11). Here you will have to decide if you want to continue the upgrade without validation or if you want to choose Validate In Pre-Production Collection. For a production environment, we recommend that you select Validate In Pre-Production Collection before releasing the new client version to production.

FIGURE 1.11
Client update options

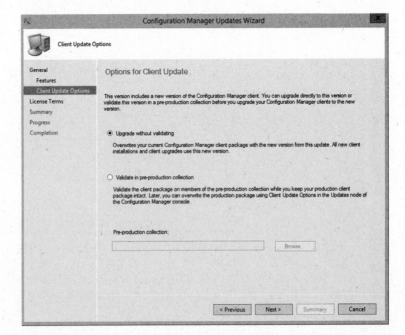

Then you will accept the licensing and review the update in the Summary section. Finally, click Next to finish the update wizard. This process will take some time; you can monitor the progress on the monitoring workspace as shown in Figure 1.7.

This update process is simpler than earlier updates or cumulative updates process.

Summary

With this understanding of Configuration Manager Current Branch, you have a foundation for the upcoming chapters. In the next chapter, you will learn about planning a Configuration Manager infrastructure.

Chapter 2

Planning a Configuration Manager Infrastructure

Properly planning a Configuration Manager Current Branch (BC) infrastructure is crucial in utilizing the software to its full potential. This is even more the case with Microsoft System Center Configuration Manager with its new and improved features.

The first step is to define a project plan with the phases defined in the Microsoft Solution Framework. The Microsoft Solution Framework will guide you to set up a project plan with the following phases:

- ◆ Envision: Gather deployment intelligence.
- ◆ Plan: Plan and design the Configuration Manager environment.
- ◆ Develop: Build the proof-of-concept and the new environment.
- ◆ Stabilize: Perform a pilot with multiple key users.
- ◆ Deploy: Migrate the users to the new infrastructure.

More information about the Microsoft Solution Framework can be found at the Microsoft TechNet documentation library.

In this chapter, you will learn to

- ◆ Plan and design a Central Administration Site
- ◆ Plan and design an effective Configuration Manager infrastructure
- ◆ Identify the enhancements to the distribution point site system role
- ◆ Prepare your current Configuration Manager 2007 environment for the migration to Configuration Manager
- ◆ Prepare your current Configuration Manager 2012 environment for the upgrade to Configuration Manager

Gathering Deployment Intelligence

When you want to implement a new Configuration Manager infrastructure in your environment or you want to migrate from Configuration Manager 2007 or Configuration Manager 2012, you need to write a plan of approach. The installation of Configuration Manager looks like a

Next, Next, and Finish installation, but without a solid plan you will not use most of it. It's crucial to describe your current environment and define a goal you want to reach or make a business case for your project. The following sections describe the process in detail.

THREE PILLARS OF CONFIGURATION MANAGER

Configuration Manager is built on three pillars:

◆ Empower Users

◆ Unify Infrastructure

◆ Simplify Administration

The Empower Users pillar means that Configuration Manager gives the users the ability to be productive from anywhere on whatever device they choose.

The Unify Infrastructure pillar means that Configuration Manager gives the IT department the ability to reduce the cost of the IT management infrastructure. This is done by the simplified Configuration Manager infrastructure and the integration of other technology in Configuration Manager, for instance, by embedding Forefront Endpoint Protection and most of the features of Microsoft System Center Mobile Device Management.

The Simplify Administration pillar means that Configuration Manager will give Configuration Manager administrators a less-complex infrastructure to manage and, with the role-based administration feature, more effectiveness.

Since the positioning of Configuration Manager in the IT environment has changed and has become more important, planning the Configuration Manager environment is essential for an effective implementation of Configuration Manager.

Determining What You Need to Accomplish

Before installing Configuration Manager in your environment, it's wise to define the business case and scope of your project. Ask yourself, "What do we need to accomplish with the implementation of Configuration Manager?" and try to answer this question with the help of your colleagues.

While planning a Configuration Manager environment you can schedule a workshop to define the scope and expectations of your project. You want the results to be accepted by your colleagues or customer. You also need to think from the users' perspective since Configuration Manager 2012 placed the user in the center. User-centricity is new but can be very powerful and well adopted by your organization or customer. During the workshop try to answer the following questions:

◆ Does the Configuration Manager environment need to have high availability?

◆ How is your IT management organized? Do you need role-based administration, or are all the administrators allowed to perform every task?

◆ How is your organization organized?

◆ Do you need to implement or do you support a full application life-cycle model?

- What kind of devices are you going to support? Which level of support do you want to provide?

- Are there relationships between users and systems?

- Do you deploy operating systems? If so, where do you need to deploy them?

- Would you like to implement self-service for the end users?

- Are you going to use one set of client settings, or is there a need for client settings based on collections of users or devices?

- Will you need to use the remote management features of Configuration Manager? If so, for what devices?

- Is there a need to use hardware and software inventory and asset intelligence?

- Is there a service-level agreement available that must be met after the implementation?

Describing the Network

When planning a Configuration Manager infrastructure, you want to look at your current network design. Collect as much information as you can about your current Configuration Manager 2007 infrastructure, your Active Directory, and your network design; this can help you make the right design decisions.

Think about the following when describing the network:

- Make a diagram of your network. The diagram must include the following: LAN and WAN infrastructure, network size per location, available bandwidth, network latency, and the use of firewalls.

- Do Configuration Manager clients need to connect to the Configuration Manager site from the Internet?

- Are you allowed to extend Active Directory with the Configuration Manager schema?

- Document your IPv4 and IPv6 number plan.

- Describe your Active Directory forest structure and possible Active Directory trusts.

- Describe your Active Directory organizational unit structure; where are your assets?

- Describe your security demands. Does Configuration Manager need to be configured to support HTTP or HTTPS intranet connections or both? Is a public key infrastructure available?

- Describe your servers and roles; if you want to manage your servers with Configuration Manager, it's good to define different maintenance windows per groups of servers.

- Do you already use Windows Server Update Services in your environment? Can it be replaced by Configuration Manager?

- Is the Configuration Manager Site server with the Service Connection point allowed to access the Internet?

Describing Your Migration Needs

With the migration feature in Configuration Manager you need to really think about how you want to migrate the investments you made in Configuration Manager 2007.

There is only one supported scenario for migrating to Configuration Manager; this is a side-by-side scenario. You need to list which collections, applications, software update deployments, operating systems, and other objects you want to migrate.

Define up front how long you want to keep the two environments operational since you need to administer two Configuration Manager infrastructures and possibly re-migrate objects you migrated earlier in the process.

Upgrading to Configuration Manager CB from Configuration Manager 2012 is an in-place upgrade. The upgrade needs to be planned since it comes with downtime while upgrading the Configuration Manager 2012 infrastructure.

Configuration Manager as a Service

The way Configuration Manager Current Branch is maintained has changed drastically. In the past Microsoft released a new version of Configuration Manager every x years, as well as service packs and cumulative updates to fix issues and to add support for new features. To be able to cope with the quickly evolving mobility world and the release cycles of Windows 10, Configuration Manager will receive updates and new features via the servicing channel.

Every quarter Microsoft will release a new version of Configuration Manager, which will be the Current Branch version, and this version will be supported for only 12 months. Versioning of System Center Configuration Manager has changed with the new release cycle. For instance, when Microsoft released the new Configuration Manager CB in February 2016, the version of the Current Branch was 1602. The 16 is the year, and the 02 is the number of the month. So, we all know what will happen if Microsoft ships a version in July 2020 and December 2020—yes, we will have 2007 and 2012 again. This version is considered the last major version. Every major update, as well as smaller updates and fixes, will become available via the new servicing channel.

The Configuration Manager media is currently based on the 1606 version, Microsoft will update the baseline in the future since 1606 is officially supported for one year. After installing the baseline version, you need to upgrade the site to the latest Current Branch version via the Updates and Servicing Node, which is covered in Chapter 4.

TECHNICAL PREVIEWS OF CONFIGURATION MANAGER

Every month Microsoft releases a technical preview of Configuration Manager. With this technical preview Microsoft is allowing the community and companies to test features that may or may not ship in the Current Branch release and provide feedback.

Technical previews are not allowed to be used in production environments, so if you want to be able to test new features before they are shipped in Current Branch, you need to create a lab environment.

Planning the Configuration Manager Environment

To plan, design, and implement a Configuration Manager environment, you need to take several steps to be able to implement it in the right way for your business. Configuration Manager can be installed and configured in many different ways, and you must make many design decisions.

Plan a workshop with your Configuration Manager team to make decisions about the following subjects:

♦ System requirements

♦ Active Directory considerations

♦ Hierarchies and sites

♦ Site boundaries and boundary groups

♦ Site system roles

♦ Site communications

♦ Site security

♦ Discovery of your resources

♦ Client settings and client deployment

♦ Content management

♦ Role-based administration

♦ Migration

♦ Disaster recovery

System Requirements

When planning your Configuration Manager infrastructure, you need to define what kind of hardware and software your infrastructure will use and what kind of devices you want to manage via the Configuration Manager infrastructure. This section describes the hardware and software requirements for the Configuration Manager infrastructure.

CONFIGURATION MANAGER CLIENT REQUIREMENTS

Configuration Manager supports managing various clients with various operating systems. In addition to the Windows operating systems, Configuration Manager also supports mobile device operating systems. In the tables in this section you will find the supported client operating systems.

HARDWARE

The minimum and recommended hardware requirements for the Configuration Manager clients are shown in Table 2.1. Refer to the processor and RAM requirements for the operating systems of the devices.

TABLE 2.1:   Hardware requirements/recommended

COMPONENT	REQUIREMENT	RECOMMENDED
Free disk space for client	500 MB	In addition to the required 500 MB, another 5 GB of free space for the client cache
RAM for operating system deployment	384 MB	
Software center	500 MHz processor	
Remote control	Pentium 4 HT 3 GHz or higher and 1 GB of RAM for best experience	
Out-of-band management	Support for Intel vPro technology or Intel Centrino Pro and a supported version of Intel AMT	

OPERATING SYSTEM

Configuration Manager supports various operating systems for desktops, laptops, and mobile devices. Windows versions ranging from Windows 7 to Windows 10 and Windows Server are supported by Configuration Manager. The exact versions and editions are found in the tables of this section.

Windows 7

Table 2.2 shows you the Windows 7 editions that are supported by Configuration Manager.

TABLE 2.2:   Supported Windows 7 versions

WINDOWS 7 VERSION	X86	X64
Enterprise Edition	✓	✓
Ultimate Edition	✓	✓
Professional Edition	✓	✓
Enterprise Edition Service Pack 1	✓	✓
Ultimate Edition Service Pack 1	✓	✓
Professional Edition Service Pack 1	✓	✓

Windows 8 and Windows 8.1

Table 2.3 shows you which editions of Windows 8 are supported by Configuration Manager and how.

TABLE 2.3: Supported Windows 8 versions

VERSION	X86	X64	CLIENT
Windows 8 Enterprise Edition	✓	✓	Full / OMA-URI
Windows 8 Pro	✓	✓	Full / OMA-URI
Windows 8.1 Enterprise Edition	✓	✓	Full / OMA-URI
Windows 8.1 Pro	✓	✓	Full / OMA-URI
Windows RT	✓	✓	OMA-URI
Windows 8.1 RT	✓	✓	OMA-URI

Windows 10

Windows 10 was released in late 2015. Table 2.4 shows you which editions are supported by Configuration Manager and how.

TABLE 2.4: Supported Windows 10 versions

VERSION	X86	X64	CLIENT
Windows 10 Enterprise Edition	✓	✓	Full / OMA-URI
Windows 10 Pro	✓	✓	Full / OMA-URI

Windows Embedded Operating Systems

Besides all full client operating systems, Microsoft also has embedded operating systems that are supported by Configuration Manager. Some limitations apply for Windows Embedded Operating Systems:

◆ On Windows Embedded systems that do not have write filters enabled, all client features are supported.

◆ Application Catalog is not supported on Windows Embedded devices.

◆ On clients with Enhanced Write Filters, RAM File Based Write Filters, or Unified Write Filters, all client features except power management are supported.

In Table 2.5 all Windows Embedded Operating Systems are listed.

TABLE 2.5: Supported Windows Embedded Operating Systems

VERSION	X86	X64	CLIENT
Windows Embedded Standard 2009	✓		Full
Windows XP Embedded SP3	✓		Full
Windows Fundamentals for Legacy PCs (WinFLP)	✓		Full
Windows Embedded POSReady 2009	✓		Full
WEPOS 1.1 with SP3	✓		Full
Windows Embedded Standard 7 with SP1	✓	✓	Full
Windows Embedded POSReady 7	✓	✓	Full
Windows Thin PC	✓	✓	Full
Windows Embedded 8 Pro	✓	✓	Full
Windows Embedded 8 Standard	✓	✓	Full
Windows Embedded 8 Industry	✓	✓	Full
Windows Embedded 8.1 Industry	✓	✓	Full

Windows Server 2008

Windows Server 2008 comes in different editions and for different platforms. Table 2.6 provides the complete list of supported versions and editions.

TABLE 2.6: Supported Windows Server 2008 versions

WINDOWS SERVER 2008 VERSION	X86	X64
Standard Edition Service Pack 2	✓	✓
Enterprise Edition Service Pack 2	✓	✓
Datacenter Edition Service Pack 2	✓	✓
R2 Standard Edition (core and full)		✓
R2 Enterprise Edition (core and full)		✓
R2 Datacenter Edition (core and full)		✓
R2 Standard Edition Service Pack 1 (core and full)		✓
R2 Enterprise Edition Service Pack 1 (core and full)		✓
R2 Datacenter Edition Service Pack 1 (core and full)		✓

Windows Server 2012 (R2)

The new flagship of Microsoft Windows Server 2012 R2 comes in different versions. Table 2.7 shows you which editions are supported by Configuration Manager.

TABLE 2.7: Supported Windows Server 2012 R2 versions

VERSION	X64
Windows Server 2012 Standard	✓
Windows Server 2012 Datacenter	✓
Windows Server 2012 R2 Standard	✓
Windows Server 2012 R2 Datacenter	✓
Windows Server 2012 Core installation	✓
Windows Server 2012 R2 Core installation	✓

DATACENTER RELEASES ARE SUPPORTED BUT NOT CERTIFIED

The Datacenter versions of Windows Server 2008 and Windows Server 2008 R2 are supported but not certified for Configuration Manager 2012.

Apple Mac OS X

Configuration Manager supports a broad range of Windows, Linux, and Mac devices. Table 2.8 lists the supported Mac OS X operating systems. Configuration Manager supports Mac management via a full client or via the MDM channel.

TABLE 2.8: Supported Mac OS X versions

VERSION	SUPPORTED	CLIENT
Mac OS X 10.6	✓	Full
Mac OS X 10.7	✓	Full
Mac OS X 10.8	✓	Full
Mac OS X 10.9	✓	Full / MDM
Mac OS X 10.10	✓	Full / MDM
Mac OS X 10.11	✓	Full / MDM

Linux and Unix Operating Systems

The Linux and Unix operating systems are the odd-men-out operating systems that are supported by Configuration Manager, since they are server-based operating systems only. In Table 2.9 you can see which versions are supported.

TABLE 2.9:   Supported Linux and Unix versions

VERSION	VERSION	SUPPORTED
Red Hat Enterprise Linux	4 x86	✓
Red Hat Enterprise Linux	4 x64	✓
Red Hat Enterprise Linux	5 x86	✓
Red Hat Enterprise Linux	5 x64	✓
Red Hat Enterprise Linux	6 x86	✓
Red Hat Enterprise Linux	6 x64	✓
Red Hat Enterprise Linux	7 x64	✓
Solaris	9 SPARC	✓
Solaris	10 x86	✓
Solaris	10 SPARC	✓
Solaris	11 x86	✓
Solaris	11 SPARC	✓
SUSE Linux Enterprise Server	9 x86	✓
SUSE Linux Enterprise Server	10 x86 SP1	✓
SUSE Linux Enterprise Server	10 x64 SP1	✓
SUSE Linux Enterprise Server	11 x86 SP1	✓
SUSE Linux Enterprise Server	11 x64 SP1	✓
SUSE Linux Enterprise Server	12 x64 SP1	✓
CentOS	5 x86	✓
CentOS	5 x64	✓
CentOS	6 x86	✓
CentOS	6 x64	✓
CentOS	7 x64	✓

TABLE 2.9: Supported Linux and Unix versions *(continued)*

VERSION	VERSION	SUPPORTED
Debian	5 x86	✓
Debian	5 x64	✓
Debian	6 x86	✓
Debian	6 x64	✓
Debian	7 x86	✓
Debian	7 x64	✓
Debian	8 x86	✓
Debian	8 x64	✓
Ubuntu	10.4 LTS x86	✓
Ubuntu	10.4 LTS x64	✓
Ubuntu	12.4 LTS x86	✓
Ubuntu	12.4 LTS x64	✓
Ubuntu	14.04 LTS x86	✓
Ubuntu	14.04 LTS x64	✓
Oracle Linux	5 x86	✓
Oracle Linux	5 x64	✓
Oracle Linux	6 x86	✓
Oracle Linux	6 x64	✓
Oracle Linux	7 x64	✓
HP-UX	11iv2 IA64	✓
HP-UX	11iv2 PA-RISC	✓
HP-UX	11iv3 IA64	✓
HP-UX	11iv3 PA-RISC	✓
AIX	5.3 Power	✓
AIX	6.1 Power	✓
AIX	7.1 Power	✓

Operating Systems for Mobile Phones and Handheld Devices

Configuration Manager supports management for several mobile phones and handheld devices. The level of support and the features vary per platform and client type, but each platform supports inventory, settings management, and software deployment. The support can be divided into two levels:

◆ Depth management

◆ Light management

Devices that are supported through depth management are mobile devices that are enrolled into Configuration Manager via the Service Connector Point or via the on premise MDM functionality for Windows 10 and Mac OS X. To be able to support the light management of devices, you need to connect the Configuration Manager environment to a Microsoft Exchange Server 2010 (SP1) or higher on-premises or online environment. In Chapter 18, "Enterprise Mobility and Configuration Manager," you can find the supported features and the supported mobile devices and learn how to enroll the mobile devices into Configuration Manager.

CONFIGURATION MANAGER SITE SERVER REQUIREMENTS

The Configuration Manager site server roles can be installed on different kinds of hardware and software platforms. This section will help you to identify the hardware and software options you have when planning your site servers.

HARDWARE

In Table 2.10 you will find the minimum and recommended hardware requirements for Configuration Manager site systems. Be sure that the hardware supports a 64-bit operating system. The only exception is for the distribution point site role; this role can be installed on a limited list of 32-bit operating systems. The following requirements are based on the requirements of Windows Server 2008 R2.

TABLE 2.10: Hardware requirements/recommended (up to 100,000 clients)

COMPONENT	RECOMMENDED
Processor	8 cores (Intel Xeon 5504 or comparable CPU)
RAM	32 GB or more
Free disk space	550 GB hard disk space for the operating system, SQL Server, and all database files

In many cases you will need fewer servers than with earlier versions and have less resource waste.

SOFTWARE REQUIREMENTS FOR SITE SYSTEM ROLES

To be able to install and configure Configuration Manager site system roles on your servers, the operating system must comply with some requirements. Site system roles are roles that can be installed and configured on Configuration Manager site systems. This section will describe the requirements for installing the different site system roles.

Operating Systems

Depending on the roles you want to install, you can choose which operating system you want to install the site system role on. Every site system role has certain requirements for which operating system it can be installed on. For instance, a management point site system role can be installed only on a 64-bit Windows Server operating system in contrast to the distribution point site system role, which is supported on a large number of operating systems. This section helps you to identify the operating system requirements for site system roles.

Site System Roles with the Same Operating System Requirements

Most site system roles require the same operating systems. The following site server roles have the same OS requirements:

◆ Central administration site

◆ Primary site server

◆ Secondary site server

◆ Site database server

◆ SMS provider

◆ Enrollment point

◆ Enrollment proxy point

◆ Fallback status point

◆ Management point

◆ Application Catalog web service point

◆ Application Catalog website point

◆ Asset Intelligence synchronization point

◆ Endpoint Protection point

◆ Reporting services point

◆ Software update point

◆ State migration point

◆ System health validator point

◆ Service connection point

◆ Certificate registration point

The operating system versions in Table 2.11 support installing the site roles mentioned here.

TABLE 2.11: Supported operating systems

OPERATING SYSTEM	X86	X64
Windows Server 2008 R2 Standard Edition		✓
Windows Server 2008 R2 Enterprise Edition		✓
Windows Server 2008 R2 Datacenter Edition		✓
Windows Server 2008 R2 SP1 Standard Edition		✓
Windows Server 2008 R2 SP1 Enterprise Edition		✓
Windows Server 2008 R2 SP1 Datacenter Edition		✓
Windows Server 2012 Standard		✓
Windows Server 2012 Datacenter		✓
Windows Server 2012 R2 Standard		✓
Windows Server 2012 R2 Datacenter		✓

The site system roles are not supported on a Core installation of Windows Server 2008, Windows Server 2008 R2, Windows Server 2008 Foundation, Windows Server 2008 R2 Foundation, Windows Server 2012, or Windows Server 2012 R2 editions.

Some of the site server roles can be installed on different operating systems than the ones required for the roles listed previously. The following site server roles can be installed and configured on many more operating systems:

◆ Distribution point

◆ Client status reporting host system

The operating systems that are supported for the distribution points are listed in Table 2.12.

TABLE 2.12: Supported operating systems for distribution points

OPERATING SYSTEM	X86	X64
Windows Server 2008 R2 Standard Edition		✓
Windows Server 2008 R2 Enterprise Edition		✓
Windows Server 2008 R2 Datacenter Edition		✓
Windows Server 2008 R2 SP1 Standard Edition		✓
Windows Server 2008 R2 SP1 Enterprise Edition		✓

TABLE 2.12:   Supported operating systems for distribution points   *(continued)*

OPERATING SYSTEM	X86	X64
Windows Server 2008 R2 SP1 Datacenter Edition		✓
Windows Storage Server 2008 R2 Workgroup		✓
Windows Storage Server 2008 R2 Standard		✓
Windows Storage Server 2008 R2 Enterprise		✓
Windows Server 2012 Standard		✓
Windows Server 2012 Datacenter		✓
Windows Server 2012 Core		✓
Windows Server 2012 R2 Standard		✓
Windows Server 2012 R2 Datacenter		✓
Windows Server 2012 R2 Core		✓
Windows 7 Professional Edition (with or without SP1)	✓	✓
Windows 7 Enterprise Edition (with or without SP1)	✓	✓
Windows 7 Ultimate Edition (with or without SP1)	✓	✓
Windows 8 Professional	✓	✓
Windows 8 Enterprise	✓	✓
Windows 8.1 Professional	✓	✓
Windows 8.1 Enterprise	✓	✓
Windows 10 Professional	✓	✓
Windows 10 Enterprise	✓	✓

When using Windows 7, Windows 8, Windows 8.1, and Windows 10 platforms, only the standard distribution point is supported. Enhanced features like PXE or Multicast are not supported.

Prerequisite Software Requirements

The following software must be installed and, if needed, configured before you can install Configuration Manager Current Branch:

◆ Windows Server Update Services 3.0 SP2 (when using Software Updates feature)

◆ Microsoft .NET Framework 3.5 SP1 (or later)

- ◆ Microsoft .NET Framework 4.5.2 (of Windows Server 2012)

- ◆ Active Directory schema extended with Configuration Manager 2012 classes

- ◆ Latest Windows ADK supporting the latest Windows 10 operating system

The following SQL Server versions are supported:

- ◆ SQL Server 2008 SP2 (Standard or Enterprise) with a minimum of Cumulative Update 9

- ◆ SQL Server 2008 SP3 (Standard or Enterprise) with a minimum of Cumulative Update 4

- ◆ SQL Server 2008 SP4 (Standard or Enterprise)

- ◆ SQL Server 2008 R2 (Standard or Enterprise) with SP1 with a minimum of Cumulative Update 6

- ◆ SQL Server 2008 R2 (Standard or Enterprise) with SP2

- ◆ SQL Server 2008 R2 (Standard or Enterprise) with SP3

- ◆ SQL Server 2012 (Standard or Enterprise) with a minimum of Cumulative Update 2

- ◆ SQL Server 2012 (Standard or Enterprise) with SP1

- ◆ SQL Server 2012 (Standard or Enterprise) with SP1

- ◆ SQL Server 2014 (Standard or Enterprise) with no Service Pack

- ◆ SQL Server Express 2008 R2 with SP1 with a minimum of Cumulative Update 6 (secondary sites only)

- ◆ SQL Server Express 2008 R2 with SP2 (secondary sites only)

- ◆ SQL Server Express 2008 R2 with SP3 (secondary sites only)

- ◆ SQL Server Express 2012 and a minimum of Cumulative Update 2 (secondary sites only)

- ◆ SQL Server Express 2012 with SP1 (secondary sites only)

- ◆ SQL Server Express 2012 with SP2 (secondary sites only)

- ◆ SQL Server Express 2014 (secondary sites only)

The collation of the SQL Server and the site databases must be SQL_Latin1_General_CP1_CI_AS to be able to install Configuration Manager 2012 R2.

As with earlier versions of Configuration Manager, several roles and features of Windows Server need to be installed and configured:

- ◆ Background Intelligent Transfer Service (BITS)

- ◆ Remote Differential Compression

- ◆ IIS7 (with IIS6 Management compatibility, ASP.NET, Static Content Compression, and the common IIS and security features)

We'll discuss more on the installation of Configuration Manager in Chapter 4, "Installation and Site Role Configuration."

Extending the Active Directory Schema

When you are migrating from Configuration Manager 2007 or upgrading Configuration Manager 2012 and you already have extended the Active Directory schema, you do not have to extend it again. The Active Directory schema of Configuration Manager 2007 and Configuration Manager 2012 is the same for Configuration Manager. The schema extensions for Configuration Manager are unchanged.

When planning the extension of the Active Directory schema for Configuration Manager, you need to take into account that several site roles require the extension.

Extending Active Directory is not part of the installation process; when extending you can publish the Configuration Manager site information into Active Directory automatically. Extending the Active Directory schema is done by executing a separate executable; you can find more about this procedure in Chapter 4.

Extending the Active Directory schema is optional, but for some features extending it is required. Table 2.13 provides the list of Configuration Manager features that require an extended Active Directory schema or need it optionally.

TABLE 2.13:   Configuration Manager features that require an extended Active Directory schema

FEATURE	SCHEMA EXTENSION	DESCRIPTION
Client installation	Optional	When installing or pushing a new Configuration Manager client, the client will default search Active Directory for information about the Configuration Manager 2012 environment. Searching Active Directory provides such information as where the management point resides and the Configuration Manager site name.
		If you don't want to extend Active Directory, you can install the client with installation parameters such as SMSMP, or you can publish the management point in DNS and in WINS.
Automatic site assignments/global roaming	Optional	If you don't want to extend Active Directory, you need to publish the management point in WINS. Otherwise, the Configuration Manager client won't find the management point and cannot communicate with the site servers.
TCP port configuration for client-to-server communication	Optional	When you install a Configuration Manager client, it is configured with information about the TCP ports that are used to communicate with the site servers.
Network Access Protection	Required	Configuration Manager publishes health state information to Active Directory; this way the system health validator point can validate whether a client is healthy.

Microsoft best practice is to extend Active Directory with the Configuration Manager schema. Also be sure that the primary site servers have access to the Systems Management container in Active Directory.

Hierarchies and Sites

When planning for a Configuration Manager infrastructure, you need to have a clear understanding of what your global network infrastructure looks like; also, you need to take into account your business needs. The Configuration Manager architecture is simplified from earlier versions and consists of the following site types:

◆ Central Administration Site

◆ Primary site

◆ Secondary site

Next to the site types, a distribution point can have an essential role in the Configuration Manager hierarchy. A Configuration Manager hierarchy consists of Configuration Manager sites that are linked directly or indirectly and have a parent-child relationship, as shown in Figure 2.1.

FIGURE 2.1
A Configuration
Manager hierarchy

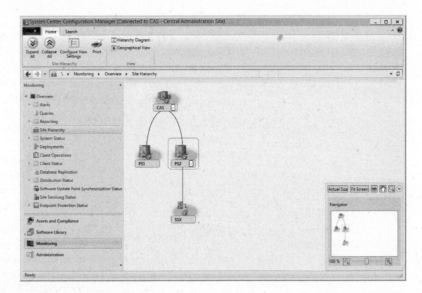

CENTRAL ADMINISTRATION SITE

The Central Administration Site (CAS) is the top-level site in a Configuration Manager hierarchy and is the recommended location for all administration and reporting for a Configuration Manager hierarchy. It has limited site roles available, has no clients assigned, and doesn't process client data.

The CAS supports only primary sites as child sites. When you are using two or more primary sites, a CAS is always the first site you need to install. A primary site that is installed before implementing a CAS can be attached to the CAS. A SQL server is needed for data that is gathered from the hierarchy. The data includes such information as inventory data and status messages from the hierarchy. You can configure the discovery of objects in the hierarchy from the CAS by assigning discovery methods to run in individual sites in the hierarchy.

The following site roles can be configured for Central Administration Sites:

- System health validator point
- Software update point
- Asset Intelligence synchronization point
- Reporting Services point
- Endpoint Protection point
- Certificate Registration point
- Service connection point

A Central Administration Site can support up to 25 child primary sites. The choice for a Central Administration Site is permanent; a primary site cannot be detached anymore.

PRIMARY SITE

The primary site serves clients in well-connected networks. A primary site can have a CAS as its parent tier. A primary site cannot have another primary site as its parent tier. Since role-based administration is a real feature, no separate primary sites are needed for security, administrative, or data-segmentation purposes.

Extra primary sites can be added for the following reasons:

- Managing clients directly
- Providing a local point for administration
- Supporting more than 175,000 clients (up to 150,000 desktop clients, and up to 25,000 Mac or Windows 7 CE devices)

The following are design rules for primary sites:

- Primary sites can be stand-alone or members of a hierarchy.
- A primary site cannot change its parent site relationship after the installation.
- A stand-alone primary site can be assigned to a Central Administration Site after the installation.
- Primary sites that are installed as children of a CAS will configure database replication to the parent site automatically.
- Primary sites use database replication for the communication to their child and parent sites.
- Primary sites can have only a central administration point as a parent site.
- Primary sites can support one or more secondary sites as child sites.

- Primary sites process all client data from their assigned Configuration Manager clients.

- A primary site can support up to 10 management points for load balancing.

- A primary site can support up to 250 secondary sites.

The following site roles can be configured for primary site servers:

- Management point

- Distribution point

- Software update point

- System health validator point

- State migration point

- Fallback status point

- Out-of-band service point

- Asset Intelligence synchronization point (only on stand-alone primary site)

- Reporting Services point

- Application Catalog web service point

- Application Catalog website point

- Enrollment proxy point

- Enrollment point

- Certificate registration point

- Endpoint Protection point (only on stand-alone primary site)

- Service connection point (only on stand-alone primary site)

SECONDARY SITE

A secondary site is installed through the Configuration Management console. The site can be used to service clients in remote locations where network control is needed. You can use secondary sites for servicing site roles such as software update points, PXE-enabled distribution points, and state migration points and if you need tiered content routing for deep network topologies.

Reassigning a secondary site to another primary site is not possible; you need to delete the secondary site and reinstall it from the Configuration Manager console.

The following are design rules for secondary sites:

- When installing a secondary site, it will automatically install SQL Server Express if a local SQL Server is not available.

- Secondary sites that are installed as children of a primary site will configure database replication to the parent site automatically.

◆ Secondary sites use database replication for the communication to their parent sites and receive a subset of the Configuration Manager database.

◆ Secondary sites support the routing of file-based content between secondary sites.

◆ When installing secondary sites, a management point and a distribution point are installed automatically.

◆ Upward and downward flow of data is required.

The following site roles can be configured for secondary site servers:

◆ Management point

◆ Distribution point

◆ Software update point

◆ State migration point

DISTRIBUTION POINTS

Distribution point is the Configuration Manager role that stages packages to clients. The distribution point role is more enhanced than in earlier versions. The following are design rules for distribution points on a remote site without a local primary site or secondary site server present:

◆ The bandwidth of your network is sufficient to communicate and send and receive information such as client inventory, client policies, reporting status, or discovery information to or from a management point.

◆ Background Intelligent Transfer Service does not provide enough bandwidth control for your network environment.

◆ You need to stream virtual applications to clients at a remote location.

◆ You need to use the multicast protocol for deploying operating systems to clients at a remote location.

◆ You need downward flow of data.

If these rules do not apply and a primary site or secondary site is also not needed, your clients can probably use a remote distribution point.

A distribution point cannot be connected to a central administration point; it always communicates with a primary site or a secondary site.

The distribution point role now supports the following:

◆ Scheduling and throttling of data synchronization

◆ PXE

◆ Multicast

◆ Content library

◆ Content validation

◆ State-based distribution point groups

◆ Prestaged content

◆ BranchCache

These are described in detail in the following sections.

Scheduling and Throttling

Whereas in Configuration Manager 2007 you needed a secondary site to be able to manage the synchronization of data on the distribution points, you are now able to control content distribution by using bandwidth, bandwidth throttling, and scheduling options. With scheduling you are able to define periods for restricting synchronization traffic to the distribution point. You can configure synchronizations per day, per hour, and by priority. With throttling you are able to configure options like the following:

Unlimited When Sending To This Destination   When you choose this option, all available bandwidth will be used for distribution point synchronization traffic.

Limited To Specified Maximum Transfer Rates By Hour   Configure per hour the percentage of the bandwidth that is allowed to be used for distribution point synchronization traffic.

Pulse Mode   When you choose this option, you can define the block size of the data that needs to be synchronized and the time delay between each block that is sent to the distribution point.

Scheduling and throttling are available only on site systems with only the distribution point site role installed.

PXE

To be able to install operating systems in your environment, you need to configure PXE support. PXE support allows you to boot into a boot image that is used to initiate operating system deployment for Configuration Manager clients. With Configuration Manager, this role is moved from the site server to a server with the distribution point available. Per site, up to 250 PXE-enabled distribution points are supported.

Multicast

The multicast support is used to deploy operating systems while conserving network bandwidth by simultaneously sending data to multiple clients instead of sending data to each client using a separate session.

Best practice is that the same distribution point is not used for multicast and unicast distributions at the same time.

Content Library

The way of storing data on the distribution point has changed drastically; where Configuration Manager 2007 stored a lot of duplicate content, Configuration Manager stores content only once. The content is stored in the content library (SCCMContentLib). This library is divided in three parts:

Data Library (DataLib)   The data library holds INI files with metadata information about each file in the file library.

File Library (FileLib)   The file library holds the actual files of the packages. It provides single-instance storage of files on the site server and distribution point.

Package Library (PkgLib)   The package library stores information about the content in each package.

The content library replaces the compressed content on the Configuration Manager 2007 distribution points and replaces the smspk$x$$ share (where x represents the volume name hosting the share), the place where the compressed content was stored.

For site-to-site replication of distribution point content, compressed copies of the content are still used. The compression method is new and has a higher compression rate. A new component called PkgXferMgr performs the distribution.

The location of the distribution point share can be spanned over different drives. Drives will have a priority set for file storage, instead of the drive with the most space being used like in earlier versions.

Content Validation

A new feature in Configuration Manager is the ability to validate the content on a distribution point (see Figure 2.2). When validating the content on a distribution point, the validation process will check to see if the content on the distribution point is the same as the content in the source of the application or package. Validating the content can be scheduled for the distribution point or done per package.

Per application on the distribution point, you are able to validate, redistribute, or remove the content. If the content is not valid, it will then be reported in the Content Status node in the Monitoring workspace of the Configuration Manager console. Content validation is done by a scheduled task on the distribution point.

FIGURE 2.2
Managing the content on the distribution point

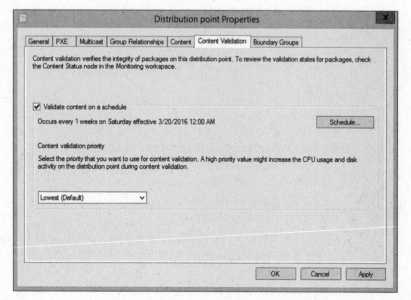

State-Based Distribution Point Groups

In Configuration Manager 2007, distribution point groups were just for administrative purposes to easily target software, but in Configuration Manager, the concept has changed. The distribution point groups are state based; this means that when you add a distribution point to a group, it will receive all the content that has previously been assigned to the distribution point group.

Content Prestaging

A new feature that replaces the courier senders and the package preload tool used in earlier versions of Configuration Manager is called Content Prestage. The courier senders and the package preload tool were used to provide distribution points with content from a physical medium (DVD, tape, external disk, and so on) instead of synchronizing the content over the WAN. The feature allows you also to deploy a remote distribution point without using the WAN to let it synchronize with the site server in the hierarchy. With Content Prestage you are able to save content to an offline media device and load it locally on the remote distribution point.

BranchCache

Since Configuration Manager 2007 SP2, distribution points also support a feature of Windows Server 2008 R2 called BranchCache. BranchCache is used to reduce WAN utilization and enhance access to content at the central office from branch office locations. When BranchCache is enabled, a copy of content retrieved from a server is cached in the branch office. When someone else wants to retrieve the same content, the client will retrieve the content from the cache available in the branch office; this way the WAN is not used to get the content again from the centrally located server. This BranchCache feature caches HTTP, HTTPS, BITS, or SMB-based content on both distributed cache and local cache locations. A distributed cache is a cache location on a Windows 7 client that is configured to use BranchCache. A local cache is a location on a Windows 2008 R2 server in the branch office where BranchCache is enabled.

There is no special configuration option in Configuration Manager to enable BranchCache since it is not a feature of Configuration Manager. The only thing you need to configure is that your deployments are enabled for downloading and running the applications locally.

BranchCache is often used in WAN environments with a lot of latency and with slow data links between the sites.

BranchCache works only in a combination of Windows 7 clients and Windows Server 2008 R2 and higher.

Site Boundaries and Boundary Groups

In Configuration Manager you can define one or more network locations called *boundaries*. A boundary in Configuration Manager can be based on the following types:

IP Subnet A boundary can be a subnet ID, which is automatically calculated while entering the IP subnet and subnet mask.

Active Directory Site When you are using Active Directory sites in your Active Directory domain, you can configure the boundary to use an Active Directory site.

IPv6 Prefix   If you are configuring Configuration Manager in an IPv6 environment, you can configure a boundary to use an IPv6 prefix. An IPv6 prefix is a fixed part of the IPv6 address or the network ID.

IP Address Range   Instead of using an IP subnet, you can configure the boundary to use an IP address range. The IP address range can be defined according to your needs.

The boundaries can contain devices that you want to manage with Configuration Manager. Each boundary must be a member of one or more boundary groups, which are collections of boundaries. Boundaries are available for the Configuration Manager hierarchy, whereas boundaries in Configuration Manager 2007 were site specific.

New for clients is that before clients can identify an assigned site or locate content on a distribution point, a boundary must be associated with a boundary group. The boundary group is used for clients to find their assigned site, and they are used to locate content. In a boundary group you can associate site system servers that have distribution points or state migration points installed so that the client can find software like applications, operating system images, and software updates. Boundary groups can be added to keep boundaries organized in a logical way.

Boundary creation can be done by hand, but when you enable the Active Directory Forest Discovery feature, you can create Active Directory site boundaries and IP subnet boundaries automatically at the same time. This process can be configured to run periodically. When migrating from Configuration Manager 2007, boundaries and boundary groups are also automatically created during the migration process.

CONFIGURING NETWORK SPEED

In Configuration Manager 2007, you needed to configure the network speed for your location. In Configuration Manager, you need to configure the network speed on the Content Location property per distribution point in a boundary group.

A boundary group can be assigned to a specific site and can have one or more content locations. A distribution point can be added to one or more boundary groups. The boundary groups will provide the clients with a list of distribution points to download the content from.

DO NOT OVERLAP BOUNDARIES

When planning boundary groups, avoid overlapping the boundaries. This is allowed in Configuration Manager and earlier versions, but when you use automatic site assignment, the site that a client will be assigned to is unpredictable. So do not use overlapping in combination with automatic client assignment.

Site System Roles

Site system roles are roles that can be installed on Configuration Manager site servers. Depending on the size of your site and hardware, you can assign multiple roles to one site system server. Some site system roles are installed while installing Configuration Manager or when adding a secondary site to the Configuration Manager infrastructure. Others can be installed in the Configuration Manager console.

The following list provides an overview (in alphabetical order) of all the site roles and what they are used for. More information about the site system roles can be found in Chapter 4.

Application Catalog Web Service Point The Application Catalog web service point publishes software information from the software library to the Application Catalog website. This site role is available hierarchy wide.

Application Catalog Website Point The Application Catalog website point publishes the available software for a user, depending on the user rights. The Application Catalog website allows, for instance, users with mobile devices, connected via Exchange ActiveSync to remotely wipe their device or request software that is available for distribution but that may or may not need approval from the system administrator. This site role is available hierarchy wide.

Asset Intelligence Synchronization Point The Asset Intelligence synchronization point synchronizes the Asset Intelligence Catalog information with the System Center online service. This site system role can only be installed on the Central Administration Site server in a hierarchy or a stand-alone primary site server. Synchronization of the Asset Intelligence information can be scheduled or run manually. This site role is available hierarchy wide.

Certificate Registration Point The certificate registration point communicates with the server that runs the Network Device Enrollment Service of Active Directory Certificate Services to manage device certificate requests that use the Simple Certificate Enrollment Protocol (SCEP).

Component Server A component server is automatically installed with all site system roles except the distribution point and is used to run Configuration Manager services.

Distribution Point Distribution point is the Configuration Manager role that stages packages such as application content, software packages, software updates, operating system images, and boot images to clients. The distribution point role in Configuration Manager 2012 also supports PXE, scheduling, bandwidth throttling, multicast, and content validation. This site role is available only in the site.

Endpoint Protection Point The Endpoint Protection role integrates the former Forefront Endpoint Protection with Configuration Manager 2012. The role is configured at the Central Administration Site or a stand-alone primary site. With the System Center Endpoint Protection role you can secure your clients and servers from viruses and malware. To be able to use the Endpoint Protection point, you need to accept the license terms and configure the default membership for the Microsoft Active Protection Service.

Enrollment Point When implementing mobile device management or secure out-of-band management, an enrollment point is needed. Public key infrastructure (PKI) certificates are required to complete the enrollment of the mobile device, Mac devices that are managed via the Configuration Manager client, and Windows 10 devices managed via MDM on premises. This site role is available only in the site.

Enrollment Proxy Point   When implementing mobile device management, an enrollment proxy point is needed to manage enrollment requests from mobile devices. Mobile device enrollment will need a PKI to secure the over-the-air communication with the mobile devices, Mac devices that are managed via the Configuration Manager client, and Windows 10 devices managed via MDM on premises. This site role is available only in the site.

Fallback Status Point   When a client becomes unmanaged or the management point is unable to communicate with the client, a fallback status point will point out unmanaged clients and helps you monitor the client installation. This site role is available hierarchy wide.

Management Point   The management point provides policy and content location information to Configuration Manager clients. It also receives configuration data from Configuration Manager clients.

The server locator point functionality as it is known in Configuration Manager 2007 is moved to the management point. If the Configuration Manager client is no longer able to retrieve site information from Active Directory or WINS, the management point is used to provide this information.

This site role is available only in the site.

Reporting Services Point   For reporting you need a Reporting Services point; this role integrates with SQL Server Reporting Services. You can create and manage reports for Configuration Manager. This site role is available hierarchy wide.

Site Database Server   The site database server hosts the Microsoft SQL Server database. This database is used to store information about assets and site data.

SMS Provider   This is installed automatically when you install a Central Administration Site and/or when you install a primary site. The SMS provider is the interface between the Configuration Manager 2012 console and the Configuration Manager 2012 database. Secondary sites do not install SMS providers.

Software Update Point   The software update point is used for integration with Windows Server Update Services so that software updates can be deployed and managed with Configuration Manager. This site role is available only in the site.

State Migration Point   When a computer receives a new operating system, the user state will be stored at the state migration point. The state migration point receives the user state from User State Migration Toolkit 4.0, which is executed in an operating system deployment task sequence. This site role is available only in the site.

Service Connection Point   The Service Connection Point is installed by default and used for the servicing of Configuration Manager. When managing mobile devices via Microsoft Intune you also need the Service connector point to be able to retrieve status messages and inventory messages from the mobile devices that are enrolled in Microsoft Intune. While installing a new Configuration Manager environment you have the option to install the Service Connection Point in online or offline mode. Updates of Configuration Manager are automatically downloaded via the Service Connection Point.

Best Practices for Site System Design

When planning and designing a Configuration Manager site hierarchy, you also need to place your site system roles on the right server. Depending on the role and the size of the site, the role can consist of other roles on one or more site servers. This section will provide information about some best practices for capacity planning of Configuration Manager.

CAPACITY PLANNING OF CONFIGURATION MANAGER

Table 2.14 lists the maximum recommendations for planning and designing your Configuration Manager infrastructure. The actual figures depend on your available hardware, your network infrastructure, and also your demands.

TABLE 2.14:   Site system planning figures

SITE SYSTEM	NUMBER	DESCRIPTION
Clients (desktops that run Windows, Linux, and UNIX)	700,000	This is the maximum number of clients supported for the entire Configuration Manager hierarchy.
Mac and Windows CE 7.0 devices	25,000	The Configuration Manager hierarchy supports up to 25,000 Mac OS X and Windows CE devices.
Devices via on-premise MDM	100,000	The Configuration Manager hierarchy supports up to 100,000 devices that are enrolled via on-premise MDM.
Cloud-based devices	300,000	The Configuration Manager hierarchy supports up to 300,000 cloud-based devices.
Primary site	25	A Central Administration Site supports up to 25 child primary sites.
Primary site	150,000	A primary site supports up to 150,000 clients.
Secondary site	250	There is a maximum of 250 secondary sites per primary site.
Secondary site	15,000	A secondary site can support communications from up to 15,000 clients.
Management point	15	A primary site can support up to 15 management points.
Management point	25,000 10,000	One management point can support up to 25,000 clients. Plus one of both, 10,000 devices enrolled via on-premise MDM or 10,000 devices that run Mac OS X or Windows CE 7.0.
Distribution point	4,000	A distribution point is capable of supporting up to 4,000 clients.
Distribution point	250	A site can hold up to 250 distribution points.

TABLE 2.14:   Site system planning figures *(continued)*

SITE SYSTEM	NUMBER	DESCRIPTION
Pull distribution point	2,000	Each primary and secondary site supports up to 2,000 pull distribution points. A primary site supports up to 2,250 distribution points, when 2,000 of those are configured as pull distribution points.
Distribution point	5,000	Each primary site can hold up to 5,000 distribution points with the primary site combined with the secondary sites.
PXE-enabled distribution points	250	Up to 250 PXE-enabled distribution points are supported per primary site.
Software update point Software update point	25,000 150,000	If the software update point runs on the WSUS server and other site roles coexist, the software update point supports up to 25,000 clients. If the software update point runs on the WSUS server and no other site roles coexist, the software update point supports up to 150,000 clients.
System health validator point	100,000	The system health validator point in Configuration Manager supports up to 100,000 clients or one per hierarchy if fewer than 100,000 clients.
Fallback status point	100,000	The fallback status point in Configuration Manager supports up to 100,000 clients or one per site.
Application Catalog website point	400,000	One Application Catalog website point supports up to 400,000 clients, but for better performance, plan for 50,000 clients per point.
Application Catalog web service point	400,000	One Application Catalog web service point supports up to 400,000 clients. Best practice is to place the website point and web service point on the same server and plan for 50,000 clients per point.
Packages and applications per distribution point	10,000	Each distribution point supports up to 10,000 packages and applications.

HIGH AVAILABILITY/LOAD BALANCING

If there is a need for a highly available Configuration Manager infrastructure in your environment or you want to load balance some site system roles, there are some options that you can implement. The following high-availability options are offered:

Adding Extra Management Points   When you add extra management points, you are providing load balancing for the management points but also a form of high availability.

When one management point fails, the second management point will take over and provide connectivity.

Adding Extra Distribution Points   When you add extra distribution points, you are providing load balancing for the distribution points but also a form of high availability. When one distribution point fails, the second distribution point will take over and provide access to the content, if configured in the same boundary or if fallback distribution has been configured.

Adding Extra SMS Providers   When you add extra SMS providers, when one SMS provider is unavailable the Configuration Manager console can still access the Configuration Manager database.

Clustering Configuration Manager Database   Per site you can place your Configuration Manager database on a Windows 2008 R2 or higher failover cluster.

When you place site system roles such as software update points or distribution points on dedicated servers, you spread the risks and load of the site system servers.

SQL Considerations

While planning the Configuration Manager infrastructure you also need to plan the SQL environment. The planning figures in Table 2.15 are valid for your SQL environment.

TABLE 2.15:   Site system planning figures

EDITION	NUMBER	DESCRIPTION
Standard	50,000	The standard edition of SQL supports up to 50,000 clients in the hierarchy when it is collocated with a CAS server or remote from the site server.
Standard	50,000	The standard edition of SQL supports up to 50,000 clients in the site when it is collocated with a primary site server.
Standard	100,000	The standard edition of SQL supports up to 100,000 clients in the site when it is remote from the site server.
Enterprise	400,000	The enterprise edition of SQL supports up to 400,000 clients in the hierarchy when it is collocated with the CAS server.

Consider the following design rules for your SQL environment:

◆ If you use a remote database server, ensure that the network between the site server and the remote database server is a high-available and high-bandwidth network connection.

◆ Each SMS provider computer that connects to the site database increases network bandwidth requirements. The exact bandwidth is unpredictable because of the many different site and client configurations.

◆ SQL Server must be located in a domain that has a two-way trust with the site server and each SMS provider. Best practice is to place SQL Server in the same domain as the SMS provider and SMS site servers.

◆ Clustered SQL Server configurations for the site database server when the site database is collocated with the site server are not supported.

Site Communications

The method of replicating data between sites has changed since Configuration Manager 2012. Synchronization of site information between sites is done by database replication, based on SQL Server Service Broker. The Data Replication Service is used to replicate the Configuration Manager database between the SQL Server databases of other sites in a Configuration Manager hierarchy. Global data and site data are replicated by database replication.

When you install a new site in the hierarchy, a snapshot of the parent site database is taken. The snapshot is transferred by server message blocks (SMB) to the new site, where it is inserted into the local database by bulk copy procedure (BCP).

For application or package content, file-based replication is still used, and it uses addresses and senders to transfer data between the sites in the hierarchy. The SMB protocol (TCP/IP port 445) is still used for file-based replication.

Table 2.16 lists the changes regarding the replication of Configuration Manager data.

TABLE 2.16: Site replication of Configuration Manager 2012 data

DATA	EXAMPLES	REPLICATION TYPE	DATA LOCATION
Global data	Collection rules, package metadata, software update metadata, deployments—anything created by administrators or scripts	SQL	Central Administration Site, all primary sites, subsets on secondary sites
Site data	Collection membership, inventory, alert messages—any data created by clients in normal operations	SQL	Central Administration Site and originating primary site
Content	Software package installation sources, software update sources, boot images	File based	Primary sites, secondary sites, and distribution points

Site Security Mode

Configuration Manager 2007 had two security modes: mixed mode and Native mode. In Configuration Manager 2007, mixed mode was the default mode, which used port 80 to communicate with the clients. Configuration Manager 2007 in Native mode was the more secure mode, which integrated PKI to secure client/server communications. The security mode in Configuration Manager 2007 was site wide.

Since Configuration Manager 2012, the concept of Native and mixed modes has been replaced and simplified. You are now able to decide per individual site system role whether clients can connect through HTTP or HTTPS. Instead of configuring a site as mixed or Native mode, you must configure the site role to use HTTP (port 80), HTTPS (port 443), or both. This way, you are more flexible if you want to implement a PKI to secure intranet client communications.

To allow secure communications between your clients and site servers, a PKI needs to be present in your environment, and certificate templates need to be created to be able to enroll certificates for the Configuration Manager site systems and the Configuration Manager clients. The following site roles can be configured in HTTP or HTTPS mode:

- Management point
- Distribution point
- Enrollment point (HTTPS only)
- Enrollment proxy point (HTTPS only)
- Application Catalog web service point
- Application Catalog website point
- Software update point (SUP)

Internet-based clients and mobile devices always use secure HTTPS connections. For Internet-based clients, you need to install a site system server in a demilitarized zone (DMZ) and configure the Internet-facing site roles to accept HTTPS client communications and connections from the Internet. When you configure Configuration Manager to be accessible from the Internet, you can support your clients from the Internet. If you have a lot of mobile workers, managing your Configuration Manager clients is essential. Mobile devices communicate over the air via the Internet to your Configuration Manager environment. For this reason, the communication between the Configuration Manager environment and mobile devices must be secure.

Discovery of Your Resources

The methods of resource discovery have not changed since Configuration Manager 2007. You can use multiple ways to discover different types of resources in the network. You define which resources you want to discover, how often, and using which scope. The following methods are available:

Heartbeat Discovery Used to send a discovery data record from the client to the site periodically; it's a method to renew client data in the Configuration Manager database. Heartbeat discovery is available for primary sites.

Active Directory Forest Discovery Used to discover Active Directory forests from the Active Directory Domain Services. It discovers site server forests plus any trusted forests and supports boundary creation on demand and automatically. Active Directory forest discovery can be configured only on a CAS or a primary site.

Active Directory Group Discovery   Used to discover group membership of computers and users from the Active Directory Domain Services. Active Directory group discovery is available for primary sites.

Active Directory System Discovery   Used to discover computer accounts from the Active Directory Domain Services. Active Directory system discovery is available for primary sites.

Active Directory User Discovery   Used to discover user accounts from the Active Directory Domain Services. Active Directory user discovery is available for primary sites.

Network Discovery   Used to discover resources on the network such as subnets, SNMP-enabled devices, and DHCP clients. Network discovery is available for primary sites and secondary sites.

Be sure to plan the resource discovery well. For instance, if there is no need to discover the whole Active Directory, plan the resource discovery to discover only resources in dedicated Active Directory organizational units. This way you keep the Configuration Manager environment free of unwanted objects. Discovered resources can be added to collections, which can be used to deploy applications or compliancy settings to the resources, for example. You will find more information about discovering your resources in Chapter 5, "Client Installation."

Client Settings and Client Deployment

With Configuration Manager you are able to create different client user and client device settings packages for different collections. Besides the default client agent settings that are available for the entire hierarchy, you can create custom client settings that you can assign to collections. Custom client settings override the default client settings. The resultant settings can be an aggregation of default and one or more custom settings.

Implementing client settings is the easiest step to reduce the infrastructure; there is no need for primary sites for different client settings.

Depending on the implementation or migration scenario, different ways of deploying the Configuration Manager client to the devices are supported. Configuration Manager still supports the client push mechanism and pushing clients via the WSUS infrastructure. Deploying the client with a third-party application deployment environment or Active Directory is of course also possible. Read more about installing Configuration Manager clients and client settings in Chapter 6.

Content Management

Managing content in Configuration Manager can be done on different levels and in different parts of the Configuration Manager console:

Distribution Points/Distribution Point Groups   Per distribution point or distribution point group you are able to see, redistribute, validate, or remove content easily. Content validation can be done automatically based on a schedule. When adding a new distribution point to a distribution point group, all the applications or packages assigned to a distribution point group will be automatically copied to the new distribution point.

Content-Related Objects   Objects that have content have a Content Locations tab where you can manage the content and see on which distribution point the content is available. From the object you are also able to validate, redistribute, and remove the content from the distribution points. Objects that have content are applications, packages, boot images, driver packages, operating system images, operating system installers, and software update deployment packages.

Monitoring In the monitoring workspace of the Configuration Manager console you can monitor your applications and packages in the Content Status node. You can also monitor the distribution point group status and distribution point configuration status.

Role-Based Administration

In Configuration Manager, role-based administration is a feature that brings you "Show me what's relevant for me" based on security roles and scopes. Configuration Manager comes with 15 standard roles, and you can also create custom roles.

Role-based administration is based on the following concepts:

Security Roles What types of objects can someone see, and what can they do to them?

Security Scope Which instances can someone see and interact with?

Collections Which resources can someone interact with?

As part of role-based administration you are able to limit collections; every collection is limited by another. Assigning a collection to an administrator will automatically assign all limited collections.

While planning role-based administration, explore the 15 standard roles and assign the rights to your administrators depending on the part of Configuration Manager they need to manage.

The 15 different roles from which you can choose are these:

- Application administrator
- Application author
- Application deployment manager
- Asset manager
- Company resource access manager
- Compliance settings manager
- Endpoint protection manager
- Full administrator
- Infrastructure administrator
- Operating system deployment manager
- Operations administrator
- Read-only analyst
- Remote tools operator
- Security administrator
- Software updates manager

Role-based administration allows you to map organizational roles of administrators to security roles. Hierarchy-wide security management is done from a single management console.

You can add Active Directory user accounts to Configuration Manager in the Configuration Manager console. In the Administration workspace you will find Administrative Users under Security; here you can add the user accounts from your users who need to have access to Configuration Manager. After adding the user accounts you can assign them the proper role.

Migration

In Configuration Manager the migration feature is used to migrate your Configuration Manager 2007 investments or investments made in another Configuration Manager environment to the new user-centric platform. With the migration feature you can migrate the following objects:

◆ Collections (not valid for Configuration Manager 2007)

◆ Deployments (not valid for Configuration Manager 2007)

◆ Software distribution deployments

◆ Task sequence deployments

◆ Application deployments

◆ Software update deployments

◆ Software update list deployments

◆ Baseline deployments

◆ Boundaries

◆ Boundary groups (not valid for Configuration Manager 2007)

◆ Global conditions (not valid for Configuration Manager 2007

◆ Software distribution packages

◆ Applications (not valid for Configuration Manager 2007)

◆ Virtual application packages (not valid for Configuration Manager 2007)

◆ App-V virtual environments (not valid for Configuration Manager 2007)

◆ Software updates

◆ Deployments

◆ Deployment packages

◆ Deployment templates

◆ Software update lists

◆ Software update groups (not valid for Configuration Manager 2007)

◆ Automatic deployment rules (not valid for Configuration Manager 2007)

◆ Operating system deployment

- Boot images

- Driver packages

- Drivers

- Upgrade packages

- Task sequences

- Settings management

Configuration baselines

Configuration items

- Asset Intelligence

Catalog

Hardware requirements

User-defined categorization list

- Software metering rules

- Saved searches (not valid for Configuration Manager 2007)

- Configuration Policies

Disaster Recovery

When planning a new Configuration Manager infrastructure, be sure to also make a disaster recovery plan. Since Configuration Manager is an important part of your IT infrastructure, you will need to be sure that when a disaster occurs, your Configuration Manager infrastructure will not be affected.

To protect yourself from failure, you can make your environment highly available. This can be done by implementing the following options:

- Installing more than one primary site server in a site

- Placing the Configuration Manager databases on a SQL cluster

- Installing more than one site role per site

It is recommended that you test your disaster recovery plan in a test environment so you can document the disaster recovery process and know what to expect while recovering your Configuration Manager environment.

You can read more about disaster recovery in Chapter 16, "Disaster Recovery."

Designing Your Configuration Manager Environment

After you've gathered your information about the new Configuration Manager infrastructure, you can design the new infrastructure. When designing a new Configuration Manager infrastructure, you need to keep a couple of things in mind. Whereas in SMS 2003 and Configuration

Manager 2007 you could easily design an infrastructure based on bandwidth, languages, or administrative purposes, in Configuration Manager the hierarchy is simplified and modernized. For most cases you can do more with less. Of course, you still need to identify your network locations and the bandwidth between your locations. Keep in mind that Configuration Manager has the goal of simplifying your Configuration Manager infrastructure by flattening the hierarchy and by server consolidation.

NONCRITICAL DESIGN ISSUES

The design of Configuration Manager was changed; for this reason, the following items are no longer critical decision points for designing a site hierarchy:

◆ Support of multiple languages

◆ Different client settings per region

◆ Decentralized administration of your Configuration Manager infrastructure

◆ Logical data segmentation

◆ Content routing for deep hierarchies

When designing a Configuration Manager infrastructure, you will need to review your gathered intelligence and translate this into a design. Things you need to take in account are the following:

Physical Locations of Your Environment   As we said, the first step is to translate your network infrastructure information into information that can be used for the design of the Configuration Manager infrastructure. Ask yourself the following questions:

◆ Where are my locations?

Are my locations in the same country? If so, larger locations often are well-connected sites, and smaller locations usually have less bandwidth available.

◆ Are my locations on the same continent?

If your locations are on the same continent, you need to place a management point at your site, and you can create a secondary site for each location. If a location is not on the same continent, it is wise to create a primary site for that location.

◆ What is the available bandwidth?

For well-connected locations it is often unnecessary to create a Configuration Manager site for that location. If there is a need for local content, you can install a distribution point on such locations since the distribution point now has throttling and bandwidth control.

◆ How many users are working at the location?

One primary site can handle 160,000 clients. Depending on your hardware performance and bandwidth, you can implement one primary site for your entire Configuration Manager infrastructure. Consider using BranchCache for small locations or just a distribution point.

◆ What kind of traffic needs to flow down in the network?

Depending on the data that needs to flow down for administrative or political reasons, it might be necessary to implement a primary site at a location that should normally not be a primary site because of the size or available bandwidth.

Central Administration Site or Not?   When you need more than one primary site in your Configuration Manager infrastructure, you also need a Central Administration Site. The placement of this CAS can be a design choice, but often you will place this site at the data-center or the location where the IT department resides. Configuration Manager clients do not connect to a CAS.

High Availability Considerations   If you need a highly available Configuration Manager site or infrastructure, you can install multiple roles (management point, provider, and so on) of the same role in one site without the need for network load balancing. The Configuration Manager client automatically finds the right management point if one is offline. You also can cluster the SQL database.

Client Settings   As we said, client settings are no longer a reason to implement a primary site. Multiple client settings can be assigned to collections of users or computers. While designing, try to define different client settings for the groups of users or computers as needed. Otherwise, just use the default client settings.

Boundary Management   Boundaries and boundary groups are fundamentals of your Configuration Manager infrastructure. Be sure to identify all the boundaries so that all the Configuration Manager clients can be managed.

Virtualization   Microsoft supports the virtualization of Configuration Manager site servers. Before implementing, always check the Microsoft website for the latest versions and supported third-party virtualization software.

Managing Untrusted Environments   In the past you could manage untrusted domains by supplying accounts with rights. With Configuration Manager you can manage other forests without the need of two-way trusts, but without the trusts fewer features are supported; one of them is, for instance, user-based targeting of software.

Another way is to install site roles in an untrusted domain, but it cannot be a primary site role. You can provide some services but not all of them.

Naming the Configuration Manager Sites   After determining your sites in your Configuration Manager infrastructure, you need to name the Configuration Manager sites. Like in earlier versions, you use a three-character-length code. The site code can contain only standard characters (A–Z, a–z, 0–9, and the hyphen, "-") and must be unique for your Configuration Manager infrastructure. In earlier versions of Configuration Manager you were not able to use Microsoft reserved names: SMS, CON, PRN, AUX, NUL, OSD, SRS, or FCS. This is still the case.

Planning the Configuration Manager Hierarchy

When designing your Configuration Manager hierarchy you need to create an implementation plan for where to install which server with what kind of roles. The deployment information you gathered in an earlier stage will provide the requirements for where you need to install the Central Administration Site, primary sites, secondary sites, and distribution points. To come up with the right design, follow these design steps:

1. Define a naming convention if one doesn't already exist.

2. Determine whether a CAS is needed and where to place this site in your environment. The CAS is the topmost site in your Configuration Manager hierarchy.

3. Define the placement of the primary sites, secondary sites, or just distribution points; remember that tiering primary sites is no longer possible. Look at your WAN and keep the design rules in mind and which roles you need in a specific site.

4. Look at the logical and physical connections between your Configuration Manager sites so you can decide whether addresses need to be configured to manage the traffic between the sites.

5. Assign the boundaries that represent your Configuration Manager sites, and be sure that no boundaries overlap each other.

6. Depending on the Configuration Manager sites, high-availability demands, and other requirements, you can place the site system roles where they are needed.

Designing a good Configuration Manager hierarchy is a must for an effective and solid Configuration Manager infrastructure. Always check the proposed design, and if possible let someone else review the design.

Planning Configuration Manager Site Systems

After designing and planning the Configuration Manager hierarchy, the next step is to plan and design your site systems. This is done by analyzing your requirements per site, gathered during the deployment intelligence phase, described in the section "Gathering Deployment Intelligence." Depending on the expected load and the number of connecting users, you can place roles on different servers or group them on one server.

When planning a highly available Configuration Manager infrastructure, you will need to plan several site roles on more than one server. Not all roles can be installed on every site, so be sure that you determine this while planning the hierarchy.

For detailed information on all the Configuration Manager site system roles and the installation of these roles, see Chapter 4.

Planning Configuration Manager Clients

The clients managed by Configuration Manager are an essential part of the Configuration Manager infrastructure. You need to plan the deployment of your Configuration Manager clients while migrating from Configuration Manager 2007/2012 or while building a new Configuration Manager because the deployment can be carried out in different ways. Planning your Configuration Manager client agent settings is also essential. In Configuration Manager you can create more than one client settings package.

CLIENT INSTALLATION PLANNING

Like in earlier versions, you are able to deploy the Configuration Manager client via different methods. Depending on your scenario, you can choose different ways to deploy the Configuration Manager client to clients:

◆ When clients are managed by a third-party desktop management tool, you can choose to install the client via the current desktop management tool or install it via the supported ways in Configuration Manager, via client push and software updates. Or you can choose to deploy a new operating system to the clients with the operating system deployment feature of Configuration Manager.

◆ When clients are managed with Configuration Manager 2007/2012, you can migrate the clients to the new Configuration Manager management point.

◆ Unmanaged clients can receive a client via the supported ways in Configuration Manager, via client push and software updates. Or you can choose to deploy a new operating system to the clients with the operating system deployment feature of Configuration Manager.

Every solution has its pros and cons, but try to find out which method is the best for your environment. For instance, installing a Configuration Manager client on an unmanaged client can result in lots of legacy and unmanaged software in your environment. Installing a new operating system on thousands of clients can be a lot of work and very expensive.

You can read more about client installation methods and best practices in Chapter 6.

CLIENT AGENT PLANNING

A Configuration Manager client consists of agents that support several Configuration Manager features. There is one default Client Settings package with settings for all manageable agents. With Configuration Manager you are able to create custom client settings and deploy them to clients on collection levels to users or devices.

Planning your client (agent) settings is more complex, because you have the ability to assign client settings to collections. For this reason it's important to analyze the needs of groups of devices and the users. You can read more about client settings methods and best practices in Chapter 6.

Determining How to Deploy Configuration Manager

After you have verified your site design in your test lab, you should plan an initial pilot deployment of Configuration Manager on a small section of your network. Monitor the deployment progress and any potential client problems with your first-level support department.

With the lessons that you learn during your pilot deployment, you'll be able to decide which method of Configuration Manager installation to use for your site deployment. Your goal will be to accomplish the deployment as efficiently as possible while preserving the functionality of any previous methods of system management that you already have in place for as long as needed. The deployment method you use will then help you decide whether you will need additional hardware or personnel resources to do that.

There are several starting points for an implementation of the new Configuration Manager infrastructure. When a Configuration Manager 2007 infrastructure is already in place, you will probably choose to migrate the environment via the side-by-side migration feature, which is available in Configuration Manager. If you have a Configuration Manager 2012 infrastructure in place, you can easily upgrade to the latest version. If you have a version older than Configuration Manager 2007, then you have only two options since direct migration of earlier versions is not supported:

- Build a *greenfield* (new) Configuration Manager infrastructure.

- Migrate first to Configuration Manager 2007 and then perform a side-by-side migration.

If you don't have any Configuration Manager infrastructure in place, you need of course to build a new environment without migrating any assets. An in-place upgrade like that supported in earlier versions is not supported by Configuration Manager.

In the next chapter you will read more about the migration options and the dos and the don'ts when migrating assets from Configuration Manager 2007.

Building a Proof-of-Concept Environment

After your plan and design phase is finished, you need to verify your design in a test or *proof-of-concept* (POC) environment. In this environment you can test your future Configuration Manager environment and create, if necessary, a detailed migration plan. The POC environment can also be used to train your Configuration Manager administrators so that they become familiar with the new environment and will accept the new Configuration Manager 2012 environment.

Be sure to create a test plan up front as a guideline for your proof-of-concept phase of the project. A few test steps that you want to take are shown here; depending on your demands, you can shorten or lengthen the list:

- Deployment of the Configuration Manager clients

- Deployment of applications, software updates, and settings

- Deployment of operating systems

- Synchronization of data between sites

- Migration of objects from Configuration Manager 2007

If all tests are successful, you can start implementing the new Configuration Manager infrastructure in the production environment. Be sure to keep the POC environment so that you will have a test lab for testing future changes in the Configuration Manager environment or for testing your disaster-recovery plan.

 Real World Scenario

IMPLEMENTING A NEW CONFIGURATION MANAGER INFRASTRUCTURE

Sports Clothes United Inc. develops and sells sportswear to retailers and their own shops all over the world. The head office is located in San Francisco. The company is growing fast, and they are now using a third-party deployment tool for applications and operating systems.

You as a consultant or Configuration Manager administrator are asked to develop a real desktop management environment where user experience is the key to the success of the project and acceptance.

continues

continued

DEPLOYMENT INTELLIGENCE

As we said, Sports Clothes United is using a third-party deployment tool, and the assets and investments made in the years they were not using it are not compatible for migration. The company has four locations with offices and factories spread over the United States and China, and they are planning to open offices in Europe soon. The proposed Configuration Manager environment must be scalable and support future expansions.

Currently Sports Clothes United has major offices and factories in San Francisco, Houston, Shanghai, and Suzhou. The corporate systems are available from a datacenter in Washington, D.C. The local stores in the United States connect through an MPLS network to the nearest office. In China the offices and plants are connected through a 2-MB fiber connection. The United States and China are connected through a 10-MB fiber connection.

The following locations serve local or remote clients:

◆   Washington, D.C.: no clients connecting

◆   Houston: 1,000 clients connecting

◆   Shanghai: 3,000 clients connecting

◆   Suzhou: 100 clients connecting

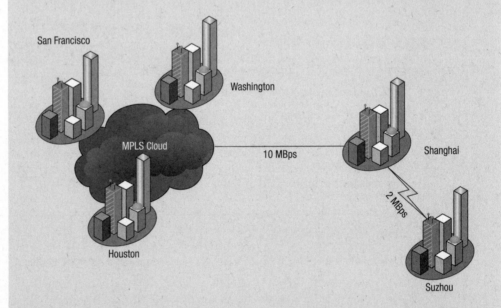

At this time Sports Clothes United isn't able to support their users at the level they want. The corporate IT department is professionalizing their processes, and they currently cannot service their internal customers according to the service-level agreement. To be able to do this they want to have the following features in their new Configuration Manager infrastructure:

◆ Software inventory

◆ Hardware inventory

◆ Software distribution to any (mobile) workplaces

◆ Zero-Touch operating system deployment of Windows 7 Multi-Language

◆ Wake On LAN

◆ User self-service portal to request or install applications

◆ Deployment of software updates

◆ Compliancy settings management to control the workplace

◆ Role-based administration for delegation of tasks

◆ Software metering to control licenses

◆ Remote administration to support internal customers

◆ Support for mobile device management

For software updates in the United States, a local software update point must be present in every major location.

One of the major requirements in managing applications is that the new environment must support people bringing their own devices to work. Supporting this new way of working is the key to success because it will promote internal customer satisfaction. The assets owned by Sports Clothes United must be able to receive a corporate image, and applications installed via Microsoft Installer Package (MSI) and assets that are brought in or are owned by the employees must be able to receive a virtualized version of that same application. Support for Virtual Desktop Infrastructure (VDI)– and Server Based Computing (SCB)–based environments is also a must-have.

Deployment Planning

With the information and requirements gathered during the deployment intelligence phase of your project, you now need to translate the information requirements to a design and a deployment plan.

One of the best practices is not to create a primary site that covers more than one continent. Since Sports Clothes United currently has locations in two continents and is planning one or more in Europe, you will need to place a primary site in North America and one in Asia.

Because of the fact that the company needs two or more primary sites, a Central Administration Site is needed. The datacenter in Washington, D.C. can be used for the CAS. No clients will connect to this site.

The locations in San Francisco and Shanghai are chosen as primary sites because of the size of the location in Shanghai and the availability of the corporate IT in San Francisco. The Houston site will be a secondary site because of the requirement that all sites in the United States need a local software update point. The site in Suzhou will receive a local distribution point with PXE, bandwidth control, and throttling enabled and configured.

continues

continued

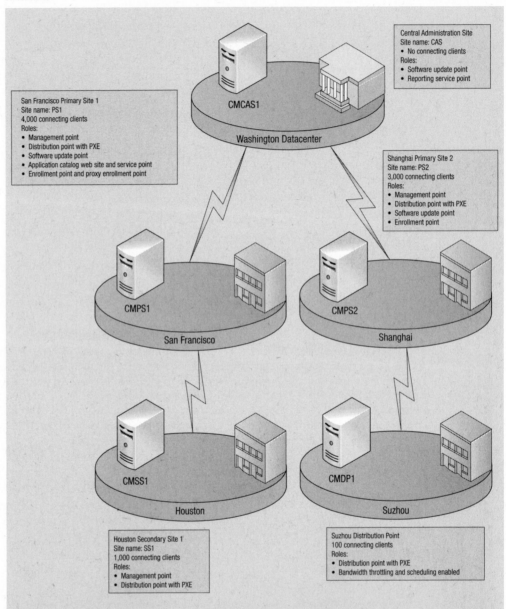

Central Administration Site
Site name: CAS
• No connecting clients
Roles:
• Software update point
• Reporting service point

San Francisco Primary Site 1
Site name: PS1
4,000 connecting clients
Roles:
• Management point
• Distribution point with PXE
• Software update point
• Application catalog web site and service point
• Enrollment point and proxy enrollment point

Shanghai Primary Site 2
Site name: PS2
3,000 connecting clients
Roles:
• Management point
• Distribution point with PXE
• Software update point
• Enrollment point

Houston Secondary Site 1
Site name: SS1
1,000 connecting clients
Roles:
• Management point
• Distribution point with PXE

Suzhou Distribution Point
100 connecting clients
Roles:
• Distribution point with PXE
• Bandwidth throttling and scheduling enabled

The basic proposed Configuration Manager hierarchy is shown here.

This Configuration Manager infrastructure can be a greenfield environment, and the transition will be done after a pilot phase has proven that the requirements have been met.

The Bottom Line

Plan and design a Central Administration Site.   One of the first questions you will ask yourself while starting to design and plan a new Configuration Manager hierarchy is "Do I need a Central Administration Site?" The answer to this question is essential for your final design.

Master It   Determine when a CAS is needed.

Plan and design an effective Configuration Manager infrastructure.   When planning and designing a new Configuration Manager infrastructure, it is important to plan your site placement appropriately. The design rules for primary sites have changed from how they were in Configuration Manager 2007.

Master It   Understand the reasons for not needing an additional primary site implementation.

Identify the enhancements to the distribution point site system role.   Distribution points in older versions were used to provide local points for accessing content and later also for App-V streaming. In Configuration Manager distribution points do a lot more.

Master It   Distribution points have been enhanced. What roles and components are merged with the new distribution point, and what's new?

Prepare your current Configuration Manager 2007 environment for migration to Configuration Manager.   An in-place upgrade of Configuration Manager 2007 to Configuration Manager is not supported. Configuration Manager has a migration feature within the feature set to enable side-by-side migration.

Master It   How can you as a Configuration Manager administrator or consultant prepare a current Configuration Manager 2007 environment for migration to Configuration Manager?

Chapter 3

Migrating to Configuration Manager

In the past, an upgrade or migration of Systems Management Server (SMS) 2003 to Configuration Manager 2007 was typically not an easy process. You could migrate the environment side-by-side manually or by using scripts, but at the end of the process you were not able to monitor the migration of the objects. In many cases, a new Configuration Manager 2007 infrastructure was created next to the old SMS infrastructure and the objects that were needed in the new Configuration Manager 2007 infrastructure were re-created by hand.

Configuration Manager 2012 introduced a migration feature that allowed an administrator to easily migrate objects from a Configuration Manager 2007 source hierarchy to a Configuration Manager 2012 hierarchy. Configuration Manager 2012 SP1 added the ability to migrate objects not only from a Configuration Manager 2007 source site but also from a Configuration Manager 2012 source site. This migration ability is carried forward in the current version of Configuration Manager.

The migration feature in Configuration Manager will assist you with:

◆ Migrating objects and clients from Configuration Manager 2007, Configuration Manager 2012, and Configuration Manager Current Branch

◆ Minimizing WAN impact

◆ Flattening the Configuration Manager infrastructure by reducing the number of primary sites

◆ Maximizing the reusability of 64-bit–capable hardware

◆ Sharing and reassigning your distribution points

In this chapter, you will learn to

◆ Determine what you are able to migrate with the migration feature

◆ Discover which migration approach is supported

◆ Ascertain what kind of interoperability is supported during the migration

Introducing Migration

The migration feature in Configuration Manager has specific terminology:

Client Information   Client information includes various items, such as the client's globally unique identifier (GUID), the inventory, and the client status information. Every Configuration Manager client has an ID that is unique in the Configuration Manager environment.

Client Migration   The process of upgrading the Configuration Manager client of the source hierarchy to the new Configuration Manager hierarchy is called *client migration*. This process can be initiated in different ways, but during the migration process the old Configuration Manager client will be uninstalled and the new Configuration Manager client will be installed.

Content   The content consists of the application and package binaries and files. The source files of the applications and packages should be accessible to the Configuration Manager site via a Universal Naming Convention (UNC).

Data Gathering   One of the first steps in the migration process is that the Configuration Manager hierarchy discovers all the objects in the source Configuration Manager environment. The source Configuration Manager environment can be a Configuration Manager 2007 SP2 site, a Configuration Manager 2012 site, or a Configuration Manager Current Branch site, and the data-gathering process is defined as part of the configuration of the migration feature.

Data gathering is an ongoing migration process and discovers all the objects or changes in the source Configuration Manager infrastructure. During the migration period, this process is scheduled by default to run every four hours.

Migration Jobs   Migration jobs are used to migrate specific objects from the source Configuration Manager hierarchy to the new infrastructure. Migration jobs can be scheduled for the future or started instantly.

Monitoring Migration   While migrating assets from the source Configuration Manager to the target Configuration Manager, it is useful to be able to monitor the migration process. Monitoring your migrations can be done from the Configuration Manager console, specifically in the Administration workspace under Migration ➤ Migration Jobs. You will be able to see which migrations completed, which failed, and which are in progress or need to be completed.

Objects   Objects subject to migration include packages, applications, software update deployments, driver packages, OS images, configuration items, and other objects within Configuration Manager.

Server Settings   Server settings are the site role settings and site properties in the Configuration Manager hierarchy.

Shared Distribution Points   Shared distribution points are distribution points that are active in the source Configuration Manager hierarchy. Enabling shared distribution points allows you to use the source Configuration Manager distribution points in the new Configuration Manager infrastructure. During the migration process, the upgraded Configuration Manager clients can receive the content from the shared distribution points. The shared distribution points are configured as read-only since they are still managed by the source Configuration Manager hierarchy. After the shared distribution points are reassigned to the target Configuration Manager hierarchy, they will be fully managed by the new hierarchy.

Source Hierarchy The source hierarchy is the Configuration Manager 2007 or Configuration Manager 2012 or later hierarchy from which you want to migrate objects to the new Configuration Manager infrastructure. The source hierarchy is the topmost site of the source Configuration Manager hierarchy.

Source Sites Source sites are the sites in the source hierarchy that hold Configuration Manager data that you want to migrate to the target Configuration Manager site. You need to configure account settings per source site to be able to connect to each source site.

Migration Functionality in Configuration Manager

Configuration Manager includes a migration feature that allows you to migrate your objects from a source Configuration Manager site to a target Configuration Manager site. Migrating objects is done via migration jobs, but first you need to designate a source hierarchy to be able to gather information from the source hierarchy and to create migration jobs.

Source Hierarchy

When migrating an existing Configuration Manager hierarchy to a new Configuration Manager hierarchy, you need to specify a source hierarchy. You must use the topmost Configuration Manager primary site server as the source hierarchy, as shown in Figure 3.1.

During the creation process, you supply a user account that has access to the SMS provider of the source site. This account needs read permission to all the objects in the source site—be sure to test the connection and the permissions. You can use the WBEMTEST utility to ensure that the account can successfully access the source hierarchy. For SQL access, you can use the same account, you can specify a different user, or you can use the local system account of the Configuration Manager central administration site (CAS) or standalone primary site to connect to the source Configuration Manager site database. The user account needs read and execute permissions.

After you specify the source hierarchy, the data-gathering process may take several hours, depending on how many objects are found in the source hierarchy.

Once the data-gathering process has finished discovering, it may have discovered other sites in the hierarchy. For those sites, you will need to supply credentials with the right permissions per discovered site to be able to access the objects in the discovered sites in the hierarchy.

Data-Gathering Process

The initial data-gathering process can take a while depending on your source hierarchy. It will gather all information about the configured site, the object data, and information about other child sites in the hierarchy. It will also set up the connection between the source Configuration Manager site and the target Configuration Manager site. The data-gathering process must complete before you can proceed with creating migration jobs or configuring credentials for other sites. Depending on the size of the source hierarchy, the data-gathering process may take a few minutes or it could take several hours to complete. The more objects you have in the source hierarchy, the longer the data-gathering process will take.

FIGURE 3.1
Specifying the
Configuration
Manager source
hierarchy

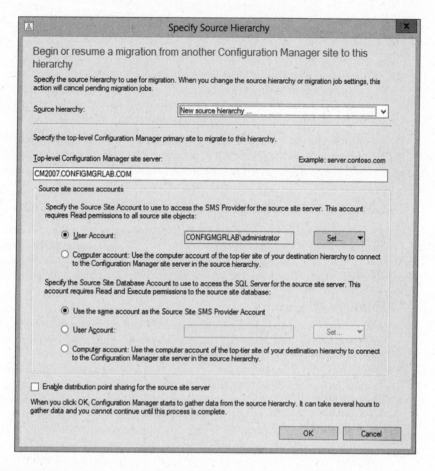

The data-gathering process runs every 4 hours by default, but you can change this interval to 1 hour, 2 hours, 4 hours, 8 hours, 12 hours, 18 hours, or 24 hours. The process runs periodically to keep the data accurate and current for the migration, and the gathered information is stored in the Configuration Manager database for reporting purposes. If the source hierarchy contains a large number of objects, you may consider setting the interval to 24 hours to ensure that the initial data-gathering process completes successfully.

The data-gathering process can be stopped by using the Stop Gathering Data action on the ribbon of the Configuration Manager console. While gathering data, you can check migmctrl.log located in the Logs folder in the Configuration Manager installation path to monitor the progress. The Logs folder can also be accessed via the %SMS_LOG_PATH% environment variable.

Migration Job Types

The migration of Configuration Manager objects from the source hierarchy is done by creating migration jobs. Configuration Manager supports three types of migration jobs, as explained in the following section.

Collection Migration

With the Collection Migration job type, you can migrate all of the objects that are related to collections, including all objects that are related to members of the collection. When you choose this option, you are able to exclude specific kinds of objects.

You are not able to migrate all Configuration Manager objects via the Collection Migration option since not all objects are related to collections. Collection Migration is available only when migrating from Configuration Manager 2007.

With Collection Migration, you can migrate the following related objects:

- Advertisements
- Software distribution packages
- Virtual application packages
- Software update deployments
- Software update deployment packages
- Operating system deployment boot images
- Operating system deployment images
- Operating system deployment operating system installers
- Task sequences
- Configuration baselines
- Configuration items

If you deselect one of these objects, then the object is placed in an exclusion list. The exclusion list can be managed from the administrative console and can be used as a reference when you want to migrate certain objects. Objects on the exclusion list are still available for migration in jobs that you create in the future. They will not be automatically selected when listed in the exclusion list.

Object Migration

With the object migration job type, you are able to migrate individual objects or object types that you select. This way, you can easily migrate your operating system deployment objects—for instance, to test the operating system deployment feature in Configuration Manager.

With object migration, you can migrate the following object types:

- Collections (from Configuration Manager 2007 only)
- Deployments (from Configuration Manager 2012 and later only)
  - Software distribution deployments
  - Task sequence deployments
  - Application deployments
  - Software update deployments
  - Software update list deployments
  - Baseline deployments

- ◆ Boundaries

- ◆ Boundary groups (from Configuration Manager 2012 and later only)

- ◆ Global conditions (from Configuration Manager 2012 and later only)

- ◆ Software distribution packages

- ◆ Applications (from Configuration Manager 2012 and later only)

- ◆ Virtual application packages (from Configuration Manager 2007 only)

- ◆ App-V virtual environments (from Configuration Manager 2012 and later only)

- ◆ Software updates

  - ◆ Deployments

  - ◆ Deployment packages

  - ◆ Deployment templates

  - ◆ Software update lists

  - ◆ Software update groups (from Configuration Manager and later only)

  - ◆ Automatic deployment rules (from Configuration Manager 2012 and later only)

- ◆ Operating system deployment

  - ◆ Boot images

  - ◆ Driver packages

  - ◆ Drivers

  - ◆ Images

  - ◆ Installer

  - ◆ Task sequences

- ◆ Settings management

  - ◆ Configuration baselines

  - ◆ Configuration items

- ◆ Asset Intelligence

  - ◆ Catalog

  - ◆ Hardware requirements

  - ◆ User-defined categorization list

- ◆ Software metering rules

- ◆ Saved searches (from Configuration Manager 2012 and later only)

OBJECTS MODIFIED AFTER MIGRATION

With the Objects Modified After Migration option, you can re-migrate objects from the source Configuration Manager hierarchy that have been migrated before and that have been changed in some way at the source hierarchy. The wizard shows you only the objects that have been changed.

You can use the Objects Modified After Migration option to migrate the following object types:

- Boundaries

- Software distribution packages

- Software update deployment packages

- Software update deployment templates

- Software update lists

- Operating system deployment boot images

- Operating system deployment driver packages

- Operating system deployment drivers

- Operating system deployment images

- Operating system deployment operating system installers

- Task sequences

- Configuration baselines

- Configuration items

- Asset Intelligence Catalogs

- Asset Intelligence hardware requirements

- Asset Intelligence software lists

- Software metering rules

To successfully re-migrate virtual application packages, you first need to delete any virtual application packages from the target Configuration Manager infrastructure.

These objects are all described in detail in the following sections.

COLLECTIONS

Collections can be migrated, but there are a couple of things that you need to take into account when migrating collections to the new Configuration Manager infrastructure.

In the new Configuration Manager infrastructure, subcollections and linked collections do not exist. Also collections with *both* users and devices are not supported and will not be migrated. In Figure 3.2, the Collections That Cannot Be Migrated dialog shows that mixed query collections, mixed collection hierarchies, or collections limited to multiple other collections in Configuration Manager 2007 cannot be migrated.

FIGURE 3.2
Collections that
cannot be migrated
are automatically
discovered.

Some rules regarding the migration of collections apply:

◆ If you build a hierarchy of collections in Configuration Manager 2007, the related empty collections are migrated to folders. This way, your collection organizational structure is preserved.

◆ Empty collections are migrated as folders (migrating only from Configuration Manager 2007).

◆ Direct membership collections are migrated as is and also when the direct membership is a Configuration Manager client in the source hierarchy that has not yet migrated to the new Configuration Manager site.

◆ Underlying collections with a mixed collection in the hierarchy cannot be migrated.

◆ To successfully migrate, a collection must contain either users/user groups or systems, but not both.

◆ Collections that are limited to multiple collections in Configuration Manager 2007 cannot be migrated.

◆ Collections that are limited to blocked collections in Configuration Manager cannot be migrated.

In Configuration Manager 2007 collections created in a central site were replicated down to the child sites. Collections created in a child site were replicated only within the site where the collection was created. This way, the collections were limited to the child site. In Configuration Manager 2012 and beyond, the collection definitions are globally replicated. The migration feature in Configuration Manager will assist you in preventing the unintentional increase of the scope of migrated collections during the migration process. A dialog like the one shown in Figure 3.3 will help you limit the collection scope.

FIGURE 3.3
Limit collections
for which the scope
will possibly be
increased.

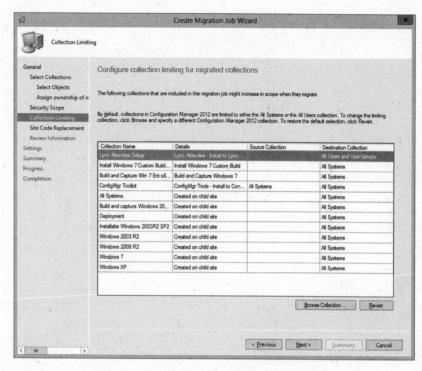

If you used site codes in the collection queries at the source Configuration Manager hierarchy, you will be prompted to replace the site code during the migration of the collections. It is mandatory for the new Configuration Manager hierarchy to use the new site codes. In Figure 3.4, you can see that site code PS7 is replaced with PS1. With the pull-down option you can choose whatever site code you want to replace.

With the collection migration job type, you will be assisted with the migration of the collections and the migration of the related Configuration Manager objects from the source hierarchy. The feature will preserve customer investments in collections and advertisements.

ADVERTISEMENTS AND DEPLOYMENTS

Advertisements are migrated from Configuration Manager 2007 and converted into deployments and the settings are preserved. During the collection migration job, you can choose to automatically enable the deployment after the migration but by default the deployment is not enabled. Advertisements from Configuration Manager 2007 are migrated only if they are associated with a collection migration job and the Configuration Manager administrator has chosen to migrate all the depended objects in addition to the collection itself. Deployments already deployed in Configuration Manager are migrated to the target Configuration Manager environment.

When an advertisement is migrated and converted, the deployment will *not* deploy the software again to computers or users where the software was already deployed in the source site. The reason for that is that the package IDs of the software packages and advertisements are preserved as part of the migration to the target Configuration Manager hierarchy. Since clients retain execution history, and it is tracked by the package ID, clients will not rerun a migrated package deployment after they have been migrated to the new hierarchy.

FIGURE 3.4
Replacing the
discovered
source site
code with the
new site code

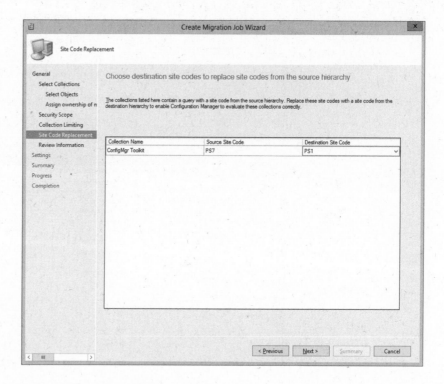

BOUNDARIES AND BOUNDARY GROUPS

While you are migrating boundaries from Configuration Manager 2007, boundary groups are automatically created by the migration process and are enabled only for content lookup. This way, you will avoid boundary overlap in Active Directory, and it will prevent new Configuration Manager clients from getting assigned to the new Configuration Manager environment unexpectedly. When migrating from a Configuration Manager 2012 or later source hierarchy, you are able to migrate both the available boundaries and boundary groups.

When Distribution Point Sharing is enabled, boundaries associated with the distribution points in the source Configuration Manager hierarchy are migrated automatically.

GLOBAL CONDITIONS

Global conditions are available only in Configuration Manager 2012 and later—they do not exist in Configuration Manager 2007. Custom global conditions that you have created are the only global conditions that can be migrated from the source Configuration Manager hierarchy to the target Configuration Manager hierarchy.

SOFTWARE DISTRIBUTION PACKAGES

During the migration from Configuration Manager 2007, software distribution packages are not converted to the new application model; they are migrated as packages. The tool is no longer being updated or supported, but depending on your migration scenario, you may be able to use the Microsoft System Center Package Conversion Manager tool to convert these packages to the application model. Refer to this site for further information on the Package Conversion Manager tool: https://www.microsoft.com/en-us/download/details.aspx?id=34605.

Also note that the CAS or primary site in a standalone scenario always needs access to the Configuration Manager UNC package source path to be able to distribute and deploy the package. For this reason, you will need to replace any local package source paths in Configuration Manager 2007 with UNC paths.

APPLICATIONS

Applications created in Configuration Manager are migrated with their deployment types, requirement rules, detection methods, deployments, dependencies, and all other configured settings. Like all objects with content, the source path needs to be a UNC path.

VIRTUAL APPLICATION PACKAGES

Virtual application packages are converted to the new application model. After the migration of the packages, you will need to create a deployment. In Chapter 7, "Application Deployment," you'll learn how to create deployments for your virtual applications.

To be able to use virtual applications in Configuration Manager, you need to upgrade the App-V client to at least version 4.6 SP1 with the hotfix that is described in Knowledge Base article 2645225: https://support.microsoft.com/en-us/kb/2645225.

The App-V client 4.6 SP2 and SP3 are supported as well; however, App-V 5 and App-V 5.0 SP1, SP2 and App-V 5.1 are supported only in Configuration Manager 2012 SP1 and later.

Also note that when Distribution Point Sharing is enabled the streaming of App-V packages is not supported.

APP-V VIRTUAL ENVIRONMENTS

App-V 5 has been supported since Configuration Manager 2012 SP1. A feature that comes with this support is the ability to create an App-V virtual environment, which creates a connection between two separate App-V applications. You can migrate those virtual environments to another Configuration Manager hierarchy.

SOFTWARE UPDATES

Software updates can be migrated with the three different migration jobs in Configuration Manager. You must be sure that all the updates that are available within the source Configuration Manager site are also available in the target Configuration Manager site and ensure that the software update point is configured. Procedures that use the WSUSUTIL utility to synchronize the software update data between Configuration Manager sites are documented on various blogs and websites. Microsoft does not support using WSUSUTIL to synchronize data between a source and a destination Configuration Manager hierarchy. Before migrating the software update objects you should ensure that the classifications, products, and languages that are configured on the software update point in the target hierarchy match those that were configured in the source hierarchy. Failure to do so may cause the migration of the software update objects to fail.

For the conversion of the Software Update objects, the following rules apply:

◆ Update lists are converted to update groups.

◆ Software update deployments are migrated to deployments and update groups.

◆ While migrating from Configuration Manager 2012 or later, software update groups can also be migrated.

◆ Automatic deployment rules can be migrated from a Configuration Manager 2012 or later site.

OPERATING SYSTEM DEPLOYMENT

The following operating system deployment–related objects can be migrated to Configuration Manager:

◆ Boot images

◆ Driver packages

◆ Drivers

◆ Images

◆ OS installers

◆ Task sequences

Note that not all operating system deployment–related objects are supported for migration to Configuration Manager:

◆ Migration of Microsoft Deployment Toolkit task sequences is not supported.

◆ The default Configuration Manager 2007 boot images are not migrated because the new Windows Assessment and Deployment Kit (ADK) that is supported in Configuration Manager supplies the version-matched boot images.

CUSTOMIZED BOOT IMAGES

Boot images that have been customized cannot be migrated. The migration process will replace the customizations made in the boot image with the default settings from the Configuration Manager boot images. A new boot image ID is assigned to each boot image. The newly created boot image can be accessed only from Configuration Manager distribution points.

When migrating a boot image that has drivers embedded, be sure that the drivers remain available from the Configuration Manager 2007 source location so that they can accessed by the Configuration Manager from the specified source location.

Configuration Manager removes all of the references to operating system client packages from the migrated task sequences. After the migration of the task sequence is finished, you can edit them in the Configuration Manager console to restore references to the local client installation packages in the target Configuration Manager hierarchy.

When migrating the operating system deployment functionality, you need to be sure that the dependent Configuration Manager site roles are installed and configured. The state migration point needs to be configured if it will be used, and the distribution points should have PXE support enabled if PXE will be used. You can read more about configuring operating system deployment in Chapter 9, "Operating System Deployment."

SETTINGS MANAGEMENT

Configuration baselines and configuration items created by you as an administrator or created by an independent software vendor are supported for migration by the migration feature of Configuration Manager.

When you need to re-migrate configuration items or baselines, any changes to the objects will be added as revisions of the objects.

Existing configuration packs can also be added to Configuration Manager through the import feature. If the source was a Configuration Manager 2007 site, the packs will be converted to the schema used in Configuration Manager. Keep in mind the following rules when migrating configuration baselines and configuration items:

♦ When migrating a configuration baseline, its assignment will not be migrated at the same time. You must migrate the configuration baseline assignment separately by using the collection migration job type.

♦ Configuration items in Configuration Manager 2007 might have rules that are not supported by Configuration Manager. When you migrate configuration items that have unsupported rule operators, Configuration Manager will convert them to equivalent values.

♦ If the objects and settings of an imported configuration item are not visible in the Configuration Manager 2007 console, also known as incomplete or uninterpreted configuration items, they are not supported by Configuration Manager. As a result, you will not be able to migrate these configuration items.

ASSET INTELLIGENCE CUSTOMIZATIONS

You can migrate Asset Intelligence customizations made for classifications, labels, families, and hardware requirements to Configuration Manager. When migrating Asset Intelligence customizations, always assign the Configuration Manager site that is the closest to the Configuration Manager 2007 site that owns the Asset Intelligence content because of WAN traffic that can occur during the migration. Gathered Asset Intelligence data is not migrated to Configuration Manager.

SOFTWARE METERING RULES

Software metering rules can be migrated and all rules that are available in the source Configuration Manager hierarchy can be migrated. After the migration, all of the migrated software metering rules are disabled by default.

SAVED SEARCHES

In the Configuration Manager administrative console, saved searches can be migrated.

SEARCH AND ADMINISTRATIVE FOLDERS

Administrator-created folders for administrative duties are migrated if chosen while migrating collections or objects. Be sure to enable the Transfer The Organizational Folder Structure For Objects From The Source Hierarchy To The Destination Hierarchy option when migrating objects from Configuration Manager 2007 to Configuration Manager. You can set this option in the process of creating a migration job and scheduling when the migration job is to run.

REPORTS

When you want to migrate reports from Configuration Manager 2007, use SQL Reporting Services to export custom reports as RDL files and then import them into the new Configuration Manager site. The Configuration Manager migration feature does not support migrating reports. Note that you will also need to update the data source for the reports once they have been imported.

Objects Not Supported for Migration

Not all objects can be migrated by the migration feature in Configuration Manager. You can create workarounds for some objects, but for others you cannot. Table 3.1 shows whether workarounds are available for objects that cannot be migrated

TABLE 3.1: Workarounds for objects that cannot be migrated

OBJECT	WORKAROUND
Queries	Export the queries in Configuration Manager to a MOF file and import the MOF file into Configuration Manager.
Security rights for the site and objects	No workaround available.
Configuration Manager 2007 reports from SQL Server Reporting Services	Export your reports from SQL Server Reporting Services and import them into the SQL Server Reporting Services servicing the Configuration Manager site.
Configuration Manager 2007 web reports	No workaround available.
Client inventory and history data	No workaround available.
AMT client provisioning information	No workaround available.
Files in the client cache	No workaround available.

PRESERVING YOUR CUSTOM *SMS_DEF.MOF* INVESTMENTS

The migration of hardware inventory from a Configuration Manager 2007 site is not supported, but you can import your custom SMS_DEF.MOF files into the new Configuration Manager infrastructure. Analyze and test the custom MOF edits before importing them into the production environment and ensure that there are no conflicting data types. You will need to carefully select only those classes that you want to migrate because many of the objects from the source hierarchy might already be defined at the target Configuration Manager hierarchy.

Distribution Point Sharing

In the process of migrating your Configuration Manager objects and clients in your source hierarchy to Configuration Manager, you can use distribution point sharing. This feature allows Configuration Manager clients to retrieve content for migrated packages that are hosted on the Configuration Manager distribution points in the source hierarchy. Distribution point sharing is configured on a site-by-site basis. You enable this option when configuring the source hierarchy by selecting the Enable Distribution-Point Sharing For This Source Site option or by configuring the source hierarchy later by enabling the Configure option in the ribbon for the source hierarchy object.

After the data-gathering process is finished, you will see the distribution points, including branch distribution points and distribution point shares. Boot images and App-V applications are not supported on shared distribution points. You will need to migrate those objects in the standard manner and make them available on a Configuration Manager distribution point in the target hierarchy. As mentioned earlier, associated boundaries are migrated when you enable distribution point sharing.

A shared distribution point can be reassigned to another site without the need to reinstall the distribution point and redistribute the content.

INTEROPERABILITY WITH CONFIGURATION MANAGER 2007

The migration feature in Configuration Manager gives you a level of interoperability while migrating a Configuration Manager 2007 infrastructure.

Once you specify a source hierarchy for the new Configuration Manager hierarchy, the data-gathering process will run every four hours by default to collect the information about the source hierarchy. During the migration period, the source hierarchy is configured in the target Configuration Manager site and the two Configuration Manager environments are connected to each other, providing a sort of interoperability.

Re-migrate Updated Objects   The migration process doesn't move objects from the source Configuration Manager environment but instead copies and, if necessary, converts the objects to Configuration Manager standards. The original objects remain in the source Configuration Manager site and can still be used and changed. If a change is made to an original object in the source hierarchy, the data-gathering process will detect the change and you can re-migrate the updated object.

Distribution Point Sharing   Enabling distribution point sharing allows you to share a distribution point that is available in a Configuration Manager 2007 site with Configuration Manager. The migrated or new Configuration Manager clients are able to retrieve content from a shared distribution point.

Planning a Migration

This section describes the steps required to prepare the migration from a source Configuration Manager hierarchy to a target Configuration Manager hierarchy. The newly designed Configuration Manager infrastructure must be in place. Consult Chapter 4, "Installation and Site Role Configuration," for information on how to install and configure the Configuration Manager environment that you designed in Chapter 2, "Planning a Configuration Manager Infrastructure."

As you define your project phases and the steps you need to take to migrate to the new Configuration Manager infrastructure, you need to plan your migration.

Preparing Your Migration

Regardless of when you want to migrate to Configuration Manager, you should prepare your source Configuration Manager infrastructure in advance to allow a smooth migration, as follows:

◆ Be sure that your new Configuration Manager infrastructure is in place and configured correctly.

◆ If you will be migrating from Configuration Manager 2007, verify it is at least running Configuration Manager 2007 Service Pack 2.

◆ Use UNC paths for the package source path and avoid using local paths. A distributed file share may be helpful while migrating objects from one site to another site.

◆ Avoid mixing users and devices in collection definitions since this is no longer supported in Configuration Manager

◆ Avoid using collections with multiple query rules that limit different collections.

◆ Use different site codes in the new Configuration Manager than in the source Configuration Manager infrastructure; the site codes must be unique.

Planning Your Migration Strategy

A documented and well-thought-out plan may be very useful when performing a Configuration Manager migration. Your project should be based on a solid foundation or methodology such as the Microsoft Operations Framework (MOF).

A thorough project plan should include some or all of the following phases as well as tasks for each phase:

Phase 1: Define and capture phase

◆ Create a project plan.

◆ Document the current environment.

◆ Conduct an initial risk review.

◆ Create business test cases.

◆ Finalize the business proposal.

Phase 2: Build phase

- Conduct a planning workshop.
- Install a proof-of-concept lab.
- Conduct server and workstation testing.
- Procure hardware.

Phase 3: Test phase (pilot)

- Draft a communication plan for the following groups:
    - Executive/management
    - Project team
    - Site (users)
- Build and deploy hardware and software.
- Implement change control for the pilot phase.
- Perform a pilot with the new environment.

Phase 4: Production deployment phase

- Implement change control for the production development phase.
- Deploy your new environment.

Effective communication is essential during the migration process. Ensure that users understand the changes that are taking place in the environment and also ensure that the additional benefits that will be delivered have been communicated. Use the project to highlight the capabilities of Configuration Manager as well as illustrate the business value and insight that Configuration Manager will provide. Don't be afraid to highlight the hard work of the migration team and the value that a project of this magnitude brings to the business.

Performing the Migration

Two main upgrade strategies are available to deploy Configuration Manager:

Side-by-Side Migration   A side-by-side migration creates a new Configuration Manager infrastructure that runs alongside the current Configuration Manager infrastructure. Using the migration feature, the administrator is able to stagger the migration of the clients and objects over a period of time if needed.

Wipe and Load   The wipe-and-load approach may be useful if the end goal is to start over with a new hierarchy and there is no need to migrate data from the old Configuration Manager hierarchy.

In this section, you will learn more about these two approaches.

Using the Side-by-Side Migration Strategy

In a side-by-side migration, an existing Configuration Manager implementation can function while client systems are gradually moved from the source hierarchy to the new hierarchy. This enables you to do the following:

◆ Use new server hardware

◆ Use current versions of the Windows Server operating system, SQL Server, and so forth.

◆ Modify or redesign your Configuration Manager hierarchy.

◆ Migrate objects and clients and retain historical client data.

The migration process may take some time, depending on the complexity of the environment and the number of objects that will be migrated.

UNDERSTANDING THE MIGRATION PROCESS

After preparing the Configuration Manager infrastructure, as described in the "Planning a Migration" section earlier in this chapter, you can proceed with the migration process. The migration process has several steps, depending on your source infrastructure:

Configure the Migration Feature   You configure the migration feature by creating a source hierarchy in the Configuration Manager hierarchy. You need to connect the Configuration Manager infrastructure to the topmost site of the source Configuration Manager infrastructure.

You must also configure the gathering process. You need to configure the schedule and supply administrative access for the gathering process.

Once the gathering process is complete and other source sites have been discovered, you must configure credentials for each of the additional source sites.

Share Distribution Points   Sharing distribution points allows you to postpone their migration. It also reduces network traffic when you enable this feature on remote locations. Shared distribution points can be reassigned to the target Configuration Manager site.

Create Migration Jobs   Migration jobs are used to migrate objects from the source hierarchy to the target hierarchy. You can create one or more jobs, depending on your source infrastructure.

When creating migration jobs, you can choose to exclude objects, assign content ownership, set the security scope, limit the collections, and change site codes in your query definitions.

The migration job does not migrate the actual content of your Configuration Manager objects. Configuration Manager will retrieve the content from the original source file location.

Migrating content can be started instantly but can also be scheduled to start later. When using a distributed file share as a content source, you do not need to migrate the content source location.

Monitor Migration Jobs   In the process of migrating your Configuration Manager objects to the new hierarchy, you should actively monitor the migration. When you select the migration job, you can monitor the migration by selecting objects in the job. Besides the in-console monitoring, Configuration Manager records migration actions in the `migmctrl.log` file located in the Logs (%SMS_LOG_PATH%) folder in the Configuration Manager installation path.

If a migration job fails and other jobs are still running, you should review the details in the `migmctrl.log` file as soon as possible. Migration actions are continually added to the file and overwrite the old details.

In the Configuration Manager console, you are able to monitor the migration by looking at the Migration dashboard, shown in Figure 3.5.

FIGURE 3.5
The Migration dashboard

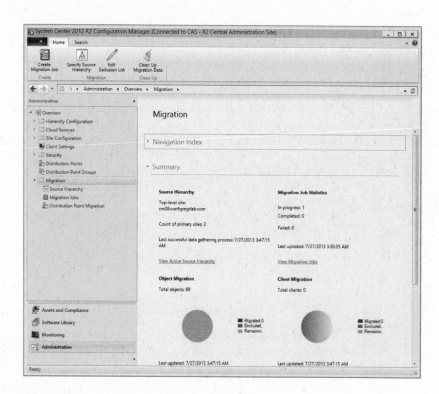

Report Migration Results   With the reporting feature within Configuration Manager, you can report information about the migration of the Configuration Manager objects to the target site. The following reports are available in the Migration category:

◆   Clients in Exclusion List

◆   Dependency on a Configuration Manager Collection

◆   Migration Job Properties

◆   Migration Jobs

◆   Objects That Failed to Migrate

You will find more information about reporting in Chapter 12, "Reporting."

Reassign Distribution Points   When upgrading or reassigning distribution points, you want to avoid having a large amount of data flowing through the WAN. For this reason, you can migrate distribution points in two ways: automatic and manual. Configuration Manager supports upgrading or reassigning the following distribution points:

◆   Branch distribution point

◆   Server share distribution point

◆   Standard distribution point

When you choose automatic migration, you need to enable distribution point sharing and reassign the distribution point from the Configuration Manager console. During the migration process, the distribution point is removed from the source database and the new distribution point is installed on the server. If you are migrating from Configuration Manager 2007, the content of the distribution point is copied to the new content library of Configuration Manager after the installation. Verify that these servers have adequate disk space available. During the upgrade process, a copy of the content in the distribution package share will be created and converted to the Configuration Manager content library. As a best practice, the disk that is being used for the package share should have at least double the size of the package share in order to accommodate the conversion. If the site server is a Configuration Manager 2007 secondary site, the secondary site will be automatically uninstalled before the Configuration Manager distribution point is installed. The migration job will pause until the next data-gathering job to check if the secondary site is completely uninstalled.

One distribution point upgrade migration job is performed at a time, and other subsequent jobs are queued.

After upgrading the Configuration Manager 2007 distribution point, you will need to manually delete the old content after verifying that deployments are working properly.

Upgrade Configuration Manager 2007 Secondary Sites   Upgrading Configuration Manager 2007 secondary sites is possible only by uninstalling the secondary site role and then installing the new secondary site from the new Configuration Manager hierarchy.

Migrate Clients   The migration of the clients is done using the same methods as for deploying a new Configuration Manager client. The first step in the migration is to uninstall the old Configuration Manager client and install the Configuration Manager client. During this process, the Configuration Manager data—for instance, advertisement history and the GUID of the client—is preserved.

Upgrade the Administrative Console   The administrative console can be installed on Windows servers and workstations. To manage the new Configuration Manager hierarchy, you will need to ensure you have the correct console version installed.

Perform Post-Migration Tasks   After migrating all the old Configuration Manager content, you must perform post-migration tasks. The first task is to stop the data-gathering process, clean up the migration data, and remove the source hierarchy. Then once you have verified that all of the required data has been migrated, you can remove the old Configuration Manager infrastructure from your environment.

The step-by-step details of these procedures are provided in the following sections.

Configuring the Migration Feature

Configuring the migration feature can be done with the following steps. First, you will need to specify the source hierarchy:

1. In the Configuration Manager console choose the Administration workspace.

2. Expand Overview ➢ Migration in the Administration workspace, and choose Source Hierarchy.

3. Choose the Home tab of the ribbon and select Specify Source Hierarchy.

4. In the Specify Migration Source screen, select New Source Hierarchy At The Source Hierarchy.

5. Specify the top-level Configuration Manager site server of your source Configuration Manager hierarchy by filling in the fully qualified domain name (FQDN) of the server.

6. Specify the site access account for the SMS provider of the source site server. Verify the connection of an existing or new account before submitting.

   The account needs read permissions to all source site objects.

7. Specify the site access account for the SQL server of the source site server.

   The Windows user account needs read and execute permissions to the site database. This can be the same account that has access to the SMS provider.

8. If you want to share the distribution points in the source hierarchy, enable the option Enable Distribution Point Sharing For The Source Site Server.

9. Click OK to save the configuration and to start the data-gathering process. You'll see the Data Gathering Status dialog, as shown in Figure 3.6.

FIGURE 3.6
The first data-gathering process is complete.

After the first data-gathering process has finished, all other primary sites in the hierarchy are discovered. In Figure 3.7 you see another primary site that has been discovered, but the data-gathering process has not run yet. The next step is to configure the credentials for the Configuration Manager source site to be able to gather the data.

FIGURE 3.7
Additional sources
site discovered
during the data-
gathering process

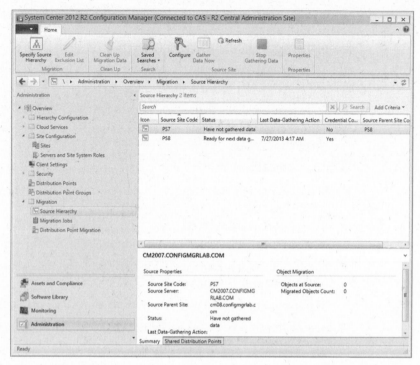

FIGURE 3.7
Additional sources
site discovered
during the data-
gathering process

1. In the Configuration Manager console, choose the Administration workspace.

2. Expand Overview ➤ Migration in the Administration workspace, and choose Source Hierarchy.

3. Select the site with the status Have Not Gathered Data.

4. On the Home tab of the ribbon, select Configure in the Source Site section.

5. Specify the site access account for the SMS provider of the source site server.

   The account needs read permissions to all source site objects.

6. Specify the site access account for the SQL server of the source site server.

   The Windows user account needs read and execute permissions to the site database. This can be the same account as the account that has access to the SMS provider.

7. Optionally, if you want to share the distribution points in the source hierarchy, select the option Enable Distribution Point Sharing For The Source Site Server.

8. Click OK to save the configuration and to start the data-gathering process.

   After configuring the credentials for the additional sites, the gathering process will start to gather all the objects in the Configuration Manager source site.

You can also configure the source hierarchy via native Configuration Manager PowerShell support:

1. In the Configuration Manager console, access the PowerShell console via the blue pull-down menu, and select Connect Via Windows PowerShell.

2. Type in the following PowerShell command; in this example, the topmost primary site server is called cm08.configmgrlab.com and the user that is used to connect to the SQL and SMSProvider is the administrator account.

```
Set-CMMigrationSource -SourceSiteServerName "cm08.configmgrlab.com"
-SmsProviderAccount "configmgrlab\administrator" -SqlServerAccount
"configmgrlab\administrator" -EnableDistributionPointSharing $True
```

3. After the command has completed, you will see that the sites have been discovered and that the first gathering process has been started.

ENABLING DISTRIBUTION POINT SHARING

The distribution points from a selected Configuration Manager site can be shared on a per-site basis in the Configuration Manager console:

1. In the Configuration Manager console, open the Administration workspace.

2. Expand Overview ➤ Migration in the Administration workspace, and select Source Hierarchy.

3. Select the site for which you want to enable distribution point sharing.

4. Select the Home tab of the ribbon, and choose Configure.

5. In the Source Site Credentials dialog box choose the Enable Distribution-Point Sharing For This Source Site option.

6. Click OK.

After enabling distribution point sharing, the gathering process will start to gather all the objects and distribution point data in the Configuration Manager source site. Once the site servers are protected, the boundaries related to the site servers of the distribution points are migrated also.

CREATING MIGRATION JOBS

As mentioned earlier, you can create three different migration jobs. Depending on your purpose, you need to use one of the following three procedures. The three different migration jobs are designed to provide support for migrating collections with all the related objects and to provide support for migrating one or more objects or objects that are changed after being migrated.

Creating a Collection Migration Job

You can use a collection migration job to migrate the collections with objects that are associated with the specific collections. This job is available only when migrating from Configuration Manager 2007 to Configuration Manager 2012 or later. To create a collection migration job, follow these steps:

1. In the Configuration Manager console, select the Administration workspace.

2. Expand Overview ➤ Migration in the Administration workspace, and choose Migration Jobs.

3. Select the Home tab of the ribbon, and choose Create Migration Job.

4. Give the migration job a name and description.

5. Select Collection Migration as the job type, and click Next.

6. Select the collections that you want to migrate, as shown in Figure 3.8, and select Migrate Objects That Are Associated With The Specified Collections.

   Another option instead of "pick and choose" is to search for the collection(s) that you want to migrate. This is done by clicking the Search button and searching for the collection based on the collection name, site code, collection ID, or status. You can review the collections that cannot be migrated by clicking the View Collections That Cannot Migrate button, also shown in Figure 3.8.

7. After searching or selecting the collections, click Next.

8. Review the objects that will be migrated, make changes if necessary, and click Next.

9. Select the destination site that will be the owner of the objects, and click Next.

10. Configure the security scope, and click Next.

11. Limit the collections if needed, and click Next.

FIGURE 3.8
Selecting the collections that need to be migrated

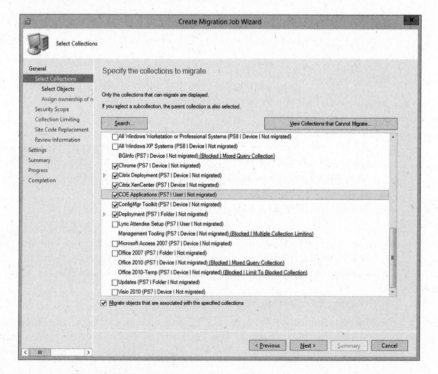

12. Replace the site code, and click Next.

13. Review the migration job information, optionally save it to a file, and click Next.

14. Select the schedule, configure the conflict handling and additional settings for the migration job, and click Next.

15. Confirm the settings on the Summary screen, and click Next.

16. Click Close to monitor the migration of the collections and the related objects.

Creating an Object Migration Job

Object migration jobs are used for migrating one or more Configuration Manager objects to Configuration Manager 2012 or later. This method is supported for both Configuration Manager 2007 and Configuration Manager 2012 and later source hierarchies. To create an object migration job, perform the following steps:

1. In the Configuration Manager console, select the Administration workspace.

2. Expand Overview ➢ Migration in the Administration workspace, and choose Migration Jobs.

3. Select the Home tab of the ribbon, and choose Create Migration Job.

4. Give the migration job a name and description.

5. Select Object Migration as the job type, and click Next.

6. Select the objects that you want to migrate, as shown in Figure 3.9.

FIGURE 3.9
Select the objects that need to be migrated.

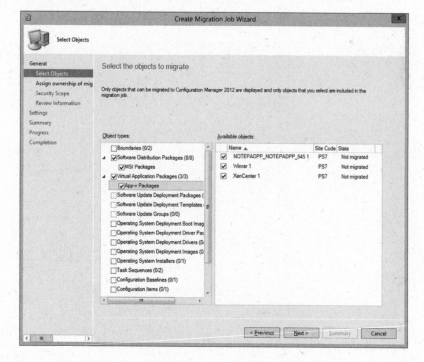

7. Click Next.

8. Select the destination site that is going to be the owner of the objects, and click Next.

9. Configure the security scope, and click Next.

10. Review the migration job information, optionally save it to a file, and click Next.

11. Select the schedule, configure the conflict handling and additional settings for the migration job, and click Next.

12. Confirm the settings on the Summary screen, and click Next.

13. Click Close to monitor the migration of the objects.

Creating an Object Modified after Migration Job

During a lengthy migration process, objects in the source Configuration Manager infrastructure may change. The migration feature allows you to re-migrate objects that have been modified. Follow these steps to create an Object Modified After Migration job:

1. In the Configuration Manager console, open the Administration workspace.

2. Expand Overview ➢ Migration in the Administration workspace, and choose Migration Jobs.

3. Select the Home tab of the ribbon, and choose Create Migration Job.

4. Give the migration job a name and description.

5. Select Object Modified After Migration as the job type, and click Next.

6. Select the objects that you want to re-migrate, as shown in Figure 3.10, and click Next.

FIGURE 3.10
Select the changed objects that need to be re-migrated.

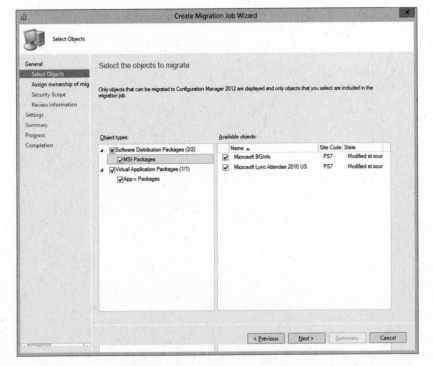

7. Select the destination site that will be the owner of the objects, and click Next.

8. Configure the security scope, and click Next.

9. Review the migration job information, optionally save it to a file, and click Next.

10. Select the schedule, and click Next.

11. Confirm the settings on the Summary screen, and click Next.

12. Click Close to monitor the migration of the changed objects.

UPGRADING DISTRIBUTION POINTS

Migrating distribution points can be done in two ways:

◆ Automatically

◆ Manually

The procedures for both options are described in the following sections.

Migrating Distribution Points Automatically

Migrating a distribution point can be done automatically by removing the distribution point from the source Configuration Manager site and adding it to the target site. You must remove the other roles such as software update points, PXE service points, or state migration points before proceeding. To be able to migrate the distribution point, you must enable the site for distribution point sharing.

You can upgrade the distribution point by following this procedure:

1. In the Configuration Manager console, choose the Administration workspace.

2. Expand Overview ➤ Migration in the Administration workspace, and choose Source Hierarchy.

3. Select the source site and choose the Shared Distribution Points tab in the information pane at the bottom of the console.

4. Select the Configuration Manager distribution point that you want to migrate or reassign to the new Configuration Manager site.

5. Select the Distribution Point tab of the ribbon, check to see if the distribution point is eligible for reassignment, and choose Reassign Distribution Point. If the distribution point is not eligible for reassignment, site roles other than those described earlier are active on the selected distribution point. In some cases, the distribution point will not be eligible because the IIS prerequisites are missing or not installed on the distribution point or the distribution point has insufficient disk space.

6. In the Reassign Shared Distribution Point Wizard, choose the site code where the distribution point must connect after upgrading. At this point, if the distribution point must be available from the Internet, configure it by filling in the FQDN for the site system for use on the Internet. Click Next.

7. Configure the distribution point settings by choosing whether the setup must install and configure IIS, if it is required, and configure whether the distribution point can handle prestaged content. Click Next.

8. Configure the drive settings for the distribution point that will be upgraded, and click Next.

9. If you want to use the pull distribution point method to pull the content from another distribution point, you can enable this option. Otherwise, click Next.

10. Configure PXE support if needed, and click Next to configure content validation for this distribution point. Click Next to proceed.

11. Configure boundary group membership for the new Configuration Manager distribution point, and click Next.

12. Be sure you have enough free space to proceed with the upgrade. Check to see if the required space meets the available space on your configured drives, as shown in Figure 3.11. When you are migrating a distribution point, the content located at the distribution point is copied and converted to the new content library. Click Next if you are sure enough space is available.

FIGURE 3.11
Be sure you have enough disk space for converting packages to the new content library.

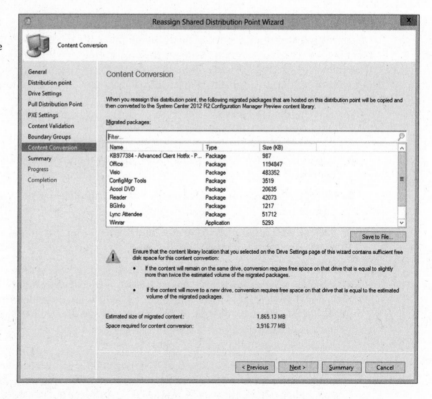

13. Review the Summary screen, and click Next to process the upgrade.

You can monitor the migration process in the `migmctrl.log` file in the Logs (%SMS_LOG_PATH%) folder in the Configuration Manager installation folder and in the Application log in the event viewer on the target server. Also, the target server contains a folder called `..\SMS_DP$\SMS\Logs\` and a file called `SMSDPPROV.LOG` where you can find possible errors in the installation of the distribution point. You can also view the status in the Distribution Point Migration node, as shown in Figure 3.12. Refreshing the screen will update the status of the upgrade.

FIGURE 3.12
Monitor the
upgrade status.

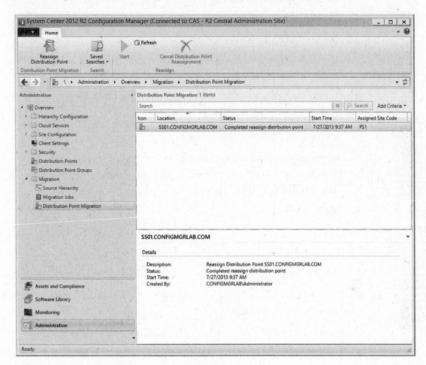

The content is copied and converted to the new content library with single-instance storage. Be sure to delete the old content from the old distribution point since the old content is not removed automatically.

Refer to Chapter 4 for more in-depth information about installing and configuring distribution points.

Migrating Distribution Points Manually

The manual migration of a Configuration Manager 2007 distribution point is done in two general steps:

1. Uninstalling the current distribution point from the Configuration Manager 2007 environment

2. Installing the distribution point with prestaged content in the new Configuration Manager environment

This scenario can be used for all distribution points, including branch distribution points, distribution point shares, and normal distribution points. For in-depth distribution point installation and configuration instructions, please consult Chapter 4.

To uninstall a distribution point from Configuration Manager 2007, follow these steps:

1. In the Configuration Manager 2007 console, open the site under Site Database\Site Management*<the site>*\Site Settings, expand Site Systems, and select the site system with the distribution point.

2. Select ConfigMgr distribution point or distribution point share, and click Delete in the Actions area of the console.

To uninstall a distribution point from Configuration Manager 2012 or later, follow these steps:

1. In the Configuration Manager console, open the Administration workspace.

2. Expand Overview ➤ Site Configuration in the Administration workspace, and choose Servers And Site System Roles.

3. Select the site server with the distribution point that you want to remove, select the Distribution Point role in the Site System Roles pane, and choose Remove Role in the Site Role tab of the ribbon.

4. Click Yes to remove the distribution point.

To install a distribution point with prestaged content in Configuration Manager, perform the following procedure:

1. In the Configuration Manager console, open the Administration workspace.

2. Expand Overview ➤ Site Configuration in the Administration workspace, and choose Servers And Site System Roles.

3. Select the Home tab of the ribbon, and choose Create Site System Server.

4. Click Browse, and search for the server on which you want to install the distribution point.

5. Select the site code in which you want to install the site server.

6. Supply, if needed, the FQDN for use on the Internet.

7. If the server is in a different Active Directory forest, select Require The Site Server To Initiate Connections To This System.

8. Supply the site system installation account, and click Next.

9. Configure the Proxy settings, and click Next.

10. Select the Distribution Point option, and click Next.

11. Select Install And Configure IIS If Required By Configuration Manager, supply a description, and configure how the client computers are allowed to communicate with the distribution point.

12. Import, if necessary, the certificate, or choose the option Create Self-Signed Certificate.

13. Enable the option Enable This Distribution Point For Prestaged Content, and click Next.

14. Configure the Drive settings, and click Next.

15. Click Next on the Pull Distribution Point page, since you are retrieving the content from a prestaged source.

16. Configure PXE, and click Next.

17. Configure Multicast, and click Next.

18. Configure Content Validation, and click Next.

19. Configure Boundary Groups, and click Next.

20. Review the Summary screen, and click Next.

21. Click Close.

Since the distribution point is enabled for prestaged content, you can now create prestaged content packages that you need to deploy on the new distribution point. Content that can be prestaged includes the following:

◆ Applications

◆ Packages

◆ Software deployment packages

◆ Driver packages

◆ Operating system images

◆ Operating system installers

◆ Boot images

◆ Task sequence—content referenced by the task sequence

Creating prestaged content packages can be done as follows:

1. In the Configuration Manager console, choose the Software Library workspace.

2. Select a content item that needs to be prestaged (application, package, etc.), right-click, and select the Create Prestaged Content File option.

3. Follow the Create Prestaged Content File Wizard to select the location to store the prestaged content file, provide the filename, and also specify whether associated application dependencies should be included in the prestaged content file. Click Next.

4. Select the distribution point that will serve as the source for the prestaged content file. Click Next.

5. Confirm the settings in the wizard and click Next to finish the wizard.

The next step is to extract the created PKGX files to the remote distribution point:

1. Open a command prompt in administrative mode on the server that serves as the new distribution point.

2. Switch the command prompt to the directory where you find the `ExtractContent.exe` command-line utility at `..\SMS_DP$\sms\Tools`.

3. Copy the PKGX file you just created to a folder on the new server holding the distribution point role.

4. Execute the following command, and you will receive results like those shown in Figure 3.13.

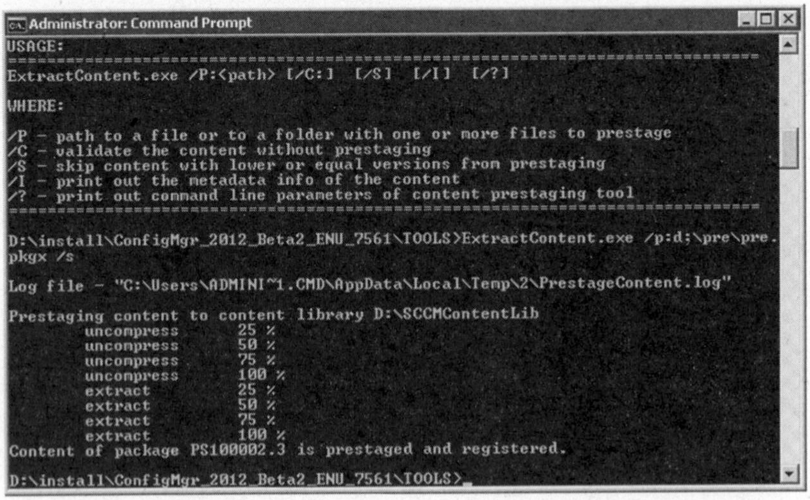

FIGURE 3.13
Extracting the prestaged package file to the new distribution point

```
ExtractContent.exe /p:<location of the prestaged file>\<prestagedfile>.pkgx /c
```

The extraction to the distribution point will be processed in the background. For troubleshooting purposes or to follow the process, you can monitor the PrestageContent.log file, which you can find in the temp folder of your user account.

UPGRADING SECONDARY SITES

Secondary sites need to be manually uninstalled from the Configuration Manager 2007 environment; there is no upgrade path for the scenario. While planning your new Configuration Manager hierarchy, consider replacing a secondary site with a distribution point. Chapter 2 describes when you can consider replacing a secondary site with a distribution point.

1. Right-click the secondary site and click Delete.

2. Click Next.

3. Select Deinstall The Site, and click Next.

4. Review the information about the secondary site to be deinstalled (Figure 3.14), and click Finish.

FIGURE 3.14
Deinstalling the
secondary site
from Configuration
Manager 2007 SP2

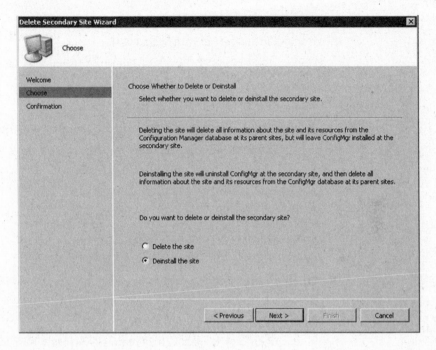

After the deletion process is finished, you can install the Configuration Manager secondary site server role.

MIGRATING CLIENTS

The Configuration Manager clients on the source hierarchy need to be migrated also. The process of client migration consists of uninstalling the Configuration Manager client on the devices in the source hierarchy and installing the new Configuration Manager client version.

You can migrate the clients via the following methods:

◆ Client push installation

◆ Software distribution

◆ Group Policy

◆ Windows Software Update Services (WSUS)

◆ Manual installation

◆ Integration with operating system deployment

Chapter 5, "Client Installation," offers more information about client installation. Remember that only the following clients are supported for Configuration Manager:

◆ Windows 7 SP1 Professional, Enterprise, Ultimate (x86 and x64)

◆ Windows 8 Pro, Enterprise (x86 and x64)

- Windows 8.1 Pro, Enterprise (x86 and x64)

- Windows 10 Enterprise, Pro (x86 and x64)

- Windows Server 2008 SP2 Standard, Enterprise, Datacenter (x86 and x64)

- Windows Server 2008 SP2 Server Core (x86 and x64)

- Windows Server 2008 R2 Server Core (RTM, SP1) (x64)

- Windows Storage Server 2008 R2 Workgroup, Standard, Enterprise (x64)

- Windows Server 2008 R2 SP1 Standard, Enterprise (x64)

- Windows Server 2012 Standard, Datacenter (x64)

- Windows Server 2012 Server Core (x64)

- Windows Server 2012 R2 Standard, Datacenter (x64)

- Windows Storage Server 2012 R2 (x64)

- Windows Server 2012 R2 Server Core (x64)

The list of supported operating systems for the Configuration Manager clients is also available here:

```
https://technet.microsoft.com/en-us/library/mt589738.aspx
```

Also, the Configuration Manager client requires Microsoft .NET Framework. If the computer does not have Microsoft .NET Framework 3.0, 3.5, or 4.0, then .NET Framework 4 is automatically installed on the computer. Note that a computer restart may be required in order to complete the .NET Framework 4.0 installation.

Using the Wipe-and-Load Strategy

The wipe-and-load strategy is the most basic and straightforward of any of the approaches. Generally speaking, this strategy is intended for environments in which the following apply:

- You still use SMS 2003 or Configuration Manager 2007 as a single-server solution.

- None of the existing data (that is, collections, inventories, packages, and so on) needs to be retained.

Although this approach may seem like the path of least resistance, you need to stay aware of a few pitfalls:

Client Manageability If you take the wipe-and-load approach, the quickest way to remove the existing client software from the computers is to perform a software distribution to run the ccmclean.exe Microsoft Resource Kit utility for SMS 2003 or Configuration Manager 2007 on all SMS 2003 or Configuration Manager 2007 clients. This poses the potential problem that the clients will remain unmanaged until the server (current or new future hardware) is rebuilt and Configuration Manager is installed and configured properly in the new hierarchy. Depending on the environment this may not be an issue, but you should perform a risk analysis to determine the likelihood that any mission-critical application updates or zero-day exploit patches would need to be deployed during the wipe-and-load timeframe. If the risk can be minimized or negated, then a wipe-and-load operation might be possible.

Implementation Timeframe   Rebuilding a server and installing or configuring all the components that are required to support a Configuration Manager installation is no small task. Not to mention that if you have a strict change-control process, this might hinder your forward momentum significantly. All these factors equate to dollars—money spent rebuilding, installing, configuring, and testing a server that was already up and running in production.

The bottom line is this: The wipe-and-load option may be the path of least resistance, but weigh your options carefully before selecting a strategy.

Upgrading the Configuration Manager Console

As with the Configuration Manager site server itself, you must consider the upgrade of all the Configuration Manager administrative consoles to the new Configuration Manager administrative console version. This potentially is an area for automation or an unattended installation routine.

Any of the setup functions (primary site, secondary site, or administrative console) can be scripted with an initialization file to answer key questions of a setup routine and provide an automated Configuration Manager console setup.

The following steps will enable you to perform an unattended installation of the Configuration Manager administrative console:

1. Ensure that administrator workstations meet the minimum requirements for the Configuration Manager administrative console. To use the Installation Prerequisite Checker to verify the workstation, you can run `prereqchk.exe /ADMINUI` from the command line. You can find this file in the installation source on the DVD (SMSSetup\Bin\x64).

2. Advertise the setup of Configuration Manager with the following command, substituting the *<msiexec /I \SMSSETUP\BIN\i386\AdminConsole.msi /qn>* with the name and location of the file:

   `msiexec /I \SMSSETUP\BIN\i386\AdminConsole.msi /qn`

The unattended installation will not remove the old Configuration Manager 2007 console. You can remove the console by uninstalling it via the Programs And Features option in Control Panel.

The following steps enable you to perform a GUI installation of the Configuration Manager administrative console:

1. Ensure that administrator workstations meet the minimum requirements for the Configuration Manager administrative console. To use the Installation Prerequisite Checker to verify the workstation, you can run `prereqchk.exe /ADMINUI` from the command line. You can find the file at the following folder on the System Center Configuration Manager DVD: \SMSSETUP\BIN\x64\.

2. Insert the System Center Configuration Manager DVD, browse to the \SMSSETUP\BIN\i386\ folder, and double-click `AdminConsole.msi`.

   The Configuration Manager Console Setup Wizard appears.

3. Click Next.

4. Supply the site server name, and click Next.

5. Browse to the installation location, and click Next.

6. Choose whether you want to join the Customer Experience Improvement Program (CEIP), and click Next.

7. Click Install.

8. Review any fatal errors, other errors, or warnings that are presented (although part of your homework was to run the Installation Prerequisite Checker and address all errors), or review `ConfigMgrAdminUISetup.log` and `ConfigMgrPrereq.log` on the root of the system drive to see which errors need to be addressed.

9. Click Finish to start the newly installed Configuration Manager administrative console.

Post-Migration or Installation Considerations

Once you have performed the selected installation, it is imperative to maintain its health moving forward. The obvious choice for performance and availability monitoring is Microsoft System Center Operations Manager; for this you need to install the Configuration Manager Management Pack in Operations Manager. More information about support for Operations Manager can be found in the book *Mastering System Center 2012 Operations Manager* (Sybex, 2012). However, Configuration Manager does include some built-in monitoring features that can be quite useful in ensuring that your hierarchy is running properly.

1. First, review the site status from within the System Status node in the Monitoring workspace in the Configuration Manager console.

2. Review all of the site system roles to ensure that they are identified properly as well as the component status.

3. If there are any critical or red components, right-click the targeted component and select Show Messages ➤ Error.

    This produces all of the error status messages, which highlight the problems within the site.

You'll find more detailed troubleshooting coverage in Chapter 17, "Troubleshooting."

Another area of concentration should be the site settings. With the new functionality and roles within Configuration Manager, a plethora of settings need to be set up and configured. A more detailed and in-depth view of site settings is provided in Chapter 4.

After you review the new environment, you need to clean up Configuration Manager by doing the following:

◆ Stop the data-gathering process.

◆ Clean up the migration data.

STOPPING THE DATA-GATHERING PROCESS

You stop the data-gathering process by following the next procedure. You need to first stop the data-gathering processes in all of the child sites in the source hierarchy:

1. In the Configuration Manager console, open the Administration workspace.

2. Expand Overview ➤ Migration in the Administration workspace, and choose Source Hierarchy.

3. Select the site with data-gathering enabled.

4. Select the Home tab of the ribbon, and choose Stop Gathering Data.

5. Click Yes when the Stop Gathering Data dialog appears.

6. Repeat this for all sites in the hierarchy.

CLEANING UP MIGRATION DATA

The next step in the post-migration task is to clean up the migration data, as follows:

1. In the Configuration Manager console, choose the Administration workspace.

2. Expand Overview ➤ Migration in the Administration workspace, and choose Source Hierarchy.

3. Select the topmost source hierarchy site with data-gathering disabled.

4. Select the Home tab of the ribbon, and choose Clean Up Migration Data.

5. Verify that you have the right source hierarchy, and click OK when the Clean Up Migration Data dialog appears (Figure 3.15).

FIGURE 3.15
Cleaning up the migration data of the source hierarchy

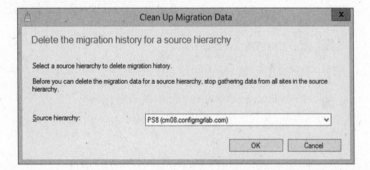

Real World Scenario

MIGRATING TO CONFIGURATION MANAGER

Sports Clothes United Inc. develops and sells sports clothing to retailers and their own shops all over the world. The head office is located in San Francisco. The company is growing so fast that they acquire a new company called Fit Clothes. Fit Clothes has its own Configuration Manager 2007 R3 SP2 environment.

You as the Configuration Manager administrator are asked to migrate the Fit Clothes Configuration Manager 2007 R2 SP2 environment to the new Configuration Manager infrastructure.

MIGRATION SCOPE

The corporate IT department investigated the Configuration Manager 2007 R3 SP2 environment of Fit Clothes and came to the conclusion that only the packages, advertisements, and collections need to be migrated to the Configuration Manager environment of Sport Clothes United.

continues

continued

Your assignment is to migrate these objects from the Configuration Manager 2007 environment to the Sport Clothes United Configuration Manager hierarchy.

MIGRATION APPROACH

You need to migrate objects from the Configuration Manager 2007 hierarchy so you decide to use the migration feature of Configuration Manager. Before performing the migration, you decide to test your migration approach in a test Configuration Manager hierarchy and verify that the steps you plan to take will succeed. Here are the steps you intend to perform:

1. Define the topmost Configuration Manager 2007 site as the source hierarchy.

2. Configure credentials to be able to gather data from the source site(s).

3. Use the collection migration to migrate your collections with the associated packages and advertisements.

4. Stop the data-gathering process, and clean up the migration data.

5. Uninstall Configuration Manager 2007 from the source hierarchy.

Once you have completed those steps, you will have migrated the required Configuration Manager 2007 assets to the Sports Clothes United Configuration Manager hierarchy.

The Bottom Line

Determine what you are able to migrate with the migration feature. The migration feature in Configuration Manager allows you to migrate the old Configuration Manager investments to a new Configuration Manager hierarchy side by side.

Master It With the migration feature, you cannot migrate objects like the following:

◆ Queries

◆ Security rights for the site and objects

◆ Configuration Manager reports from SQL Server Reporting Services

◆ Configuration Manager 2007 web reports

◆ Client inventory and history data

◆ AMT client-provisioning information

◆ Files in the client cache

Identify what objects you *can* migrate.

Discover which migration approach is supported. Configuration Manager provides migration features that can be used for your migration of Configuration Manager 2007 to the current version.

Master It With the earlier upgrades or migrations of Configuration Manager in your mind, what migration approaches are supported when migrating from previous versions of Configuration Manager?

Ascertain what kind of interoperability is supported during the migration.   Interoperability like that supported in earlier versions is no longer supported; nevertheless, the migration feature of Configuration Manager supports some interoperability during the migration process. Depending on the size of your Configuration Manager source hierarchy, the migration can take some time.

> **Master It**   Interoperability like you were used to in SMS 2003 and Configuration Manager 2007 is no longer supported. Give two examples of interoperability features in the current version of Configuration Manager.

Chapter 4

Installation and Site Role Configuration

Previous chapters have already begun pulling back the covers on the changes in Configuration Manager. This chapter explores Configuration Manager sites, hierarchies, and site system roles and provides a walkthrough of building a hierarchy.

In this version of Configuration Manager, you can see the advances Microsoft has made toward the cloud. This version focuses on the ability to manage not just on-premise clients but also those clients in Microsoft Azure or mobile clients. The integration with Microsoft Intune and the ability to host roles in Azure are great parts of this new version. Once you finish reading this chapter, you will understand some of those benefits and the advantages they can provide to your current infrastructure.

Another change introduced with System Center 2012 Configuration Manager was hierarchy simplification, which lets customers understand the need for having a central administration site or just a standard primary site server. In the new version of Configuration Manager, a central administration site supports some one million clients and a primary site supports about 250,000 clients. Many customers are moving to a primary site and starting to use more distribution points or secondary sites when needed. This chapter explores each of these roles and how they can be useful for your hierarchy.

In this chapter, you will learn to

◆ Understand Configuration Manager sites and the new approach to hierarchy design

◆ Construct a Configuration Manager hierarchy

◆ Determine when to expand a hierarchy and when to simply add a site system role for additional service

◆ Deploy and configure the various site system roles available per site

Understanding Site Types

It doesn't take long when working with any of the versions of Configuration Manager to be introduced to the concept of a site server. Site servers exist to provide service to Configuration Manager clients. Site servers understand which clients they should serve by defining management boundaries, which may be Active Directory sites, IP subnets, or IP address ranges. Depending on the size and organization of your Configuration Manager environment, you may need more than a single site to manage all of your clients in the enterprise. When more than one site is needed, it is common to establish a site hierarchy, which will facilitate centralized management of all Configuration Manager clients.

A specific design goal of Configuration Manager is to reduce the number of sites needed in a hierarchy and to reduce complexity. Further discussion of this goal will come shortly.

Site servers fall into one of two categories: a standalone primary or a central administration site. A standalone site is best for smaller deployments and can be used to manage devices without the need for additional sites. A central administration site is best for large-scale deployments and provides a central point of administration. Let's take a closer look at each:

Standalone Primary   A standalone primary was originally defined as having the following characteristics:

- It has its own database hosted on SQL Server to maintain configurations.

- It is the only site type where clients can be directly assigned.

- It has the ability to host child sites—either other primary sites or secondary sites.

Both the first and last characteristics are no longer items that distinguish a primary site. In the new version of Configuration Manager, primary site servers *do* still have their own copy of SQL running, but secondary sites do as well. Further, a primary site *can* have child sites, but those child sites can *only* be secondary sites. Now only primary sites can be assigned to the central administration site—secondaries need not apply!

Secondary Site Server   A secondary site server has historically been identified by a few characteristics:

- It does not make use of a SQL database.

- There is no way to directly administer a secondary site; all administration would have to come from an administration console connected to a primary site somewhere above the secondary.

The former condition is no longer true—secondary sites now *do* have a database. When installing a secondary site, you have a choice of either using an existing instance of SQL or, if SQL is not present on the target server, installing and using SQL Express. The latter observation remains true—secondary sites cannot be administered directly through the console.

Also, the historical justification for secondary sites has primarily been to provide local content access for clients residing in or roaming into its defined boundaries and to help control network traffic for content moving between the secondary site and its assigned parent primary site. Secondary sites are still used for that purpose today (although the argument is far less compelling).

So, secondary sites are still available in Configuration Manager, but before you plan to install one, check out the various bandwidth-control features of Configuration Manager. One key addition is that it is now possible to control, or throttle, network bandwidth between a site and its remote distribution points within the site. This one addition in Configuration Manager makes it worth considering whether secondary sites are necessary. If secondary sites were in use in an environment for the sole purpose of controlling network bandwidth for content distribution (some content is *huge*), then the ability to throttle content delivery between a site and a remote distribution point introduced in Configuration Manager will be of interest.

Other reasons for having a secondary site include the ability to throttle non-content site-to-site communications. This results in a much reduced data size compared to content, but if throttling is still of concern to you, then a secondary site may be justified. (In previous versions of Configuration Manager, this content would consist of files that contained status information, site configuration information, client information, and so on. In Configuration Manager this content is still transferred between sites but is split between traditional file-based transfer and SQL replication.)

When it comes to secondary sites—or any other site type for that matter—*think* before following the same old pattern for a hierarchy. Configuration Manager *is* about hierarchy simplification and does a nice job of increasing site efficiency!

Central Administration Site   Another type of site that has been around in previous versions of Configuration Manager is the central site server. A central site server is the one at the top of a hierarchy and is used to centrally administer the entire Configuration Manager implementation. Because of its role in hierarchy-wide management, a central site typically should not have clients directly assigned. Further, because all information in the hierarchy resides at the central site, this is typically the key site in the hierarchy where reporting is configured.

The central site server is no longer present in the new version of Configuration Manager. It has been replaced by a new type of site server known as a central administration site (CAS). The CAS is much like the central site server except that it cannot have any clients assigned (it's not even an option), some site functions are not available (such as most of the discovery options), and the CAS must be the first site server installed on your hierarchy. However, if you decide not to install the CAS until your organization has reached a desired limit of clients, you can later expand your standalone primary site into a CAS only once.

As we mentioned, sites manage clients. To facilitate client management and depending on the services being delivered, several different functional roles must be in place at the site. These functional roles are either added to the site server itself or configured on external servers. Either way, the servers that host these support roles are known as site systems. The option for distributed site servers to fulfill various functions allows for very flexible and scalable designs. Ultimately, the decision on where to place these site systems or whether to use external site systems at all is up to the administrator. And, if these roles need to be moved to other servers after installation, or other servers need to be added, that is easy to do. This work is performed in the Administration workspace, under Site Configuration of the Configuration Manager console, as shown in Figure 4.1.

FIGURE 4.1

The Administration workspace within the Configuration Manager console

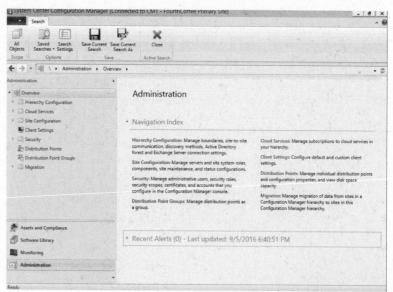

HIERARCHY DESIGN AND IMPLEMENTATION

Now that we've discussed the types of sites available in Configuration Manager, it's natural to begin thinking about implementation details. Hopefully it is clear that Configuration Manager introduces significant changes in terms of site and hierarchy design. Administrators who have experience with previous versions might be tempted to set up Configuration Manager in the same design that is currently being used. That approach might work, but it would be a mistake and would likely mask many of the features for simplified management that are available in Configuration Manager.

One of the major design pillars for Configuration Manager was hierarchy simplification. With that in mind, during the design phase remember that a standalone hierarchy is capable of supporting up to 175,000 clients and devices, and in a Central Administration hierarchy configuration it is able to support up to 1,025,000 devices, 700,000 desktop device, 300,000 cloud-based devices, or 100,000 on-premises MDM and 150,000 clients or devices per primary site, and in order to support this you most use SQL Server Enterprise Edition. This means that for many organizations the Configuration Manager design might be handled with only a single primary site along with additional servers to support various roles in the environment. It's interesting to note that even in Configuration Manager 2007 a primary site was also able to support 100,000 clients. That type of scale often was not realized because of the need for additional sites for political or load reasons. The design of Configuration Manager removes virtually all technical reasons for adding additional site servers unless the addition is driven by scale.

For up-to-date information on client supportability, visit

https://docs.microsoft.com/en-us/sccm/core/plan-design/configs/size-and-scale-numbers

Implementing Site Servers

The terms *site* and *site server* are often used interchangeably. In reality this shouldn't be the case. A Configuration Manager site encompasses all servers that are used to deliver the services offered by the site. Said another way, a Configuration Manager site can consist of one to several servers. The size of the site will dictate how many servers are needed to deliver service to clients. In smaller environments, it may be that only a single server is necessary to host all components needed to deliver the site's services. In larger environments, multiple servers may be required. With the new design of Configuration Manager, the expectation is that the number of total sites needed for an environment will decrease, but the number of supporting servers for a site might increase.

A site server is the one server in a site that orchestrates delivery of service to clients. This server will interact with any other servers that are in place supporting the site's ability to deliver services. These additional servers are known as site systems. (A site server is also a *site system*.)

As services are added to a site and assigned to a server, the list of site system roles will increase. A quick glance at the Configuration Manager console will reveal the site systems that are in use to support a site and also what services those site systems are delivering on behalf of the site. An example is shown in Figure 4.2. Note that two systems are shown related to site code PRI. One is the site server itself and the other is a site system server providing service for the site.

FIGURE 4.2
Site systems and roles

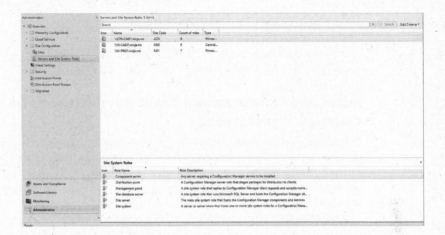

Software Requirements

Before further discussing Configuration Manager, it is beneficial to install the required software. There are a few prerequisites for installing a site server. For a full list of these prerequisites, go to

https://docs.microsoft.com/en-us/sccm/core/plan-design/configs/site-and-site-system-prerequisites

These prerequisites may also apply to site systems that may be installed. Depending on the services, those servers will offer the following:

♦ All site servers must be members of a Windows Active Directory domain (Windows Server 2003 functional level or above if using the discovery filter for stale computer records).

♦ The site servers must be deployed on 64-bit hardware. Configuration Manager is a native 64-bit application, and there is no version that can be installed on 32-bit systems. (32-bit systems are supported as Configuration Manager clients and some site systems.)

♦ .NET Framework 3.5 SP1 and 4.0 must be installed.

♦ Microsoft XML Core Services 6.0 or greater must be installed.

♦ Microsoft Remote Differential Compression must be installed.

♦ SQL Server 2012 R2 or 2014 SP1 is required to host the ConfigMgr database.

And don't worry; if a required software happens to be missed along the way, the Configuration Manager prerequisite checker, which runs as part of the installation wizard, will let you know. The details of the checks that are performed during prerequisite validation are recorded in ConfigMgrPrereq.log, located in the root of the C: drive of the server where Configuration Manager is being installed. If it would be helpful to run the prerequisite checker outside of the Configuration Manager setup wizard, it is available as a separate executable located in the \SMSSETUP\BIN\X64 folder of the installation media. The filename is PREREQCHK.EXE.

Pre-requirements Automation

The community is really great when it comes to tools and automation of common tasks, and one of the tools we like to use is call the ConfigMgr Prerequisites tool. And for the following section we have invited Nickolaj Andersen, the author of the tool, to describe the tool.

PREPARING YOUR WINDOWS-BASED ENVIRONMENT FOR CONFIGURATION MANAGER

Before you start to install the first site in your deployment of Configuration Manager, it's critical that you've prepared the server that will eventually become, for instance, your primary site server as well for Active Directory. If this task has not been successfully completed, you'll see warnings or even errors during the prerequisite check step of the installation wizard, ultimately not allowing the site installation process to proceed.

Preparing your environment for a successful deployment of Configuration Manager should not be an obstacle or time consuming. Many of the issues that might occur during the initial installation process can often be resolved by making sure that the correct prerequisites are in place.

On TechNet Library, you'll find all of the required software and Windows feature prerequisites well documented. Refer to the following documentation for a list of what's required when preparing for your deployment:

```
https://docs.microsoft.com/en-us/sccm/core/plan-design/configs/site-and-site-
system-prerequisites
```

If this is the first time you're installing a Configuration Manager deployment, you should familiarize yourself with the overall process of preparing for the installation.

However, this procedure can be completed more rapidly with the right tools. The tool is called the ConfigMgr Prerequisites Tool and it's available for free to download from the TechNet Gallery (see Figure 4.3).

```
https://gallery.technet.microsoft.com/ConfigMgr-2012-R2-e52919cd
```

FIGURE 4.3
ConfigMgr
Prerequisites Tool
version 1.4.2 running
on Windows Server
2012 R2

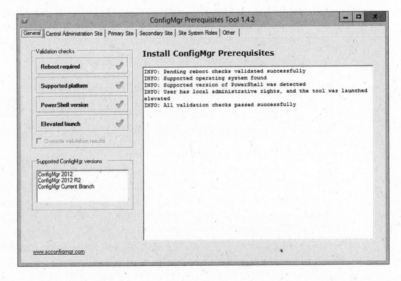

Upon the launch of the ConfigMgr Prerequisites Tool, four different validation checks are performed:

- Pending reboot
- Running on a supported operating system (platform)
- PowerShell version
- Elevated launch

If any of the validation checks fails, you have the option to override the validation results. However, we recommend that you assess the validation check warnings before you start using the tool.

CONFIGMGR PREREQUISITES TOOL DOCUMENTATION

The ConfigMgr Prerequisites Tool will allow you to install the required software and Windows features for the following site types:

- Central administration site
- Primary site
- Secondary site

And the following site system roles:

- Management Point
- Distribution Point
- Software Update Point
- State Migration Point
- Application Catalog
- Enrollment Point (and Enrollment Proxy Point)

In addition to what's mentioned here, the tool will allow you to

- Extend Active Directory
- Install the Windows Assessment and Deployment Kit (ADK)
- Create the System Management container in Active Directory
- Delegate permissions to the System Management container
- Create NO_SMS_ON_DRIVE.SMS files to prevent unwanted volumes from being used by Configuration Manager

CONFIGMGR PREREQUISITES TOOL REQUIREMENTS

Before you start using this tool, you need to make sure that your Windows-based server complies with the requirements. This tool has been written completely in PowerShell; therefore you must be running at least PowerShell 3.0. Supported Windows Server operating systems are the following:

◆ Windows Server 2012

◆ Windows Server 2012 R2

By default, these Windows Server operating systems ship with a supported version of PowerShell for this tool. There's no need to install Windows Management Framework 3.0 (which includes PowerShell 3.0). For older Windows Server operating systems, such as Windows Server 2008 R2, there's an older version of the ConfigMgr Prerequisites Tool (version 1.2.1) available for download on the same TechNet Gallery page mentioned earlier.

When you've downloaded and extracted the script file (`Install-ConfigMgrPrereqsGUI_ 1.4.2.ps1`) embedded in the zip container, you should elevate a PowerShell console and browse to the fully qualified location of where you extracted the script. Due to the fact that the tool performs various activities like installing Windows features, it will not function properly unless you elevate the PowerShell console.

For some of the activities performed by the tool, it's necessary that you be able to provide access when prompted to the Configuration Manager installation media. This behavior is intentional because the tool relies on external executables available in the `SMSSETUP\BIN\X64` folder of the installation media. Those activities are for when you extend Active Directory and download prerequisites—for example, a primary site that is used by the Configuration Manager installation process.

Once you've launched the tool for the first time, you'll see that it consists of several tabs indicating the different site types, site system roles, and additional preparation options that we've previously talked about. Each tab has been constructed so that they will install the required prerequisites for a specific scenario. Exceptions to this rule are when installing the Windows Assessment and Deployment Toolkit (Windows ADK) and preparing for a software update point (since it requires Windows Server Updates Services to be installed and configured). Both of these exceptions are available under the Other tab.

Additionally, the tool provides certain help messages for each selection on the different tab pages, giving you guidance and information on what will happen if chosen for installation.

It's important to make a note that the ConfigMgr Prerequisites Tool does not fully support remote execution. This means that you'd have to launch the tool locally on the designated Windows-based server that you want to prepare for a Configuration Manager deployment, or on management servers with proper access to the Windows-based infrastructure, such as Active Directory.

General Tab

This is the tab that will be shown upon launching the tool. In this view you're presented with the results of the validation checks in both graphical form and a more detailed explanation for each validation check. In the event of any of the validation checks are not met, all other tab pages are automatically disabled. You do, however, have the option to override the result of these checks, thus enabling the tab pages, but we highly recommend that you proceed with caution and that you attempt to correct the errors given instead of overriding the results. An example when you would override the results could be that you've restarted the Windows-based server several times, making sure that there's no pending reboot, but the tool reports that the server in fact still needs to be rebooted.

Central Administration Site Tab

The first site type tab is the Central Administration Site tab. In situations when your deployment of Configuration Manager requires a CAS, select this tab to install the necessary Windows features. You're also given an option to select to download the prerequisite files required by the Configuration Manager installation wizard. If you select to download these files at this stage, you'll be asked to provide access to the Configuration Manager installation media. During this step, the tool requires an external executable called SETUPDL.EXE, available in SMSSETUP\BIN\X64 in the installation media folder structure. If you do not choose to download the prerequisite files, you'll have that opportunity during the Configuration Manager installation wizard.

When you click the Install button, the Configuration Manager Prerequisites Tool will attempt to install the necessary Windows features. During this operation, each feature will be assessed to determine whether it should be installed. Once the tool completes this operation, a validation process will enumerate all features to assess if they were in fact installed or if they're missing.

Primary Site Tab

For single-site Configuration Manager deployments, the Primary Site tab should be used. Just like the Central Administration Site tab, the required Windows features will be installed and you also have the option to download the prerequisite files required for the installation wizard. If the prerequisites files are selected for download, a prompt asking where to save the files appears. You'll also be prompted to provide access to the Configuration Manager media, when the Download Prerequisite Files check box is selected.

When you click the Install button, the same process used for the Central Administration Site with Windows feature installation assessment and validation will be taken.

Secondary Site Tab

If your deployment of Configuration Manager will require a secondary site, the Secondary Site tab will allow you to install the required Windows feature prerequisites. However, it does not install SQL Server Express, since that's taken care of by the installation of a secondary site through the Configuration Manager console. Each Windows feature required for a secondary site will be assessed and validated after an attempt to install it has been performed by the tool, just like for a primary site and a central administration site.

Site System Roles Tab

If you're an administrator who has previous experience with Configuration Manager, you are familiar with site system roles, which provide different functionality to a site. For instance, the Management Point role handles the communication between the Configuration Manager clients and the site. The ConfigMgr Prerequisites Tool provides you with the ability to prepare and install the required Windows features and configure them accordingly for the site system role to function properly. You must add the computer account of the parent site server (your primary site server) to the local Administrators group of the server that will function as your new site system server hosting the site system role. This means that if you would, for instance, prepare and install an additional distribution point on a remote server called SERVER1 that should belong to your primary site called PRIMARY1, the computer account of your primary site server PRIMARY1 should be added to the local Administrators group on the new remote server designated as your new distribution point, SERVER1.

There are some limitations to where the ConfigMgr Prerequisites Tool will make some assumptions for you. Say you want to install the Application Catalog Site System role within the tool. Since this role consists of two separate site system roles in Configuration Manager that are required for the Application Catalog to function properly, the tool will prepare for both roles.

As mentioned earlier, the following site system roles are supported for preparation in terms of Windows feature installation and configuration by the ConfigMgr Prerequisites Tool:

◆ Management Point

◆ Distribution Point

◆ Application Catalog

◆ Enrollment Point

◆ Enrollment Proxy Point

◆ State Migration Point

As for those site system roles that are not listed but are present in Configuration Manager, the tool does not provide assistance in preparation for such an installation. However, in general those roles do not require any significant Windows feature installations other than what's in the Windows Server 2012 (and above) operating system by default.

Other Tab

Even though the name of this tab may not be the most intuitive, it provides you with the options to perform tasks such as

◆ Extending Active Directory

◆ Installing and configuring WSUS

◆ Installing Windows ADK

◆ Creating and adding access to the System Management container in Active Directory

◆ Creating NO_SMS_ON_DRIVE.SMS files on volumes that should not be considered by Configuration Manager for various purposes

EXTEND ACTIVE DIRECTORY

You should consider extending the schema in your Active Directory forest before you install Configuration Manager. During this phase, it's required that the account you've launched the Configuration Manager Prerequisites Tool with be a member of the Schema Admins domain group. You're also required to provide the tool with the name of your domain controller hosting the Schema Master FSMO Flexible single master operation role. In addition, you'll be prompted to provide access to the SMSSETUP\BIN\X64 folder on the System Center Configuration installation media. A file called extadsch.exe will be copied to the specified domain controller and executed locally on that server.

INSTALL WSUS

When preparing for the installation of a software update point (SUP) site system role on a remote Windows server, Windows Server Update Services (WSUS) is a prerequisite that needs to be in place and properly configured. WSUS requires a database where it stores metadata about all the software updates it synchronizes, its configuration, and more. This database can be in the form of either a Windows Internal Database (WID) or a SQL Server database. In the ConfigMgr Prerequisites Tool, you'll be required to make a selection of either WID or SQL.

When WID is chosen, a Windows Internal Database instance will be installed locally on the Windows server the ConfigMgr Prerequisites Tool is running on, eventually the Windows-based server that will become a remote software update point. The SQL Server name and SQL Server instance fields are not enabled when the Database Options combo box is set to WID.

For the SQL database option, it's a bit different. When the SQL database option is selected, you're required to at least provide the hostname or FQDN of a Windows-based server running SQL Server. In some SQL Server environments, you also need to specify a particular SQL Server instance name. If you want to create the WSUS database in the default instance, leave the SQL Server instance field empty.

Whether you've chosen WID or SQL, the required Windows features for WSUS will be installed. Once that installation of those features has finished, WSUS post-configuration will be started and will configure WSUS with the selected database option. You're also prompted to provide the tool with a folder for storing WSUS content. We recommend that you do not store this content folder on the system volume, since it can grow quite large over time, depending on the selected update classifications, software updates, languages, and more that you configure to synchronize from Microsoft Update.

INSTALL WINDOWS ADK

Windows Assessment and Deployment Toolkit (Windows ADK) is a key component prerequisite for Configuration Manager when it comes to operating system deployment (OSD). The ConfigMgr Prerequisites Tool will perform an unattended installation of the following components from Windows ADK:

◆ Deployment tools

◆ Windows Preinstallation Environment (Windows PE)

◆ User State Migration Tool (USMT)

Since Windows ADK can be installed either online or offline, the ConfigMgr Prerequisites Tool has been built to support both, to include the possibility of performing an installation where no active Internet connection is available. For an Online installation, you're required to select whether to download and install Windows ADK version 10 or greater. When the Online installation method is chosen, adksetup.exe is downloaded directly from the Microsoft Download Center and placed in C:\Downloads; from there the installation is initialized. For Offline scenarios, the administrator must download the redistributable files for Windows ADK beforehand, and these files must be available locally on the Windows-based server.

In either scenario, the ConfigMgr Prerequisites Tool waits for installation of Windows ADK to finish by regularly checking if there's an adksetup.exe process running before it returns any output.

SYSTEM MANAGEMENT CONTAINER

If you've chosen to extend your Active Directory schema, it's required that you create the System Management container. This container is used by the site for storing published data such as boundary information for the Configuration Manager client to look up. You have the option to create this container manually or let the ConfigMgr Prerequisites Tool create it for you. You can do so by putting a check mark in the Create The System Management Container check box. When performing any of the configuration options available for the System Management container, the tool will check if the current user is a member of the Domain Admins group.

Before the ConfigMgr Prerequisites Tool can create the System Management container, you are asked to provide an Active Directory security group. This group should contain your primary site server computer account, and if your deployment will require a CAS, the group should contain all of your primary site server computer accounts.

When you click the Search button, a new window will appear where you're able to search for security groups by entering the name of your group (the samAccountName property is used for matching the entered group name when enumerating security groups). A list of results matching what you've entered in the Search For An Active Directory Group text field will be shown in the data grid view. Make sure to select the correct security group. The selected security group will always be shown in the bottom text field, just to give you an indication of what group the tool will use when configuring the System Management container. At this stage, if you've selected to also create the container, the tool will attempt to create the container and add the selected security group with Full Control for this object and all descendant objects.

Should you decide to manually create the container, be aware that this is not an organizational unit (OU) and cannot be created with Active Directory Users and Computers. Instead you should use ADSI Edit to create the container. Remember to select the proper object type, *container*, and place the System Management container in the root of your structure. It's also vital that you name the container correctly, or the prerequisite checker for Configuration Manager will not be able to check for the container presence.

NO SMS ON DRIVE

Configuration Manager is famous for spreading itself out over all available volumes. This behavior may at times seem legacy, but it's a feature that has been in the product for a very long time. Configuration Manager selects the volume that has the largest amount of space available at the time of execution, during the processing of various tasks. If you want to have total control over this behavior, you can create a file called NO_SMS_ON_DRIVE.SMS in the root of a volume you want to exclude from the volumes Configuration Manager will enumerate through. If this file exists on a particular volume, Configuration Manager will honor that the administrator has chosen to not have site content data stored on the volume. The ConfigMgr Prerequisites Tool gives you the option to automatically create this file on the volumes of your choosing.

USING THE CONFIGMGR PREREQUISITES TOOL

The following examples describe real-world scenarios where the ConfigMgr Prerequisites Tool is used in preparation of the Windows-based infrastructure needed for a successful deployment of Configuration Manager.

This step-by-step process assumes that your environment meets the requirements of the ConfigMgr Prerequisites Tool for the tasks that are performed.

Scenario 1: New Deployment of a Primary Site

For this scenario we're preparing a Windows-based server running Windows Server 2012 R2 with the latest security patches installed. For a successful installation of Configuration Manager, the following steps need to be taken before the installation can begin:

◆ Install prerequisites for a primary site server

◆ Prepare the Active Directory environment

◆ Install the Windows Assessment and Deployment Toolkit

You need to have the Configuration Manager installation media at hand and access to the Internet from the Windows-based server where you will be running the tool.

INSTALL PREREQUISITES FOR A PRIMARY SITE SERVER

To begin, follow these steps:

1. Open an elevated PowerShell console and launch the ConfigMgr Prerequisites Tool by running the following command from within the directory where the tool is located:

```
.\Install-ConfigMgrPrereqsGUI_1.4.2.ps1
```

2. Select the Primary Site tab, put a check mark in the Download Prerequisite Files check box, and click Install. Depending on the performance of the server, this process will take some time. The current operation is shown in the log window to give you an indication of what's currently being processed.

3. When prompted to select a folder where the prerequisite files should be downloaded to, browse to `C:\Temp\CMPrereqs`. Create the folder if necessary.

4. In the second prompt, browse to the location of the Configuration Manager installation media and select the `SMSSETUP\BIN\X64` folder to start the download of the prerequisite files.

Once the download of the prerequisite files operation has completed, the validation operation of each Windows feature will begin. If any of the Windows features failed to become installed, it will be shown in the log window.

PREPARE ACTIVE DIRECTORY ENVIRONMENT

To begin, follow these steps:

1. Select the Other tab and click Extend Active Directory.

2. In the Schema Master Server Name text field, enter the hostname or FQDN of the domain controller holding the Schema Master FSMO role. Click the Extend button to initiate the Active Directory schema extension operation. When prompted, browse to the location of the Configuration Manager installation media, selecting the `SMSSETUP\BIN\X64` folder. If the extension operation either was successful or failed, it will be indicated in the log window.

3. Still under the Other tab, select System Management Container.

4. Put a check mark in the Create The System Management Container option.

5. Click Search, and in the new window that appears, type the name of an Active Directory group that has the primary site server as a member, in the Search For An Active Directory Group text field.

6. Click Search again, and select the Active Directory group for the results. Make sure that the Selected Active Directory Group text field is populated with the group you want.

7. Click OK.

INSTALL WINDOWS ASSESSMENT AND DEPLOYMENT TOOLKIT

To begin, follow these steps:

1. Select the Other tab and click Install Windows ADK.

2. In the Installation Methods combo box, select whether to perform an Online or Offline based installation of Windows ADK. When no Internet connection is available on the Windows-based server, select the Offline installation method. Be aware, though, the installation files for Windows ADK would have to be available, meaning you'd have to download them from another system.

3. For System Center Configuration Manager Current Branch, select Windows ADK 10 or ADK 10 1607 in the Version combo box. For previous versions of Configuration Manager, select Windows ADK 8.1.

4. Click Install.

With all of these steps successfully performed, your Windows-based infrastructure, site server, and Active Directory have been prepared for the installation of a primary site.

Scenario 2: Preparation for Installing a Remote Distribution Point

In situations when you need to prepare a Windows-based server distribution point (or other site system roles for that matter), you can use the ConfigMgr Prerequisites Tool to speed up the deployment process.

INSTALL PREREQUISITES FOR A REMOTE DISTRIBUTION POINT ROLE

For a remote distribution point, no installation media or other required software is necessary. You only need the ConfigMgr Prerequisites Tool on the Windows-based site system server that you want as your remote distribution point.

1. Open an elevated PowerShell console and launch the ConfigMgr Prerequisites Tool by running the following command from within the directory of where the tool is located:

```
.\Install-ConfigMgrPrereqsGUI_1.4.2.ps1
```

2. Select the Site System Roles tab, and click Distribution Point in the left pane.

3. In the Add Site Server To Administrators Group text field, add the hostname or FQDN of the parent site server (for instance, your primary site or secondary site server).

4. Click Install.

Once the required Windows features for the selected site system have been installed, in this case for a distribution point, you can go ahead and deploy your site system role through the Configuration Manager console.

Implementing a Central Administration Site

Installing Configuration Manager begins by installing the first site. A very important question should be answered before launching the Setup Wizard: Is it expected that more than a single primary site will need to be included in the deployment? If the answer is *yes*, then the very first site that needs to be installed is the central administration site. The CAS is the top site in the hierarchy and is used solely for administration of the entire hierarchy. No clients or client-related functions are possible at the CAS. This is critical to understand. If there is any expectation of joining multiple primary sites in a hierarchy relationship, then the CAS must be the first server installed. If it's not installed, then you should plan to expand the standalone primary site to a CAS at a later time.

For those of you who have worked with previous versions of Configuration Manager, your initial reaction may be that multiple sites *are* needed because they were needed in the current implementation (whatever version that is) of Configuration Manager. Not so fast! Remember that one of the design goals of Configuration Manager is hierarchy simplification. A Configuration Manager site is more efficient in many ways, not the least of which is the ability to throttle traffic to remote distribution points (thus often eliminating the need for secondary sites). This one tweak by itself will go a long way to reducing the number of sites. Further, a single site has been able to scale to support 200,000 clients for some time now. Often, this kind of scale for a single site was not realized because of the need for additional sites due to network conditions, security considerations, and the like. With Configuration Manager and hierarchy simplification along with other improvements, expect to see primaries carrying much more of a client load than might have been seen in previous versions.

For the examples given here, installation will proceed assuming a three-tier hierarchy is to be built. The hierarchy will consist of a CAS, two primary sites, and a single secondary site.

With the decision made as to how many sites are needed for the hierarchy, the first site to be installed is the CAS. Before starting the Setup Wizard, make sure SQL is installed and available. Also, install the Windows Assessment and Deployment Kit for Windows 10 first (it's required).

 Real World Scenario

Choosing Local or Remote Installation

A SQL Server installation can be either local or remote. Arguments rage about the best approach. This argument is helped in Configuration Manager by some support boundaries. A standalone primary site server on appropriate hardware is able to support more than 175,000 clients. However, if you going to install and configure a hierarchy and will have child primary sites, the version of SQL Server does affect the client supportability. In this case, if you choose a SQL Standard Edition for your site server, this one will be limited to 50,000 clients. This is mostly due to the load that SQL replication introduces. Still, while the performance differences between a remote versus a local SQL server when properly configured are slight, if a site will host fewer than 50,000 clients, using collocated SQL is still preferred and is considered most efficient. One reason for this is that when SQL is running on the same system, it is possible to take advantage of the shared memory

continues

continued

> protocol. One consideration for local SQL, however, is the default memory settings. SQL by default is configured to consume all available RAM. This is a good configuration for standalone SQL because RAM is more efficient than disk memory.
>
> When sharing a server, setting a maximum amount of RAM for SQL consumption and thereby reserving the rest for Configuration Manager, the operating system, and other applications such as virus scanners is an optimal configuration. SQL does a very good job of managing RAM and not overconsuming and starving other applications. But there is a cost, however slight, because SQL pages information out of RAM to make room for the needs of other applications. Setting a maximum from the beginning avoids this problem, and with the amount of RAM available on servers today, there shouldn't be an issue with specifying a maximum RAM value for SQL.

Finally, it's time for installation! The installation process is wizard driven and does a good job of keeping you on track. The most difficult part of the installation is knowing what options to choose. The example will explain how to configure the various options and what they mean. Let's get started:

1. Insert the installation media, and Autorun should cause the initial installation screen to be displayed.

   If this is not the case, or if you're running from a location other than the supplied media, simply double-click the `splash.hta` file, which will display the initial installation screen.

   The splash screen provides options for accessing various documentation and assistance—even links to the Configuration Manager community. There are also links to access server readiness components and links to download Configuration Manager updates that are required during the installation process. These latter links are nice additions to Configuration Manager, providing an easy way to download updates and move them to a server that is being installed that may not have Internet access to download the updates during setup. Other links include options to just install the Configuration Manager console and to download System Center Updates Publisher—a tool that anyone using software updates should take a look at. Clicking the Install link at the top left of the screen launches the Setup Wizard and opens the Setup Wizard Welcome page.

2. Review the information on the Before You Begin page, and click Next to continue to the Getting Started page.

   On the Getting Started page, the various install options are presented. The options available here will be based on the state of the system where the install is being run. If a system already has Configuration Manager installed, only the options to uninstall or perform a site reset may be available. If you're running the wizard on a system without Configuration Manager, you'll have the options shown in Figure 4.4.

   This is the point in the wizard where the decision you made earlier is configured—whether to install a standalone primary site or to install a central administration site. This installation will be for a CAS.

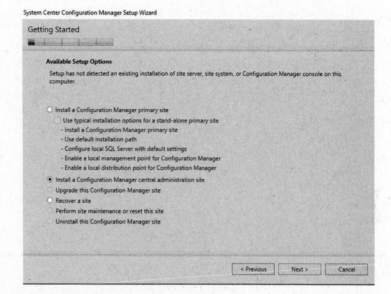

FIGURE 4.4
Setup Wizard: Getting
Started page, when
installing on a system
without Configuration
Manager

3. With that option selected, click Next to continue to the Product Key page. Decide whether
to install as an evaluation or to supply a product key. Once you've entered the key, click
Next to continue to the Microsoft Software License Terms page.

Note: Beginning with the October 2016 release of the version 1606 baseline media for
System Center Configuration Manager, you can specify the Software Assurance expira-
tion date of our licensing agreement as a convenient reminder to you on that date. If you
do not enter this during setup, you can specify it later within the Configuration Manager
Console. Also on this media you will have the option to select Current Branch or Long
Term Servicing Branch, as you can see in Figure 4.5.

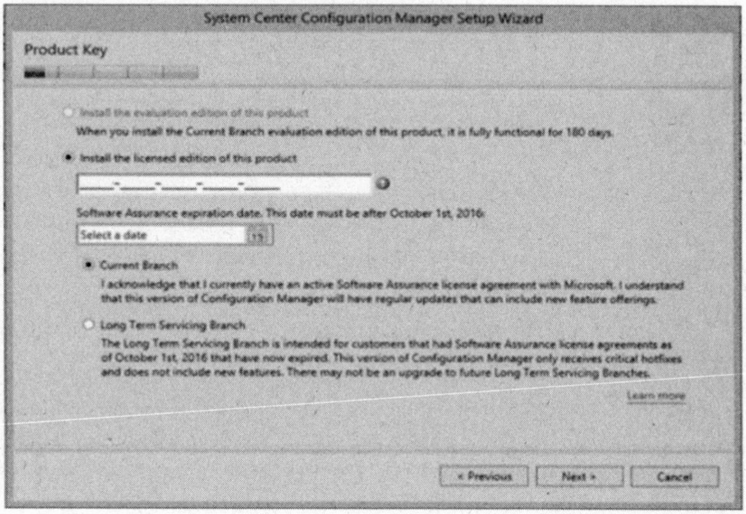

FIGURE 4.5
Setup Wizard: Product
Key after October 2016
Release

4. On the Microsoft Software License Terms page, review the information. If you agree, select I Accept These License Terms and click Next to proceed to the Prerequisite Licenses page.

5. On the Prerequisite Licenses page, review the information. This page requires you to accept the license terms for SQL Server Express, SQL Server Native Client, and Microsoft Silverlight. If you agree, select the appropriate box to accept the terms for each, and click Next to proceed to the Prerequisite Downloads page, shown in Figure 4.6.

FIGURE 4.6
Setup Wizard:
Prerequisite
Downloads page

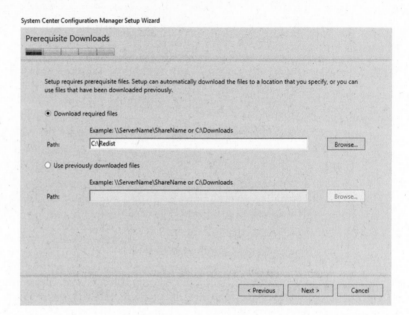

6. On the Prerequisite Downloads page, decide whether to download the updates or, if the updates have been previously downloaded—either from another site installation or using the link on the initial splash page—select the second option.

In both cases, a path for the updates should be specified. For the example, the updates have been previously downloaded and will be installed from the path shown.

7. Once you've completed this screen, click Next, which, depending on the selection made, will initiate the update download process or update evaluation. Once this step is complete, the wizard moves on to the Server Language Selection page.

When migrating from a previous version of Configuration Manager, it might be useful to have both consoles installed on a system. Doing so is fully supported.

8. Choose the languages you want to support. The default is English. Once you've completed this screen, click Next to go to the Client Language Selection page. On the Client Language Selection page, configure additional languages that should be supported from a client perspective. The default here is English. Once you've done this, click Next to proceed to the Site And Installation Settings page, shown in Figure 4.7.

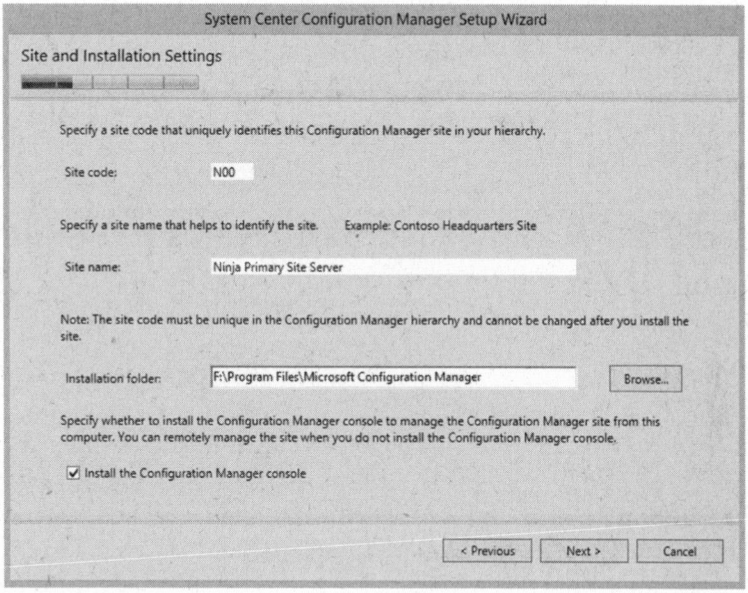

FIGURE 4.7
Setup Wizard: Site And
Installation Settings
page

On the Site And Installation Settings page, several options are available. The first
required option is the Site Code field. The site code can be any three-character alphanumeric code but cannot contain any special character such as a dash or ampersand. In fact,
to ensure no mistake is made here, the wizard won't even accept special characters for the
site code. Next is the Site Name field. Choose a descriptive name and enter it into this box.
Finally, input the installation path where Configuration Manager should be installed.

Setting the correct path is a critical part of installing Configuration Manager. The default
path is on the C: drive, and for the example, we will use the E: drive for best practice.

SELECTING A DISK FOR INSTALLATION

In production environments, you should avoid installing Configuration Manager on a disk shared
by other disk-intensive applications, including the operating system, SQL databases, or the page
file. Doing so may degrade Configuration Manager performance.

The last option is a choice of whether to include the Configuration Manager console as
part of the installation. This option is commonly used and is checked by default. If you
don't want this option, remove the check mark. If you need the administrative console at
a later time, you can easily add it.

9. Click Next to proceed to the Central Administration Site Installation page, where you
can choose from two options: Install As The First Site In A New Hierarchy or Expand An
Existing Stand-Alone Primary Into A Hierarchy. For this example, choose Install As The
First Site In A New Hierarchy.

10. Click Next to proceed to the Database Information page, as shown in Figure 4.8.

FIGURE 4.8
Setup Wizard:
Database Information
page

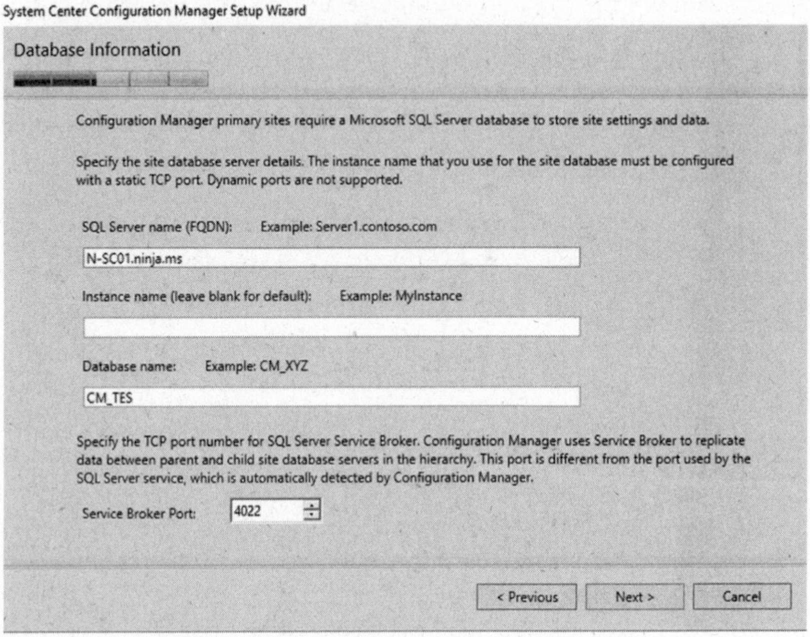

11. On the Database Information page, configure the SQL Server information.

For the example, SQL is installed on the same server where the Setup Wizard is being run, so the default location that shows up for SQL Server is the local server. If you're installing SQL on a remote server, enter the name of that remote server in the SQL Server Name box.

An option to name the database is also provided. If a different database name is preferred, modify the default entry as needed.

12. Click Next to proceed to the Destination page, where you select the destination where the database will be installed. It is important to ensure that this destination has enough space to store the Configuration Manager database.

13. Click Next to proceed to the SMS Provider Settings page, where an option is given to specify where the SMS Provider should be installed.

You may ask, what is the SMS Provider? Detailed information on the SMS Provider can be found here:

`http://technet.microsoft.com/en-us/library/bb680613.aspx`

But in short, the SMS Provider is the resource the Configuration Manager console uses for most of its access to data residing in the Configuration Manager database.

In the example, the central administration site and SQL are installed on the same server, so it only makes sense that the SMS Provider be collocated on that same server. If the SQL Server being used for the CAS were remote, then you'd need to choose whether to place the SMS Provider on the CAS or on the SQL Server. Typically, the provider would be placed on the SQL Server in that configuration for best performance. It is also possible that the SMS Provider could be placed on a totally separate server. In practice, it is an uncommon condition where using a separate server to host the SMS Provider is warranted. More information regarding SMS Provider placement is available in the "Plan for the SMS Provider" document available here:

```
https://docs.microsoft.com/en-us/sccm/core/plan-design/hierarchy/plan-for-the-
sms-provider
```

14. Configure the location, and then click Next to proceed to the Service Connection Point Setup page. You choose either Yes, Let's Get Connected (Recommended), or Skip This For Now.

The Service Connection Point is introduced in the Current Branch 1511 to support the new servicing model of Configuration Manager. It's very important to have the role enabled on those servers that will have Internet connectivity. This is known as the online mode in the Service Connection Point.

15. Click Next to proceed to the Customer Experience Improvement Program page. Review the information and decide whether to participate in the program.

16. With the selection made, click Next to proceed to the Settings Summary page, as shown in Figure 4.9.

FIGURE 4.9
Setup Wizard: Settings Summary page

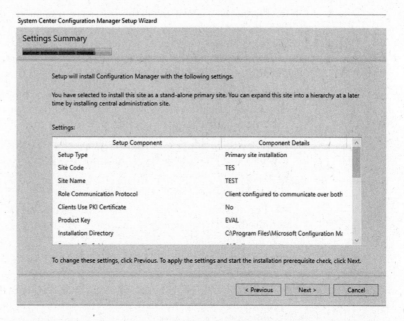

17. On the Settings Summary page, review the configured settings, and if corrections are needed, use the Previous button to move back in the wizard and correct any mistakes.

18. Once all settings are as desired, click Next to proceed to the Prerequisite Check page, shown in Figure 4.10.

FIGURE 4.10
Setup Wizard:
Prerequisite Check
page

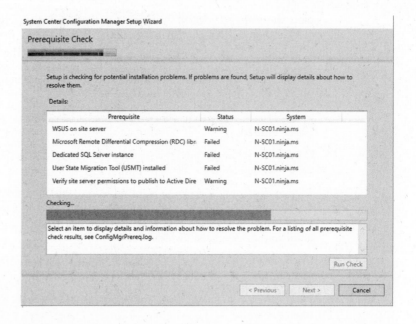

On the Prerequisite Check page, the wizard immediately starts the Prerequisite Wizard to verify that all components required for a successful installation are present. Note that in the figure one item is flagged with a Warning status. Missing prerequisites that are not vital to successful installation will be listed with a warning to raise awareness of their absence. Common warning conditions listed are as follows:

Schema Extensions   This warning alerts administrators to the possibility that Active Directory schema extensions may not be installed. In most cases, extending the Active Directory schema is advantageous, but in some corner cases it can cause confusion.

WSUS SDK On Site Server   This warning alerts administrators to the fact that there is no installation of Windows Server Update Services (WSUS) on the CAS. In most environments Configuration Manager is used to deploy software updates. Software update functionality requires WSUS components to be installed. When they aren't, the warning results.

AD Permissions   In order to publish to Active Directory, the site server must have permissions. This warning is an alert to administrators that required permissions may not be in place.

SQL Memory Usage   By default SQL Server is configured to consume all available memory and to manage the memory so that other applications have what they need and SQL has the rest. Where a server is dedicated to SQL, when other enterprise applications share a system (which is the case when Configuration Manager is collocated with SQL Server), there can be some performance degradation due to memory management. In such cases you should place a limit on the amount of memory available to SQL. You can do so directly in the SQL interface.

SQL Server Process Memory Allocation   This warning alerts administrators that on the CAS SQL Server should be allocated no less than 8 GB of memory.

Having the listed components installed may or may not be appropriate for a specific scenario, depending on the ultimate configuration of the server. If only warning messages are listed, then it is OK to proceed with the install. These warning scenarios can be fixed later if need be. If any critical prerequisites are missing, then Setup cannot proceed.

19. Fix anything that shows a Critical status, and run the prerequisite check again by clicking Run Check. If more information is needed about a particular prerequisite, click any specific item to see more detail.

20. Once all prerequisite issues are resolved, click Begin Install to proceed to the Install page and begin installation. Figure 4.11 shows the page after installation is finished.

FIGURE 4.11
Setup Wizard: Install page: installation complete

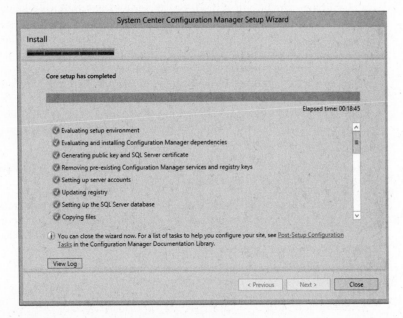

The wizard will remain on the same page, and each phase of the installation will be listed, along with its status, as the installation proceeds. Depending on hardware, the installation will take several minutes or longer. One of the longest steps is installing the boot image package used for operating system deployment.

21. Once the install completes, scroll through the list of installed components, verifying that each has completed successfully.

22. Review the details of the installation procedure by clicking View Log.

The setup process is recorded in two logs: ConfigMgrSetup.log and ConfigMgrPrereq.log. If you're installing the administrative console, that portion will be recorded in ConfigMgr AdminUISetup.log. Lastly, the wizard progress is recorded in ConfigMgrSetupWizard.log. All of these logs are located in the root of the C: drive where Configuration Manager was installed.

23. When you're ready, click Close to exit the wizard.

And that's it; the CAS is now installed. Feel free to explore the console at this stage if you like. The next step is to install a primary child site and attach it to the Central Administration Site. Proceed to the next section when ready.

Implementing a Primary Site

The next step in building a hierarchy is to install a primary site. Remember that primary sites can exist either standalone or in association with other sites in a structure known as the site hierarchy. If you're planning a primary site as part of a hierarchy—which is the case for our example—that primary site must be installed and joined to the CAS. Said another way, a primary site in Configuration Manager must be a child site of the CAS in a hierarchy. This implies that there can be only a single tier of primary sites in the hierarchy. That implication is correct. Unlike previous versions of Configuration Manager, where it was possible to build hierarchies multiple layers deep with primary sites, the new version of Configuration Manager allows only a single tier of primary sites. This change was made specifically to help simplify hierarchies and increase the efficiency and speed of data moving from one site to another. With Configuration Manager, it is possible to have up to four tiers of hierarchy if secondary sites are used. More on that soon, but for now, let's install the primary child.

The Setup Wizard is very similar when installing a primary child site. There are only a few differences. Since we've already discussed the setup process for a CAS, we'll examine only the specific steps that are different for installing a primary site:

1. As before, ensure that the server where the primary site will be installed meets all prerequisites and is ready to receive the installation.

2. When you're ready, launch the splash page, choose to install, and move through the wizard using the information we've already discussed until you arrive at the Getting Started page. Accept the license agreement and continue until you see available setup options, as shown in Figure 4.12.

FIGURE 4.12
Setup Wizard: Getting
Started page for a
primary site

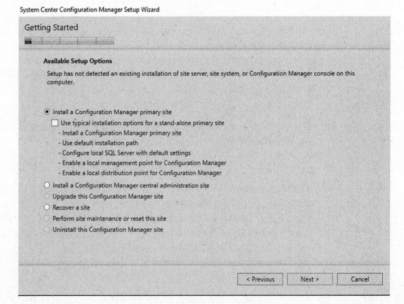

INSTALLING STANDALONE VS. INCLUSION IN A HIERARCHY

If you're installing a standalone primary site and if the option Use Typical Installation Options For A Single Server Installation is selected, then certain pages of the Setup Wizard will be skipped, including the ability to change the directory in which Configuration Manager is installed. This option would be similar to the simple install option available with Configuration Manager 2007. While this option exists, my experience is that most Configuration Manager administrators prefer to see each option as the wizard proceeds to ensure nothing is configured in error.

It is possible to select the option Use Typical Installation Options For A Single Server Installation even when the intent is to join the new primary site to a hierarchy. At this stage of the installation process, Setup doesn't have sufficient information to know the intent. If the option is selected, there will be no option to join to a central administration server.

This is the first place where the setup process will differ from what has already been described.

3. On this page, ensure that the option Install A Configuration Manager Primary Site is selected, but do *not* choose Use Typical Installation Options For A Single Server Installation because this installation isn't for a standalone primary site. Click Next, and proceed through the wizard as before until you arrive at the Prerequisite Components page.

4. On the Updated Prerequisite Components page, select the option Use Previously Downloaded Updates From The Following Location, and specify the update folder used when installing the CAS.

   Since the updates are already downloaded and local, this setting should prevent any download delays. Click Next to continue.

5. Continue through the wizard until you arrive at the Primary Site Installation page. There, you can choose to install the primary site in a standalone configuration or join it to the CAS.

6. The example installation is to be part of a hierarchy, so do the following:

   a. Select the Primary Site Will Be Joined To An Existing Hierarchy option.

   b. Specify the name of the central administration site server.

   c. Click Next to proceed to the Database Information page, shown in Figure 4.13.

   If you had selected the Use Typical Installation Options For A Single Server Installation option on the Getting Started page, this screen of the wizard would have been suppressed.

7. Configure the settings on the Database Server page as before.

8. Continue through the wizard as before until you arrive at the Client Computer Communication Settings page, shown in Figure 4.14.

9. On the Client Computer Communication Settings page, decide whether clients will require secure HTTP communications or whether they can use either secure or nonsecure HTTP communication.

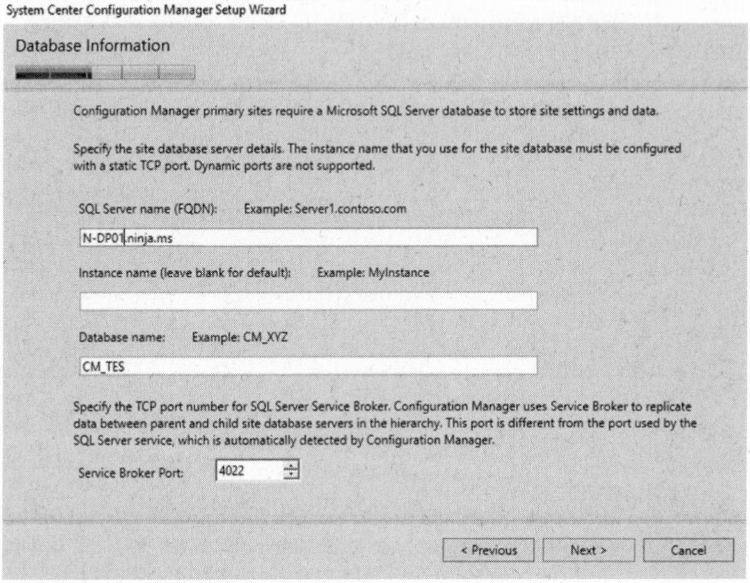

FIGURE 4.13
Setup Wizard:
Database Information
page for a primary site

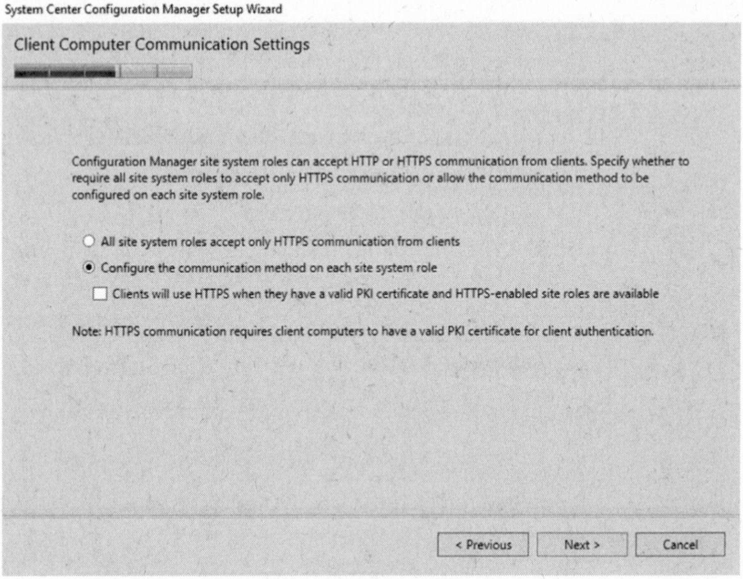

FIGURE 4.14
Setup Wizard:
Client Computer
Communication
Settings page for a
primary site

For the example, choose the latter option, and ensure that the box for Clients Will Use HTTPS When They Have A Valid PKI Certificate And HTTPS-Enabled Site Roles Are Available is selected. Setting this option ensures that when secure communications are possible, they are used.

10. Click Next to proceed to the Site System Roles page, shown in Figure 4.15.

FIGURE 4.15
Setup Wizard: Site
System Roles page for a
primary site

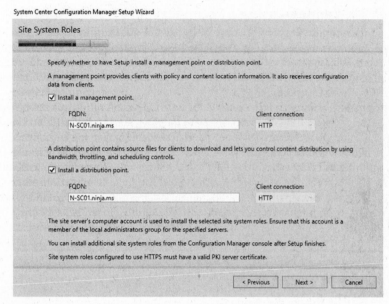

11. On the Site System Roles page, configure whether or not Setup should attempt to install a management point and/or a distribution point and, if so, on what server they should be installed and what communication protocol they should be using—either HTTP or HTTPS.

Remember, site system roles do not have to be configured on the site server itself. Often the Management Point role is configured on the site server and the Distribution Point role is configured on both the site server and remote servers. For our example, the management point and distribution point will be configured on the site server to use HTTP communication.

FURTHER INDICATION OF CENTRAL ADMINISTRATION SITE UNIQUENESS

Notice that the option to specify a management point and a distribution point was not a part of the Central Administration Site Setup Wizard. This is another aspect of the fact that the central administration site is different from a standard primary site. As already mentioned, the CAS cannot host clients, and therefore there is no need for a management point or distribution point.

---

12. Once this is configured, click Next, and complete the wizard as previously described and allow the primary site server to complete installation. Be sure to fix any relevant prerequisite failures!

If all goes well, the site should be installed. It's time to move to our next type of site: the secondary site.

Implementing a Secondary Site

Secondary sites historically have been used to allow local access to distribution points across slower WAN links. The secondary site installation allowed communication of content from its primary parent site to be compressed and the sender to throttle communication across sensitive or slow WAN links. Such a configuration was the most compelling reason for a secondary site installation in the past.

There are other reasons to maintain secondary sites in a hierarchy. One such reason would be if WAN links are too fragile to tolerate client traffic as policy data is retrieved from the management point and discovery and inventory data is uploaded to the management point. An example of such a condition would be a facility, such as a cruise ship, relying on unstable satellite connections for communications. In such a case, a secondary site may still be needed.

The procedure for installing a secondary site in previous versions has been to either push the secondary site installation across the network or install the secondary site from installation media. You may have noticed that the Setup Wizard has no option to allow for installing a secondary site from media, which leaves only the first option—remote install of the secondary site—available in Configuration Manager. A remote install does *not* mean that media will need to be pushed to the target server. If media is available locally, then it can be used, or if not available locally, the needed content can be pushed. For our example, a secondary site will be installed as a child of the primary site just completed.

Initiate the secondary site from the Configuration Manager administrative console. The installation can be initiated from either the CAS or the primary server. For the example, and since central administration is most commonly used, you'll start the installation from the CAS.

1. If the administrative console is not open on the CAS, open it by selecting Start ➤ All Programs ➤ Microsoft System Center ➤ Configuration Manager ➤ Configuration Manager Console.

2. Once it is open, select the Administration workspace, and then expand Site Configuration ➤ Sites.

3. Select the primary site you just installed, and from the Home tab of the ribbon, choose Create Secondary Site, as shown in Figure 4.16. This action launches the Create Secondary Site Wizard.

FIGURE 4.16
Secondary site
installation

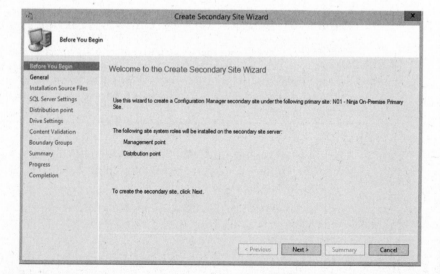

Note in the wizard that a management point and a distribution point will be installed on the secondary site. This is an important distinction because with previous versions administrators had a choice of whether to install a management point, known as a proxy management point, at a secondary site. In Configuration Manager there is no choice. As already mentioned, if you choose a secondary site configuration, it is assumed the WAN is too fragile to tolerate any unthrottled traffic and that local access to policy is required.

4. Review the remaining information on this page, and click Next to proceed to the General page, shown in Figure 4.17.

FIGURE 4.17
Create Secondary Site
Wizard: General page

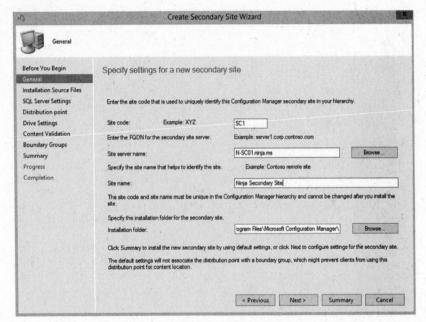

5. On the General page, provide information for the site code and the site name as well as the name of the site server where the secondary site will be installed and a path for the installation.

6. Click Next to proceed to the Installation Source Files page. Select whether to transfer the source files over the network, to use source files at a given network location, or to use source files already staged on or near the remote system being selected for the secondary site installation.

   The latter option allows for scenarios where the network link is insufficient or too unstable to reliably transfer data. For our example, data will be transferred across the network.

7. With the Copy Installation Source Files Over The Network From The Parent Site Server option selected, click Next to proceed to the SQL Server Settings page, shown in Figure 4.18.

FIGURE 4.18
Create Secondary Site
Wizard: SQL Server
Settings page

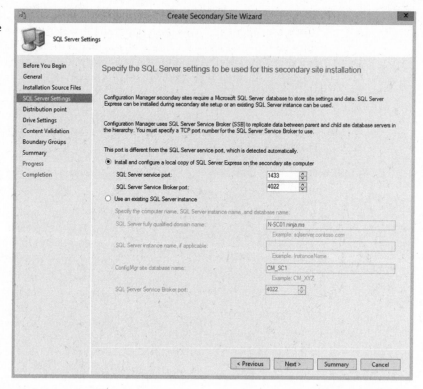

8. On the SQL Server Settings page, either choose to install and configure SQL Express for the secondary server or, if an instance of SQL Server already exists on the destination server, choose the second option and enter details to configure the secondary site accordingly.

SQL AND SECONDARY SITE SERVERS

SQL may already be installed on the secondary site to support other applications, or it may be installed to support components needed by Configuration Manager, such as Windows Server Update Services. If it is, you may choose to install the secondary site database to the existing instance of SQL or choose to install SQL Express instead. If a full version of SQL is already installed, choosing to install SQL Express will result in another instance of SQL running.

Administrators with experience using previous versions of Configuration Manager may see the option to provide a database name and wonder whether they need to take manual action on the destination secondary site server to create the database. There's no need for concern. The installer will take the supplied database name and create the required database automatically.

For our example, SQL is already installed on the destination server, so follow these steps:

a. Select Use An Existing SQL Server Instance.

b. Supply SQL connection details.

c. Click Next to proceed to the Distribution Point page, shown in Figure 4.19.

FIGURE 4.19

Create Secondary Site
Wizard: Distribution
Point page

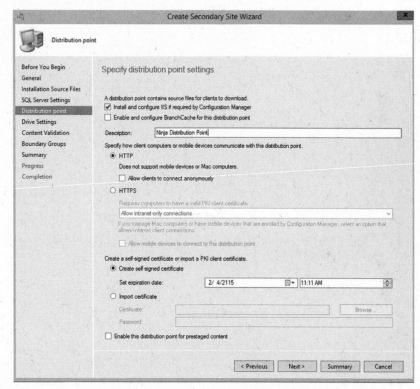

9. On the Distribution Point page, choose the security options for how clients will communicate and also whether the distribution point will be enabled for prestaged content.

10. Click Next to proceed to the Drive Settings page, shown in Figure 4.20.

On the Drive Settings page, configure how you would like your disk drives to be configured for use by the distribution point.

Click Next to proceed to the Content Validation page, shown in Figure 4.21.

On the Content Validation page, configure whether validation should take place and on what schedule and with what priority.

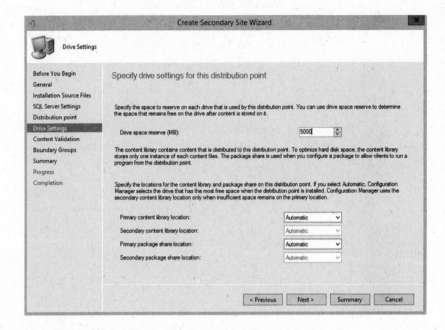

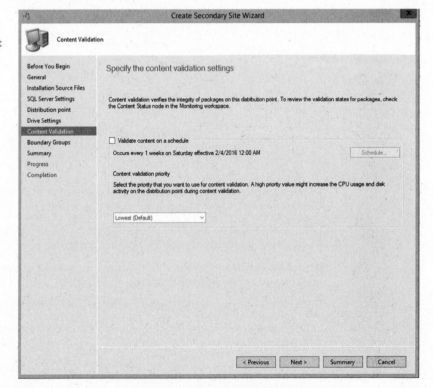

11. Click Next to proceed to the Boundary Groups page. This page provides an opportunity to choose which boundary group the secondary site distribution point should join. There is no requirement to join a boundary group at this stage, and since none have yet been created during the install and further discussion of boundary groups is beyond our focus at the moment, we'll bypass configuring any options on this page.

12. Click Next to proceed to the Summary page, shown in Figure 4.22. This page displays the choices made in the Create Secondary Site Wizard.

FIGURE 4.22

Create Secondary Site
Wizard: Summary page

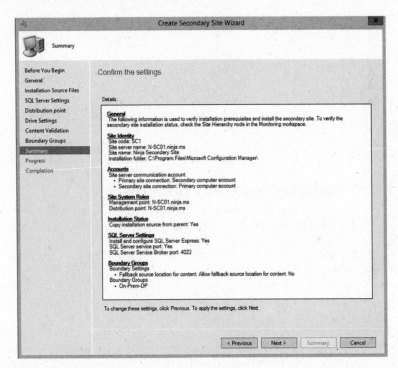

13. Review the summary, and click Previous if you need to make any corrections. When finished, click Next to begin the secondary site installation.

A progress page will come up while the secondary site installation job is being submitted, followed by the Completion page, which shows the installation details in roughly the same way as they appeared on the Summary page.

Installing a secondary site requires checking for prerequisites. This is done behind the scenes as a part of the installation. It is possible to review the prerequisite checks during the secondary site installation in the console. Simply right-click the pending secondary site and select Show Install Status. The Secondary Site Installation Status screen is shown in Figure 4.23.

Finally, a hierarchy is born! All that's left is to double-check the installations.

FIGURE 4.23
Right-click the secondary site and choose Show Install Status to see this screen.

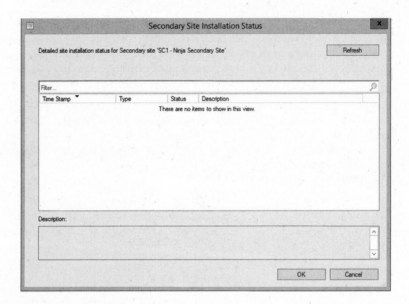

Verifying Proper Site Installation

It seems that all sites in our example installed successfully. The Administration console for the CAS shows all sites listed as expected and in an active state, as shown in Figure 4.24.

FIGURE 4.24
Administration console showing the Sites node

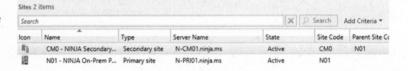

Based on this view alone, everything appears healthy. To make sure that this is truly the case, it's worth taking a look at a few key locations to verify. The locations to check may differ depending on the type of site being installed and the associated services chosen. We'll use the primary site as an example, but the topics generally apply to all types of sites. The areas discussed next are being presented to help with site installation validation. Providing the information in no way implies that it is OK to modify the described settings. In many cases Microsoft doesn't support modifying the settings, and doing so can result in a damaged site.

REGISTRY VALIDATION

A couple of registry locations are important for validating proper site installation. The locations that we discuss are not exhaustive of all registry keys that are added as part of site installation but rather are intended for use in spot-checking installation success.

```
HKEY_LOCAL_MACHINE\SOFTWARE\Microsoft\SMS
```

It may be obvious but the SMS registry key is created as a result of site installation and should appear similar to Figure 4.25. The Identification key is selected to show some of the details about the site.

FIGURE 4.25
Post-installation
Identification key

The CCM registry key is a shared key and will be present either when the management point component of a site server is installed or when a Configuration Manager client is present on the system. If both are present, then the registry key is shared. The CCM key in this case is present because the installed site is a primary site, and the management point was installed as part of installing the site. If the management point is remote, the key won't necessarily be present on the site server. Note also that the client elements are missing from the registry key since the client is not yet installed at the site. This is shown in Figure 4.26.

FIGURE 4.26
Post-installation
CCM key

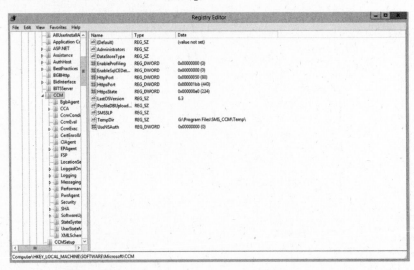

The central administration server will not have the CCM key unless a client is installed on the system. The server cannot host any clients and therefore cannot have a management point installed.

```
HKEY_LOCAL_MACHINE\SOFTWARE\Microsoft\CCM
```

The `ConfigMgr10` registry key results from the console installation. Installing the console as part of the installation is optional, so this key may not be present. The key is shown in Figure 4.27.

```
HKEY_CURRENT_USER\Software\Microsoft\ConfigMgr10
```

FIGURE 4.27
Post-installation
`ConfigMgr10` key

The `Services` registry key is host to an abundance of keys for the various services running on the system. There will be a number of keys beginning with `SMS_` after a successful install. The number and type will depend on the type of site in question. This key is shown in Figure 4.28.

```
HKEY_LOCAL_MACHINE\SYSTEM\CurrentControlSet\Services
```

FIGURE 4.28
Post-installation
`Services` key

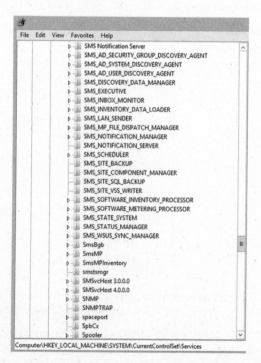

FILE SYSTEM VALIDATION

Site installation files are located in a couple of different file locations. Pick the disk where Configuration Manager was installed and navigate to ..\Program Files\Microsoft Configuration Manager. The folder will look similar to Figure 4.29. In addition, for sites with management points navigate to Program Files\SMS_CCM. The folder will look similar to Figure 4.30.

FIGURE 4.29
Microsoft Configuration
Manager installation
folder

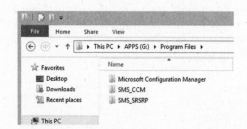

FIGURE 4.30
Management point
SMS_CCM installation
folder

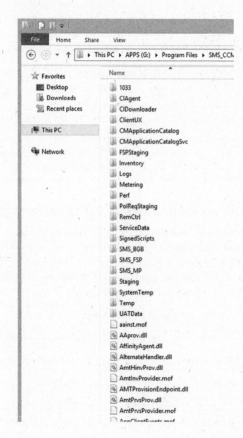

GROUP VALIDATION

The idea of a site hierarchy has been mentioned several times. In order to have a site hierarchy, the individual sites must be able to communicate. Detailed discussion about how this is done is beyond the scope of this chapter, except to mention one thing: Communication between sites requires a security context. In Configuration Manager, such configuration is facilitated using groups configured on the site servers during installation. Several groups are created during site installation, but only a single group, the SMS_SitetoSiteConnection_*<site code>* group, is used to configure the security context for site-to-site communication. When sites attempt communication, the default option is to do so with computer accounts. In the example hierarchy, this would mean that when the CAS attempts to communicate with the primary site, it will attempt a connection using the computer account of the Central Administration account. This communication will fail unless the central administration site's computer account is part of the SMS_SiteToSiteConnection_N01 group. Said another way, any site that needs to communicate with the primary site must have its computer account as a part of the SMS_SiteToSiteConnection_N01 group. This group is shown in Figure 4.31.

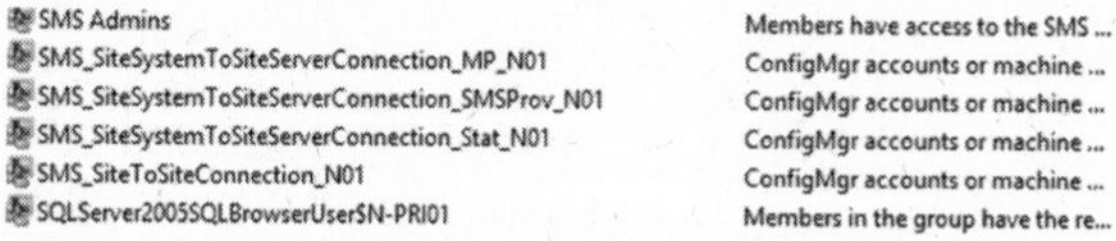

FIGURE 4.31

SMS_ groups added as part of installation

SMS Admins	Members have access to the SMS ...
SMS_SiteSystemToSiteServerConnection_MP_N01	ConfigMgr accounts or machine ...
SMS_SiteSystemToSiteServerConnection_SMSProv_N01	ConfigMgr accounts or machine ...
SMS_SiteSystemToSiteServerConnection_Stat_N01	ConfigMgr accounts or machine ...
SMS_SiteToSiteConnection_N01	ConfigMgr accounts or machine ...
SQLServer2005SQLBrowserUser$N-PRI01	Members in the group have the re...

ADDING COMPUTER ACCOUNTS AS ADMINISTRATORS

OK, it's not really true to say that the computer accounts must be members of the SMS_SiteToSiteConnection_<site code> group. Simply adding the computer accounts as administrators of the various servers would achieve the same purpose and is not recommended. Taking this approach grants more rights than are necessary to the computer accounts and is not a recommended method.

If you prefer not to use the computer accounts as administrators, then it is possible to configure specific credentials to facilitate site-to-site communication. Simply substitute those credentials for the computer account in the same group.

WINDOWS MANAGEMENT INSTRUMENTATION VALIDATION

We've already mentioned the SMS Provider, which is used to interact with the site server database, so ensuring that the installation created information in Windows Management Instrumentation (WMI) as required is important. The current discussion is not intended to be a detailed WMI discussion; simply ensuring that the namespaces were created as required is enough. To verify, follow these steps:

1. Open Computer Management.

2. Select Configuration and then WMI Control.

3. Right-click WMI Control and select Properties.

4. Select the Security tab and expand Root.

A successful installation will result in the SMS namespace being created along with the child namespace site_<site code>, as shown in Figure 4.32.

FIGURE 4.32
WMI namespace
validation

SERVICES VALIDATION

The services have already been validated in the registry, but it's also a good idea to take a look at them in the Services list to ensure all are present and in the proper state of operation. This is shown in Figure 4.33.

FIGURE 4.33
Services validation

DATABASE VALIDATION

A site can't work without its database, so it stands to reason that the site couldn't be installed successfully without the database being installed successfully. Very true, but it's still worth a look for familiarity if nothing else. To view the database, launch SQL Management Studio and follow the steps listed. In our example, SQL is located on the same server as the site.

1. Connect to the database.

2. Open the server.

3. Expand Databases, and the CM_N01 example database should be present. This is shown in Figure 4.34.

CMTRACE

Configuration Manager introduces an updated version of CMTrace. The updated utility is available in the Tools folder on the Configuration Manager media.

The CMTrace utility is very flexible, and administrators will find it to be useful for examining logs other than those from Configuration Manager.

FIGURE 4.34
Database validation

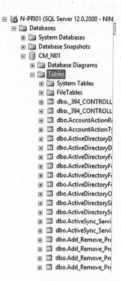

Unattended Installation

In some cases it may be of interest to perform a scripted install of Configuration Manager. This chapter won't go into depth about how this process works, but suffice it to say that the most difficult part of installing a site often is the *answer file* used during installation. Configuration Manager makes this easier: when a site is installed through the UI, an unattended installation file is created as part of the process. This unattended file is called ConfigMgrAutoSave.ini and it's located in the temp directory for the user installing the product. The file is easily modified to perform scripted installs of other sites.

The unattended files generated in the example are shown to give an idea of how these are constructed based on different site types. When you're using the unattended file to initiate a site installation, a command line similar to the following should be used:

```
Setupwpf.exe /script <path to script>\ConfigMgrAutoSave.ini
```

This command line should be initiated from within this directory:

```
<Configuration Manager Source>\SMSSetup\BIN\x64
```

The content of the unattended files is shown in Listing 4.1 and Listing 4.2. Note that single lines may wrap for readability.

LISTING 4.1:   Central administration site unattended file

```
[Identification]
Action=InstallCAS
[Options]
ProductID=
SiteCode=CAS
SiteName=Demo Hierarchy - Central Administration Site
SMSInstallDir=C:\Program Files\Microsoft Configuration Manager
```

```
SDKServer=cmcas.contoso.com
PrerequisiteComp=0
PrerequisitePath=C:\SCCM2012Updates
MobileDeviceLanguage=0
AdminConsole=1
JoinCEIP=0
[SQLConfigOptions]
SQLServerName=cmcas.contoso.COM
DatabaseName=CM_CAS
SQLSSBPort=4022
SQLDataFilePath=C:\Program Files\Microsoft SQL Server\MSSQL10_50.MSSQLSERVER\ ↵
MSSQL\DATA
SQLLogFilePath=C:\Program Files\Microsoft SQL Server\MSSQL10_50.MSSQLSERVER\ ↵
MSSQL\DATA
[CloudConnectorOptions]
CloudConnector=1
CloudConnectorServer= cmps1.contoso.com
UseProxy=0
ProxyName=
ProxyPort=

[SystemCenterOptions]
SysCenterId=HAF5ly+ED00m2PdqZs6JmjCBDVAUKdjlQsD60Wihe+s=

[HierarchyExpansionOption]
```

LISTING 4.2:   Primary site unattended file

```
[Identification]
Action=InstallPrimarySite
[Options]
ProductID=
SiteCode=PS1
SiteName=Test Hierarchy - PS1
SMSInstallDir=C:\Program Files\Microsoft Configuration Manager
SDKServer=cmps1.contoso.com
RoleCommunicationProtocol=HTTPorHTTPS
ClientsUsePKICertificate=1
PrerequisiteComp=1
PrerequisitePath=\\cmcas\c$\sccm2012updates
MobileDeviceLanguage=0
ManagementPoint=cmps1.contoso.com
ManagementPointProtocol=HTTP
DistributionPoint=cmps1.contoso.com
DistributionPointProtocol=HTTP
DistributionPointInstallIIS=0
AdminConsole=1
```

```
JoinCEIP=0
[SQLConfigOptions]
SQLServerName=cmps1.contoso.com
DatabaseName=CM_PS1
SQLSSBPort=4022
SQLDataFilePath=C:\Program Files\Microsoft SQL Server\MSSQL10_50.MSSQLSERVER\ ↵
MSSQL\DATA
SQLLogFilePath=C:\Program Files\Microsoft SQL Server\MSSQL10_50.MSSQLSERVER\ ↵
MSSQL\DATA
[CloudConnectorOptions]
CloudConnector=1
CloudConnectorServer=cmps1.contoso.com
UseProxy=0
ProxyName=
ProxyPort=

[SystemCenterOptions]
SysCenterId=HAF5ly+ED00m2PdqZs6JmjCBDVAUKdjlQsD60Wihe+s=

 [HierarchyExpansionOption]
CCARSiteServer=cmcas.contoso.com
```

Installing Site System Roles

The process just discussed results in a hierarchy with three sites: a central administration site, a primary site, and a secondary site. But just installing the sites doesn't mean that installation is complete. In order to provide service to clients that will be *interacting* with these sites, you must first decide what services will be provided and then configure the additional site components that facilitate providing the needed services. These site components are also known as *site system roles*. The ones available for a given site will depend on the site type:

Central Administration Site

- Asset Intelligence synchronization point

- Certificate registration point

- Endpoint protection point

- Reporting Services point

- Software update point

- System Health Validator point

- Service connection point

Primary Site

- Application Catalog web service point

- Application Catalog website point

- ◆ Certificate registration point

- ◆ Enrollment point

- ◆ Enrollment proxy point

- ◆ Fallback status point

- ◆ Out of band service point

- ◆ Reporting Services point

- ◆ State migration point

- ◆ System Health Validator point

Secondary Site

- ◆ Software update point

- ◆ State migration point

- ◆ Management point

- ◆ Distribution point

Notice that the term *interacting* was used in regard to clients and site servers. Administrators familiar with Configuration Manager may have expected the term *assigned* to be used instead. This term was used on purpose because in Configuration Manager clients can only be assigned to primary sites but are able to interact with any site their boundaries match. This concept is known as *roaming* and describes how clients are able to interact with secondary sites and other primary sites if they're within defined boundaries for those sites. Roaming is beyond the scope of discussion for this section.

A common element in installing all site system roles is the Add Site System Roles Wizard. Before launching the wizard to add the role, you must first decide whether the role will be added to an existing server or a new server. In the example hierarchy just built, that means a choice of adding the new role to a site server itself or creating a new server on which to add the role (both are shown in Figure 4.35).

- ◆ If you're adding to an existing server, simply right-click that server under the Servers and Site System Roles node of the console, and choose Add Site System Roles.

- ◆ If you're adding a new server to host a site system role, that process is initiated by selecting the Create Site System Server action from the Home tab of the ribbon.

A single remote site system server cannot host roles from multiple sites!

Both methods will result in the Create Site System Role Wizard launching. For the example, site system roles are being added to the primary site, which already exists. The first page of the wizard is shown in Figure 4.36.

On this page of the wizard you have the opportunity to provide a server name. This option will be available only if you're creating a new site system server. In addition, options are available to supply the FQDN of the server if it will be addressable from the web. The goal of the option Allow Only Site Server Initiated Data Transfers From This Site System is to designate that communication to site systems should be initiated from the site server itself, rather than the site system pushing data back to the site server. This adds additional security and also accommodates scenarios where trusts aren't in place for cross-forest authentication.

FIGURE 4.35
Use the Create Site
System Server button
on the ribbon to
create a new server;
use the context menu
to assign a new role
on an existing server.

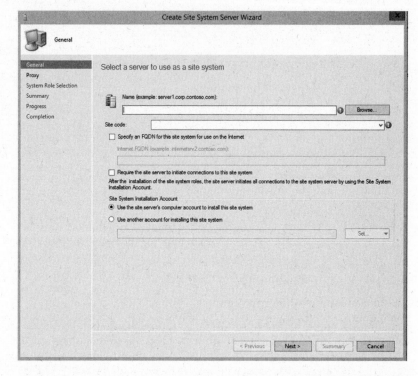

FIGURE 4.36
Add Site System Roles
Wizard: General page

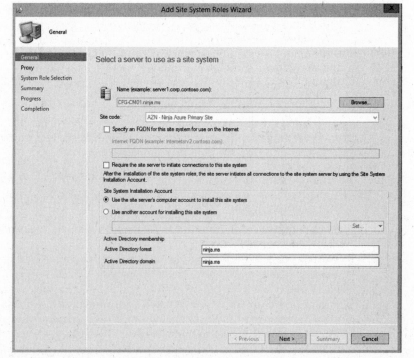

Administrators accustomed to previous versions of Configuration Manager may note that the option to set the site system as a protected site system is no longer available on the first page of the Create Site System Role Wizard. Site system protection only applied to distribution points and state migration points. Because of the new design of Configuration Manager, where distribution points and state migration points are protected by default (more on that shortly), the option to do so was not needed in the wizard.

Clicking Next on the wizard will move you to the page where you select which site system roles should be added to the target server. Once you select the roles and continue moving through the wizard, you must configure the various options for the role-specific pages that will be displayed. Those pages will be discussed shortly for each type of site system.

As previously stated, the available site system roles for a given server depend on the type of server being configured. Each available site system role is described next.

Understanding Configuration Manager Site System Roles

The various site system roles available for each site type can be seen using the administrative console and focusing on the site in question. The list of available site systems that might be installed at the CAS, for example, can be obtained by following these steps:

1. Open the console and navigate to Administration ➤ Overview ➤ Site Configuration ➤ Servers And Site System Roles.

2. Select the site type of interest, right-click, and choose Add Site System Roles.

3. In the wizard, move to the System Role Selection page.

4. Compare the roles available on this page to the roles already installed for the site, as shown in the console.

5. Generate a full list of available roles for a given site.

You can use the same approach for obtaining lists of available site systems for a primary site and a secondary site. Table 4.1 shows the available sites for each site type.

TABLE 4.1:　　Available site system roles by site type

SITE SYSTEM ROLES	CENTRAL ADMINISTRATION SITE	PRIMARY SITE/ STANDALONE	SECONDARY SITE
Component server	×	×	×
Distribution point		×	×
Management point		×	×
Site database server	×	×	×
Site server	×	×	×

TABLE 4.1:   Available site system roles by site type   *(continued)*

SITE SYSTEM ROLES	CENTRAL ADMINISTRATION SITE	PRIMARY SITE/ STANDALONE	SECONDARY SITE
Site system	×	×	×
System Health Validator point	×	×	
State migration point		×	×
Fallback status point		×	
Out of band service point		×	
Reporting Services point	×	×	
Application Catalog web service point		×	
Application Catalog website point		×	
Mobile device enrollment proxy point		×	
Mobile device and AMT enrollment point		×	
Asset Intelligence synchronization point	×	×	
Endpoint Protection point	×	×	
Software update point	×	×	×
Windows Intune Connector	×	×	
Certificate registration point	×	×	

Notably missing from the list of roles at the central administration site is the Management Point role and the Distribution Point role. This might seem strange at first until you again factor in that a CAS is not intended to support any clients; it is solely for the purpose of administration.

Also notably missing are the PXE Service Point role for operating system deployment and the Server Locator Point role used to help clients during site assignment and management point lookup. Don't worry; neither role is gone. The PXE service point is now available as a component of the Distribution Point role, and the server locator point has been merged into the Management Point role.

Another interesting aspect is that one of the site system roles listed for each site is the site server itself. That may seem odd, but in truth the site server function is but one role, albeit the key one, for a site. Note also that these roles can be placed on the same server or they can be placed on dedicated servers. The decision is driven by client count and load on a given role. For some site systems types such as distribution points (discussed shortly), it's quite possible that the same role will be needed on multiple servers to support a single site.

Now, let's discuss what each site system role does, the services it delivers, how it can be used, and some tips on troubleshooting each role.

Component Server

A *component server* is a unique site system role in Configuration Manager. This role cannot be manually added, nor can it be manually removed. This role is managed by the site server itself and will exist on any server that is running the SMS_Executive service within the hierarchy. This service runs specified threads that support other roles, such as a management point.

Distribution Point

The role of the *distribution point* has been expanded in Configuration Manager. In previous versions, this site system was nothing more than a glorified file server, storing files for access by clients requiring content.

The role of the distribution point is still to store file content and make it available to clients, but the way in which it does this has been updated. The first thing that we should mention is that the distribution point is designed to support both classic package distribution and the new application distribution mechanism introduced in Configuration Manager. The legacy style distribution point, which is noted by a file folder named SMSPKG<*driveletter*>$, remains but is used only for packages set to Run From Distribution Point, and this is the only deployment mechanism that bypasses the requirement to use Background Intelligent Transfer Service (BITS). Beyond that, the updated distribution point structure is used universally. While the function of the distribution point in Configuration Manager remains the same, making content available to clients, the structure and function of the distribution point to provide its service have been substantially updated:

♦ There is no option to use the distribution point without making use of BITS.

♦ The distribution point structure is no longer just a file store. Now, files are stored in a cache that takes advantage of single-instance storage, supports automated integrity checks, and more.

♦ The branch distribution points are gone and replaced with the fact that a standard distribution point is now fully supported on a supported Windows 7 workstation system—no client required. The workstation system is still subject to the connection limitation for a given operating system. In Windows 7 the connection limit is set to 20.

Bottom line: This isn't your grandpa's distribution point anymore! First things first—the distribution point must be installed.

It may be that the distribution point role is already installed. One of the default settings when installing a primary or secondary site is to also add the Distribution Point and Management Point roles. If the role has not yet been added or if an additional distribution point is needed, then this component won't yet be present on the server and will need to be added.

1. In the Create Site System Server Wizard, shown in Figure 4.37, select the Distribution Point role, and click Next to proceed to the Distribution Point page of the wizard, as shown in Figure 4.38.

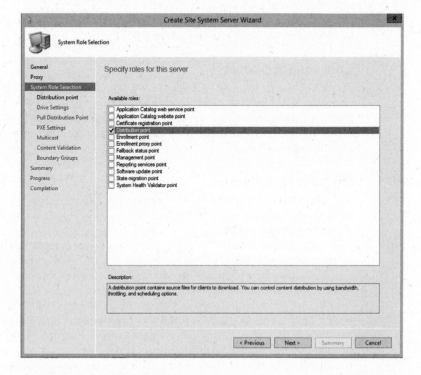

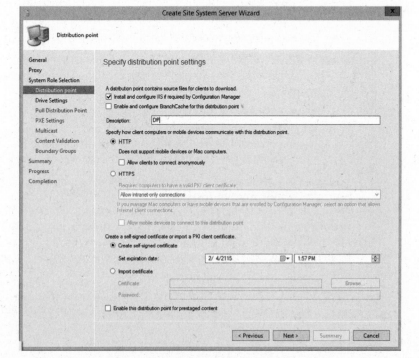

2. On the Distribution Point page of the wizard, configure a few options:

   ◆ The first option, Install And Configure IIS If Required By Configuration Manager, is not selected by default, but you must select this option prior to proceeding as a best practice to ensure the IIS was configured correctly. This option highlights the fact that with Configuration Manager it is not possible to create a non-BITS-enabled distribution point. This fact may influence distribution point placement but is a welcome modification. Also in this section you can select Enable And Configure BranchCache For This Distribution Point. BranchCache is a feature introduced with Windows Server 2008 R2 that allows systems within the same subnet and separate from a content source to share downloaded content locally rather than each system having to download them. You can also enter any information as a description of this distribution point; it's a good idea to configure this to verify what this distribution point is for.

   ◆ Next on the page is the choice of whether clients should communicate with the distribution point using HTTP or HTTPS traffic. When clients use BITS to pull information from the distribution point, as is required by Configuration Manager, the clients do not directly connect to the distribution point structure but rather initiate a BITS session through IIS.

   ◆ Other options on this page allow the administrator to decide whether the distribution point will use self-signed certificates or certificates imported from a different source, such as a certificate authority. If the installation supports Internet scenarios, a certificate would be imported at this step.

   ◆ The last option on the page allows configuration of a distribution point to support prestaged media. Prestaged media is a feature of Configuration Manager and addresses scenarios where administrators would prefer to deliver content in bulk to a distribution point rather than having it copied over the network.

3. Once you've configured all options on this page, click Next to proceed to the Drive Settings page, shown in Figure 4.39.

   Configuration Manager 2012 R2 introduced the ability to control distribution point drive selection and allocate reserved storage when configuring the distribution point. Mechanisms did exist in previous versions of Configuration Manager to make similar configurations effective, notably the use of the no_sms_on_drive.sms flag file, but having these options in the console allows more effective and granular administrator control. A couple of options are presented here:

   ◆ First is the ability to preconfigure the amount of drive space that should be reserved for the distribution point.

   ◆ The next set of options, which are perhaps more important, let you choose which drives should be used for the content libraries and package share locations. In our example, there is only a single drive on the site server, so leaving the options set to Automatic makes sense.

      Also, since there is only a single drive on the server, it doesn't make sense to set a secondary content location, so that option is grayed out. If multiple drives are available and the setting is left at Automatic, then the system will pick the drives to use the same way it has done historically—using the NTFS drive with the most available space as a first choice, and so on.

FIGURE 4.39
Create Site System
Server Wizard: Drive
Settings page

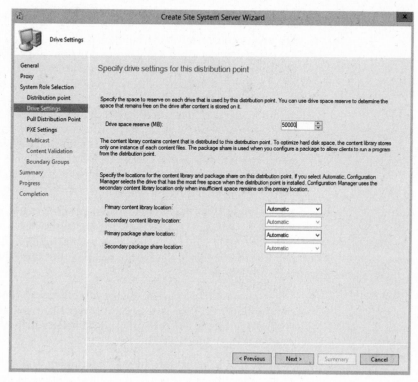

4. Select the Pull Distribution Point page of the wizard if you need this option for your distribution point. The use of pull distribution points can help reduce the processing load on the site server when you deploy content to a large number of distribution points at one site.

   Configure the distribution point to be a pull distribution point by selecting Enable This Distribution Point To Pull Content From Other Distribution Points, as shown in Figure 4.40.

   ◆ Click Add, and then select one or more of the available distribution points to be source distribution points.

   ◆ Click Remove to remove the selected distribution point as a source distribution point.

5. Once the settings are configured, click Next to proceed to the PXE Settings page of the wizard, shown in Figure 4.41.

   The PXE Settings page of the wizard lets you choose whether the distribution point being configured should also act as a PXE server for operating system deployment. Because of the dependency the PXE server has on the distribution point to deliver boot images, having this setting as part of the distribution point makes sense. For the example we won't install a PXE point; it can be added later as needed.

FIGURE 4.40
Create Site System
Server Wizard:
Pull Distribution
Point page

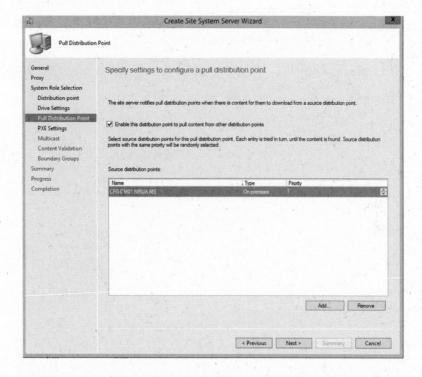

FIGURE 4.41
Create Site System
Server Wizard: PXE
page

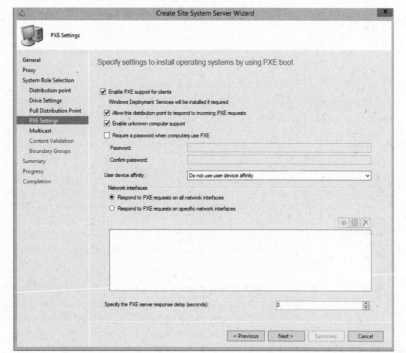

6. Review the settings on this page and click Next to proceed to the Multicast page of the wizard, shown in Figure 4.42.

FIGURE 4.42
Create Site System
Server Wizard:
Multicast page

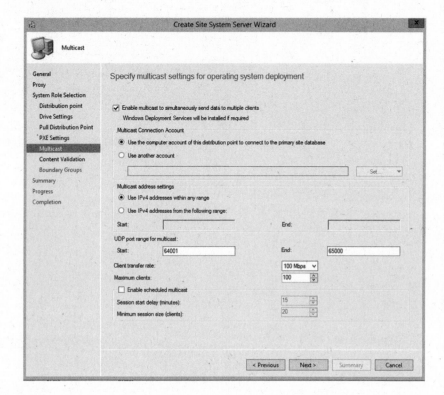

The Multicast page of the wizard allows administrators to specify whether or not the distribution point being configured should support multicast. Multicast is used with operating system deployment and is a very efficient protocol for delivering images to multiple systems simultaneously. The example distribution point will not be used for multicast support for now, so don't select this option. It can be added later as needed.

7. Review the settings on this page, and click Next to proceed to the Content Validation page, shown in Figure 4.43.

The Content Validation page of the wizard allows administrators to specify whether content should be periodically validated on the distribution point and, if so, on what schedule and at what priority. When Validate Content On A Schedule is selected, the default evaluation period is once per week and at a low priority, to ensure other activities on the server are not disrupted.

This is a significant feature update for Configuration Manager! Most readers who have used distribution points in previous versions of Configuration Manager will have encountered a scenario where content will be distributed to distribution points, work fine for a period of time, and then start to show errors, typically a hash mismatch problem.

This might happen for several reasons, often due to on-demand virus scanning of the distribution points, but when encountered, the problem is disruptive until fixed. The ability to do content validation and proactively identify problems is a welcome change indeed! Further, the updated structure of the distribution point should help keep content in a good state. More on the distribution point structure shortly.

FIGURE 4.43
Create Site System Server Wizard: Content Validation page

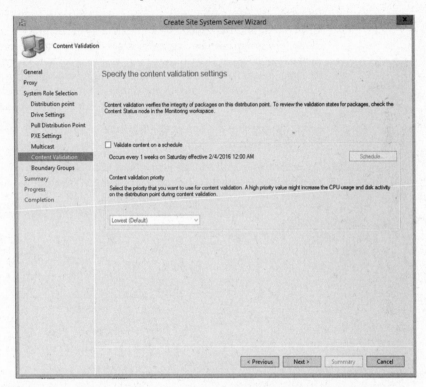

8. Once you've configured these settings, click Next to proceed to the Boundary Groups page of the wizard, which allows the administrator to choose the boundary group(s) of which the distribution point should be a member. While it is not a strict requirement that a distribution point be a member of any boundary group in order to be created, the distribution point may not be accessible by any client until it is added to the appropriate boundary group(s). Detailed discussion of boundary groups is beyond the focus of this chapter, but based on the tight dependency between distribution point function and boundary groups, a bit of discussion is appropriate here.

Boundary groups were introduced in Configuration Manager 2012 and serve two purposes: client assignment and content access. The latter item is the one of concern for distribution point access. We mentioned earlier that on the Create Site System Server Wizard's General page, the option to specify a site system as protected was removed. In Configuration Manager, when a distribution point (or state migration point in operating system deployment) is added to a boundary group, by definition the distribution point is protected and only those clients that are within the boundaries defined by the boundary group are able to retrieve content from the distribution points that have membership in the boundary group. Further, a distribution point can have membership in multiple boundary groups. By taking this new approach, administrators are afforded additional control to easily specify which distribution points are available to service clients depending on which subnets the clients happen to be located near.

But what if a client requires access to content but is not within boundaries defined by any boundary group, such as a laptop in a hotel room? That scenario is also addressed. Boundary groups can be flagged as accessible to systems when the system is in a location where no other distribution point can be resolved. This is known as *fallback* and is enabled by default for the boundary group, as noted at the bottom of the Boundary Groups page. For the example, the distribution point has been added to a boundary group that was previously created for the example primary site.

9. Once the boundary group configuration is complete, click Next to review the Summary page of the wizard.

10. After confirming all settings, click Next to finish the wizard and implement the distribution point deployment. The successful completion is shown in Figure 4.44.

FIGURE 4.44
Create Site System
Server Wizard:
Summary page

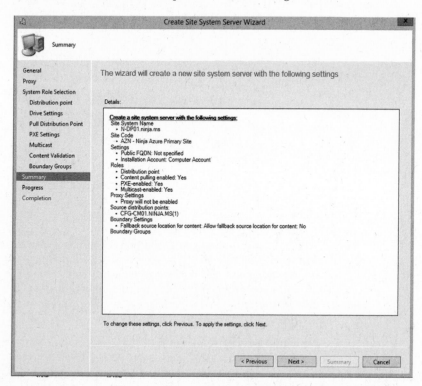

As mentioned earlier, the Configuration Manager distribution point structure has changed. After installation is complete and after a couple of applications have been deployed, open the drive hosting the distribution point and check for a few folders, as shown in Figure 4.45.

Program Files
SCCMContentLib
SMSPKG
SMSPKGG$
SMSPKGSIG
SMSSIG$
WSUS

FIGURE 4.45
Distribution point structure

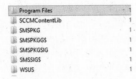

The same folders you might expect from previous versions are still present to support distribution of classic software packages configured to Run From Distribution Point: `SMSPKG`, `SMSPKG`*`<driveletter>`*`$`, `SMSSIG$`, and `SMSPKGSIG`. In addition to these folders, another is present called `SCCMContentLib`. This folder contains the new structure for the distribution point and is worth further discussion.

Historically, opening the distribution point folder will reveal a list of folders named with package IDs and, within the folder, the contents of the package. That still is the case, but the structure is far different. Remember that the new distribution point structure in Configuration Manager is designed to take advantage of single-instance storage and also to be a bit more stable. Looking inside the `SCCMContentLib` folder reveals three additional folders, `DataLib`, `FileLib`, and `PkgLib`, shown in Figure 4.46.

This PC ▸ APPS (G:) ▸ SCCMContentLib ▸
Name
DataLib
FileLib
PkgLib

FIGURE 4.46
`SCCMContentLib` structure

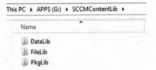

The `PkgLib` folder is the starting place to examine the new structure, and it contains files with names that match the package ID from the site, shown in Figure 4.47.

N000000A
N0000001
N0000002
N0000006

FIGURE 4.47
`PkgLib` folder structure and INI files

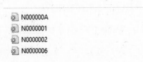

Note that these files are INI files. Looking inside reveals the packages that are associated with the package ID. From here, copy and paste the two `Content_` GUIDs and navigate to the `DataLib` folder, shown in Figure 4.48. For the example, use `Content_3b898e35-9ecc-45e2-9231-ee3f30b2a3aa.1`.

0a972ee5-35dd-484f-84b9-236ccc5b4a22
0d9fb39e-b95a-46d7-a5a0-2c435b268793
0d91bd37-4d81-4fb1-a96b-1be800238f94
0f017ab9-f9bc-4538-a5d1-ff67cab113b8
1b9e0474-477a-4150-a9c6-5429cc2fbf7b
1d6c7217-acdc-40d4-908d-789e27ef6bf9
1d4069f2-75b0-41b2-b8f3-7b7edfc25678
1ee6893c-2a3a-4711-9fbb-a827976017dd
1fc26f41-d126-4c78-a68e-b24bf3971864
02bc4623-8e42-4864-ab76-b12fdce80904
2a38c074-0026-4a5d-b9aa-3a3f10504922

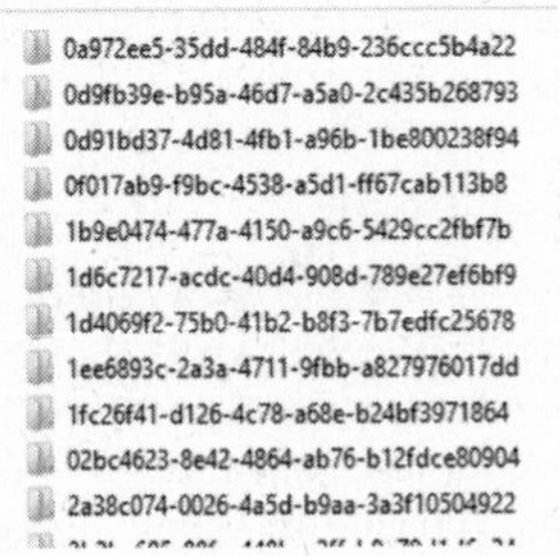

FIGURE 4.48
`DataLib` folder structure, GUID folder, and configuration file

In the DataLib folder there are two entries that match; the first is a folder and the second is a configuration file. Looking at the GUID folder first, it looks like the location of the package content. But not so fast! The filenames here will match the filenames from the source file folder, but a quick glance at the file sizes and file extension will show that these are just configuration files. Taking a look at the client.msi file reveals details about the actual file, including file size, in this case 37294080 bytes, and the hash value for the file. The first four characters of the hash value here are key to finding the actual file. In the example, the hash value of interest is 00FD. More on this shortly.

In addition to the source file structure, there is another configuration file matching the GUID in question; it is at the root of DataLib. Opening it shows a hash value for the folder itself.

Armed with information gained from this folder, it's time to visit the FileLib folder, shown in Figure 4.49.

FIGURE 4.49

FileLib folder
structure

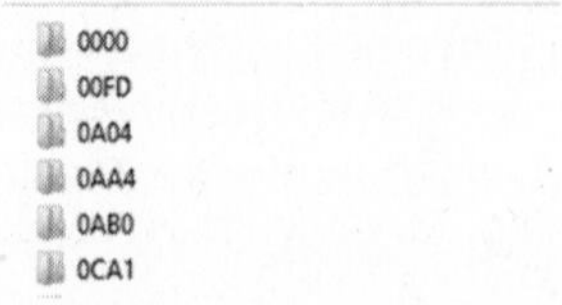

Within the FileLib folder is a series of other folders with names that at first appear cryptic—only four characters. Aha! Remember that we just mentioned that the first four characters of the hash value for the client.msi file were important. In this folder there is a subfolder named C6BB. A quick look inside that folder reveals a file with the exact size of the client.msi file—37,294,080 bytes. Bingo! This is the location of the actual client.msi file, simply renamed and placed into this single-instance storage format. You could also take the file out of the FileLib and rename its extension to **.msi** and it can be used to trigger the install if necessary.

SOFTWARE REQUIREMENTS

Configuration Manager distribution points require the following:

◆ All site servers must be members of a Windows 2012 R2 or higher Active Directory domain.

◆ Distribution points require Background Intelligent Transfer Service (BITS) version 2.0 or higher and cannot be installed or used without it.

◆ The Web Server (IIS) role.

◆ Distribution points may be installed on any supported server or client operating system.

◆ All Configuration Manager distribution point systems using BITS bandwidth throttling require BITS 2.0 or higher in the Server Operating System.

Management Point

A *management point* is the primary point of contact between the Configuration Manager clients and the site server. All site servers that host clients must have at least one management point installed; this includes primary site servers and secondary site servers. A management point installed at a secondary site server is known as a proxy management point. Clients use the management point to retrieve and send all data to and from their assigned site server; this includes retrieving settings and configuration via the policy and forwarding operational data such as inventory, state messages, status messages, discovery information, and more. In addition, clients will send requests to the management point requesting help locating content they may need, such as finding which distribution points are available to the client and contain needed software update or software package content, or even the location of a software update point used in software update scanning.

Once a management point receives data from the client, it will be further analyzed and converted into a form acceptable by the site server and then forwarded to the site server for further processing. This also includes content location requests, but in these cases there is no data to forward to the site server. Instead, the management point will execute queries against the site database and return that information to requesting clients.

Here are a few things to remember about management points:

♦ Every primary and secondary site must have a management point specified.

♦ The central administration site cannot host a management point.

♦ Management points require access to the site database for certain operations.

♦ Management points require a local installation of IIS to be installed.

♦ Management points make use of BITS when moving content, depending on size, to help avoid impacting network utilization.

Also of interest for management points is that they no longer have a dependency on WebDAV. Add to this that management points are now treated similarly to distribution points in that they can be placed where needed to support clients. In previous Configuration Manager releases, the only way to host multiple active management points at a site was by using a network load balancer as a front end. Now management points are simply looked up by clients—similar to distribution points—and the best choice at a site is returned to the client. This statement may cause you to ask how exactly clients learn about possible management points. There are a couple of ways. It's possible to specify a single or multiple management points on the command line when installing the client using the SMSMP= switch. If Active Directory publishing is enabled, clients will be able to look up the management point list from there as well. During client installation, and during ongoing client operation, they will learn which management point is optimum for their use through boundary groups—again, much the same as distribution points.

Another big shift for management points is that now the server locator point functionality is included in this role.

It may be that the Management Point role is already installed. One of the default settings when installing a primary or secondary site is to also add the management point role. If the role was not yet added as part of setup, then you will need to add it.

1. In the Add Site System Roles Wizard, select to add the Management Point role, and click Next to proceed to the Management Point page, as shown in Figure 4.50.

♦ The first choice on this page allows administrators to choose how clients should communicate with this management point, either by HTTP or by HTTPS.

♦ Administrators are also able to specify whether they want to receive an alert in the console indicating when the management point is unhealthy.

If this option is selected, administrators can find alerts generated in the Monitoring workspace of the console.

2. Click Next to continue to the Management Point Database page shown in Figure 4.51.

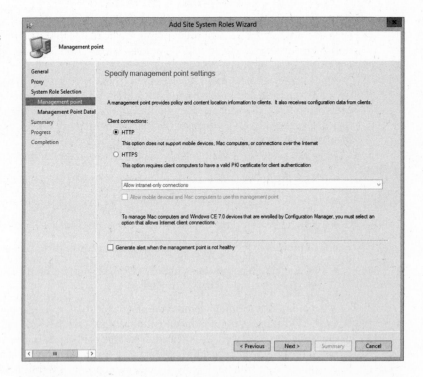

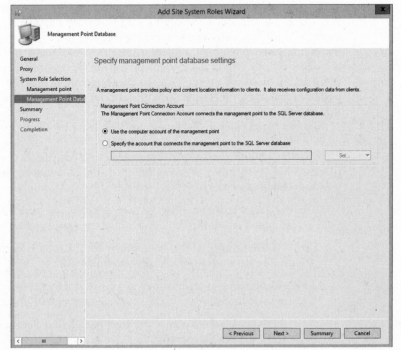

PROXY MANAGEMENT POINTS

Proxy management points are the same as standard management points except that they are located at a secondary site. In previous versions of Configuration Manager, it was the administrator's choice whether to include a proxy management point at secondary sites. In the new version there is no choice; proxy management points are automatically installed on every secondary site server.

Proxy management points exist to help reduce the impact on the WAN when clients are operating outside the boundaries of their assigned primary site but within the boundaries of a secondary site that is a child of their assigned primary site. A client in this configuration will consider the proxy management point to be its local management point but will always consider the management point from its assigned primary site to be the assigned management point. The difference between the two is that the client is able to use the local management point to find local distribution points via content location requests and also as a point for offloading data, such as inventory and state messages, on its way to the parent site's database. The client will still use its assigned management point to retrieve all policy changes.

Proxy management points can significantly reduce the load on WAN traffic by processing data from and providing client policy to those clients that fall within their roaming boundaries. Data flow between Configuration Manager clients and the Configuration Manager hierarchy is as follows:

1. Clients send discovery data, inventory data, status data, and software-metering data to the proxy management point in XML format.

2. The proxy management point processes the submitted XML file and converts it into the appropriate file type, and the file is placed in the associated Inbox directory on the secondary site server.

3. The secondary site server processes the data as it would under normal circumstances and forwards it up the hierarchy to its parent site.

Proxy management points also retrieve policy information from the database of the primary site and forward the data to Configuration Manager clients. Proxy management points allow the client to function locally when roaming to a secondary site, while further allowing administrators to control the replication of client data from the secondary site to the primary parent by means of standard sender throttling.

HOW CLIENTS FIND MANAGEMENT POINTS

During installation and general operation, Configuration Manager clients obtain management point locations in much the same way as they look up distribution points. Configuration Manager allows for multiple active management points per site. Periodically, clients will poll for which management point they should be using. The determination is made by evaluating boundary groups in relation to the client, very similar to the mechanism used to find distribution points. If a client roams outside of its assigned site's boundaries, then the lookup is a bit more complex but is needed to allow clients to access local management point servers where possible. There is also a lookup mechanism for management points in Active Directory.

LOCATING MANAGEMENT POINTS IN AD

In an environment that provides Active Directory services, Configuration Manager clients locate management points by following these steps:

1. The client searches the Active Directory global catalog for a local site code with a matching Active Directory site name, IP network, or IP address range that has been previously registered by a site server.

2. If a match is not found or if required content is not available at the local site, then the client uses the site code of its assigned site.

3. The client then queries Active Directory again to find the appropriate management point for the site code identified in the previous steps.

   For this reason, management points should be installed prior to Configuration Manager client deployment, but the client will be able to access the management point once it becomes available.

4. If there is only one management point for the site, the client gets the name of that management point from Active Directory and then connects to it.

OVERLAPPING BOUNDARIES AND MANAGEMENT POINT LOCATION

The fact that the client will always query Active Directory first when attempting to locate management points is one of many reasons why overlapping site boundaries is unsupported and will wreak havoc on an environment. When sites publish their information to Active Directory and that information is inconsistent, as in the case of overlaps, the client may not choose the correct management points for use when looking up content locations. The result may be failed software deployment in the environment, not to mention the implications for proper client assignment if installing clients.

AUTOMATIC MP QUERY

When installing the Configuration Manager client, you must either set it to determine the SMS site automatically or specify site assignment as part of the command line for the installation. During installation and after being assigned to a site, the client will look up the appropriate management point it should be using. The client gets this list either by command line during installation, by querying Active Directory, or by learning about additional management points and adjusting after installation.

In addition, a new option has been added to Configuration Manager to specify a default site a client should be assigned to if it is unable to find a site by normal lookup mechanisms. This fallback ability helps ensure clients do not get installed and immediately orphaned because they cannot find a site.

You can see this in the `LocationServices.log` file of the Configuration Manager client, located at `%Windir%\CCM\Logs`.

SERVER LOCATOR POINT FUNCTIONALITY

As mentioned, the server locator point functionality has been merged into the Management Point role. But what is a server locator point used for? Server locator points are used within a Configuration Manager hierarchy to provide services for client site assignment, location of client installation files, and location of management points when clients cannot access that information within Active Directory. The role helps those clients in workgroups and untrusted forest as well. Thus, merging this role with the Management Point role is a natural fit.

LOGGING

Logs of management point activity can exist in one of two locations, depending on which was installed first: the Configuration Manager client or the management point. The management point and the client share a common framework and thus both run under the SMS Agent Host service, CCMExec. However, the management point runs under a thread of SMS Executive. This is potentially confusing at first because it is possible to have just a management point installed without the client component, but the service name will still be SMS Agent Host.

If the management point is installed on a server first, the logs will be located in the `.\SMS_CCM\Logs` directory. When the Configuration Manager client has already been installed on the server, the logs are located in the `%Windir%\CCM\Logs` directory along with the client-side logs.

Default logging is good for both the client and the management point, but there are some log details that won't be seen unless verbose and debug logging are enabled. Some of the information that is accessible with this extra level of logging is so useful that it is common practice to configure verbose and debug logging as a standard across the environment. There is additional overhead because more data is written to the logs, but it is minimal and should cause no impact to the operation of the system.

Enabling verbose and debug logging requires two registry changes. First, you enable verbose logging by navigating to

`[HKEY_LOCAL_MACHINE\software\microsoft\ccm\logging\@global]`

and changing the value `LogLevel` to 0 (which will require a permissions change on the @GLOBAL key). To enable debug logging, create a registry key called `DebugLogging` directly under

`[HKEY_LOCAL_MACHINE\SOFTWARE\Microsoft\CCM\Logging]`

Inside this registry key create a string value named `Enabled` and set its value to `True`.

SOFTWARE REQUIREMENTS

Configuration Manager management points require the following:

◆ All site servers must be members of a Windows 2012 R2 or higher Active Directory domain.

◆ The Web Server (IIS) role in Windows Server 2012 R2 or higher.

Site Database Server

Every Configuration Manager implementation will have at least one server running the site Database Server role. The simplest implementation will have a single server running all the Configuration Manager roles as well as Microsoft SQL Server 2012 R2 or higher. As noted earlier, at least one database repository is required to store all the client information and site configurations.

A Configuration Manager site database server requires the following:

◆   All site servers must be members of a Windows 2012 R2 or higher Active Directory domain.

◆   Microsoft SQL Server 2012 R2 or higher is the only version of SQL Server supported for hosting the Configuration Manager database. (There may also be cumulative update requirements; for the latest list, check the TechNet documentation.)

◆   The SQL database service is the only SQL Server component required to be installed to host the site database.

Site Server

A *site server* is a unique site system role in Configuration Manager. This role cannot be manually added, nor can it be manually removed. This role is managed by the site server itself and will exist on any server that is serving as a site server in the hierarchy. When a site is installed, whether a central administration site, primary site, or secondary site, it will be shown as having the site server role.

This role manages all functions of the site and interacts with all remote systems hosting site system roles for the site. The overall health of the site server role can be reviewed in the Monitoring node of the console and also by examining the site server logs generated.

Site System

A *site system* is a unique site system role in Configuration Manager. This role cannot be manually added nor can it be manually removed. This role is managed by the site server itself and will exist on any server that is serving as a site system in the hierarchy. The site server itself will always be a site system as will any remote servers that are deployed to host various roles to provide services needed by the site.

The overall health of the site system server can be reviewed in the Monitoring node of the console. The specific nodes to review as well as the specific log files will be dictated by the specific functions being performed by the site system server.

State Migration Point

The state migration point is a Configuration Manager site system role that provides a secure location to store user state information as part of an operating system deployment. User state is stored on the state migration point while the operating system deployment proceeds and is then restored from the state migration point to the new computer at the appropriate time during imaging. Each state migration point site server can be a member of only one Configuration Manager site, but each site may have multiple state migration points if needed.

If the state migration point role has not yet been added, you will need to select it, as shown in Figure 4.52.

1.   Choose the site where the state migration point will be located, and select the role in the Add Site System Roles Wizard.

2.   Click Next to proceed to the State Migration Point page of the wizard, shown in Figure 4.53.

This page allows configuration of the state migration point.

FIGURE 4.52
Add Site System
Roles Wizard: State
migration point
selected

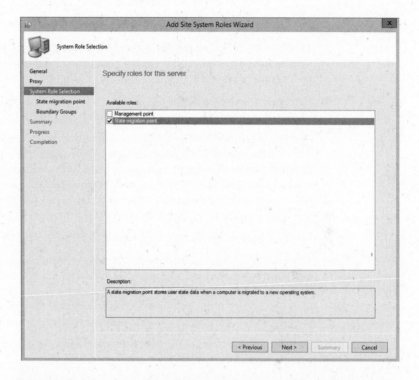

FIGURE 4.53
Add Site System
Roles Wizard: State
Migration Point page

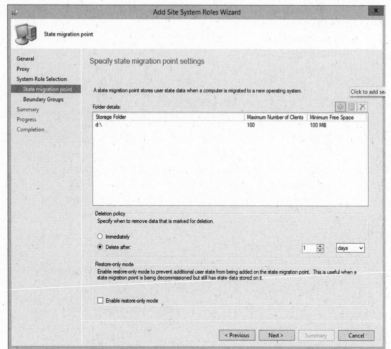

3. First, choose the folder that will host user data sent to the state migration point.

   This includes choosing the drive, the folder name, the maximum number of clients that may be served by the state migration point, and also the minimum amount of disk space that should be reserved.

4. Configure the Deletion Policy to show how long user state data is held following a successful operating system deployment before being deleted.

   This raises an important point. When user state data is stored on the state migration point, it is with the intention that the state data will be restored to either the same system or a different system as imaging nears completion. If the state data is never restored, it is never marked as eligible for deletion because there might have been problems during the imaging process, and allowing deletion would remove potentially needed data from the system. This is particularly true if the deletion settings specify to remove data immediately.

5. Finally, flag the state migration point as being in restore-only mode.

   This special setting, disabled by default, allows administrators to configure a state migration point so that it doesn't receive new state data but is available for use in already stored state data. Typically you would set this option if you have a state migration point server that is scheduled for maintenance or replacement; you could also use this option if you are building a new state migration point but you don't want it to go into service yet.

6. Once the configuration settings are complete, click Next to proceed to the Boundary Groups page of the wizard, shown in Figure 4.54.

FIGURE 4.54
Add Site System Roles
Wizard: Boundary
Groups page

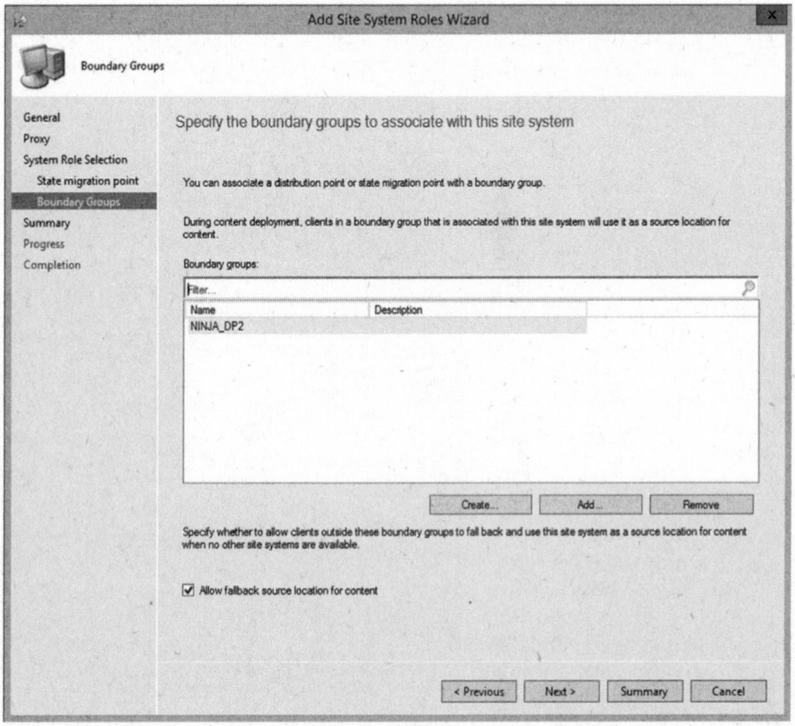

Like the distribution point, the state migration point needs to be added to an appropriate boundary group to make it available for use by clients. If the state migration point is being installed on a server that already hosts the Distribution Point role, then the boundary group may be prepopulated.

7. Make any needed changes and click Next to continue through the wizard and finish.

Software Requirements

Configuration Manager state migration points must be members of a Windows 2012 R2 or higher Active Directory domain.

Fallback Status Point

The Fallback Status Point role helps address today's greater security requirements while enabling a mechanism to catch clients that are not communicating properly. When deploying clients it is critical to know if problems are being encountered. Typically these problems are reported to the management point in the form of status or state messages. When installing the client, there is a time when it is not possible to send data to the management point. In addition, there may be problems reaching the management point even after install. In such cases, if the client does not have a mechanism to notify the site of problems, it will become orphaned and unusable. The Fallback Status Point role provides an administrator with insight into the installation and management of a client and works well because the location of the fallback status point is configurable on the command line when client installation is initiated.

A fallback status point is similar to a proxy server that proxies client status messages up to the site server. Two types of messages may occur: the normal messages that appear during client installation and assignment or those identifying unhealthy Configuration Manager clients. In either scenario, the fallback status point fills the gap and shows the administrator that there are client issues that need to be addressed.

Because of the potential security threat of an unknown client or client status, it is recommended that the fallback status point be placed on a separate site server that is not a site already. It can be a low-end server, because of the relatively small number of potential requests it should receive. As in any design decision, the criterion of scale versus risk should be investigated before a decision is made.

Through detailed reporting, an administrator can gain knowledge and take proactive measures to ensure that availability remains in its highest state. These reports include detailed client information on capable and incapable client communication.

Installation of a fallback status point is not a requirement for a site but it is recommended. Typically there is one fallback status point installed per site that hosts clients.

If the Fallback Status Point role has not yet been added, you will need to select it.

1. Choose the site where the fallback status point will be located, and select the status point in the Add Site System Roles Wizard.

2. Click Next to proceed to the Fallback Status Point page of the wizard, shown in Figure 4.55.

There is little configuration to be done for the fallback status point. The only option is to configure the number of state messages that are allowed to be processed during the given time window. Typically the default values are fine.

FIGURE 4.55
Add Site System Roles
Wizard: Fallback
Status Point page

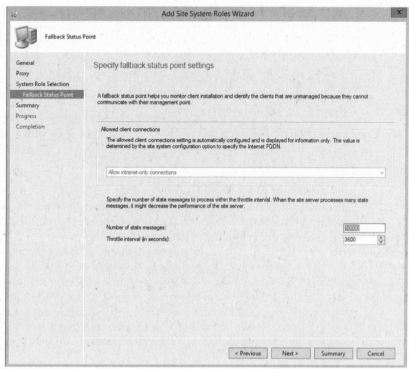

3. Make any needed changes, and click Next to complete the wizard.

SOFTWARE REQUIREMENTS

♦ Configuration Manager fallback status points require that all site servers be members of a Windows 2012 R2 or higher Active Directory domain.

♦ The Web Server (IIS) role is required.

Reporting Services Point

The Reporting Services point provides integration between Configuration Manager and SQL Server Reporting Services (SSRS) to facilitate report publishing and rendering. SSRS integration just makes sense. Most people don't enjoy reading through line after line of tabular reports and would prefer to encapsulate that same data in a graphical format. SSRS can handle most any reporting scenario with ease.

If the SSRS role has not yet been added, you will need to select it in the Add Site System Roles Wizard.

1. Choose the site and server where the Reporting Services point will be located.

If a central administration site is in place, then it is a good choice as a site to host this site system role. It is also possible to install this role on a primary site or to install it in multiple locations. Which options you choose depends on the overall configuration of the hierarchy and reporting needs.

2. Select the role in the Add Site System Roles Wizard. Click Next to proceed to the Reporting Service Point page of the wizard, shown in Figure 4.56.

FIGURE 4.56

Add Site System Roles Wizard: Reporting Services Point page

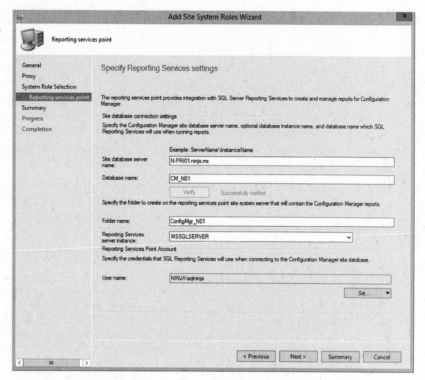

3. On the Reporting Services Point page, provide the server name that is hosting the Configuration Manager database instance and also the database name.

   The server listed here can be the same server hosting the Reporting Services server instance or a remote server.

4. Click Verify to confirm connectivity.

5. Configure the reporting server component by providing the folder name where the reports will be stored along with the specific SQL Server instance hosting the Reporting Services and the authentication method that will be used for security validation.

   Note that for this section there is no option to specify a server name because it is assumed the site system where the role is being configured is the server hosting the SSRS instance.

6. Once these configurations are complete, click Next.

SOFTWARE REQUIREMENTS

♦ The Configuration Manager Reporting Services point requires that all site servers be members of a Windows 2012 R2 or higher Active Directory domain.

♦ SQL Server Reporting Services 2012 R2 or higher is needed.

Application Catalog Web Service Point and Application Catalog Website Point

A significant change in Configuration Manager is its user-centric focus. One component of user-centric focus, and a feature that has been much anticipated, is the ability for users to browse a web page–hosted catalog of published applications available for installation in the environment. These published applications may be either available without restriction to users or configured to require administrative approval prior to installation. Only software deployed to users will appear in the Application Catalog.

Two site system roles work in tandem to provide the Application Catalog service: the Application Catalog web service point and the Application Catalog website point. At first glance, the difference between these two site system roles may not be apparent.

Application Catalog Website Point The Application Catalog website point is the site system providing the software catalog service to users.

Application Catalog Web Service Point The Application Catalog web service point is the site system role that serves as a connection point between the Application Catalog web service point site systems and the Configuration Manager site, providing software information to the website for presentation to users.

ABOUT THE EXAMPLE

For the example, the Application Catalog web service point and the Application Catalog website point are presented together. It should not be implied, however, that these site system roles will necessarily be configured on the same server in all cases. While both site system roles are required to facilitate Software Catalog services, it is not necessary that they be configured together.

If the Application Catalog Website Point and Application Catalog Web Service Point roles have not yet been added, you will need to select them in the Add Site System Roles Wizard, as shown in Figure 4.57.

1. Choose the site and server where the Application Catalog website point and Application Catalog web service point will be located.

   The exact servers chosen depend on the overall configuration of the hierarchy and mobile management needs.

2. Select the roles in the Add Site System Roles Wizard. Note that the order of the next couple of figures could be different depending on how you choose to install the roles. The net result is the same.

3. Click Next to proceed to the Application Catalog Website Point page of the wizard, as shown in Figure 4.58.

4. On the Application Catalog Website Point page, configure the name for the website to be used.

   Also note the web application name suggested. If the name of the web application is modified on the Application Catalog Web Service Point page, this URL will need to be modified accordingly.

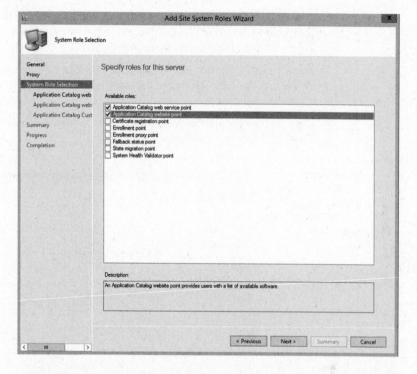

5. Also on this page, choose whether the web service will support HTTP or HTTPS traffic and, if you select HTTPS, whether the web service will allow only intranet-connected clients or also allow Internet-connected clients.

   Supporting Internet clients requires the use of certificates. In addition, if mobile devices will be supported in the environment, enabling the website to support HTTPS-connected clients is required.

6. Once all configuration is complete, click Next to proceed to the Application Catalog Website Point page, as shown in Figure 4.59.

FIGURE 4.59
Add Site System Roles Wizard: Application Catalog Website Point page

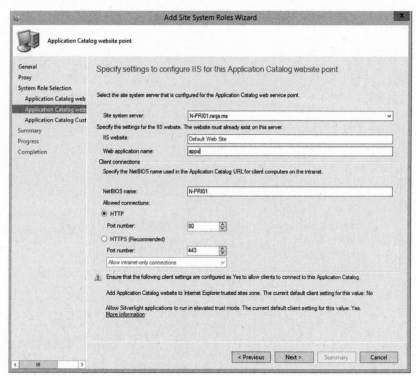

7. On the Application Catalog Website Point page, configure the web application name for the website to be used and whether the website will use HTTP or HTTPS.

8. Once all configuration is complete, click Next to proceed to the Application Catalog Customizations page. Here administrators are able to provide some minor customization as to the presentation of the catalog (organization name and website theme). Make any modifications desired and click Next to complete the wizard.

SOFTWARE REQUIREMENTS

The Configuration Manager Application Catalog website point and Application Catalog web service point require the following:

◆ All site servers must be members of a Windows 2012 R2 or higher Active Directory domain.

◆ .NET 4.0 must be installed.

◆ The Web Server (IIS) role is required.

◆ IIS 6 Management Compatibility is required.

Enrollment Point and Enrollment Proxy Point

Mobile devices have become commonplace in IT environments. With the increase in device numbers and increasing power and function of these devices, providing management capabilities in the enterprise is becoming more of a focal point for administrators. Configuration Manager provides two types of management for mobile devices: "lite" management and depth management.

Lite Management   Lite management is provided to any device that is capable of interfacing with Exchange Server through the ActiveSync connector. Such devices include Windows Phone and iPhone and Android devices. Configuration Manager provides an Exchange Server connector that works with Exchange ActiveSync–connected devices and facilitates settings management, general inventory, and remote wipe capabilities.

Depth Management   Depth management is available for legacy Windows phone platforms, such as Windows Mobile 6.x as well as Nokia Symbian devices, and it allows for a more robust management experience, including the ability to install a native Configuration Manager client on a device. Depth-managed devices provide all of the features of lite management (though not through Exchange ActiveSync) but also include support for software distribution and over-the-air enrollment. Further, inventory options available for depth-managed clients are more extensive and flexible than those provided through lite management.

Depth-managed devices require a client to be installed, along with certificates to provide access to the various Configuration Manager systems. Once the client is installed, the device acts similar to a PC, looking up and making use of management points for retrieving policy, sending data such as inventory, and also making use of distribution points for software deployments.

SITE SYSTEMS AND MOBILE DEVICES

Site systems that will interact with mobile devices must be configured to support HTTPS communication. Mobile devices use certificates for authentication and must be able to use these certificates to validate against management points and distribution points (and optionally, Application Catalog servers).

The process of placing the client and certificates on the mobile device, known as enrollment, requires the use of two site system roles: the mobile device enrollment proxy point and the enrollment point. These site systems work in tandem to facilitate enrollment, provisioning, and management of mobile devices. At first glance, the difference between these two site system roles may not be apparent.

Enrollment Proxy Point   This is the site system role typically placed in the DMZ and is the initial point of communication for devices. It is also the location where mobile devices find and download the mobile version of the Configuration Manager client. Once the client is installed, and as a part of enrollment, the mobile device enrollment proxy point will communicate with the enrollment point, typically located inside the protected network, to retrieve needed certificates and present them to the device being enrolled.

Configuring multiple enrollment proxy points at a single site to support multiple DMZ configurations is supported.

Enrollment Point   This is a site system role typically installed inside the protected network, and it serves as an interface between the enrollment proxy point and the Enterprise Certificate Authority as certificate requests are presented from mobile devices and generated certificates are sent back to mobile devices.

TIDBITS ABOUT SITE SYSTEM ROLES

It is *not* required that these site system roles exist on the same site system server. If you're using lite management of mobile devices, neither of these site system roles is required. Enrollment proxy point is recommended to live in a DMZ scenario so it can be exposed over the Internet.

ABOUT THE EXAMPLE

For the example, the mobile device enrollment proxy point and enrollment point are presented together. It should not be implied, however, that these site system roles will necessarily be configured on the same server in all cases. While both site system roles are required to facilitate depth management of mobile devices, they are not required to be configured together.

If the Enrollment Proxy Point or the Enrollment Point roles have not yet been added, you will need to select them in the Add Site System Roles Wizard.

1. Choose the site and server where the enrollment proxy point and enrollment point will be located.

   The servers you choose depend on the overall configuration of the hierarchy and mobile management needs.

2. Select the roles in the Add Site System Roles Wizard System Role Selection Page. Click Next to proceed to the Enrollment Point page of the wizard.

3. On the Enrollment Point page, shown in Figure 4.60, configure the name for the website to be used.

   If you make any changes, then the virtual directory name in the URL configured for the enrollment proxy point must be updated as well. You can also specify which account will be used for database communication. Of the two site system roles, this is the only one that needs to access the database directly.

FIGURE 4.60

Add Site System Roles
Wizard: Enrollment
Point page

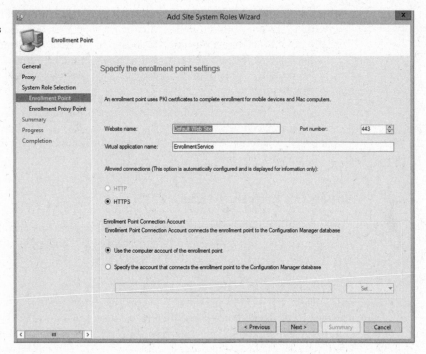

4. On the Enrollment Proxy Point page, configure the name for the website to be used, as shown in Figure 4.61.

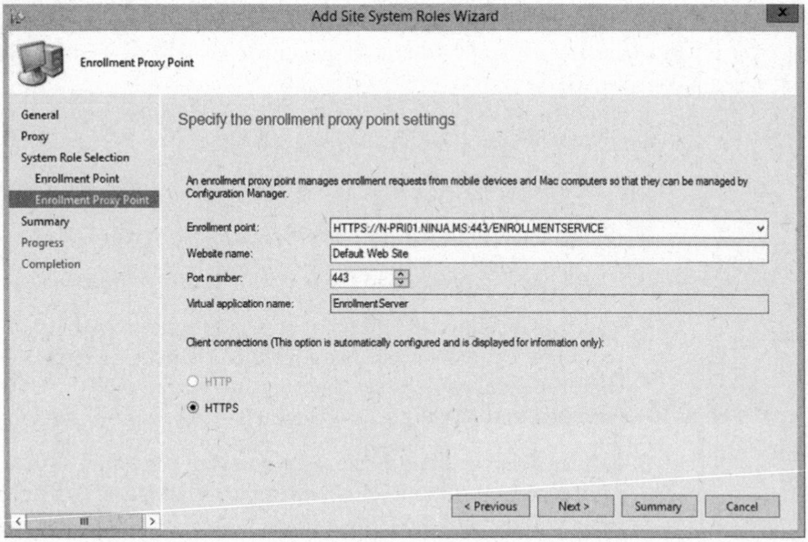

FIGURE 4.61

Add Site System Roles
Wizard: Enrollment
Proxy Point page

Note that the website must support SSL communication and that a default URL pointing to the enrollment point is already present. This URL is configurable and will need to point to whichever location is chosen to host the Enrollment Point role. Note also that the end of the URL refers to the `EnrollmentService` virtual directory. This is the default name. If a nondefault name is chosen for the virtual directory, the URL will need to match.

Note also that there is a virtual application name listed on the current page that is similar in name. Don't be confused by the similarity; the virtual directory name here is the one used to configure the mobile device enrollment proxy point and is not changeable.

5. Once all configuration is complete, click Next.

Software Requirements

♦ The Configuration Manager enrollment proxy point and enrollment point require that all site servers be members of a Windows 2012 R2 or higher Active Directory domain.

♦ The Web Server (IIS) role must be installed.

Software Update Point

The Software Update Point role is integral to the software update mechanism and is responsible for synchronizing all patches from Microsoft Update and making them available in the Configuration Manager interface for deployment. The software update point requires that Windows Software Update Services be installed on the same server where the software update point is being installed and requires that the instance of WSUS be dedicated to interfacing with the software update point and providing service to Configuration Manager. Also, administrators should not perform any administrative work on the WSUS console itself. All administrative work should be done through the Configuration Manager console. You will find that the options available in the Configuration Manager console are very similar to what are found in the WSUS console.

If the software update point has not yet been added, you will need to select it in the Add Site System Roles Wizard, as shown in Figure 4.62.

1. Choose the server where the WSUS component is installed.

2. Select the role in the Add Site System Roles Wizard.

3. Click Next to proceed to the Software Update Point page of the wizard.

4. On the Software Update Point page, configure whether to use ports 80 and 443 for client communications or the customized 8530 and 8531. Determine what kind of client connection type you expect, whether they are intranet-only, Internet-only, or both. Click Next to proceed to the Proxy And Account Settings page of the wizard.

5. A proxy server should be used when synchronizing software updates and also when downloading content with auto deployment rules. Also, choose whether alternate credentials will be used to connect to the WSUS server. If a proxy server is needed, supply the needed information for the proxy server. This is shown in Figure 4.63.

FIGURE 4.62
Add Site System
Roles Wizard: System
Role Selection page
with Software
Update Point selected

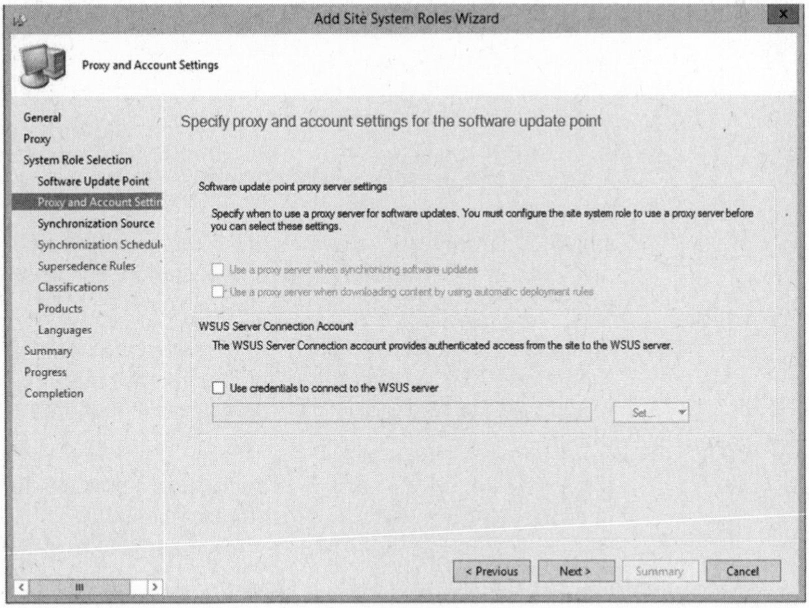

FIGURE 4.63
Add Site System
Roles Wizard:
Proxy And Account
Settings page

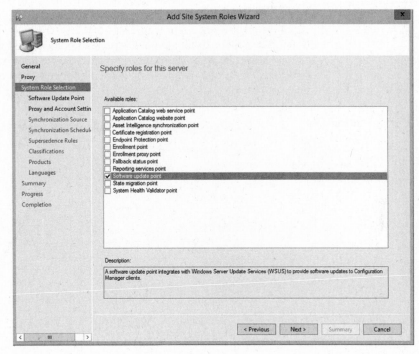

6. Once all configuration is complete, click Next to proceed to the Synchronization Source page of the wizard, shown in Figure 4.64. If software update services will be used in Configuration Manager, at least one software update point is required. Note that a stand-alone software update point on properly sized hardware is capable of supporting 125,000 clients in Configuration Manager. However, if the role is collocated with Configuration Manager it can only support 25,000 clients.

FIGURE 4.64
Add Site System
Roles Wizard:
Synchronization
Source page

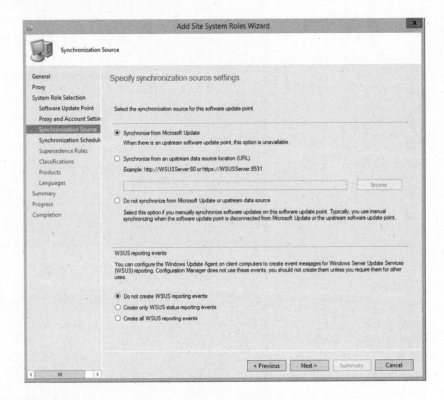

7. On the Synchronization Source page, configure the location that the software update point will use for obtaining update information. Typically, this setting will be to synchronize from Microsoft Update from the Internet.

   If this software update point is installed at a child site in a hierarchy, then the option to choose here will be to synchronize from an upstream update point. In this case the CAS would host the top-level software update point and the primary site would synchronize from it.

   If the software update point is on the CAS and the CAS does not have access to the Internet, then it's possible to synchronize manually. If this is the case, choose the option Do Not Synchronize From Microsoft Update Or Upstream Data Source.

8. In the WSUS Reporting Events section, choose whether or not to create any or all WSUS reporting events.

9. Once all configuration is competed, click Next to proceed to the Synchronization Schedule page. Choose whether or not synchronization should proceed on a schedule. It is not required that the software update point be configured to synchronize automatically, but in most environments a recurring schedule is ideal. The schedule is up to you; just remember that Microsoft publishes new patches the second Tuesday of every month and from time to time will have out-of-band patch releases. If you are using Endpoint Protection in Configuration Manager, it is recommended to perform synchronization no less than daily (or as often as three times per day).

10. If you would like an alert when synchronization fails (a good idea), select that option as well.

11. Once all configuration is complete, click Next to proceed to the Supersedence Rules page shown in Figure 4.65.

FIGURE 4.65

Add Site System Roles Wizard: Supersedence Rules page

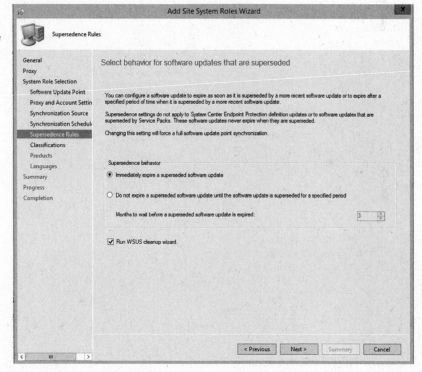

12. On the Supersedence Rules page, choose the behavior that happens when a new update is available and synchronized that replaces an existing update. The first option, Immediately Expire A Superseded Software Update, caused frustration in many environments—not because an update was superseded, but because the action of superseding also caused the original update to be expired. When an update is expired, it can no longer be deployed. While it is a good idea to stop deploying a superseded update when it has been replaced, the truth is that testing cycles in many environments do not easily allow for this kind of rapid change. For that reason, the second choice (Months

To Wait Before A Superseded Software Update Is Expired) was made available in Configuration Manager. Note that the superseded update is still superseded; it just isn't expired and can still be deployed. You should leave this configuration as Immediately expire a superseded software update for best practice.

13. Select the Run WSUS Cleanup Wizard option to help maintain the WSUS folder and keep the database up-to-date with the changes performed by the synchronization. That way, all updates that are superseded or deleted will be removed from the database and source, as shown in Figure 4.65.

14. Once all configuration is complete, click Next to proceed to the Classifications page, shown in Figure 4.66.

FIGURE 4.66
Add Site System Roles Wizard: Classifications page

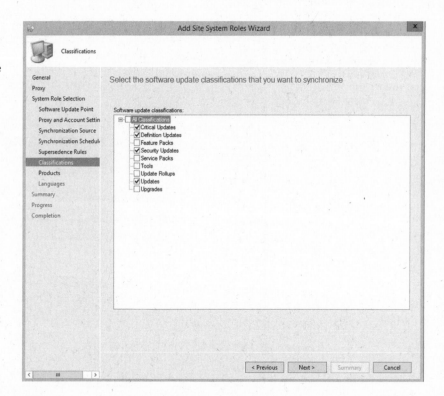

15. On the Classifications page, choose the classifications of updates that should be retrieved from Microsoft Update and made available in Configuration Manager for deployment.

16. Once all configuration is complete, click Next to proceed to the Products page, shown in Figure 4.67.

17. On the Products page, choose the products or product families that should be included when retrieving updates from the categories just configured. The expanded list is shown in the figure.

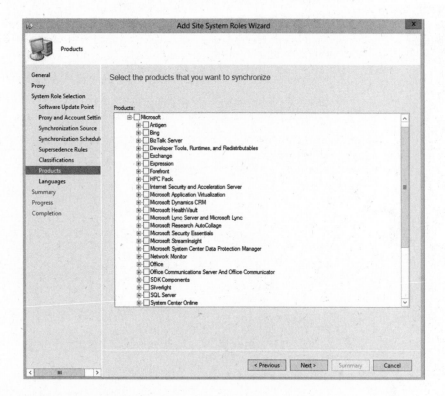

FIGURE 4.67
Add Site System
Roles Wizard:
Products page

18. Once all configuration is complete, click Next to proceed to the Languages page. Here, choose all languages that are in use in your environment. This will ensure that the appropriate language-specific patches are included during synchronization as well.

19. Once all configuration is complete, click Next and proceed through the remaining wizard pages to complete the configuration.

SOFTWARE REQUIREMENTS

The Configuration Manager software update point requires that all site servers must be members of a Windows 2012 R2 or higher Active Directory domain. In addition, the software update point requires WSUS 3.0 SP2 and Internet Information Services to be installed.

Endpoint Protection Point

If you will be using Configuration Manager for Endpoint Protection services, then you must install the Endpoint Protection Point role. This role is available only at the CAS and requires that separate licensing be in place. Installing this role is very easy and simply enables the use of Endpoint Protection in the hierarchy.

If the Endpoint Protection point has not yet been added, you will need to select it in the Add Site System Roles Wizard:

1. Choose the server where the Endpoint Protection point will be located.

2. Select the role in the Add Site System Roles Wizard. Note that when you attempt to place a check mark in the role, you will see a popup notifying you of default configurations that will be set.

3. On the Endpoint Protection page, accept the license agreement.

4. Once all configuration is complete, click Next to proceed to the Microsoft Active Protection Service page, shown in Figure 4.68.

FIGURE 4.68
Add Site System Roles Wizard: Microsoft Active Protection Service page

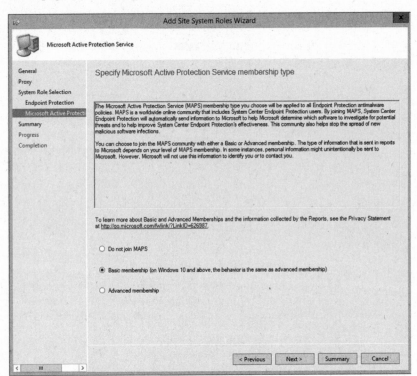

5. On the Microsoft Active Protection Service page, read the description of the Active Protection Service membership, and choose what type of membership you would like, if any.

6. Once all configuration is complete, click Next through the wizard to complete installation.

SOFTWARE REQUIREMENTS

The Configuration Manager Endpoint Protection point requires that all site servers be members of a Windows 2012 R2 or higher Active Directory domain.

Asset Intelligence Synchronization Point

If you will be using Configuration Manager for Asset Intelligence information, then you will likely want to install the Asset Intelligence Synchronization Point role. This role is available at the CAS or standalone primary; the role will assist in the latest Software Information as part of the System Center Online Catalog. Installing this role enables synchronizing of catalog updates from the Internet and also allows you to upload custom catalog requests and categorization information to Microsoft.

If the Asset Intelligence synchronization point has not yet been added, you will need to select it in the Add Site System Roles Wizard.

1. Choose the server where the Asset Intelligence synchronization point will be located.

2. Select the role in the Add Site System Roles Wizard.

3. On the Asset Intelligence Synchronization Point Settings page, select whether to use this system as the active system and, if you have a certificate, the UNC path where it can be found. Note that the use of a certificate is not required. This is shown in Figure 4.69.

FIGURE 4.69

Add Site System Roles Wizard: Asset Intelligence Synchronization Point Settings page

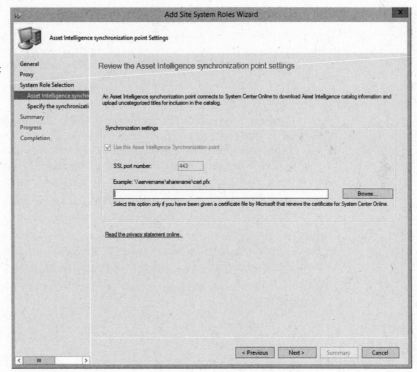

4. Once all configuration is complete, click Next to proceed to the Specify The Synchronization Schedule page. Here, configure the schedule you would like to use for synchronizing the catalog and also sending your update requests for the catalog to Microsoft. Typically, the default schedule is appropriate.

5. Once all configuration is complete, click Next through the wizard to complete installation.

SOFTWARE REQUIREMENTS

The Configuration Manager Asset Intelligence synchronization point requires that all site servers be members of a Windows 2012 R2 or higher Active Directory domain.

The Bottom Line

Understand Configuration Manager sites and the new approach to hierarchy design. Configuration Manager has three types of sites: the central administration site, which is new, and the primary and secondary sites, which should be familiar to you. Although two of the three site types are familiar, their use and approach to hierarchy design—or whether a hierarchy is needed at all—are quite different now.

Master It Describe the purpose of each site type and map each to specific management needs.

Construct a Configuration Manager hierarchy. The site hierarchy in Configuration Manager consists of the site types just described. The approach to design is very different from the previous version, with the number of primary sites being limited to a single tier. The chapter walked through configuring a hierarchy with all three site types.

Master It Describe a Configuration Manager site hierarchy. Detail components needed for site-to-site communication and security settings.

Determine when to expand a hierarchy and when to simply add a site system role for additional service. A major design goal of Configuration Manager is simplified hierarchy design. Administrators familiar with previous versions may be tempted to retain old hierarchy approaches when designing Configuration Manager. Taking such an approach will often lead to inefficient designs and additional server cost and in some cases simply won't work.

Master It Understand the changes in sites and site components that lend themselves to hierarchy simplification and enable parity management with fewer site servers.

Deploy and configure the various site system roles available per site. There are many roles available to enable management at a site. Understanding each role and the service it delivers is critical to getting the most out of your investment in Configuration Manager.

Master It Review critical system roles and understand the services that are enabled through each.

Chapter 5

Client Installation

Once you have the Configuration Manager sites and site servers installed and configured, the next logical step is to plan the client deployment. The client deployment success rate very much depends on your knowledge of the internal network infrastructure combined with the ability to understand the components involved in the process. Once you fully understand the process, installing a large number of clients over a short period of time may be no problem. On the other hand, if you do not truly understand the process, installing a single client can be a very time-consuming experience.

No one solution for deploying the Configuration Manager client fits all organizations. Most likely you will find yourself using a mix of the various installation techniques described in this chapter.

This chapter covers the prerequisites for installing clients, a walk-through of the different client installation methods, and information needed for troubleshooting the installation process.

In this chapter, you will learn to

◆ Configure boundaries and boundary groups

◆ Select the relevant discovery methods

◆ Employ the correct client installation methods

◆ Manage Unix/Linux and Mac devices

◆ Ensure client health

Creating Client Settings

To manage a device with Configuration Manager, you must first have the client software installed. Regardless of the device and operating system on that device, we always use the term *client* when we refer to the software on the managed computer that interacts with the Configuration Manager site servers. A client consists of different agents that you can enable or disable. During the installation, the full Configuration Manager client is installed, and you use the Client Settings section of the Administration workspace to control the agent settings and configuration. In Configuration Manager, client settings are global data and thus are no longer separately controlled by each primary site. Furthermore, you can create multiple custom client settings and assign them to individual collections. As a best practice, you should typically configure custom client settings only as exceptions to the default client settings. There may be several reasons why you would need to configure multiple client settings—for example:

◆ You want to control the ability to initiate a remote session against servers.

◆ You want to disable the remote tools agent on all computers in the HR department.

◆ You want different inventory frequencies on servers and desktops.

A set of default client settings is always configured when you install Configuration Manager. In Figure 5.1 you can see an example of where two custom client settings have been created and deployed to collections. Notice the number in the Deployments column; it indicates the number of collections that are affected by the custom client settings. Figure 5.2 shows the new client settings interface. You can assign your own custom client settings to any user or device collection. The same settings can be assigned to multiple collections, and one collection can have multiple assignments. In the event of a conflict, the custom setting with the lowest priority number will be applied.

FIGURE 5.1
Client settings

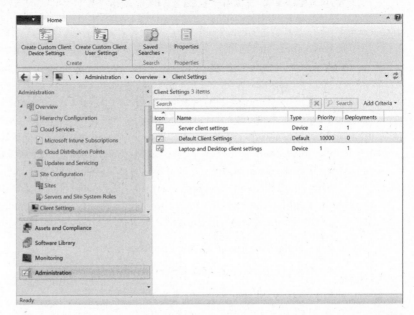

FIGURE 5.2
Creating custom client settings

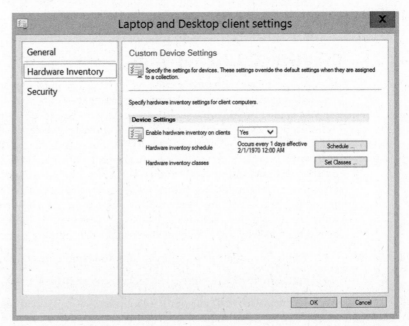

Real World Scenario

CONFIGURE DIFFERENT CUSTOM CLIENT SETTINGS FOR ALL SERVERS

As the Configuration Manager administrator, you have been requested to ensure that only members of the global group Server Administrators can use Remote Tools on servers. Follow these steps to do so:

1. Open the Configuration Manager administrative console.

2. Select the Administration workspace and browse to Client Settings.

3. On the Home tab of the ribbon, click Create Custom Client Device Settings.

4. Type **Remote settings for servers** in the Name column.

5. From the list of custom settings, select Remote Tools.

6. In the left column, select the Remote Tools settings and click Set Viewers.

7. Click the yellow starburst, and in the New Permitted Viewer window, enter the name of the user or group that should be given access in the User or group name field. This should be in the form of *domain\group name* (or *domain\user name*)—for example, **Contoso\Server Administrators**.

8. Click OK three times.

   Notice the number shown under Permitted Viewers.

9. Click OK to save the custom client settings.

10. Back in the administrative console, select the newly created custom settings, and click Deploy on the ribbon.

11. Select the All Servers device collection, and click OK.

The individual client agent settings will be discussed in detail in later chapters. Figure 5.2 shows a client settings group that includes a custom setting for hardware inventory. You can view the list of all possible settings by selecting Default Client Settings and selecting Properties in the ribbon. Here is a short description of each of the agent settings:

Background Intelligent Transfer   This setting allows you to control the BITS protocol. BITS is the protocol being used by the client when it is downloading and uploading information to the management point and also when it is downloading packages from the distribution points.

Cloud Services   This setting determines whether client computers are allowed to access cloud distribution points.

Client Policy   The Client Policy settings control how often the client agent will contact the management point for a policy refresh:

- ◆ Client Policy Polling Interval (Minutes) defines how often the client will request a new machine policy. It can be any value between 3 minutes and 1440 minutes. Best practice (and the default value) is 60 minutes.

- ◆ Enable User Policy On Clients: Use this setting if you have configured Configuration Manager to discover users and intend to deploy applications and programs to users.

- ◆ Enable User Policy Request From Internet Clients: Use this setting if you have any Internet-facing site systems and you want to support user-centric scenarios for Internet-based clients.

Compliance Settings This option is used to enable the settings-management feature formerly known as Desired Configuration Management in Configuration Manager 2007.

Computer Agent Here you define most of the basic Configuration Manager client settings:

- Deployment Deadline settings are used to control when users will be reminded about future deployments.

- Default Application Catalog Website Point: Use this setting to define how clients will connect to the Application Catalog. It can be either automatic, a specific server, or a specific website. If you select Automatic, the management point will supply the client with a random catalog, which is not guaranteed to be the one nearest the user.

- Add Default Application Catalog Website To Internet Explorer Trusted Sites Zone will add the selected website to the trusted site zone. This will ensure that users are prompted to enter their account credentials when accessing the Application Catalog website.

- Organization Name is the name that will be displayed in the Software Center.

- Use New Software Center: Enable this option to utilize the new version of the Software Center application, which shows both computer and user-targeted deployments.

- Install Permissions can be configured to control the permissions required to start any deployment on the client. You can choose from All Users, Administrators, Primary Users, or No Users. This setting is particularly valuable when you are controlling terminal servers.

- Suspend BitLocker PIN Entry Or Restart is used to control whether you want to suspend the PIN requirements after running a deployment that requires a system restart.

- PowerShell Execution Policy: By default PowerShell scripts will run in the context of a service. If you want to run a PowerShell script within a task sequence, you should select Bypass, which is the same as running the PowerShell script unrestricted.

- Show Notifications For New Deployments controls the default UI experience for the logged-on user when a deployment is received or about to start.

Computer Restart This setting allows you to control when restart notifications are shown.

Endpoint Protection Here you enable or disable the System Center Endpoint Protection agent. The settings are configurable only when you have enabled the Endpoint Protection Site System role:

- Manage Endpoint Protection Client On Client Computers: Configure this setting to True to start managing Endpoint Protection in the hierarchy.

- Install Endpoint Protection Client In Client Computers: When this setting is True, the Endpoint Protection client will automatically be installed. Notice that the client is already deployed during the initial Configuration Manager client installation.

- Automatically Remove Previously Installed Antimalware Software Before Endpoint Protection Client Is Installed: When this is True, an attempt to uninstall some predefined antimalware application will be performed.

- ◆ Suppress Any Required Computer Restart After The Endpoint Protection Client Is Installed: If configured to True, no restart will be performed, not even if a previous antimalware application is uninstalled first.

- ◆ Allowed Period Of Time Users Can Postpone A Required Restart To Complete The Endpoint Protection Installation (Hours): This option is configurable only if the setting to suppress computer restart is False. The number of hours will be the maximum number of hours a restart can be postponed by the user before a restart of the computer will be forced.

- ◆ Disable Alternate Sources (Such As Microsoft Windows Update, Microsoft Windows Server Update Services, Or UNS Share) For The Initial Definition Update On Client Computers: Configure this setting to False if you want to allow multiple update sources to be considered for the first definition update.

Enrollment   This setting provides configuration options for enrolling mobile devices and Mac computers. It can be used to define the polling interval for mobile device legacy clients as well as defining whether end users are allowed to enroll mobile devices and Mac computers.

Hardware Inventory   This option is used to scan for and report hardware installed on the computer. You can specify custom agent settings for different collections but only define hardware to collect in the default client settings. Unlike Configuration Manager 2007, there is no unique sms_def.mof file per site; instead you use the Custom Client Settings interface to specify the inventory data classes.

Metered Internet Connections   This setting can be used to control costs if client computers are utilizing an Internet service provider that charges based on the amount of data that is used.

Network Access Protection (NAP)   Use this option to enable Network Access Protection compliance on systems as well as to schedule when scans will occur. Notice that NAP requires that you have installed and configured Network Policy and Access Services in Windows Server 2008 (or higher).

Power Management   This setting enables power management for all clients in the hierarchy and allows you to control whether end users can exclude their own devices from being part of a power management configuration. You configure each of the Power Management settings by collection.

Remote Tools   This is used to control the Remote Tools and Remote Assistance settings for Windows XP and later systems.

Software Deployment   Use this option to configure whether notifications should be shown when deployments are about to run. Schedule Re-evaluation For Deployments determines how often the Configuration Manager client will trigger the re-evaluation process. The process will automatically install required software that is not already installed and remove software that is supposed to be uninstalled.

Software Inventory   This option is used to discover what software is installed on the computer. You can control which file types the agent will scan for and where. Furthermore, you can use the settings to collect software files. Collected files are not stored in the database but will be stored on the site server. Even though it might be tempting to collect files, you should think twice before enabling this feature because it can easily lead to network congestion.

Software Metering This option enables software metering and controls how often clients will upload the software-metering data from WMI to the management point.

Software Updates This setting enables software updates, controls how often clients will perform a scan for software updates, and determines whether all required updates should be installed upon the deployment deadline.

State Messaging This setting controls how often state messages are forwarded from the client to the management point.

User And Device Affinity This setting controls the calculations that are being used to determine when a user(s) is being considered a primary user(s) for a device.

Windows PE Peer Cache This setting allows Windows PE clients to obtain content from a peer on the local network instead of a distribution point. This setting only applies to operating system deployments.

Supported Operating Systems

The following are the more common operating systems that are supported for the Configuration Manager client. The complete list of supported operating systems is available at https://technet.microsoft.com/en-us/library/mt589738.aspx.

Windows:

Remember that only the following clients are supported for Configuration Manager:

- Windows 7 SP1 Professional, Enterprise, Ultimate (x86 and x64)
- Windows 8 Pro, Enterprise (x86 and x64)
- Windows 8.1 Pro, Enterprise (x86 and x64)
- Windows 10 Enterprise, Pro (x86 and x64)
- Windows Server 2008 SP2 Standard, Enterprise, Datacenter (x86 and x64)
- Windows Server 2008 SP2 Server Core (x86 and x64)
- Windows Server 2008 R2 Server Core (RTM, SP1) (x64)
- Windows Storage Server 2008 R2 Workgroup, Standard, Enterprise (x64)
- Windows Server 2008 R2 SP1 Standard, Enterprise (x64)
- Windows Server 2012 Standard, Datacenter (x64)
- Windows Server 2012 Server Core (x64)
- Windows Server 2012 R2 Standard, Datacenter (x64)
- Windows Storage Server 2012 R2 (x64)
- Windows Server 2012 R2 Server Core (x64)
- Windows Storage Server 2012 (x64)
- Windows 10 Enterprise LTSB (x86, x64)
- Windows Server 2016—Standard, Datacenter

  NOTE: Windows Server 2016 is supported beginning with Configuration Manager version 1606 with the hotfix rollup from KB3186654 (or the baseline version of 1606 which released in October of 2016).

Also, the Configuration Manager client requires Microsoft .NET Framework and if the computer does not have Microsoft .NET Framework 3.0, 3.5 or 4.0, then .NET Framework 4 is automatically installed on the computer. Note that a computer restart may be required in order to complete the installation of .NET Framework 4.0.

The following are the prerequisites for Windows-based clients:

◆ Microsoft Windows Installer version 3.1.4000.2435 or later

◆ Microsoft Background Intelligent Transfer Service (BITS) version 2.5

◆ Microsoft Task Scheduler service

The following are the prerequisites for Windows-based clients downloaded during the client installation:

◆ Microsoft Windows Update Agent version 7.0.6000.363 or later

◆ Microsoft Core XML Services (MSXML) version 6.20.5002 or later

◆ Microsoft Remote Differential Compression (RDC)

◆ Microsoft .NET Framework 4.0 Client Profile

◆ Microsoft Silverlight

◆ Microsoft Visual C++

◆ Windows Imaging APIs 6.0.6001.18000

◆ Microsoft Policy Platform 1.2.3514.0

◆ Microsoft SQL Server Compact 3.5 SP2 components

You'll find additional information here:

```
https://technet.microsoft.com/en-us/library/gg682042.aspx?f=
255&MSPPError=-2147217396
```

Depending on your scenario, it's possible that some of these items may not be required. For example, if you are managing Windows servers and you prefer that these devices not utilize the Software Center or Application Catalog, you may prevent the installation of Silverlight by utilizing the /skipprereq:Silverlight.exe syntax as part of the client install command. Configuration Manager provides client support for Linux/Unix computers as well as Macintosh computers. The following are the supported operating system versions for these platforms:

Linux/Unix:

◆ Red Hat Enterprise Linux (RHEL) Version 4 (x86 & x64), Version 5 (x86 & x64), Version 6 (x86 & x64), Version 7 x64

◆ Solaris Version 9 (SPARC), Version 10 (SPARC & x86), Version 11 SP1 (x86 & SPARC)

◆ SUSE Linux Enterprise Server Version 9 x86, Version 10 SP1 (x86 & x64), Version 11 SP1 (x86 & x64), Version 12 x64

◆ CentOS Version 5 (x86 & x64), Version 6 (x86 & x64), Version 7 x64

◆ Debian Version 5 (x86 & x64), Version 6 (x86 & x64), Version 7 (x86 & x64)

◆ Ubuntu Version 10.4 LTS (x86 & x64), Version 12.04 LTS (x86 & x64), Version 14.04 (x86 & x64)

◆ Oracle Linux Version 5 (x86 & x64), Version 6 (x86 & x64), Version 7 x64

◆ HP-UX, Version 11iv2 (IA64 & PA-RISC), Version 11iv3 (IA64 & PA-RISC)

◆ AIX Version 5.3 (Power), Version 6.1 (Power), Version 7.1 (Power)

Macintosh:

◆ Mac OS X 10.6 (Snow Leopard)

◆ Mac OS X 10.7 (Lion)

◆ Mac OS X 10.8 (Mountain Lion)

◆ Mac OS X 10.9 (Mavericks)

◆ Mac OS X 10.10 (Yosemite)

◆ Mac OS X 10.11 (El Capitan)

Discovering Network Objects

Discovery is the process by which Configuration Manager finds objects in the computer infrastructure and keeps them up to date in the Configuration Manager database. Objects can be users, groups, computers, and network devices that have an IP address if Network Discovery is being used. All discovery processes will generate one data discovery record (DDR) for each discovered object. For an administrator it is nice to know how many computers you have (and where they are) before you start deploying clients. To find out, you must understand the various discovery methods and when they should be used. Discovery also plays an important part in creating the collections that will support features like application deployment, updates deployment, and operating system deployment.

The only discovery method enabled by default is Heartbeat Discovery, described in a later section. Before configuring any other discovery method, you must ask yourself a few basic questions:

◆ What is being discovered by the method?

This is essential knowledge before configuring any of the methods. If you do not understand what's being discovered, chances are that you will discover the wrong information.

◆ Why do you need the data?

If you can't answer this question, most likely you do not need to configure the discovery method.

◆ How often do you need to refresh the discovery data?

Configuration Manager natively supports delta discovery, which eliminates the reason for running frequent full discovery processes.

◆ What is the duration of the discovery process?

Not knowing the duration of each discovery method may result in backlogs and incorrect discovery schedules. Having knowledge about the log files generated by each discovery process can give you precise data and help you configure the correct schedules.

◆ What is the impact of configuring the method?

The discovery methods use different techniques to gather a DDR. Active Directory methods will query the nearest domain controller, whereas Network Discovery uses protocols like RIP and OSPF to get the information.

To configure discovery methods, perform the following steps:

1. Open the Configuration Manager administrative console.

2. Select the Administration workspace, navigate to Hierarchy Configuration, and choose Discovery Methods.

3. You can then modify each of the discovery methods by selecting the discovery method and choosing Properties from the ribbon.

Active Directory Discovery Methods

Each of the Active Directory discovery methods requires a target and a schedule. The target can be a single object, an organizational unit (OU), a security/distribution group, or an entire domain. While it might not make much sense to search for a single object, specifying individual OUs or groups versus the entire domain is often considered a best practice. Especially in the pilot phase, it is an easy way to limit the number of objects you are working with. A new feature in Configuration Manager allows you to specify the account being used to run the discovery process. If none is specified, the process will run under the security context of the site server. In order to run a successful discovery, the account you specify must have Read permission on the object.

Figure 5.3 shows the Active Directory Container dialog that you use to define the locations where you want to search. When you click Browse next to the Path field, you will see the dialog shown in Figure 5.4. This dialog allows you to select the criteria for the LDAP query. You can select any container or OU within the tree view. Unlike with previous versions of Configuration Manager, you can now browse to other domains and forests.

FIGURE 5.3
New Active Directory Container search criteria

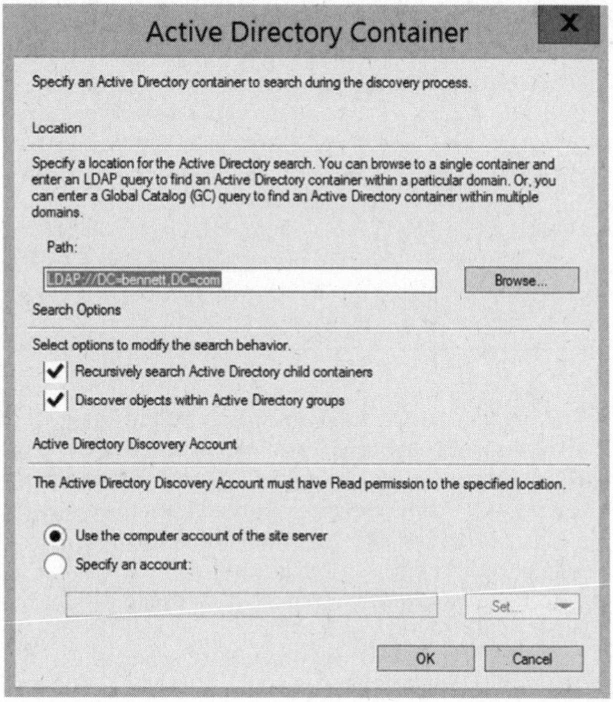

Active Directory Container   X

Specify an Active Directory container to search during the discovery process.

Location

Specify a location for the Active Directory search. You can browse to a single container and enter an LDAP query to find an Active Directory container within a particular domain. Or, you can enter a Global Catalog (GC) query to find an Active Directory container within multiple domains.

Path:

`LDAP://DC=bennett,DC=com`   Browse...

Search Options

Select options to modify the search behavior.

✔ Recursively search Active Directory child containers

✔ Discover objects within Active Directory groups

Active Directory Discovery Account

The Active Directory Discovery Account must have Read permission to the specified location.

● Use the computer account of the site server
○ Specify an account:

   Set... ▼

OK   Cancel

FIGURE 5.4
The Select New
Container dialog box

Real World Scenario

DISCOVERY PATHS AND ACTIVE DIRECTORY ORGANIZATIONAL UNITS

It is important to know that Configuration Manager will query all objects in the specified paths every time. If you delete an old computer object from the Configuration Manager database but not from Active Directory, the same computer object will be added to the Configuration Manager database after the next discovery process unless you have configured the option to exclude computer objects that have not recently logged on or changed their password. Failure to exclude computers can have an effect on the automatic client push installation attempts because Configuration Manager will initiate a client push attempt on computers that do not have the client installed. These might be the most important reasons why you should plan the discovery processes carefully; make sure that you have an OU structure in Active Directory where you can store objects that are no longer active and exclude those OUs from the specified LDAP path. Failure to do so might lead to errors related to failed client push installation attempts and discovery of unwanted objects, creating unnecessary overhead on the primary site server.

Once you choose the start location for the query, the default behavior of the query is to search all of the child objects beneath the starting point. If you do not want to search through the child OUs, you can clear the Recursively Search Active Directory Child Containers check box. This is a good way to limit the data returned from the query.

The option Discover Objects Within Active Directory Groups is especially useful in scenarios where you want the Active Directory System Group Discovery method to find computer objects within Active Directory groups. Many organizations have a unique OU where they store computer groups.

Figure 5.5 shows all discovery methods available in a primary site. Let's look at each of these methods in detail.

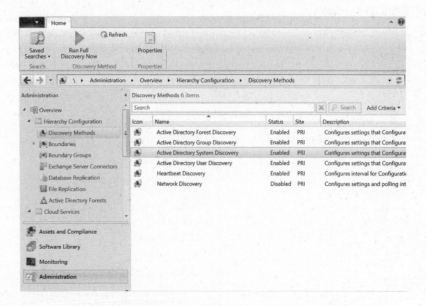

FIGURE 5.5
Discovery methods

ACTIVE DIRECTORY FOREST DISCOVERY

This discovery method was introduced in Configuration Manager 2012 and can be very helpful in environments where the Configuration Manager administrator is not always informed about IP infrastructure changes. The method returns information about domains, IP ranges, and Active Directory sites. Furthermore, as shown in Figure 5.6, you can configure the method to automatically create boundaries for the objects being discovered (IP ranges or Active Directory sites only), thus saving yourself hours of work.

FIGURE 5.6
Configuring Active
Directory Forest
Discovery

By default the discovery process runs once a week and will only discover those forests that are created as Active Directory Forest objects in the Administration workspace. The local forest is automatically created as part of the site installation process. Figure 5.7 shows how you can specify a new forest and define how to connect to the forest, via either the site server computer accounts or a specific account.

FIGURE 5.7
Defining a new Active Directory forest

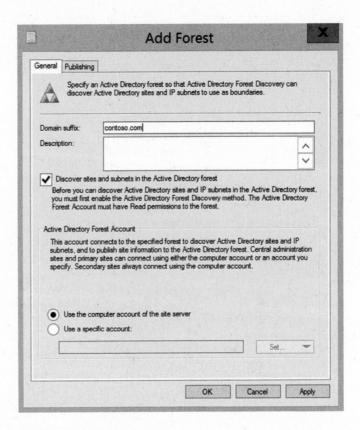

You can monitor this discovery process by reading the `ADForestDisc.log` on the site server.

ACTIVE DIRECTORY GROUP DISCOVERY

This discovery method will discover any local groups, global groups, and universal security groups. You can search for objects within a specific group or perform the search for all groups in a specific location. The information is not really used in a client installation scenario. But once you have the client deployed, you will find the Active Directory security group very useful, especially in user target deployments. You can limit the number of objects returned in the discovery process by configuring the values on the Option tab.

You can monitor this discovery process by reading the `ADsgdis.log` on the site server.

ACTIVE DIRECTORY SYSTEM DISCOVERY

This is the key discovery method for finding devices. In essence you configure one or more LDAP paths to Active Directory and query a domain controller for all objects in those paths. The device attributes returned by the domain controller depend on what you have configured. By default these attributes will be returned:

- ObjectGUID
- Name
- SAMAccountName
- ObjectSID
- PrimaryGroupID
- DNSHostName
- UserAccountControl
- LastLogonTimestamp
- DistinguishedName

In Figure 5.8 you see some of the default object attributes and some of the available attributes that could be added if needed. These attributes can be specified for AD System Discovery and AD User Discovery. The information you specify will be added to the discovery data and used in queries and reports like any other discovery information. You can monitor this discovery process by reading the `ADSysDis.log` on the site server.

FIGURE 5.8
Custom Active Directory system attributes

ACTIVE DIRECTORY USER DISCOVERY

This discovery method is not used at all in the client deployment process but plays an important part in the user-centric application model. With the method enabled, you will get a list of users to whom you can target different deployments such as applications. By default these attributes will be returned:

◆ ObjectGUID

◆ Name

◆ UserAccountControl

◆ SAMAccountName

◆ ObjectSID

◆ PrimaryGroupID

◆ DNSHostName

◆ Mail

◆ DistinguishedName

◆ UserPrincipalName

You can monitor this discovery process by reading the ADusrdis.log on the site server.

HEARTBEAT DISCOVERY

This discovery method is enabled by default (and should typically never be disabled) and differs from the other methods (see Figure 5.9). It is the responsibility of the client to initiate the discovery process. Failure to do so can result in unwanted client installation attempts and cause the client to be marked as inactive in the Configuration Manager console. The discovery process will not discover any new objects; instead it rediscovers existing objects. You can look at this method as a way to send a keep-alive package from the client to the management point. The heartbeat record is used for the following purposes:

◆ Determine whether a client is marked active or inactive.

◆ Update the Client column from No to Yes in the console when the client is installed.

◆ Re-create the client record in a database if you accidentally deleted the object.

◆ Have an impact when the Clear Install Flag site maintenance task will delete the client install flag in the database. If the install flag is removed and Automatic Client Push is enabled, a new client installation attempt will begin.

FIGURE 5.9
Heartbeat Discovery
Properties

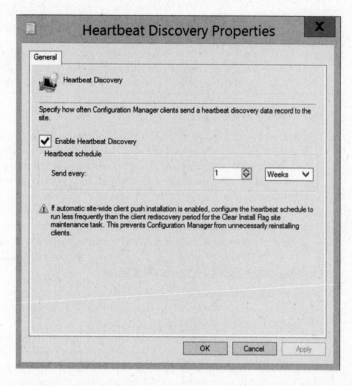

How often should you run the discovery method? By default clients will send an updated DDR to the management point every seven days, and you can change this to occur more frequently, perhaps daily, if needed to meet your requirements. As with any Configuration Manager changes, monitor the environment for any performance or file backlog issues if you make changes to the default settings. These are some of the attributes that will be returned:

- ClientInstalled
- ClientType
- ClientID
- ClientVersion
- NetBIOSName
- IPSubnet
- Domain
- ADSiteName
- IPAddress
- MACAddress

You can monitor this discovery process by reading the InventoryAgent.log on the client.

HEARTBEAT DISCOVERY AND MODIFYING COMPUTER NAMES

The Heartbeat Discovery process is responsible for updating changes in the computer name to the database. If you are starting a process where you need to rename a large number of computers, consider modifying the default schedule from seven days to a more frequent interval.

NETWORK DISCOVERY

Use the Network Discovery method only when no other discovery method can find the needed resources. This may be useful for Mac devices on your network but will also discover any device with an IP address, including printers and routers. It is considered to be the "noisiest" method and will use protocols like RIP or OSPF to discover objects. Most often you'll need to use this method only if you have a number of workgroup clients in your environment. Network Discovery is used to discover many different types of objects. Not only can you find computers that are on the network, but you can discover any device that has an IP address as well.

You can monitor the Network Discovery process by reading the Netdisc.log on the server.

DISCOVERY SCHEDULING OPTIONS

Each method also has a way of scheduling when the discovery will run, as shown in Figure 5.10. The schedule determines when the site server will initiate a full discovery. You can also configure delta discovery runs by default every 5 minutes and will only discover any changes made to the objects. Unlike in Configuration Manager 2007 R3, the process will discover when you modify existing objects, such as adding an existing computer account to an existing group. Using delta discovery along with the collection property Use Incremental Updates For This Collection, all changes will be reflected in the collection within 10 minutes: 5 minutes for the delta discovery and 5 more minutes for the incremental collection update.

FIGURE 5.10
Active Directory System
Discovery polling
schedule

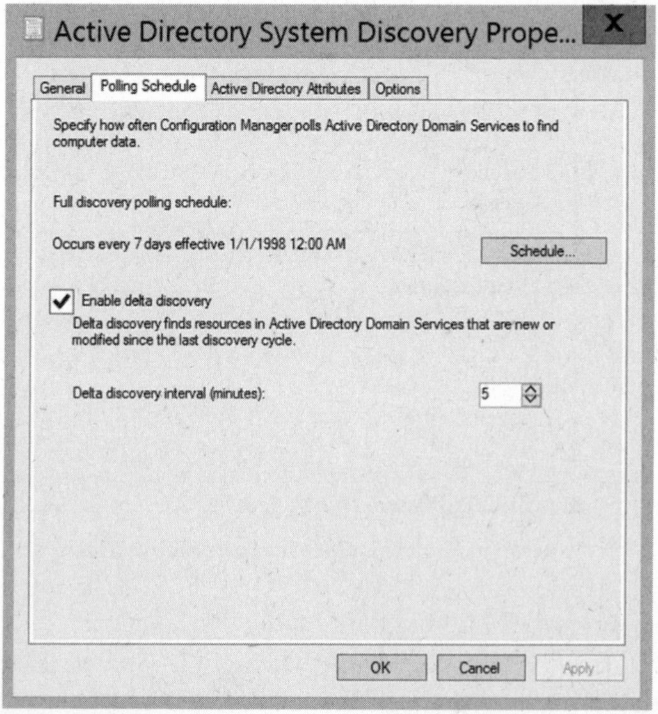

If you need to modify the schedule, click the Schedule button to display the Custom Schedule window, as shown in Figure 5.11.

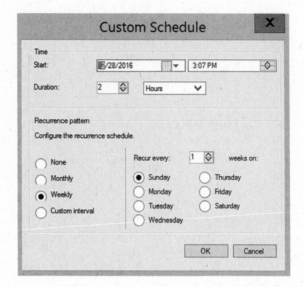

Configuring Boundaries and Boundary Groups

After a client has been installed, it must be assigned to a Configuration Manager site before it can be managed. Once assigned, the client will start receiving the default client policies, using the local resources of the site such as management points, distribution points, and software update points. During the installation, you can configure command-line properties to automatically assign the client a fixed site code or let an auto-assignment process begin. Note that clients will never be assigned to secondary sites, only primary sites.

Configuring boundaries has long been the way you assigned a client to a client site, and boundary groups were added to products to provide even more control over site assignments. In essence you still use boundaries, but they have no real value until they have been added to a boundary group. A boundary group is basically a collection of individual boundaries grouped together for one or two purposes:

Site Assignment   Used to control which sites clients are assigned to

Content Lookup   Used to control which distribution points will be used by the client

Figure 5.12 shows an IP address range that has been defined for an IP range boundary, and Figure 5.13 shows a boundary group that is configured for site assignment.

FIGURE 5.12
Creating a boundary

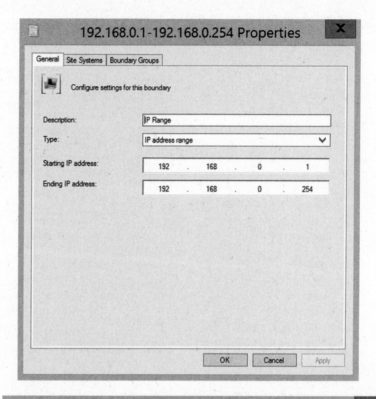

FIGURE 5.13
Boundary group config-
ured for site assignment

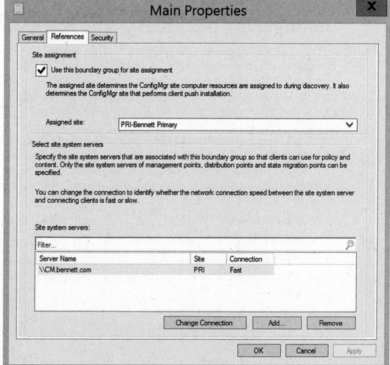

Boundaries are basically address ranges; the following range types are supported:

◆ IP subnet

◆ Active Directory site

◆ IPv6 prefix

◆ IP address range

Even though all four boundary types are supported, there will be scenarios where one or more of the types will not work correctly. There are known issues with IP subnets and network IDs that might cause clients not to be assigned even if they fall within the boundary defined. Furthermore, AD site boundaries are not supported in IP supernetting environments. If you experience problems, you can always configure IP ranges.

 Real World Scenario

CONFIGURING A BOUNDARY AND A BOUNDARY GROUP

As the Configuration Manager administrator, you have been requested to create an AD boundary and ensure it is used to assign clients to the primary site. Follow these steps:

1. Open the Configuration Manager administrative console.

2. Select the Administration workspace and browse to Overview ➢ Hierarchy Configuration ➢ Boundaries.

3. On the ribbon click Create Boundary.

4. Type **HQ** in the Description field, and under Type select Active Directory Site.

5. Click Browse, select the Active Directory site, and click OK.

6. Click OK to create the boundary.

7. Navigate to Boundary Groups, and on the ribbon click Create Boundary Group.

8. In the Name field type **HQ**, click Add, select the newly created boundary, and click OK.

9. Select the References tab.

10. Check the box Use This Boundary Group For Site Assignment. Select a primary site and click OK.

Client Installation Methods

You need to ask yourself a few questions as an important part of your client deployment planning:

◆ How are you going to deploy the client?

Basically you can choose between a manual installation and an automatic installation. The automatic installation method comes in different flavors.

◆ Where are you deploying the client?

You need to know which environments need a client. Many organizations plan only for client support in the local domain just to realize later in the process that they also need to support workgroup clients, clients in DMZ, and clients in other forests.

◆ When do you want to deploy the client?

You need to decide whether you want to deploy all clients at once or in a controlled manner.

You have several deployment methods to choose from; most organizations find themselves using a mix of different methods. It is important to know that there is no right or wrong method, but methods used in different scenarios have different requirements. Regardless of the installation method, you need to know the different command-line properties and when to use them. Gaining knowledge about the command-line properties will ensure that you can install clients in different environments such as workgroups, other forests, and DMZs.

Command-Line Properties

Several command-line properties are used to control the installation. Before you start the deployment, you will need to know two things:

◆ What command-line properties are you going to use?

◆ How are you going to provision the command-line properties?

The installation process will always run ccmsetup.exe and client.msi; both of these processes can be controlled using command lines. Any needed prerequisites will be installed and controlled by ccmsetup.exe. When you specify command-line properties, you should do so like this:

```
CCMSetup.exe [CCMsetup properties] [client.msi setup properties]
```

For an updated list of command-line properties, you should look at the TechNet article at this URL:

```
http://technet.microsoft.com/en-us/library/gg699356.aspx
```

The following are ccmsetup.exe command-line properties:

/source The /source switch is used to identify the location of the client.msi installer file and other client source files. You can specify the switch multiple times to provide additional source file locations to provide for redundancy. Usage: ccmsetup.exe /source:folderpath.

/MP The /MP switch is used to specify the management point that will be used as a source location. As with the /source switch, you can specify multiple management points by including the switch multiple times. The setting is not used to control the management point that will be used during the site assignment process. Usage: ccmsetup.exe /MP:*Server*.

/retry:<minutes> The /retry switch is used to retry values used to determine how often a client will try to download the installation files. The client will attempt to download the files until it reaches the values specified in downloadtimeout. Usage: ccmsetup.exe /retry:30.

/downloadtimeout:<minutes> The /downloadtimeout switch controls the number of minutes the ccmsetup process attempts to download the needed client installation files. By default the ccmsetup process will try downloading files for one day. Usage: ccmsetup /downloadtimeout:120.

/noservice   The /noservice switch is used to specify that the logged-in user's account is the service account for the installation of the client. For this switch to work, the user account will need to have rights to install software; otherwise the installation will fail. Usage: ccmsetup /noservice.

/Service   The /Service switch is used to install the client software using the security context of the local system account. For this to work, Active Directory has to be in use within your network, and the computer's Active Directory account must have access to the installation directory where the client installation files are stored. Usage: ccmsetup /Service.

/Logon   The /Logon switch is used to determine if a Configuration Manager client exists on the system. If a Configuration Manager client is already installed, the installation process will stop. Usage: ccmsetup.exe /Logon.

/forcereboot   The /forcereboot switch is used to determine if the ccmsetup process needs to perform a restart of the computer in order to finish the installation. Usage: ccmsetup.exe /forcereboot.

/BITSPriority:<Priority>   The /BITSPriority switch controls the Background Intelligent Transfer Services (BITS) download priority when downloading the client installation files. You can specify these values:

- Foreground
- High
- Normal
- Low

Usage: ccmsetup.exe /BITSPriority:Foreground.

/Uninstall   The /Uninstall switch is used to silently uninstall the Configuration Manager client. Usage: ccmsetup.exe /Uninstall.

/UsePKICert   The /UsePKICert switch is used to specify that the client will use a PKI certificate that uses client authentication for communication. If no certificate can be found, the client will use a self-signed certificate and communicate using HTTP. Usage: ccmsetup.exe /UsePKICert.

/NoCRLCheck   The /NoCRLCheck switch is used to specify that the client will not check the certificate revocation list before establishing HTTPS communication. This example will enable HTTPS communication and not check for any revocation lists. Usage: ccmsetup.exe /UsePKICert /NoCRLcheck.

/config:<configuration file>   The /config switch is used to specify the name of a user-defined configuration file. The configuration file replaces the default mobileclient.tcf file. It is a very good idea to modify an existing mobileclient.tcf file whenever you want to create a custom configuration file. That way you ensure that the syntax used in the file is correct. Usage: ccmsetup.exe /config:C:\Windows\ccmsetup\mysettings.txt.

The following are Client.msi command-line properties:

Patch   This property allows you to apply client patches during the installation. As of this writing, there are no Configuration Manager client patches. Usage: patch=\\Server\Share\clientpatch.msp.

CCMALWAYSINF   This property with a value of 1 allows you to determine that the client will always be Internet based, thus never connecting to the intranet site systems. Usage: CCMALWAYSINF=1.

CCMCERTISSUERS   This property specifies the list of certificate issuers trusted by the Configuration Manager site. Notice that the list is case-sensitive. Usage: CCMCERTISSUERS= ="CN=CM Root CA; OU=SRV; O=CM, Inc; C=US".

CCMCERTSEL   This property allows you to control the certificate selection criteria used when the client has more than one certificate to choose from. When specifying the criteria you can search for the exact subject name (type **subject:** prior to the SN) or a partial match in the subject name (type **subjectstr:** prior to part of the subject name, object identifier, or distinguished name). Usage: CCMCERTSEL="subject:Server1.CMSITE.COM".

CCMCERTSTORE   This property allows you to specify an alternative certificate store. You should use the command line only if the certificate is not found in the default store. Usage: CCMCERTSTORE="CMSITECERT".

CCMFIRSTCERT   With this property configured to 1, the client will automatically select the certificate with longest validity period. Usage: CCMFIRSTCERT=1.

CCMHOSTNAME   This property is used to specify the management point for Internet-based managed clients. Usage: CCMHOSTNAME="MPServer.CMSITE.COM".

SMSPUBLICROOTKEY   This property allows you to specify the trusted root key if, for some reason, it cannot be retrieved from Active Directory. You can open the mobileclient.tcf file and copy the trusted root key. Usage: SMSPUBLICROOTKEY=

02000000A400005253413100080000010001008186332BF592B793C8B7F7C01FB32CB811465DE
B71095C4442DE45661CE25031FE2B6F8D9C1C71C6C0BB335C3B5747035E028C43C35E4F8DF1E0
CB8B42289A8B9F9A3143964817DCC50F0D5DB9A879705AD0F4063F4F30242472A933FE8B452BE
E608147D9ECED79CA9422D5441894D152C54B0ABB920741BA0B5582482EA1231FAB0BD67AAAB8
2DEC50BDCE7D91FCCFB2C3F6C03C8C67C31B5F083A98860389E8D2FD93C4C5BAE6124A4977EA7
6B5A89AE2917687782783E003C5F215C767782C0F79A1C1E1F4D14E8B69325C8CC33C574BE774
CEA9579AD765A864DB0FBBBBB854D4390473E72014111EFDFC11DDDF46EF7B1F03EF1D60A3AB
DAA52E8868A0.

SMSROOTKEYPATH   This property allows you to reinstall the trusted root key from a file. Usage: SMSROOTKEYPATH="D:\NewRootKey\Rootkey.txt".

RESETKEYINFORMATION   This property allows you to remove the old trusted root key. This is often used when you move clients from one Configuration Manager site hierarchy to another. Usage: RESETKEYINFORMATION=TRUE.

CCMAdmins   This property allows you to configure which admin accounts are for the client. If there is more than one account, separate the accounts with a semicolon. Usage: CCMAdmins= account1;account2;....

CCMAllowSilentReboot   After the installation is complete, if a reboot is required, this property will cause the machine to reboot without saving any user changes. It needs to be specified only if the silent reboot is to be used. A value of 1 forces the reboot if required. Usage: CCMAllowSilentReboot.

CCMDebugLogging   This property enables or disables debug logging. A value of 1 enables logging; a value of 0 disables logging. Usage: CCMDebugLogging=0 | 1.

CCMEnableLogging   This property turns logging on or off. If this property is not included, then logging is disabled. Usage: CCMEnableLogging=True.

CCMInstallDir   This is the directory where the client software will be installed. Usage: CCMInstallDir=*C:\ConfigMgr*.

CCMLogLevel   This property is used to control the amount of logging activity. A value of 0 is verbose logging. A level of 1 logs all information, warning, and error conditions. A level of 2 logs warning and error conditions. A value of 3 logs error conditions only. When included, you must also use CCMEnableLogging. Usage: CCMLogLevel=0 | 1 | 2 | 3.

CCMLogMaxHistory   This property controls the total number of previous log files within the Logs directory. When included, you must also use CCMEnableLogging. Usage: CCMLogMax History=*NumberOfLogFilesToKeep*.

CCMLogMaxSize   This property controls the maximum log file size. When included, you must also use CCMEnableLogging. Usage: CCMLogMaxSize=*LogSizeBytes*.

DisableCacheOpt   When this property is included in the text box, it disables the Cache configuration setting within the Systems Management properties in Control Panel. Users will not be able to manipulate the settings—only administrators will be allowed to. Usage: DisableCacheOpt=True.

DisableSiteOpt   When this property is included in the text box, it disables the Site Code configuration setting within the Systems Management properties in Control Panel. Users will not be able to manipulate the settings—only administrators will be allowed to. Usage: DisableSiteOpt=True.

SMSCacheDir   This property controls the directory where the cache is created. Usage: SMSCacheDir=*directorypath*.

SMSCacheFlags   This property can be used to control how much space the cache can occupy and the location where the cache will be stored. When used in conjunction with the SMSCacheDir property, you have control over where the cache is stored. The flags are as follows:

   SMSCacheFlags=PercentDiskSpace   Used to control the size of the cache by allocating the total cache size as a percentage of the disk size. Cannot be used with PercentFreeDiskSpace.

   SMSCacheFlags=PercentFreeDiskSpace   Used to control the size of the cache file by allocating the total cache size as a percentage of the free space on the disk. Cannot be used with PercentDiskSpace.

   SMSCacheFlags=MaxDrive   Used to place the cache on the largest drive in the system. Cannot be used with MaxDriveSpace.

   SMSCacheFlags=MaxDriveSpace   Used to place the cache on the drive with the most free space. Cannot be used with MaxDrive.

   SMSCacheFlags=NTFSOnly   Used to control the placement of the cache drive on volumes formatted with NTFS.

   SMSCacheFlags=Compress   Used to compress the files within the cache.

   SMSCacheFlags=FailIfNoSpace   Used to stop installation of the client if there is not enough space on the drive for the cache.

SMSCacheSize   This property controls the amount of space in megabytes that the cache will consume or in percentage if used in combination with PERCENTDISKPACE or PERCENTFREEDISKSPACE. Usage: SMSCacheSize=*CacheSizeInMB*.

SMSConfigSource This property controls where the configuration source files are stored. Usage: SMSConfigSource=R | P | M | U.

SMSDIRECTORYLOOKUP This property controls whether WINS lookup is allowed when the client is trying to locate the management point and the site code. Usage: SMSDIRECTORYLOOKUP=NOWINS.

CCMHTTPPort This is the HTTP port used by the client to communicate with the site systems. Usage: CCMHTTPPort=80.

CCMHTTPSPort This is the HTTPS port used by the client to communicate with the site systems. Usage: CCMHTTPSPort=443.

SMSMP This property is used to configure the initial management point that the client communicates with. Usage: SMSMP=Server1.CMSITE.COM.

FSP This property specifies that a fallback status point is used. Usage: FSP=Server1.CMSITE.COM.

DNSSUFFIX This property specifies the DNS domain of the management point. With this option clients will search DNS for the .srv record that includes the DNS suffix of the management point. Usage: DNSSUFFIX=CMSITE.COM.

SMSSiteCode This property controls the site code that is assigned to the client. Usage: SMSSiteCode=Auto | SiteCode.

CCMEVALINTERVAL This property controls how often in minutes the client evaluation process runs. By default the process is configured to run once a day. Usage: CCMEVALINTERVAL=1440.

CCMEVALHOUR This property controls when the client evaluation process runs (by the hour). By default the process is configured to run at midnight. Usage: CCMEVALHOUR=14.

For example, suppose you wanted to push the client to systems, using the following options:

◆ Install the cache in the \Cache directory on the largest drive.

◆ Enable verbose logging.

◆ Keep five log files.

◆ Automatically discover the site code.

Your entry within the Property text box would look like this:

```
SMSSITECODE=AUTO SMSCACHEDIR=CACHE SMSCACHEFLAGS=MAXDRIVE SMSENABLELOGGING=TRUE
CCMLOGLEVEL=0 CCMLOGMAXHISTORY =5
```

PROVISIONING COMMAND LINES

You can provision command lines in three different ways:

◆ Manually type the command lines during the installation.

◆ Publish them to Active Directory.

◆ Configure a Group Policy with the ConfigMgrInstallation.adm template.

If the AD schema is extended, you can type the command lines in the Installation Properties for the client push installation method. All properties you enter here will be published to Active

Directory and used by any client that can access Active Directory during the installation. Notice that this applies only if you start the installation using `ccmsetup.exe` with no other command lines.

For those scenarios where clients cannot access the information in Active Directory, you can provision the command lines using a Group Policy with the `ConfigMgrInstallation.adm` template. The template is found on the Configuration Manager installation media in `.SMSSetup\TOOLS\ConfigMgrADMTemplates`.

Manually Installing the Client

This installation method might sound like a very time-consuming method; however, you will find yourself installing clients manually for several reasons. You can manually install the client by running `CCMSetup.exe` from the site server or from any management point. The file is located in the `Program Files\Microsoft Configuration Manager\Client` folder.

To manually install a client in an environment where the AD schema has been extended, do the following: From Start ➤ Run, type `\\`**ConfigMgr Server\SMS_<sitecode>\Client\ccmsetup.exe**.

To manually install a client on a workgroup computer, follow these steps:

1. Make sure you can access the client installation files or copy them to the local client.

2. Open a command prompt as administrator.

3. Run `ccmsetup.exe smssitecode=PS1 /Source:C:\CMClient smsmp=SCCM4.SCCMLAB.Local fsp=SCCM4.SCCMLAB.Local DNSSUFIX=SCCMLAB.Local`.

This will install the Configuration Manager client from the local source `C:\CMClient` and assign it to primary site PS1 using SCCM4 as the management point and fallback status point. The client must be able to resolve the site system names; otherwise the installation will fail. You can use the Hosts and LMHOSTS files to provide the needed naming resolution support.

To support a DMZ installation where the client is not able to resolve the needed hostnames, you configure these settings in the LMHOSTS and Hosts files (in the example the site server is named SCCM4.SCCMLAB.LOCAL with 192.168.1.2 as the IP address). You can find the files in `%windir%\System32\drivers\etc\`. There must be exactly 15 characters between the first " and the \ in the LMHOSTS file.

Add these entries to the LMHOSTS file:

```
192.168.1.2 SCCM4 #PRE
192.168.1.2 "SMS_MP    \0x1A" #PRE
```

Add this entry to the Hosts file:

```
192.168.1.2 SCCM4.SCCMLAB.local
```

Client Push

Client push is one of the most used installation methods because it requires very little work. All you need to do is to specify one or more client push installation accounts along with some client push installation settings. Before you use client push, you need to understand the preinstallation phase:

◆ When one of the discovery processes is running, a client configuration request (CCR record) will be generated for each object that does not have a client installed.

◆ Using the client push account, the Client Configuration Manager (CCM) component will make a connection to the client and copy the two files `ccmsetup.exe` and `mobileclient.tcf` to `\\Client\Admin$\CCMSetup`.

♦ Once the files have been successfully copied to the client, the server will verify that the CCMsetup service is starting successfully on the client before it disconnects.

♦ From this point on, the local client is responsible for installing the Configuration Manager agent.

LINUX/UNIX OR MAC COMPUTERS

The client push installation feature of Configuration Manager does not support client installation on Linux/Unix or Mac computers. The client for these platforms must be installed manually or via a remote scripting solution.

All this information from the preinstallation phase is recorded in the CCM.log file on the site server. It is not uncommon to see errors in the log file for reasons like these:

♦ A local firewall is running on the client and no firewall rules have been created. This will generate an error message like this: ---> Failed to connect to \\Client\admin$ using machine account (67).

♦ The client push account does not have the correct permissions to access IPC$ and Admin$. This will generate an error message like this: Unable to connect to remote registry for machine name "client ", error 5. Error 5 may also indicate that the computer is not online, the Windows Firewall is not configured properly, and others.

♦ The client is not running. This will generate an error message like this: ---> Failed to connect to \\Client\admin$ using machine account (67).

♦ Configuration Manager is unable to locate the client because of naming resolution errors. This will generate an error message like this: The network path was not found (53).

If the client Configuration Manager component fails to start the installation on the client, it will retry the installation once an hour for seven days. All retry attempts are stored in \Program Files\Microsoft Configuration Manager\inboxes\ccrretry.box. If you want to re-initiate the client installation attempt on these devices, you can cut and paste the files in the ccm.box folder. This may be useful as you troubleshoot client push installation issues.

To configure the client firewall correctly, you need to enable

♦ File and Printer Sharing

♦ Windows Management Instrumentation (WMI)

To configure the client push installation account correctly, you need to assign it local administrative permissions on the client.

When you create the account, make sure you add it to the group within your Active Directory structure that has the proper security rights on each machine within the site. Once the account(s) are created, you can configure them as client push installation accounts in the Configuration Manager console. If none of the specified client push accounts are able to connect to the client, the site server will attempt to connect using the site server computer account. With that in mind, you can also assign the correct permissions to the site server computer account, thus eliminating the need for multiple client push accounts.

CONFIGURING CLIENT PUSH SETTINGS

Once the discovery methods have been configured, you will need to configure the client push settings. In the Configuration Manager Administrator console, follow these steps:

1. Select the Administration workspace.

2. Browse to Overview ➢ Site Configuration ➢ Sites.

3. Choose Client Installation Settings ➢ Client Push Installation on the ribbon.

Selecting the check box Enable Automatic Site-Wide Client Push Installation means that whenever a computer is discovered within a defined site boundary group, the client will be automatically installed.

Figure 5.14 shows the Client Push Installation Properties, and this is where you can enable and configure automatic client push installation. It is important to know that client push can be performed in several ways. Use the General tab to configure the options for the fully automated client push feature of Configuration Manager. For a collection-based or client-based client push, you only need to configure settings on the Accounts and Installation Properties tabs.

FIGURE 5.14
The General tab of
Client Push Installation
Properties

The Accounts tab, shown in Figure 5.15, allows you to specify the accounts to use to install the Configuration Manager client. Configuration Manager will try the accounts in order until it finds an account with administrative rights on the destination computer. It will always try using the site server's computer account last if one or more accounts are listed and try the site server's computer account only if no accounts are listed. A maximum of 10 user accounts can be specified here.

FIGURE 5.15
The Accounts tab of
Client Push Installation
Properties

In the Installation Properties tab of Client Push Installation Properties, shown in Figure 5.16, you control how the client is installed by entering installation properties within the text box. The properties that you enter here will be published as command lines in Active Directory. You can enter all available `client.msi` command lines.

FIGURE 5.16
The Installation
Properties tab of Client
Push Installation
Properties

To manually push the client install out from within the Configuration Manager administrative console, the target client system(s) needs to be discovered and visible in the Assets and Compliance workspace. Once a system is available, you can push the client to the individual system, or you can push the client to all of the systems within the collection. The simplest way to do this is with the Install Configuration Manager Client Wizard. To initiate the wizard, select a discovered system or collection and choose Install Client from the ribbon. This will open the Install Configuration Manager Client Wizard.

Although the properties and the installation account cannot be modified from the wizard, as Figure 5.17 shows, you can change some of the client push installation options on an individual basis. Especially notice that you can select which site you want to use to install the client. The site choice also affects from which server the client will download the needed software.

FIGURE 5.17
Client push Install Configuration Manager Client Wizard settings

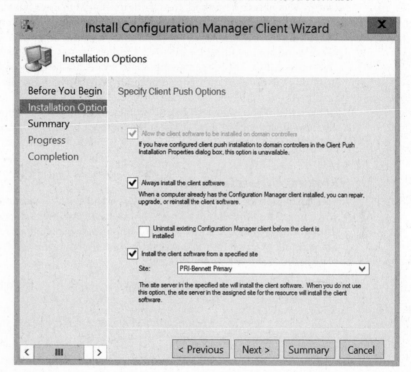

From this page you can also choose to always install the client software. This will force the installation of the client, even if another client is already installed.

You can use the canned reports in the Client Push category to monitor the client push attempts. The reports will provide you with information about all client push attempts divided into days and installation status.

Group Policy

You can use a software installation GPO to install the client. For GPO installations you must use the ccmsetup.msi file. This file can be found in the folder .\Program Files\Microsoft Configuration Manager\bin\i386 on the site server. You cannot specify any command-line properties when publishing the client; instead the command lines that are published to Active Directory will be used. If you are installing the client in another forest, you can use a Group Policy based on the `ConfigMgrInstallation.adm` template to provision the command lines locally on the client in the registry before installing the client.

Software Update

This installation method requires that you have an existing WSUS server in the environment and that it is also configured as the software update point. (A Windows client can only be configured with a single WSUS server. For that reason you need to make sure that the WSUS server specified in the GPO is the same as the one being used as the software update point.) Once you enable this method, the Configuration Manager client will be published to WSUS as a required infrastructure update. You cannot specify any command-line properties when publishing the client; instead the command lines that are published to Active Directory will be used. If you are installing the client in another forest, you can use a Group Policy based on the `ConfigMgrInstallation.adm` template to provision the command lines in the registry before installing the client. You can monitor publishing between the site server and WSUS server by reading the `wcm.log` file on the site server.

Note that if you ever need to uninstall Configuration Manager for any reason, make sure you have disabled this client installation method. Failure to do so will leave the Configuration Manager client in WSUS as a required infrastructure update.

Software Distribution

You can deploy the client using the Software Deployment feature. This method is often used when upgrading the client to a new service pack. You will notice that a new installation of Configuration Manager ships with a Configuration Manager client package and a Configuration Manager client Upgrade package. If you want to create your own Configuration Manager client software package, follow these steps:

1. Open the Configuration Manager console and navigate to the Software Library workspace.

2. Select Overview ➤ Application Management ➤ Packages and click Create Package From Definition on the ribbon.

3. Under Name, select Configuration Manager Client Upgrade and click Next.

   If you do not see the definition, verify that you have selected Microsoft as the publisher.

4. Select Always Obtain Files From A Source Directory and click Next.

5. In the source directory type `\\<server>\sms_<sitecode>\Client` where *<server>* is the name of the Configuration Manager site server and *<sitecode>* is the site code.

6. Click Next and finish the guide.

You have now created a software package containing the client software that you can deploy using the deployment methods described in later chapters.

Logon Script Installation

Logon scripts have been used by companies for many years to apply settings to users and their systems. The parameters that you can use are the same as those described earlier in this chapter. When installing the client using this method, remember to add the /Logon command line to ccmsetup.exe; otherwise, the client installation will begin every time the user logs on to a system. Some administrators prefer to use a combination of the client push and logon script methods.

Imaging

If you are using the Operating System Deployment feature of Configuration Manager, there is a step in the task sequence that will install the Configuration Manager client. The task sequence step Set Up Windows And Configuration Manager is required and will install the Configuration Manager client correctly in both the reference image and the real image. If you are using another imaging solution and need the Configuration Manager client installed in the reference image, follow these steps:

1. Manually install the client.

2. Stop the SMS Agent Host service by running **NET STOP CCMEXEC**.

3. Remove the trusted root key and any other unique certificates. Remove the trusted root key by running **CCMSetup RESETKEYINFORMATION = TRUE**.

4. Run **SYSPREP.EXE**.

5. Capture the image.

Installing Linux/Unix Clients

Beginning with Configuration Manager 2012 SP1, Configuration Manager supports Linux and Unix computers as Configuration Manager clients. The Linux/Unix Configuration Manager client supports hardware and software inventory as well as software distribution. The client push feature of Configuration Manager cannot be used to install the client, and these computers are treated as workgroup-based devices. As a result, you must manually install the Configuration Manager client on Linux/Unix devices, or you can use a shell script that installs the client remotely.

The client installation process leverages a script named Install, which is included in the downloaded media for the Linux/Unix client. This installation media is available at www.microsoft.com/en-us/download/details.aspx?id=39360.

The Install script supports command-line properties, some of which are required and others are optional. For example, you must specify the management point for the site that the Linux/Unix client will utilize. Once the client is installed, you can use the Client Settings feature in the Configuration Manager console to configure the client agent as you would for Windows-based clients.

You must use the correct client installation package for the Linux/Unix computer that the Configuration Manager client will be installed on. Several versions of Linux/Unix can utilize the Universal Agent, whereas other versions will use a client installation package that is specific to each operating system version and platform. See the Supported Distributions of Linux and

UNIX section in the Supported Configurations for Configuration Manager article on TechNet to determine which installation package to use:

http://technet.microsoft.com/en-us/library/gg682077.
aspx#BKMK_SupConfigLnUClientReq

You can utilize the same installation process and command-line properties, regardless of which installation package is used. Also, the client installation package contains all of the files required to completely install the Configuration Manager client, and the computer will not download additional files from the management point or another source location during the install process.

As shown in Figure 5.18, the client installation command line will reference the Install script that is included with the client installation package and will also specify the management point, the assigned site, any optional installation configurations, and the client installation package file.

FIGURE 5.18
Linux/Unix client
installation

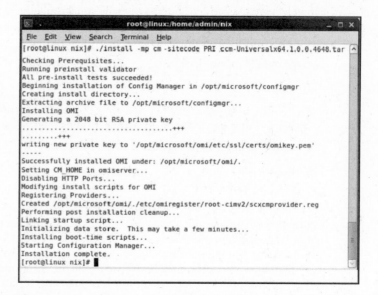

To install the client on a Linux/Unix computer, follow these steps:

1. Copy the Install script file and the client installation .TAR file to a folder on the Linux/Unix computer.

2. Use root credentials to run the command to enable the Install script to run: chmod +x install.

3. Under the root credentials, run the command with the required parameters and optional items, if needed:

./install -mp <management point> -sitecode <sitecode> <property #1>
<property #2> <client installation package>

4. Once the client installation is complete, you can validate the status of the installation via the log file /var/opt/microsoft/scxcm.log. You can also verify that the computer registered with Configuration Manager properly by viewing the Devices node in the Assets and Compliance workspace in the Configuration Manager console.

If optional command-line properties are needed during the install, they must be specified in the command before the statement that identifies the client installation package file that will be used. Also, the client installation package file must be specified last in the command line. Table 5.1 describes the available command-line options. You can use the property -h to display this list of properties that are available.

TABLE 5.1: Available command-line options

PROPERTY	REQUIRED OR OPTIONAL	COMMENTS
-mp	Required	This is the FQDN of the management point server that the client will use for initial contact, but it does not specify the management point that the client will use after being assigned to a site. If the management point is configured to accept only HTTPS connections, you must also use the -UsePKICert property.
-sitecode	Required	This specifies the Configuration Manager primary site server that the client will be assigned to.
-fsp	Optional	This is the FQDN of the fallback status point server that the client will utilize to submit state messages.
-dir	Optional	This provides an alternate location for the client installation package. The default location is /opt/microsoft.
-nostart	Optional	This prevents the automatic start of the Configuration Manager client service after the client installation process is completed. After the client install process is complete, you must manually start the client service. The default option is to start the service after the client installation process is complete.
-clean	Optional	This is used to remove all client files and data from a previously installed client before the new installation starts.
-keepdb	Optional	This specifies that the local client database should be retained and reused when the client is reinstalled. The default option is to delete the database when the client is reinstalled.

TABLE 5.1:   Available command-line options   *(continued)*

PROPERTY	REQUIRED OR OPTIONAL	COMMENTS
-UsePKICert	Optional	This specifies the full path and filename for the PKI certificate in the Public Key Certificate Standard format. Use the -certpw command-line parameter to provide the password associated with the PKCS#12 file. If the certificate is not valid or cannot be located, the client will use HTTP and use a self-signed certificate. Also, you must use this property if you use the -mp option to specify a management point that is configured to accept only HTTPS client connections.
-certpw	Optional	This specifies the password associated with the PKCS#12 file that was specified with the -UsePKICert property.
-NoCRLCheck	Optional	This specifies that the client should not check the certificate revocation list when it communicates over HTTPS. The default is that the client will check with the CRL before establishing an HTTPS connection.
-rootkeypath	Optional	This specifies the path and filename for the trusted root key.
-httpport	Optional	This specifies the port that the client uses to communicate with the management point via HTTP. The default value is 80. Note: After installing the client, you cannot change the port configuration. To change the port you will need to reinstall the client and specify the port to utilize. Use the -keepdb option to retain the client database and files.
-httpsport	Optional	This specifies the port that the client uses to communicate with the management point via HTTPS. The default value is 443. Note: After installing the client, you cannot change the port configuration. To change the port you will need to reinstall the client and specify the port to utilize. Use the -keepdb option to retain the client database and files.
-ignoreSHA256validation	Optional	This specifies that the client installation will skip SHA-256 validation. Use this option if you're installing a client on an operating system that does not support SHA-256.

TABLE 5.1:   Available command-line options   *(continued)*

PROPERTY	REQUIRED OR OPTIONAL	COMMENTS
-signcertpath	Optional	This specifies the full path and filename for the exported self-signed certificate of the site server.
-rootcerts	Optional	This allows you to specify additional root certificates that the client may need to validate site servers.

Installing a Mac Client

Configuration Manager also supports the management of Apple Mac computers as clients. The client for the Mac operating system allows you to discover, retrieve inventory, manage settings, and also deploy applications and security updates via Configuration Manager.

The management of Mac computers in Configuration Manager requires the use of public key infrastructure (PKI) certificates. Configuration Manager can utilize Microsoft Certificate Services with an enterprise certification authority (CA), or you can request and install computer certificates outside Configuration Manager as long as the certificate meets the requirements of Configuration Manager. It is worth noting that Mac-based Configuration Manager clients always perform certificate revocation checking and cannot be disabled. If Mac clients cannot confirm the certificate revocation status via the certificate revocation list (CRL), they will not be able to connect to the Configuration Manager site servers. Mac devices will also require that the Configuration Manager enrollment point and enrollment proxy point site system roles are installed and configured.

Mac computers are automatically assigned to the Configuration Manager site that will manage them and are installed as Internet-only clients, even if the Mac computer will communicate only on an internal or intranet network. Thus, you will need to ensure that the site systems in the assigned Configuration Manager site are configured to allow client connections from the Internet. You may consider using a separate site server that is configured for HTTPS and Internet-only connections as the enrollment point, enrollment proxy point, management point, distribution point, and so forth that will service the Mac devices. This avoids the need to configure the existing SCCM infrastructure to use HTTPS if the environment is not already configured for HTTPS.

The following is the process for installing the Configuration Manager client on a Mac computer:

1. Ensure that the proper certificates have been prepared and deployed. A web server certificate must be deployed to the management point, distribution points, the enrollment point, and the enrollment proxy point. Also, a client authentication certificate must be deployed to the management point and distribution point. If you need guidance on preparing a Configuration Manager site for supporting PKI and Internet-based clients, refer to the definitive article "Step-by-Step Example Deployment of the PKI Certificates for Configuration Manager: Windows Server 2008 Certification Authority" at http://technet.microsoft.com/en-us/library/gg682023.aspx.

2. Open the Configuration Manager console and select the Administration workspace.

3. In the Administration workspace, choose Client Settings and then select Default Client Settings. You must modify the default client settings in order to configure the enrollment process. These settings cannot be applied via a custom device settings group.

4. Right-click Default Client Settings and select Properties.

5. Select Enrollment and set Allow Users To Enroll Mobile Devices And Mac Computers to Yes.

6. Select Enrollment Profile and click Set Profile.

7. In the Mobile Device Enrollment Profile window, click Create.

8. In the Create Enrollment Profile window, enter a name for the enrollment profile and configure the site code for the Configuration Manager site that will manage the Mac computers.

9. Click Add and in the Add Certification Authority For Mobile Devices window select the certification authority that will issue certificates to Mac computers. Click OK.

10. In the Create Enrollment Profile window, select the Mac computer certificate template that was previously created and click OK.

11. Click OK to close the Enrollment Profile window, and click OK to apply the settings to the default client settings.

12. Download the Mac installation media client files and install the Mac client. The Mac client applications are contained in a file named `ConfigmgrMacClient.msi` and can be obtained at `https://www.microsoft.com/en-us/download/details.aspx?id=47719` `www.microsoft.com/en-us/download/details.aspx?id=36212`.

13. On a Windows computer, run the `ConfigmgrMacClient.msi` file and extract the files that are included in the MSI.

14. Copy the `Macclient.dmg` file from the extracted files to the Mac computer.

15. Run the `Macclient.dmg` file on the Mac computer to extract the Mac client installation files. This will create a `Tools` folder and will contain several Mac client tools and files, including ccmsetup and `cmclient.pkg`.

16. For Configuration Manager you have two options for enrolling the Mac client. You can use the CMEnroll tool that is included in the extracted media from the previous step, or you can use the Mac Computer Enrollment Wizard.

Here are the steps for the CMEnroll process:

a. To use the CMEnroll process, open the folder where the extracted files were stored and enter the following command line: **Sudo `./ccmsetup`**. Wait for the Completed Installation message to appear. Do not restart the computer.

b. Open the folder where the extracted files were stored and enter the following command line: **Sudo `./CMEnroll` -s** *<enrollment proxy server>* **- ignorecertcha-invalidation -u** *<user name>*. The username must match an active account in Active Directory that has been granted Read and Enroll permissions on the Mac client certificate template. Also, this command will prompt for the password for the super user account first and then prompt for the password for the Active Directory user account. Make sure you use the correct passwords.

c. Wait for the message stating that the Mac client has been successfully enrolled, and then restart the computer.

Here are the steps for the Mac Computer Enrollment Wizard process:

a. To use the Mac Computer Enrollment Wizard, click Next at the welcome page. The Mac Computer Enrollment Wizard is shown in Figure 5.19.

FIGURE 5.19
Mac Computer
Enrollment Wizard

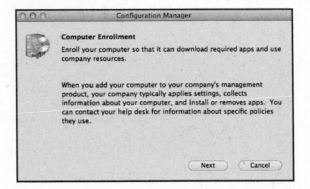

b. Enter the required information. The username can be in domain\username format or username@domain.

c. The username and the password must match an Active Directory account that has been granted Read and Enroll permissions on the Mac client certificate template.

d. Enter the password that is associated with the specified user account.

e. For server name, enter the name of the enrollment proxy point server.

f. Click Next and complete the wizard.

Once the client installation is complete, you can verify that the Mac computer registered properly by viewing the Devices node in the Assets and Compliance workspace in the Configuration Manager console. If you have Macs that are workgroup clients, you will need to give the Configuration Manager client access to the certificate in KeyFinder on the Mac.

Verifying Client Installation

While the installation is in progress, you can view the installation program running within Task Manager or monitor the installation by reading the log files. In Task Manager you will see `ccmsetup.exe` running. As it completes, you will see `ccmsetup.exe` replaced by the agent host program `ccmexec.exe`.

You can also verify that the client has obtained the correct site code and is communicating with the management point, as follows:

1. Open Control Panel, and you will find a new icon named Configuration Manager.

2. Double-click this icon, and the Configuration Manager Properties screen will appear.

3. Click the Site tab to find the site code within the Currently Assigned To Site Code box, as shown in Figure 5.20.

FIGURE 5.20
Verifying that the site code has been obtained

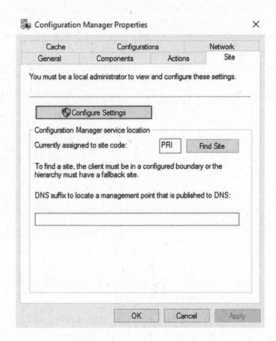

Within the Actions tab of the Configuration Manager Properties screen, you should also find several actions listed by default; other actions will appear in this list as the client agents are enabled. The default actions are Application Deployment Evaluation Cycle, Discovery Data Collection Cycle, Hardware Inventory Cycle, Machine Policy Retrieval & Evaluation Cycle, User Policy Retrieval & Evaluation Cycle, and Windows Installer Source List Update Cycle.

Now, unless you have a very small environment, you will not be able to manually verify the installation of each client. Instead you will use the following reports in the Site - Client Information category:

◆ Client Deployment Success Report

◆ Client Deployment Status Details

◆ Client Assignment Status Details

◆ Client Assignment Success Details

The reports require that you have specified a fallback status point in the command line for the client installation.

Troubleshooting a Client Installation

To troubleshoot a client installation, you will need to understand the three phases in the process. You can troubleshoot each of the phases in real time by reading the correct log files with CMtrace.exe.

The Preinstallation Phase This phase is described in the "Client Push" section of this chapter. A useful log file in this phase is ccm.log on the site server.

The Installation Phase This phase begins when ccmsetup.exe reads the mobileclient. tcf file and starts downloading the required files needed to complete the installation. Useful log files in this phase are ccmsetup.log and client.msi.log, both found in the %windir%\ ccmsetup folder on the client.

The Post-installation Phase This phase is also known as the assignment phase, where the client is being added as a managed client to a primary site. Useful log files in this phase are clientidstartupmanager.log, clientlocation.log, and locationservices.log, all found in the %windir%\ccm\logs folder on the client.

Once you have identified where the problem is, you will be able to select the correct log file for further troubleshooting.

Ensuring Client Health

Client status and automatic client remediation are some of the new features in Configuration Manager. In previous versions of Configuration Manager/Systems Management Server, organizations were forced to spend numerous hours creating custom client health solutions, and even more organizations did not even implement a client health process. In Configuration Manager an automatic remediation process runs daily on every client, and reports and alerts tell you if the number of active clients is dropping to a number below the defined service-level agreements for the company.

Automatic Client Remediation

During the client installation, a schedule remediation task is created in Windows. Figure 5.21 shows the scheduled task in Task Scheduler. The process ccmeval will run daily and perform all the checks that are specified in the ccmeval.xml file found in the %windir%\ccm folder. There are more than 20 different checks. If the evaluation process fails, the client will automatically be repaired. All ccmeval status messages will be forwarded to the management point. You can monitor the process by reading the ccmeval.log and CcmEvalTask.log files found in %windir%\ccm\logs and the ccmsetup-ccmeval.log file found in %windir%\ccmsetup\.

FIGURE 5.21
CCM evaluation task

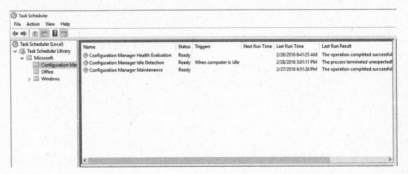

You can monitor the client remediation process in the Configuration Manager console. Navigate to the Monitoring workspace and select Client Status ➤ Client Check.

Determining Client Health

To determine the overall client health, Configuration Manager uses multiple objects such as these:

◆ Discover records

◆ Hardware inventory

◆ Software inventory

◆ Status messages

◆ Policy requests

◆ Active Directory integration

As the administrator, you will define when a client goes from being considered active to inactive. To configure the client activity settings, follow these steps:

1. Navigate to the Monitoring workspace.

2. Select Client Status.

3. From the ribbon, click Client Status Settings to open the window shown in Figure 5.22.

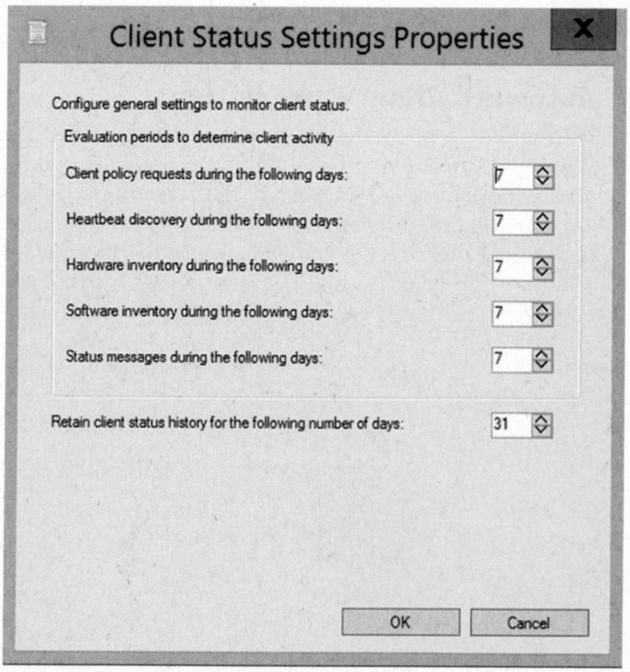

FIGURE 5.22
Client Status Settings
Properties—General
tab

Client Status Settings Properties

Configure general settings to monitor client status.

Evaluation periods to determine client activity

Client policy requests during the following days: 7

Heartbeat discovery during the following days: 7

Hardware inventory during the following days: 7

Software inventory during the following days: 7

Status messages during the following days: 7

Retain client status history for the following number of days: 31

OK   Cancel

There are no correct or incorrect settings; it all depends on the client behavior in your network. Do you have only workstations that are supposed to be started daily, or do you have a large number of laptops that are infrequently connected to the network? Don't be too aggressive when configuring the settings. If you configure the wrong values, you might find yourself chasing ghosts and trying to troubleshoot clients that for obvious reasons are not connected to the network.

Monitoring Client Status

The client status data is displayed in the Monitoring workspace. When you click the Client Status node, you will see both the client activity and the client check data. If you click any of the different states, you will be taken to the Assets and Compliance workspace, where you will see all the devices that are in the selected state.

You can also use the canned reports in the Client Status category. They will provide you with valuable information about the overall health status and the client agility.

Client Status Summary   Can be used as the main client health report. It will give an overview of the client health and client activity data.

Inactive Client Details   Will list all inactive clients along with information about the last health check.

Client Status History   Will provide a very good historic view for the last 30–90 days.

Client Time To Request Policy   Will display how many clients have requested policies during the last 30 days.

Configuring Alerts

Having a mixed environment with laptops, desktops, and servers often means that you have different activity requirements. You can configure individual thresholds per collection and that way have different settings for the unique computer roles in your environment. Figure 5.23 shows the alerts settings that are configured for a collection.

FIGURE 5.23
Configuring alert settings on a collection

CONFIGURING CLIENT HEALTH ALERTS FOR THE ALL SERVERS COLLECTION

As the Configuration Manager administrator, you have been requested to ensure that alerts are generated if any servers become unhealthy. To do so, follow these steps:

1. Open the Configuration Manager administrative console.

2. Select the Assets and Compliance workspace, and browse to Device Collections.

3. Select your All Servers collection, and click Properties on the ribbon.

4. Select the Alerts tab, click Add, and select each of the three Client Status checks.

5. Click OK.

6. In Conditions select each of the Client Status checks and configure the threshold and alert severity.

7. Click OK to save the settings.

To monitor the alerts, do the following:

1. Navigate to the Monitoring workspace.

2. Select Alerts.

3. In the Search field, type **Client** and click Search.

You will now see a list of all client remediation, client health, and client activity alerts.

Automatic Client Upgrade

Configuration Manager provides the ability to automatically upgrade the Configuration Manager client software on Windows-based devices to the latest version when the site determines that the Configuration Manager client version that is being used is lower than the version that is being used in the hierarchy. The configuration options are shown in Figure 5.24.

Configuration Manager automatically creates a client upgrade package and deploys the content to all of the distribution points in the hierarchy (except for cloud-based distribution points). As changes are made to the client package—for example, adding a client language pack—Configuration Manager will automatically update the package and update the distribution points. If automatic client upgrade is enabled, all clients will install the new client language pack automatically. The automatic upgrade feature was originally intended for upgrading relatively small numbers of Configuration Manager clients, but with the performance improvements introduced in Configuration Manager 2012 it is possible that the automatic client upgrade feature is the primary method you will use for upgrading clients.

The client upgrade feature also provides the ability to deploy preproduction client version to a specified collection for testing purposes. This may be useful if you want test a new Configuration Manager client version heavily before it is deployed to the entire infrastructure. For additional information on how to configure and utilize this feature, refer to https://technet.microsoft.com/en-us/library/mt612863.aspx.

FIGURE 5.24
Automatic Client
Upgrade configuration

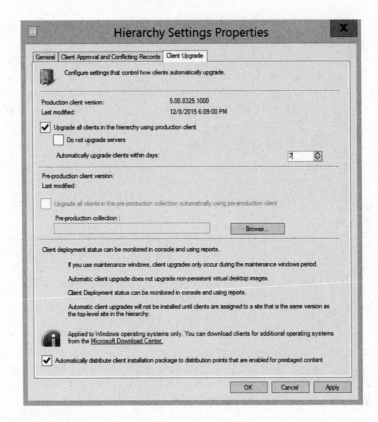

The following is the process to configure the automatic client upgrade feature:

1. Open the Configuration Manager console and select the Administration workspace.

2. Select Site Configuration and then select Sites.

3. In the Home tab of the ribbon, click Hierarchy Settings.

4. In the Site Settings Properties window, select the Client Upgrade tab.

5. If you want to enable the automatic client upgrade feature, select the Upgrade All Clients In The Hierarchy Using Production Client check box.

6. A window will appear confirming that you have chosen to enable automatic upgrade of all clients in the hierarchy and reminding you that all clients in the hierarchy will be upgraded. Click OK.

7. Configure the number of days in which the client computers must upgrade the client software. The clients will be upgraded at a random interval over the specified number of days. This will help prevent performing a large number of client upgrades at the same time. The default value is 7. You also have the option to not upgrade clients on servers.

8. Make sure the option Automatically Distribute Client Installation Package To Distribution Points That Are Enabled For Prestaged Content is enabled if you want the client installation package to be copied to distribution points that are enabled for prestaged content.

9. Once the settings are configured, click OK to save the settings and close the Site Settings Properties window. Clients will receive the updated setting during their next policy polling check.

The Bottom Line

Configure boundaries and boundary groups.   Before starting any client installation, verify that you have configured a boundary group for site assignment.

> **Master It**   Let Configuration Manager Forest Discovery automatically create the boundaries and add them to the correct boundary groups.

Select the relevant discovery methods.   You configure discovery methods in the Configuration Manager console. The Active Directory discovery methods all require a schedule and an LDAP path. There are schedules for delta and full discovery. In Configuration Manager, delta discovery will also find changes to existing objects; this eliminates the need to run a full discovery more than once a week.

> **Master It**   Always know what you want to discover and where. Based on that knowledge, configure the needed discovery methods.

Employ the correct client installation methods.   When configuring the client installation methods, make sure you know the pros and cons for each method. Some require firewall settings; others require local administrative permissions. You need to make sure that all the required settings are in place. Do not start any installation until you have the needed site systems, boundary groups, and command lines specified.

> **Master It**   Configure the correct command-line properties and ensure they will work for all environments (local forest, workgroup, and DMZ). Create multiple client push installation accounts, and ensure that you have a good understanding of the three phases (preinstallation, installation, and post-installation).

Manage Unix/Linux and Mac devices.   Configuration Manager provides support for managing Unix/Linux and Mac computers as devices. You are now able to manage your entire computer infrastructure from a single management console.

> **Master It**   Understand the installation methods available for deploying the Configuration Manager client to the Unix/Linux computers and Mac computers. Remember that client push cannot be used for these devices.

Ensure client health.   Client status might not be the first task you think about when implementing a system like Configuration Manager. But it is crucial to the daily administration that you can trust the numbers you see in the reports and in the console. One way to ensure that is by making certain that all clients are healthy and are providing the server with up-to-date status messages and discovery information.

> **Master It**   Discuss the different environments that exist in your organization, and use that information when configuring client health alerts. Make sure that you know the client activity during a normal period and that you have a set of defined SLAs for each of the environments (laptops, road warriors, servers, call center, and so forth).

Chapter 6

Client Health

Maintaining healthy Configuration Manager clients is critical for delivering Configuration Manager services and meeting required service-level agreements. When clients in the environment are not healthy, the accuracy and dependability of Configuration Manager services are degraded, resulting in systems that are either completely or partially unmanaged.

Client health has been a challenge historically with Configuration Manager, and many tools or processes have been developed to help identify and repair broken clients. The most recent offering from Microsoft was the Client Status Reporting tool, which arrived in Configuration Manager 2007 R2. While good, many of these tools fall short in that client health problems must be managed manually, and automatic remediation is not generally part of the process. Since Configuration Manager 2012 R2 the game changed in a dramatic way by not only detecting health problems via a thorough set of diagnostics but automatically remediating the problems as well. Before continuing, we must point out that no solution is 100 percent effective, and there will be problems that can't be resolved automatically. However, the majority of client problems that happen now are likely due to external issues that are not related to Configuration Manager specifically. The inclusion of client health evaluation/remediation by default in Configuration Manager significantly enhances the stability of deployments. While this solution won't address every potential issue, it goes a long way to reducing administrator workload in keeping systems active and healthy.

This chapter details the client health mechanism in Configuration Manager Current Branch. In this chapter, you will learn to

- ◆ Detail client health evaluations in Configuration Manager Current Branch
- ◆ Review client health results in the Configuration Manager console

Understanding the Client Health Mechanism

Managing client health issues involves detecting potential issues and fixing problems as they arise. Configuration Manager clients can become unhealthy for any number of reasons, often because of external issues such as WMI failure, DCOM permissions, service failures, and more. Configuration Manager uses an automated mechanism to detect the most common client health issues and automates the process of fixing the problem. Although this mechanism will go a long way toward helping maintain healthy clients, there will likely still be situations where manual intervention is required, but those situations should be greatly minimized.

Any tool used to effectively validate and potentially repair client health issues, by definition, must be able to execute independently without relying on a healthy client to operate. Further, such a tool must execute locally to mitigate any potential network issues. The client health tool in Configuration Manager addresses this requirement nicely by running as a scheduled task—set apart from the client itself. The next section reviews the elements of this scheduled task for implementing the client health scanning.

Scheduled Task

The client health tool operates as a scheduled task. The required scheduled task is automatically created when the Configuration Manager client is installed and set to run daily or a bit past midnight. Figure 6.1 shows the scheduled task created on a client system.

FIGURE 6.1
Scheduled task created by a client installation

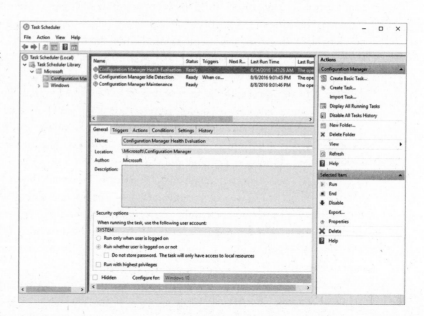

DIFFERENCES BETWEEN PLATFORMS

All platforms supported for use with the Configuration Manager client also support the client health scheduled task, but there are differences in the way various configurations may appear between platforms. The example discussion focuses on a Windows 10 workstation.

The overview of the scheduled task shown in Figure 6.1 provides helpful information, including the last runtime and next runtime for the task and whether the task was successful.

CLIENT HEALTH VS. PROBLEM-FREE EXECUTION

A successful task doesn't necessarily mean that the Configuration Manager client is healthy; it simply means that the client evaluation tool was able to execute without encountering a problem.

Notice that this view also provides various tabs that allow you to view the underlying configuration for the scheduled task. To make any changes to the task, you must select the properties for the task, which will present the same information but in an editable format, as shown in Figure 6.2 and described in the following sections.

FIGURE 6.2
Properties window for the scheduled task

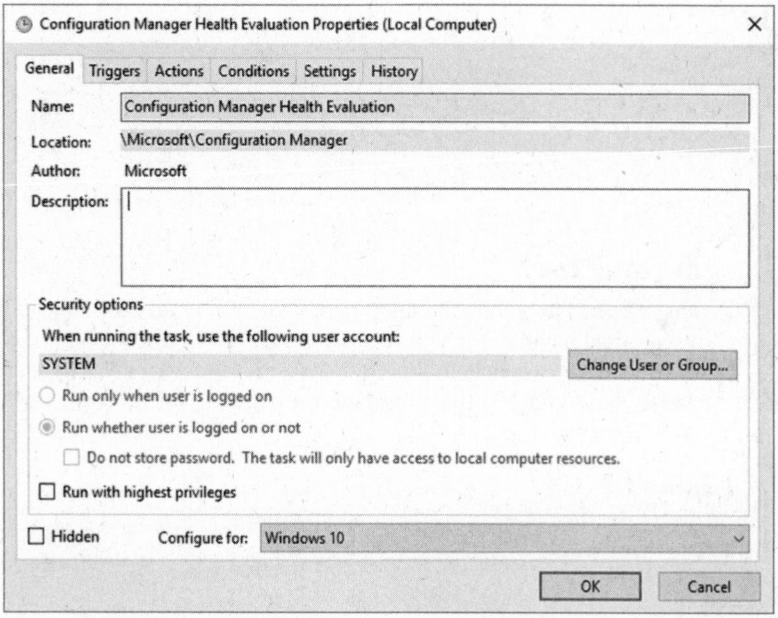

TRIGGERS TAB

The Triggers tab of the scheduled task, shown in Figure 6.3, is the place where you might adjust the run schedule for the scheduled task. By default, no trigger is configured. The schedule is written into the registry; looking at the location HKEY_LOCAL_MACHINE\SOFTWARE\Microsoft\CCM\CcmEval in the registry will show you what the LastEvalStartTime and EvaluationInterval are. By default, the EvaluationInterval is 1440 minutes, or 24 hours.

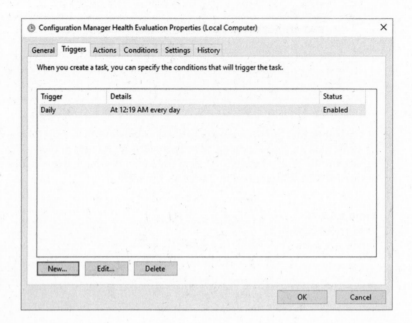

FIGURE 6.3
Triggers tab for the
scheduled task

ACTIONS TAB

The Actions tab of the scheduled task, shown in Figure 6.4, shows the command line that is to
be executed when the scheduled task runs. As you can see from the figure, the task executes
CCMEval.exe, which is in the %WINDIR%\CCM directory. We'll discuss CCMEval in more detail
shortly. No command-line parameters are needed for this executable.

FIGURE 6.4
Actions tab for the
scheduled task

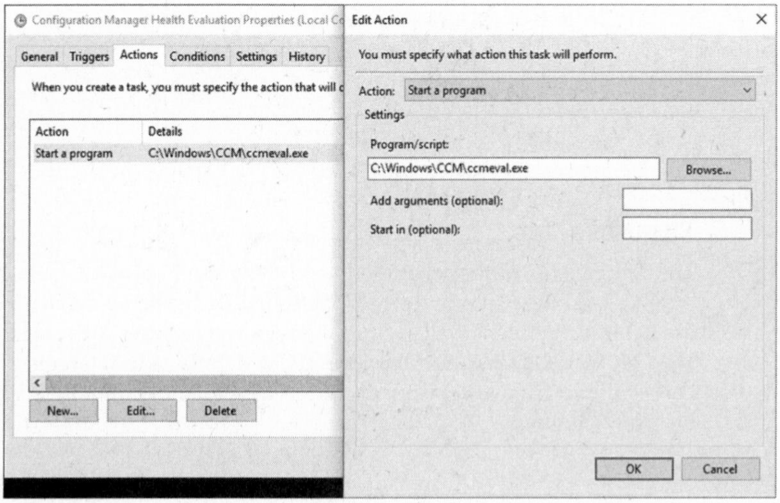

CONDITIONS TAB

The Conditions tab, shown in Figure 6.5, allows administrators to specify conditions that must be met before starting the task. There are no conditions set on this tab by default.

FIGURE 6.5
Conditions tab for
the scheduled task

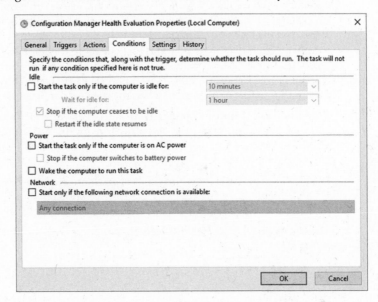

SETTINGS TAB

The Settings tab, shown in Figure 6.6, specifies various settings for the task. The default values configured are as follows:

FIGURE 6.6
Settings tab for
the scheduled task

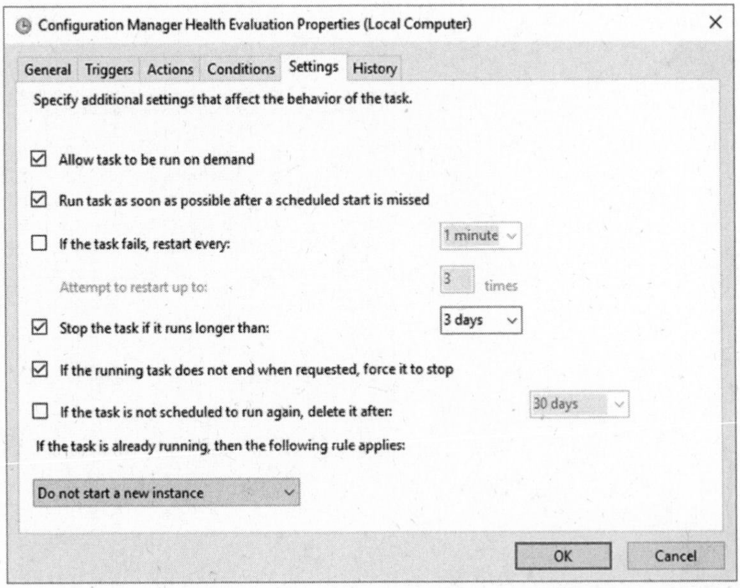

Allow Task To Be Run On Demand   This setting specifies that the task can be started by administrators as needed, such as in troubleshooting scenarios, outside the scheduled start time.

Run Task As Soon As Possible After A Scheduled Start Is Missed   This setting specifies the run behavior for the task if the system isn't able to run it on the defined schedule. As an example, if the system is powered off overnight and cannot run the task at the assigned time, then the task will be initiated the next time the system is started. The CCMEval process is lightweight but in this scenario is just one more thing for a system to do during startup, a process already loaded with significant activity. To avoid additional system load during startup caused by running this task, it may be worth considering rescheduling the start time for the task so that it takes place when the system is anticipated to be available.

Stop The Task If It Runs Longer Than   This setting ensures that a hung task doesn't continue to run long term. The default setting for this is 3 days, and it's unlikely that the CCMEval task will run into issues causing the process to hang. Having this set as a fail-safe, though, is a good idea.

If The Running Task Does Not End When Requested, Force It To Stop   This setting works with the previous setting and will force the CCMEval thread to terminate if it remains in a hung state even after termination is requested.

The last setting, Do Not Start A New Instance, prevents multiple instances of CCMEval from spinning up.

History Tab

The History tab, shown in Figure 6.7, allows administrators to review the execution history for the task. This tab has no configurable settings.

FIGURE 6.7
History tab for the scheduled task

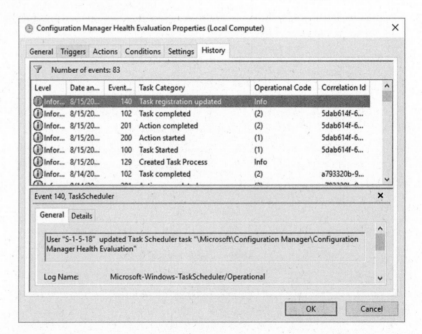

CCMEval Process

The task to execute CCMEval runs on a daily schedule by default. It is fully possible to change this schedule, but it's not recommended. If needed, the task can be run manually for trouble-shooting or other purposes, as previously alluded to.

With the understanding that client health checking and remediation for Configuration Manager clients is handled by CCMEval, it's natural to wonder what this process actually does. That's the next part of the discussion.

CCMEval is an executable that exists in the %WINDIR%\CCM folder on all Configuration Manager clients, as shown in Figure 6.8.

FIGURE 6.8
CCMEval executable in the %WINDIR%\CCM folder

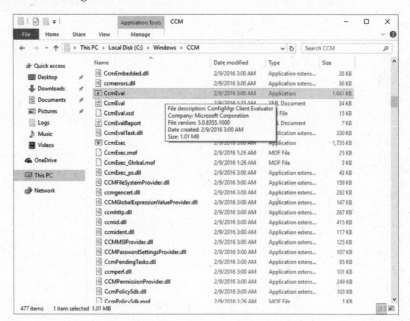

Note that in addition to CCMEval.exe you have CCMEval.xml, CCMEval.xsd, CCMEvalReports.xml, CCMEval.dll, and CCMEval.log. These support files for the CCMEval process are used as follows:

CCMEval.exe   This is the executable file used to drive the health evaluation and remediation process on Configuration Manager clients.

CCMEval.xml   This is the control file that defines the tests and remediation actions that will be taken as a result of test conditions. This file will be discussed in some detail shortly.

CCMEval.xsd   This file defines the schema used to validate client health evaluation and report data.

CCMEvalReports.xml   This is a header file used for building reporting information for-warded to Configuration Manager servers.

CCMEval.dll   This is a library file for use with CCMEval.exe.

CCMEval.log   This file records the progress of health check and remediation activities and is located in the Windows\CCM\logs folder.

Understanding the health check and remediation mechanism provided by CCMEval requires reviewing the work that is done during a CCMEval cycle along with the various checks that are performed. You can mine this information by reviewing `CCMEval.xml` along with `CCMEval.log`, and it will help you understand what is happening behind the scenes. Table 6.1 lists the checks and potential remediation outcomes that take place when problems are found during evaluation.

TABLE 6.1: CCMEval evaluation tasks and potential remediation actions

EVALUATION TASK	POTENTIAL REMEDIATION ACTION
Verify client check recently run	Run client check.
Verify that prerequisites of client are installed	Install prerequisites of client.
Integrity test WMI repository	Reinstall client.
Verify if client service is running	Start the client service (SMS Agent Host).
Verify WMI service exists	No remediation.
Verify if the client is installed correctly	Reinstall client.
Verify/remediate WMI service startup type	Sets the Windows Management Instrumentation service's startup type to automatic.
Verify/remediate WMI service status	Sets the Windows Management Instrumentation service to a running state.
WMI repository read/write test	Remediation of this client check is performed only on computers that run Windows Server 2003, Windows XP (X64), or an earlier version.
Verify/remediate client WMI provider	Restart the Windows Management Instrumentation service. This remediation is performed only on computers that run Windows Server 2003, Windows XP (X64), or earlier versions.
WMI repository integrity test	Checks that Configuration Manager client entries are present in WMI; if not, it will reinstall the Configuration Manager client.
Verify BITS exists	No remediation.
Verify/remediate BITS startup type	Sets the BITS service to the expected startup type.
Verify SMS Agent Host service exists	No remediation.
Verify/remediate SMS Agent Host service startup type	Sets the client (SMS Agent Host) service startup type to automatic.

TABLE 6.1: CCMEval evaluation tasks and potential remediation actions *(continued)*

EVALUATION TASK	POTENTIAL REMEDIATION ACTION
Verify/Remediate SMS Agent Host service status	Starts the SMS Agent Host service.
WMI Event Sink Test	Checks whether the Configuration Manager-related WMI event sink is lost and then restarts the client service.
Microsoft policy platform WMI integrity test	Checks the integrity of policy platform WMI data structures.
Verify/remediate Microsoft Policy Platform service existence	Installs Microsoft Policy Platform.
Verify/remediate Microsoft Policy Platform service startup type	Resets the service startup type to manual.
Verify/remediate anti-malware service startup type	Resets the service startup type to automatic.
Verify/remediate anti-malware service status	Starts the anti-malware service.
Verify/remediate Windows Update service startup type	Resets the startup type to automatic or manual.
Verify/remediate Windows Update service startup type on Windows (8)	Resets the service startup type to manual or automatic (trigger).
Verify/remediate Configuration Manager Remote Control service startup type	Resets the service startup type to automatic.
Verify/remediate Configuration Manager Remote Control service status	Starts the Remote Control service.
Verify/remediate Configuration Manager wake-up proxy service startup type	Resets the Configuration Manager Wake-up Proxy service startup type to automatic; this remediation is performed only if the Power Management: Enable Wakeup Proxy client setting is set to Yes on supported operating systems.
Verify/remediate Configuration Manager wake-up proxy service status	Starts the Configuration Manager Wake-up Proxy service; this client check is made only if the Power Management: Enable Wakeup Proxy client setting is set to Yes on supported client operating systems.
Verify that the Microsoft SQL CE database is healthy	Reinstalls the Configuration Manager client.

Figure 6.9 shows a portion of the `CCMEval.xml` file that contains the rules that are used during the client health/remediation evaluation cycle.

FIGURE 6.9
`CCMEval.xml` example

```
<?xml version="1.0"?>
- <ClientHealth Version="1.1" xmlns:ns="http://schemas.microsoft.com/SystemsManagementServer/2008/05/ClientHealth">
  - <HealthCheck Type="Services" ID="4AB7D77D-3BB0-4EAB-BEFD-7C0F7DA10296" Description="Verify WMI service exists.">
      <Applicability ClientVersion="ALL" OS="ALL" Platform="ALL"/>
      <PARAM Description="Services Check" Order="1"> ServiceExists </PARAM>
      <PARAM Description="Service Name" Order="2"> Winmgmt </PARAM>
    </HealthCheck>
  - <HealthCheck Type="Services" ID="518C0699-03F8-4F38-85C4-4D319EAEFC05" Description="Verify/Remediate WMI service startup type."
    DependsOn="4AB7D77D-3BB0-4EAB-BEFD-7C0F7DA10296">
      <Applicability ClientVersion="ALL" OS="ALL" Platform="ALL"/>
      <PARAM Description="Service Check" Order="1"> ServiceStartupType </PARAM>
      <PARAM Description="Service Name" Order="2"> Winmgmt </PARAM>
      <PARAM Description="Expected Service Startup State" Order="3"> Automatic </PARAM>
    - <Remediate>
        <PARAM Description="Services Remediation" Order="1"> ServiceStartupType </PARAM>
        <PARAM Description="Service Name" Order="2"> Winmgmt </PARAM>
        <PARAM Description="Desired Service Startup State" Order="3"> Automatic </PARAM>
      </Remediate>
    </HealthCheck>
  - <HealthCheck Type="Services" ID="7F4B6E15-2221-455B-9615-93C379E470D5" Description="Verify/Remediate WMI service status."
    DependsOn="4AB7D77D-3BB0-4EAB-BEFD-7C0F7DA10296">
      <Applicability ClientVersion="ALL" OS="ALL" Platform="ALL"/>
      <PARAM Description="Service Check" Order="1"> ServiceStatus </PARAM>
      <PARAM Description="Service Name" Order="2"> Winmgmt </PARAM>
      <PARAM Description="Expected Service Status" Order="3"> Active </PARAM>
    - <Remediate>
        <PARAM Description="Services Remediation" Order="1"> ServiceStatus </PARAM>
        <PARAM Description="Service Name" Order="2"> Winmgmt </PARAM>
        <PARAM Description="Desired Service Status" Order="3"> Running </PARAM>
      </Remediate>
    </HealthCheck>
```

Figure 6.10 is an example of the `CCMEval.log` file after an evaluation cycle is complete. Experienced administrators may notice that after the health-checking cycle is complete, the report is sent back to the site in the form of a state message. We mentioned earlier that an effective client health tool must function independently and not rely on a client function for any of its operation. State messages are commonly sent by the Configuration Manager client, so you might question whether the health evaluation tools simply offload the resulting state report to the client or handle it independently. The latter is true; the client health mechanism forwards the state message directly to the client's management point using its own mechanism. This is also noted in the log snippet in the figure.

FIGURE 6.10
`CCMEval.log` sample

```
CcmEval - Notepad
File Edit Format View Help
<![LOG[==========[ ccmeval started in process 2644 ]====================================]LOG]!><time="08:07:56.220-60" d
<![LOG[ccmeval version: 5.0.8325.1000]LOG]!><time="08:07:56.733-60" date="02-10-2016" component="CcmEval" context="" typ
<![LOG[Loading manifest file: C:\Windows\CCM\CcmEval.xml]LOG]!><time="08:07:57.086-60" date="02-10-2016" component="CcmE
<![LOG[Successfully loaded ccmeval manifest file.]LOG]!><time="08:08:07.380-60" date="02-10-2016" component="CcmEval" co
<![LOG[Begin evaluating client health rules.]LOG]!><time="08:08:09.941-60" date="02-10-2016" component="CcmEval" context
<![LOG[Successfully retrieved all client health checks.]LOG]!><time="08:08:09.949-60" date="02-10-2016" component="CcmEv
<![LOG[Evaluating health check rule {4AB7D77D-3BB0-4EAB-BEFD-7C0F7DA10296} : Verify WMI service exists.]LOG]!><time="08:
<![LOG[Evaluating health check rule {518C0699-03F8-4F38-85C4-4D319EAEFC05} : Verify/Remediate WMI service startup type.]
<![LOG[Evaluating health check rule {7F4B6E15-2221-455B-9615-93C379E470D5} : Verify/Remediate WMI service status.]LOG]!>
<![LOG[Evaluating health check rule {14E6774A-1795-4E09-B17D-B6F36A124205} : WMI Repository Read/Write Test.]LOG]!><time
<![LOG[Evaluating health check rule {690A959D-6210-4930-865F-E3BB82F02133} : Verify/Remediate client WMI provider.]LOG]!
<![LOG[Evaluating health check rule {A81778B5-9A1E-4A52-9C6E-6939CEFAA118} : WMI Repository Integrity Test.]LOG]!><time=
<![LOG[==========[ ccmeval started in process 4624 ]====================================]LOG]!><time="08:09:14.290-60" d
<![LOG[ccmeval version: 5.0.8325.1000]LOG]!><time="08:09:14.471-60" date="02-10-2016" component="CcmEval" context="" typ
<![LOG[Loading manifest file: C:\Windows\CCM\CcmEval.xml]LOG]!><time="08:09:14.474-60" date="02-10-2016" component="CcmE
<![LOG[Successfully loaded ccmeval manifest file.]LOG]!><time="08:09:14.480-60" date="02-10-2016" component="CcmEval" co
<![LOG[Begin evaluating client health rules.]LOG]!><time="08:09:14.481-60" date="02-10-2016" component="CcmEval" context
<![LOG[Successfully retrieved all client health checks.]LOG]!><time="08:09:14.486-60" date="02-10-2016" component="CcmEv
<![LOG[Evaluating health check rule {4AB7D77D-3BB0-4EAB-BEFD-7C0F7DA10296} : Verify WMI service exists.]LOG]!><time="08:
<![LOG[Evaluating health check rule {518C0699-03F8-4F38-85C4-4D319EAEFC05} : Verify/Remediate WMI service startup type.]
<![LOG[Evaluating health check rule {7F4B6E15-2221-455B-9615-93C379E470D5} : Verify/Remediate WMI service status.]LOG]!>
<![LOG[Evaluating health check rule {14E6774A-1795-4E09-B17D-B6F36A124205} : WMI Repository Read/Write Test.]LOG]!><time
<![LOG[Evaluating health check rule {690A959D-6210-4930-865F-E3BB82F02133} : Verify/Remediate client WMI provider.]LOG]!
<![LOG[Evaluating health check rule {A81778B5-9A1E-4A52-9C6E-6939CEFAA118} : WMI Repository Integrity Test.]LOG]!><time=
```

CCMEVAL–CUSTOMIZABLE? PORTABLE?

Contoso has some 25,000 clients, who they monitor on a daily basis to ensure they are healthy. In the past, Contoso used to spend 10 hours a week troubleshooting the clients that were not reporting to the site. Now, with Configuration Manager and client health, Contoso only spends about two hours reviewing the reports, alerts, and client statuses. When there is a problem, most clients automatically remediate by themselves using the CCMEval and CCMrepair task. If this doesn't fix the problem, Contoso will focus their efforts only on those clients that are failing. This is a good example of how client statuses save hours of work by implementing Configuration Manager.

After taking a peek at the CCMEval.xml and CCMEval.log files, a common question to ask is whether customers are able to customize or add to these checks. Unfortunately, changes to these files are not supported, so if any modifications are attempted, they are solely at the risk of the administrator and may cause problems. Remember, the content of this file impacts every Configuration Manager client in the organization.

Another question that commonly follows is whether it's possible to port the CCMEval process to work on earlier versions of Configuration Manager clients. The answer is no. CCMEval is solely for use on Configuration Manager client systems.

Real World Scenario

DON'T WANT TO CHECK AND REMEDIATE THE CLIENT AUTOMATICALLY?

If you do not want to automatically remediate a broken or not properly working client, open the registry of the computer that you do not want to automatically remediate; then navigate to HKEY_LOCAL_MACHINE\Software\Microsoft\CCM\CcmEval\NotifyOnly and change the value of the NotifyOnly key to True. (Change the key back to False if you later want to enable automatic remediation.) Changing the registry can be done via a configuration item (CI); configuration items and configuration baselines are discussed in Chapter 13, "Compliance Settings."

Another option is to use the /NotifyOnly parameter while installing the client via CCMSetup.exe.

Client Health Evaluation: Results

Client health evaluation results are accessible in the Configuration Manager console in several areas. First, client health is reported on a device level by reviewing collection membership. Any collection in which the device is a member will provide the same health information. To view health results for a device, simply select it in the console, and the bottom of the screen will reveal five tabs: Summary, Client Check Detail, Malware Detail, Antimalware Policies, and Client Settings. All of these tabs contain useful health information, but for client health evaluation, the Summary, Client Activity and Client Check Detail are the main ones to review.

Summary   The Summary tab, shown in Figure 6.11, reports the latest client health information as Pass or Fail and also reports whether the last remediation attempt was successful.

FIGURE 6.11
Summary tab for
specific device

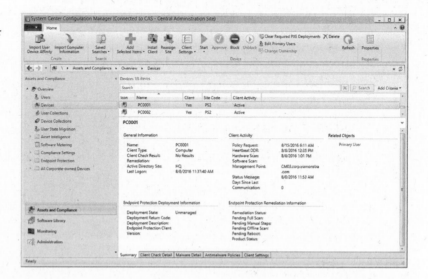

Client Activity section in the Summary tab The Client Activity tab, shown in Figure 6.12, reports the last time the client requested policy, sent a heartbeat, reported hardware or software inventory, and sent a status message. The Days Since Last Communication field reflects how long the site has gone without hearing from the client. All of this information taken together gives a good idea about client health, but it's important to also factor in systems that may be powered off for extended periods or are offline because of network or other issues. The Management Point field documents the management point in use by the client. This information can help identify potential issues with boundaries, roaming, and the like.

FIGURE 6.12
Client Activity Detail
tab for specific device

Client Activity

Policy Request:	8/15/2016 6:11 AM
Heartbeat DDR:	8/8/2016 12:35 PM
Hardware Scan:	8/8/2016 1:01 PM
Software Scan:	
Management Point:	CM03.corp.viamonstra .com
Status Message:	8/8/2016 11:53 AM
Days Since Last Communication:	0

Looking at the icons of the computer objects in Figure 6.11 you see that both the computers are online. If a device is offline, a gray cross will be shown instead of the green check. When the online status is unknown, a question mark is shown.

Client Check Detail The Client Check Detail tab, shown in Figure 6.13, provides summary information about the device's last health evaluation scan. The specific evaluation rules and remediation status are reflected in the summary.

FIGURE 6.13
Client Check Detail
tab for specific
device

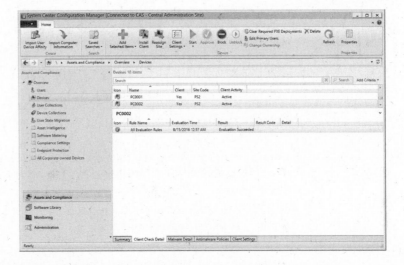

Configuring Client Health

Now that you understand the main functions of the client health mechanism and what can be
remediated with CCMEval, it's time to configure client health. Before you can monitor the client
status and remediate problems that are found in your hierarchy, you must configure your site
to specify the parameters that are used to mark clients as inactive and configure options to alert
you if client activity falls below a specified threshold. You can also disable computers from automatically remediating any problems that client status finds.

1. In the Configuration Manager console, choose Monitoring.

2. In the Monitoring workspace, select Client Status, and then right-click it and choose
   Client Status Settings.

3. In the Client Status Settings Properties, shown in Figure 6.14, configure the following settings:

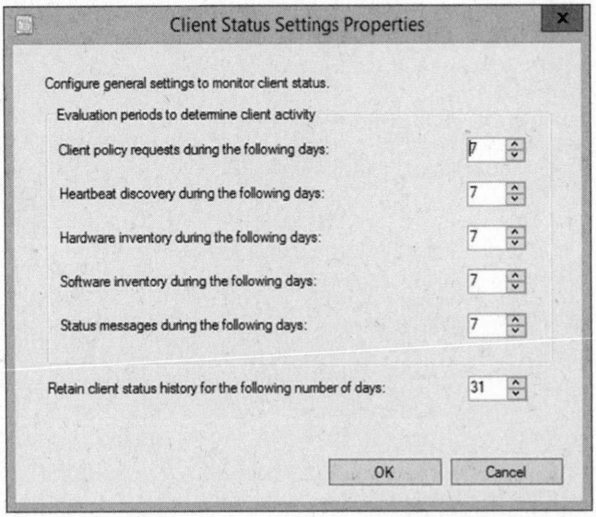

FIGURE 6.14
Client Status Settings
Properties

Client Status Settings Properties

Configure general settings to monitor client status.

Evaluation periods to determine client activity

Client policy requests during the following days: 7

Heartbeat discovery during the following days: 7

Hardware inventory during the following days: 7

Software inventory during the following days: 7

Status messages during the following days: 7

Retain client status history for the following number of days: 31

OK   Cancel

◆ Client Policy Requests During The Following Days: Specify the number of days a client has requested policy. The default value is 7 days.

◆ Heartbeat Discovery During The Following Days: Specify the number of days the client computer has sent a heartbeat discovery record to the site database. The default value is 7 days.

◆ Hardware Inventory During The Following Days: Specify the number of days the client computer has sent a hardware inventory record to the site database. The default value is 7 days.

◆ Software Inventory During The Following Days: Specify the number of days the client computer has sent a software inventory record to the site database. The default value is 7 days.

◆ Status Messages During The Following Days: Specify the number of days the client computer has sent status messages to the site database. The default value is 7 days.

◆ Retain Client Status History For The Following Number Of Days: Specify how long you want the client status history to remain in the site database. The default value is 31 days.

4. Once you finish configuring each item, click OK.

Monitoring: Client Status

The Monitoring workspace of the Configuration Manager console is the place to view Client Check and Client Activity information summarized for all clients in the hierarchy. This information is located under the Client Status node.

The Client Check node shown in Figure 6.15 shows a collective view of client health in the hierarchy. The number of devices that have passed or failed or are in an unknown status for health evaluation are reflected in a pie chart, and the accompanying legend details issues that have been found for those systems failing health evaluation. There is also a line graph showing trending information for client health. For more detail, simply click the section of interest from the pie chart, the pie chart legend, or the line graph, which will open a view of all devices in the selected category.

FIGURE 6.15
Client Check node in the Monitoring workspace of the Configuration Manager console

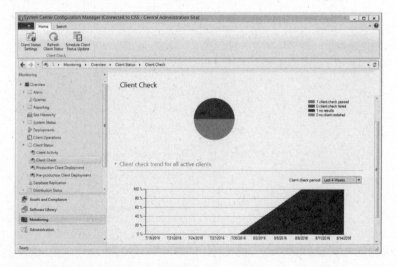

Monitoring: Client Activity   The Client Activity node shown in Figure 6.16 shows a collective view of client activity in the hierarchy. Devices are represented in a pie chart as either active or inactive. In the example, all clients are active. Having 100 percent active clients would be a *great* result in a production environment but likely will not often be achieved because of environmental issues, systems being powered off for extended periods, network issues, and the like. This view also provides a line graph for trend analysis. To view specific systems that are in an active or inactive state, simply click the area of the pie chart or pie chart legend of interest to drill down for additional detail.

FIGURE 6.16
Client Activity node in the Monitoring workspace of the Configuration Manager console

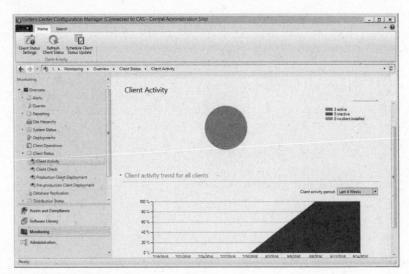

Reporting: Client Status   Configuration Manager provides a wealth of information through the reports available in the console. Reports are grouped by category and, as shown in Figure 6.17, there are seven reports specifically geared to client status information. Combining the reports with the ability to create report subscriptions, as detailed in Chapter 12, "Reporting," gives administrators significant flexibility to pick reports that best serve their needs and render or deliver automatically.

FIGURE 6.17
Client Status reports

Alert: Client Health

Part of being a Configuration Manager administrator is that you don't have enough time to perform all of your daily, weekly, and monthly tasks. The monitoring aspects of client health are a very good method of keeping you informed about what is going on with your clients. With

Configuration Manager you have the ability to configure alerts for each collection. If you use this method to find out what is going on with your clients, then you can focus on those critical systems. To configure the alerts that will be displayed on the Monitoring workspace, perform the following steps on those critical collections:

1. In the Configuration Manager console, select Assets And Compliance.

2. In the Assets And Compliance workspace, choose Device Collections.

3. In the Device Collections node, select the collection for those critical systems and right-click Properties.

4. In the Properties dialog box, click the Alerts tab, as shown in Figure 6.18, and then click Add.

FIGURE 6.18
Client health collection alerts

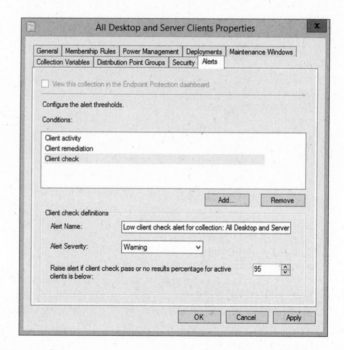

5. In the Add New Collection Alerts dialog box, choose the alerts that you want generated when the client status thresholds fall below a specific value. Then click OK.

6. In the Conditions list, select each client status alert and then specify the following information:

   ◆ Alert Name: Accept the default name or enter a new name for the alert.

   ◆ Alert Severity: From the drop-down list, choose the alert level that will be displayed in the Configuration Manager console.

   ◆ Raise Alert If Client Check Pass Or No Results Percentage For Active Clients Is Below: Specify the threshold percentage for the alert.

7. Click OK.

The Bottom Line

Detail client health evaluations in Configuration Manager Current Branch. Health evaluations and remediations take place daily on every Configuration Manager client in the hierarchy. This information is updated at the site and is available for review on every client and also summarized for every client across the hierarchy.

Master It List the health evaluations and remediations that take place on Configuration Manager clients.

Review client health results in the Configuration Manager console. Client health data is available in several locations of the console to allow access to health for individual devices and summarized data for all clients in the hierarchy.

Master It List the locations in the console where individual client health and summarized client health data are accessible.

Chapter 7

Application Deployment

The ability to deploy applications has long been a primary function of Configuration Manager. The Application Deployment feature, available since Configuration Manager 2012, is the new approach for software deployment and allows administrators to deploy almost any kind of content to Configuration Manager clients, affecting potentially thousands of systems or users.

The list of content deployable through Application Deployment includes virtually anything—from full applications (i.e., Office) to scripts and batch files. Beyond simply specifying *what* to deploy is also the ability to detail *how* to deploy, including whether an application should be delivered to systems so it is available for all users versus specific users or whether the application should be a full installation on the target system versus a virtualized version using App-V.

With so much flexibility and power comes a great amount of responsibility. Configuration Manager provides robust ability to define and control Application Deployment to systems and users. When properly used, the experience with Application Deployment will be very positive, but it is also possible to make mistakes with this feature and deliver the mistakes to potentially thousands of systems or users. This underscores the need to completely understand the feature and its various options and also the need for proper testing before introducing a change to such a potentially large number of systems or users. This need for proper understanding and testing is not unique to Configuration Manager but applies to any product of enterprise scale.

This chapter will detail the various options and features of Application Deployment in Configuration Manager.

In this chapter, you will learn to

♦ Explain the options available for Application Deployment

♦ Detail the various components required for Application Deployment

♦ Understand the role of and manage distribution points

What's New in Application Deployment?

The label *Application Deployment* describes the new approach being taken in Configuration Manager for deploying content. Software Distribution, as it has been historically known, has not been removed from the product; it is still present in the console and represented by the Packages node of Application Management. Also note the Applications node, which is where configurations using the new approach are centered; see Figure 7.1.

Applications and
Packages nodes

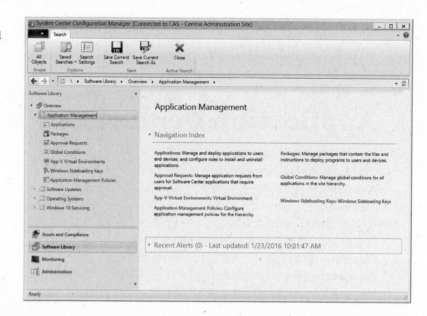

Classic Software Distribution works very much the same way as it did in Configuration Manager 2007/2012. Classic Software Distribution might be seen as available only to facilitate migration and to allow administrators the ability to deploy content the old way while learning the new approach in Configuration Manager. Classic Software Distribution remains very useful in certain scenarios. Remember that the new Application Deployment approach is designed to deploy applications, and it offers very rich configurations. The Application Deployment model, however, may not be a good option for every potential deployment. Consider a scenario where an administrator simply needs to deploy a command line to systems. The Application Deployment model isn't well suited for such a task, and instead administrators should use either classic Software Distribution or a task sequence.

With proper deference given to classic Software Distribution, it is much the same as it was in Configuration Manager 2007, so the discussion in this chapter will be solely focused on the new Application Deployment features.

If you need a full review of the classic Software Distribution model, an excellent discussion is available in the book *Mastering Microsoft System Center Configuration Manager 2007 R2* (Sybex, 2009).

Note the difference in terminology, as shown in Table 7.1.

TABLE 7.1:   Terminology differences

APPLICATION DEPLOYMENT	CLASSIC SOFTWARE DISTRIBUTION
Application	Package
Deployment type	Program
Deployment	Advertisement

Because Application Deployment is such a paradigm shift from classic Software Distribution, a bit of discussion about what exactly has changed is warranted.

Distribution Point Changes

Distribution points are key components for any kind of content delivery in Configuration Manager. Understanding the features of this role will directly relate to the efficiency of your design and satisfaction with the product.

Workstations as Distribution Points   Branch distribution points were first introduced in Configuration Manager 2007, and as of Configuration Manager 2012 they were gone! They were replaced with the ability to directly configure any Windows 7 up to Windows 10 workstation as a distribution point. This may seem like simply a cosmetic difference—and in some ways that is true, but not totally; there are some significant differences.

The ability to specify a workstation as a distribution point directly means that instead of having a client component to fill the Distribution Point role, as was the case with Configuration Manager 2007 branch distribution points, the client doesn't even have to be present!

One limitation of distribution points located on workstation systems is the limit of 20 simultaneous connections. This is a workstation operating system limitation rather than a limit imposed by Configuration Manager. Another, not trivial thing is that the workstations that are configured as a distribution point may not be turned off, since they cannot service other clients when turned off.

Single-Instance Storage   The traditional distribution point structure and function are still available for very specific classic Software Distribution scenarios, namely, if a legacy package is configured to run from a distribution point. For every other kind of content deployment, whether classic Software Distribution or the Application Deployment model, the distribution point engine is completely new. The change also brings some changes in administration, but they are well worth it!

Content storage on traditional distribution points often requires substantial hard drive space. The distribution point model takes advantage of single-instance storage, which results in less hard drive space required for content. Take note of the following:

- ◆ Administrators or users are not able to connect to a known distribution point and execute an install remotely.

- ◆ The Run From Distribution Point option is not available for Application Deployment (but is still available with classic Software Deployment).

- ◆ The single-instance storage change increases security by obscuring the content and making it difficult for the content to be downloaded and used other than for the intended purpose.

Distribution Point Content Validation   Many Configuration Manager administrators have faced the problem where content initially deploys to distribution points but later becomes corrupt, preventing further deployment until the corruption is resolved. Often the only way administrators have known about the corruption is through failed deployments. Configuration Manager offers the ability to proactively check content for corruption on both classic and new distribution points and, when found, notify the administrator so proactive corrective action may be taken. After enabling Content Validation, a scheduled task on the Distribution Point is created based on the schedule configured. In the Task Scheduler the task can be started on demand.

Remote Distribution Point Throttling   A common reason for maintaining secondary sites in a Configuration Manager hierarchy is to support locations where it is important to ensure that network bandwidth usage is tightly controlled when sending content to locations with slow, overloaded, or unreliable WAN connections.

Configuration Manager allows throttling of bandwidth directly between a site and its remote distribution points, helping eliminate the need for secondary sites to achieve this goal.

Hierarchy simplification was a design goal since Configuration Manager 2012; the design goals have not been changed since. This one added feature helps achieve the simplification goal by drastically reducing the need for secondary sites in most Configuration Manager hierarchies.

Distribution Point Selection   The ability to specify which distribution points are available to clients, an option known as *protected distribution points*, has been available in previous versions of Configuration Manager.

Since Configuration Manager 2012, all distribution points are protected by default. The only way clients are able to access a distribution point is if the distribution point is part of a boundary group that matches the client's current boundary. There is a fallback mechanism to allow clients to access distribution points when the client is in an unknown boundary. Allowing fallback is configured per distribution point and per deployment.

Prestaged Content   Managing content in bulk on distribution points has historically been challenging for Configuration Manager administrators. When replacing a distribution point server or even renaming, replacing, or modifying hard disks, administrators were faced with the need to redistribute all content to the new server. If connectivity to the server in question was either unreliable or slow, the challenge was even more pronounced.

An initial thought to solve the problem might be to simply copy content from the current to the replacement server. A quick evaluation of this option reveals that it is not a workable choice because a simple file copy does not result in the needed database and other adjustments to reflect the new location of the content. Because of this, administrators either had to use external tools, such as preloadpkgonsite.exe, or suffer through overloading the network while copying potentially gigabytes of content.

Configuration Manager 2012 introduced an option allowing content to be prestaged on distribution points. There is a specific wizard used to accomplish this—as will be seen later in the chapter—but the net effect is that in situations where bandwidth is challenging, content can now be natively staged locally on systems without such strain on network links. The same is true for Configuration Manager Current Branch.

Distribution Point Groups   The process of either adding or replacing a distribution point in Configuration Manager is fairly straightforward, but what about the content? If the distribution point being replaced is the storage point for many applications, administrators historically have been faced with either constructing a script to parse through applications and adding them to the new distribution point in bulk or working through applications one by one and enabling the new distribution point. Either task is time consuming!

The use of distribution point groups was possible in Configuration Manager 2007 but was not often used by administrators. Since Configuration Manager 2012 the use of distribution point groups was revamped, and they offer easy management of distribution points by allowing distribution points that should store similar content to be treated collectively. Simply choose a distribution point group when deploying or removing content, and all distribution points within that group will receive or remove the content. Better still, when a new distribution point is added to the group or removed, then all applicable content targeted to the group will also be added or removed.

User-Centric Focus   In previous versions of Configuration Manager, it was possible to target a deployment to users, but this ability was not robust and seemed like an afterthought. In Configuration Manager Current Branch, the user is the focus—or at least can be.

Yes, it is still possible to target deployments to systems, and many administrators will continue to do this because, in many cases such as server management, that is the best approach. Plus, the ability to target users for deployments and to do so with great specificity is a paradigm shift since Configuration Manager 2012. Don't overlook this feature, though, because it offers the ability to significantly enhance a user's experience with and impression of Configuration Manager.

User-centric focus allows administrators to define deployments that function differently based on the location of the user. Consider, for example, a user who is logged on to and using their main computer (known as a primary device in Configuration Manager terminology). Deployments can be configured to recognize this and, in such cases, install software directly onto the user's device, including mobile devices managed directly or via Windows Intune— more on that in Chapter 18, "Enterprise Mobility and Configuration Manager." Conversely, if the user happens to be logged on to a device in another location, such as in a remote office, this can be recognized and the deployment can be delivered automatically as a virtualized application instead, allowing the deployment to be made available quickly and without persisting the installation. This allows the user the same experience regardless of which system they are actually logged on to and using, and it's all seamless.

Software Center   The Configuration Manager Software Center is an updated replacement to the Run Advertised Program option available in previous versions of Configuration Manager. The Software Center is the central location where users are able to view available or required deployments targeted for their user or system and to also make their own custom changes, such as to specify working hours or whether Configuration Manager operations should be suppressed while presentations are taking place, or even whether their computer should honor assigned power-management settings.

The only required deployments visible in Software Center will be those that are configured with the ability for users to interact.

Application Catalog   Configuration Manager gives administrators the option to publish deployments into a web-based Application Catalog. The Application Catalog web page is accessible to any user and is filtered to list only deployments specifically targeted to the given users. Through the catalog, users are able to request available software that is of interest. Entries in the Application Catalog can be configured as freely available or as requiring approval. Note the Approval Requests node under Application Management in Figure 7.1. When software is configured to require approval, the user is able to request the software, but an administrator will need to manually approve the request before deployment will continue. Administrators approve pending requests in the Approval Requests node.

Applications: Application References

The Application References mechanism allows administrators to view what dependency and supersedence relationships are associated with a given application. The best way to describe this is by example.

Dependency Assume two applications, Foxit Reader and .NET Framework 3.5. It is possible to specify a dependency so that Foxit Reader requires that .NET Framework 3.5 be present on a target device. If .NET Framework 3.5 isn't present on the device when you attempt to deploy Foxit Reader, you can configure it to automatically deploy as part of the Foxit Reader deployment. If not, Foxit Reader will fail to install until .NET Framework 3.5 is present.

The dependencies themselves are configured on the Dependencies tab of the properties for the application deployment type. The References tab on the application properties dialog box displays the information for the application as a whole.

Supersedence Assume two applications, Foxit Reader and Adobe Acrobat 9 Pro. It is possible to specify a supersedence relationship to define that Foxit Reader supersedes Adobe Acrobat 9 Pro. Doing so effectively links the two applications and establishes a path for replacing one application with another, either by upgrade or by uninstalling the superseded application and replacing it with the current application

Be careful when building relationships between applications. Relationships will prevent an application from being deleted, and excessive numbers of relationships will increase complexity and potential confusion.

Deployment Types

Deployment types in Configuration Manager Current Branch directly influence the flow of application deployment. There are a couple of new options available to help control this flow, as described here:

Deployment Types Deployment types specify how a particular application should be deployed. As shown in Table 7.1 earlier, think of deployment types as similar to programs in classic Software Distribution but with much greater flexibility and specificity. Several deployment types are available.

- Windows Installer (`.msi` file)
- Windows app package (`.appx` and `.appxbundle` files)
- Windows app package in the Windows Store
- Script Installer
- Microsoft Application Virtualization version 4
- Microsoft Application Virtualization version 5

- Windows Phone app package (`.xap` file)

- Windows Phone app package in the Windows Phone Store

- Windows Mobile Cabinet (`.cab` file)

- App Package for iOS (`.ipa` file)

- App Package for iOS from the Apple App Store

- App Package for Android (`.apk` file)

- App Package for Android on Google Play

- Mac OS X (`.cmmac` file)

- Web Application (URL)

- Windows Installer through MDM (`.msi` file)

Beyond these predefined types, it is possible to manually define whatever other type of deployment may be needed.

Native Uninstall Support   Previous versions of Configuration Manager allowed for software deployment but no native support for software uninstall. Uninstall was possible but required a separate program definition. Configuration Manager Current Branch allows specifying options for both install and uninstall within a single deployment type. There is no requirement to use both, but they are available. When you create an application using the wizard, some deployment types—such as MSI-based deployments—will automatically create the uninstall option.

Detection Method   Previous versions of Configuration Manager allowed administrators to define a deployment but no mechanism to determine if that deployment had already taken place by another mechanism. The result was that software could get reinstalled even if it was already present. Configuration Manager allows administrators the ability to define rules to determine if the deployment is already in place on a system and, if so, to simply exit without triggering a reinstall. This mechanism may seem similar to what historically has been seen with software patching. The two mechanisms are very similar.

If a required application is being removed by the user, based on the detection method the installation can be triggered again while an Application Deployment Evaluation Cycle is performed. The Application Deployment Evaluation Cycle checks if all deployments are installed by evaluating the detection method; if the application is not in place the installation will be done again. The same applies to uninstallations that are required and the user reinstalls the application manually.

Requirements   In previous versions of Configuration Manager, it was common practice to build collections of systems matching specific criteria or filters and then to target advertisement(s) to those collections. In Configuration Manager, collections remain a requirement for deployment targeting, but the need to build a new collection or multiple new collections to provide filtering for a single deployment should be reduced. Administrators now have the ability to specify deployment requirements per deployment type. These requirements ensure that a specific deployment type is not executed unless specific criteria are met.

Once defined, requirement rules are reusable. Requirement Rules can be static rules but also scripts based on PowerShell, VBScript, or JScript that are created by administrators.

TARGETING

Historically Microsoft recommended that you avoid targeting the All Systems collection when deploying software. Doing so meant that the software would be received and executed by every device that is part of the All Systems collection, which is every device at a site and potentially every device in the hierarchy when a deployment is configured as required. It is still a good idea to avoid targeting the All Systems collection, but with deployment type requirements properly configured, it would be possible to safely do so if needed. Deployments can of course also be configured as available, which allows users to get their apps from the Software Center.

Dependencies   The ability to specify dependencies between different deployments has been available since the release of SMS 2.0. Until Configuration Manager 2012, however, these dependencies were not so straightforward, and creating multiple dependencies often resulted in confusion.

Dependencies since Configuration Manager 2012 became a much more elegant solution. Administrators can configure other applications on which the one being configured depends. Single dependencies may be specified or multiple. When adding dependencies, it is possible also to select whether a given dependency will be automatically installed in the event it is absent. Setting Auto Install for a dependency is not a requirement but can help ensure that deployments execute error free.

Adding dependencies essentially joins the current application with whatever dependency is being specified, so later, if a dependent application is removed, a warning will be displayed about potentially breaking a dependency relationship.

Although dependencies are a big step forward for controlling and predicting application deployment results, there is still no way to define order of installation for dependencies. Typically this fact isn't a big deal, but if multiple dependencies are configured for an application, it could be a concern. If you have to know the exact order of execution for a deployment and its related dependencies, consider using a task sequence instead.

Return Codes   A successful install of most applications will result in a return code of either 0 or 3010 being generated. These return codes mean success or success pending reboot, respectively. In previous versions of Configuration Manager, if a return code other than these two is returned, then the application deployment is considered to have failed. Depending on the software manufacturer, a return code other than 0 or 3010 may actually be informative about the state of a deployment other than simply indicating success or failure. The number of such applications is relatively small, but when encountered they can be frustrating because a successful install will appear to have failed. The task sequence engine in Configuration Manager 2007 was the first place where administrators were able to account for exit code variations. In Configuration Manager Current Branch this ability has been brought forward to Application Deployment as well, fully allowing administrators to define what specific exit codes from an application actually mean and responding accordingly when reporting status.

Deployment Settings Action   Previous versions of Configuration Manager allowed deployments to be built that would be installed on clients. Configuration Manager also allows for that but introduces the ability to force an application uninstall on clients. This action will cause the uninstall command line configured on the deployment type to be executed.

Deployment Settings Purpose   The deployment purpose can be configured as either available or required. These options are similar to specifying a deployment as optional or mandatory in previous versions of Configuration Manager, but with a twist. When a deployment is configured as required, the application will be forced onto the client. This is the same behavior as previous versions when selecting a mandatory deployment. The twist is that on a schedule, the deployment is reevaluated, and if the application is found to be missing, it is forced back onto the client system.

Alerts   New to Configuration Manager is the ability to specify alerts when deployments fail to reach a certain threshold of success, specified as a percentage. The next question that often is asked when discussing this new alerting functionality is whether this ability is intended to replace monitoring by the System Center Operations Manager Configuration Manager management pack. The answer is a resounding no. The scope of the Configuration Manager management pack is more encompassing than what can be achieved by native Configuration Manager alerting. The alerting feature in Configuration Manager was introduced to allow administrators some ability to raise awareness of issues independently without System Center Operations Manager. In environments with System Center Operations Manager, the Configuration Manager management pack should be the primary monitoring resource, with the internal Configuration Manager alerting engine acting as a supplement.

Dependencies for Application Deployment

The Application Deployment feature makes use of several different dependencies. These dependencies must all be configured correctly for application deployment to be successful.

Management Point

The management point is the key interface between clients and their assigned site. Through management point policy updates, clients learn about assigned settings and activity requested by the site, and they also return data to the site, such as inventory or discovery data. It is through management point policies that clients are made aware of pending application deployments and associated settings, and it is through the management point that clients return status after attempting to run an application deployment. The management point is also responsible for providing the list of available distribution points to the client when the client requests content for a particular application deployment.

Thus, having a functioning management point is crucial not only for proper client operation but also for proper application deployment. Chapter 4, "Installation and Site Role Configuration," includes a full discussion of management point setup and configuration.

Distribution Point

The distribution point role is crucial for application deployment in that it is the location where all remote content that should be accessed and used during application deployment is stored.

If a distribution point is not available to clients when you attempt to initiate an application deployment, the deployment will fail when the application contains content. Multiple distribution points may be present in the primary site, including workstation-class machines running Windows 7 or greater. Distribution points installed for a site but on servers other than the site server, also known as remote distribution points, may be configured for content throttling in the distribution point's properties. Chapter 4 discusses distribution point setup and configuration.

APPLICATION DEPLOYMENT FAILURE

It is possible that an application deployment may fail even if content is available on some or all of the distribution points. In such cases, verify that at least one distribution point within the client's boundary is configured with content, and if the distribution point is running on a workstation system, ensure that it is not exceeding its connection limit. In addition, check whether the errors have been encountered when staging content to distribution points. You have the ability to configure failback distribution point; if the content is available on the failback distribution point, the application deployment will not fail.

BITS-ENABLED IIS

In previous releases of Configuration Manager it was optional to enable Background Intelligent Transfer Service (BITS) for a distribution point. In Configuration Manager BITS is required.

Default Client Settings

A word about client settings: The default list of client settings applies to all clients in the Configuration Manager hierarchy. It is possible to override the default settings and specify different values for specific sites or specific systems via collection targeting.

This flexibility gives administrators complete control of which settings apply to devices and removes the technical limitation that often resulted in multiple sites or hierarchies, such as scenarios where servers and workstations needed separate management settings. The flexibility offered with client settings applies generically throughout Configuration Manager, but several settings that are available have a specific impact on Application Deployment, as discussed in the following sections.

BACKGROUND INTELLIGENT TRANSFER SERVICE

BITS settings are part of the default client settings and are shown in Figure 7.2. In some environments clients are installed and managed across slow or heavily utilized WAN links. In such cases it may be important to ensure that clients are able to sense a heavy load on the network and, during critical times, respond by reducing the amount of data that is being transferred, a process also known as *throttling*. Throttling controls are found throughout Configuration Manager to help reduce WAN impact. The BITS client settings specifically allow administrators to configure clients to limit the amount of network bandwidth they utilize when transferring content. This content includes application deployment data, along with several other types of information.

FIGURE 7.2
BITS settings

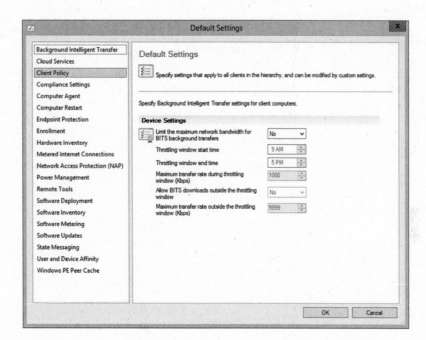

COMPUTER AGENT

Computer Agent settings are part of the default client settings and are shown in Figure 7.3. These settings apply to all deployments, including software updates and operating system deployments, and allow the administrator control over the user experience while deploying content.

The Computer Agent settings can be set up in different ways, depending on the types of clients in your environment. Types of clients can be laptops, desktops, kiosks, RDP clients, or VDI clients. In Table 7.2 you will find the options that can be configured with the Computer Agent settings.

FIGURE 7.3
Computer Agent
settings

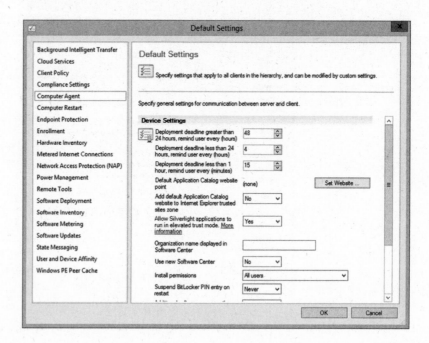

TABLE 7.2: Computer Agent settings

OPTION	DESCRIPTION
Deployment Deadline Greater Than 24 Hours, Remind User Every (Hours)	Every required deployment has a deadline; when this deployment has been received by the client, you can configure how often the user must be notified when the deadline is further away than 24 hours. This reminder will help the user to run the deployment at the time it is most suitable for them.
Deployment Deadline Less Than 24 Hours, Remind User Every (Hours)	When a deployment comes within the period of 24 hours before the deadline, you can remind the user more often, every x hours.
Deployment Deadline Less Than 1 Hour, Remind User Every (Minutes)	If the user hasn't run the deployment within one hour before the deadline, you can remind the user every x minutes. If the deadline is reached, the installation will start.
Default Application Catalog Website Point	When using the Application Catalog to allow users to select and install the applications they need, you are able to configure one of the available Application Catalog website points or a URL that can, for instance, be available through a network load balancer.

TABLE 7.2: Computer Agent settings *(continued)*

OPTION	DESCRIPTION
Add Default Application Catalog Website To Internet Explorer Trusted Sites Zone	To be able to install applications via the Application Catalog website, your Internet browser needs to trust the website. With this setting you can automatically configure the Application Catalog website to be recognized by the trusted sites zone within Internet Explorer. Adding the website to this zone will also take care of pass-through authentication to the website.
Allow Silverlight Applications To Run In Elevated Trust Mode	This setting is new for SP1 and R2 and must be enabled when using those versions. The Application Catalog website is a Silverlight application that needs to run in elevated trust mode.
Organization Name Displayed In Software Center	You can customize the Software Center by adding the company name.
Use New Software Center	The new Software Center is also able to give access to user-targeted applications. This new Software Center relies on the Application Catalog website.
Install Permissions	The Install Permissions option allows you to configure how users can initiate the installation of software, software updates, and task sequences. This option comes with four levels:
	◆ **All Users**
	When this option is selected, all users who are logged on to the client can initiate an installation of software, software updates, and task sequences via the Software Center.
	◆ **Only Administrators**
	When this option is selected, only users who are local administrators and who are logged on to the client are able to initiate an installation of software, software updates, and task sequences via the Software Center.
	◆ **Only Administrators And Primary Users**
	When this option is selected, only users who are local administrators or are the primary user of the client that they are logged on to are able to initiate an installation of software, software updates, and task sequences via the Software Center.
	◆ **No Users**
	When this option is selected, no users are able to initiate the installation of software, software updates, and task sequences via the Software Center. This option is often used when a user logs on to a Remote Desktop Services server that is shared with other users.

TABLE 7.2:   Computer Agent settings *(continued)*

Option	Description
Suspend BitLocker PIN Entry On Restart	If you need to enter a BitLocker PIN when logging on to your clients, this option can bypass this requirement when the client needs to restart after a software installation.
Additional Software Manages The Deployment Of Applications And Software Updates	This option allows you to disable the deployment of applications and software updates on servers that are, for instance, used for Citrix XenApp, XenDesktop, or another shared VDI desktop solution that is using a shared image without disabling the Configuration Manager client. Tooling of the vendor will control the installation of the available deployments.
PowerShell Execution Policy	PowerShell scripts can be used to deploy software but also to check for the existence of software or to detect configuration items and check them for compliance. With this setting you can configure the execution policy for PowerShell scripts that run via the Configuration Manager client.
Show Notifications For New Deployments	You can enable or disable notification for new deployments that become available when a user is logged on to a client.
Disable Deadline Randomization	This option checks whether the client uses an activation delay of up to two hours to install required software updates and applications when the deadline is reached. By default the activation delay is disabled. For VDI environments it can help to not have to install an update on all VDI desktops at the same time. Disabling deadline randomization in big environments can negatively impact the performance of the VDI environment as well as the network, distribution points, and site servers.

COMPUTER RESTART

Computer Restart settings are part of the default client settings and are shown in Figure 7.4. These settings apply to all deployments, including software updates and operating system deployments, and allow administrators to define countdown settings to be used in the event a computer must be restarted as a result of application deployment.

FIGURE 7.4
Computer Restart
settings

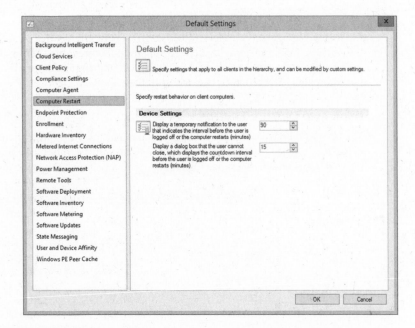

FIGURE 7.4
Computer Restart
settings

SOFTWARE DEPLOYMENT

The Software Deployment settings are also part of the default client settings and are shown in Figure 7.5. The only option here allows administrators to determine what schedule should be used for reevaluating deployments.

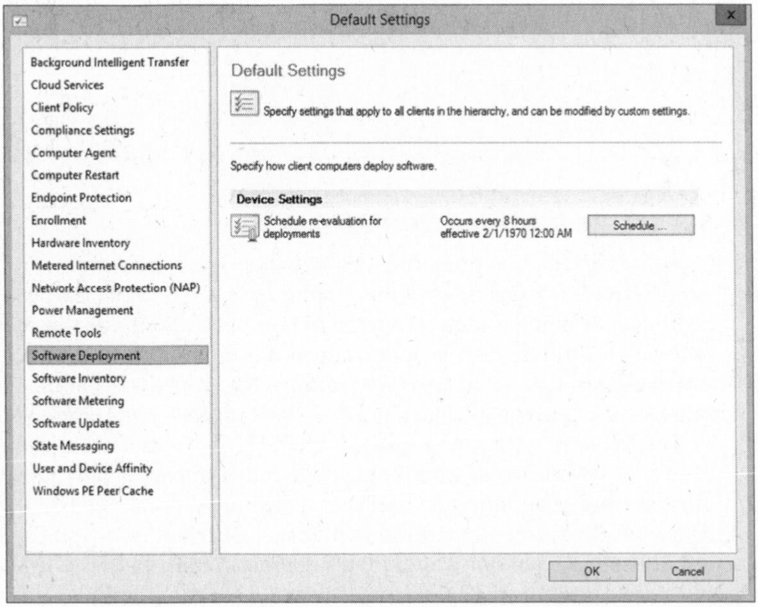

FIGURE 7.5
Software
Deployment
settings

When you, as a Configuration Manager administrator, decide to uninstall, for instance, an expensive version of Autodesk AutoCAD from your clients and a user then decides to reinstall the same version, they may make it so you are no longer compliant with your licenses.

When reevaluating the client, Configuration Manager will see that AutoCAD is installed on the client and will automatically uninstall it again.

USER AND DEVICE AFFINITY

The User and Device Affinity settings are also part of the default client settings and are shown in Figure 7.6. These settings specify options that Configuration Manager will use when attempting to determine whether a user is logged on to a primary device or logged on elsewhere.

FIGURE 7.6
User and Device
Affinity settings

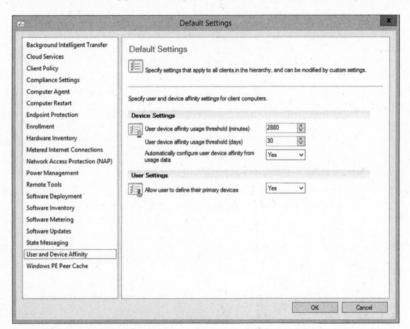

SOFTWARE DISTRIBUTION PROPERTIES

Software Distribution properties are accessible from the Administrative node by selecting Administration ➤ Overview ➤ Site Configuration ➤ Sites. In the Sites node, select a site server hosting distribution points. From the ribbon, select Configure Site Components and then Software Distribution. This option allows administrators to configure concurrent package distribution settings and also retry settings if a failure is encountered. These settings are the same as what were available in previous versions of Configuration Manager.

The Network Access Account, shown in Figure 7.7, is used to define an account that can be used for network access when content is needed during deployment from a network location other than the Configuration Manager distribution point or when the computer account cannot be used to access the Configuration Manager distribution point. The Network Access Account also is used in scenarios where clients are installed in an untrusted scenario, such as workgroup systems or machines in an untrusted forest. This account is also important for use in operating system deployment; without a network access account, the operating system deployment would fail instantly. With Configuration Manager you can create more than one network access account per site. When a client tries to access content and cannot use its local computer account, it will first use the last network access account that was able to successfully connect to the distribution point. Configuration Manager supports adding up to 10 such accounts. The ability to add more than one network access account to one site offers an option to simplify the Configuration Manager hierarchy, since the account could be one of the reasons for installing more than one primary site.

FIGURE 7.7
Network access account in Software Distribution Component Properties

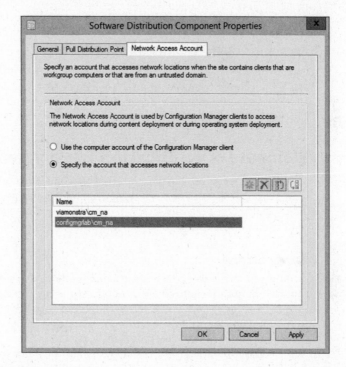

DATA REPLICATION

Previous versions of Configuration Manager made use of standard site-to-site communications for sending all data between sites via file replication. Configuration Manager still uses site-to-site communications for some data, but for configuration data, such as application deployment configurations, that data is replicated between sites using SQL Server features. Thus, ensuring that the SQL data replication structure for Configuration Manager is healthy is vital to guaranteeing consistent data throughout the hierarchy. Configuration Manager uses its own replication service, called Data Replication Service (DRS), to replicate data through the SQL Server Service Broker to and from other Configuration Manager databases in a Configuration Manager hierarchy.

SITE-TO-SITE COMMUNICATIONS

The mechanism for site-to-site communications has been part of Configuration Manager for many versions. This mechanism is much the same in Configuration Manager but its scope is limited to sending data such as application deployment content. The SQL Server Service Broker is used for transferring site settings information between sites.

COLLECTIONS

Collections remain integral to application deployment. Collections are the ultimate target for all deployments, and so the proper use of collections, including dynamic versus static collections and including versus excluding rules, are important to successful application deployment. Proper use of collections is crucial for successful application deployment, but collections are necessary to many functions in Configuration Manager beyond just application deployment. For that reason, collection management and strategy are not discussed in this chapter but are discussed in more detail in Chapter 15, "Role-Based Administration."

BOUNDARIES/BOUNDARY GROUPS

Boundaries and boundary groups are the mechanisms Configuration Manager clients use to locate available distribution points for content access. Configuring these settings correctly will allow for efficient application deployment. Boundaries and boundary groups are detailed in Chapter 2, "Planning a Configuration Manager Infrastructure."

Elements of Application Deployment

Several components are integral to successful configuration of Application Deployment in Configuration Manager. Some of these components are specific to Application Deployment and others apply more generally. In either case, a proper understanding and configuration of these components is important.

Applications

Administrators build applications in Configuration Manager to describe software that is to be deployed. Administrators create an application to specify details regarding the application, such as the manufacturer, an internal contact for support, information that should appear in the Application Catalog, details regarding the action an application will take, or whether the application being built supersedes a previous version.

A sample application is shown in Figure 7.8. The process of building an application will be detailed shortly.

Deployment Types

The act of creating an application by itself does not specify sufficient instruction for carrying out deployment of the application. Deployment types provide additional detail for how a given application should be handled in various situations, such as what type of action to take when the application is being deployed to various types of devices or users. In addition, a deployment type describes mechanisms to detect whether an application is already installed or whether command lines are needed to remove an application. The deployment type is created when building an application through the Create Application Wizard, so the difference between the application itself and the deployment type may not be clear. Figure 7.8 shows the General Information tab for the application definition. The Deployment Types tab, which will list all configured deployment types for the application, is also visible in Figure 7.8. Figure 7.9 shows the properties of a sample deployment type. The process of building deployment types will be detailed shortly.

FIGURE 7.8
Sample application
properties

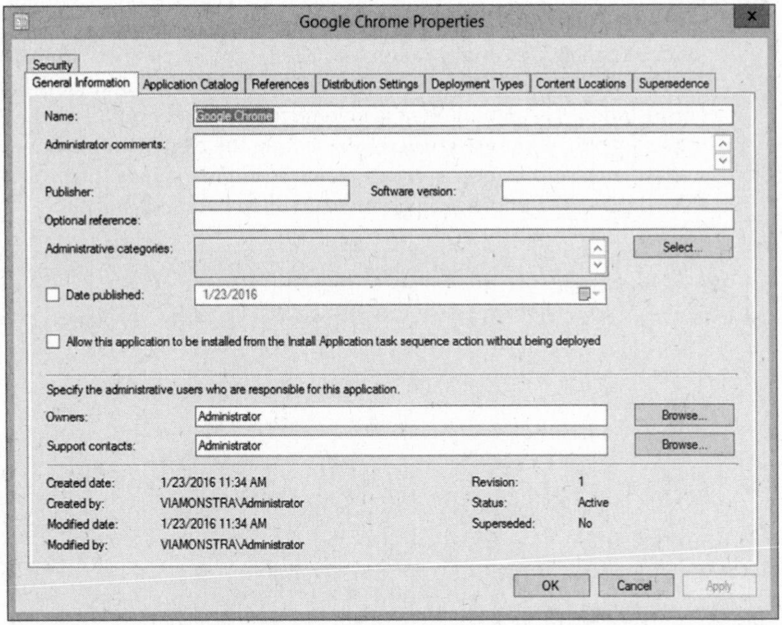

FIGURE 7.9
Sample deployment
type properties

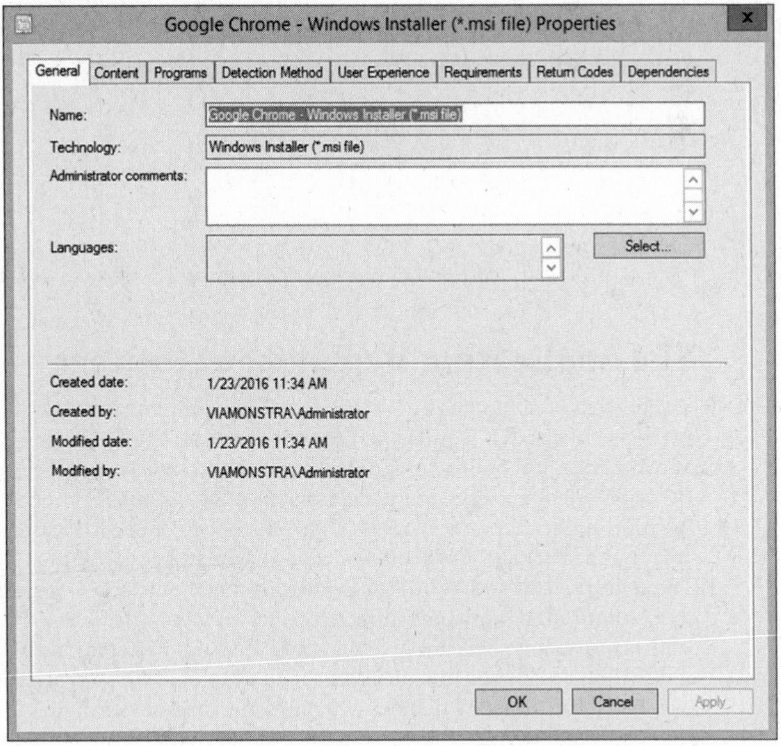

Deployments

A deployment in Configuration Manager is the mechanism that associates applications and deployment types with a collection of devices or users so that the application can be installed or uninstalled. The deployment is not created as part of building the application and deployment type. Deployments are created by selecting the Deploy option from the ribbon when focused on a particular application in the console. Figure 7.10 shows the properties of a sample deployment. The process of building deployments will be detailed shortly.

FIGURE 7.10
Sample deployment properties

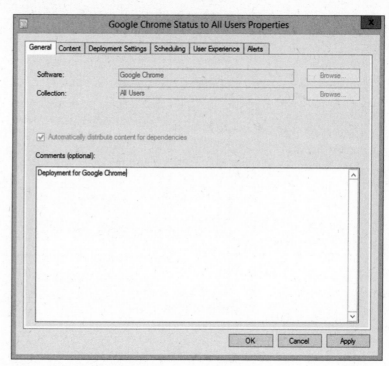

The Application Deployment Process

The process of deploying applications in Configuration Manager has some similarity to previous versions but also has significant differences and additional options. One such example is the use of collections. It remains a requirement to have an application deployed to a collection in order for deployment to begin, but the use of collections is much changed from previous versions. In the past, application-specific collections of systems, and rarely users, would be created ahead of creating the package, program, and advertisement (classic Software Distribution terminology). The collections would be built according to specific criteria to define the scope of the distribution.

Configuration Manager Application Deployment introduces the concept of requirements. With requirements it is possible to define the rules of deployment within the deployment itself rather than build specific collections to do the same thing. When requirements are used instead of collections to specify deployment rules, the load of evaluation is effectively moved from the site server to individual client systems. Add to this that once a requirement rule is defined, it is retained and reusable for other deployments.

The use of requirements is optional, but they are both effective and efficient ways to validate deployment requirements. Administrators should consider strongly whether the old-style collection sprawl, which tends to junk up the console over time and can get fairly confusing to look at, continues to be justified.

The best way to discuss the application deployment process is to create a sample application, deployment type, and deployment and then to demonstrate its execution in the environment. To start, a view of the Software Library ➤ Overview ➤ Application Management ➤ Applications node of the console is instructive.

Create Application Wizard

The Create Application Wizard creates an application and the first of potentially several deployment types. When you're getting started with Application Deployment in Configuration Manager, the console will be not be populated with any deployments.

A Word about Packages

If you're migrating from Configuration Manager 2007/2012, any packages are considered legacy (but still fully functional) in Configuration Manager and are migrated to the Packages node.

To get started with Application Deployment, you can either import an application from another Configuration Manager hierarchy by clicking the Import Application button or click Create Application. Both options are on the ribbon.

To build the sample application deployment, click Create Application to launch the Create Application Wizard. The general page of the Create Application Wizard is shown in Figure 7.11.

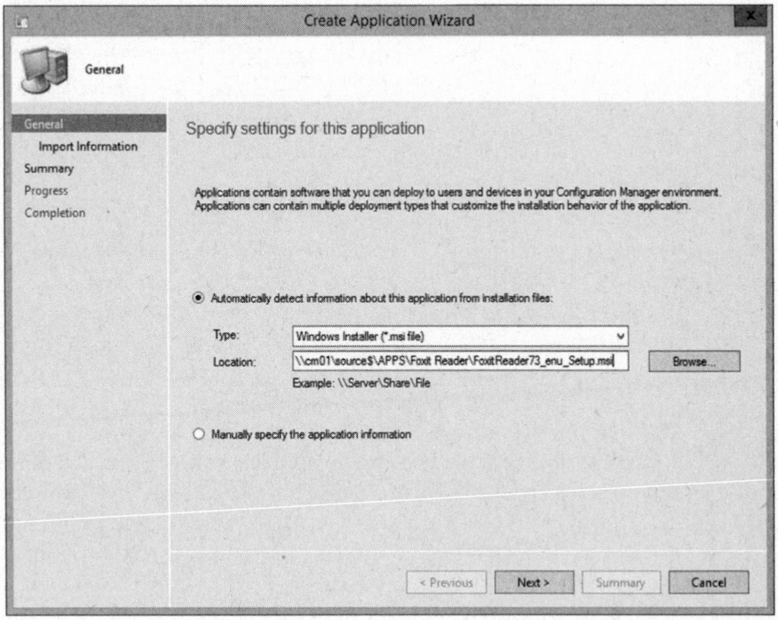

FIGURE 7.11
General page of the
Create Application
Wizard

The General page lets you choose either Automatically Detect Information About This Application From Installation Files or Manually Specify The Application Information. The quickest mechanism for configuring the sample application is to allow information to be automatically detected. This is particularly efficient when deploying an MSI file. The option you choose on this page is dictated by preference and the type of application being defined. Using the option to manually define the information may be more appropriate depending on the type of content being deployed. Choosing this option simply requires manual entry of data that is otherwise supplied by the automatic option. In either case, reviewing all settings after they're initially configured with the wizard is a good idea.

For the sample application deployment, select the automatic option and choose Windows Installer (*.msi file) in the Type field. Then click Next to proceed to the Import Information page of the wizard, shown in Figure 7.12. This page of the wizard is displayed while information is being gathered from the specified source, in this case the `FoxitReader73_enu_Setup.msi` file.

FIGURE 7.12
Import Information page of the Create Application Wizard

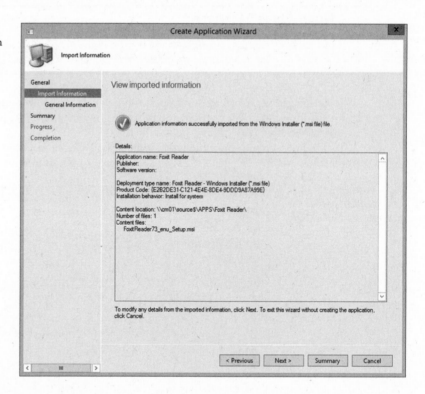

Once the Next option becomes available, click it to proceed to the General Information page of the wizard, shown in Figure 7.13.

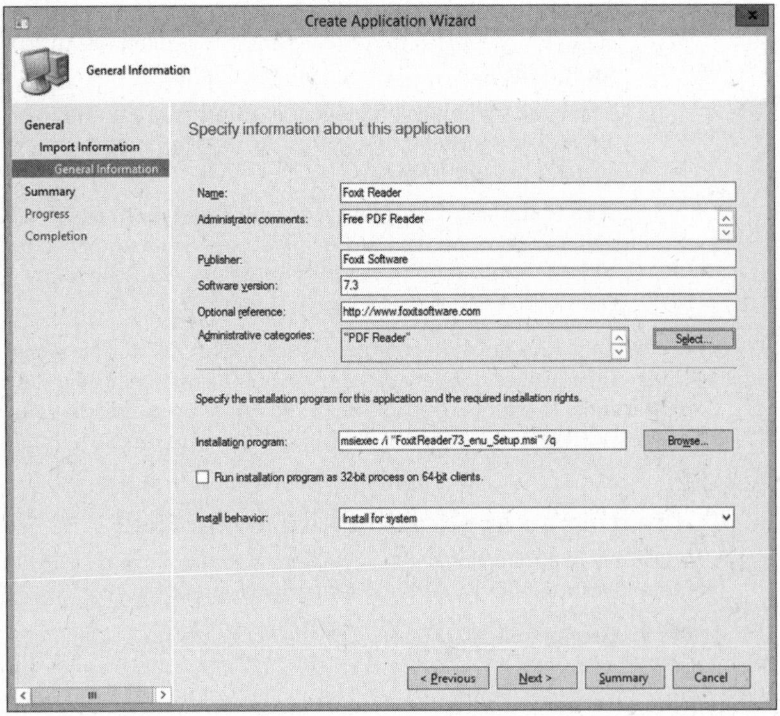

FIGURE 7.13
General Information
page of the Create
Application Wizard

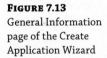

On the General Information page specify the requested information as follows:

Required Information   The import process should have completed the required fields of the General Information page, leaving only the optional fields to be completed.

   Name   The name of the application being created.

   Installation Program   The command line of the program to initiate application installation.

   Install Behavior   Options for this setting allow administrators to specify whether the deployment will be targeted to Install For User, Install For System, or Install For System If Resource Is Device, Otherwise Install For User.

Optional Information   The information supplied as part of the optional fields is available for user review when applications are published in the Software Center or Application Catalog.

   Administrator Comments   Allows you to include any comments to further describe or detail the application.

   Publisher   Allows you to specify the software publisher.

   Software Version   Allows you to specify the software version.

   Optional Reference   Allows you to specify additional reference information for the application.

Administrative Categories   Allows you to group applications together by user-defined categories that make sense in a given organization. Multiple categories may be specified.

There are two types of categories: administrative and user. The dialog here allows specification of administrative categories. Specifying user categories is done on the Catalog node of the application.

Run Installation Program As 32-Bit Process On 64-Bit Clients   When installing a 32-bit application on a 64-bit operating system you need to enable this option to be sure that the application is installed in the *<drive:>*\Program Files (x86)\ folder. Also, the Wow6432Node in the registry is used.

When you've finished entering information, click the Next button to proceed to the Summary page of the wizard. Review the summary information, and if it's correct, click Next to create the application. If errors are encountered, the wizard will display them. If the application is created successfully, exit the Create Application Wizard and return to the main console.

Creating an Application with PowerShell

Creating an application can also be done with the PowerShell cmdlets. The workflow of creating an application with PowerShell consists of four steps:

1. Create the application.

2. Create a deployment type.

3. Distribute the content.

4. Deploy the created application.

In this example, we want to create an application called Google Chrome; it is located at the source$ share and will be deployed to the All Users collection.

Let's first create the application by calling the New-CMApplication cmdlet:

```
New-CMApplication -name "Google Chrome" -Owner "Corporate IT" -Keyword
"Alternative Test Browser"
Add-CMDeploymentType -MsiInstaller -ApplicationName "Google Chrome"
-InstallationFileLocation
"\\cm01\source$\Apps\MSI\Chrome\GoogleChromeStandaloneEnterprise.msi"
-ForceForUnknownPublisher $True
Start-CMContentDistribution -ApplicationName "Google Chrome"
-DistributionPointGroupName "All Content"
Start-CMApplicationDeployment -CollectionName "All Users" -Name
"Google Chrome" -DeployPurpose Available
```

Options for Application Deployment: The Ribbon

Now that an application is defined in the console, additional options appear on the ribbon. Let's take a quick pause to explore the options, as shown in Figure 7.14.

FIGURE 7.14
Ribbon options for application deployment

Wow, that's a lot of new options! Yes, and this is the first place that you start to see some of the new choices available for applications in Configuration Manager.

Revision History   The Revision History option tracks all changes that have been made to an application. This tracking not only creates a record of changes but also allows you to revert to a previous version if you've made a mistake. For the sample Foxit Reader application, we made a simple change to the administrator comments text, resulting in a new version being created. You can view the change by selecting the revision of interest, selecting the record, and clicking View. Notice in Figure 7.15 that the words *for Microsoft Windows* have been added to the administrator comments in the right figure of Figure 7.15. If for some reason you don't want this change, you can simply pick the revision that is correct and click Restore to revert the application.

FIGURE 7.15
Viewing revision history

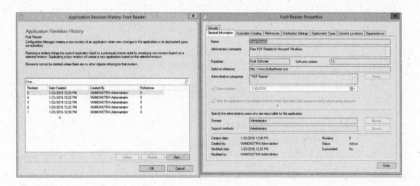

While this example is of a minor change, it does illustrate the power of revision tracking.

Create Prestaged Content File   We've already discussed the challenges of managing distribution point content when replacing or adding distribution points in previous versions of Configuration Manager. The challenges are made worse when the distribution points are positioned across a slow or busy WAN connection from the site server. Historically, solutions for staging content in bulk without saturating such a WAN connection included utilities such as `preloadpkgonsite.exe`, scripts, or other third-party tools. But all of these tools came with their limitations and challenges. Configuration Manager introduces Prestaged Content as a mechanism to manage this type of scenario natively. When a distribution point supports Prestaged Content, administrators are able to choose applications that should be made available in a Prestaged Content file, along with all dependencies, which can then be copied locally onto the remote distribution point without the need for substantial WAN communication. Configuring Prestaged Content support requires setting the option on the distribution point and then using the Create Prestaged Content File Wizard to generate a file containing the content of interest. The Create Prestaged Content File Wizard is shown in Figure 7.16.

FIGURE 7.16
Create Prestaged
Content File Wizard

Update Statistics Application statistics like those shown in Figure 7.14 are not updated in real time; summarizing jobs will take care of that. If you want to trigger an update of the statistics, use the option Update Statistics.

Create Deployment Type A deployment type for the sample Foxit Reader application has already been created by the Create Application Wizard. We'll review this shortly. For a given application it is possible to create multiple deployment types. Selecting this button from the ribbon launches a wizard that walks through the configurations needed for creating new deployment types to augment deployment of the selected application.

Retire/Reinstate   The option to retire an application allows administrators to effectively mark an application as no longer deployable without deleting it from the console. There are a few advantages to this approach:

◆ The application deployment status is not removed.

◆ If questions arise about the application configuration, the configuration may easily be reviewed.

◆ If it becomes necessary to reinstate the application to an active status, it is possible to do so by simply selecting the Reinstate option.

Delete   It is pretty obvious what this option does, but it's still worth a bit of discussion. As you will see shortly, it is possible (and likely) that applications will be tied to each other through dependencies and supersedence relationships. When these relationships exist, or when there is a deployment defined for an application, the deletion option will fail to work. This prevents you from potentially removing an application that is critical to the function of another. Although this is good, it is important to understand and be able to resolve these relationships. The View Relationships option helps detail all configured links for a given application.

Simulate Deployment   This is a cool option in Configuration Manager that allows administrators to perform a test deployment of a configured application that will function only to validate associated relationships and report back on what kind of success might be expected. Nothing is actually executed on the machine where the simulated deployment is deployed to. After testing the simulated deployment, the deployment needs to be deleted to be able to deploy the actual application to the same collection. The Simulate Application Deployment Wizard is shown in Figure 7.17.

FIGURE 7.17
Simulate Application
Deployment Wizard

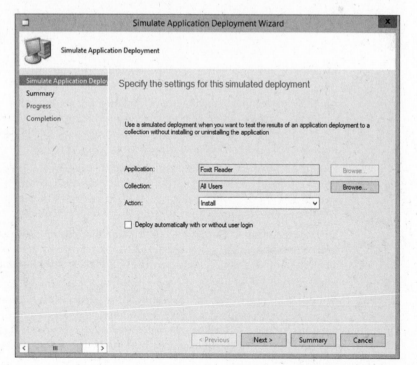

Export Configuration Manager allows you to share almost any configuration, including application definitions, between Configuration Manager hierarchies if you do not want to use the migration feature. The Export button on the ribbon launches a wizard to walk through the steps to complete the export. The wizard is shown in Figure 7.18.

FIGURE 7.18
Foxit Reader properties in the General tab of the Export Application Wizard

The content created by the Export Application Wizard is available for import into another Configuration Manager hierarchy using the Import Application button from the ribbon.

Another potentially interesting use of this functionality is as an extra level of backup for data configured in the site. Consider retiring an application as an example. It could be that the application is ready to be purged from the console, but you would like to keep a copy around for those scenarios where it might be needed again. Exporting before deletion is the perfect answer!

Deploy Creating an application and associated deployment type(s) does not result in any action taking place. To trigger action, a deployment is needed. Deployments are *not* created as part of the Create Application Wizard and must be configured through the Deploy Wizard, as will be shown for the Foxit Reader sample application shortly.

Distribute Content Deploying applications requires that content needed for the application be distributed to target systems/users. To make content available to clients, it must be staged on a distribution point. We'll review the options to distribute content for the Foxit Reader sample application shortly.

At this stage we will just say that though this option is useful to stage content to distribution points, using it isn't strictly required. By defining distribution point groups to include collection mappings, when a collection is targeted with a deployment the content needed will automatically deploy to the defined distribution points—a nice option to save a couple of extra mouse clicks!

Move This option allows administrators to move applications between defined folders. This helps keep things organized as the number of defined applications increases.

Set Security Scope Security scopes are more of a topic for security, covered in detail in Chapter 16, "Disaster Recovery." The role security scopes play with applications is interesting, though, and merits a brief discussion.

A significant change since Configuration Manager 2012 is in how security is handled, both in terms of assignment of user roles and the ability to mark certain objects, such as applications, as being part of one or more defined security scopes. Configuration Manager console users may also be assigned to one or more security scopes; by so doing, you limit the users' visibility of the Configuration Manager environment, including applications, to just those items that are part of their assigned scope(s).

Categorize As already noted when creating the sample Foxit Reader application, it is possible to create and assign categories to applications for the purposes of organization or grouping. Managing categories can be done as part of the application creation, but that is cumbersome, so the Categorize option on the ribbon is available to enable easier category management.

Properties This option will open the Properties dialog for selected objects in the console and is useful for editing settings made through the various wizards.

Exploring the Sample Application

The wizard operations are complete. The result? An application and an associated deployment type. That was easy! But what options did the wizard actually set for these items, and what options are available? To take a look, select the application, and from the ribbon, select Properties. The Foxit Reader 7.3 application property screen opens to the General Information tab, as shown in Figure 7.19.

FIGURE 7.19
Foxit Reader 7.3
Properties—General
Information tab

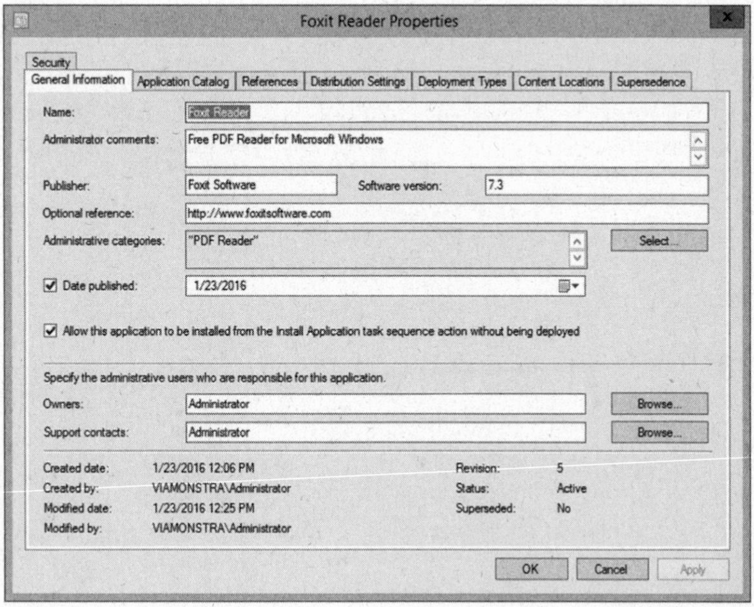

Most of the options on the General Information tab have already been discussed. In addition to those already mentioned, a few additional options are available:

Date Published   The published date allows administrators to note when the application was published. This date defaults to the current date if not selected and modified.

Allow This Application To Be Installed From The Install Application Task Sequence Action Without Being Deployed   This option is not selected by default. If the application should be deploy able via a task sequence, you must select this box. If the option isn't selected, the task sequence will fail, or you will not be able to select the application while creating a new task sequence.

Owners   This option allows administrators to define who the owner is for the given application. This information is then displayed in Software Center and also in the Application Catalog.

Support Contacts   This option allows administrators to define who users should contact if problems are encountered with the application. This information is then displayed in Software Center and also in the Application Catalog. The Browse button allows you to select users from Active Directory if desired, or you may enter users manually.

The bottom section of the General tab provides summary information for the application, including its status, whether it is superseded by another application, and the current revision number.

Selecting the Application Catalog tab details options related to publishing the application in the Application Catalog. Some options here will be provided already. If you're publishing in the catalog, you'll likely need to modify or supply some of the default options. Remember, publishing in the Application Catalog and Software Center is not actually accomplished on this tab. Rather, this tab collects information to be used *if* the application is published in the catalog. Associating your deployment, described soon, with a collection of users or user groups will result in the application showing up in the catalog. This information is shown in the Application Catalog and Software Center for applications that are deployed as Available. Options for the Foxit Reader sample are shown in Figure 7.20.

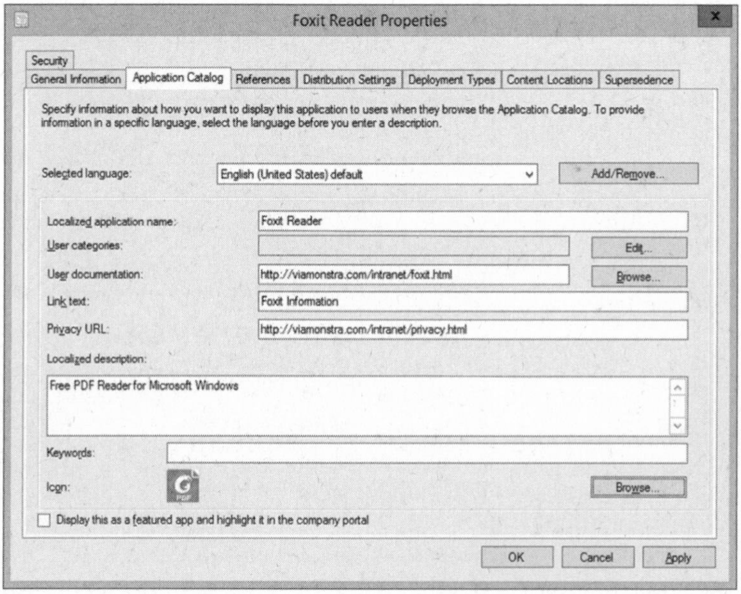

FIGURE 7.20
Foxit Reader 7.3 Properties— Application Catalog tab

Selected Language This option allows administrators to add or remove languages that should be supported by the application in the catalog and also to specify which language should be displayed.

Localized Application Name This option presents the application name localized by the current language selected.

User Categories User-targeted applications and device-targeted applications maintain separate category lists for grouping purposes. If publishing this application for users, administrators have the option to select an existing user category for describing the application or to create a new one. Users can also use them to filter applications in the Application Catalog and Software Center.

User Documentation With this option, administrators are allowed to specify a path that is available to the user for additional information on the application. This path may be a web page that the user might visit or a link to an online document.

Link Text This option allows administrators to specify what text is displayed in the catalog instructing users how to obtain additional documentation.

Privacy URL An application can have a privacy policy. As an administrator, you can configure the URL that redirects you to the website with the privacy policy.

Localized Description This section allows users to specify text, localized to the language selected, to be displayed as the application description in the catalog.

Keywords When multiple applications and categories are present in the catalog, locating specific content may be difficult. To help with the location process, administrators have the option to specify search keywords for an application that will aid users in finding its location.

Icon Administrators can choose from a substantial list of custom icons that might be associated with the application.

Display This As A Featured App And Highlight It In The Company Portal An application can be configured as a featured app in the company portal.

Selecting the References tab will display any other defined applications that either depend on the one being configured or any applications that supersede the one being configured. Also, depending on virtual environments, if available, are displayed on the References tab. In the case of the sample Foxit Reader application, no dependency or superseding application is defined.

The next tab is the Distribution Settings tab; here you can configure the distribution settings for the application. Configure the distribution priority or the prestaged distribution point settings.

The Deployment Types tab, as shown in Figure 7.21, lists all defined deployment types for the application. It is possible to configure multiple deployment types to cover all potential deployment scenarios for the application. Deployment types will be discussed in detail shortly.

The Content Locations tab, as shown in Figure 7.22, will list all distribution points or distribution point groups that have been configured to host the content. In the sample Foxit Reader application, distribution points have not yet been defined but will be shortly. If they are defined, this tab allows you to validate, redistribute, or remove the content from the distribution points or distribution point groups.

FIGURE 7.21
Foxit Reader 7.3
Properties—
Deployment
Types tab

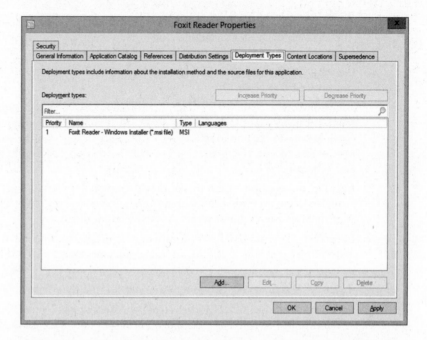

FIGURE 7.22
Foxit Reader 7.3
Properties—
Content
Locations tab

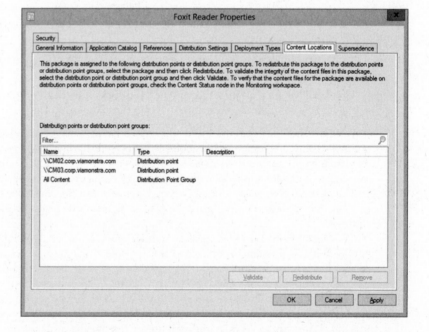

The Supersedence tab, as shown in Figure 7.23, lists any application that the current one supersedes. The ability to build links between applications that supersede each other is much like the experience that is seen with patches and brings significant benefit. (This is discussed in detail in the section "Supersedence" later in this chapter.) The sample Foxit Reader application does not currently have any superseding relationships defined. By clicking Add on this page, you can define the application that is superseded by the one being configured and also specify the new deployment type to use and whether the previous application should be uninstalled prior to installing the current version. This gives you great flexibility in controlling how deployments take place, especially when upgrading from previous versions.

The Security tab allows administrators to specify users who may access the application and their effective rights to the application.

FIGURE 7.23
Foxit Reader 7.3 Properties— Supersedence tab

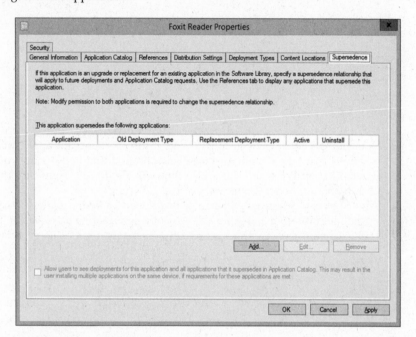

Exploring the Deployment Type

In addition to creating the sample application, the Create Application Wizard created one deployment type. This was already noted briefly and is shown in Figure 7.21.

The current sample application has only a single deployment type configured. This is shown in Figure 7.24. Note from this same figure that deployment types have as part of their definition an assigned priority. When multiple deployment types are present, it is possible to rank how they should be evaluated in relationship to each other using the Priority option. The priority for a deployment type may be increased or decreased from either the context menu brought up by right-clicking the deployment type or from the Deployment Type option on the ribbon, which is also identified in Figure 7.24.

FIGURE 7.24
Displaying
deployment type
properties

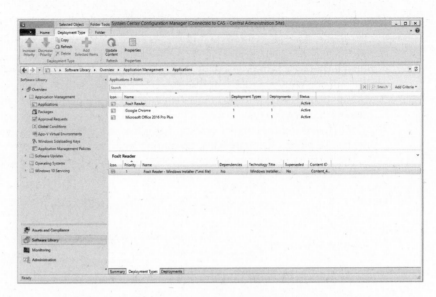

You have several options when creating a deployment type. To access the sample deployment type, either navigate to it through the properties of the application and click Edit, or simply select the sample Foxit Reader application, and in the bottom of the screen select the Deployment Types tab. This is also shown in Figure 7.24. Right-click the only deployment type available and select Properties.

Selecting Properties will display the properties for the deployment type with the General tab showing, as shown in Figure 7.25. All of the information displayed on the General tab except for the Administrator Comments text was supplied by the Create Application Wizard.

FIGURE 7.25
Sample deployment
type properties—
General tab

Name   This is the name of the deployment type. Supplying a descriptive name for each deployment type helps administrators know the intended use of each deployment type configured.

Technology   This describes what type of item is being deployed and will change based on whether an MSI (as in this case), script, or other deployment type is being deployed.

Administrator Comments   This field allows administrators to provide any needed additional information regarding the deployment type.

Languages   This field allows administrators to optionally select the specific language for the deployment type.

The bottom section of the General tab provides additional information as to the creation and modified dates for the deployment type.

Selecting the Content tab of the deployment type properties, as shown in Figure 7.26, will list various options specific to configuring content.

FIGURE 7.26

Sample deployment type properties— Content tab

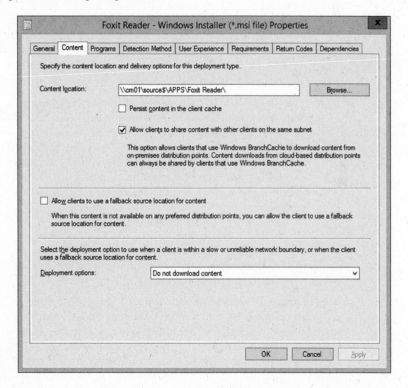

Content Location   The Content Location option allows administrators to specify the location on the network where Configuration Manager can find the content to be deployed. The path listed for this option must be specified in UNC format. This is considered the source location of the application.

Persist Content In The Client Cache   This option, disabled by default, flags that the content being deployed should remain in the client cache rather than being marked eligible for deletion. You should consider this option if the content being deployed will be reused. An example might be a script that runs periodically against clients. In such a case it is more efficient and predictable to persist the script in the client cache so it is available locally each time it is scheduled to run. If this option is not selected, after the script content runs successfully the first time, it will be eligible for deletion from the client cache if space is needed and will need to be downloaded again at the next runtime.

Allow Clients To Share Content With Other Clients On The Same Subnet This option, enabled by default, allows clients (Windows Vista and higher) on the network segment to leverage BranchCache capabilities of the operating system and act as a location cache for content that other clients on the same network segment may need. When a local peer client is detected that already has content available, clients needing the content will simply download it locally rather than from a distribution point. Of course the BranchCache feature needs to be installed and configured on the distribution point to be able to use this feature.

There are multiple scenarios where this type of configuration is helpful. Consider the following:

♦ Clients reside in a small office with no local distribution point and limited bandwidth. When applications are configured to support shared content, when a single client in the office has downloaded the content, either in total or in part, then it will be possible for other clients in the same office to access the content locally rather than traversing the network.

♦ Clients reside in a small office with a local distribution point hosted on a workstation system and limited bandwidth. In this scenario a local distribution point exists. Depending on the total number of workstations acting as distribution points and the total number of clients, it may still be useful to enable shared content distribution. When a distribution point is configured on a workstation, there is a limit of 20 simultaneous connections possible. If this small office had 100 Configuration Manager clients all needing to run an application at the same time, connections to the distribution point may be exceeded. Having content persisted in the cache of various client systems would present another option for content download.

When an administrator is planning the Configuration Manager implementation, having the ability to factor in shared content distribution as an option may allow fewer distribution points to be installed at a given location.

Allow Clients To Use A Fallback Source Location For Content. In Configuration Manager, protected distribution points will be common. When clients are connected to the corporate network directly, and if Configuration Manager distribution point access is properly configured, there should be little problem finding a distribution point that is available for use. If a client connects remotely from a boundary not configured in Configuration Manager boundary groups, the client may not be able to find a distribution point that is accessible to it because of boundaries. Setting this option, disabled by default, to allow those clients to communicate with an unprotected distribution point is important to successful application deployment. It probably goes without saying, but to be clear, setting this option by itself is only part of the equation. Distribution points themselves must be configured to be used for fallback, which is not enabled by default. When using alternative third-party content providers like 1E, this feature is crucial to get, for instance, 1E Nomad to work.

Deployment Options   When configuring boundary groups in Configuration Manager, administrators are able to designate each included distribution point that is part of the boundary group as being across either a fast or a slow connection. This option allows administrators to define how application deployment will proceed. The default option is Do Not Download Content, which means the client will delay content download until it moves inside a boundary noted as being fast. The other option is Download Content From Distribution Point And Run Locally, which will allow content to be downloaded regardless of connection quality. Remember that clients attempt to download content using BITS, which works to ensure that transfers complete successfully, even across unreliable or slow network conditions.

The Programs tab of the deployment type properties, as shown in Figure 7.27, lists program installation and uninstallation options.

FIGURE 7.27
Sample deployment
type properties—
Programs tab

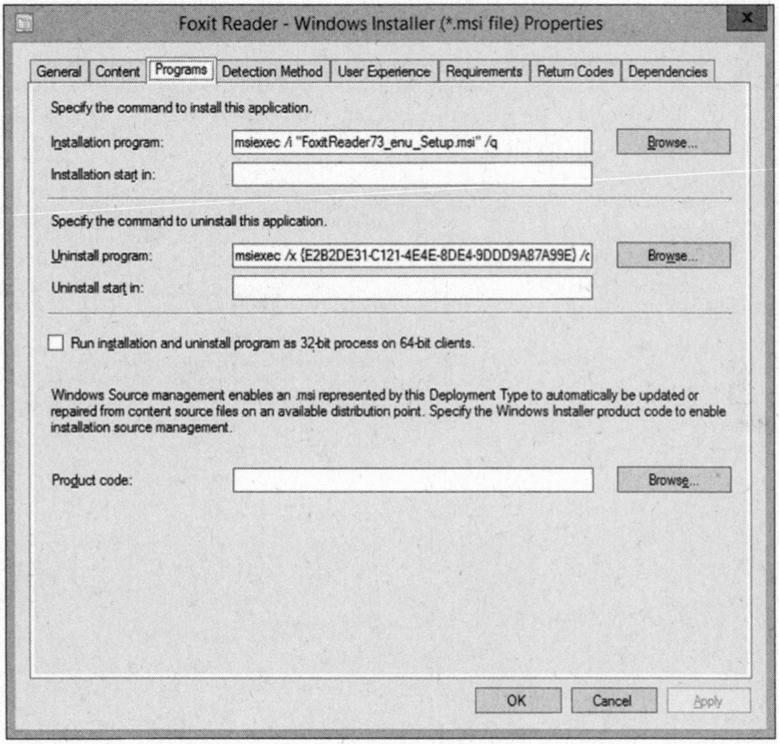

Installation Program   This option allows administrators to specify the command line to be used for program installation. This command line will be initiated from the source content downloaded from the distribution point, as specified earlier.

Installation Start In   This option allows administrators to specify a specific directory that installation should be initiated from. This option is useful when the root of the content folder on the distribution point does not contain the files needed to initiate an installation. In such a case it would be possible to specify which folder within the content does contain the needed information.

Uninstall Program   This option allows administrators to specify a command that is useful to uninstall the given application. If you're using an MSI, as in the example, the uninstall command is straightforward. It would also be possible to include a script to automate removal of any type of application install.

Uninstall Start In   This option is the same as for Installation Start In discussed previously.

Run Installation And Uninstall Programs In 32-Bit Process On 64-Bit Clients   This option allows administrators to toggle that 32-bit applications should be handled within their own 32-bit process when running on a 64-bit system.

Product Code   This option is specifically for use when deploying MSI applications. The design of MSIs allows for application self-repair and also installation of additional features if the application user selects functions that require them. In order for MSIs to work properly, they must be configured to know where the original source files are located. This option serves that purpose.

Selecting the Detection Method tab of the deployment type's properties, as shown in Figure 7.28, lets you see options for use in detecting whether an application being deployed is already present on the target device.

FIGURE 7.28

Sample deployment type properties— Detection Method tab

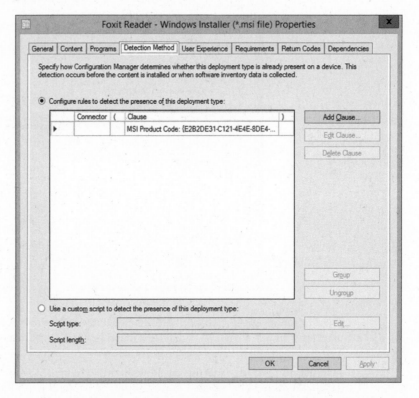

An important feature for application deployment in Configuration Manager is the ability to configure detection logic to determine if an application is already present or not on the target device. Depending on the deployment an application will be installed if it is not present or nothing will happen if the application is already present on the device. This option is much like what is already part of software update deployment but has been brought into the Application Deployment feature. Properly configuring the detection methods will prevent reinstallation of an application, which you would normally want to avoid; it is also pivotal to verifying dependencies and other configured relationships, for instance. When you're using an MSI, as in the example Foxit Reader application, this information is supplied automatically and is straightforward. Regardless of the type of application being installed, it is possible to configure a useful detection mechanism. Clicking Add Clause opens the Detection Rule dialog box, which is used to add criteria needed to detect whether the application is already installed. We'll more fully explore this wizard later in this chapter. Also note the option to execute a custom script to detect an already installed application. In most cases, the available options for detection will suffice, but if not, the script option allows almost any scenario for detection to be handled.

The User Experience tab of the deployment type's properties, as shown in Figure 7.29, lists options that allow administrators to define the experience users will have during application deployment.

FIGURE 7.29
Sample deployment type's properties—User Experience tab

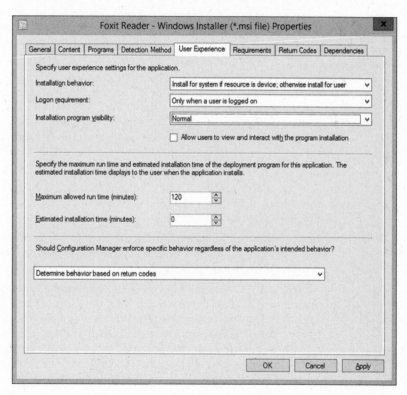

Installation Behavior This option allows administrators to define whether the application will be a deployment for a system or for a user. A third choice allows administrators to define the deployment for a system if the resource is a device but for a user otherwise. Selecting a deployment to a user will gray out the next option so that a deployment can only be executed when a user is logged on.

When a deployment is configured for a system, this indicates that the deployment will take place under the security context of the local system account. When a deployment is configured for a user, this indicates that the deployment will take place under the security context of the logged-on user. Configuration Manager is not able to execute an application installation with elevated rights like local administrator natively.

Logon Requirement   This option allows administrators to configure whether a user needs to be present during a deployment. When a deployment is identified as being for a user, this option is grayed out. When a deployment is identified as being for a system, three choices are available:

> **Only When A User Is Logged On**   This option requires a user to be logged on to the client system before a deployment will proceed, even when the deployment is identified as being for a system.

> **Whether Or Not A User Is Logged On**   This is by far the most commonly used option because it allows a deployment to proceed without the user being present.

> **Only When No User Is Logged On**   This option ensures that no application deployment takes place when a user is logged on to the system. This option would be useful in a scenario where it is crucial to ensure that users are not disrupted for application deployment, such as when a retail kiosk system is in use by a customer.

Installation Program Visibility   Options here allow administrators to configure whether the program will run Maximized, Normal, Minimized, or Hidden. The default option is Hidden. Ultimately these choices come into play only if an application is deployed to a user or to a system and the option Allow Users To View And Interact With The Program Installation is chosen. Deployments targeted to a system execute in the context of the local system account, so without that option, users wouldn't be aware of any information displayed on the screen during installation since it is not happening in their logged-on context.

Allow Users To View And Interact With The Program Installation   This option, only available when Only When A User Is Logged On is selected for the Logon Requirement, is enabled by default and cannot be disabled when the installation is identified as being for a user, but it can also be enabled when the installation is identified as being for a system.

> **User**   When an application is being deployed to a user, the installation proceeds under that user's credentials, and thus the user is able to interact with the application unless it is being deployed silently.

> **System**   When the application is being deployed to a system, the installation proceeds under the local system's credentials. Since the user's credentials aren't in use, this effectively hides any interaction from the user. Setting the option to Allow Users To View And Interact With The Program Installation causes the system to pass the local system's interactive experience through to the logged-on user. While this option is not often used in production environments, it can be a useful troubleshooting option so that administrators are able to watch an application as it installs and identify any problems that might occur.

Maximum Allowed Run Time (Minutes)   This option allows administrators to configure a maximum amount of time that an application install is able to run before being forcibly terminated. Typically the default setting of 120 minutes is more than sufficient, but in some cases application deployment errors may cause a deployment to appear hung, which will cause the installation to run past the configured window and be terminated. An example of such a situation would be if the application requires user input but is hidden from the user either because of the settings just discussed or because the application was set to run silently. In such cases, using the option Allow Users To View And Interact With The Program Installation would help identify the problem.

In many environments administrators didn't think to adjust this setting, and in many cases this presented no issue. With the introduction of maintenance windows in Configuration Manager 2007, however, this setting took on great importance. If maintenance windows are defined for the environment, the Configuration Manager client will first check to see if it is in a maintenance window before attempting to execute the application. If the client is within a maintenance window, then the amount of time configured for the install (this setting) will be compared against the time remaining in the maintenance window. If insufficient time remains, the application deployment is canceled and attempted at the next opportunity. From this alone it is clear that configuring a realistic value for this setting is critical when making use of maintenance windows in the environment. It's important to set this even when maintenance windows are not in play. Leaving it set to the default 120 minutes means it will take 2 hours for the application deployment to time out if there is an issue with the way the application was configured and/or deployed. Most applications require no more than 15–30 minutes to install. Thus the 120-minute default should be changed accordingly to avoid the maintenance window issue and to avoid waiting long periods of time for an application deployment to time out.

Estimated Installation Time (Minutes)   This option allows administrators to specify how long they anticipate that an application will take, at most, to complete the install. This setting has been an option in previous versions of Configuration Manager.

The bottom part of the User Experience tab allows administrators to configure how the Configuration Manager client should respond after the application deployment is complete. Four options are available:

Determine Behavior Based On Return Codes   This is the default option and likely makes the most sense in most scenarios. When this option is selected, the action taken by the Configuration Manager client will be determined by application return codes. Some return codes indicate that the application was successful, whereas others indicate the application was successful but requires a reboot. Still others may indicate some sort of failure. Administrators are able to specify custom return codes, discussed next, for applications that do not adhere to standards.

No Specific Action   This option simply allows the Configuration Manager client to exit after the application install is complete, without any further action.

The Software Install Program Might Force A Device Restart   This option indicates to the Configuration Manager client that once the application deployment completes, the application itself will force a reboot if necessary.

Configuration Manager Client Will Force A Mandatory Device Restart   This option causes the Configuration Manager client to force the device to reboot following an application installation.

Selecting the Requirements tab of the deployment type's properties, as shown in Figure 7.30, lists options that administrators can use to define requirements that must be met before the application installation is attempted. This page is a starting point, allowing administrators to review requirements already configured or add additional requirements.

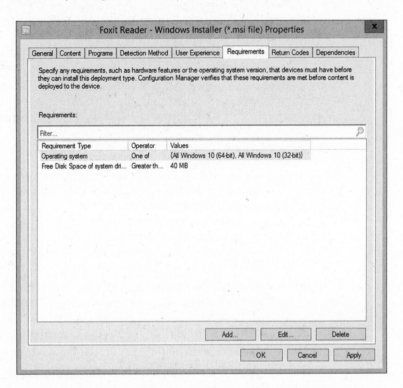

FIGURE 7.30
Sample deployment type's properties— Requirements tab

The addition of deployment rules is a significant modification in Configuration Manager and will be described later in this chapter. For now, suffice it to say that rules are intended to either (1) take the place of building unique collections with criteria per deployment that need to be managed by the site server, or (2) move the responsibility for rules checking to the client system instead. This practice will allow administrators to shift their thinking about how many collections they need to maintain, but they will need some learning time to fully acclimate to this change!

Selecting the Return Codes tab of the deployment type's properties, as shown in Figure 7.31, allows administrators to define possible return codes for the application and how they should be interpreted by the Configuration Manager client. The default values are shown in the figure. Administrators choose whether the default values are sufficient or they need to augment them.

In most cases, the default return codes will be sufficient, but in some cases, applications introduce their own return codes in an effort to help identify certain conditions that may exist at deployment time. A return code of 1, for example, may indicate a successful deployment but one that needs some sort of post-deployment action. If a return code of 1 was not added to this list, then the Configuration Manager client would interpret it as a failed deployment.

FIGURE 7.31
Sample deployment
type's properties—
Return Codes tab

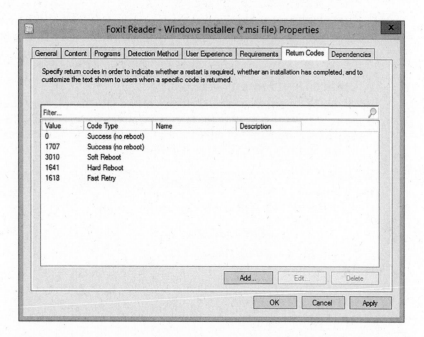

FIGURE 7.31
Sample deployment
type's properties—
Return Codes tab

Selecting the Dependencies tab of the deployment type's properties, as shown in Figure 7.32, allows administrators to define any software items that must be installed prior to the current application being installed.

FIGURE 7.32
Sample deployment
type's properties—
Dependencies tab

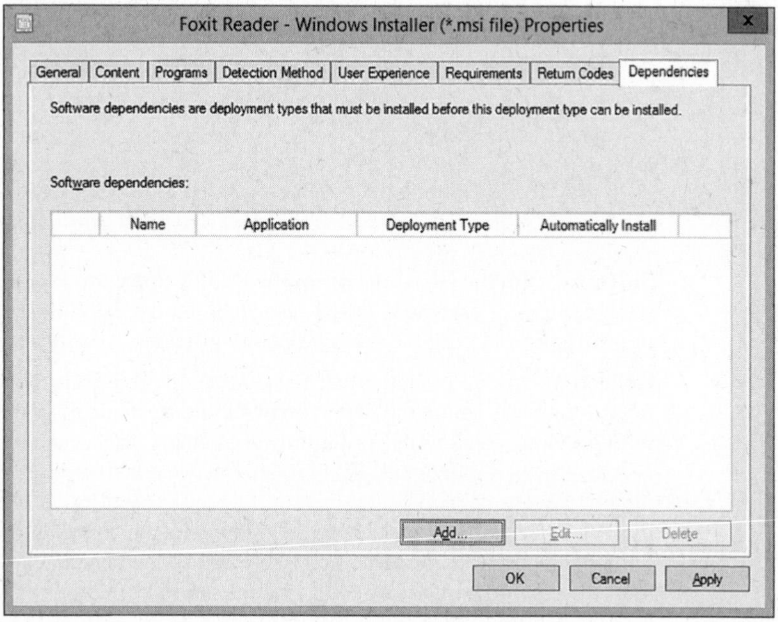

Dependencies will be detailed later in the chapter, but a quick look at the column headers reveals that along with specifying dependencies, administrators are able to specify whether a given dependency, if absent, should be automatically installed as part of the application deployment.

Create Deployment Wizard

The Create Application Wizard worked to build the sample Foxit Reader application and deployment type but did nothing to create an actual deployment. To create the deployment, click Deploy from the ribbon to launch the Deploy Software Wizard. The General page of the Deploy Software Wizard is shown in Figure 7.33.

FIGURE 7.33
Deploy Software Wizard—General page

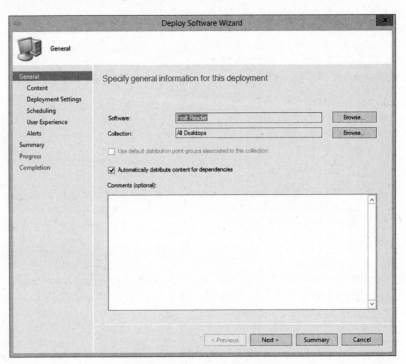

Software On the General page of the Deploy Software Wizard, the software to be deployed likely is already specified, in this case Foxit Reader 7.3. If the provided selection is incorrect or is missing, clicking the Browse button will allow you to select the correct application.

Collection A deployment must be associated with a collection. A collection is a group of devices or users where the deployment should be made available. Administrators familiar with previous versions of Configuration Manager are accustomed to building collections specific to a given deployment. This can still be done in Configuration Manager, or it is possible to target a generic collection and rely on the requirement rules, mentioned earlier and discussed in more detail later in this chapter, to determine which systems actually run the deployment. In practice, a hybrid approach will likely be used, where a collection is built containing systems that should be targeted with an application but without the various deployment criteria such as minimum disk space, minimum processor, minimum software version, and so on. These latter options will be managed as part of the application's Requirements settings.

Use Default Distribution Point Groups Associated To This Collection   In Configuration Manager it is possible to associate collections with a distribution point group. If this is done, the option shown would be available for selection and would result in the deployment being automatically distributed to distribution points based on collections chosen. The benefit of being able to link a collection with a distribution point group allows administrators additional flexibility. As an example, it would be possible to build collections per machine type per a given geography or office location. Then, when building distribution groups, the relevant collections and distribution points that serve those collections could be grouped together, facilitating more efficient management.

Automatically Distribute Content For Dependencies   If dependencies are defined for an application and if those dependencies have not been deployed to the distribution points selected for the deployment being configured, selecting this option will ensure that the content for the dependency is made available in the event it is needed.

Comments   The Comments section allows administrators to optionally add any information that may be pertinent for the deployment.

The Content page is shown in Figure 7.34. On the Content page, administrators are able to view currently assigned distribution points and distribution point groups. If the content is not already on any of the distribution points, you can add the content to distribution points or distribution point groups. You can also select additional distribution points or distribution point groups that are appropriate locations to stage the content for client access.

FIGURE 7.34
Deploy Software
Wizard—Content
page

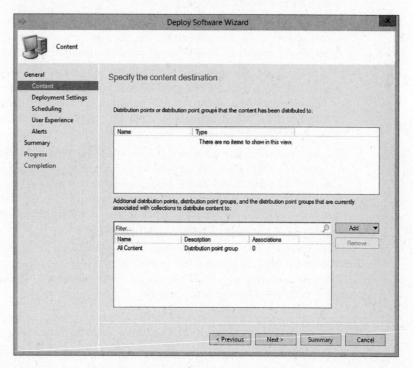

When you've finished with the settings on the Content page, click Next to continue to the Deployment Settings page, as shown in Figure 7.35.

FIGURE 7.35
Deploy Software
Wizard—Deployment
Settings page

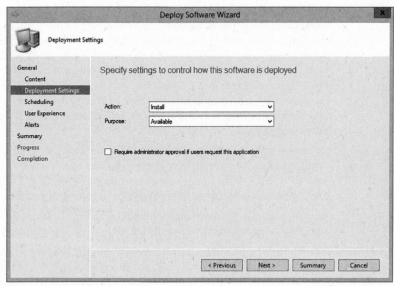

Action This setting is where administrators choose whether the deployment will act to install or uninstall the application.

Purpose This setting is where administrators choose whether the application simply is made available for manual installation, such as through the Software Center or the Application Catalog, or whether the application installation will be required.

If set to Required, the application will be enforced on targeted systems/users on the schedule specified. A change since Configuration Manager 2012—with the Required setting in place, the Configuration Manager client will periodically check to see if the application remains installed. If the application has been removed, it will be deployed again. As shown when discussing client settings earlier, the default detection cycle is to every 7 days.

Require Administrator Approval If Users Request This Application If this application is targeted to a collection of users or user groups, this option becomes available and allows administrators to flag this application as one that will be listed as needing approval in the Application Catalog. Require Administrator Approval can, for instance, be used when a license is required to be allowed to install the application. The administrator can check if the licenses are available before approving the installation.

When you've finished with the settings on the Deployment Settings page, click Next to continue to the Scheduling page, shown in Figure 7.36.

The options available on the Scheduling page are dependent on the setting chosen for Purpose on the Deployment Settings page:

◆ When Purpose is set to Available, then the only scheduling option available will be one that allows administrators to schedule application availability.

◆ When Purpose is set to Required, then the administrator will additionally be able to schedule the deadline for installation, either as soon as possible or for a specific time.

FIGURE 7.36
Deploy Software
Wizard—Scheduling
page

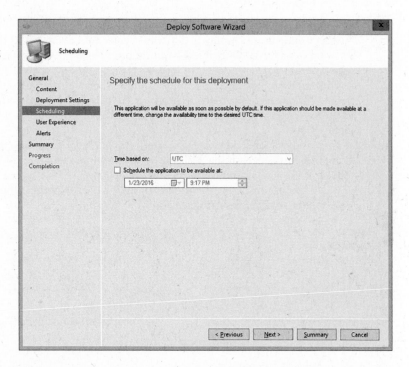

When you've finished with the settings on the Scheduling page, click Next to continue to the User Experience page, shown in Figure 7.37.

FIGURE 7.37
Deploy Software
Wizard—User
Experience page

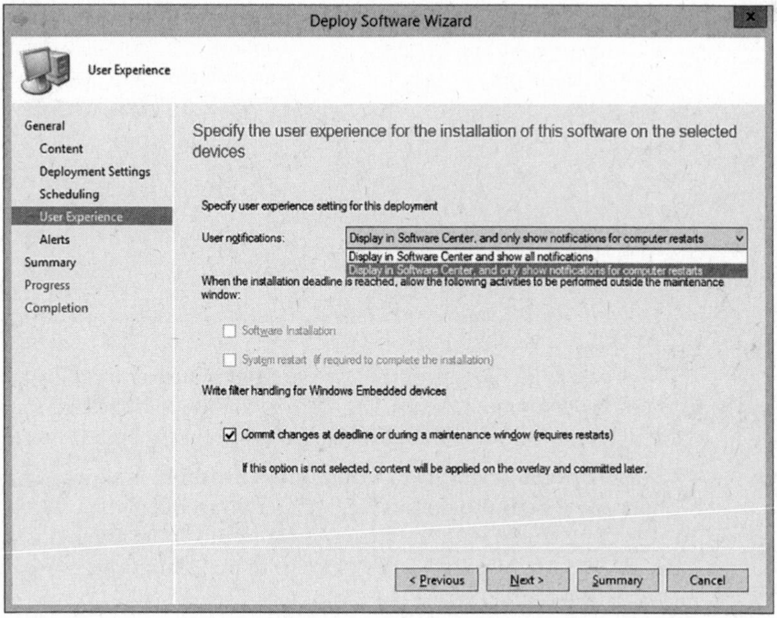

The User Experience page allows administrators to configure user notifications. Available options are Display In Software Center And Show All Notifications or Display In Software Center, And Only Show Notifications For Computer Restarts. These options are self-explanatory.

The options for specifying activity to allow when an installation deadline has been reached are gray when the deployment is set with a Purpose of Available. When the deployment is set with a Purpose of Required, the options Software Installation and System Restart are configurable.

For Windows Embedded devices, support is added for handling the write filters. You are able to commit the changes at the deadline or during a maintenance window, or the content will be applied in the overlay and committed in a later stage.

When you've finished with the settings on the User Experience page, click Next to continue to the Alerts page, shown in Figure 7.38.

FIGURE 7.38

Deploy Software Wizard—Alerts page

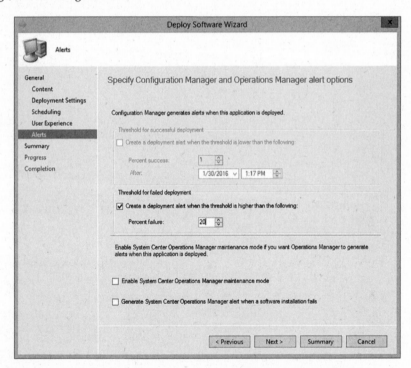

The Alerts page allows administrators to configure criteria for when to generate alerts in response to deployment status. The alerting ability provided in Configuration Manager is new and provides an additional mechanism for awareness of deployment health.

Create A Deployment Alert When The Threshold Is Lower Than The Following This option allows administrators to specify a threshold of expected deployment success for a given deployment within a specific time frame. If the deployment success has not met or exceeded the configured threshold within the configured time, an alert will be generated to notify the administrator.

Create A Deployment Alert When The Threshold Is Higher Than The Following This option allows administrators to specify a threshold for a deployment that, if exceeded, will cause an alert to be triggered. This option would be useful in a scenario where a certain number of licenses have been purchased for an application. If a sufficient number of users install the application to cause the number of available licenses to reach near depletion, the administrator would be alerted and have the opportunity to either order additional licenses or scale back the usage of the application.

Enable System Center Operations Manager Maintenance Mode This option allows integration between Configuration Manager and Operations Manager. By selecting this option, when a deployment begins on a client, and if the client is also an Operations Manager agent, the agent will be placed in maintenance mode. After the deployment completes, the Operations Manager agent will be triggered to exit maintenance mode.

Generate System Center Operations Manager Alert When A Software Installation Fails This option causes an alert to be generated in Operations Manager to raise immediate awareness when the installation of an application fails.

MONITORING DEPLOYMENTS WITH SYSTEM CENTER OPERATIONS MANAGER

Although Operations Manager maintenance mode is beyond the scope of our discussion, one thing does need to be mentioned. This option does not cause true Operations Manager maintenance mode to start. Instead, the Health Service on the Operations Manager agent is simply paused for the duration of the application deployment. Once deployment completes, the health service resumes from that point in time without accounting for any problems that might have happened during application deployment, such as a system reboot. This is an effective approach to suppress noise in Operations Manager but will not be reflected as maintenance mode in the Operations Manager console.

UPDATED INTEGRATION FEATURE

In Configuration Manager 2007, this maintenance mode integration was not reliable. Configuration Manager has been updated so that this integration works as intended, regardless of platform.

When you've finished with the settings on the Alerts page, click Next to continue to the Summary page. Review the settings on the Summary page. If they're all acceptable, click Next to save the configuration and then exit the wizard.

Application Deployment—Client Experience

The ultimate goal of Application Deployment is to take action on Configuration Manager clients. The work described so far involves creating an application deployment, a deployment type, and a deployment. Our current sample was configured to be available and was targeted to a collection of devices. The current configurations will simply make the application available for install in the Software Center on all targeted clients.

As configured, the application will by default *not* show up in the user-centric Application Catalog. Inclusion in the Application Catalog requires that the application be deployed to a collection of users or user groups. To make the sample Foxit Reader application also show as available in the Application Catalog, a second deployment needs to be added. The only difference for this deployment is that a collection of users will be chosen rather than systems. The new deployment is shown in Figure 7.39.

FIGURE 7.39
Second deployment added, targeted to a user collection

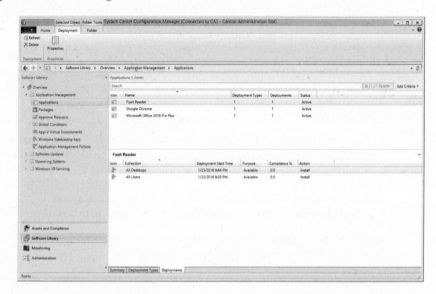

With the second deployment added, the application now shows as available in both the Software Center and the Application Catalog. Take a look at the way the applications are presented in both and the descriptive information that is available. Looking at Figure 7.19 and Figure 7.20, you can see that the information you have supplied is presented in the Software Center in Figure 7.40 and the Application Catalog in Figure 7.41. It's good to understand how these configurations map between the different components so that when you configure an application, the user will have meaningful and descriptive information to review.

FIGURE 7.40
Foxit Reader in the Software Center

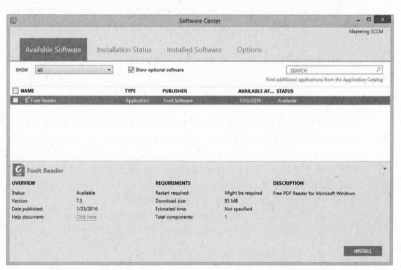

FIGURE 7.41
Foxit Reader in
the Application
Catalog

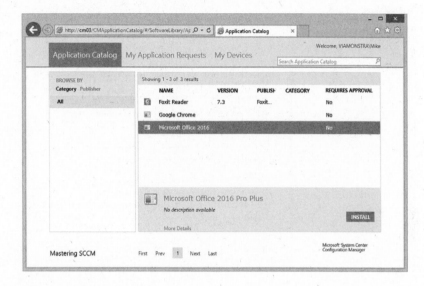

CLIENT APPLICATION INSTALLATION

When an application is configured to be required, it will be installed regardless of whether
the user requests it in the Software Center or selects it in the Application Catalog. In some
cases, applications may be marked as required but also as visible in the Software Center and
Application Catalog, but that is not automatic. For applications that should be optional for the
user, simply mark them as being available, and depending on other configurations such as
requirements, they will appear for the user in the Software Center. If the application is targeted
to a user collection, it will also appear in the Application Catalog.

Bottom line, the Software Center is available on each Configuration Manager client and
allows users to have control over at least some of their own experience with Configuration
Manager. As the name implies and as already discussed, the Software Center presents a list of
applications to users that are available for install, along with a good amount of potential detail
to help users understand the application. But the Software Center is more than just a tool to
install applications. Click the Installed Software node, and you'll see that it is also useful for
tracking software that has been installed on the system historically.

The Options node, also part of Software Center and shown in Figure 7.42, allows users to
specify their own work information and maintenance settings. Think of these settings as a user-
controlled maintenance window. By specifying business hours, users are configuring their system so that they are not disrupted by application installs or system reboots in the middle of the
day. Maintenance settings work with Work Information settings to specify when the computer
will be available for software installations. Ultimately, the Configuration Manager administrator retains full control even at this level because, when necessary, application deployment can be
configured to proceed regardless of the settings specified.

Also available on the Options tab is the ability to configure local remote control settings and
whether power management policy will apply to the system. But those topics are beyond the
scope of software distribution, so we won't discuss them here.

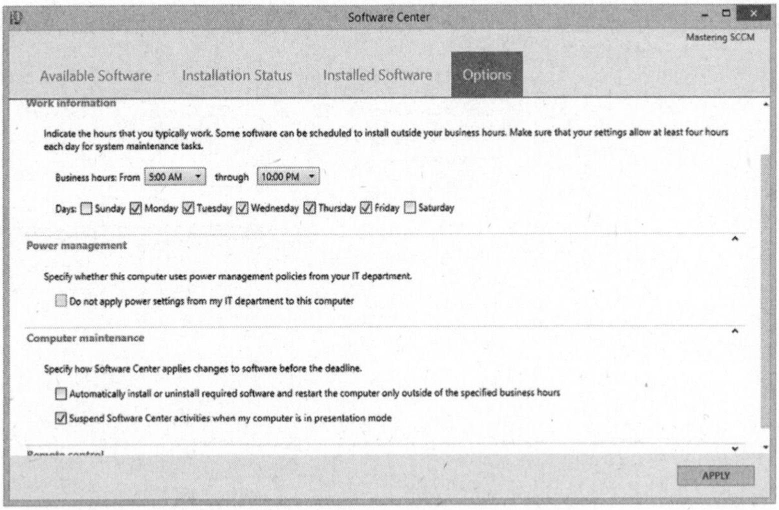

FIGURE 7.42
Software Center
Options tab

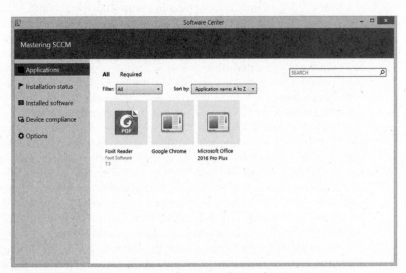

USING THE SOFTWARE CENTER FOR USER TARGETED APPS

New in Configuration Manager is the ability to access applications from the Software Center that are deployed to users collections. To be able to do so, you need to change the Use New Software Center option to Yes, as shown in Figure 7.3 and Table 7.2 earlier in this chapter.

After enabling the Use New Software Center option, the Software Center will have a new look and feel (see Figure 7.43). Remember that both the site roles Application Catalog website point and the Application Catalog web service point are a prerequisite for this new Software Center experience.

FIGURE 7.43
The new Software
Center

In Figure 7.43 you also see the PowerShell-created Google Chrome app that is deployed to the All Users collection earlier in this chapter.

> ### 🌐 Real World Scenario
>
> #### APPLICATION DEPLOYMENT—BEYOND THE LAB
>
> Stepping through creation of the sample application is enough to start the wheels turning about ways this new model could be used in production. There is tremendous flexibility in the new Application Deployment model, but don't jump too far too fast. Spend time with the model and understand how things work before spinning up deployments in production. Remember, a lab environment is much more forgiving—and doesn't result in the need to explain problems to management!
>
> In addition, there are many layers to the Application Deployment model. Explore each layer completely—from the rules-based Requirements engine to the ability to link applications together, known as references, creating a tie between applications that is useful for application upgrade. There is also the ability to verify that prerequisites are in place before deploying a given application. And don't forget a real gem of the new model, the ability to create multiple deployment types that can work with each other to detect information about the environment for the current deployment and deliver a version of the application best suited for each scenario; this includes deployments to devices, users, or both.
>
> If you have trouble finding the right parameters for the setup of the application or the detection methods, a tool called Setup Commander can help you create the deployment type with the right parameters and detection methods for lots of common software based on MSI setups and older legacy setups. Look for more information at www.setupcommander.com.

Application Deployment—Advanced Configurations

The steps just discussed demonstrated how to configure a basic application, deployment type, and deployment. These building blocks are pivotal to understanding the Configuration Manager Application Deployment model, but in some ways they just scratch the surface of what is possible. We've already mentioned several additional and more complex configurations but have not discussed them in any detail. This section takes a step back and reviews these additional configurations. With Application Deployment, all of the various configurations and options that are possible are simply too numerous to cover individually. The hope is that with the discussion provided you will be able to see the possibilities, flexibility, and power available.

SUPERSEDENCE

This example builds on the previous one by adding an additional deployment that is configured to deploy Adobe Acrobat 9 Pro. In this example the Configuration Manager admin must cut costs and replace the paid version of Adobe Acrobat 9 Pro with Foxit Reader, which is free. This introduces the first point of discussion: *supersedence*. In the definition of the application it is possible to configure a relationship where one application supersedes another application. This type of relationship is extremely valuable to maintain control of the application upgrade process and also to define how one application should operate during the upgrade process—but that's jumping a bit too far ahead.

Configuring a supersedence relationship is easy. Simply do the following:

1. Open the properties of the application where a supersedence relationship is to be defined and click the Supersedence tab.

2. Click Add, and click Browse.

3. Select the application that the current one should supersede, and then click OK two times.

The result is shown in Figure 7.44.

FIGURE 7.44
Supersedence
relationship added
to Foxit Reader
application

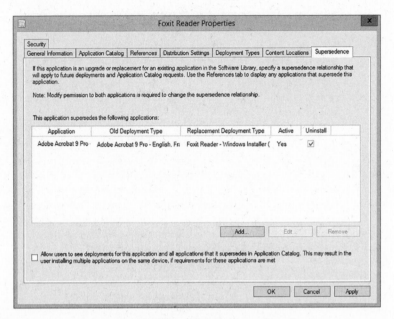

Notice that when defining a supersedence relationship it is possible to specify whether the application being replaced should first be uninstalled. When selecting to uninstall an application, make sure that the uninstall command-line setting for the previous application has been configured properly to accommodate the uninstall. A further configuration allows specifying which deployment type from the current application will be used during deployment.

To see the results of creating the supersedence relationship, simply look at the properties for the Adobe Acrobat 9 Pro application and select the References tab. There are three options for viewing data on this tab: Applications That Depend On This Application, Applications That Supersede This Application, and Virtual Environments That Contain This Application. For the current purpose, select the second option, which will show that the Foxit Reader application now supersedes the Adobe Acrobat 9 Pro application. This is shown in Figure 7.45.

FIGURE 7.45
Supersedence
reference

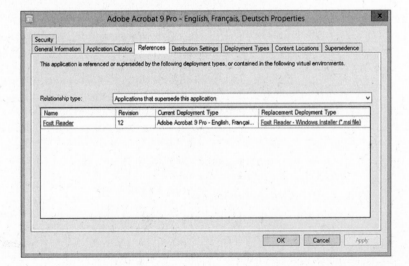

DEPENDENCIES

Going back to the deployment type for the sample Foxit Reader application, it's time to configure a dependency. The dependency option specifically allows administrators to define software that must be installed before the current application can be deployed. The dependency option is not a vehicle to specify any other kind of requirement. As shown in Figure 7.46, the sample Foxit Reader application is configured to require that .NET Framework 4.5 be installed first. If this requirement isn't met, and depending on the setting for the Automatically Install option, either the application installation will fail or the application installation will pause while .NET Framework installation completes.

FIGURE 7.46
Dependency
configuration

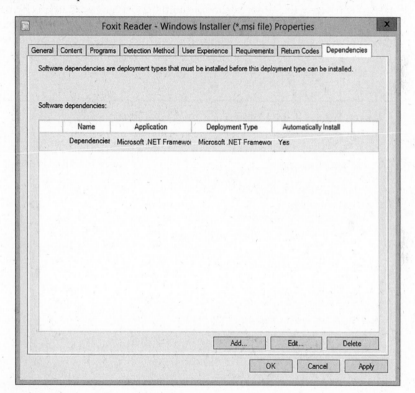

DETECTION METHOD

The ability to detect whether a dependency is installed depends on whether settings to do so are specified in the Detection Method tab for an application. Dependencies also allow administrators to configure potentially complex dependency relationships to ensure that all needed applications are present before proceeding with a deployment.

Detection methods are also useful to determine whether a given application has already been deployed to a target system. If so, there is no need to deploy it again, and the application deployment will simply exit.

If a user, for instance, removed the application from the computer and the Application Deployment evaluation cycle detects that an application is not installed, the application will be installed (again).

You can create detection configurations to check the filesystem, a registry location or value, an MSI GUID, or a combination of these settings to determine if a given application is present. When you use the wizard to build an application deployment based on an MSI, as in the Foxit Reader example, the detection information is supplied by default. Figure 7.28, shown earlier, is a view of the Detection Method tab.

Besides the standard detection methods, custom PowerShell, JScript, or VBScript scripts can also be used to detect whether an application is installed.

Requirements

When deploying an application, administrators may wish to specify rules to govern the application install. The Requirements tab of the deployment type allows deployment rules to be configured, from simple to complex. You can build rules to check attributes related to the device or user being targeted or build custom rules to cover most any scenario. The conditions that are available for both device and user-targeted applications are shown in Table 7.3.

TABLE 7.3:   Rule options

DEVICE	USER
Active Directory site	Primary device*
Configuration Manager site	
CPU speed	
Disk space	
Number of processors	
Operating system	
Operating system language	
Organizational unit (OU)	
Ownership	
Total physical memory	
Windows Store Global Condition	

The primary device and its use for application deployment will be discussed along with user affinity.

The mechanisms available for building custom rules are as follows:

Active Directory query

Assembly

Filesystem

IIS Metabase

Registry key

Registry value

Script

SQL query

WQL query

XPath query

As is noted by the combination of the rule options shown, literally any possible scenario can be covered by specifying the right type of rule.

For the sample Foxit Reader application, the only systems that should install it are those that run Windows 7 or newer and already have the superseded application, Adobe Acrobat 9 Pro, installed. Figure 7.47 shows the completed Requirements node, which details the checks that must pass before proceeding with application deployment.

FIGURE 7.47
Requirements node completed

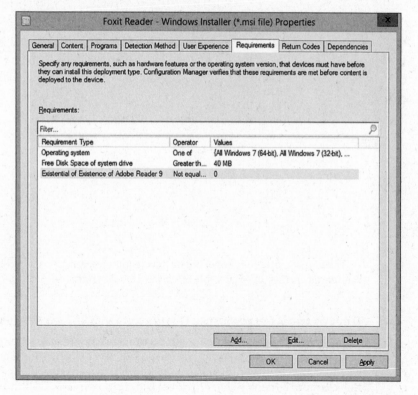

It's interesting to note regarding the Requirements tab that when Configuration Manager clients receive notification of a new application and if that application has a list of requirements, those requirements will be evaluated upon receipt of the deployment policy, and if the requirements for deployment are not met, the application will not be displayed as available for deployment on the target system. Applications are evaluated periodically to determine if the conditions specified by the requirements have changed.

The rules available for use in the Requirements tab are visible in the Software Library ➤ Overview ➤ Application Management ➤ Global Conditions node of the console. The list will also include any custom requirements that may be created. This is shown in Figure 7.48. Note that the custom global condition just created is stored in the list and selected.

Global conditions can also be created from the node shown in Figure 7.48, when selecting the Create Global Condition option in the Home tab of the ribbon in the Configuration Manager console. The custom-created global conditions can be used in other applications throughout the hierarchy.

FIGURE 7.48
Global
Conditions
node

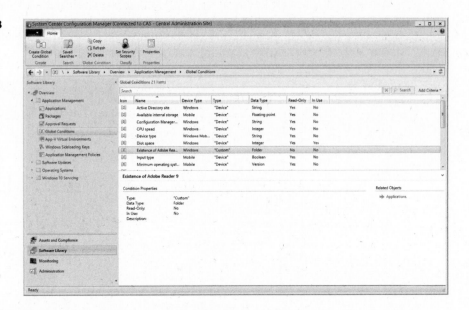

When retrieving the properties of the custom-created global condition, you can review the references and see in what application the global condition is used, as shown in Figure 7.49.

DEPLOYING APPLICATIONS OTHER THAN MSI AND SCRIPTS

Not only MSI files, executables, or scripts can be deployed to users or devices. Configuration Manager has more deployment types available. Since Chapter 18, "Enterprise Mobility and Configuration Manager," is all about mobile device management, we focus here on the applications that can be deployed to Windows, Unix/Linux, or Mac OS X–based devices.

FIGURE 7.49
Reviewing the
references of the
Custom Global
Condition

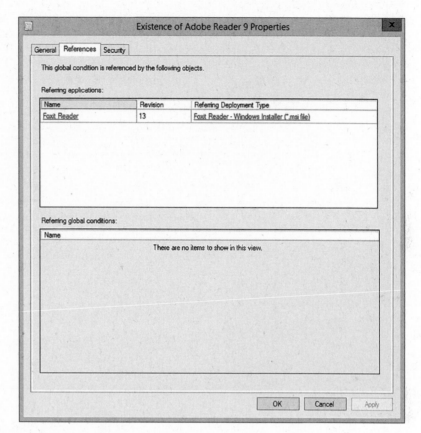

Application Virtualization 4.6/5

When you have sequenced an App-V 4.6 or App-V 5 application, you can deploy this application to devices depending on the requirement rules. Both App-V clients need to be deployed separately and are not included with Configuration Manager.

In Configuration Manager you can create virtual environments for App-V 5. App-V applications in a virtual environment share the same filesystem and registry; this way the applications can interact with each other. You can create App-V virtual environments in the Software Library ➤ Overview ➤ Application Management ➤ App-V Virtual Environments node of the console, as shown in Figure 7.50.

Windows App Package

Deploying Windows app packages for Windows 8.x, Windows 10, or Windows RT devices can be done in two different ways:

♦ Install the application from the online Windows Store

♦ Install the application from the distribution point, called *sideloading* the application

FIGURE 7.50
App-V virtual
environment for
Office 2010 and
Visio 2010

FIGURE 7.50
App-V virtual
environment for
Office 2010 and
Visio 2010

When you want to install a Windows app from the Windows Store, you need to browse to the application via the Windows app package browser in the Windows Store and then select it as the Deployment Type. Browse to the app and click OK to select it to be used for the deployment type, as shown in Figure 7.51.

To be able to sideload a Windows 8 line-of-business (LoB) application, you need a trusted certificate to sign the application, since it is not signed by the Windows Store. This can be a trusted certificate from your own certificate authority or one from the trusted root CA such as VeriSign, GlobalSign, or Symantec. Using an external trusted root is a best practice. A LoB universal application can be developed in-house or by a software vendor hired by your organization.

You also need product activation keys for every device you want to sideload an application to. These keys can be acquired at the Microsoft Volume License website. Once you have the sideloading product activation keys, you need to add them to Configuration Manager. You can add these keys in the Software Library ➤ Overview ➤ Application Management ➤ Windows Sideloading Keys node of the console. Click Create Sideloading Key to enable sideloading of applications for Windows RT, Windows RT 8.1, and Windows 8. This opens the Specify Sideloading Key dialog shown in Figure 7.52.

FIGURE 7.51
Select an application
from the Microsoft
Store.

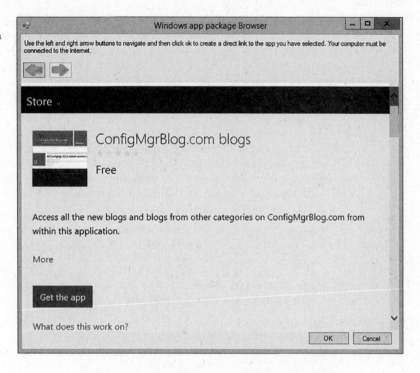

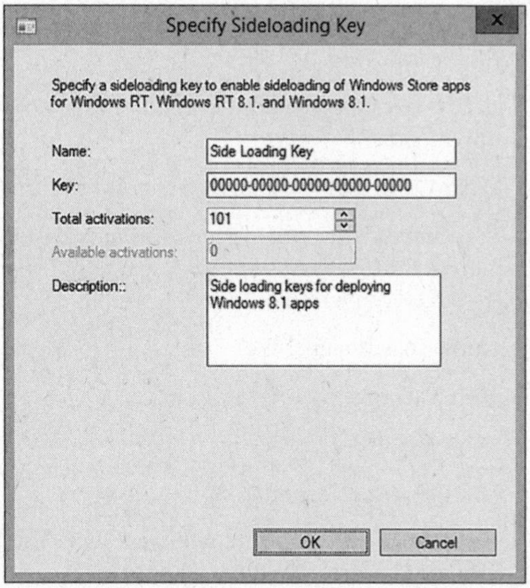

FIGURE 7.52
Adding sideloading
keys

If you want to create and deploy a custom-developed application, you need to acquire a
Microsoft developer license. Once you have the license, you can create a custom application,

sign it, and sideload it via Configuration Manager. Sideloading is only required for Windows RT and Windows 8/8.1. Windows 8/8.1 Enterprise devices that are domain joined do not require sideloading. They only require a Group Policy object (GPO) that enables the "Allow all trusted apps to install" setting on the device. Windows 8/8.1 Pro devices, on the other hand, that are domain-joined do require sideloading. Windows RT and non-domain joined Windows 8/8.1 Pro or Enterprise also require sideloading.

Mac OS X

Configuration Manager supports the deployment of Mac OS X applications to the supported Mac OS X versions described in Chapter 2. Deploying an application to a Mac is somewhat different than deploying it to a Windows device using the new application model. Deploying the Mac OS X application is done with the new Mac OS X deployment type but has the following limitations:

◆ You need to first convert the Mac application package to a format that Configuration Manager recognizes and supports. You can convert the Mac application package with the CMAppUtil tool that comes with the Configuration Manager client for the Mac OS X platform.

◆ Applications cannot be deployed to users but only to devices. Predeploying software to the user's primary device is not supported.

◆ Mac applications support simulated deployments, allowing you to test your requirement rules.

◆ Global conditions are not supported when you create deployment types for Mac OS X computers.

◆ All deployments must have a purpose of Required. There is no Software Center available for the Mac OS X.

◆ BITS is not supported on Mac computers. When a download of the content fails, the entire download will restart.

◆ Wake On LAN via the deployment is not supported on Mac computers.

The first step if you want to deploy an application to a Mac OS X computer is to convert the application to the Configuration Manager–supported CMMAC format. The following application packages can be converted:

◆ Apple Disk Image (.dmg)

◆ Meta Package File (.mpkg)

◆ Mac OS X Installer Package (.pkg)

◆ Mac OS X Application (.app)

For example, we want to deploy Firefox, which comes in DMG format (Firefox 23.dmg). The Configuration Manager client for the Mac includes the tool CMAppUtil. This tool can be found in the Tools folder after extracting the compressed file.

Running the following command will result in a Firefox23.0.cmmac file, as shown in Figure 7.53.

```
./CMAppUtil -c firefox23.0.dmg -o ./ -a
```

FIGURE 7.53
The DMG file is converted to a CMMAC file.

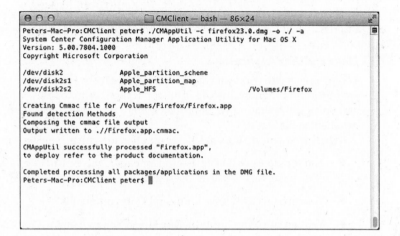

```
Peters-Mac-Pro:CMClient peter$ ./CMAppUtil -c firefox23.0.dmg -o ./ -a
System Center Configuration Manager Application Utility for Mac OS X
Version: 5.00.7804.1000
Copyright Microsoft Corporation

/dev/disk2              Apple_partition_scheme
/dev/disk2s1            Apple_partition_map
/dev/disk2s2            Apple_HFS                        /Volumes/Firefox

Creating Cmmac file for /Volumes/Firefox/Firefox.app
Found detection Methods
Composing the cmmac file output
Output written to .//Firefox.app.cmmac.

CMAppUtil successfully processed "Firefox.app",
to deploy refer to the product documentation.

Completed processing all packages/applications in the DMG file.
Peters-Mac-Pro:CMClient peter$ █
```

After you import the CMMAC file for Firefox, all the necessary information, including the detection method, is automatically configured. Figure 7.54 shows the detection method configured for detecting the application bundle `org.mozilla.firefox` version 23.0.

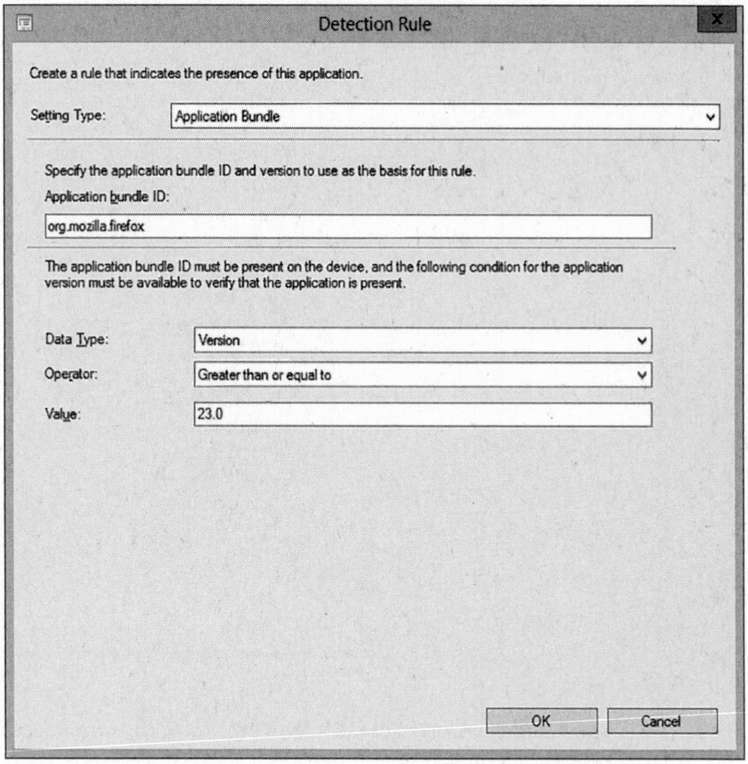

FIGURE 7.54
Detection method for a Mac OS X application

Detection Rule

Create a rule that indicates the presence of this application.

Setting Type: Application Bundle

Specify the application bundle ID and version to use as the basis for this rule.

Application bundle ID:

org.mozilla.firefox

The application bundle ID must be present on the device, and the following condition for the application version must be available to verify that the application is present.

Data Type: Version

Operator: Greater than or equal to

Value: 23.0

OK   Cancel

As mentioned, the application needs to be deployed to the Mac OS X device; it will be installed when the Configuration Manager client connects to the primary site.

Linux and Unix Applications

When you need to deploy an application to a Linux or Unix server, you will need the classic packages and programs instead of an application. With the classic packages you can deploy new software, operating system patches, and software updates for programs that are already installed on the server.

When deploying a Linux or Unix application to a server, you need to keep the following in mind:

◆ You should learn how to use and manage Linux or Unix, or you can ask the administrator of those servers to deliver the scripts that can be used to deploy the software or updates.

◆ You can run only native Linux and Unix commands.

◆ You can run only scripts that are already located on the Linux or Unix server.

◆ You can create a program for specific operating systems by selecting the option This Program Can Run Only On Specified Platforms, as shown in Figure 7.55.

FIGURE 7.55
Select the platform for which the program is created.

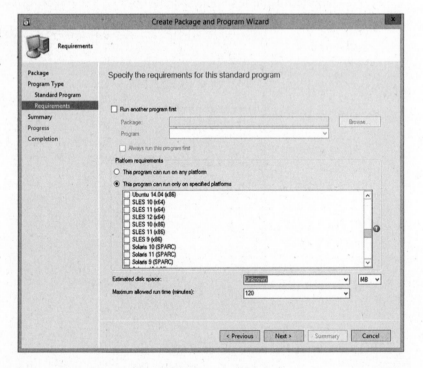

◆ The Configuration Manager client for Linux and Unix does not support the deployment of scripts that make user environment configuration changes.

◆ The Network Access account is used to download the content from the distribution points.

◆ Only deployments with a Required purpose are supported.

◆ Include file types in the scripts that are supported on the destination operating systems.

MORE MAC OS X SUPPORT

If you want to deploy native Mac OS X apps without needing to wrap it, you may want to have a look at Parallels Mac Management (PMM) for Configuration Manager. With PMM you are able not only to deploy native Mac OS X apps but also to manage more settings and deploy Mac OS X operating systems.

Web Application

A web application is a link to a website; this deployment type installs a link on the device of the user.

User Device Affinity

As already described, the Application Deployment model in Configuration Manager is extremely flexible and gives administrators many options for delivering content. Configuration Manager provides flexibility in delivering applications to users so that users, regardless of what device they are using, will have a consistent experience. As an example, if a user is logged on to their primary device, then an application may be configured to be installed on the target system, whereas if a user is simply logged on to a shared computer, they may instead receive a virtualized copy of the application. If the user is logged on to a mobile device and a mobile version of an application is available, further options to accommodate software deployment are available there as well. Whatever the case, the user's experience is that their required software is available, but the administrator has control over how the software is provided.

In order for a user to be properly detected as logged on to their primary device rather than a shared device, a mechanism must be in place to guide that decision. User Device Affinity settings provide that mechanism.

User Device Affinity allows a user to be associated with their primary device(s). User Device Affinity associations are configured in one of several ways:

◆ The user can configure that a device should be considered a primary device in the Application Catalog.

◆ The administrator can configure the My Devices option in the Application Catalog, shown in Figure 7.56.

◆ You can use a file to map a user to their primary device(s) and then import this file to Configuration Manager.

◆ You can choose the option Import User Device Affinity settings, which is available in the Assets and Compliance node of the console. The Import User Device Affinity Wizard is shown in Figure 7.57.

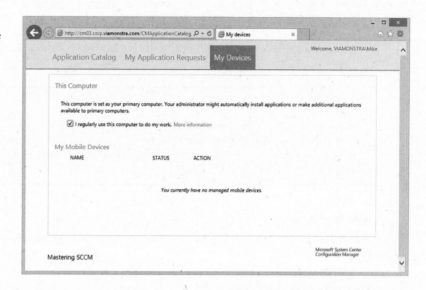

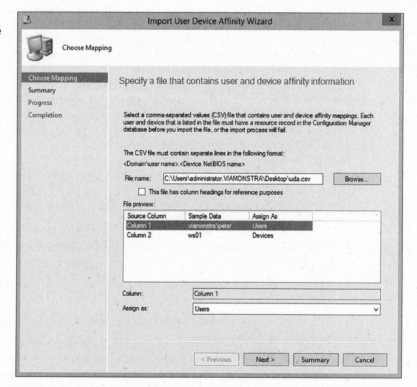

- You can configure Configuration Manager to automatically build user-to-primary device mappings based on information collected about devices used by a user. With this method administrators retain control over whether to automatically accept the detected settings.

- Configuration Manager can be configured to automatically detect primary device mappings through usage data, as shown in Figure 7.58. The default setting does not allow you to automatically configure the user device affinity. Note that the required inventory class in the Hardware Inventory, SMS_SystemConsoleUsage, is enabled by default. Configuration Manager reads data about user logons from the Windows Event log. To be able to automatically create user device affinities, logon events in the Windows Event log need to be enabled via the local security policy via Windows Group Policy. Audit account logon events and Audit logon events need to be enabled.

FIGURE 7.58
Configuring automatic user device affinity detection

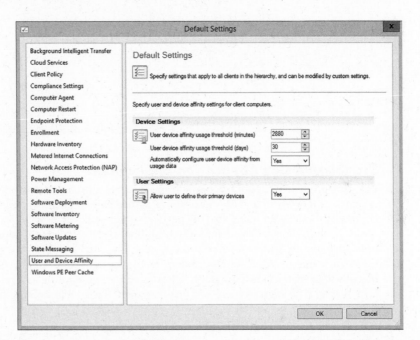

- The Configuration Manager administrator can manually create relationships between users and device(s) by using the Edit Primary Devices node in the console. This is shown in Figure 7.59.

- Specific to mobile devices, when a user enrolls a device, a relationship is automatically created between the user and the mobile device.

Also note that the User and Device Affinity settings are not limited to specifying one primary device per user. Very often a single user may have more than one primary device, such as a computer, as well as a mobile device. It's also possible that a given device will be the primary device for multiple users, such as in a shared workstation scenario. Configuration Manager handles any of these device-to-user mapping scenarios.

FIGURE 7.59
Edit Primary
Users

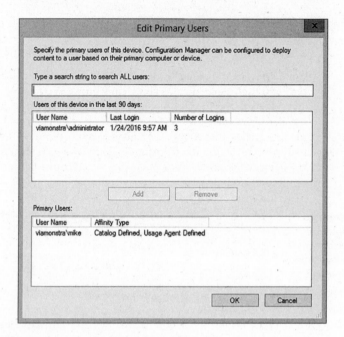

FIGURE 7.59
Edit Primary
Users

Troubleshooting Application Deployment

With any product, in-depth troubleshooting requires a good understanding of the overall system to know where to look and common things that might go wrong. Configuration Manager is a large product with many moving parts, so understanding how to troubleshoot effectively comes with experience. The depth of troubleshooting attempted will depend on available time and your experience level with the system. The latter will grow over time. Chapter 17, "Troubleshooting," discusses the troubleshooting options for Configuration Manager in general. It is useful to spend a few paragraphs discussing troubleshooting as it relates to Application Deployment. The intention here will be to augment the troubleshooting discussion from Chapter 17.

MONITORING

Configuration Manager is built to help administrators stay updated on the progress of various work and to flag when a problem is encountered; the Monitoring section of the console is designed specifically with that purpose in mind. Figure 7.60 shows the Deployments node of the Monitoring section.

The Deployments node allows administrators to see at a glance the progress of deployments in the environment. The top section of the screen is just a summary. Note that the sample Foxit Reader deployment is listed twice, one instance being the deployment targeted to users and the other instance targeted to systems. In this node it might be possible that a given deployment is shown as 100 percent compliant, yet no systems may have attempted to run the Foxit Reader application yet. Why might that be the case? In this case, compliance reflects that 100 percent of the targeted systems have accepted the deployment and reported back with a status.

FIGURE 7.60
Deployments
node of the
Monitoring
section

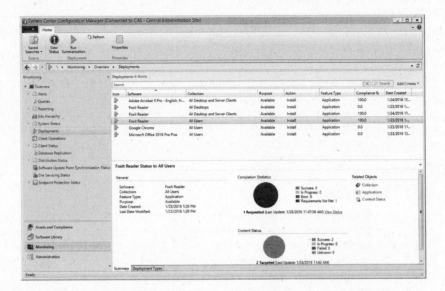

This would mean that the systems reporting back have evaluated the deployment and found it to fail the deployment validation—so status is reported back but no install is attempted. Taking this type of logic further, consider if this application had been delivered to a collection with six systems, but we receive status back for only two. Does that mean the other four are having issues? Maybe but not necessarily. If the application requirements exclude deployment to the other four systems, then they won't even show up. Remember what was mentioned earlier about how it is feasible to deploy everything to the All Systems collection provided sufficient requirements are in place for an application? This is an example of how that would work. To restate, deploying to the All Systems collection is not recommended, but it would be possible.

From the Summary view it is also possible to review the target collection, the state of the software, and the status of deployed content (see Figure 7.61).

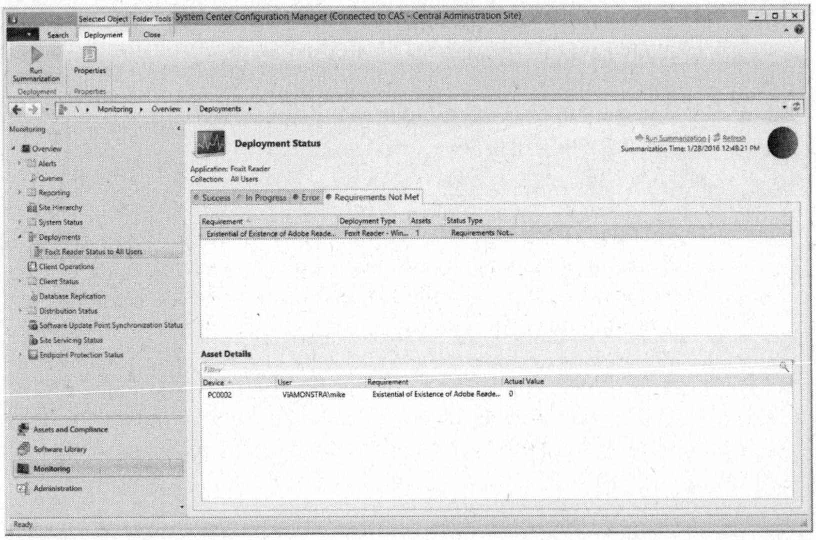

FIGURE 7.61
Deployment
status

Log Files

Configuration Manager provides an extensive set of log files to aid administrators in trouble-shooting scenarios. The information provided by the log files is significant, but even more detail is possible if you configure verbose or debug logging (covered in Chapter 17).

Logs in Configuration Manager are very beneficial for experienced administrators to quickly pinpoint a problem. For beginning administrators, though, the logs may be intimidating. Experience will help increase your comfort level with logs. A few suggestions will help keep things on track:

◆ Determine which logs to review.

Configuration Manager processes generally can be broken into processing that happens on the server and processing that happens on the client. The management point is in the middle and can have elements that interact with both the server and the client. The place to start reviewing log information depends on where the processing problem seems to be happening: server side or client side.

◆ Be patient.

The logging system in Configuration Manager is extensive, and finding the right log to review at first might be challenging. Many different Configuration Manager client components are required when trying to process an application deployment. These components pass information back and forth as the work gets done. With experience it becomes easier to know which log to start with, and it's well worth learning. Never fear, though; if it gets too time consuming to dig through the information provided, Microsoft support is just a phone call away.

◆ Watch the time stamp.

Following data in the log files boils down to following the time stamps. As logs update, their time stamps do too. A quick look at which logs have been active recently will help you identify logs that might be good candidates for review after an action is attempted and a failure encountered.

◆ Use CMTrace.

The log files are viewable with Notepad, but it's definitely not the best environment. The CMTrace utility (formerly known as Trace32) available in Configuration Manager is perfect for viewing Configuration Manager logs—and many other types of text logs as well. Trace includes an error-lookup capability, the ability to filter by keyword or processing thread, the ability to merge log files to view the entire conversation between components (remember the time stamp discussion?), and so on. The utility has been updated for Configuration Manager.

The Bottom Line

Explain the options available for Application Deployment.   The new Application Deployment model is a significant and welcome change for deploying software in the enterprise. There are many new components including a rules-based Requirements engine, the ability to detect whether the application is already installed, the option to configure application dependencies and relationships, and more.

> **Master It**   List several configuration options available for applications and deployment types.

Detail the various components required for Application Deployment.   Success with Application Deployment requires that several other Configuration Manager components be available and properly configured. The list includes management point(s), distribution point(s), IIS, BITS, the client itself, and possibly more.

> **Master It**   List the components required for configuring an application deployment.

Understand the role of and manage distribution points.   The role of distribution points has not changed significantly in that this is the role that makes content available to Configuration Manager devices and users. The options available for implementing the role have changed significantly with the inclusion of throttling control content flow from site server to remote distribution points, the single-instance storage approach for placing content on distribution points, the ability to detect content corruption, and the requirement that all distribution points be BITS enabled.

> **Master It**   Discuss the differences between implementing a distribution point role on the site server locally and remotely.

Chapter 8

Software Updates

Ever since the I Love You (ILoveyou) worm hit the Internet in May 2000 and the Nimda worm hit the Internet in September 2001, patch management has become a very important part of maintaining network security. Those worms revealed the importance of patch management because it was vulnerabilities in Windows that had allowed the worm to spread so fast around the world, and Microsoft had released patches for these vulnerabilities several months earlier.

At the time, patching an operating system was a labor-intensive task. Windows Update was available, but you still had to run it manually on each machine that needed updates. This meant connecting to the Internet, which was really too dangerous for corporate networks while ILoveyou and Nimda were spreading. As a result, network administrators and PC support staff ended up traveling to all their computers with a CD full of updates to get them patched up and safe again.

Microsoft released Software Update Services in 2002, and Systems Management Server (SMS) 2.0 got some patch-management functionality through an add-on feature pack. However, it wasn't until SMS 2003 that a truly functional patch-management solution was released for the corporate enterprise. SMS 2003 used Microsoft Update technology to detect and install its updates, and it allowed reporting to show the progress. This was not without its problems; as more and more patches became available for Microsoft's operating systems and applications, this patch solution became more taxing on server and workstation resources.

The Software Updates feature in Configuration Manager 2007 was rewritten from the ground up and made the software update process even more effective by leveraging the Windows Server Update Services (WSUS) product and incorporating its capabilities into patch management and also by taking some of the load off Configuration Manager clients in the process. With the introduction of Configuration Manager, Microsoft made configuring, deploying, and maintaining the software update role much easier than before. With the latest versions, a couple of new features are available.

In this chapter, you will learn to

- ◆ Plan to use Software Updates
- ◆ Configure Software Updates
- ◆ Use the Software Updates feature to manage software updates
- ◆ Use automatic update deployment to deploy software updates

Highlights in Software Updates

After integrating Windows Server Update Services in Configuration Manager 2007 as the Software Updates feature, Microsoft further enhanced the feature in the successors. With Configuration Manager you can manage your software updates more easily and quickly. The following great components are available when looking at the Software Updates feature:

Software Update Groups When you want to organize your software updates in your environment effectively, you need to use software update groups. With automatic deployment rules, you can add new updates automatically, or you can add them yourself manually. The deployment of software update groups can also be done automatically or manually.

With software update groups, you are also able to retrieve compliance information from devices for the software updates without deploying them.

Automatic Deployment Rules Software update administrators will have a ball with this feature. With automatic deployment rules, you can automatically deploy software updates. You can specify criteria for software updates, and the software updates are automatically added to the software update group. When creating an automatic deployment rule, you can, for instance, use all Windows 10 updates released since the last Patch Tuesday; this way the Windows 10 updates will be automatically added to the software update group. When a deployment for the software update group is available, the software updates will be automatically rolled out to your clients. With Configuration Manager Current Branch you are able to reuse an Automatic Deployment Rule by redeploying it to another collection.

Software Update Filtering The new Configuration Manager console has a good search engine; this search engine is also used for searching or filtering software updates. While defining a search, you can add a set of criteria that makes it easy to filter and find the updates you need. You can save the defined criteria when you are finished and use the criteria at future software update deployments.

With the results of the search, you can select those software updates and add them to an existing or new software update group. You can also see the compliance information about the selected updates.

Software Update Monitoring The in-console monitoring feature is also implemented in the Software Updates feature. The Configuration Manager console provides monitoring information about software updates and running processes. For instance, you can view the following information:

- Compliance and deployment information about key software updates
- Detailed state messages for the deployments and software update assets
- Error codes with additional information for software updates
- State messages for software update synchronizations
- Alerts for software update issues

Besides information in the Configuration Manager console, you can also use the software update reports that are available out of the box.

Managing Superseded Software Updates   In Configuration Manager, software updates automatically expired after being superseded. This was done in the full software update synchronization process. You could not deploy superseded software updates because they were expired, and Configuration Manager doesn't allow you to deploy expired software updates.

Configuration Manager lets you choose to manage superseded software updates. You can also choose to configure a specific period of time in which the software update doesn't automatically expire after being superseded. This way, you can deploy superseded software updates if necessary.

HOW TO MANAGE EXPIRED UPDATES

If software updates are expired, you can easily identify them and remove the membership of the software update groups. After you remove the membership, the WSUS cleanup wizard will remove the expired updates from the distribution points, when the option is selected on the Software Update Point. This allows you to remove the expired updates from your distribution points in the Configuration Manager hierarchy.

Increased User Control over Installation of Software Updates   The Empower Users pillar of Configuration Manager fits perfectly in the Software Updates feature. Configuration Manager allows users to have more control over when software updates are installed on their devices (Figure 8.1). Users can schedule or reschedule software installations or updates via the Software Center during nonworking hours.

FIGURE 8.1
Defining business hours in the Software Center

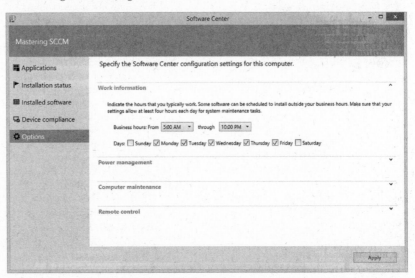

Software Update Files Are Stored in the Content Library   The content of software updates is also stored in the content library of Configuration Manager. The single-instance storage of the content library is also used for software updates. Before content files are downloaded, Configuration Manager checks to see if the content file is already in the content library. If the content file is available, it will use that file for the new software update.

Administrative Access Especially for the Software Update features, a role for software update management is defined in role-based administration. You can delegate the deployment of software updates to your systems to the security officer, for instance. Or you can delegate it to a local administrator by limiting the scope of the role assignment.

Software Update Deployment Template In ConfigMgr Current Branch you can only create deployment templates with the Automatic Deployment Rules wizard or the Deploy Software Updates Wizard. The deployment template stores many of the deployment properties that will not change when you create new deployments.

Prerequisites for Software Updates

Before you can plan and set up the Software Updates feature, you need to be familiar with its components so that you can determine which ones to install and configure for your environment. Table 8.1 provides a list of these components.

TABLE 8.1:   External prerequisites to the Configuration Manager Software Updates feature

PREREQUISITE	DESCRIPTION
Windows Server Update Services (WSUS) 3.0 SP2 or later on Windows Server 2008 R2	Software Updates requires WSUS 3.0 or later to be installed before setting up the Software Update Point Site system role because it is used for update synchronization and compliance assessment on clients.
Windows Server Update Services (WSUS) 4 or later on Windows Server 2012 and Windows Server 2012 R2	Software Updates requires WSUS 4.0 or later to be installed before setting up the Software Update Point Site system role because it is used for update synchronization and compliance assessment on clients.
WSUS Administrator Console	The WSUS Administrator Console is required on the Configuration Manager site server when WSUS is not on the site server itself. The console is required in order to communicate with a remote WSUS server.
Windows Update Agent (WUA) 3.0 or later	The WUA 3.0 client or later is required, in addition to the Configuration Manager client, to connect to the WSUS server so it can retrieve the list of software updates that need to be scanned for.
Background Intelligent Transfer Service (BITS) 2.5	Microsoft highly recommends that BITS be enabled and configured for a Configuration Manager site and that distribution points also be BITS enabled. Because software updates are downloaded to the local client cache before they are installed, having BITS enabled will allow clients to continue a download of updates if a client is disconnected from a distribution point.
Windows Installer 3.1	Certain updates, such as ones for Microsoft Office, require Windows Installer 3.1 or they will not be detected during a scan for compliance.
Site server communication to the software update point (SUP)	There may be configuration settings that need to be examined depending on your software update point infrastructure and Configuration Manager settings. We will go into that in more detail in the section on planning the software update point installation.

Of course, you will also need to configure a SQL Reporting Services (SRS) reporting point before you can use the Software Updates reports. We'll go into more detail on configuring a reporting point in Chapter 12, "Reporting."

Elements of Software Updates

Before you can plan to implement the Software Update process, you need to become familiar with the various elements of the process and their roles in the overall picture.

Software Update Point

As discussed in Chapter 4, "Installation and Site Role Configuration," the *software update point* is a site system role that is required for managing software updates in Configuration Manager. Each Configuration Manager CAS or primary site must have at least one software update point that is able to synchronize with a source like Microsoft Update before it can deploy software updates to Configuration Manager clients. The Software Update Point role can only be configured on a server that already has Windows Server Update Services (WSUS) 3.0 SP2 or 4.0 installed. The software update point software provides the bridge between the WSUS components and Configuration Manager. It allows synchronization with the WSUS database to download the latest software update information from Microsoft Update and locally published updates.

When the Software Update Point Site system role is created and configured as the software update point that synchronizes with a synchronization source, the software update point components are installed and enabled. The WSUS Control Manager component configures the associated WSUS server with the settings that were chosen when you set up the Software Update Point Site system role.

When you are deploying a CAS, you need to install the software update point in the CAS first.

The software update point settings can be changed from the Software Update Component Properties window via the Configuration Manager console:

1. Choose the System Center Configuration Manager console ➤ Administration ➤ Overview ➤ Site Configuration ➤ Sites.

2. Select the site for which you want to change properties.

3. Choose Configure Site Components ➤ Software Update Point.

The software update point settings can modify the Software Update Point Site system server, the synchronization source, the schedule, and the products, classifications, and languages for which software updates will be synced with the database. You will find more details on these settings later in the chapter.

The first time the software update point completes its synchronization, the Software Updates client agent components are activated from a dormant state. They will connect on a schedule to WSUS on the software update point server to start a scan for update scan compliance, as described earlier in the chapter.

Software Updates Agent

The Software Updates Agent is part of the Configuration Manager client. You can configure the Software Updates Agent with the client settings. With Configuration Manager you can create different client agent settings for groups of computers, so you are able to assign different settings for different groups of computers and servers. For instance, you can configure client settings for computers in such a way that all mandatory software updates that reach their deadline are installed immediately. For servers you can configure a different setting.

Software Updates Metadata

A software update has two parts: the software update file(s) and the metadata. The metadata is contained in the Configuration Manager database and provides information about the software update, including its name, description, products supported, update class, size, article ID, download URL, rules that apply, and so on.

Most important, the metadata for each software update defines what products are applicable to the update. A product (for example, Windows 10) is a specific edition of an OS or application. A product family (for example, Microsoft Windows) is a base OS or application from which single products come. You can select a product family or individual products when choosing what will be synced by Configuration Manager.

> **MULTIPLE PRODUCT UPDATES**
>
> If an update is applicable to many products, and at least a few of those products from a product family have been chosen for synchronization, then all the updates will appear in the Configuration Manager console.

The metadata for each update also defines the update's *classification*. This represents the type of software an update will modify on clients. There can be many different classifications for any given product family, which we will go over in the "Planning to Use Software Updates in Configuration Manager" section later in this chapter. The metadata also defines what languages the update file is applicable to, and it provides a summary of the software update in one or more languages.

Software Update Files

The software update files are the actual files that the client downloads, such as an EXE, a Windows Installer file (MSI), a Microsoft Update Standalone Package (MSU), or a Windows Installer patch (MSP), and then installs to update a component or application. The software update file might be stored on a WSUS server that is configured to be a software update point, or source location for all of your packages, but it is always stored on distribution points for the site when the software update is downloaded or deployed. The process is as follows:

1. Software update files are retrieved from either the upstream server or Microsoft Update.

   An upstream server is a software update point higher in the Configuration Manager hierarchy.

2. The updates are then copied to distribution points when the software update is downloaded using the Download Software Updates Wizard or deployed to clients using the Deploy Software Updates Wizard.

   Both methods are covered in detail later in this chapter.

3. Both methods download the software update files to a temporary location on the site server hard drive.

4. The site server creates and stores a compressed package file containing the software update.

5. It decompresses the package file.

6. Then it copies the update file to the content library on the distribution point.

Software Update Objects

The Software Updates node in the Configuration Manager console is divided into four nodes, as shown in Figure 8.2.

In these nodes you will find the items that are related to the Software Updates feature. Table 8.2 lists the items that are related to Software Updates.

TABLE 8.2:   Software Updates related items

OBJECT	DESCRIPTION
All Software Updates	Every software update has a configuration item object that is created during the software update sync cycle.
Software Update Groups	These are fixed sets of software updates that can be used for delegated administration and creating software update deployments.
Deployment Packages	These host the software update source files.
Automatic Deployment Rules	Automatic deployment rules give you the ability to automatically download and deploy software updates to all or a subset of your devices.
Deployment Template	This stores many of the deployment properties that may not change from one deployment to the next and are used to save time and ensure consistency when creating deployments. The deployment template is stored within the Configuration Manager database and is accessible only when creating a deployment or an automatic deployment rule.
Search	This feature provides an easy way to retrieve a set of software updates that meet the search criteria; the searches can be saved in the Configuration Manager database.

As noted in some of the preceding descriptions, software update deployment and deployment package objects are replicated from the site where they were created to all sites in the Configuration Manager hierarchy. The objects replicated to a child site will be read-only. Even though the properties for these objects must be modified at the site where they were created, the actions available for deployments at child sites are the same as those at the site where they were created. Also, deployment packages can be used to host the software updates that are deployed on the child sites.

Software Update Groups

A software update group in Configuration Manager contains a set of software updates. Software update groups offer several benefits for deploying and monitoring software updates and are part of Microsoft's recommended Software Updates workflow.

Using a software update group allows you to automate the process of deploying software updates with automatic deployment rules. Tracking the compliance state for the software updates in deployments is an important task for Configuration Manager admins. If deployments are made without update groups, it's very hard to get the overall compliance state for the same set of software updates that have been sent out with multiple deployments. When update groups are used instead, you can use the Compliance 1 - Overall Compliance report for the set of updates in the software update group or the Compliance 3 - Update Group (Per Update) report to get a list of the updates in an update group and the overall compliance of each. This is a great reason to use software update groups as a part of your software update procedure.

Deployment Templates

Deployment templates can store many of the software update deployment properties, and they can be created for consistency, to save time, or to fit your software update procedures. You can create a deployment template in the process of creating a deployment or automatic deployment rule and save the settings in a template. Table 8.3 shows the deployment properties that are saved in a deployment template.

TABLE 8.3: Deployment template properties

SETTING	DESCRIPTION
Collection	Indicates the collection that will be targeted for the software update deployment. This setting is optional when you make a deployment template.
Deployment Settings	Configured deployment settings such as Send Wake-up Packets or Verbosity Level are saved in the deployment template.
Deployment Schedule	Sets whether the user will be notified of pending updates, the installation progress for updates, whether the client evaluates the deployment schedule in local or Coordinated Universal Time (UTC), and the timeframe between when an update is available and when it is mandatory on clients.
User Experience	Hides software update installation and notifications. Sets the system restart behavior when an update installs on a client and needs to restart to finish. Also allows a system restart to be completed outside a maintenance window.

TABLE 8.3:   Deployment template properties   *(continued)*

Setting	Description
Alerts	Sets if alerts are generated for the in-console alerting feature. Sets whether Operations Manager alerts are disabled while updates install and/or send an alert if the install fails.
Download Settings	Sets how clients will interact with the distribution points when they get a software update deployment.
Deployment Location	Sets whether to download the software updates from the Internet or a network file share.
Language Settings	Sets the language of the software updates that need to be downloaded and deployed.

Creating deployment templates in advance for typical deployment scenarios in your environment allows you to create deployments using templates that populate many of the properties that are most often static for the particular deployment scenario. Using the deployment template also reduces the number of wizard pages to work through in the Deploy Software Updates Wizard by up to seven pages, depending on what information you have already populated. This not only saves time but also helps to prevent mistakes when setting up a deployment.

Deployment Packages

A *deployment package* is the method used to download software updates (either one or several) to a network shared folder, which must be manually created before it is used, and copy the software updates source file to distribution points defined in the deployment. The Deployment Package can also be created as part of the Deploy Software Updates Wizard, discussed later in this chapter.

Software updates can be downloaded and added to deployment packages prior to deploying them by using the Download Software Updates Wizard. This wizard provides admins with the capability to provision software updates on distribution points and verify that this part of the deployment process works properly.

When downloaded software updates are deployed using the Deploy Software Updates Wizard, the deployment automatically uses the deployment package that contains each software update. When software updates are selected that haven't been downloaded or deployed, a new or existing deployment package must be specified in the Deploy Software Updates Wizard, and the updates are downloaded to the package when the wizard is finished.

There is no hard link between a deployment and a specific deployment package. Clients will install software updates in a deployment by using any distribution point that has the software updates, regardless of the deployment package. Even if a deployment package is deleted for an active deployment, clients will still be able to install the software updates in the deployment—as long as each update has been defined in at least one other deployment package and is present on a distribution point that the client can get to. To help prevent software update deployment failures, you should make sure that deployment packages are sent to a group of distribution points that can be accessed by all the clients you are targeting.

Deployment package access accounts allow you to set permissions to specify users and user groups who can access a deployment package folder on distribution points. Configuration Manager makes these folders available to everyone by default, but you can modify this access if required for a specific security need.

Configuration Manager client computers also have the option of selective download: A deployment package might contain both updates that are required for a client and some that are not, but the client can determine which software updates are applicable and retrieve only those files. This allows admins to have multiple updates in a single deployment package and use it to target clients that might need only some of those updates.

Deployments

While it is deployment packages that host the update files, it is *software update deployments* that actually deliver software updates to clients. The Deploy Software Updates Wizard is used to create deployments and can be started using several methods, which we will detail later in the chapter. Table 8.4 lists all the pages in this wizard and describes the settings that can be configured in each one to create a software update deployment.

TABLE 8.4:   Deploy Software Updates Wizard settings

PAGE	DESCRIPTION
General	Provides the name of and comments about the deployment; the update or update group and collection also need to be supplied.
Deployment Settings	Defines if the deployment is required or optional and sets the verbosity level. Also configures whether to send wake-up packets.
Scheduling	Sets whether the user will be notified of pending updates and/or the installation progress for updates, if the client evaluates the deployment schedule in local or Coordinated Universal Time, and the timeframe between when an update is available and when it is mandatory on clients.
User Experience	Defines whether users will receive notice of installations of software updates and what happens when an installation deadline is reached. Defines the system restart behavior when an update installs on a client and needs to restart to finish. Defines whether the Windows Embedded write filter is enabled or bypassed for this deployment.
Alerts	Sets the in-console alert handling of Configuration Manager and sets if System Center Operations Manager (SCOM) alerts are disabled while updates install and whether to send an alert if the install fails.
Download Settings	Sets how clients will interact with the distribution points when they get a software update deployment. Defines whether clients should use Microsoft Updates for content download if the updates are not present on the preferred distribution point, or whether to download software update content when on a metered Internet connection.

TABLE 8.4:   Deploy Software Updates Wizard settings   *(continued)*

PAGE	DESCRIPTION
Deployment Package	Shows the deployment package that will host the software updates for the deployment. This setting won't appear if the updates have already been downloaded to a package.
Download Location	Lets you choose to download the updates from the Internet or from a source on the local network.
Languages Selection	Lets you select the languages for which the software updates that will be in the deployment are downloaded.

If an update in a deployment has Microsoft Software License Terms that have not been accepted yet, then a Review/Accept License Terms dialog box will appear before the Deploy Software Updates Wizard and give you a chance to review and accept the license terms. When you accept the terms, then you can deploy the updates. If you don't accept the terms, the process is canceled.

Automatic Deployment Rules

A great Software Updates feature in Configuration Manager is Automatic Deployment Rules. This feature lets you define rules for specific types of software updates that can be downloaded and added to a software update group automatically. If a software update group is enabled for deployment, the updates are automatically deployed to your workstations. The Automatic Deployment Rules feature can be used for two common scenarios:

- Automatically deploying Endpoint Protection definition and engine updates
- Patch Tuesday security patches

For both scenarios, two out-of-the-box templates are available to assist you in creating the automatic deployment rules. When you create an automatic deployment rule, you need to define whether you want to add the updates to an existing software update group or automatically create a software update group.

When you deploy Endpoint Protection (System Center Endpoint Protection) definition and engine updates, you can add these updates to an existing software update group. The reason for this is that only four definition updates are available per agent for Endpoint Protection. Three of them are superseded, and only one is active. Every fifth definition update will be expired and fall out of the software update group. Configuration Manager is able to run the automatic deployment rule up to three times a day, in line with the definition updates publishing frequency. An automatic deployment rule can have deployments to one or more collections; depending on the availability and deadlines, you are able to deploy one automatic deployment rule on different times with different deadlines.

If you want to deploy the Tuesday patches automatically, it is recommended that you create a new software update group every Patch Tuesday. This keeps your software updates organized.

You can automatically select software updates based on the following parameters:

- Article ID
- Bulletin ID
- Custom severity
- Date released or revised
- Description
- Language
- Product
- Required
- Severity
- Superseded
- Title
- Update classification
- Vendor

Running an automatic deployment rule for a longer time can result in a very large package size. You are able to change the deployment package in an automatic deployment rule to limit the size of the package.

AUTOMATIC DEPLOYMENT OF PATCH TUESDAY SOFTWARE UPDATES

The Automatic Deployment Rules feature allows you to automate the deployment of software updates. You can use it to automatically deploy the Patch Tuesday software updates for test purposes or prepare the deployment in production. Depending on your requirements, you can configure an automatic deployment rule for Windows 10 Patch Tuesday updates by creating an automatic deployment rule with the following steps:

1. Create a new software update group each time the rule runs. This way, you are able to group the update groups per Patch Tuesday cycle, and you will limit the size of the software update deployment.

2. Select Enable The Deployment after this rule has run.

3. Select a collection with your test systems where you want to automatically test the Patch Tuesday patches.

4. Supply the following search criteria for the rule:

   - Product: Windows 10
   - Date Released Or Revised: Last 1 Day
   - Update Classification: Security Updates

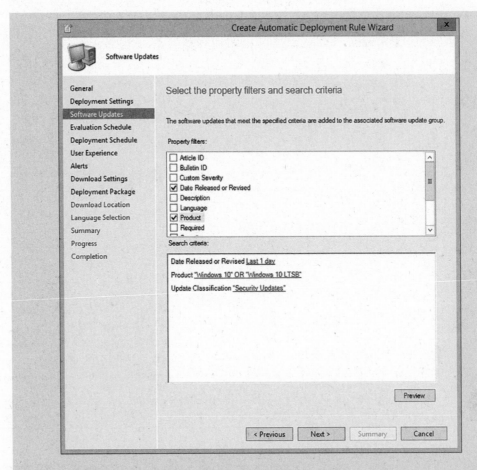

5. Before going further, preview the number of updates that will be initially discovered. This way, you can test your criteria before going into production and, for instance, accidentally deploying hundreds of updates automatically.

6. Evaluation Schedule: Be sure the evaluation runs after the Software Update Synchronization Schedule on the second Tuesday of every month.

7. Deployment Schedule: Enable the availability of the deployment for four hours after the deployment is created so that you are sure that the deployment has been distributed throughout your Configuration Manager hierarchy. Configure whether you want the deadline for the deployment.

After you configure the rest of the automatic deployment rule, the rule will create a software update deployment every second Tuesday of the month.

If you want to also automatically deploy the patch Tuesday updates to more than one collection with a different deadline, deployments can be added. Adding a deployment can be done by selecting the automatic deployment rule and clicking Add Deployment from the ribbon in the Configuration Manager console.

continues

continued

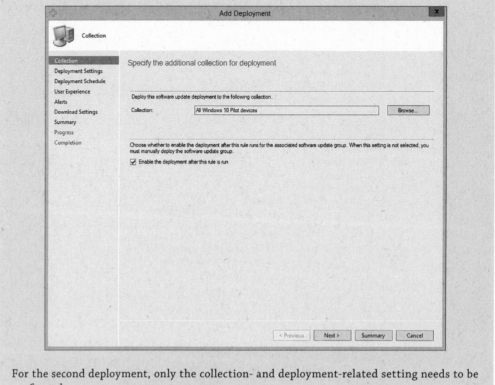

For the second deployment, only the collection- and deployment-related setting needs to be configured.

System Center Updates Publisher

The System Center Updates Publisher was built on the custom updates framework that was introduced in Systems Management Server 2003 R2. Updates Publisher is a standalone tool that enables independent software vendors or line-of-business developers to import custom software update catalogs, create and modify software update definitions, export update definitions to catalogs, and publish software update information to a configured WSUS server. By using Updates Publisher to define software updates and publish them to the WSUS server, the Software Updates feature in Configuration Manager is able to synchronize the custom update from the WSUS server database to the site server database. This will allow you to enable client computers to scan for custom update compliance and to provide administrators with the ability to deploy the custom updates to client computers. More information about SCUP can be found at https://technet.microsoft.com/en-us/library/hh134747.aspx#PublishToServer2012.

The Software Update Process in Configuration Manager

As you'll see throughout the hands-on portions of this chapter, the biggest parts of the software update process are planning and configuration. After you've completed those, Configuration Manager itself performs three main operational phases: synchronization, scanning for compliance, and deployment.

Synchronization

Synchronization is the process of retrieving the metadata for software updates that meet the configured criteria; it can be retrieved from the upstream Windows Server Update Services (WSUS) 3.0 SP2 server, the WSUS 4.0 server, or Microsoft Update. The WSUS Synchronization Manager component on the software update point works with WSUS to complete the synchronization process. The highest site (central administration site) in the Configuration Manager hierarchy that has a software update point synchronizes with, for instance, Microsoft Update; this is done either on a schedule you set up or manually by using the Synchronize Software Updates action on the All Software Updates node in the Configuration Manager console. (We go into more detail on how to do that later in the chapter.) When a sync cycle is started at the CAS, the WSUS Synchronization Manager makes a request to the WSUS service to start a sync cycle. The software update's metadata is then synchronized from Microsoft Update, and any changes are inserted into the WSUS database.

When WSUS finishes its sync cycle, WSUS Synchronization Manager starts syncing with the WSUS database and inserts any changes into the site server database. When that process is finished, the WSUS Synchronization Manager component (SMS_WSUS_SYNC_MANAGER) creates a status message with an ID of 6702.

DIFFERENCE BETWEEN SCHEDULED AND MANUAL SYNCHRONIZATION

A scheduled synchronization does a full sync, but the Run Synchronization action does only a delta sync. Updates are marked as expired if they are superseded by another software update or marked as expired in the update catalog. They are marked as expired only during the scheduled synchronization.

When a sync is run on a schedule, all changes to the software update metadata since the last scheduled sync are put into the site database. This includes metadata that is new (products, languages, and so on), modified, or removed. A manually run sync will be faster than a scheduled one because it downloads only delta changes to what already exists in the database. When adding or removing a classification or product, a full sync will take place when executing a manual sync.

When a software update sync finishes at the CAS, a sync request is sent out to all of its child sites. When a child site gets that request, it will first sync itself from its parent site and then send out a request to any child sites that are configured as software update points. This continues on down the hierarchy until all child sites have been synchronized.

With an Internet-based software update point (which is also used in Network Access Protection scenarios), a sync request is sent to it right after the software update point that synchronizes with the synchronization source is finished with its syncing request. The process for both is the same except that the upstream server of the Internet-based software update point is automatically configured to be the first software update point for the site, and the site server database is not updated when the Internet-based software update point finishes its sync cycle.

If the synchronization fails, there is a retry interval of 60 minutes. The WSUS Synchronization Manager component will schedule the sync to run again 60 minutes after the process fails and start over. WSUS Synchronization Manager will create a status message with an ID of 6703 in the case of a sync failure.

Compliance

When software update synchronization completes at each site, a sitewide machine policy is created that allows client computers to retrieve the location of the WSUS server and to start a scan for software update compliance. When a client receives that machine policy, a compliance assessment scan is scheduled to start at a random time within the next two hours. When the scan runs, a component of the client Software Updates Agent clears the previous scan history, sends a request to find the WSUS server that should be used for the scan, and then updates the local Group Policy with the WSUS server location.

The scan request is then passed to the Windows Update Agent (WUA). The WUA then connects to the WSUS server that it just got information about, downloads a list of the software updates that have been synced with the WSUS server, and scans the client computer for the updates in the list. A component of the Software Updates Agent then sees that the scan for compliance is finished and sends a state message for each software update that had a change in compliance state since the last scan. Those state messages are then sent to the client's management point in bulk every five minutes. The management point will then forward the state messages to the site server, where they are inserted into the site server database.

Supersedence occurs when a new software update has the same fixes as a previous update but may have fixed issues with the update and/or added new fixes. In SMS 2003, when new software updates supersede ones that had the same fixes, they may both be marked as needed when only the new one is necessary. In Configuration Manager Software Updates, you can configure the supersedence behavior; you can choose to expire a superseded update or to expire the update after a configurable number of months at the software update point. When new software updates are released that supersede others, Microsoft Update is refreshed with that information. When client computers are scanned for compliance, the new updates produce a compliance state by the client, but the older updates do not. The only time this is not the case is when a service pack contains a required update. The WUA will then return a compliance state on both, which allows admins to deploy individual updates or service packs as needed. Table 8.5 shows details on the four states of compliance for Software Updates.

TABLE 8.5: Software Updates compliance states

STATE	DESCRIPTION
Required	The software update is applicable to the client, which means any of the following conditions could be true:
	◆ The update has not been deployed to the client.
	◆ The update has been installed, but the state of the update hasn't been updated in the database yet.
	◆ The update has been installed, but the client requires a reboot before it finishes.
	◆ The update has been deployed but is not yet installed.
Not Required	The update isn't applicable on the client.
Installed	The update is applicable on the client, and it has already been installed.
Unknown	This state usually means that the software update has been synced to the site server, but the client hasn't been scanned for compliance for that update. The unknown state can also mean that the client has not sent a state message for compliance of a particular update. In which case, if you suspect that the client should have installed an update and is reporting unknown, you can force the client to send up its state messages.

Deployment

The compliance assessment data is then used to determine which software updates are required on client computers. When you create a software update deployment with the Deploy Software Updates Wizard, as described later in this chapter, the software updates in the deployment are downloaded from the location specified on the Download Location page of the wizard to the configured package source, if they haven't been downloaded already. When the wizard finishes, a deployment policy is added to the machine policy for the site. The updates are then copied from the package source to the shared folders on the distribution points set up in the package, where they will be available for clients.

When a client in the target collection of the deployment receives the machine policy, the software update client component starts an evaluation scan. Updates that are still required on the client are then added to a class in Windows Management Instrumentation (WMI). Any updates that are mandatory deployments are downloaded as soon as possible from the distribution point to the local cache on the client. The updates in the optional deployment category are not downloaded until they are manually started. If an optional deployment has a deadline that makes it mandatory, the client will download the update as soon as it registers the change in deployment status.

> **SOFTWARE UPDATES IN CONFIGURATION MANAGER ARE ALWAYS DOWNLOADED TO THE CLIENT**
>
> Like in Configuration Manager 2012, software updates are always downloaded to the local client cache before they are run in Configuration Manager Current Branch. You don't have the option to have them run from a distribution point as you did in Configuration Manager 2007.

If the client can't find the location of the distribution point through Location Services (via requests of the management point), it will keep trying to find a distribution point for up to 5 days before it stops. If the client can't connect to the distribution point to which it has been referred as a source of the software updates in order to download the updates, it will try for up to 10 days before it stops trying. When you start updates manually, the client will try every hour for each distribution point for up to 4 hours before it fails.

When an update deployment has a deadline that becomes available for deployment on a client, the Available Software Update icon will show up in the notification area to tell a user that the deadline is coming up. By default, these display notifications will show up on a periodic basis until all mandatory updates have been installed. They will be displayed every 48 hours for deadlines more than 24 hours away, every 4 hours for deadlines less than 24 hours away, and every 15 minutes for deadlines less than an hour away.

Just imagine the phone calls you'd get if you left things that way! Fortunately, Microsoft has given you the option to turn these notifications off with the client agent settings that let you hide all software update deployments from users. This setting doesn't affect regular software deployment settings, but it will keep display notifications, notification area icons, and software update installation progress boxes from appearing at all. However, this will also mean that you can send out only mandatory software update deployments to your clients. We recommend doing this anyway because users will more than likely delay deployments until they become mandatory.

Unless you hide your update deployments, users will be able to open the Express/Advanced dialog to start up the installation of all mandatory software updates at once. They will also be able to open the Available Software Updates dialog, where they can choose to install whatever is available.

When the deadline passes on a mandatory update, a scan will start on the client to make sure that the updates are still required; the local client cache will be checked to make sure the updates are still available, and then the updates will be started. When that is done, another scan will start to make sure that the updates are no longer required on the client. Finally, a state message is sent to the management point saying that the updates are now installed.

LIMIT OF 1,000 SOFTWARE UPDATES IN A DEPLOYMENT

Be sure to limit the number of software updates in your software update deployments. Configuration Manager supports up to 1,000 software updates per deployment. When using automatic deployment rules, be sure that the criteria you use will not return more than 1,000 software updates as a result.

Planning to Use Software Updates in Configuration Manager

Now that you have seen what's new in Configuration Manager Software Updates, the prerequisites, and the major components of the process, you can plan the use of Software Updates in your environment.

To do so, you can use the same process of deployment intelligence that you used to plan the deployment of Configuration Manager itself in Chapter 2, "Planning a Configuration Manager Infrastructure." Using this method will help you ensure that you get everything out of Software Updates that your company requires to keep your computer resources up to date with the latest software upgrades and patches.

Deployment intelligence for Software Updates has three phases:

◆ Determine what needs to be accomplished with Software Updates.

◆ Determine what's on the network now and what has been used in the past.

◆ Test in an isolated lab.

Determining What Needs to Be Accomplished

This may seem like a no-brainer, because the first thing that probably comes to mind is "deploy patches," but with Configuration Manager you can do a lot more than just deploy security patches, as you will soon learn.

This part of the planning will also let you decide how you want to configure your test environment, your software update point infrastructure, and the settings for the Software Updates servers and client agent.

PLANNING FOR SOFTWARE UPDATE POINT INFRASTRUCTURE

Software update points can be used in a hierarchy or in standalone sites. In both cases you need to plan the placement of the software update point. Determine whether you need more than one software update point in a site.

Planning Software Update Points in a Hierarchy

When you have a Configuration Manager hierarchy, the CAS server is at the top of the Configuration Manager hierarchy. One software update point is configured on the CAS so that software updates can be managed. Most of the synchronization settings are configured there and propagated down to the rest of the sites in the hierarchy. The software update point on the CAS is what syncs with Microsoft Update or another upstream WSUS server. The software update points in the primary sites that are children of the CAS are automatically configured to synchronize with the software update point in the CAS.

When using a software update point in a primary site with secondary sites, the child sites sync with the software update point that is set up on the parent site. Secondary sites can be set up with a software update point, or clients at the secondary site can connect directly to the software update point on the parent primary site.

Planning a Software Update Point in a Standalone Primary Site

When you have only a single primary site, the software update point needs to be configured on the primary site server, and it will sync with Microsoft Update or another upstream WSUS server.

Planning to Add More than One Software Update Point per Primary Site

With Configuration Manager you are able to install more than one software update point per primary site. When installing more than one software update point in your primary site, you can create a form of high availability for deploying software updates. By adding software update points, you provide the ability for clients to switch between software update points when one is unavailable. Switching software update points is based on a software update point list; this list allows the client to randomly select a software update point when the configured software update point is not available. Configuration Manager can provide a client with a different list, depending on the type of client:

Intranet-Based Clients   Intranet-based clients will receive a list of software update points that are configured to allow connections from the intranet only combined with those that allow connections from the Internet and intranet.

Internet-Based Clients   Internet-based clients will receive a list of software update points that are configured to allow connections from the Internet only combined with those that allow connections from the Internet and intranet.

The software update points that are in the same Active Directory forest are prioritized above the ones that are not in the same forest but are part of the same Configuration Manager infrastructure.

When using software update point switching, keep the following in mind. When a client is assigned to one software update point, it stays assigned to this software update point until it fails and becomes unavailable. Then the client will automatically connect to a different software update point. It stays assigned to this new software update point until it fails and becomes unavailable, even if the first software update point becomes available again. The following process is used to switch a software update point:

1. When an initiated or scheduled software update scan fails, the client waits 30 minutes and retries the scan using the same software update point.

2. After the scan fails four times at an interval of 30 minutes (2 hours total), the client waits another 2 minutes before switching to another software update point based on the software update point list.

3. When the software update scan is successful, the client will be connected to the new software update point going forward.

When using this default method in a large environment and one software update point becomes unavailable for a longer time, all clients will be connected to one software update point. This may cause unnecessary extra load on the software update point. Another, better way is using network load balancing (NLB); this way, the clients will connect to the virtual IP address of the network load balancer instead of directly to the site server.

If you are going to have more than 25,000 clients connecting to WSUS on a software update point, new software update points can be added.

Planning for Internet

When your site is in secure (HTTPS) mode, you have the option to configure a software update point to accept connections from clients on both the intranet and the Internet, from only clients on the intranet, or from only clients on the Internet. When Internet-based client connectivity is not accepted on the primary software update point used for clients in the intranet, you can set up separate Internet-based software update points if needed.

This site system server role must be assigned to a site system server that is remote from the site server and the software update point. When the Internet-based software update point doesn't have connectivity to the first software update point for the site, you will have to use the export and import functions of the WSUSUtil tool to sync the software update metadata.

PLANNING FOR THE SOFTWARE UPDATE POINT INSTALL

Before setting up the Software Update Point Site system role in Configuration Manager, you must consider several requirements depending on your Configuration Manager infrastructure, such as when the software update point will be configured to communicate using Secure Sockets Layer (SSL), or when the site server is in secure mode, and so on. You must take additional steps before the software update point in the hierarchy will work properly.

As discussed earlier in the chapter, Software Updates requires that the last version of Windows Server Update Services be installed on all site systems servers that will be configured for the Software Update Point Site system role. There can be many site systems with the Software Update Point Site role, but only one site system can be configured as the software update point. Also, when the software update point is not on the site server itself, the WSUS administrative console is required on the site server, which lets the site server communicate with the WSUS components on the software update point. You can configure an account to connect to a remote WSUS server or a WSUS server in another forest.

During the WSUS install, you can choose to use the default or a custom website to host the WSUS components. If WSUS is going to be installed on a primary Configuration Manager site system, Microsoft recommends that you choose a custom website so that IIS hosts the WSUS services in a dedicated website instead of sharing the site with Configuration Manager site systems or other applications.

You can use a WSUS server that was active in your environment before Configuration Manager was implemented. When the WSUS server is configured as the first software update point, the sync settings are then specified. All of the software update metadata from the WSUS server will be synced to the Configuration Manager database regardless of the sync settings for the software update point. Be sure to disable the Group Policies that point the clients to the WSUS server.

When your Configuration Manager site server is in secure mode or when the software update point is configured to use SSL, a web server certificate must be assigned to the website used by WSUS. When you use a custom website for WSUS, per Microsoft's recommendation, the WSUS website must be assigned a web server certificate where the Subject Name or Subject Alternate Name field contains the Internet fully qualified domain name (FQDN). The upstream WSUS server must be set with the same certificate, or SSL communication will fail between the servers. The certificate must also reside in Trusted Root Certification Authorities in the Computer certificate store on each client computer, or it will fail to scan for software update compliance.

When the site server is in secure mode, the web server certificate that is used for the Configuration Manager site systems can also be used by the WSUS website. Also, when the WSUS uses the same website as the Configuration Manager site server, and the site is in secure mode, the default website might already be assigned the right web server certificate. The certificate would still need to be configured on the upstream WSUS server, but it should already be configured on Configuration Manager clients.

If there is a firewall between the Configuration Manager software update point and the Internet, a software update point and its upstream server, or an Internet-based software update point and the software update point for the site, the firewall might have to be configured to accept the HTTP and HTTPS ports used for the WSUS website. By default, a WSUS server that is configured for the default website uses port 80 for HTTP and 443 for HTTPS communication, whereas one configured for a custom website uses port 8530 for HTTP and 8531 for HTTPS communication.

If your company doesn't allow these ports and protocols to be open for all addresses on the firewall between the software update point and the Internet, you can restrict access to the following URLs so that WSUS and Automatic Updates can communicate with Microsoft Update.

```
http://windowsupdate.microsoft.com

http://*.windowsupdate.microsoft.com

https://*.windowsupdate.microsoft.com

http://*.update.microsoft.com

https://*.update.microsoft.com

http://*.windowsupdate.com

http://download.windowsupdate.com

http://download.microsoft.com

http://*.download.windowsupdate.com

http://test.stats.update.microsoft.com

http://ntservicepack.microsoft.com
```

If there is an Internet-based software update point, or there are child sites with a software update point, these addresses might also need to be added to a firewall between the servers:

```
http://<FQDN for software update point on child site>

https://<FQDN for software update point on child site>

http://<FQDN for software update point on parent site>

https://<FQDN for software update point on parent site>
```

PLANNING THE SOFTWARE UPDATE SERVER SETTINGS

There are software update point settings and general site settings that have an impact on software updates in Configuration Manager. These settings configure the first software update point and determine which updates are synchronized, whether there are maintenance windows for installing updates, how much time software updates have to complete, and so on.

The software update point settings configure which site system server is the software update point that is used to synchronize with Microsoft Update or another source. You can also configure which site system server is the Internet-based software update point if one is specified at the site, the sync source, the sync schedule, the products, the classifications, and the languages for which software updates will be synchronized. After starting the Add Site Systems Roles Wizard, you will be faced with several decisions to make about how you want the software update point configured for your environment.

General Settings

At the general settings page you are able to set which ports and, if needed, which proxy server and proxy account are used.

Software Update Point This setting will determine which ports are used for connectivity to the site system server that is assigned the Software Update Point Site role and whether SSL is used when synchronizing data from the software update point and when clients connect to the WSUS server on the software update point. Ports 80 and 443 are set as the default for client communications, and SSL is not set by default.

Proxy and Account Settings If a proxy server will be required by your environment in order to synchronize this software update point, you will have the opportunity to determine whether to use a proxy server for synchronizing software updates, to use a proxy server to download content using an automatic deployment rule, or both. You will also be able to specify alternate credentials in order to make authenticated connections from the site to the WSUS server if desired.

Synchronization Settings

The sync settings for the software update point specify the sync source and whether WSUS reporting events are created during the sync process.

Synchronization Source The sync source for the first software update point at the central site is configured to use Microsoft Update, but it can be changed to use a custom upstream data source location (a URL), or you can choose not to synchronize with any of the two sources. The software update point on child sites is automatically configured to use the software update point on its parent site as the sync source. When there is an Internet-based software update point, the software update point for the site is automatically set to be the sync source. When you choose not to sync with a sync source, you can use the export and import functions of the WSUSUtil tool instead to get the updates you need.

WSUS Reporting Events   The Windows Update Agent on clients can create event messages that are used for WSUS reporting. These events are not used in Configuration Manager, so the Do Not Create WSUS Reporting Events setting is checked by default. When these events are not created, the only time clients should connect to the WSUS server is during software update evaluation and compliance scans. If these events are needed outside of the Configuration Manager reporting for software updates for some reason, then you will need to modify this setting for your specific needs.

Synchronization Schedule   The sync schedule can be configured only at the software update point on the central Configuration Manager site (CAS or standalone primary site). When this schedule is configured, the software update point on the central site will start syncing with the configured synchronization source at the scheduled date and time. The custom schedule allows you to sync software updates on a date and time when the demands from the WSUS server, site server, and network are low and less likely to interfere with regular network traffic. You can also run a sync cycle manually from the central site from the Update Repository using the Run Synchronization action in the Configuration Manager console.

After the software update point successfully syncs with the synchronization source, a sync request is sent to the Internet-based software update point, if there is one, and to the software update point on child sites. This process repeats throughout the hierarchy until it is successful.

Supersedence Rules   You can configure a software update to expire as soon as it is superseded by a more recent software update. You also can set an update to expire that is superseded after a specific period of time. Supersedence settings are not applicable for System Center endpoint definition updates. Definition files are automatically expired after four newer definition updates are released. Supersedence settings are also not applicable for software updates that are superseded by a service pack; these software updates will never expire after they are superseded.

Update Classifications   Updates are defined with classifications that help to organize the different types of updates. During the sync process, the software updates metadata for the specified classification will be synchronized. Table 8.6 shows the classifications of updates that can be synced with Configuration Manager.

TABLE 8.6:   Update classes

UPDATE CLASS	DESCRIPTION
Critical updates	Broadly released fixes for specific problems addressing bugs that are critical but not security related.
Definition updates	Updates to virus or other definition files.
Feature packs	Feature packs often bring more functionality to a product; they are also deployed via software updates.
Security updates	Broadly released fixes for specific products, addressing security issues.

TABLE 8.6:   Update classes *(continued)*

UPDATE CLASS	DESCRIPTION
Service packs	Cumulative sets of all hotfixes, security updates, and updates created since the release of the product. Service packs might also contain a limited number of customer-requested design changes or features.
Tools	Utilities of features that aid in accomplishing a task or set of tasks.
Update rollups	Cumulative set of hotfixes, security updates, critical updates, and updates packaged together for easy deployment. A rollup generally targets a specific area, such as security, or a specific component, such as IIS.
Updates	Broadly released fixes for specific problems addressing non-critical, non–security-related bugs.

You will need to decide if you are going to deploy some or all of these categories or even choose specific updates from each category in your environment. The update classification settings are configured only on the highest software update point in the Configuration Manager hierarchy. They are not configured anywhere else because they synchronize the metadata from the upstream sync source using the class settings from the central site. When you choose update classes to sync, remember that the more classes you choose, the longer it will take to sync the software update metadata.

Products   The metadata for each update sets the product or products for which the update is applicable. A product is a specific edition of an operating system (such as Windows 8) or application, whereas a product family is the base operating system or application to which the individual products belong (such as Microsoft Windows). You can choose a product family or individual products within a product family.

When updates are applicable to several products and at least one of the products is one you have chosen to update, all of the products will appear in the Configuration Manager console even if they haven't been selected.

The Products settings, like other software update settings, are configured only on the software update point highest in the Configuration Manager hierarchy.

Languages   This setting allows you to configure the languages for which the summary details will be synced for a software update and the update file languages that will be downloaded for the software update.

Software Update File   The languages configured for the Software Update File setting provide the default set of languages that will be available when downloading updates at the site server. When you're on the Language page of the Deploy Software Updates Wizard or Download Software Updates Wizard, the languages configured for the first software update point are automatically selected, but they can be modified each time updates are downloaded or deployed. When the wizard finishes, the software update files for the configured languages are downloaded, if they are available, to the deployment package source location and copied to the distribution points configured for the package.

The Software Update File language settings should be configured with the languages that are most often used in your environment. For example, if your clients use English and Spanish for the operating systems or applications and not much else, then select those languages in the Software Update File column and clear the others. This will allow you to use the default settings on the Language Selection page of the wizards most of the time, and it also prevents unneeded update files from being downloaded. This setting is configured at each software update point in the Configuration Manager hierarchy.

Summary Details During the sync process, the Summary Details information (Software Update metadata) is updated for the languages selected. The metadata provides information about the software update, such as name, description, products supported, update class, article ID, download URL, applicability rules, and so on.

When selecting the Summary Details languages, you should select only the languages needed in your environment. The more languages that are selected, the longer it will take to sync the Software Update metadata. The metadata is displayed in the location of the operating system where the Configuration Manager console is running. If localized properties for the software are not available, the information displays in English.

Maintenance Windows

Maintenance windows provide admins with a way to define a period of time that limits when changes can be made on the systems that are members of a collection. Maintenance windows restrict when the software updates in deployments can be installed on client computers, as well as restrict operating system and software distribution deployments. In Configuration Manager you can create maintenance windows that apply specifically to software updates, as shown in Figure 8.3. This way, you are able to create more granular maintenance windows for software updates that may have a higher priority, for instance, than an application deployment. You can create more than one maintenance window.

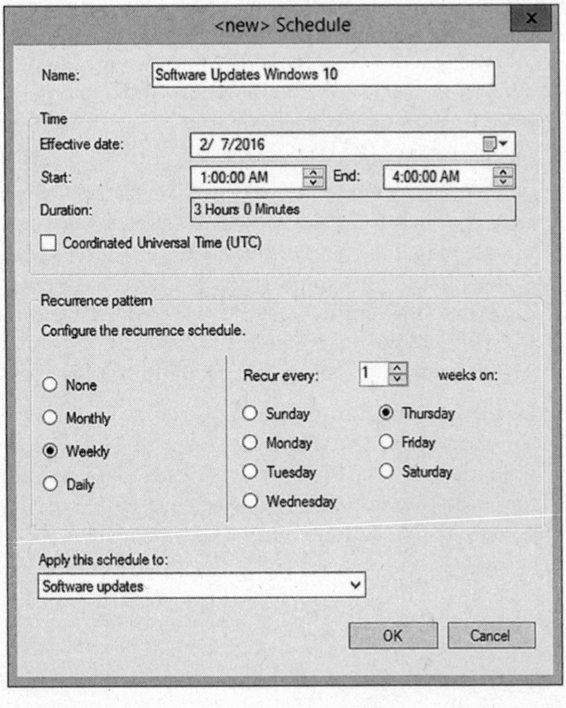

FIGURE 8.3
Creating a maintenance window

Client computers determine whether there is enough time to start a software update install through the following settings:

Restart Countdown The length of the client restart notification (in minutes) for computers in the site. The default interval is 15 minutes, and it is a global site setting that can be changed in the Client Settings dialog box, in the Computer Restart setting.

System Restart Turnaround Time The length of time given for computers to restart and reload the operating system. This setting is in the site control image and has a default of 10 minutes.

Maximum Run Time The amount of time estimated for a software update to install on a client. The default is 10 minutes for updates and 60 minutes for a service pack. This timeframe can be changed for each software update on the Maximum Run Time tab of the properties of a software update.

When you use these settings to determine the available time in a maintenance window, each software update has a default of 35 minutes. For service packs, the default is 85 minutes. When you plan for maintenance windows in your deployments, take these defaults into consideration. When planning software update deployments, be aware of the collection's maintenance window and how many updates are in a deployment so that you can calculate whether clients will be able to install all the updates within the maintenance window or the installation of updates will span multiple maintenance windows.

When a software update installation completes but there is not enough time left in the maintenance window for a restart, the computer will wait until the next maintenance window and restart before starting any more update installs.

If more than one update is to be installed on a client during a maintenance window, the update with the lowest maximum runtime installs first, then the next lowest installs, and so on. Before installing each update, the client will verify that the available maintenance window is long enough to install the update. Once an update starts installing, it will continue to install even if the install goes beyond the maintenance window.

When you create a software update deployment, there are two settings that can allow maintenance windows to be ignored:

Deadline Behavior - System Restart (If Necessary) You can set this option to indicate whether you want to allow system restarts outside configured maintenance windows. By default, this setting is disabled. This setting comes in handy when you want your software update install to complete on clients as soon as possible. When this setting is not enabled, a system restart will not be triggered if the maintenance window ends in 10 minutes or less. This could prevent the install from completing and leave the client in a vulnerable state until the next maintenance window. This setting is available on the User Experience page of the Create Automatic Deployment Rule Wizard or the Deploy Software Updates Wizard.

Deadline Behavior - Software Updates Installation This setting determines whether software updates in the deployment are installed at the deadline regardless of a configured maintenance window. It is disabled by default. This setting comes in handy when you have software updates that must be installed on clients as soon as possible, such as security patches to fix a vulnerability that is being exploited on the Internet. This setting is available on the User Experience page of the Create Automatic Deployment Rule Wizard or the Deploy Software Updates Wizard.

Software Update Properties

Each software update has a properties box with tabs that provide configuration settings to enable software updates and configure the update settings on clients:

Maximum Run Time Tab   This tab allows you to set the maximum amount of time a software update has to complete installing on clients, in minutes. If the maximum runtime value has been reached, a status messages is created and the deployment is no longer monitored. This setting is also used to determine whether the update should be started within a configured maintenance window. If the maximum runtime value is greater than the time left in the maintenance window, the software update installation is not initiated until the start of the next maintenance window.

Keep in mind that if a maximum runtime value is set for more time than the configured maintenance window of a collection it targets, it will never run on those clients. This setting can be configured only on the site synchronized with Microsoft Update, which is more than likely the CAS, and the default is 60 minutes for service packs and 10 minutes for all other types. Values can range from 5 to 9,999 minutes.

Custom Severity Tab   This is a nice addition to Software Updates that allows you to assign custom severity values for software updates if the default value doesn't meet your organization's needs. The custom values are listed in the Custom Severity column in the Configuration Manager console. The software updates can be sorted by custom severity values, the search criteria can be created based on these values, and queries and reports can be made that filter on these values—whatever suits your needs. This setting can be configured only on the site that syncs with Microsoft Update.

PLANNING FOR SOFTWARE UPDATES CLIENT SETTINGS

The Software Updates client settings in Configuration Manager can be configured sitewide (by default), and you can configure client settings for specific collections. There are Software Updates client agent settings and general settings that affect when updates are scanned for compliance and how and when updates are installed on clients. The client agent settings specific to software updates are configured in the Software Updates Client Agent properties, and the sitewide general or collection-based settings related to software updates are configured within the Computer Client Agent properties. The software update installation schedule can be modified from Configuration Manager Software Center on the client. You may also need to configure Group Policy settings on the client computer depending on your environment.

COMPUTER CLIENT AGENT SETTINGS

The properties for this client agent are found in various sections that provide configuration settings that affect the software update reminders and the customization for software update deployments on clients. In Figure 8.4, you see the relevant custom settings categories.

FIGURE 8.4
Computer client agent settings for software update deployment

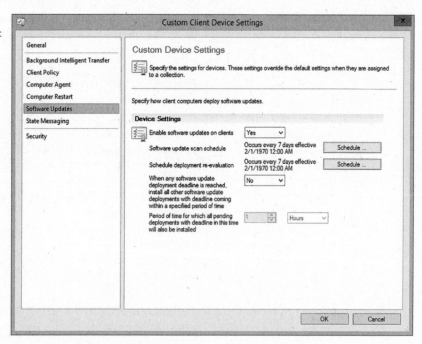

Background Intelligent Transfer Service Section

The settings in this section specify if bandwidth throttling is configured for the site. These settings apply to Configuration Manager clients when they use BITS to download software update files from distribution points. BITS is often used in environments with slow connections between offices or when mobile users log in remotely to save bandwidth.

Client Policy Section

In the Client Policy section you can specify a polling interval, whether user policy should be allowed on clients, and whether to carry out user policy requests from Internet clients. The Policy Polling Interval (Minutes) setting controls how often clients retrieve the machine policy. This setting is relevant to software updates in that when new deployments are created, the machine policy is updated with the deployment information. Clients can take up to the policy polling interval to get those changes, depending on when they last got the policy. The default for this setting is 60 minutes.

Computer Agent Section

On this tab you can provide custom information about the updates that will appear on clients.

Reminder Settings   The settings specify how often notifications are displayed on client computers when a deployment deadline is approaching for software updates. The reminder intervals can be configured for when the deadline is more than 24 hours away, when the deadline is less than 24 hours away, and when the deadline is less than an hour away.

Default Application Catalog Website Point   You can configure the default application catalog website point so that the users can define their own working hours when going to the default application catalog website.

Organization Name   This setting specifies the name of the organization authoring the software update install. By default this text box displays "IT Organization." The organization name appears in software update display notifications, the Available Software Updates dialog box, and the Restart Countdown dialog box on clients where software updates are deployed. Microsoft recommends that you customize this field with something related to your organization.

Computer Restart Section

These settings configure the start countdown timeframe and restart final notification when a software update is installed on client computers. By default, the initial countdown is 90 minutes, and a final notification is displayed when 15 minutes remain before the restart will occur.

State Messaging Section

In the State Messaging section you can specify a reporting cycle for state messages. The State Message Reporting Cycle (Minutes) setting specifies how often clients send state messages to the management point. The software update client creates state messages for scan, software updates compliance, deployment evaluation, and deployment enforcement. The default setting for this is 15 minutes.

CLIENT CONFIGURATION MANAGER PROPERTIES

The Configuration Manager Properties dialog box in the control panel of a Configuration Manager client provides software update actions and configuration settings. When you browse to the Actions tab, you can choose the following actions that are applicable for software updates, shown in Figure 8.5:

FIGURE 8.5
The Actions tab of the Configuration Manager client properties

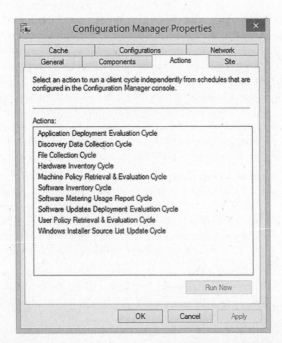

Software Updates Deployment Evaluation Cycle   When this action is started, active deployments will be evaluated after the scan cycle is executed.

Software Updates Scan Cycle   This starts a software updates scan when run.

SOFTWARE SETTINGS OPTIONS

Configuration Manager 2012 introduced the Software Center, which is part of the Configuration Manager client. With the Software Center users can install or request software, but the users are also able to configure some settings that allow them to manage your software update deployment. A user can configure the Work Information and Computer Maintenance settings, shown previously in Figure 8.1:

Work Information   You, as a user, can configure your business hours and business days. Once you define the hours and days, the software updates will be installed outside your work hours. Users can define business hours per hour from 12 a.m. until 11 p.m. and all hours in between, and they can choose the days by selecting a check box per day. You must reserve at least four hours each day for system maintenance tasks.

Computer Maintenance   For software update installations, users are able to choose to automatically install required software only outside the specified business hours and restart the computer if necessary, or suspend Software Center activities when the computer is in a presentation mode.

GROUP POLICY SETTINGS

These settings in Group Policy are required for the Windows Update Agent on client computers to connect to WSUS on the software update point and successfully scan for software update compliance:

Specify Intranet Microsoft Update Service Location   When the software update point is created for a site, clients receive a machine policy that provides the software update point server name and configures the Specify Intranet Microsoft Update Server Location local policy on the local computer. The WUA retrieves the server name set with Set The Intranet Update Service For Detecting Updates and then connects to that server when it scans for software update compliance. When a domain policy has been created for the Specify Intranet Microsoft Update Service Location setting, it will override local policy, and the WUA might connect to a server other than the software update point. If that happens, the client computer might scan for software update compliance based on different products, classes, and languages. Microsoft recommends that this domain policy *not* be configured for Configuration Manager clients; as mentioned earlier, you should disable the Group Policy settings when you already use a WSUS infrastructure in your environment.

Allow Signed Content From Intranet Microsoft Update Service Location   Before the WUA on clients can scan for updates that were created and published with the System Center Updates Publisher, the Allow Signed Content From Intranet Microsoft Update Service Location Group Policy setting must be enabled. When the policy setting is enabled, the WUA will accept updates received through an Internet location if the updates are signed in the Trusted Publishers certificate store on the local computer.

Configure Automatic Updates   The Automatic Updates feature allows clients to receive security updates and other important downloads. It is configured through the Configure Automatic Updates Group Policy setting of Control Panel on the local computer. When

Automatic Updates is enabled, clients will receive update notifications (if you have notifications enabled) and download and install required updates. When Automatic Updates coexists with Configuration Manager Software Updates, each might display notification icons and pop-up display notifications for the same update. Also, when a restart is required, each might display a Restart dialog box for the same reason.

Self-Update   During a Configuration Manager client install, the Windows Update Agent is installed on a client computer if it is not already installed. When Automatic Updates is enabled, the WUA on each client automatically does a self-update when a newer version becomes available or when there are problems with the component. When Automatic Updates is not configured or is disabled, the WUA is still installed during Configuration Manager client installs. If the WUA install fails or becomes corrupt, or a new version of WUA is available, you must create a software distribution to update the agent on clients. If the WUA fails on a client, the scan for software update compliance also fails until it is fixed.

Role-Based Administration

For administering software update deployment, a special role is defined in the Role-Based Administration feature within Configuration Manager. An administrator who is added to the Software Update Manager role has the permissions delegated that are shown in Table 8.7.

TABLE 8.7:   Permissions of the Software Update Manager role

OBJECT	PERMISSION
Alerts	Read, Modify, Delete, Create, Run Report, Modify Report
Boundary	Read
Boundary groups	Read
Client Agent Settings	Read
Collection	Read, Read Resource, Deploy Client Settings, Deploy Software Updates, Modify Client Status Alert
Deployment template	Read, Modify, Delete, Create
Distribution point	Read, Copy to Distribution Point
Distribution point group	Read, Copy to Distribution Point, Create Association to Collection
Query	Read
Site	Read
Software update groups	Read, Modify, Delete, Set Security Scope, Create
Software update package	Read, Modify, Delete, Set Security Scope, Create
Software updates	Read, Modify, Delete, Create, Move Objects, Modify Folder, Network Access, Run Report, Modify Report

Depending on whether the scope is limited, you can deploy the software updates to all Configuration Manager clients or a limited group of Configuration Manager clients. With Role-Based Administration, an administrator who is added to the Software Update Manager role sees only the objects that are related to the role.

System Center Updates Publisher

When planning to implement the current version of System Center Updates Publisher 2011, you need to be able to identify the following items.

COMPONENTS OF SYSTEM CENTER UPDATES PUBLISHER

System Center Updates Publisher 2011 consists of the following components:

Software Update Catalog   Software Update Catalogs are used to import collections of related software updates into the System Center Updates Publisher repository.

Software Update   The repository in the System Center Updates Publisher contains software updates that you can publish or export. You can import them via the update catalogs, or you can create them yourself.

Publications   When publishing a software update to Configuration Manager, you can publish either the full content of the software update or the metadata that describes the software update.

Rules   When you publish software updates in System Center Updates Publisher, the applicability rules are used to check whether the computer meets the prerequisites for the software update. It also checks whether the software update is already installed on the computer.

WHICH VENDOR UPDATES TO DEPLOY

Currently three third-party custom software update partners publish catalogs that can be used via System Center Updates Publisher. You can import Software Update Catalogs from the following third-party hardware and software vendors: Adobe, Dell, and HP.

THE SYSTEM REQUIREMENTS

To be able to install System Center Updates Publisher, you need to be sure that the operating system complies with the following requirements:

- Windows Server Update Services 3.0 Service Pack 2 (WSUS 3.0 SP2)
- Windows Server Update Services 3.0 Service Pack 2 hotfix (KB2530678)
- Microsoft .NET Framework 4

Supported operating systems are

- Windows Vista
- Windows 7
- Windows 8.x
- Windows Server 2008

- Windows Server 2008 R2

- Windows Server 2012

- Windows Server 2012 R2

Testing in an Isolated Lab

It is important to understand how software updates will work in your environment, and one way you can do that is to set up a test lab that is as close to your production environment as possible. This section describes a minimum setup of Configuration Manager to use while you are testing or evaluating the software update components and other deployments like applications and operating systems; always test your deployment in a test environment before deploying it in the production environment.

To start, you will need at least one computer for each operating system that you use in your environment. Also, you will need computers that have other crucial line-of-business applications running on them as well.

A single client is adequate for minimum test purposes, but if you want to have a representative sample of how software updates will work with all computers used in your enterprise, then you will need to have a representative of each client configuration in your environment. For example, if you are using Windows Server 2008 R2, Windows Server 2012 R2, Windows 8.1, and Windows 10 in your organization, then you should have at least one client with each of those operating systems on it for testing. If you can't get that many machines together, at least try to get one beefed-up computer with lots of RAM. That way, you can use Windows Server 2012 Hyper-V or Windows 10 Hyper-V to set up virtual representations of the computers that you couldn't procure physically.

By doing this, you will become familiar with how the Software Updates components and the actual software update executables work with the operating systems on your network before you use Software Updates enterprise-wide. By using more than one operating system in your testing, you will be able to do the following:

- Review the specific software updates that Microsoft has published for those operating systems.

- Start becoming familiar with software update management practices for each type of computer.

- Learn how software updates work with different operating systems in a controlled environment.

- Learn how to find information about specific software updates for a specific OS when you need it.

REQUIREMENTS FOR TESTING SOFTWARE UPDATE POINTS

When you test software updates, create the Software Update Point Site role as it would be in your production site. You will need to decide if a single software update point will be created or if there will be a software update point for connectivity from client computers on the Internet, and if the software update point will be set up with an NLB cluster. The deployment intelligence that you have gathered up to this point will be crucial to helping you plan your test environment.

Configuring Software Updates

Now that we have taken the time to look at the components of Software Updates and how they fit together, and you have taken that information with your deployment intelligence and put together a plan as to how you want to set up Software Updates in your environment, we can examine how to get everything working.

Before Software Updates data can be displayed in the Configuration Manager console and software updates can be deployed to clients, you must set up and configure the software update point, as well as the rest of the components of Software Updates.

Configuring the Software Updates Client Agent

The Software Updates Agent is enabled in Configuration Manager by default, but you still have to configure the other settings of this client agent to match your plans for using Software Updates in your environment.

To configure the Software Updates Agent, follow these steps:

1. In the Configuration Manager console, choose the Administration workspace, then choose Overview ➤ Client Settings, and select the Default Client Agent Settings policy object.

2. Select the Home tab of the ribbon, and then click Properties.

3. Select Software Updates, and (as shown in Figure 8.6) configure the following settings:

FIGURE 8.6
The default settings of the Software Updates Client Agent

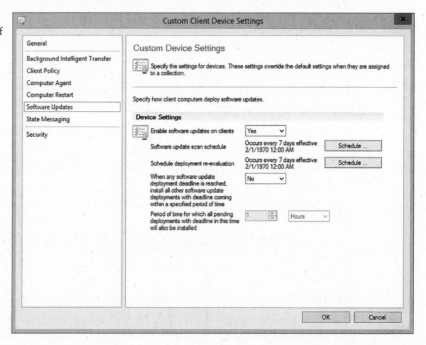

Enable Software Updates On Clients This setting defines whether the Software Updates Agent is enabled for the site; this agent is installed and enabled on Configuration Manager clients by default. Make sure that this setting is enabled. If the client agent is disabled, the client agent components are put into a dormant state but not uninstalled, and existing deployment policies will be removed from clients as well. Re-enabling the client agent starts a policy request that the components on clients be enabled and the deployment metadata be downloaded. With Configuration Manager you can configure more than one client agent settings package. Chapter 5, "Client Installation," has more information about client agent settings.

Software Update Scan Schedule This setting specifies how often the client computer scans for software update compliance. By default, a simple schedule is configured to run the scan every 7 days, and the site database is updated with any changes since the last scan. The minimum value for the scan is 1 minute and the maximum value is 31 days. This setting can be configured only after a Software Update Point Site role has been installed on a site system in the site. When a custom schedule is configured, the actual start time on client computers is the start time plus a random amount of time up to 2 hours. This keeps all the clients from starting a scan and connecting to WSUS at the same time.

Schedule Deployment Re-evaluation You can configure how often the Software Updates Agent re-evaluates software updates for installation status. When software updates that have been installed are no longer found on client computers and are still required, they will be reinstalled. This re-evaluation schedule will need to be adjusted based on company policy for update compliance, whether users have the ability to un-install updates, and similar considerations. You also have to consider that every re-evaluation cycle results in some network and client computer activity. The minimum value allowed for the deployment re-evaluation schedule is 1 minute and the maximum is one month. A simple schedule of every 7 days is set by default.

When Any Software Update Deployment Deadline Is Reached, Install All Other Software Update Deployments With Deadline Coming Within A Specified Period Of Time This setting indicates whether to enforce all mandatory software update deployments that have deadlines within a certain timeframe. When a deadline is reached for a mandatory software update deployment, an installation is started on the clients that have been targeted for the mandatory deployment. It also indicates whether to start the install for updates defined in other mandatory deployments that have a configured deadline within a specified timeframe. The benefits of this setting are that it expedites software update installs for mandatory updates and that it might increase security, decrease display notifications, and decrease system restarts on clients. This setting is disabled by default.

Period Of Time For Which All Pending Deployments With Deadline In This Time Will Also Be Installed This sets the timeframe for the software updates with a deadline to be installed if the deadline is coming within a specified period of time. The minimum value allowed is 1 to 23 hours, and the maximum is 1 to 365 days. By default, this setting is configured for 1 hour.

4. When you have finished setting things the way you want them, click OK to finish.

Installing Windows Server Update Services 4.0 Server

Windows Server Update Services 4.0 Server (WSUS) or later is required in order to use Software Updates in Configuration Manager. Installing WSUS for use with Configuration Manager is different from a standard install of WSUS without the Configuration Manager infrastructure.

The WSUS installation procedure described here can be used for both the first software update point (the main software update point installed on the CAS) and all other software update points (those for any other primary Configuration Manager sites) or for installing WSUS on a remote server that is not a Configuration Manager site server. The decision to install WSUS on the same server as your site servers or on another remote server will depend on your server resources and your plans for the software update infrastructure.

Next, you have to go through a series of steps to make a software update point the active one for the Configuration Manager hierarchy. We will detail those steps later on in the chapter.

Depending on the version of your operating system, you need to either add the Windows Server Update Services role through the Server Manager of Windows Server 2008 R2 or Windows Server 2012 or make sure that you have downloaded the latest version of WSUS at the WSUS home page:

```
http://technet.microsoft.com/windowsserver/bb332157.aspx
```

INSTALLING WSUS ON WINDOWS SERVER 2012 R2

To add the WSUS role to Windows Server 2012 R2, you need to perform the following steps:

1. Start the Windows Server 2012 R2 Server Manager from the Start screen.

2. In the Dashboard, click Manage and select Add Roles And Features to start the Add Roles and Features Wizard.

3. Click Next twice, select the server on which the WSUS role needs to be installed, and click Next again.

4. Select Windows Server Update Services, click Add Features, and click Next.

5. Click Next after reviewing the features that are automatically added. Click Next at the WSUS page to start the initial configuration of the WSUS role.

6. On the Roles Services page, deselect WID Database, select WSUS Services and Database, and click Next.

7. On the Content page, disable the Store Updates In The Following Location option and click Next.

8. Supply the SQL Server And Instance Name (if necessary) and click Check Connection. Click Next.

9. Specify an alternate source path if necessary; then click Install to begin the feature and roles installation.

10. After the installation is finished, start the Windows Server Update Services application from the Start screen to configure the WSUS role. Configure the database server where the WSUS database needs to be stored, and click Run to start the post-installation. Click Close when the post-installation is finished.

INSTALLING WSUS ON WINDOWS SERVER 2008 R2

To add the WSUS role to Windows Server 2008 R2, perform the following steps:

1. Start the Windows Server 2008 R2 Server Manager from the Administrative Tools section of the console.

2. Click Roles and select Add Roles, and then click Next at the Before You Begin page.

3. Select Windows Server Update Services, and click Next.

4. Read the introduction to WSUS, and click Next.

5. Confirm the settings, and click Install.

   Once the download is finished, you will see the welcome screen of the WSUS 3.0 SP2 Setup Wizard.

6. Click Next.

7. Click the I Accept The Terms Of The License Agreement check box, and then click Next.

   If the Microsoft Report Viewer 2008 Redistributable is not installed, the Setup Wizard gives you a warning about it.

8. Click Next.

9. The next screen will ask you to choose if and where you want updates to be stored on the WSUS server; just click Next.

10. The next page lets you choose your database options:

   ◆ If you are not installing WSUS on a Configuration Manager site, the default of Install Windows Internal Database On This Computer is probably your best option, because it installs Microsoft SQL Server 2005 Embedded Edition just for the purpose of managing WSUS. This will save you from having to purchase another full SQL Server license for WSUS and managing another instance of SQL as well.

   ◆ If you are installing WSUS on a Configuration Manager Central Administration Site or a primary site server and it has the resources to handle it, then we recommend going ahead and using the instance of the SQL Server that is already installed. (If it doesn't have enough resources, you probably shouldn't be installing WSUS on this server anyway.) Having two versions of SQL installed on the same server could cause problems in the long run, and they would be competing for the same resources.

   Depending on what you choose, WSUS will either create the Windows Internal Database or test the connection to the existing SQL Server instance.

11. After that is done, click Next.

12. On the next page of the wizard, choose how to configure the WSUS website. Microsoft recommends that you choose to make a custom website if you are using WSUS as a software update point, even if the WSUS server is remote from the Configuration Manager site system. You should definitely use the custom site option if you are installing WSUS on a Configuration Manager site so that the install will not interfere with the other Configuration Manager components that use IIS. By default, the custom WSUS website uses HTTP port 8530 and HTTPS port 8531.

13. Click Next.

14. Review the settings, and click Next to install WSUS 3.0 SP2.

15. Click Finish and then Close after the installation.

16. The WSUS configuration wizard will start up after that, but you should close it, because Configuration Manager will take care of configuring all of the settings for WSUS.

NEVER CONFIGURE WSUS USING THE WSUS CONSOLE

When you use WSUS in combination with the software update point role, you should never use the WSUS console to configure WSUS. Always use the Configuration Manager console to configure the software update point.

INSTALLING THE DOWNLOADED WSUS VERSION

To install the downloaded version of WSUS, perform the following steps:

1. Double-click the WSUS install file that you downloaded, `WSUSSetup_30SP2_x86.exe` (or `WSUSSetup_30SP2_x64.exe`), and you will see the opening page of the Windows Server Update Server 3.0 Setup Wizard.

2. Click Next, and then select Full Server Installation Including Administration Console and click Next again.

3. Click the I Accept The Terms Of The License Agreement check box, and then click Next.

   The next screen will ask you to choose if you want updates to be stored on the WSUS server and where you want to store them. You must accept the default and store a copy of these updates locally.

4. Choose where you want to keep these files, and then click Next.

   The next page lets you choose your database options.

   ◆ If you are not installing WSUS on a Configuration Manager site, the default of Install Windows Internal Database On This Computer is probably your best option, because it installs Microsoft SQL Server 2005 Embedded Edition just for the purpose of managing WSUS. This will save you from having to purchase another full SQL Server license for WSUS and managing another instance of SQL as well.

   ◆ If you are installing WSUS on a Configuration Manager primary site server and it has the resources to handle it, then we recommend going ahead and using the instance of the SQL Server that is already installed. (If it doesn't have the resources, you probably shouldn't be installing WSUS on this server anyway.) Having two versions of SQL installed on the same server could cause problems in the long run, and they would be competing for the same resources.

   Depending on what you choose, WSUS will either create the Windows Internal Database or test the connection to the existing SQL Server instance.

5. Once that is done, click Next.

6. The next page of the wizard, shown in Figure 8.6 earlier, lets you choose how to configure the WSUS website.

   Microsoft recommends that you choose to make a custom website if you are using WSUS as a software update point, even if the WSUS server is remote from the Configuration Manager site system. You should definitely use the custom site option if you are installing WSUS on a Configuration Manager site so that the install will not interfere with the other

Configuration Manager components that use IIS. By default, the custom WSUS website uses HTTP port 8530 and HTTPS 8531. Click Next.

7. Review the settings and click Next. When the wizard is done, click Finish. The WSUS configuration wizard will start up after that, but you should close it, because Configuration Manager will take care of configuring all of the settings for WSUS.

Setting Up the Software Update Point

There can be several Configuration Manager site systems with the Software Update Point Site system role, but there can be only one site system server configured as the software update point that synchronizes with a synchronization source like Microsoft Update in a Configuration Manager site. By default this is the first software update point you install in your environment. All other software update points are replicas of the first one you installed and use that one as the synchronization source.

When your Configuration Manager site is in HTTPS mode, you can have an Internet-based software update point assigned to a remote site system server that allows communication from only Internet-based client computers. Also, if the first software update point is on a network load balancing cluster, there should be a software update point installed on every server that is in the NLB cluster. When you have a CAS in your Configuration Manager hierarchy, you first need to install and configure a software update point at one of the site servers in your CAS.

SETTING UP THE SOFTWARE UPDATE POINT IN THE CENTRAL ADMINISTRATION SITE

To set up a software update point in the CAS, follow these steps:

1. In the Configuration Manager console, choose Administration Workspace ➤ Overview ➤ Site Configuration ➤ Servers And Site System Roles.

2. Decide whether to create a new site system server or add the software update point role to an existing site system. Depending on which you choose, take the next step:

   ◆ To create a new site system with a software update point, click Create Site System Server on the Home tab of the ribbon.

   ◆ To add the software update point role to an existing server, do the following:

      a. Select the site server on which you want to install the software update point role.

      b. Choose Add Site System Roles in the Home tab of the ribbon.

3. Configure the server that is to be used for a site server, and click Next.

   See Figure 8.7 for the options for this choice.

Specify An FQDN For This Site System For Use On The Internet   You will have to configure this setting for a software update point when the site server is in secure mode or when it is in mixed mode and using Secure Sockets Layer (SSL).

Internet FQDN   You must configure this setting if you are setting up a software update point that accepts Internet-based client connections or for the active Internet-based software update point. It is only enabled when selecting the option Specify An FQDN For This Site System For Use On The Internet.

FIGURE 8.7
Configure the software update point settings.

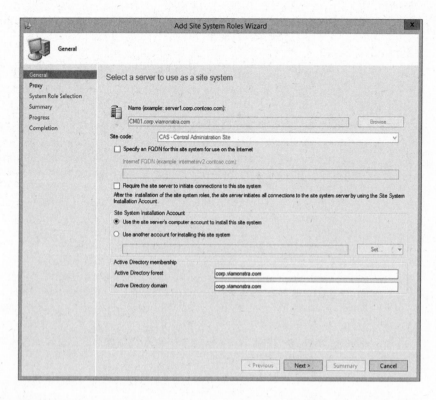

Require The Site Server To Initiate Connections To This Site System You must use this setting when the remote software update point doesn't have access to the inboxes on the site server. This will let a site system from a different domain or forest place files that need to be transferred to the site server. The site server will connect to the remote site system and get the files periodically. The Internet-based software update point might need this setting to be enabled to work.

Site System Installation Account Configure this setting when the computer account for the site server doesn't have access to the remote site system being set up as a software update point—for example, a remote SUP in a different domain than the CAS or primary site server, and no trust exists between the domains. In this case, an account from the domain where the remote SUP is located should be specified here.

Active Directory Membership Configure the site system membership by supplying the forest and domain FQDNs.

4. If you need to go through a proxy server to get to the Internet, you will need to configure the proxy server and the possible credentials. If you have Internet access without a proxy server, just click Next.

5. Select Software Update Point and click Next.

6. On the Software Update Point page (see Figure 8.8), specify the port settings that are used by the WSUS you are connecting to. By default, the port settings for a WSUS custom website (the recommended settings) are HTTP port 8530 and HTTPS port 8531. If you installed WSUS on the default website, the ports are HTTP port 80 and HTTPS port 443. Click Next.

FIGURE 8.8
Configure the
software update
point port settings.

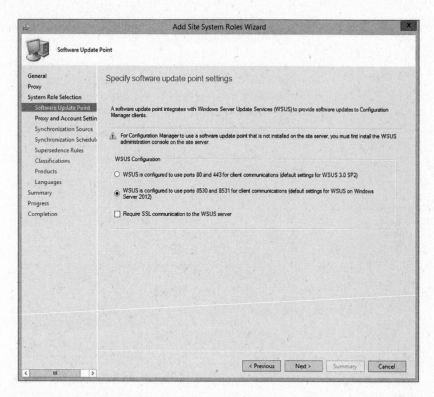

7. If your software update point is behind a proxy server on which you need to authenticate, you can enable the earlier configured proxy server access by choosing Use A Proxy Server When Synchronizing Software Updates and/or Use A Proxy Server When Downloading Content By Using Automatic Deployment Rules. If authenticated access to the WSUS server is required, you can configure a WSUS Server Connection Account. Click Next when finished configuring the proxy and account settings.

8. Choose the synchronization source for the software update point by selecting one of the following options, and then click Next:

Synchronize From Microsoft Update The software update point that is highest in the Configuration Manager hierarchy (usually the CAS) can use this setting. When an upstream software update point is in place, this option is not available.

Synchronize From An Upstream Data Source Location (URL) If you do not want to synchronize directly with Microsoft Update but with another WSUS server, you can configure an upstream data source location. Normally it will be something like https://wsusserver:8531 or http://wsusserver:8530.

Do Not Synchronize From Microsoft Update Or Upstream Data Source Use this setting when the software update point can't connect to the upstream update server. This will usually be used by an active Internet-based software update point that doesn't have access to the software update point. The software update point on the CAS can't use this setting. Synchronizing a software update point through importing and exporting updates is covered later in the chapter.

9. Configure the synchronization behavior of the software update role by selecting Enable Synchronization On A Schedule.

   This is disabled by default, and you can start a manual sync by running the Run Synchronization action in the Configuration Manager console. We recommend that you enable a schedule, because scheduled syncs perform full synchronizations, and manual syncs only do delta synchronizations of software updates.

10. Click Next after configuring the synchronization schedule.

11. Configure the supersedence behavior for updates that are about to expire, as shown in Figure 8.9. Choose one of the following:

    ◆ Immediately Expire A Superseded Update

    ◆ Do Not Expire A Superseded Software Update Until The Software Update Is Superseded For A Specified Period

FIGURE 8.9
Configure behavior for software updates that are superseded.

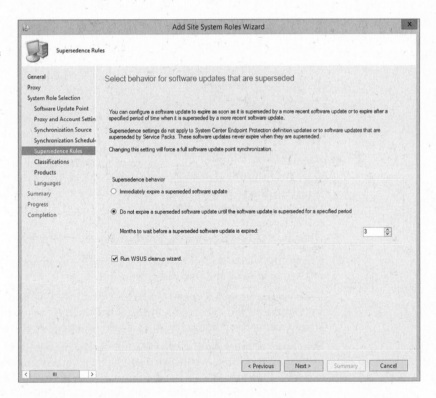

12. Enable Run WSUS Cleanup Wizard to automatically clean up the expired updates from the database.

13. Click Next and deselect all update classifications, and then click Next. You can change the classifications in a later stage.

14. Deselect all the products; you can change the products in a later stage. The number of products will change after the first synchronization with Microsoft Update has finished.

15. Select all the languages that you will be supporting with software updates, and then click Next.

16. Click Next again after reviewing the summary, and click Close after the installation is finished.

SETTING UP THE SOFTWARE UPDATE POINT IN A PRIMARY SITE THAT IS A CHILD OF A CAS

To set up a software update point in a primary site that is a child of a CAS, follow these steps:

1. In the Configuration Manager console, choose Administration Workspace ➤ Overview ➤ Site Configuration ➤ Servers And Site System Roles.

2. Decide whether to create a new site system server or add the software update point role to an existing site system. Depending on which you choose, take the next step:

◆ To create a new site system with a software update point, click Create Site System Server on the Home tab of the ribbon.

◆ To add the Software Update Point role to an existing server, do the following:

a. Select the site server on which you want to install the Software Update Point role.

b. Click Add Site System Roles on the Home tab of the ribbon.

What you do next will depend on your site settings. By default, the computer account for the site server will connect to the site system computer (if you're installing on a separate site) and install the necessary components. If the computer account of the site server has access to the site system server and the Configuration Manager site is in HTTPS mode, the settings shown previously in Figure 8.7 are optional.

3. When the computer account does not have access to the site system server or when the site is in secure mode, you will have to configure the following settings on the New Site Role page:

a. Specify the option An FQDN For This Site System For Use On The Internet.

By default, you will have to configure this setting for a software update point when the site server is in secure mode or when it is in mixed mode and using SSL.

b. Internet FQDN

You must configure this setting if you are setting up a software update point that accepts Internet-based client connections or for the active Internet-based software update point.

c. Require The Site Server To Initiate Connections To This Site System

This setting must be used when the remote software update point doesn't have access to the inboxes on the site server. This will let a site system from a different domain or forest add files that need to be transferred to the site server. The site server will connect to the remote site system and get the files every so often. The Internet-based software update point might need this setting to be enabled to work.

d. Site System Installation Account

This setting is configured when the computer account for the site server doesn't have access to the remote site system being set up as a software update point.

e. Active Directory Membership

Configure the site system membership by supplying the Forest and Domain FQDN.

4. After you have configured what you need, click Next.

5. If you have to go through a proxy server to get to the Internet, configure the proxy server and the possible credentials. If you have Internet access without a proxy server, just click Next.

6. Select Software Update Point from the list of available site roles, and then click Next.

7. On the Software Update Point page (see Figure 8.10), configure the port settings for a WSUS custom website (the recommended settings are HTTP port 8530 and HTTPS port 8531). If you installed WSUS on the default website, the ports are HTTP port 80 and HTTPS port 443.

FIGURE 8.10
Specify software
update point settings.

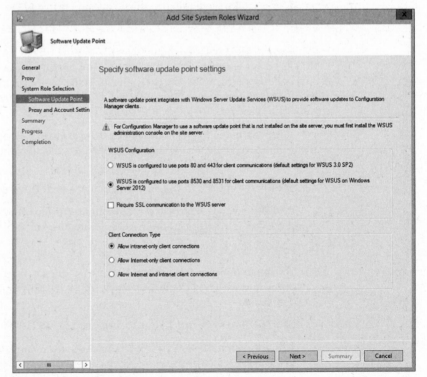

In the Client Connection Type section, you need to configure what client connections are allowed for this software update point. Decide, depending on the purpose of the software update point, whether only intranet and/or Internet client connections are allowed.

8. If your software update point is behind a proxy server on which you need to authenticate, you can enable the earlier configured proxy server access by choosing Use A Proxy Server When Synchronizing Software Updates and/or Use A Proxy Server When Downloading Content By Using Automatic Deployment Rules. If authenticated access to the WSUS server is required, you can configure a WSUS Server Connection Account. Click Next when finished configuring the proxy and account settings.

9. Review the summary, and click Next to start the installation of the software update point.

10. Click Close when the installation has finished.

11. After finishing the configuration of the software update point in the child primary site, you need to configure the supported languages for this software update point. In the Configuration Manager console, choose Administration Workspace ➤ Overview ➤ Site Configuration ➤ Sites, and select the child primary site in the hierarchy.

12. Choose Configure Site Components on the Settings section of the Home tab of the ribbon, and click Software Update Point. In Figure 8.11 you see that it is recognized as a child site and that the upstream software update point is configured automatically. Select the Languages tab and configure the languages that you need to support. Be sure to configure languages that are available on the upstream software update point. Click OK when finished.

FIGURE 8.11
Software Update
Point Component
Properties

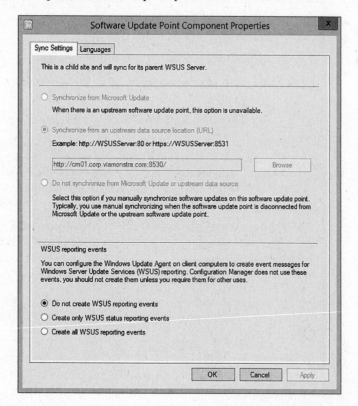

ADDING AND REMOVING A SOFTWARE UPDATE POINT WITH POWERSHELL

You are also able to add a software update point with the default Configuration Manager cmdlets in PowerShell. Adding a software update point on site server CM01 in the domain `configmgrlab`.`com` in primary site PS1 for only Intranet clients is done as follows:

```
Add-CMSoftwareUpdatePoint -SiteSystemServerName cm01.configmgrlab.com
-SiteCode ps1 -ClientConnectionType Intranet -WsusiisPort 8530 -WsusiissslPort 8531
```

Removing the same software update point can be done with the following command:

```
Remove-CMSoftwareUpdatePoint -SiteSystemServerName cm01.configmgrlab.com -SiteCode ps1
```

SETTING UP THE SOFTWARE UPDATE POINT IN A STANDALONE PRIMARY SITE

A software update point can be installed in a hierarchy or at a standalone primary site. This section describes the installation steps of a software update point on a standalone primary site.

1. In the Configuration Manager console, choose the Administration workspace, then select Overview ➤ Site Configuration ➤ Servers And Site System Roles.

2. Decide whether to create a new site system server or add the Software Update Point role to an existing site system. Depending on which you choose, take the next step:

   ◆ To create a new site system with a software update point, click Create Site System Server on the Home tab of the ribbon.

   ◆ To add the Software Update Point role to an existing server, do the following:

      a. Select the site server on which you want to install the Software Update Point role.

      b. Click Add Site System Role on the Home tab of the ribbon.

   What you do next will depend on your site settings. By default, the computer account for the site server will connect to the site system computer (if you're installing on a separate site) and install the necessary components. If the computer account of the site server has access to the site system server and the Configuration Manager site is in HTTPS mode, the settings shown previously in Figure 8.7 are optional.

3. When the computer account does not have access to the site system server or when the site is in secure mode, you will have to configure the following settings on the New Site Role page:

      a. Specify An FQDN For This Site System On The Intranet

      By default, you will have to configure this setting for a software update point when the site server is in secure mode or when it is in mixed mode and using SSL.

    b. Internet FQDN

       You must configure this setting if you are setting up a software update point that accepts Internet-based client connections or for the active Internet-based software update point.

    c. Require The Site Server To Initiate Connections To This Site System

       This setting must be used when the remote software update point doesn't have access to the inboxes on the site server. This will let a site system from a different domain or forest add files that need to be transferred to the site server. The site server will connect to the remote site system and get the files every so often. The Internet-based software update point might need this setting to be enabled to work.

    d. Site System Installation Account

       This setting is configured when the computer account for the site server doesn't have access to the remote site system being set up as a software update point.

    e. Active Directory Membership

       Configure the site system membership by supplying the forest and domain FQDNs.

4. When you have configured what you need, click Next.

5. If you have to go through a proxy server to get to the Internet, configure the proxy server and the possible credentials. If you have Internet access without a proxy server, just click Next.

6. Select Software Update Point from the list of available site roles, and then click Next.

7. On the Software Update Point page (see Figure 8.10), specify the port settings that are used by the WSUS you are connecting to and which clients are allowed to connect to the software update point. Click Next after configuring the software update point server.

    By default, the port settings for a WSUS custom website (the recommended settings) are HTTP port 8530 and HTTPS port 8531. If you installed WSUS on the default website, the ports are HTTP port 80 and HTTPS port 443.

FINDING THE PORTS USED BY WINDOWS SERVER UPDATE SERVICES

If someone else installed the WSUS server that is being used for a software update point, you may not know what ports were used during setup. If you input the wrong ports on this page of the wizard, the setup will fail. You can find the ports used by WSUS by following these steps:

1. Under Administrative Tools, click Internet Information Services (IIS) Manager.

2. Expand Sites, right-click the website that is being used for WSUS, and click Edit Bindings. A custom WSUS site is recommended, but the default website might have been used instead. The Port column will contain the number for the TCP port.

3. Look at the Browse Website list in the Actions section of the Management console; it will also contain the port list for the website.

continues

continued

8. If your software update point is behind a proxy server on which you need to authenticate, you can enable the earlier configured proxy server access by choosing Use A Proxy Server When Synchronizing Software Updates and/or Use A Proxy Server When Downloading Content By Using Automatic Deployment Rules. If authenticated access to the WSUS server is required, you can configure a WSUS Server Connection Account. Click Next when finished configuring the proxy and account settings. Otherwise, just click Next. Choose the synchronization source for the software update point by selecting one of these options:

Synchronize From Microsoft Update The software update point that is highest in the Configuration Manager hierarchy can synchronize from Microsoft Update; since you are installing it in a standalone primary site you may use this setting.

Synchronize From An Upstream Data Source Location (URL) If you do not want to synchronize directly with Microsoft Update but with another WSUS server, you can configure an upstream data source location. Normally it will be something like `https://wsusserver:8531` or `http://wsusserver:8530`.

Do Not Synchronize From Microsoft Update Or Upstream Data Source Use this setting when the software update point can't connect to the upstream update server. This will usually be used by an active Internet-based software update point that doesn't have access to the software update point. The software update point on the CAS can't use this setting. Synchronizing a software update point through importing and exporting updates is covered later in the chapter.

9. On that same page, accept the default of Do Not Create WSUS Reporting Events, and then click Next.

10. Always choose to synchronize software updates on a schedule by selecting Enable Synchronization On A Schedule.

   This option is disabled by default; you can start a manual sync by running the Run Synchronization action in the Configuration Manager console. We recommend that you enable a schedule, because scheduled syncs perform full synchronizations and manual syncs only do delta synchronizations of software updates. Synchronizing a software update point manually is not a best practice.

11. Once you have made your choice, click Next.

12. Configure the supersedence behavior for updates that are about to expire, as shown previously in Figure 8.9. Choose one of the following:

   ◆ Immediately Expire A Superseded Update

   ◆ Do Not Expire A Superseded Software Update Until The Software Update Is Superseded For A Specified Period

13. Enable Run WSUS Cleanup Wizard to automatically clean up the expired updates from the database.

14. Click Next.

15. Deselect all update classifications, and then click Next. You can change the update classifications in a later stage.

16. Deselect all the products, and then click Next. You can change the products in a later stage. The number of products will change after the first synchronization with Microsoft Update has finished.

17. Select all the languages that you will be supporting with software updates, and then click Next. You can change the supporting languages in a later stage.

18. Click Next again on the following page, and click Close.

CHECKING THE INSTALLATION OF THE SOFTWARE UPDATE POINT

After the installation of the software update point(s), it is a good idea to check some log files to be sure that the software update point(s) are installed correctly.

1. To monitor the install of the software update point, open SUPSetup.log in the <ConfigMgr Install Path>\Logs or %SMS_LOG_PATH% folder.

   When the install has finished, you will see the text "Installation Was Successful."

2. Open WCM.log in the same directory to verify that the connection to the WSUS server worked.

   When the connection to the WSUS server is made and the WSUS components are checked, you will see

   ```
   There are no unhealthy WSUS Server components on WSUS Server servername
   ```

and

```
Successfully checked database connection on WSUS server servername
```

in the log file.

Configuring Software Updates Settings and Synchronization

Software updates in Configuration Manager must be synchronized with Microsoft Update or an upstream WSUS server before information on those updates will be available to view in the Configuration Manager console. Synchronization starts at the highest level in the hierarchy that has a software update point and either has a configured schedule or is started manually using the Run Synchronization action.

When synchronization is started on a configured schedule, all changes to the Software Updates metadata since the last scheduled sync are inserted into the site database. This will include metadata for new software updates or metadata that has been modified or deleted. When a sync is started manually, only new Software Updates metadata since the last sync is inserted into the database. The manual sync process is faster since it is not pulling as much Software Updates metadata. A manual sync action is available only on parent sites.

To manually sync the software update point, do the following:

1. In the Configuration Manager console, choose the Software Library workspace, then choose Overview ➢ Software Updates ➢ All Software Updates.

2. Select the Home tab of the ribbon and click Synchronize Software Updates. Click Yes to initiate a sitewide synchronization of software updates.

The synchronization process might take longer than an hour to finish, depending on several factors, including whether a synchronization has been run before and what languages, products, and update classifications have been configured to be synchronized. You can monitor the synchronization process by looking at the log file for WSUS Synchronization Manager, wsyncmgr.log. This is located by default at %Program Files%/Microsoft Configuration Manager/Logs.

When the synchronization is complete, you will see a 6702 status message from SMS_WSUS_SYNC_MANAGER.

Beginning in Configuration Manager 2012, you can monitor the synchronization in the Configuration Manager console. To do so, follow these steps:

1. In the Configuration Manager console, choose the Monitoring workspace, then select Overview ➢ Software Update Point Synchronization Status.

2. Look at the synchronization status, the link state, and the catalog versions.

When the synchronization with Microsoft Update is complete (either from a schedule or started manually) at the highest site in the hierarchy, sync requests are sent to all child sites, and they in turn start synchronization with their configured upstream WSUS servers as soon as the request has finished processing.

The Software Updates metadata that is synced from Microsoft Update is based on the update classes, products, and languages that were selected when the software update point was first configured. A child site will synchronize whatever updates have been configured on its parent site.

After installing the software update point, we need to select the Update Classifications and Products that we want to support. To configure the update properties for software updates, follow these steps:

1. In the Configuration Manager console, choose the Administration workspace, then choose Overview ➤ Site Configuration ➤ Sites, and select the site that is the highest in the hierarchy.

2. Choose Configure Site Components on the Settings section of the Home tab of the ribbon, and click Software Update Point.

3. To configure Update Classifications, click the Classifications tab, as shown in Figure 8.12.

FIGURE 8.12
Software Update Point
Component Properties,
Classifications tab

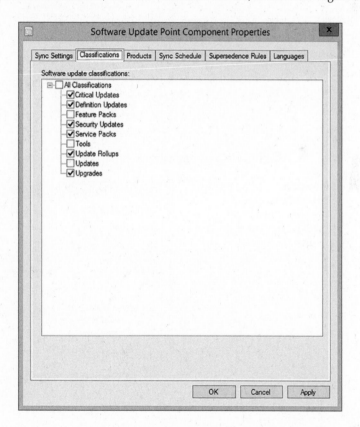

4. To configure products that are being synced, click the Products tab, as shown in Figure 8.13.

FIGURE 8.13
Software Update Point
Component Properties,
Products tab

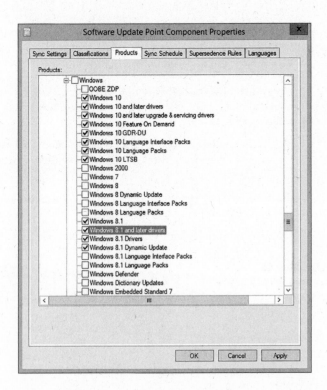

5. To configure languages that are being synced, click the Languages tab, as shown in Figure 8.14.

FIGURE 8.14
Software Update Point
Component Properties,
Languages tab

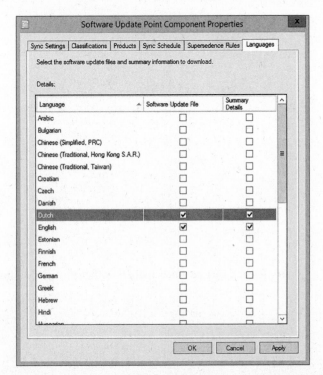

6. To reconfigure the supersedence settings, click the Supersedence Rules tab, as shown in Figure 8.15.

FIGURE 8.15
Software Update Point Component Properties, Supersedence Rules tab

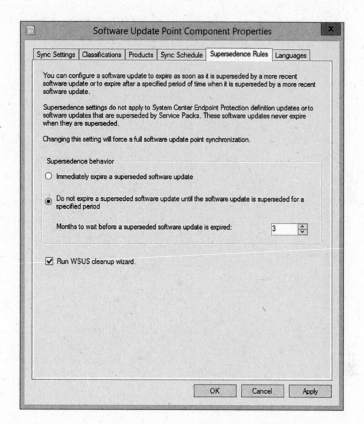

To configure the software updates synchronization schedule, follow these steps:

1. In the Configuration Manager console choose the Administration workspace, then select Overview ➤ Site Configuration ➤ Sites, and select the site that is the highest in the hierarchy.

2. Choose Configure Site Components on the Settings section of the Home tab of the ribbon, and click Software Update Point.

3. To configure the synchronization schedule, click the Sync Schedule tab, as shown in Figure 8.16.

4. To enable synchronization on a schedule, select Enable Synchronization On A Schedule, and set the schedule as you want it.

5. When you have finished, click OK to save the schedule.

Unless you change the Start value in the custom schedule, synchronization will be started as soon as possible and will repeat based on the schedule that you configured.

FIGURE 8.16
Software Update Point
Component Properties,
Sync Schedule tab

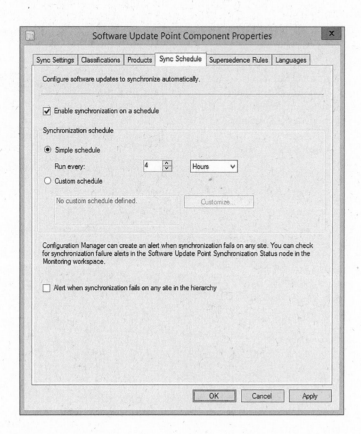

6. If you want alerts to be reported in the Alerts node of the Configuration Manager 2012 console, enable the Alert When Synchronization Fails On Any Site In The Hierarchy option.

Synchronizing Updates with Export and Import

When a software update point is not configured or cannot synchronize with its upstream server in the Configuration Manager hierarchy, the export and import functions of the WSUSUtil tool can be used to synchronize Software Updates metadata manually. The user who performs the export/import must be a member of the local Administrators group on the WSUS server, and the tool must be run locally on the WSUS server itself.

The files found in the WSUSContent folder (by default located in <WSUSInstallDrive>\ WSUS\WSUSContent) must also be copied from the upstream update server to the software update point so that locally stored updates and the license terms for the updates are available to the import server. This procedure can also be used for migrating the software update content from Configuration Manager 2007 to Configuration Manager 2012 or Configuration Manager Current Branch.

To export and import software updates from the export WSUS server to the import WSUS server, follow these steps:

1. Copy files from the export server to the import server:

   a. On the export server, go to the folder where software updates and the license terms for those software updates are stored. By default, this will be `<WSUSInstallDrive>\WSUS\WSUSContent`.

   b. Copy all of these files to the same folder on the import server.

2. Export metadata from the database of the export server:

   a. At a command prompt on the export WSUS server, go to the folder that contains `WSUSUtil.exe`. By default, this will be located at `%ProgramFiles%\Update Service\Tools`.

   b. Then enter the following:

   `WSUSUTIL.exe export packagename logfile`

   The name of *packagename* doesn't really matter, as long as it and the log file are unique in that folder. This command will export the Software Updates metadata into a file called `packagename.cab`.

   c. Move the export package that you just made to the folder that contains `WSUSUtil.exe` on the import WSUS server.

3. Import metadata to the database of the import server:

   a. At a command prompt on the WSUS server that you are importing the updates to, go to the folder that contains `WSUSUtil.exe`, which is `%Program Files%\Update Services\Tools`.

   b. Enter

   `WSUSUTIL.exe import packagename logfile`

   where *packagename* is the name of the export file that you exported in step 2.

This will import all the metadata from the exporting server and create a log file that you can use to review the status.

Preparing Software Updates for Deployment

So far in this chapter, we have planned our implementation of Software Updates and set up and configured Software Updates. Now we are finally ready to deploy Software Updates to Configuration Manager clients—well, nearly ready. We still need to find the updates to be deployed (using any of several methods), download them, and optionally create a software update group and/or an automatic deployment rule. These tasks can be done in the sequence shown here or independently of each other.

Before we get into that process, there are a few things you should keep in mind after you have set up all of the Software Updates components.

Give the process a little time to work. Don't expect to set up everything we have discussed so far and think you are going to be able to do a couple of clicks and deploy updates to your clients. You will have a little bit of lead time as updates are synced with Microsoft Update, the metadata is synced with the rest of the Configuration Manager hierarchy, and clients get requests for scans. Depending on the size of your hierarchy and the number and kind of clients you need to be scanned, this might take a while; after all, this is a process.

If you click the Software Updates node in the Configuration Manager console and don't see any results in your compliance summary, then either your clients haven't been scanned or they haven't sent their scan results. Until you see something in those reports, you don't have enough to work with to do any update deployments.

With that said, we can continue preparing for software update deployment.

Finding the Software Updates to Be Deployed

Before you can deploy any software updates to clients, you will need to figure out which ones you want or need to deploy to your clients. Configuration Manager provides several ways to do that, and each allows you to find clients that need the updates you want to focus on installed.

When you are looking for updates to deploy, avoid updates that show up in the Configuration Manager console with a yellow arrow icon. These are updates that have been superseded by another update that contains the same fixes. To avoid installing outdated components to your clients, do not include these updates in your deployments. They are no longer needed.

There are basically three methods to find needed software updates:

◆ Software Updates reports

◆ Software Updates search

◆ All Software Updates node

USING SOFTWARE UPDATES REPORTS TO FIND UPDATES

You can gather compliance information on your clients by running reports under the Software Updates - A Compliance category, because they are designed specifically for this purpose.

To use web reports from the Configuration Manager console to find required updates, follow these steps:

1. In the Configuration Manager console, choose the Monitoring workspace, then select Overview ➢ Reporting, expand Reports, and open the Software Updates - A Compliance folder.

   This will give you a list of all reports in the right pane of the console.

2. Find the report Compliance 4 - Updates By Vendor Month Year, select it, and click Run on the Home tab of the ribbon.

3. To get an idea of what update data you have collected already, do the following:

   a. Click Values for the collection All Systems.

   b. Click Values for the vendor Microsoft.

   c. Click Values for the update class Security Updates.

   d. Click Values for the current year (2016).

   e. Click Values for the current month (January)

   f. Click View Report.

You should see a report like the one shown in Figure 8.17.

Any software updates that meet those criteria will be displayed in the report. The Required column gives the number of clients that require each software update in the list. The report also shows all of the updates that have been deployed by listing an asterisk (*) in the Approved column. To get more information about any of the updates, click the information link on the far right of the report (you may have to do some side scrolling to see it), and this will pull up the latest information from Microsoft on this update.

FIGURE 8.17

A sample compliance report with values entered for Collection ID, Vendor, Update Class, and Year

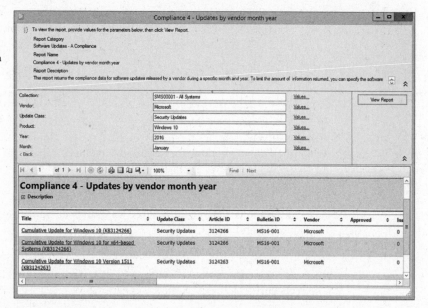

4. To get more details, click the drill-down link in the first column of the report.

This will open the Compliance 6 - Specific Software Update States (Secondary) report, and you will see a count of computers for each compliance state for that particular update.

USING THE SEARCH OPTION IN THE CONFIGURATION MANAGER CONSOLE

Beginning with Configuration Manager 2012, you also have the ability to use a powerful search engine that comes with the console. Just under the ribbon, you will find the search option.

To use the search option to show software updates, follow these steps:

1. In the Configuration Manager console, choose Software Library ➢ Overview ➢ Software Updates ➢ All Software Updates.

2. Click Add Criteria next to the Search button.

You will then see the Criteria list box, as shown in Figure 8.18.

FIGURE 8.18
Search criteria

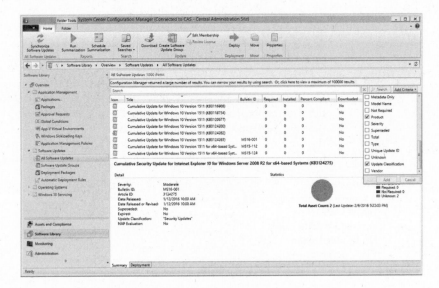

3. You want to search for all security updates for Windows 10 that are required. So first you scroll down and look for Required, Update Classification (for security updates) and Product (for Windows 10).

4. Click Add to add the criteria to the search box.

5. We only want to deploy required software updates, so select the option Is Greater Than Or Equal To and set it to 1.

6. To select the right product, click the link next to Product and select Windows 10.

7. To select the right update classification, click the link next to Update Classification and select Security Updates, as shown in Figure 8.19.

8. Click Search to activate the criteria.

9. To save the search for future use, you can click either Save Current Search or Save Current Search As in the Home tab of the ribbon of the Configuration Manager console.

You can find all the updates that need to be deployed to Windows 10 computers in this search by looking at the column labeled Required. You can sort by any column by clicking that column. From here you can download these updates, add them to an update group, or deploy them to client computers.

FIGURE 8.19
Adding search
criteria to the
search

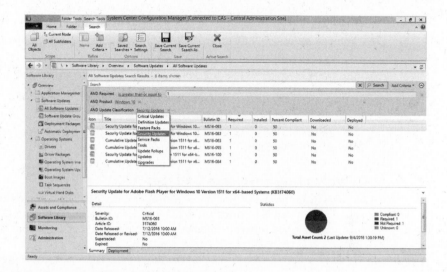

To manage and access saved searches, do the following:

1. In the Configuration Manager console, choose Software Library ➤ Overview ➤ Software Updates ➤ All Software Updates.

2. Choose Saved Searches in the Search or Home tab of the ribbon of the Configuration Manager console, and click Manage Searches For Current Node.

3. Select the search you need, as shown in Figure 8.20, and click OK to make the search active. You can also rename or delete a saved search.

FIGURE 8.20
Selecting the search
you need

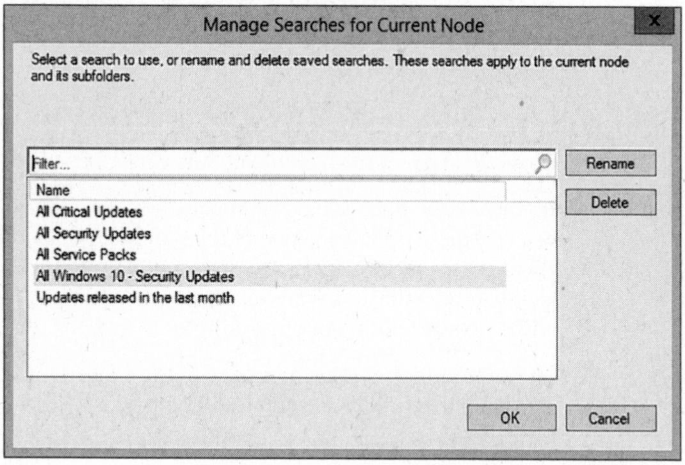

Using the All Software Updates Node

When you browse in the Configuration Manager console to the All Software Updates node, you can select the software updates you want without using the search option.

To select the updates you want, do the following:

1. In the Configuration Manager console, choose Software Library ➤ Overview ➤ Software Updates ➤ All Software Updates.

2. Browse to the update you want to deploy, or use the search option without the criteria to filter the updates.

Downloading Software Updates

As you saw in the last section, there are several ways to search for software updates that you want to download in Configuration Manager. The Download Updates Wizard allows you to download selected software updates to a deployment package before deploying updates to clients.

Software updates are downloaded from the Internet or from a shared folder on the network that the site server has access to and that can be added to new or existing deployment packages.

To download software updates to a deployment package, follow these steps:

1. In the Configuration Manager console, choose Software Library ➤ Overview ➤ Software Updates ➤ All Software Updates.

2. Choose Saved Searches in the Search section of the Home tab of the ribbon of the Configuration Manager console, and click Manage Searches For Current Node.

3. Select the created Windows 10 - Security Updates Search, and click OK.

4. Sort the updates in the list so that the updates required by the most clients are at the top by clicking the Required column twice.

5. Hold down the Shift or Ctrl key and select all the updates that have at least one client requiring that update.

6. Choose the Home tab of the ribbon, and click Download.

   This will start up the Download Software Updates Wizard, shown in Figure 8.21.

   If you already have deployment packages created (as described later in the chapter), you can add these updates to one of them in the first field by selecting Select A Deployment Package. Then click Browse to open a dialog that will allow you to select a package that is only for hosting software updates, and select one from the list. Otherwise, this option will be grayed out, as in our example.

7. The other option on this first page of the wizard is Create A New Deployment Package. There are three fields for you to fill out:

   Name   The name of the deployment package. You should pick a unique name that describes the content and limit it to 50 characters or less.

   Description   The description of the package contents up to 512 characters.

FIGURE 8.21
The Deployment
Package page of the
Download Software
Updates Wizard

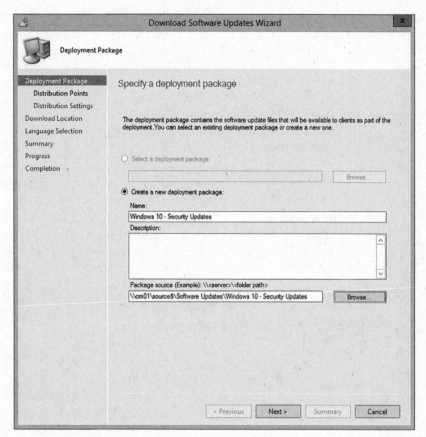

Package Source The location of the software update source files. You should manually create this share before going any further. When the deployment is created, the source files are compressed and copied to the distribution points that are associated with the deployment package. This location must be entered as a network path (such as $\backslash\backslash server\backslash sharename\backslash path$), or you can click the Browse button to find the location on the network. This location should not be used by any other deployment or software distribution package.

8. After choosing the deployment package or supplying information for a new deployment package, click Next.

   The next step is the Distribution Points page. The Add button allows you to select from the available distribution points or distribution point groups on your site that you want to use for this software update package. You can leave this blank for now, and the software update files will be downloaded to the source folder. However, the updates will not be available to deploy to clients until you add at least one distribution point.

9. After adding the distribution point(s), click Next to configure the distribution settings.

   In the Distribution Settings page, shown in Figure 8.22, the following options can be configured:

Distribution Priority   The distribution priority is used for the deployment package when it is sent to distribution points at child sites. Packages are sent in priority order of High, Medium, or Low. Packages with the same priority are sent in the order in which they are created. Unless there is a backlog, packages should process immediately no matter their priority. Medium is the default priority.

Distribute The Content For This Package To Preferred Distribution Points   When a client requests the content for this package and it is not available on any preferred distribution points for the client, specify if you want to distribute the content to the preferred distribution points.

When you enabled content prestaging on your distribution points, because the scheduling synchronization and throttling of your bandwidth do not work for you, you also need to look at the following settings:

Automatically Download Content When Packages Are Assigned To Distribution Points   Use this option when smaller software update packages are used and scheduling and throttling settings provide enough control for the distribution of the content.

FIGURE 8.22

The Distribution Settings page of the Download Software Updates Wizard

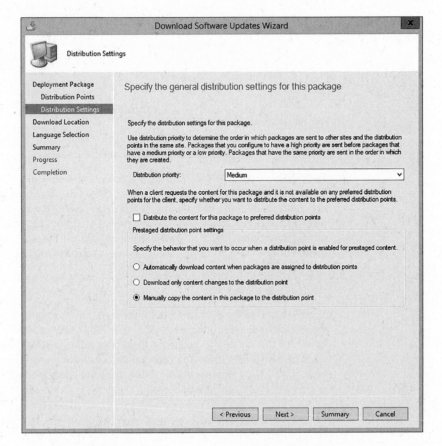

Download Only Content Changes To The Distribution Point   This option should be used when you have an initial package that is possibly large but you want to add future software updates to the content of this package.

Manually Copy The Content In This Package To The Distribution Point   Use this option when you have large packages and you don't want to use the network for distribution of the content to the distribution point. You need to prestage the content on the distribution point.

10. Click Next when you've finished configuring the distribution settings.

Next is the Download Location page, with the following options:

Download Software Updates From The Internet   This will download the updates from the location on the Internet that is defined in the software update definition. This is the default setting.

Download Software Updates From A Location On My Network   The software updates are downloaded from a local directory or shared folder that you set in the box. Use this setting when the site server doesn't have Internet access. The software updates can be downloaded from any computer that does have Internet access and stored in a location on the local network that the site server has access to.

After configuring the download location, click Next. The Language Selection page shows the languages in which the software update files will be downloaded. By default, the languages that are configured for the software update point are selected. Adding a selection here does not add it to the software update point settings.

11. Click Next.

12. Review the settings and click Next; the updates will be downloaded.

When the wizard is done, the software updates will show up under Overview ➤ Software Updates ➤ Deployment Packages ➤ *<deployment package name>* in the Software Library workspace of the Configuration Manager console.

Creating a Software Update Group

As stated earlier in the chapter, a software update group in Configuration Manager contains a set of software updates. A software update group offers several benefits when deploying and monitoring software updates and is part of Microsoft's recommended Software Updates workflow.

Tracking the compliance state for the software updates in deployments is an important task for Configuration Manager administrators. When update groups are used, you can use the Compliance 1 - Overall Compliance report for the set of updates in the update group or the Compliance 3 - Update Group (Per Update) report to get a list of the updates in an update group and the overall compliance of each. This is a great reason to use the update groups as a part of your software update procedure.

To create a software update group, follow these steps:

1. In the Configuration Manager console, choose Software Library ➤ Overview ➤ Software Updates ➤ All Software Updates.

2. Choose Saved Searches in the Search area of the ribbon of the Configuration Manager console, and click More or use the Recent Searches option.

3. Select the created Windows 10 - Security Updates Search and click OK.

4. Sort the updates in the list so that the updates required by the most clients are at the top by clicking the Required column twice.

5. Hold down the Shift key and select all the updates that have at least one client requiring that update.

6. Click Create Software Update Group, and fill in the name and description of the software update group.

7. Click Create, and the software update group will be created.

Your new software update group will appear in the Software Update Group node under Software Updates in the Configuration Manager console.

Deploying Software Updates with the Deploy Software Updates Wizard

Now that all the setup and preparation tasks have been done, you are ready to run the deployment. Before deploying software updates, make sure you've considered things like whether the maintenance windows and client restart settings will work for the different clients in your environment, how you are going to handle servers differently than workstations, and which deployments will be delegated.

To ensure the most successful software update deployments, utilize software update groups that fit the needs of your organization, and keep software updates organized so they are easier to keep track of and deploy.

The Deploy Software Updates Wizard in Configuration Manager allows you to create or modify software update deployments. You can select software updates that you want to deploy from several locations, as discussed earlier in this chapter, and you can start the deployment wizard in different ways as well.

To deploy software updates using the Deploy Software Updates Wizard, use the following steps:

1. In the Configuration Manager console, choose Software Library ➢ Overview ➢ Software Updates ➢ Software Update Groups.

2. Decide what updates you want to deploy.

   You can use any of the methods that were described in the "Finding the Software Updates to Be Deployed" section earlier in the chapter, or you can just select several updates from any of the Update Repository sections by Ctrl-clicking the updates that you want.

3. Start the Deploy Software Updates Wizard using either of the following methods:

   ♦ Right-click some selected updates or a software update group, and then click Deploy.

   ♦ Click Deploy on the Home tab of the ribbon of the Configuration Manager console after selecting some updates or a software update group.

For this example, some updates that were not already downloaded were selected before clicking Deploy.

The first page of the Deploy Software Updates Wizard is shown in Figure 8.23.

FIGURE 8.23
The General page

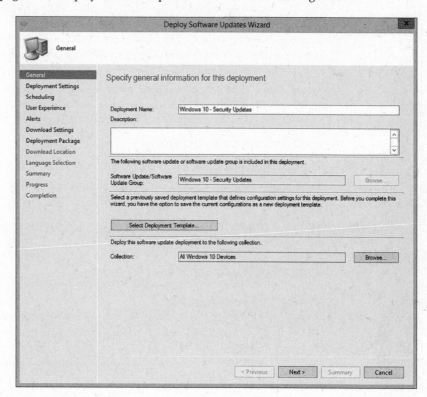

4. Configure the following options:

Select Deployment Template If you have already saved a deployment template, you can select a saved deployment template. This template holds the most common settings.

Deployment Name Give the deployment a name.

Software Update/Software Update Group This option is active only when you select one or more updates instead of an update group.

Collection Select the collection to which the deployment must deploy software updates.

5. Click Next.

The next step in creating a deployment for deploying software updates is to configure the deployment settings. The configurable settings are as follows:

Type Of Deployment Choose whether the deployment is available or required for installation. If the deployment is required, the installation of the software updates will start automatically, depending on the maintenance windows. If a deployment is available, the user is able to install the software updates. For software update deployments it is common practice to configure the deployment as required.

Use Wake-On-LAN To Wake Up Clients For Required Deployments Disabled by default, this option specifies whether at deadline Wake On LAN will be used to send wake-up packets to computers that require updates in the deployment. Be sure to configure the support of Wake On LAN in the Configuration Manager environment, your devices, and your network. See Chapter 4 for more information about configuring the support for sending wake-up packets.

Detail Level The detail level configures the state-message details that are returned by the clients for deployments. There are three levels that you can configure: All Messages, Only Success And Error Messages, or Only Error Messages.

6. Configure the settings and click Next.

The Scheduling page, shown in Figure 8.24, is next. This page has three sections:

Schedule Evaluation Select what the scheduled time must be based on: Client Local Time (the default) or UTC.

FIGURE 8.24
The Scheduling page

Software Available Time Select the date and time when software updates will be made available to clients: As Soon As Possible (the default) or Specific Time, which allows you to set a specific date and time when clients will be able to see the deployment.

Installation Deadline   Specify whether the software updates should automatically install on clients at a configured deployment deadline:

♦   As Soon As Possible

♦   Specific Time: Enabled by default, this allows you to set a date and time as a deadline for this deployment to be installed on clients.

7.   Once you have made your choices on this page, click Next.

The software updates will be available as soon as they have been distributed to the distribution points.

The next step that you need to take is to configure the user experience; the options shown in Figure 8.25 can be configured.

FIGURE 8.25
The User Experience page

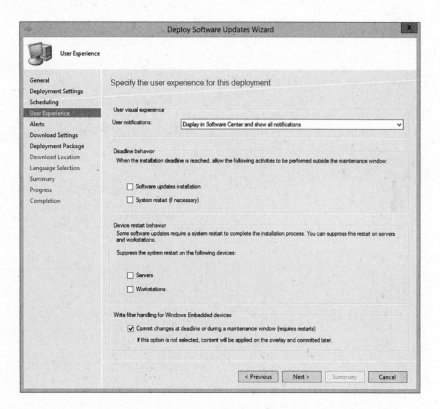

User Visual Experience   You can set several options to configure the user experience when the software updates are deployed. You can hide software update installations and notifications from your users by selecting Hide In Software Center And All Notifications or choose Display In Software Center And Show All Notifications or Display In Software Center, And Only Show Notifications For Computer Restarts if you want notifications shown to your users.

Deadline Behavior   When an installation deadline is reached, the installation can be performed outside the maintenance window, if you want. You can configure the actions by allowing an update installation and a system restart (if necessary) outside the maintenance window.

Device Restart Behavior   Installing software updates on workstations or servers can initiate a system restart. With this setting you can suppress a system restart on workstations and servers.

Write Filter Handling For Windows Embedded Devices   When using Windows Embedded devices, write filters are in place to prevent the operating system from being changed by software or the users. The software updates agent in the Configuration Manager client is able to control the write filter so that the changes (software updates) are committed at the deadline or during maintenance windows. If this option is not selected, the software updates will be applied on the overlay and committed in a later stage.

8. Click Next when you have finished configuring the user experience.

   With the alerting feature, you can retrieve alerts in the Configuration Manager console and take actions when required.

9. Configure the options shown in Figure 8.26 for your organizational needs, and click Next.

FIGURE 8.26
The Alerts page

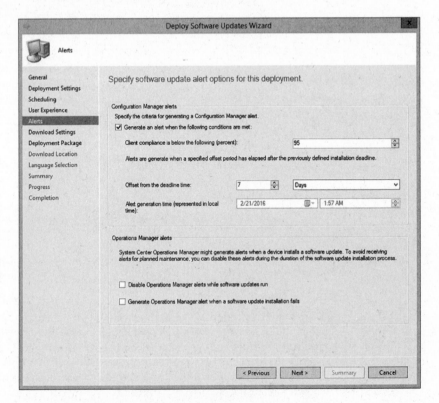

Configuration Manager Alerts   This option is disabled by default, but it is recommended that you enable this option to get more control over the compliance level of your Configuration Manager clients. When you receive an alert that your compliance level is below a selected percentage, you can proactively take action to get the compliance at the right level.

Operations Manager Alerts   Besides handling the alerting in the Configuration Manager console, you can retrieve your alerts by using Operations Manager. In this page you can disable the alerts for the duration of the software update installation.

10. Specify the download settings for your deployment. The page is divided into four sections:

Download Settings For Slow Or Unreliable Network   Define what to do if the Configuration Manager client is connected via a slow or unreliable network boundary. You can choose not to install the software updates or to download them from the distribution point and install them after downloading.

Download Settings For Non-preferred Distribution Points   Define what to do if the Configuration Manager client is connected via a network boundary with an unprotected distribution point. You can choose not to install the software updates or to download them from the unprotected distribution point and install them after downloading.

Allow Clients To Share Content With Other Clients On The Same Subnet   Select this option if you want to reduce the load on the WAN by allowing clients to download the Software Update content from other clients in the same subnet that already have downloaded and cached the content. This option uses Windows BranchCache.

If Software Updates Are Not Available On Preferred Distribution Point Or Remote Distribution Point, Download Content From Microsoft Updates   When the Configuration Manager client has already received a new list of updates that needs to be installed but the updates are not available on the preferred distribution point or a remote one, you can allow the client to download the software updates from Microsoft Update.

Allow Clients On A Metered Internet Connection To Download Content After The Installation Deadline, Which Might Incur Additional Costs   You can allow clients that are connected via a metered Internet connection (mobile data connection) to download their updates via this metered connection. Be aware if you enable this option that you might have extra costs for mobile data on your phone bill.

11. Click Next after configuring the download settings for the deployment.

The next step is to select an existing deployment package to add the software update to or create a new software update package.

12. Click the first Browse button on the Deployment Package page and select one of the existing packages, or create a new deployment package. Then configure the settings that you need for creating a new deployment package:

Name   Supply the name of the deployment package; be sure it is descriptive so you can identify the deployment package when you want to add other software updates to it.

Description   Supply the description of the deployment; be sure it is descriptive so you can identify the deployment package when you want to add other software updates to it.

Package Source   The package source is a UNC path to a location where the source of the deployment package will be stored. The UNC path must be available for the Configuration Manager site servers.

Sending Priority The sending priority is used for the deployment package when it is sent to distribution points at child sites. Packages are sent in priority order from High, Medium, or Low. Packages with the same priority are sent in the order in which they were created. Unless there is a backlog, packages should process immediately no matter their priority. Medium is the default priority.

13. After configuring the deployment package, click Next, add the distribution point from which the deployment package must be available, and click Next again.

The Download Location page appears with the following options:

The Internet This will download the updates from the location on the Internet that is defined in the software update definition. This is the default setting.

A Network Location The software updates are downloaded from a local directory or shared folder that you set here. Use this setting when the site server doesn't have Internet access. The software updates can be downloaded from any computer that does have Internet access and can be stored in a location on the local network that the site server has access to.

14. Configure where you want to retrieve the software updates from and click Next.

The Language Selection page shows the languages in which the software update files will be downloaded. By default, the languages that are configured for the software update point are selected. Adding a selection here does not add it to the software update point settings.

15. Click Next.

16. On the Summary page shown in Figure 8.27, review the options you selected.

FIGURE 8.27
The Summary page

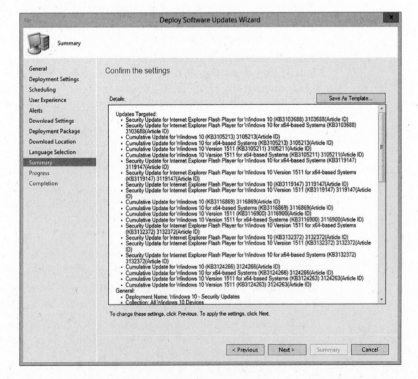

17. You can save all settings in a deployment template by clicking Save As Template.

A dialog with all the settings will appear, as shown in Figure 8.28.

FIGURE 8.28
Naming the deploy-
ment template

18. Name the deployment template and click Save.

19. After you have finished reviewing the Summary, click Next, and when the progress bar is done, click Close.

Using System Center Updates Publisher

With System Center Updates Publisher, you can deploy software updates from third-party manufacturers. This section describes how to install and use System Center Updates Publisher.

Installing System Center Updates Publisher

After downloading the System Center Updates Publisher software and complying with the requirements, you need to install it. This section describes the installation process:

1. Go to the installation source of the System Center Updates Publisher and start SystemCenterUpdatesPublisher.MSI.

2. Click Next when the Setup Wizard starts.

3. If you are not using Windows Server 2012 and did not install the WSUS 3.0 hotfix (KB2530678), click the Install Microsoft Windows Server Update Services 3.0 SP2 Hotfix button, and download and install the hotfix, as shown in Figure 8.29.

FIGURE 8.29
Download the WSUS
3.0 SP2 hotfix.

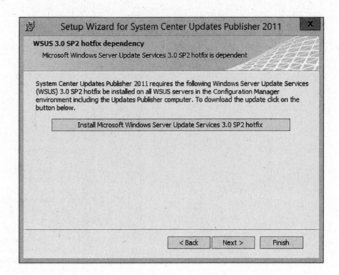

FIGURE 8.29
Download the WSUS
3.0 SP2 hotfix.

4. Click Next.

5. Select I Accept The License Agreement, and click Next.

6. Define the installation location, and click Next twice.

7. Click Finish when the installation is complete.

Configuring System Center Updates Publisher

Next, you must configure System Center Updates Publisher so that it's able to publish software updates to the WSUS 3.0 SP2 server:

1. Start the System Center Updates Publisher 2011 console from the Start menu within Windows.

   The console will start, as shown in Figure 8.30.

2. Click Configure WSUS And Signing Certificate to configure the System Center Updates Publisher options, shown in the right column of the console.

   Update Server Configure an update server by choosing Enable Publishing To An Update Server. Whether your WSUS server is installed locally or remotely, select the appropriate option to configure the WSUS server, as shown in Figure 8.31. Supply a signing certificate or create a self-signed certificate. Be sure that your computers also trust the certificates that are used to sign the software updates.

   Configuration Manager Server Configure the connection with your Configuration Manager server and test the connection. If you have installed System Center Updates Publisher on a remote server, also configure the thresholds. Be sure to enable this Configuration Manager integration setting.

FIGURE 8.30
The System Center Updates Publisher 2011 console

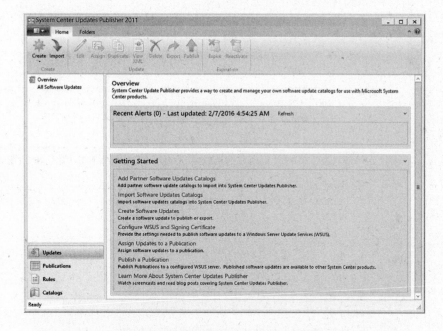

FIGURE 8.31
Enable publishing to an update server.

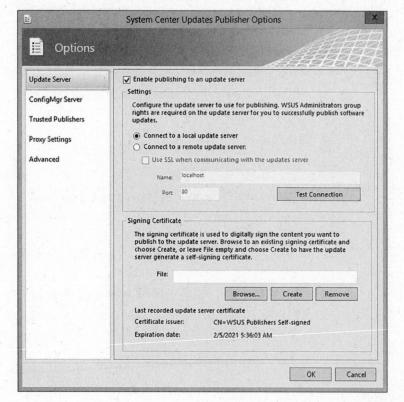

Trusted Publishers   If you accept the certificates of the publishers while importing catalogs, you can remove or view them here.

Proxy Settings   Configure the proxy settings if you need to use a proxy to connect to the Internet.

Advanced   If you are signing updates, you need to choose the Enable Add Timestamp When Signing Updates option. You can also configure security and local source publishing settings.

SELF-SIGNED CERTIFICATES AND WINDOWS SERVER 2012 R2

On Windows Server 2012 R2, you may receive an error that no self-signed certificate for WSUS has been created. This feature is disabled on Windows Server 2012 R2 by default and can be enabled by creating a registry key as a workaround:

```
Create DWORD value: EnableSelfSignedCertificates = 1 in
  HKEY_LOCAL_MACHINE\Software\Microsoft\Update Services\Server\Setup\
```

Also check whether the self-signed WSUS certificate is in the right certificate store, as described here:

https://blogs.technet.microsoft.com/sus/2009/02/05/unable-to-publish-updates-using-scup-exception-occurred-during-publishing/

Using System Center Updates Publisher

When using System Center Updates Publisher, you need to go through the following steps:

1. Add partner software updates catalogs.

2. Import updates.

3. Create rules.

4. Publish updates.

ADDING PARTNER SOFTWARE UPDATES CATALOGS

After configuring System Center Updates Publisher, the next step is to add partner software updates catalogs:

1. Start the System Center Updates Publisher 2011 console from the Start menu within Windows.

2. Click Add Catalogs in the Catalogs workspace of the System Center Updates Publisher 2011.

3. Select the partner catalogs you want to use, and add them to the Selected Partner Catalogs list, as shown in Figure 8.32.

FIGURE 8.32
Adding partner
catalogs

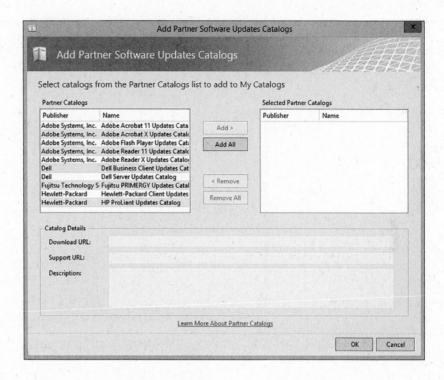

4. Click OK.

IMPORTING UPDATES

The next step after adding the partner software updates catalogs is importing the updates to System Center Updates Publisher:

1. Start the System Center Updates Publisher 2011 console from the Start menu within Windows.

2. Click Import in the Home ribbon of the Updates workspace, select the update catalogs, as shown in Figure 8.33, and click Next.

3. Confirm the settings and click Next.

   While downloading the catalogs you will see a security warning, as shown in Figure 8.34.

4. Review the certificate, select Always Accept Content From "*Publisher*," and click Accept.

5. Click Close once the import is ready.

FIGURE 8.33
Importing the
update catalogs

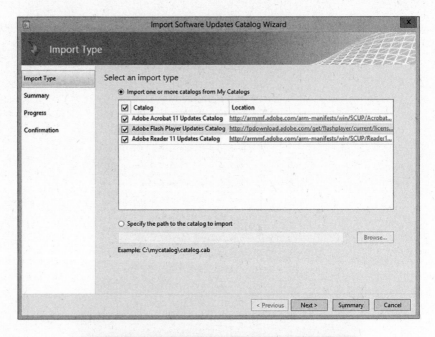

FIGURE 8.34
Accepting the catalogs

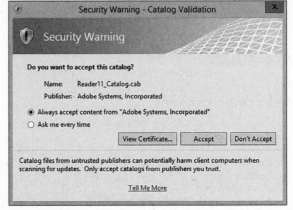

CREATING RULES

With applicability rules, you can define which updates can be deployed on what kind of operating system:

1. Start the System Center Updates Publisher 2011 console from the Start menu within Windows.

2. Click Create on the Home tab of the ribbon in the Rules workspace.

3. Supply a rule name, and click the yellow star icon to add a rule.

   You can configure different kinds of rules based on file, registry, system, or Windows Installer properties.

4. Configure the rule like the example for Windows 8 shown in Figure 8.35.

FIGURE 8.35
Configure the rule like
you want.

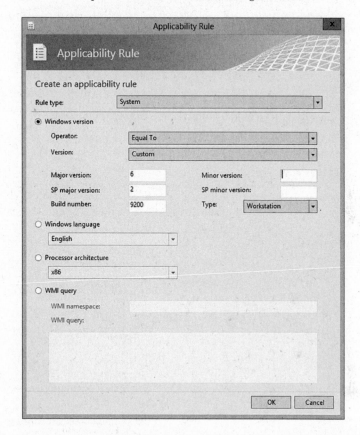

You can add AND or OR operators to the statement, as shown in Figure 8.36, and click OK.

FIGURE 8.36
Combined rule
statement

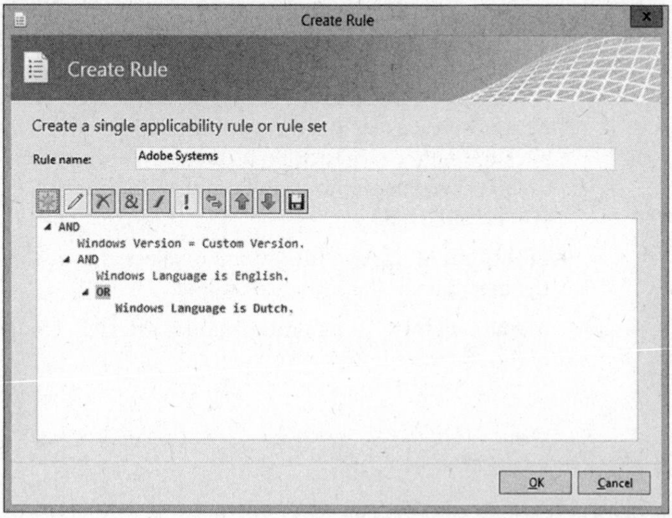

PUBLISHING UPDATES

After assigning the update catalogs, importing them, and creating rules, the next step is to publish the updates to Configuration Manager so that you can deploy the updates:

1. Start the System Center Updates Publisher 2011 console from the Start menu within Windows.

2. Choose the Updates workspace, and select the updates you want to publish.

3. Click Publish on the Home tab of the ribbon.

4. Select the publish option you want, as shown in Figure 8.37.

FIGURE 8.37
Select the appropriate publish option.

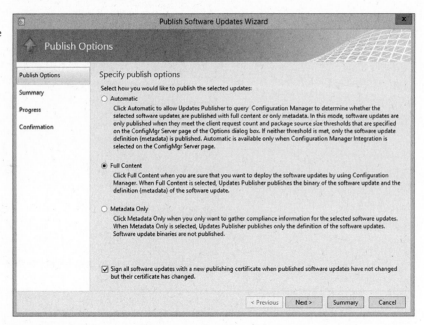

Automatic This option lets Configuration Manager determine whether the selected software updates are published with full content or metadata only. When you select this option, software updates are published only when they meet the client request count and package source size thresholds that are configured at the Configuration Manager Server section while configuring the connection. If the thresholds are not met, only metadata will be published.

Full Content When this option is selected, Updates Publisher publishes the binary and the metadata of the software update.

Metadata Only When this option is selected, Updates Publisher publishes the metadata of the software update.

5. Select Sign All Software Updates With A New Publishing Certificate When Published Software Updates Have Not Changed But Their Certificate Has Changed, and click Next.

6. Confirm the settings and click Next.

7. After the updates are published, as shown in Figure 8.38, click Close.

FIGURE 8.38
Confirmation page of the Publish Software Updates Wizard

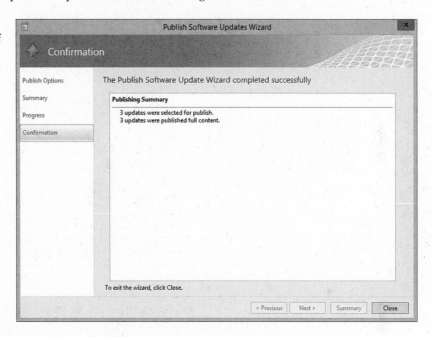

Third-Party Updates in Configuration Manager

To be able to deploy the third-party software updates with Configuration Manager, you need to configure the software update point component to also synchronize the software updates:

1. In the Configuration Manager console choose the Administration workspace, then select Overview ➤ Site Configuration ➤ Sites and select the highest site in the hierarchy.

2. Choose Configure Site Components on the Settings section of the Home tab of the ribbon, and click Software Update Point.

3. To configure the third-party software updates, click the Products tab, as shown in Figure 8.39. If the third-party updates are not yet available, manually synchronize the software updates.

4. After you synchronize the software updates, the third-party updates will become available in Configuration Manager, as shown in Figure 8.40.

These updates can be deployed like every other software update in the Software Updates feature.

FIGURE 8.39
Select the third-party updates.

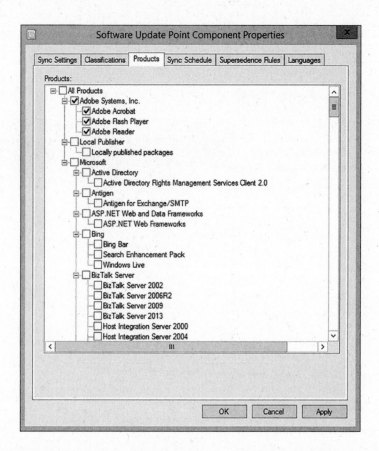

FIGURE 8.40
The third-party updates are available in Configuration Manager.

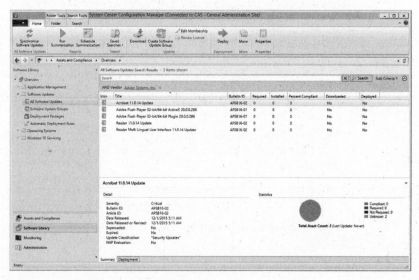

Monitoring Software Update Deployments

Configuration Manager offers in-console monitoring. You can see the compliancy level per deployment.

In-Console Monitoring

You can find in-console monitoring of software update deployment in the Configuration Manager console at several places. The error codes are explained, so you can find the solution instantly.

MONITORING PER SOFTWARE UPDATE

When you select a software update in the All Software Updates repository, the statistics of the software update appear. In the Statistics part of the summary in Figure 8.41, you are able to see how many systems are compliant, how many systems don't need the update, where the update is required, and where the status is unknown.

FIGURE 8.41

In-console statistics per update

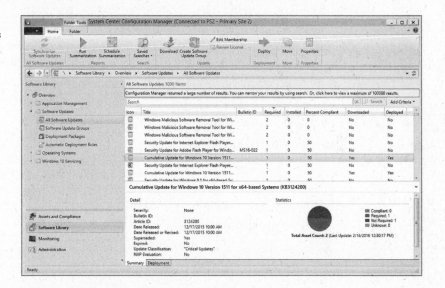

MONITORING PER DEPLOYMENT

When you deploy the updates, you can see the deployment status per deployment. The deployment status contains the following categories and subcategories. The deployment status in Figure 8.42 shows how many systems are compliant, how many systems are in the process of installing the updates, how many systems have an error, and where the status is unknown.

FIGURE 8.42
In-console statistics per update deployment

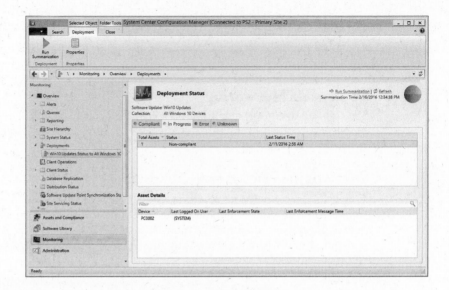

Status: Unknown This status says that the status messages of the Configuration Manager clients have not yet been received by the management point of the primary site. The following subcategories are available:

- Devices Unhealthy/Active
- Devices Healthy/Inactive
- Devices Healthy/Active

Status: Error Errors can occur when you deploy software updates. This category shows all the devices that have had an error while deploying the software updates. The following subcategories and error descriptions are available:

- Scan Tool Policy Not Found.
- Network Connection: Windows Update Agent Encountered An Error.
- Policy Platform Client: Data Is Invalid.
- Fatal Error During Installation.
- Pre Install Scan Failed.
- Software Update Still Detected As Actionable After Apply.
- Unknown Error (-2147012744).
- Class Not Registered.
- Access Is Denied.
- Unspecified Error.

Status: In Progress   The In Progress status displays all devices that are preparing for the deployment of a software update or are currently receiving a deployment. The following subcategories are available:

- Downloading Update(s)

- Downloaded Update(s)

- Installing Update(s)

Compliant   When the devices are compliant, you will see all the assets that are compliant.

When selecting a system in the Asset Details part of the Deployment Status screen, you can retrieve additional details about the system by right-clicking the system and choosing More Details. In the Asset Message dialog shown in Figure 8.43, you can view the information about the deployment.

FIGURE 8.43
Details about the software update deployment

SOFTWARE UPDATE POINT SYNCHRONIZATION STATUS

Besides examining the log files as described earlier, you can monitor the software update point synchronization status from the console.

To monitor the synchronization in the hierarchy, do the following:

1. In the Configuration Manager console, choose the Monitoring workspace, then select Overview ➢ Software Update Point Synchronization Status.

2. Examine the synchronization status, the link state, and the catalog version, as shown in Figure 8.44.

FIGURE 8.44
Software
Update Point
Synchronization
Status

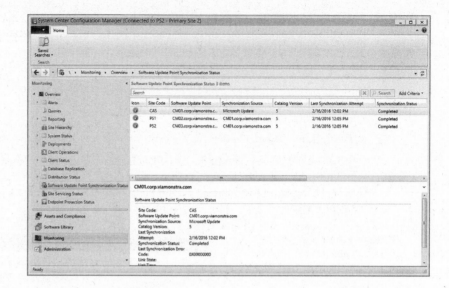

Reporting

The Configuration Manager client software performs two main phases of the software deployment process:

Evaluation Configuration Manager clients determine if the software updates in a deployment are required.

Enforcement Clients report their compliance state for the deployment.

Microsoft provides excellent reports to monitor the phases of software update deployments in Configuration Manager, and these reports are considered the best way to monitor the software update deployments. Those reports can be found in the Software Updates - C Deployment States category in the Reports node in the Configuration Manager console.

To monitor the evaluation phase of software update deployments, you should use the following three main reports:

States 2 - Evaluation States For A Deployment This report will give you a summary of the evaluation state of clients for a selected deployment and will provide information as to whether clients were able to evaluate a deployment successfully.

States 4 - Computers In A Specific State For A Deployment (Secondary) You can drill down into this report to get more information about clients in a specified deployment state.

States 7 - Error Status Messages For A Computer (Secondary) You can use this report to get all error message information for a deployment on a specific computer.

To monitor client enforcement for software update deployments, there are also three main reports that you should use:

States 1 - Enforcement States For A Deployment This report gives a summary of the enforcement state of clients for a specific deployment. It shows information on the state for installing the updates in the deployment, such as downloading the update, installing the update, successfully installing the update, and so on.

States 4 - Computers In A Specific State For A Deployment (Secondary)   You can drill down into this report to get more information about clients in a specified deployment state.

States 7 - Error Status Messages For A Computer (Secondary)   You can use this report to get all error message information for a deployment on a specific computer.

 Real World Scenario

BECOME FAMILIAR WITH WHAT NEEDS TO BE UPDATED AND IMPLEMENT SOFTWARE UPDATES

Now that you have deployed Configuration Manager and have Software Updates up and running, your manager wants you to make a concentrated effort to get clients up to date with critical security patches. He has made it clear that these are to be given priority over other updates until the numbers of required patches are down to a reasonable level, which is not the case now.

To accomplish your new software update initiative, you must first figure out what patches need to be installed on which computers.

One way to do this is to set up search criteria for each operating system that you support, listing all the critical security patches. With those search criteria, you highlight all the security patches that are required by your clients and make an update group out of them.

Once you have done that, you can either download all the updates and put them on your distribution points, or you can start a deployment directly from the update group and configure downloading those updates as part of that update.

The procedures that we detailed earlier in the chapter for configuring the different elements of Software Updates were made with that method of organization in mind.

Windows Update Servicing

There have been several changes to the method of delivering updates after October 2016. This new process is to bring more consistency and simplification to the update process. In this way, you can use the same method for all the Microsoft Windows Operating Systems. You can read more about this announcement in the following blog post: `https://blogs.technet.microsoft.com/windowsitpro/2016/08/15/further-simplifying-servicing-model-for-windows-7-and-windows-8-1/`.

Now let's dive more into what changed and how can you deliver those updates using System Center Configuration Manager.

The concept of servicing started with Windows 10 and now is being used for the following operating systems:

◆   Windows 7 SP1

◆   Windows 8.1

◆   Windows Server 2008 R2

◆   Windows Server 2012/2012 R2

The new update process consists in three main formats:

Security-Only (Quality) Updates These updates are going to be released on the normal Patch Tuesday that is the second Tuesday of every month; this update is considered a B week release.

Monthly (Quality) Rollups These updates are going to be released on the normal Patch Tuesday that is the second Tuesday of every month. This update is considered a B′ week release.

Preview (Quality) Rollups These updates are going to be released on the third Tuesday of every month; this is considered the C week release. Preview rollups are an additional monthly rollup containing a preview of upcoming non-security updates that are going to be included on the next monthly rollup.

Tables 8.8 and 8.9 give you an overview.

TABLE 8.8: Windows Update Overview

| | **PUBLISHING METHOD** | | | | | |
UPDATE TYPE	**WINDOWS UPDATE**	**WSUS**	**WUC**	**CLASSIFICATION**	**RELEASE CYCLE**	**CONTENTS**
Security Only Update		*	*	Security Updates	2nd Tuesday of each month	Only security fixes for the current month
Monthly Rollup	*	*	*	Security Updates	2nd Tuesday of each month	Security and non-security fixes for the current month and previous months
Preview Rollup	*	*	*	Updates	3rd Tuesday of each month	Preview of fixes to be released the following month as well as the previous months' fixes

TABLE 8.9: Windows Update Package Name

UPDATE TYPE	**DESCRIPTION**	**EXAMPLES**
Security Only Updates	Title always contains the phrase "Security Only" and *never* contains the word "Rollup"	October, 2016 *Security Only* Quality Update for... November, 2016 *Security Only* Update for .NET Framework...
Monthly Rollups	Title always contains the word "Security" *as well as* the phrase "Quality Rollup"	October, 2016 *Security* Monthly *Quality Rollup* for... December, 2016 *Security* and *Quality Rollup* for .NET Framework...
Preview Rollups	Title contains the phrase "Preview of Monthly Quality Rollup" and does *not* contain the word "Security"	October, 2016 *Preview of Monthly Quality Rollup* for...

It is important to note that once the software update catalog has synced with Microsoft Updates, you will see the packages as noted in Table 8.9 in the All Software Updates node under Software Library Workspace ➤ Software Updates. Once they have synced you are ready to create your Software Update Groups; it is recommended that you create these groups very like the Update Types. The software update groups should look like Figure 8.45.

FIGURE 8.45

Software Update Groups for Servicing

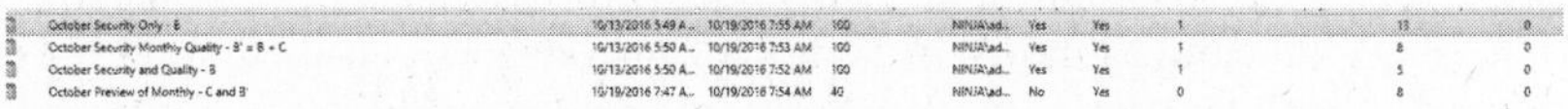

Figure 8.45 shows that we follow the example of Table 8.9 in creating our software update groups. In each of these groups you will find the updates that were released for that month; for example, the October Security Only - B software update group is shown in Figure 8.46. You can see that it only contains updates for Windows operating systems and some .Net Framework updates for the current month, as was explained in Table 8.8.

FIGURE 8.46

October Security Only - B software update group

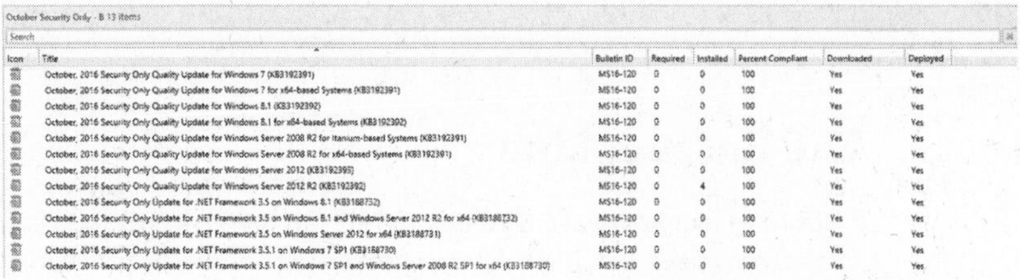

Notice that in the October Security Monthly Quality - B′ = B + C software update group, shown in Figure 8.47, contains Security Monthly Quality updates for that month and the previous month, as was explained in Table 8.8.

FIGURE 8.47

October Security Monthly Software Update Group

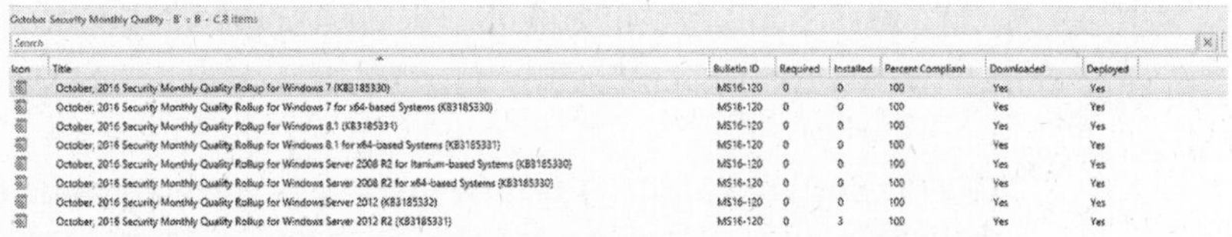

Notice that the October Security and Quality - B software update group, shown in Figure 8.48, contains Security and Quality updates for that month. This is a set of updates that are going to be released just for .NET Framework every month and should only be deployed to those systems that require the updates. It is also important to note that Internet Explorer updates will be released as part of the monthly rollups when they are required. As reference you can read more about the .Net Framework monthly rollup at the following link:

```
https://blogs.msdn.microsoft.com/dotnet/2016/10/11/net-framework-monthly-rollups-
explained/
```

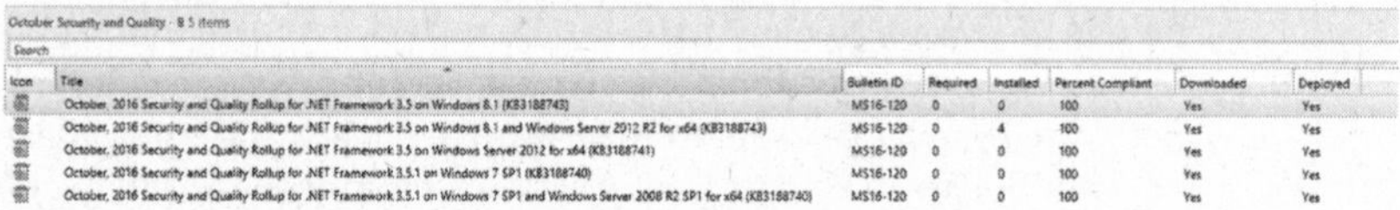

FIGURE 8.48
October Security and
Quality software
update group

Also as part of the new update process there is a new category of updates that is called the Preview, as shown in Table 8.8. This category is used to test upcoming updates ahead of time, to validate that they work before the next monthly rollup is released to everyone. As you can see in Figure 8.49, the updates are released as Preview and should only be deployed to a QA or testing environment. This group contains updates for that month and the previous month, as explained in Table 8.9.

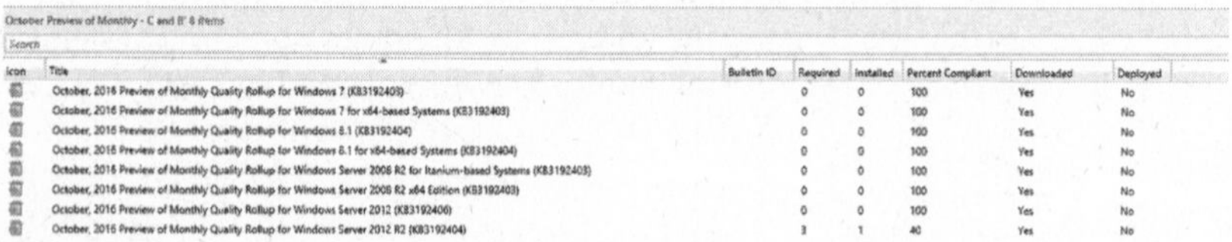

FIGURE 8.49
October Preview
of Monthly Rollup
software update
group

The Bottom Line

Plan to use Software Updates. You can use the same method of deployment intelligence that was used in Chapter 2 to gather information for planning to implement Software Updates. This will be very helpful in making sure that you get the most out of the Software Updates feature for your organization.

> **Master It** What is the first step in gathering deployment intelligence when you are planning to implement Software Updates?

Configure Software Updates. Before you can use Software Updates in your environment, you must set up and configure the various components of this feature.

> **Master It** What is the first thing you have to install before you can use Software Updates?

Use the Software Updates feature to manage software updates. The hardest thing to do in SMS 2003 relating to patch management was to programmatically prioritize software updates that are critical so they can be deployed with a higher priority than other updates.

> **Master It** What does Configuration Manager provide that can help with prioritizing software updates?

Use automatic update deployment to deploy software updates. When you deployed software in Configuration Manager 2007, you deployed software updates through a procedure that consumed a lot of time.

> **Master It** Configuration Manager Current Branch has a new feature called Automatic Deployment Rules. What kinds of updates are suitable to deploy via the automatic deployment rules?

Chapter 9

Operating System Deployment

Most IT administrators want to automate as many functions as possible in order to reproduce the same outcome consistently and quickly to as many devices as possible. Setting up a basic computer build is no exception.

In Configuration Manager 2007, the Operating System Deployment (OSD) feature became one of the most important features. With Configuration Manager you can install Windows operating systems without any user intervention. This is known as Zero-Touch deployment. When a Windows deployment is finished, the user is able to log in to the network and start working with the new operating systems and the available applications. The OSD feature is highly dependent on the Windows Assessment and Deployment Kit (ADK) for Windows 10. The Windows ADK is a prerequisite of Configuration Manager Current Branch.

In Configuration Manager Current Branch the OSD feature has matured and includes added features such as Windows 10 Servicing and the Windows 10 Upgrade task sequence. We will walk you through several Windows deployment scenarios without and with the use of the Microsoft Deployment Toolkit (MDT) 2013.

In this chapter, you will learn to

◆ Specify a Network Access account

◆ Enable PXE support

◆ Update the driver catalog package

◆ Update an image from the console

◆ Support Windows 10

What's New in Operating System Deployment

The OSD feature has not been significantly changed from Configuration Manager 2012. Some parts are enhanced, changed, or new to the feature. The following list shows the changes since Configuration Manager 2012:

◆ Support for Windows 10 upgrade packages

◆ Support for Windows 10 upgrade task sequences

◆ Support for Windows 10 servicing

Planning for OSD with Configuration Manager

Before you configure the feature, you should plan your deployment, since you can deploy different kinds of operating systems in numerous ways. To deploy your operating systems in an effective and cost-efficient way, you need to address the following items when planning your deployment:

◆ Deployment scenarios

◆ The kind of images to deploy

◆ The kind of components to use

Deployment Scenarios

You can deploy the operating system in different ways. In Configuration Manager you can deploy an operating system in three kinds of scenarios:

Bare-Metal Scenario   Installing an operating system to a new out-of-the-box client computer.

Refresh Computer Scenario   Deploying an image to an existing Windows installation to perform an upgrade or reinstall while migrating the user state to the new Windows installation.

Upgrade Scenario   Especially for Windows 10, an upgrade scenario/task sequence has been added.

The Kind of Images to Deploy

Configuration Manager Current Branch supports, as did the previous version of Configuration Manager, the deployment of two kinds of operating system installations. You can install images, based on the Windows Imaging (WIM) format, or just install operating systems by using the source of an operating system installation. Using the source of an operating system is an unattended installation and is normally used to create a WIM image with a build-and-capture task sequence. The source can be a copy of the DVD of Windows 10, Windows 8.*x*, Windows 7, Windows Vista, Windows Server 2008 (R2), Windows Server 2012 (R2), or Windows Server 2016.

Operating System Images   Operating images are often custom images that are built with the build-and-capture task sequence; the default install.wim file can also be used. This task sequence allows you to install and create an image of a customized reference operating system image. Also, the operating system images are used when you want to build and capture a custom image of a Windows 7 or higher or a Windows Server 2008 or higher operating system.

Operating System Upgrade Packages   An upgrade package is used to upgrade older Windows versions to Windows 10 operating systems or while upgrading to the latest version of Windows 10 if you have Windows 10 already.

OSD Components

The OSD feature uses different kinds of components within Configuration Manager Current Branch. We'll look at each of them.

BOOT IMAGES

Configuration Manager comes with two default boot images. These images are available for all sites in the hierarchy. There is no need to create and deploy boot images for each Configuration Manager site in the hierarchy.

When you access a standard boot image, you can configure several settings in various tabs. To access the boot image, browse to the Software Library workspace and choose Overview ➤ Operating Systems ➤ Boot Images. The tabs shown in Figure 9.1 are available.

FIGURE 9.1
Boot Image Properties

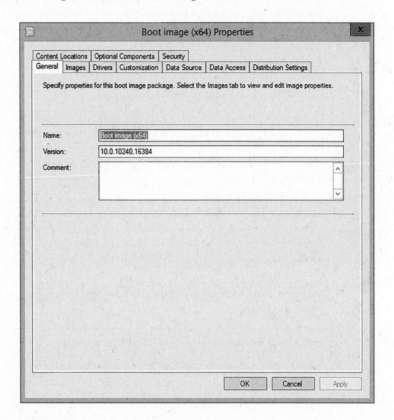

General On the General tab, you can enter or change the name, version, or comments of the boot image that's already available in Configuration Manager.

Images The Images tab provides information about the boot image. If you changed the image properties with an external tool, you can reload the original properties.

Drivers The Drivers tab provides an overview of the drivers that are injected into the boot image. You can also add drivers from the driver store to the boot image. Common drivers to add to boot images are network and SATA/SCSI drivers and any other critical drivers.

Customization If you want to customize the selected boot image, you can find some options on the Customization tab. When you're in the plan and build phases of your project and you want to test the deployment of images, you can enable command support in the

Windows Preinstallation Environment (WinPE) phase of your deployment. Pressing F8 opens a command prompt that allows you to access the filesystem and log files that are located in the _SMSTaskSequence\Logs\Smstslog directory. There is also an option to change the background that is shown during the WinPE phase.

If you want to add a prestart command hook and supporting files, you can add the command line here.

Data Source   The Data Source tab supplies the path to the boot WIM image that is used for the boot image package. The Data Source tab is also the place to enable or disable the ability to boot the image from PXE and deploy it to a PXE-enabled distribution point.

Data Access   With settings in the Data Access tab, you can configure how the package is stored on the distribution points.

Distribution Settings   Here you can define how the boot image package is distributed to the distribution points and set the priority.

Content Locations   On the Content Locations tab, you can see on which distribution points or distribution point groups the image package is available. Selecting a distribution point or distribution point group allows you to validate the copy on the location, redistribute the boot image package to the location, or remove the boot image package from the location.

Optional Components   In earlier versions, an administrator had to use MDT to create custom boot images to incorporate components such as an HTML Application (HTA). Or the administrator had to add the components to an SCCM boot image manually using Deployment Image Servicing and Management (DISM). Configuration Manager includes the ability to add optional components to the WinPE images from the Configuration Manager console.

Security   The Security tab shows you the users who have administrative permissions to the boot image object.

DECIDING WHEN TO USE WHICH BOOT IMAGE

There are two different versions of boot images that support two kinds of platforms: an x86 version and an x64 version.

You can use the x86 boot image version to deploy the following:

◆   32-bit operating system image

◆   64-bit operating system image

◆   32-bit operating system upgrade package

You can use the x64 boot image version to deploy the following:

◆   64-bit operating system image

◆   64-bit operating system upgrade package

You can define per task sequence which boot image to use.

STATE MIGRATION POINT

The state migration point stores the user data that is gathered by the User State Migration Tool (USMT) when a computer is being refreshed by a new Windows operating system. The component can be configured to store user data on different storage folders, depending on the deletion policy.

DISTRIBUTION POINTS

The distribution point is used to store the content that is related to the OSD. Since Configuration Manager 2012, two very important features have been moved to the distribution point: PXE and multicast.

When configuring a distribution point for OSD, you can adjust the following settings:

PXE Tab   As mentioned earlier, the PXE feature has been moved to the distribution point. The PXE tab allows you to enable or disable support for PXE, but a Windows Deployment Services (WDS) service must be present. As in earlier versions, you can configure PXE to respond to incoming PXE requests and unknown computer support. Configuration Manager Current Branch introduces the ability to enable Primary User Assignment, which is discussed later in this chapter. If you want to secure PXE with a password, you can configure one. When you enable a boot image for PXE and the boot image is available on the distribution point, the boot image is also copied into the RemoteInstall\SMSBoot folder of WDS. Enabling the PXE feature will also install the WDS feature if it is not yet available.

Multicast Tab   The Multicast feature has also been moved to the distribution point via PXE. You configure the options per distribution point. With multicasting, you can deploy an image to more than one workstation simultaneously. For instance, a normal deployment of operating systems in an environment with Configuration Manager for a 2 GB image to 30 devices would result in about 60 GB of network utilization. However, when you take the same deployment and use multicasting, you now see as little as about 2 GB of network utilization to deploy the same 30 devices.

Talk to your network administrator while implementing multicasting in your network.

OPERATING SYSTEM IMAGES

The operating system images are the WIM images that can be deployed to workstations or servers. An operating system image can be a captured operating system. When you access the image, you can configure several settings in various tabs. To access an operating system image, go to the Software Library workspace and choose Overview ➤ Operating Systems ➤ Operating System Image.

General   The General tab is used to supply information about the operating system image, like name, version, and comments.

Images   The Images tab gives you information about the WIM image. Information like OS version, architecture, creation date, and more is shared. If you changed the image properties using an external tool, you can reload the information from the WIM image.

Data Source   The Data Source tab supplies the UNC path to the WIM image that is used for the operating system image package.

Data Access Tab   With settings in the Data Access tab, you can configure how the package is stored on the distribution points.

Distribution Settings   Here you can define how the operating system image package is distributed to the distribution points and set the priority. You can also specify whether to allow this operating system image to be transferred using multicasting via WinPE.

Servicing   On the Servicing tab you are able to see or change the offline servicing schedule if offline servicing for an image is scheduled.

Installed Updates   The installed updates tab gives you a list with installed updates that have been installed with offline servicing.

Content Locations   On the Content Locations tab, you can see on which distribution points or distribution point groups the operating system image package is available. Selecting a distribution point or distribution point group allows you to validate the copy on the location, redistribute the operating system image package to the location, or remove the operating system image package from the location.

Security   The Security tab shows you the users who have administrative permissions to the operating system image object.

Operating System Upgrade Packages

The operating system upgrade packages are the install source of a Windows 10 operating system. With this source you are able to install or upgrade an operating system unattended. Operating system upgrade packages can also be used, for instance, while building and capturing an operating system image. When you access the package, you can configure several settings. To access an operating system upgrade package, go to the Software Library workspace and choose Overview ➤ Operating Systems ➤ Operating System Upgrade Packages. Operating system upgrade packages for Configuration Manager Current Branch are supported only for Windows 10.

General   The General tab is used to supply information about the operating system installer, like name, version, and comments.

Editions   The Editions tab allows you to see information about the selected edition in the installation source. For instance, a Windows 10 install source has more editions available; editions can be Professional or Enterprise.

Data Source   The Data Source tab supplies the UNC path to the install source of the operating system installer that is used for the operating system installer package.

Data Access   With settings in the Data Access tab, you can configure how the package is stored on the distribution points.

Distribution Settings   Here you can define how the operating system installer package is distributed to the distribution points and also set the priority.

Servicing   On the Servicing tab you are able to see or change the offline servicing schedule if offline servicing for an image is scheduled.

Installed Updates   The Installed Updates tab gives you a list of installed updates that have been installed with offline servicing.

Content Locations   On the Content Locations tab, you can see on which distribution points or distribution point groups the operating system installer package is available. Selecting a distribution point or distribution point group allows you to validate the copy on the location, redistribute the operating system installer package to the location, or remove the operating system installer package from the location.

Security   The Security tab shows you the users who have administrative permissions to the operating system installer object.

Task Sequences

Task sequences provide a mechanism to perform a series of tasks on a client computer without any user intervention. Using task sequences, you can deploy operating systems but also distribute software, configure client settings, update drivers, edit user states, and perform other tasks in support of operating system deployment. Task sequences are global data and are available for all Configuration Manager sites in the hierarchy.

You can create four different kinds of task sequences:

Install An Existing Image Package   This task sequence will install an existing WIM image to a computer via the normal distribution method, PXE, or media. This option uses a predefined sequence of steps. The steps will take care of wiping or formatting the disk, installing the operating system, installing software updates, installing applications, and setting the user state.

Build And Capture A Reference Operating System Image   This task sequence will build and capture a Windows operating system in a new WIM image. You can use this WIM image to deploy to the client computers. This option uses a predefined sequence of steps.

Install An Existing Image Package To A Virtual Hard Drive   This task sequence will install an existing image package and shut down the computer. This task sequence is used with the Create Virtual Hard Drive Wizard. The wizard creates a temporary virtual machine, creates the virtual hard disk (VHD), installs task sequence, and saves the virtual hard drive to a defined location. The Create Virtual Hard Drive Wizard is discussed later in this chapter in detail.

Upgrade An Operating System From An Upgrade Package   This task sequence will upgrade your current operating system to the one provided in the operating system upgrade package.

Create A New Custom Task Sequence   A custom task sequence is an empty task sequence for which you define your own steps.

A task sequence consists of tasks or steps grouped into the following categories:

General   In the General category, the following tasks can be configured for the task sequence:

- Run Command Line
- Run PowerShell Script
- Set Dynamic Variables
- Join Domain Or Workgroup
- Connect To Network Folder

- ◆ Restart Computer
- ◆ Set Task Sequence Variable
- ◆ Check Readiness

Software In the Software category, the following tasks can be configured for the task sequence:

- ◆ Install Application
- ◆ Install Package
- ◆ Install Software Updates
- ◆ Download Package Content

Disks In the Disks category, the following tasks can be configured for the task sequence:

- ◆ Format And Partition Disk
- ◆ Convert Disk To Dynamic
- ◆ Enable BitLocker
- ◆ Disable BitLocker
- ◆ Pre-provision BitLocker

User State In the User State category, the following tasks can be configured for the task sequence:

- ◆ Request State Store
- ◆ Capture User State
- ◆ Restore User State
- ◆ Release State Store

Images In the Images category, the following tasks can be configured for the task sequence:

- ◆ Apply Operating System Image
- ◆ Apply Data Image
- ◆ Setup Windows And Configuration Manager
- ◆ Upgrade Operating System
- ◆ Install Deployment Tools
- ◆ Prepare Configuration Manager Client For Capture
- ◆ Prepare Windows For Capture
- ◆ Capture Operating System Image

Drivers In the Drivers category, the following tasks can be configured for the task sequence:

- ◆ Auto Apply Drivers
- ◆ Apply Driver Package

Settings   In the Settings category, the following tasks can be configured for the task sequence:

- Capture Network Settings
- Capture Windows Settings
- Apply Network Settings
- Apply Windows Settings

TASK SEQUENCE MEDIA

When you use task sequence media, you can create a CD, DVD, or USB containing the files required for deploying or capturing an operating system with Configuration Manager. You can select the following kinds of media:

Standalone Media   Use this type of media to deploy an operating system without network access.

Bootable Media   Use this type of media to access the Configuration Manager infrastructure to deploy an operating system across the network.

Capture Media   Use this type of media to capture a WIM image of an operating system on a reference computer.

Prestaged Media   Use this type of media to create a file for operating system deployment that contains an operating system image and bootable media that can be prestaged on a hard disk.

DRIVER CATALOG

The driver catalog is the place to store device drivers that need to be added during a Windows deployment or to a boot image. Normally not all the device drivers need to be added, because Windows 10 supports many hardware platforms and devices. When you deploy an operating system, you can include a driver package or let WinPE discover the drivers through WMI.

You can organize your driver structure by adding the drivers for each make and model to folders or categories. This way, you can clean up old drivers in the future.

DRIVER PACKAGES

The driver packages are used to keep the drivers grouped per brand, model, operating system, and/or platform and contain the source of the drivers. These driver packages need to be distributed to the distribution point (groups) in your Configuration Manager hierarchy and can be used in the task sequences.

User Device Affinity

User device affinity helps you create relationships between users and devices. You create relationships by either adding primary devices to users or adding primary users to devices. When you deploy a new operating system to a device, Configuration Manager will check the user's collection memberships and pre-deploy the user-targeted applications. The user's primary device will attempt to install the application that is targeted to the user whether or not the user is logged on as part of the OSD process. When a user logs on for the first time after the installation of the new operating system is finished, all user-targeted apps are available and the user is able to work with the device instantly.

Configuration Manager allows you to create the following relationships:

◆ Single primary user to primary device

◆ Multiple primary devices per user

◆ Multiple primary users per device

Deployment Process

When you deploy a Windows operating system using the task sequences of Configuration Manager, you need to follow certain steps to be sure that the deployment will succeed. Generally speaking, deploying an operating system involves three major steps: prepare, build and capture, and deploy.

Prepare for OSD

The first step is preparing the Configuration Manager environment so that you can deploy the operating system. Gather the information that you need to create an image of an operating system and deploy it to client computers. Essential information includes the makes and models of the computers and the devices that need drivers. You also need to specify whether you want to add applications to the image.

Build and Capture an Operating System

After your design for the operating system is finished, you need to translate the design into a task sequence that will build and capture your operating system.

The build-and-capture task sequence creates a fully unattended installation of a Windows operating system. Depending on your design, the task sequence can take care of installing the available software updates and, if you like, applications that are part of the common operating environment. Incorporating applications into your WIM image is not a best practice, but there are situations where you'll want to add some applications to your image.

Another option is to use a reference computer and capture the reference operating system, which is created manually, using a capture media task sequence.

FAT VS. THIN IMAGES

When you deploy Windows images in your environment, think about how to deploy your common operating environment, operating system, and standard applications. You can choose to deploy your operating system and applications in an image (fat image) or just the operating system in an image (thin image) and the applications during the deployment process. A thin image is easier to maintain because you don't have to recapture your image when an application needs to be updated. However, a fat image may be quicker to deploy.

Deploy an Operating System

After capturing an operating system image, you can deploy it to one or more computers in your environment. The task sequence that you create can be used for bare-metal deployment or to refresh or upgrade a computer that is a member of an existing Configuration Manager environment. After creating a task sequence to deploy your Windows image, you can change and add tasks to suit your needs. You can also add or change the software updates, installation of applications, disk layout, domain, network settings, and much more.

MAINTAINING IMAGES

Configuration Manager supports maintaining your Windows images with software updates from the console. You can schedule offline servicing of the Windows image by adding the latest software updates and redeploying the images to your distribution points periodically. This is described in the section "Servicing Your Operating System Images and VHDs Offline" later in this chapter. We recommend that you re-create your image every quarter; this way, you will keep your images up to date and the deployment process fast and smooth.

Preparing Configuration Manager for OSD

You need to configure Configuration Manager Current Branch for deploying an operating system image. The first step in preparing for OSD is to configure the Network Access account. Then you need to install and configure the state migration point role and enable the PXE feature on the distribution points. In earlier versions, you had to manually create packages for the Configuration Manager Client and USMT; now, those packages are available by default after the installation of Configuration Manager Current Branch.

Configuring the Network Access Account

The first step is to set up an Active Directory user as the Network Access account. As mentioned in Chapter 7, "Application Deployment," you are able to create more than one Network Access account to support, for instance, multiple forests. A general rule for those accounts is to give them an easily identifiable name. For example, a domain administrator would create an account called svc-sccm-na (or whatever fits your environment's naming conventions).

Next, you will need to configure Configuration Manager to use the Network Access account. Take the following steps:

1. Open the Configuration Manager console, choose the Administration workspace, and expand Overview ➢ Site Configuration ➢ Sites.

2. Select one of the sites for which you want to configure the Network Access account, and click Configure Site Components in the settings section on the Home tab of the ribbon.

3. Select Software Distribution.

4. Select the Network Access Account tab, and set the Network Access account to the account created earlier, as shown in Figure 9.2.

5. Click OK.

The Network Access account must have access to the computer that is deployed and to the content on the distribution points. Normally a Network Access account has permission if it's a member of the Domain Users Active Directory group.

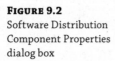

FIGURE 9.2
Software Distribution
Component Properties
dialog box

Configuring the State Migration Point Role

The next step in preparing Configuration Manager for OSD is to set up a state migration point. The state migration point is used to store user-migrated settings and data during the operating system image deployment. This state migration point is a site system role within Configuration Manager, and it will need to be assigned to a server. Follow these few steps to set up the state migration point role:

1. Open the Configuration Manager console, select the Administration workspace, and expand Overview ➢ Site Configuration ➢ Servers And Site System Roles.

2. Select the site server for which you want to install and configure the state migration point, and click Add Site System Roles on the Home tab of the ribbon.

3. On the Add Site System Roles Wizard's General page, click Next twice.

4. You will be presented with the System Role Selection page. Select State Migration Point, as shown in Figure 9.3, and click Next.

5. On the State Migration Point page, click the starburst icon to create a new storage folder.

6. Create a new storage folder in the Storage Folder Settings dialog, shown in Figure 9.4.

   This allows you to enter the path to use when storing state migration data.

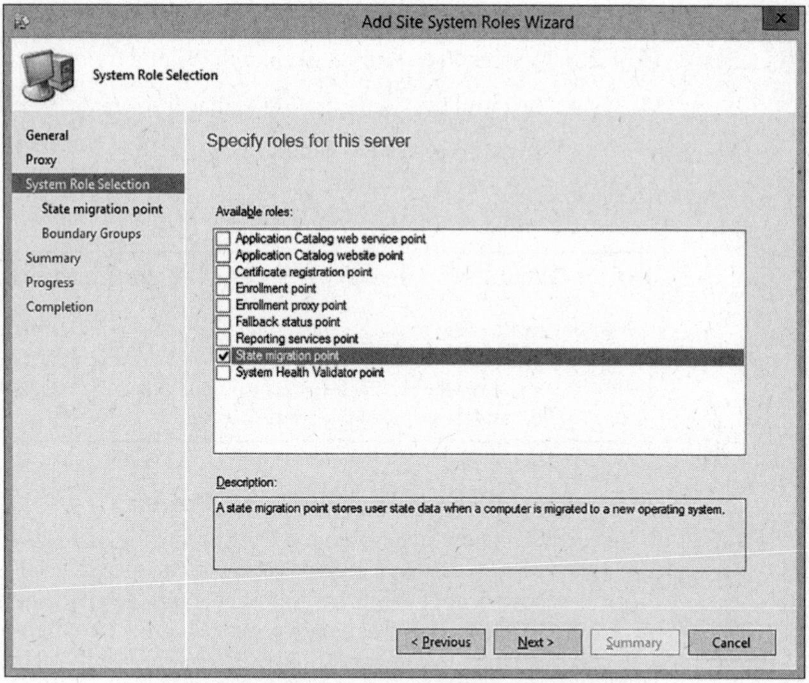

FIGURE 9.3
Add Site System
Roles Wizard—State
Migration Point page

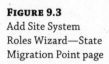
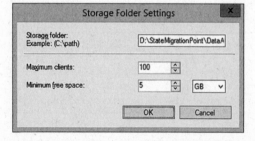

FIGURE 9.4
Designating a storage
folder

7. Under the storage folder you also have to configure the maximum number of clients that are allowed to store the data and the minimum required free space on the disk.

A way to determine the size for your state migration point is to identify the number of deployments that must take place, the average size of the user state, and how long the user state must be stored. Be sure to keep your drive from running out of free space by configuring a minimum free space for the disk where the storage folder is located.

8. Click OK to return to the State Migration Point page.

You can change the Deletion Policy setting if you think one day is too long or not long enough until the user data is removed from the state migration point.

Enabling the Restore-Only Mode option will result in the state migration point responding only to restore requests.

9. Click Next to configure boundary groups for the site system.

10. Click Next, and you will be taken to the Summary page.

11. Click Next to allow Configuration Manager to create the new site role.

    This brings up the Wizard Completed page.

12. Click Close.

DON'T CONFIGURE THE DELETION POLICY TO DELETE USER STATE IMMEDIATELY

A best practice from Microsoft is not to set the deletion policy to delete a user state immediately after it is marked for deletion. If an attacker is able to retrieve the user state before a valid computer does, the user state would be deleted before that time. Set the deletion interval to long enough to verify the successful restore of the user state data.

Configuring PXE on Distribution Points

To allow Configuration Manager to use OSD for deploying to bare-metal devices, you must configure PXE on the distribution points for which you will need to set up the Network Access account (we showed you how earlier in this chapter). You will also need to ensure that the Configuration Manager client upgrade package has been configured and is ready for deployment, as you also did earlier in this chapter. Finally, ensure that the boot image is set up as a package.

To be able to use PXE on a distribution point site server, you also have to install WDS on that server.

INSTALLING WINDOWS DEPLOYMENT SERVICES

You can install WDS through Add Or Remove Programs on Windows Server 2008 SP2 or higher machines. If you do not install the WDS feature within Windows, Configuration Manager will automatically install this feature when enabling the PXE feature on the distribution point.

The next stage in preparing Configuration Manager for OSD is to set up PXE support. Configuration Manager no longer has a PXE service point; the PXE feature is embedded in the distribution point role. You need to enable and configure the PXE feature per distribution point. Follow these few steps to set up the PXE feature:

1. Open the Configuration Manager console, select the Administration workspace, and expand Overview ➤ Distribution Points.

2. Select the site server on which the distribution point resides, and click Properties on the Site Role tab of the ribbon.

3. Select the PXE tab and click Enable PXE Support For Clients.

   When you enable the feature, you will see a Review Required Ports For PXE dialog, as shown in Figure 9.5. This dialog informs you that Configuration Manager must have some UDP ports opened on the server.

FIGURE 9.5
Review Required Ports
For PXE dialog

4. Click Yes to continue enabling PXE support for clients.

5. After enabling the feature, you can configure how Configuration Manager will allow incoming PXE requests, as shown in Figure 9.6. Click OK when you've finished.

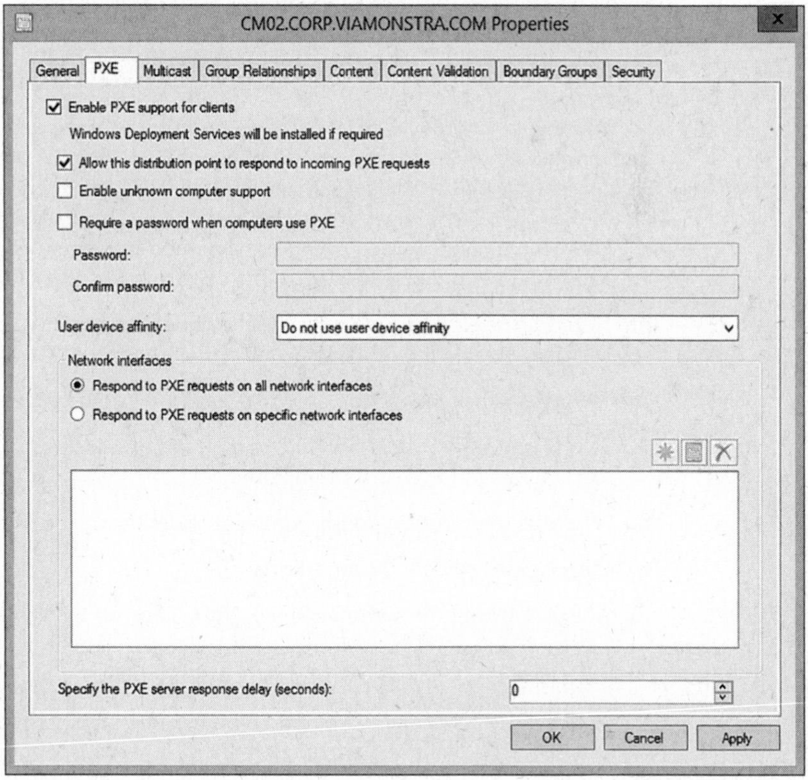

FIGURE 9.6
PXE settings page

It will take some time for the PXE feature to successfully install on the system. You can monitor the progress of the installation by checking the `distmgr.log` and `smspxe.log` files. WDS will be installed if it is not already present on this system.

DHCP AND PXE ON THE SAME SERVER

You'll need to set up some DHCP options for PXE to boot properly. Specifically, you'll have to specify options 60, 66, and 67 when the DHCP server is on the same server as your Windows deployment server. Option 60 needs to be set to PXEClient, which is only used in this scenario. Option 66 is the FQDN of the Configuration Manager server, and option 67 should be the path to `SMSBoot\<platform>\pxeboot.com`.

Distributing the Boot Image Package

The next part of preparing Configuration Manager for OSD is to distribute the boot image package to a distribution point. This boot image is used to start the computer in WinPE for capturing, prior to deploying the operating system image. This procedure, because of the size of the images, will take some time to complete:

1. From the Configuration Manager console, choose the Software Library workspace, expand Overview ➤ Operating Systems, and select Boot Images.

   You will notice two boot images for various platforms: one for x64—Boot Image (x64)—and the other for x86 devices—Boot Image (x86). For the purpose of this book, we will concentrate on the x86 boot image, but there is basically no difference in configuring one or the other. The images are configured during the installation of Configuration Manager. However, no distribution points are assigned for either of the boot images. You need to add both boot image packages to the distribution points.

2. To configure a distribution point, select Boot Images ➤ Boot Image (x86), and click Distribute Content on the Home tab of the ribbon.

3. This opens the Distribute Content Wizard's Welcome page; click Next to continue.

4. Select the distribution point you want to use on the Specify The Content Destination page by clicking Add ➤ Distribution Point.

5. Select the distribution points you want to deploy the boot image to, and click OK.

6. Click Next to review the summary.

7. After reviewing the summary, click Next. Then on the Wizard Completed page, click Close.

   It will take some time to copy the boot image package to the distribution point. Do the same for the boot image called Boot Image (x64). Every time you change the boot image, it will be re-created and distributed to the different distribution points.

Enabling Boot Images for PXE

The last part of preparing Configuration Manager for OSD is enabling both of the boot images to be available for PXE:

1. From the Configuration Manager console, choose the Software Library workspace, expand Overview ➤ Operating Systems, and select Boot Images.

2. Select the boot image for which you want to enable PXE support, and click Properties on the Home tab of the ribbon.

3. Click the Data Source tab, and enable the Deploy This Boot Image From The PXE-Enabled Distribution Point option, as shown in Figure 9.7; this is enabled by default for the default boot images.

4. Click OK.

FIGURE 9.7
Enable the boot image to boot via PXE.

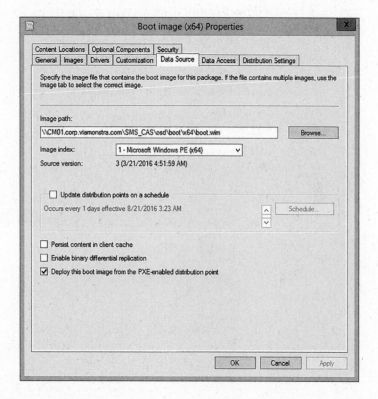

Configuration Manager will process the change and configure the WDS server to use the boot image from Configuration Manager. Configuration Manager will place the boot image in the `<drive>\RemoteInstall\SMSImages` folder.

Let's review the steps briefly for configuring Configuration Manager for OSD:

1. First, you configure the Network Access account, and then you create the client install package.

2. Second, you set up the state migration point and PXE support for Configuration Manager.

3. Finally, you deploy the boot images to the distribution points and PXE-enabled distribution points.

Adding Operating System Source

The next step after preparing Configuration Manager for OSD is to add the source content of the default operating systems.

Adding the Default Operating System Image

Adding a source of an operating system that you can use for the build-and-capture process can be done as follows:

Adding a Default *install.wim* image as an Operating System Image   Adding the default image can be done by adding the default install.wim as an operating system image to Configuration Manager. The install.wim file can found in the source of the DVD or ISO that holds the operating system. The Build And Capture Task Sequence Wizard, for instance, lets you select the operating system image directly.

You can add an install.wim file from an operating system source by following these steps:

1. From the Configuration Manager console, choose the Software Library workspace, expand Overview ➤ Operating Systems, and select Operating System Images.

2. Click Add Operating System Image, and browse to the root UNC location of the install source on your package source share. From there, browse to Sources and select the install.wim file, as shown in Figure 9.8.

FIGURE 9.8
Add an install.wim file as an operating system image.

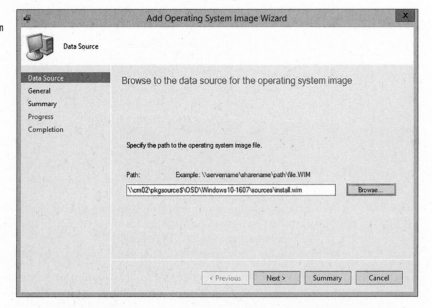

3. Click Next and supply the operating system image with a name, version, and comments if necessary, and click Next again.

4. Review the summary, and click Next.

5. When finished, click Close.

After creating the operating system image package, distribute the package to the distribution points in your hierarchy. By using this method, you can build and capture the following operating systems:

- Windows 7 SP1

- Windows 8

- Windows 8.1

- Windows 10

- Windows Server 2008

- Windows Server 2008 R2

- Windows Server 2012

- Windows Server 2012 R2

- Windows Server 2016

Adding an Operating System Upgrade Package

The operating system upgrade packages can be used to upgrade operating systems that you can deploy with Configuration Manager by using the unattended setup. With Configuration Manager and the default boot images, only Windows 10 operating system installers are supported. This operating system upgrade package cannot be used for build-and-capture task sequences.

You can add an operating system upgrade package by following these steps:

1. From the Configuration Manager console, choose the Software Library workspace, expand Overview ➢ Operating Systems, and select Operating System Upgrade Package.

2. Click Add Operating System Upgrade Package on the Home tab of the ribbon, and fill in the UNC path to the install source of the operating system, as shown in Figure 9.9.

3. Click Next.

4. Supply the operating system upgrade package with a name, version, and comments, and click Next.

5. Review the summary, and click Next.

6. When finished, click Close.

FIGURE 9.9
Creating an operating system upgrade package

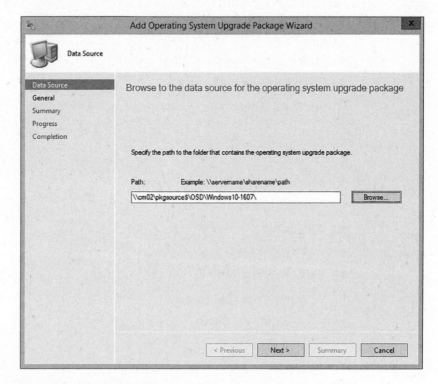

Developing a Task Sequence for Creating a Capture Image

Now we will show how to create a task sequence that will be used to capture an image of a workstation. A *task sequence* is a way for Configuration Manager to perform one or more steps or tasks on a client computer without requiring user intervention—a process known as Zero-Touch deployment. A task sequence can consist of a single step or multiple tasks grouped together to perform functions. The tasks can depend on other tasks to complete successfully or be independent of each other.

There are two options for creating task sequences for OSD:

- Task sequences used with PXE boot

- Task sequences used with boot media

Task Sequences Used with PXE Boot

When you enable PXE on the distribution points, you can simply create a build-and-capture task sequence that will take care of the build-and-capture process. Take the following steps to create a task sequence for creating an image:

1. From the Configuration Manager console, select the Software Library workspace, expand Overview ➤ Operating Systems, and select Task Sequences.

2. Click Create Task Sequence on the Home tab of the ribbon, and select the Build And Capture A Reference System Image option.

3. Give the task sequence a name (for instance, Build And Capture Windows 10 Enterprise), select a boot image that will support your operating system version and platform, and click Next.

4. Select the operating system image package, and supply a local administrator password that you will remember if you need to troubleshoot.

The local administrator account will be disabled if you do not supply a password. Do not supply a product key if you are building and capturing Windows 7, Windows 8.*x*, Windows 10, Windows Server 2008, Windows Server 2012, or Windows Server 2016 images, as shown in Figure 9.10. Supplying a product key while building and capturing will cause the process to fail with exit error 31.

FIGURE 9.10
Define which Windows operating system will be captured.

5. Click Next to move to the next page of the wizard.

6. Supply a name for the workgroup that you want to join while you are building and capturing your operating system.

Be sure to join a workgroup so that no Group Policies are applied while you are building and capturing your reference image.

7. Click Next after supplying the name of the workgroup.

8. Select the Configuration Manager client package, and supply the SMSMP=<siteservername> installation properties, as shown in Figure 9.11.

Supplying the installation properties allows you to install approved software updates via the Software Updates feature while the operating system is part of a workgroup.

FIGURE 9.11
Install the Configuration Manager client task.

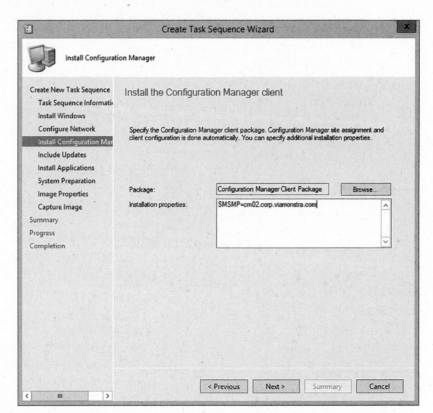

9. Click Next.

10. Decide whether you want to install software updates during the build-and-capture process.

Best practice is that you install all software updates that are approved in the Software Updates feature in Configuration Manager.

11. Click Next to be able to select the application that you want to install while building and capturing your reference operating system image, and click Next again.

12. Depending on the source of your operating system, you may need to supply a system preparation tool; click Next.

    When deploying, for instance, Windows XP SP3 Embedded (which is still supported), you need to use Sysprep to seal the operating system and make it anonymous before capturing. Windows 7, Windows Server 2008, and higher operating systems have a built-in system preparation tool.

13. Supply information about the image, such as creator, version, and description, and click Next.

14. Supply a UNC path and a filename for the captured operating system image, as shown in Figure 9.12, and click Next.

FIGURE 9.12
Captured image path
and filename

15. Supply an account with Write permission to the share where the image will be captured. Click Test Connection if you want to test whether the username and password are correct.

16. Click Next to see the summary.

17. After reviewing the summary, click Next to create the task sequence.

18. When finished, click Close.

Task Sequences Used with Media

If you do not want to enable PXE support on your distribution points or you want to capture a custom reference computer, you can also create a build-and-capture task sequence that runs from media. Follow these steps to create a task sequence, using media for creating a capture image:

1. From the Configuration Manager console, choose the Software Library workspace, expand Overview ➢ Operating Systems, and select Task Sequences.

2. From the Home tab of the ribbon, click Create Task Sequence Media. This opens the Select Media Type page, shown in Figure 9.13.

FIGURE 9.13
Create Task Sequence
Media Wizard—Select
Media Type page

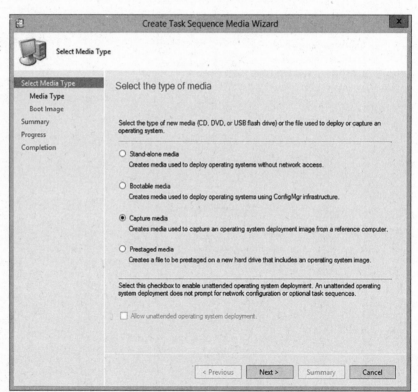

3. On the Select Media Type page, select Capture Media, and then click Next.

By selecting Capture Media, you will be creating the capture media that will be used to capture the operating system image.

On the wizard's Media Type page, shown in Figure 9.14, you can select the type of media to create.

FIGURE 9.14
Create Task Sequence
Media Wizard—
Media Type page

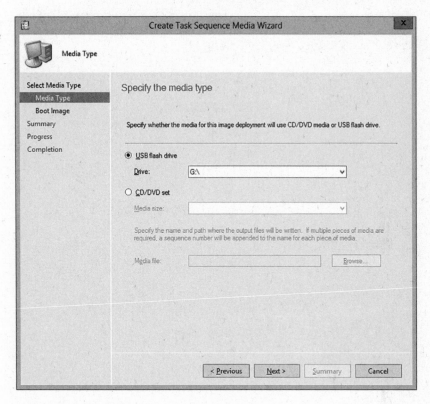

4. For this example, select USB Flash Drive, select the available drive, and click Next. Click Yes at the dialog that warns you that the device will be formatted.

5. On the Boot Image page, shown in Figure 9.15, specify the boot image and distribution point you want to use. Click Browse, select the boot image, and click Browse to select the distribution point. Click Next to continue.

6. Click Next on the Summary page, and Configuration Manager will begin creating the capture media on the USB stick.

7. Finally, you will be presented with the Wizard Completed page; click Close.

When finished, you can use the USB stick to boot up the computers that you will be using to build your operating system image. If you have selected to create an ISO file, you can now burn that ISO file to a CD and use that CD to boot up the computers in which you will be building your operating system image.

FIGURE 9.15
Create Task Sequence
Media Wizard—Boot
Image page

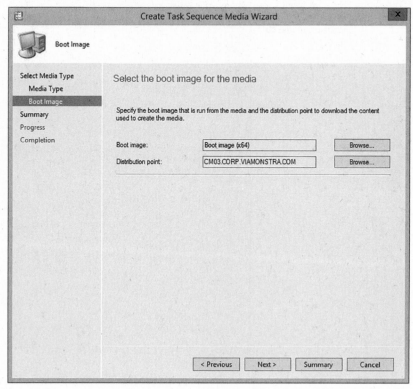

Capturing an Operating System Image

Configuration Manager supports two different ways of capturing an operating system image. You can use the fully automatic way, by using the build-and-capture task sequence, or you can capture a custom reference computer, by using the capture media created earlier.

Building and Capturing Automatically

When building and capturing an operating system image with the specially designed build-and-capture task sequence, you can fully automate the build-and-capture process. This way, you know that the result of a task sequence is always the same, and no user intervention is necessary. To cause less overhead on drivers, building and capturing images is often done with virtual machines.

To be able to use the build-and-capture task sequence created earlier, you must make the task sequence available for deployment, as follows:

1. From the Configuration Manager console, choose the Software Library workspace, expand Overview ➢ Operating Systems, and select Task Sequences.

2. Select the build-and-capture task sequence, and click Deploy on the Home tab of the ribbon.

3. Specify the collection where the reference computer resides, and select the distribution point(s) where the content needs to be deployed to.

Be sure that you create a special collection for building and capturing operating systems. So click OK, as shown in Figure 9.16, if you acknowledge that deploying a task sequence is a potential high-risk deployment and select the collection you want to deploy the build-and-capture task sequence to.

FIGURE 9.16
High-risk deployment
warning

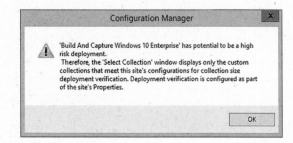

4. Click Next to proceed in the wizard.

Now you need to configure the deployment settings; for Purpose you can select either Available or Required. If you choose Available, you need to press F12 to enter the PXE boot procedure and select the task sequence in the WinPE environment. If you choose Required, the machine will boot into WinPE during the PXE boot procedure. You also need to configure in which scenario the deployment is available.

Only Configuration Manager Clients   A task sequence deployment can be made available for Configuration Manager clients only. This means that an operating system with a Configuration Manager client must be active to be able to receive and start the task sequence deployment. This option can be used best in refresh client scenarios.

Configuration Manager Clients, Media And PXE   If the task sequence that needs to be deployed must be available in all scenarios, you need to select this option.

Only Media And PXE   When a task sequence like the build-and-capture one needs to be available only for media and PXE, then you need to select this option. Another scenario is bare-metal deployment. This is the best option to use with build-and-capture task sequences.

Only Media And PXE (Hidden)   When a task sequence like the build-and-capture one needs to be available only for media and PXE, select this option. Another scenario is bare-metal deployment. This is often used for test purposes. To be able to use the hidden deployment, set the SMSTSPreferredAdvertID variable with the AdvertID of the Task Sequence as the value at the collection level where the task sequence is deployed.

Click Next.

5. Select the option Only Media And PXE, as shown in Figure 9.17, and click Next to configure the deployment settings.

FIGURE 9.17
Specify the deploy-
ment settings.

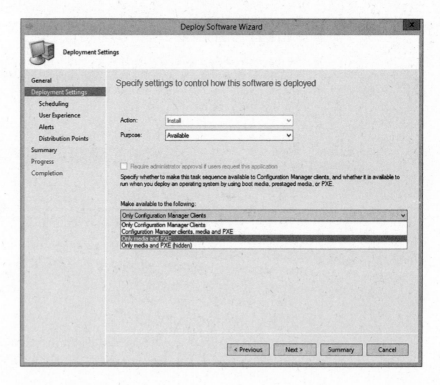

6. Configure the scheduling settings, and click Next.

7. Since you are configuring a deployment for a build-and-capture task sequence, no user experience options need to be configured, so click Next.

8. Configure Alerts options for failed deployments; you can set a threshold for alerts to be sent when the threshold is higher than a percentage of failed deployments. Click Next to proceed.

9. Configure the distribution point settings, and click Next to review the summary.

10. After reviewing the summary, click Next and then Close.

After making the build-and-capture task sequence available for deployment, you can go into action and build and capture the image. To begin, shut down your reference computer and be sure that you can boot from the network via PXE. To use the following procedure, be sure that your computer object in Configuration Manager is added to the collection where the task sequence is deployed.

1. Start your computer or virtual machine and boot into PXE.

2. At the Welcome To This Task Sequence screen, click Next.

3. Select the Build And Capture Windows 10 Enterprise task sequence, as shown in Figure 9.18, and click Next.

FIGURE 9.18
Selecting the task sequence

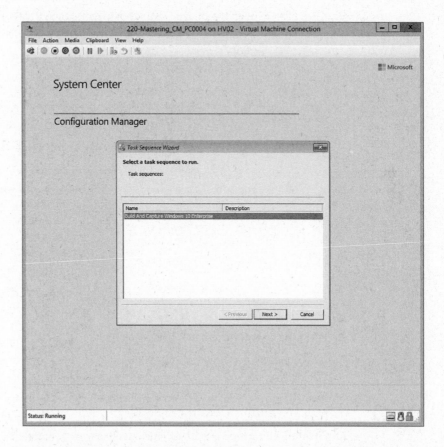

After the build-and-capture process, described earlier, has finished, you will have your captured Windows image. The computer will restart in Windows.

The captured WIM image can be used for deployment to the computers in your environment. Be sure to always test your deployment in a test environment.

Capturing a Reference Computer

When creating an image of a reference computer, you need to be aware of a few requirements. First, ensure that the computer is a member of a workgroup instead of a member of the domain. This is a required step; if the reference computer is a member of the domain, you will be required to remove it from the domain to create the image of the operating system of the computer. Second, we recommend removing the Configuration Manager client from the machine. This is not a requirement, just a recommendation and best practice.

1. To begin creating an image of the reference computer, insert the CD that was created from the ISO file you created earlier.

2. Run LaunchMedia.cmd located in the root folder on the CD. This opens the Image Capture Wizard.

3. Click Next to open the Image Destination page, shown in Figure 9.19, which allows you to specify where to copy the image when the capture is completed.

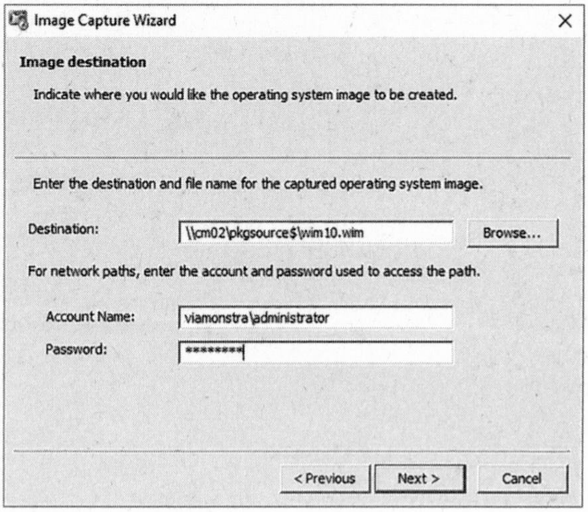

FIGURE 9.19
Image Capture
Wizard—Image
Destination page

4. Fill in the correct information, and click Next.

   As you can see, we copy the WIM file to our site server or any other server that is reachable.

   You will now be able to add some information about the image on the Image Information page. You can fill in the Created By, Version, and Description fields for the WIM file.

5. Fill in this information with as much detail as you can; then click Next.

6. On the Summary page, click Finish to begin the capture phase.

   An Installation Progress window appears, telling you that the Image Capture Wizard is working and running in the background. When the image capture is complete, a System Restart message will appear, and the system will reboot. When the system reboots, it will boot into WinPE and begin capturing the system. This process can be a lengthy one, so be patient while the operating system is being captured.

   Once the image capture is complete, you will see the Image Capture Wizard success message, shown in Figure 9.20.

7. Click OK to allow the machine to reboot and return to the operating system.

FIGURE 9.20

Image capture
success message

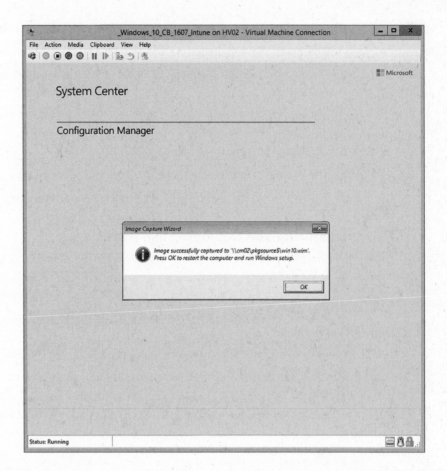

Deploying an Image

Since you've now successfully captured an image, you need to add this operating system image to Configuration Manager. Then you have to deploy this image by creating a task sequence and deploy this task sequence to the computers in your environment. Always be sure to thoroughly test the image in a separate test environment before deploying it into production.

Adding a Captured Image

The WIM file that you just created must be added as an available operating system for Configuration Manager. To deploy this image, follow this procedure:

1. From the Configuration Manager console, select the Software Library workspace, expand Overview ➤ Operating Systems, and select Operating System Images.

2. Click Add Operating System Image on the Home tab of the ribbon.

   This opens the Add Operating System Image Wizard's Data Source page.

3. Ensure that the (UNC) Path field points to the location where the WIM file was created, and click Next.

   The General page allows you to customize the Name, Version, and Comments fields for the image file.

4. Fill in the appropriate information, and click Next.

5. The Summary page will be displayed; review the information and click Next.

6. Finally the Wizard Completed screen will appear. On this page, click Close.

Distributing and Deploying the Image

Next, you need to distribute the image to your distribution points.

1. From the Configuration Manager console, choose the Software Library workspace, expand Overview ➤ Operating Systems, and select Operating System Images.

2. Select the image that you added, and click Distribute Content on the Home tab of the ribbon.

3. In the Distribute Content Wizard, click Next.

4. Click Add and select Distribution Point or Distribution Point Group.

5. In the Add Distribution Points or Add Distribution Point Groups dialog, select the distribution points or groups that you want to distribute the WIM image to, and click OK.

6. Click Next to review the summary.

7. After reviewing the summary, click Next and then Close.

Creating a Task Sequence for Deployment

Now you will need to create a task sequence for deploying the Windows operating system image. Creating a task sequence will give Configuration Manager a series of steps to perform on the new installation of the workstation:

1. From the Configuration Manager console, select the Software Library workspace, expand Overview ➤ Operating Systems, and select Task Sequences.

2. Select Create Task Sequence on the Home tab of the ribbon.

   This will open the New Task Sequence Wizard's Create A New Task Sequence page.

3. Because you have already built an image of a Windows client, select Install An Existing Image Package, and then click Next.

   This opens the New Task Sequence Wizard's Task Sequence Information page.

4. Specify the task sequence name and a comment, and specify the boot image to use during the installation of the image. Click Next after supplying the information.

   The Install Windows page, shown in Figure 9.21, allows you to specify the Configuration Manager image package containing the operating system you want to install.

FIGURE 9.21
Create Task Sequence
Wizard—Install
Windows page

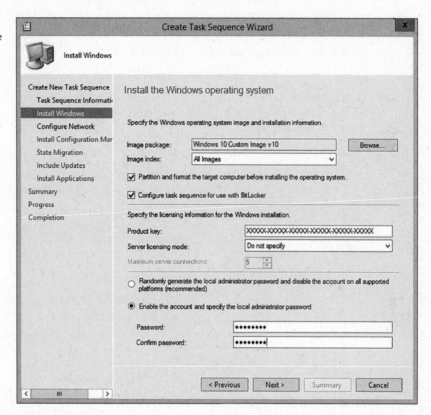

5. Click the Browse button to find the image of the operating system you want to install, and click OK.

6. If you want to partition and format the target computer before installing the operating system, leave the Partition box selected, and format the target computer before installing the operating system.

7. Keep the Configure Task Sequence For Use With BitLocker option enabled if you want to enable BitLocker during the deployment of the Windows image.

8. Enter the licensing information for the version of Windows you are installing in the Product Key field, and click Next.

9. On the Configure Network page, select the domain or workgroup to join.

If you select to join a domain, you can specify which organizational unit (OU) in which to put the computer once it joins the domain. If you select to join a domain, you will need to specify the account that has permission to join computers to a domain. Create a different account to join the computer to the domain; do not use the Network Access Account for this. You must delegate this access to the user account. Verify the account by testing the connection after configuring the account.

10. Click Next to continue.

Now all the work you did earlier will finally be put to use.

11. On the Install Configuration Manager Client page, specify any additional installation properties. Click Browse if you do not want to use the default Configuration Manager client package.

12. Click Next to continue.

The Create Task Sequence Wizard page that appears is State Migration, shown in Figure 9.22, which allows you to configure the user state migration capture.

FIGURE 9.22
Create Task Sequence Wizard—State Migration page

13. Select or deselect whether you want to capture network and Microsoft Windows settings.

14. Click Browse, if you do not want to use the default User State Migration Tool package, and then click Next.

After you've configured the state migration, the Include Updates page will appear, which allows you to specify whether the client will get mandatory, all, or no software updates after the image has been installed.

15. Configure the installation of software updates, and click Next.

Now you have the option to install additional applications by adding the configured applications to the task sequence. This is extremely useful if you have a large number of applications you want installed on each system after the operating system has been installed. Figure 9.23 shows the Install Applications page, where you can specify the additional applications.

FIGURE 9.23
Create Task Sequence
Wizard—Install
Applications page

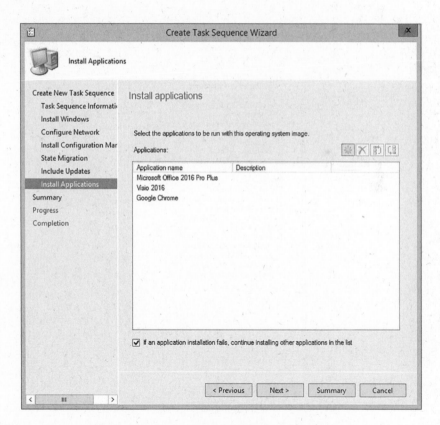

16. Select the option If An Application Installation Fails, Continue Installing Other Applications In The List if you want to let the task sequence proceed with its tasks.

17. Click Next once you have the additional applications specified.

18. Click Next on the Summary page, and Configuration Manager will complete the Create Task Sequence Wizard.

19. Click Close.

PRESERVE THE DRIVE LETTER IN YOUR IMAGE, OR NOT

A disadvantage of deploying the default INSTALL.WIM files is that Microsoft created the INSTALL.WIM image by installing the Windows 7 version to the D: drive. For this reason the Windows operating system is installed by default to the D: drive. Windows 10 installs the operating system by default to the X: drive.

You can disable this default behavior by setting a task sequence variable at the top of the task sequence.

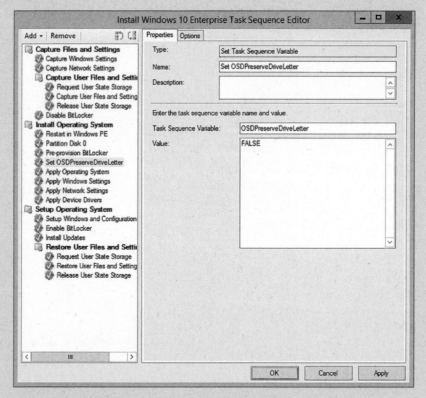

Adding the task sequence variable OSDPreserveDriveLetter = False to the task sequence allows you to install the default INSTALL.WIM image to drive C: instead of drive D: or X:.

As from Windows 10 version 1607, the OSDPreserveDriveLetter task sequence variable is not supported anymore. Just select the drive in the task sequence to which Windows 10 needs to be installed.

Deploying the Task Sequence

You have now successfully created a new task sequence to install a new operating system on a machine, join the system to the domain, and install the Configuration Manager client on the machine once it comes online. However, the task sequence won't do you any good unless you deploy it to a collection. Take the following steps to create a task sequence for the refresh scenario:

1. From the Configuration Manager console, choose the Software Library workspace, expand Overview ➤ Operating Systems, and select Task Sequences.

2. Select the task sequence you want to deploy, and click Deploy on the Home tab of the ribbon.

3. Click Deploy to open the General page of the Deploy Software Wizard.

4. Click Browse to find the collection where you want to install this operating system package-age, and then click Next to continue.

   The next wizard page is Deployment Settings, shown in Figure 9.24.

FIGURE 9.24
Deploy Software
Wizard—Deployment
Settings page

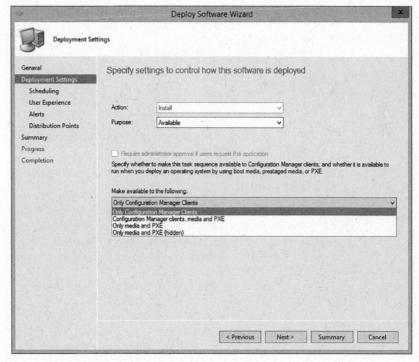

5. Supply the purpose of the deployment.

   ◆ If you want to let your users choose to reinstall their operating system, choose the Available option.

◆ If you want the installation to start automatically, choose the Required option.

Choosing the Required option enables you to send wake-up packets to the computers in the collection. Of course, you need to first configure Wake On LAN support in Configuration Manager. The task sequence you are creating is used to refresh your Windows installation, so you will be making the deployment available only for Configuration Manager clients.

6. Click Next to continue.

The next step is to configure the scheduling options for the deployment.

7. Configure the availability of the deployment and when the deployment will expire—this availability step is optional; if you want the deployment to be available directly, you do not need to configure this.

8. Define the assignment schedule, and be sure to set the rerun behavior to Rerun if the previous attempt failed.

If you do not set this option, the deployment will rerun as soon the deployment is finished, thereby creating a deployment loop.

9. Click Next to proceed.

10. On the User Experience page, specify how users are notified about the deployment and how they interact with the deployment.

We prefer to show the task sequence progress to let the end user know that the computer is being reloaded.

11. Click Next to proceed, and configure the Alerts options for this deployment.

12. Click Next, configure how to run the content for this deployment on the Distribution Points page, and click Next again.

13. Review the summary, click Next, and click Close when the wizard has finished processing the deployment.

Now you have created the deployment for the operating system deployment, and any system in the collection you specified will get the new deployment during the next policy refresh. Once the policy refresh takes place, the workstation will receive the Assigned Program About To Run notification. Once the installation begins, you will see the progress message box in Windows, as shown in Figure 9.25.

The system will automatically reboot and then begin the boot to WinPE, as shown in Figure 9.26.

The installation will take some time to complete. During this install, Configuration Manager is gathering the user state and saving the date in the USMT folder on the site server, which you configured earlier in this chapter. You can monitor the <drive>:\USMTData folder on the site server to see the user state migration data being copied to the server.

Configuration Manager will push the new operating system down to the new machine and then join it to the domain, install the Configuration Manager client, and finally copy back all the user data on the client.

FIGURE 9.25
Installation progress
message box

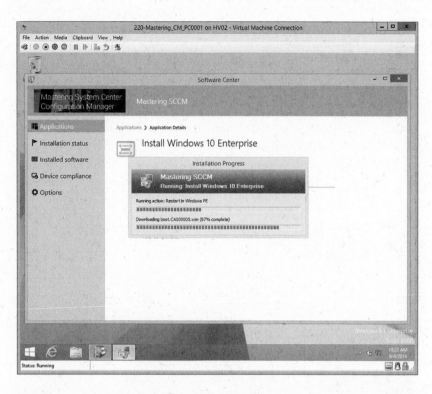

FIGURE 9.26
Booting to WinPE

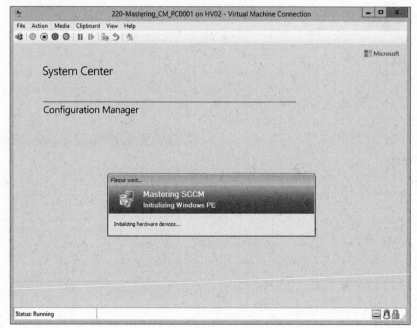

You can monitor the progress of the operating system deployment in the Deployment Status window, shown in Figure 9.27.

1. From the Configuration Manager console, choose the Monitoring workspace, expand Overview ➢ Deployments, and select the deployment that you want to monitor.

2. After selecting the deployment, click Run Summarization on the Home tab of the ribbon.

3. After the summarization is updated, click View Status on the Home tab of the ribbon to see the status of the deployment, as shown in Figure 9.27.

4. While viewing the status, you can refresh the status by clicking Run Summarization or Refresh. If a deployment is in progress, or fails as shown in Figure 9.27, you are able to identify which machines have which status.

FIGURE 9.27
Monitoring the OSD deployment status

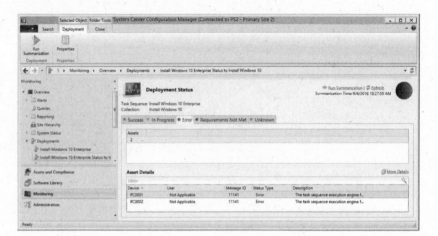

5. While monitoring the OSD deployment status, you are able to review the completed tasks by selecting More Details and selecting the Status tab of the Asset Message dialog, as shown in Figure 9.28.

FIGURE 9.28
Review the task sequence steps in the Asset Message dialog screen.

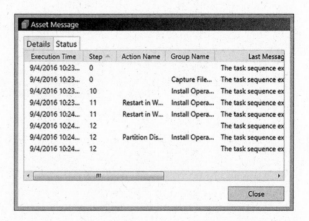

Upgrading Operating System to Windows 10

With the introduction of Windows 10, a new task sequence has been introduced to streamline the upgrade process from older operating systems to Windows 10. So when do you need this upgrade task sequence?

- If you want to keep all of the applications and its settings

- If you do not need to switch between BIOS and the Unified Extensible Firmware Interface (UEFI)

- If you do not want to refresh or completely reinstall the operating system

- If you do not need to switch between 32-bit and 64-bit operating systems

- If you want to upgrade one Windows 10 build to a newer build and you do not want to use the new servicing model

---

STILL ON BIOS? SWITCH TO UEFI AS SOON AS POSSIBLE!

If you are still using BIOS on your workstations, you definitely need to think of switching to UEFI to be able to use all of the Windows 10 security features such as Secure Boot, Device Guard, and Credential Guard. Switching from BIOS to UEFI can be automated within the task sequences. Be sure to read the following blog posts from some great OSD folks in the community!

- Johan Arwidmark (MVP): `https://ref.ms/JohanArwidmarkUEFIBlogs`

- Nickolaj Andersen (MVP): `https://ref.ms/NickolajAndersenUEFIBlog`

- Mike Terrill: `https://ref.ms/MikeTerrillUEFIBlogs`

Perform the following tasks to prepare the Upgrade Task Sequence for Windows 10:

1. From the Configuration Manager console, choose the Software Library workspace, expand Overview ➢ Operating Systems, and select Task Sequences.

2. Click Create Task Sequence on the Home tab of the ribbon, select Upgrade An Operating System From Upgrade Package, and click Next.

3. Supply the task sequence name and the description, and click Next.

4. Click Browse on the Upgrade The Windows Operating System page, as shown in Figure 9.29, and select the upgrade package you want to install. Click OK.

5. Choose the edition and supply the product key; then click Next.

6. Configure the installation of software updates, and click Next.

   Now you have the option to install additional applications by adding the configured applications to the task sequence. This is extremely useful if you have a large number of applications you want installed on each system after the operating system has been installed.

FIGURE 9.29
Select an operating
system upgrade
package.

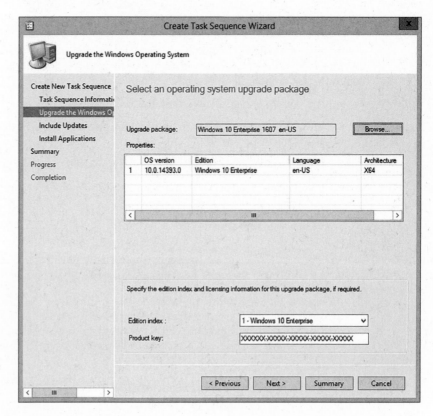

7. Select the option If An Application Installation Fails, Continue Installing Other Applications In The List if you want to let the task sequence proceed with its tasks.

8. Click Next once you have the additional applications specified.

9. Click Next on the Summary page, and Configuration Manager will complete the Create Task Sequence Wizard.

10. Click Close.

11. Deploy the task sequence to a device collection as described earlier in this chapter.

Deploying the Operating System on Bare Metal

After deploying an operating system in a refresh scenario, you also need to create a task sequence and deployment to be able to deploy an operating system to bare-metal computers. *Bare-metal* computers are computers without any operating system present.

To deploy an operating system to a bare-metal computer, you can use a CD or DVD to boot into WinPE, but you can also boot into PXE to start the WinPE image from the network. Let's see how this works with PXE. To be able to deploy an operating system to a bare-metal computer, you need to perform the following tasks:

◆ Import information about a computer.

◆ Create a task sequence.

◆ Deploy the task sequence.

Importing Computer Information

Now you are ready to set up a computer association so that Configuration Manager can identify the bare-metal machines that will receive a fresh install. You can also use the unknown computer support, which is discussed later in this chapter. To specify the computer association, open the Configuration Manager console and proceed as follows:

1. From the Configuration Manager console, choose the Assets And Compliance workspace and expand Overview ➤ Devices.

2. Click Import Computer Information on the Home tab of the ribbon.

   This will allow you to import a single computer or import many systems from a comma-separated values (CSV) file.

3. Select the option Import Single Computer, and click Next.

   This will bring up the Single Computer page, as shown in Figure 9.30.

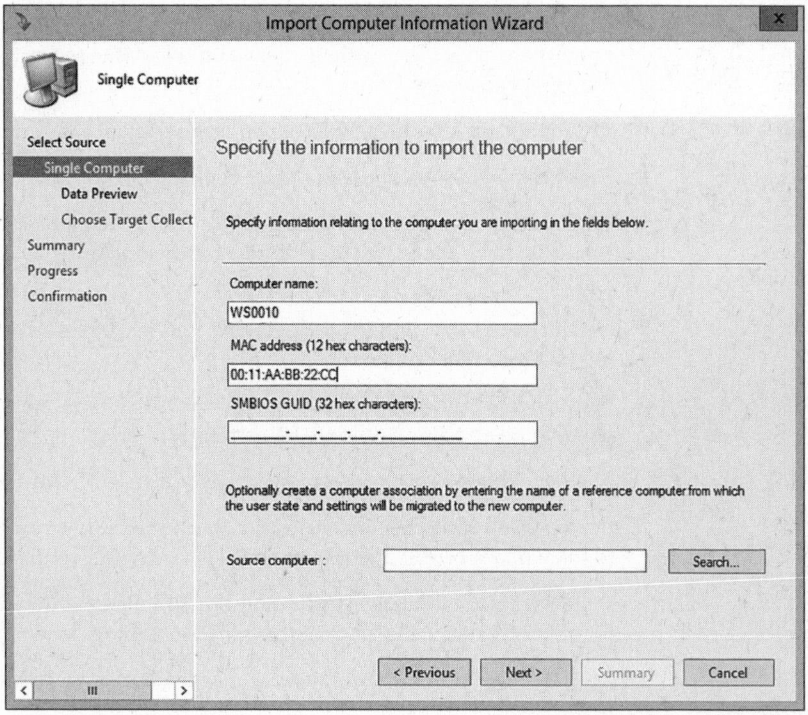

FIGURE 9.30
Import Computer
Information
Wizard—Single
Computer page

You must enter the computer name along with either the MAC address or the System Management BIOS (SMBIOS) GUID. The computer name is just how the machine will appear in the collections, not what the actual computer will be named.

4. Fill in the appropriate information, and then click Next.

5. This sends you to the Data Preview page; check the information and click Next.

   You'll then see the Choose Target Collection page.

6. Specify which collection you want to add to this new machine.

   It is extremely important to put all the bare-metal installs into the same collection, used only for bare-metal deployment.

7. Click Next.

8. After specifying the collection, you will see the Summary page. Click Next, and then click Close on the Finish page.

Creating a Task Sequence for the Bare-Metal OSD

When you deploy a bare-metal machine, it is wise to create a dedicated task sequence for this purpose. Once you create this special task sequence, you need to deploy it to a special collection in which you can place the bare-metal computers.

Creating a task sequence for deploying an image to a new machine is straightforward:

1. From the Configuration Manager console, choose the Software Library workspace, expand Overview ➢ Operating Systems, and select Task Sequences.

2. From there, click New Task Sequence on the Home tab of the ribbon of the Configuration Manager console.

   This opens the Create New Task Sequence page of the New Task Sequence Wizard.

3. Select the Install An Existing Image Package option, and click Next.

4. On the Task Sequence Information page, fill in the name, optionally add a comment, and select the boot image you want to use for the operating system deployment; then click Next.

5. On the Install The Windows Operating System page, select the image package by browsing to the correct image.

6. Because this example is deploying Windows to a bare-metal machine, enable the option to partition and format the target computer.

   The next options you can configure are the network settings.

7. On the Configure The Network page, specify whether you want to join the new machine to the domain or join a workgroup. Click Next after configuring the network settings.

   A Configuration Manager task sequence will allow you to install the Configuration Manager client during an operating system deployment.

8. On the Install The Configuration Manager Client page, add installation properties if you need to and click Next.

9. Since you are deploying Windows to a bare-metal machine, on the State Migration page, shown in Figure 9.31, deselect all the options because you do not need to worry about capturing any data from these machines. Click Next to configure the installation of software updates.

FIGURE 9.31
Create Task Sequence
Wizard—State
Migration page

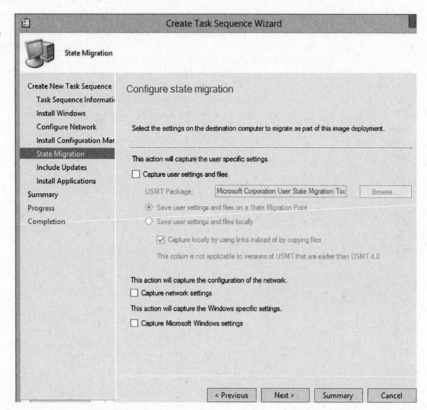

On the Include Updates page, you can now allow Configuration Manager to include software updates during the install.

10. Make the selections you desire, and click Next.

On the Install Applications page, you can add applications, such as Microsoft Office, that you want to install on the machine after the operating system has been deployed.

11. Click Next to view the Summary page.

12. After viewing the summary, click Next and then Close to complete the wizard.

Deploying the Bare-Metal Task Sequence

After creating the task sequence for bare-metal deployment, you need to deploy this task sequence, as discussed earlier. Be sure to select that the task sequence is available to only media and PXE.

USING THE UNKNOWN COMPUTER COLLECTION

You can enable support for unknown computers. Unknown computer support is a feature in Configuration Manager that allows unmanaged systems to be managed with Configuration Manager during an OSD. To do so, open the Configuration Manager console, select the Administration workspace, and expand Overview ➤ Site Configuration ➤ Servers And Site System Roles. Select the server with the distribution point where PXE is enabled, and click Role Properties in the Site Role section of the ribbon. Browse to the PXE tab in the Distribution Point Properties dialog, shown here, and select the box Enable Unknown Computer Support.

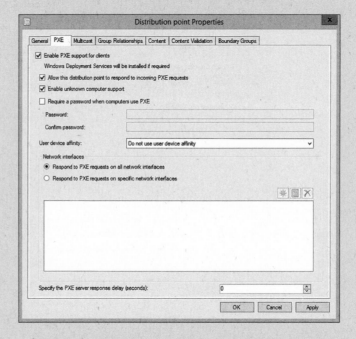

When you enable this option, you will be prompted with the caution message shown next. Assuming you are ready to proceed, click OK.

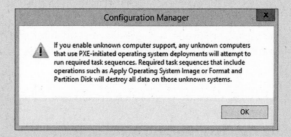

To create a task sequence for bootable media, open the Configuration Manager console, choose the Software Library workspace, and expand Overview ➤ Operating System ➤ Task Sequences. Click Create Task Sequence Media on the Home tab of the ribbon. This opens the Create Task Sequence Media Wizard's Select Media Type page.

Select Bootable Media, and click Next. Choose Dynamic Media When The Media Contacts A Management Point, which redirects the client to a different management point based on the client location in the site boundaries, or choose Site-Based Media when you want to specify a management point. Click Next to configure the media type. On the Media Type page, select the type of media you will be using, either a USB flash drive or a CD/DVD set, and then click Next. The Security page offers the Enable Unknown Computer Support option. Selecting this will allow you to target the unknown computer collection with the operating system deployment.

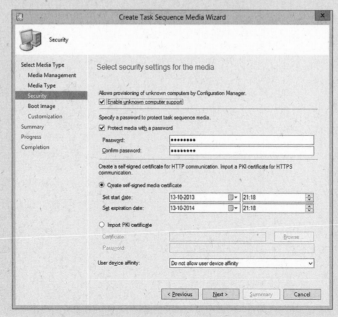

continues

continued

The next step, after configuring unknown computer support, is configuring the boot image, distribution point, associated management points, and customizations.

After creating the boot media, you can create a deployment to this collection for the OSD task sequence, and Configuration Manager will process the task sequence for the unknown computers. Be sure to enable your deployment to be accessible for boot media and PXE.

Installing Device Drivers into OSD

Now you have configured one package to perform Windows upgrades and another package to install that same Windows install package onto a bare-metal system. But what happens if you get a new system with a completely new setup, including device drivers that are not installed within the current package, so that when the machine comes online it will not be able to attach to the network?

Microsoft has provided the ability to import device drivers into Configuration Manager and add them to the boot images or driver packages so they can be installed as part of the operating system deployment task. To import Windows device drivers, take the following steps:

1. From the Configuration Manager console, choose the Software Library workspace, expand Overview ➤ Operating Systems, and select Drivers.

2. Click Import Driver on the Home tab of the ribbon of the Configuration Manager console.

   This opens the Locate Driver page, shown in Figure 9.32.

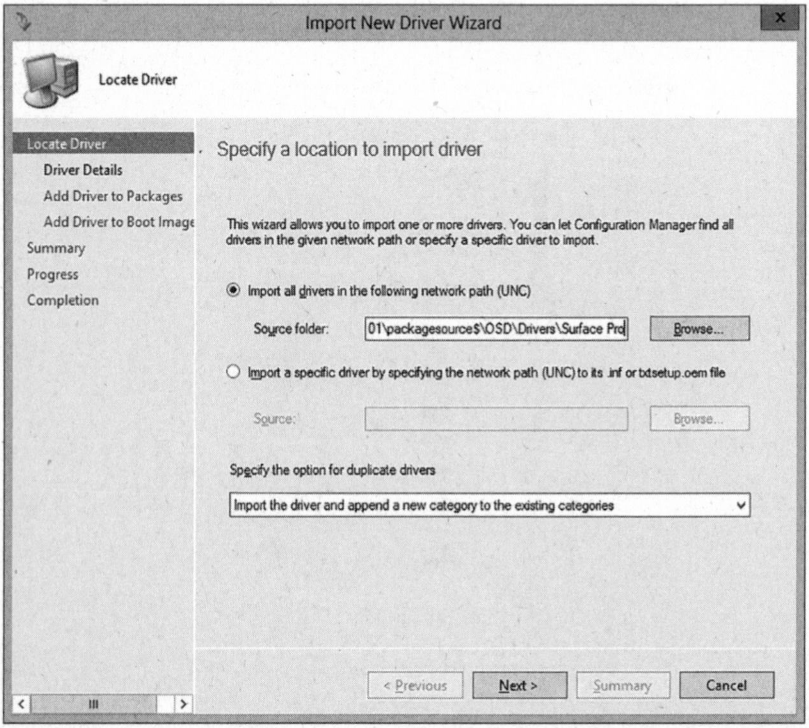

FIGURE 9.32
Import New Driver
Wizard—Locate Driver
page

3. You can specify whether you want to import all drivers or just a single device driver. When importing drivers, you could run into the fact that there are duplicate drivers, so you should configure the import behavior when duplicate drivers are detected. You can configure the following options:

- Import The Driver And Append A New Category To The Existing Categories

- Import The Driver And Keep The Existing Categories

- Import The Driver And Overwrite The Existing Categories

- Do Not Import The Driver

4. Click Next after picking the correct driver(s), and then you will be presented with the Driver Details page. Next you should assign the driver(s) to one or more categories.

WORKING WITH CATEGORIES ENABLES YOU TO MANAGE DRIVERS

If you add categories to drivers, you can manage your drivers in the store more easily. By adding the category to the search criteria, you can easily select the drivers and delete them by clicking Delete on the Home tab of the ribbon in the Configuration Manager console.

---

5. On the Add Driver To Packages page, shown in Figure 9.33, specify the package(s) you want to add this driver to, or specify a new package. If you need to create a new driver package, do the following.

FIGURE 9.33
Import New Driver
Wizard—Add Driver
To Packages page

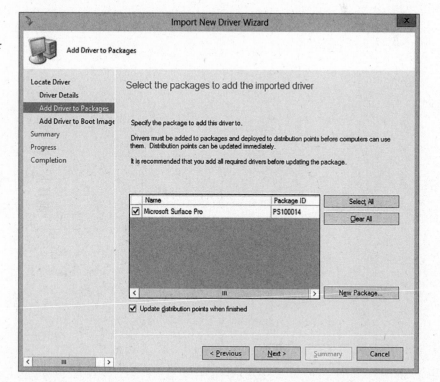

     a. Click New Package.

     b. Supply a name and a UNC path for the source of the package.

     c. Click OK.

     d. If desired, select Update Distribution Points When Finished so the driver will be available as soon as possible to your site.

6. Click Next to continue.

7. Next, select which boot images you want to add the driver to, as shown in Figure 9.34. When selecting drivers in bulk—for instance, all drivers from one model—do not add these to the boot images. Add them in a later stage, since, for instance, we do not want video, sound, and other drivers in our boot image. It is a best practice to add only the missing NIC drivers and drivers related to storage (controllers) to the boot images.

FIGURE 9.34
Adding drivers to boot images

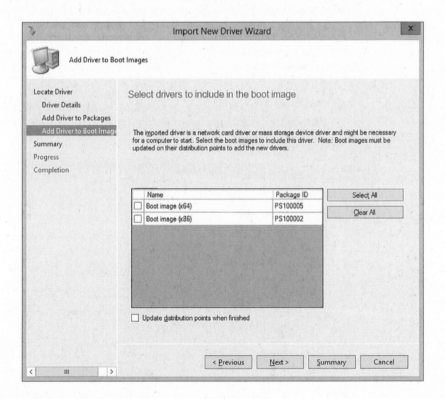

8. Click Next to open the Summary page. Review the configuration, click Next, and then click Close.

Now Configuration Manager will inject that driver package into the packages and boot images you selected. This could take some time to process.

Using User Device Affinity

As discussed earlier, user device affinity enables you to deploy user-targeted applications during the operating system deployment process. There are several ways to configure user device affinity. Let's look at the following options:

◆ Manually configure a primary user for a device.

◆ Manually configure a primary device for a user.

◆ Configure a site to automatically create user device affinities.

◆ Import user device affinities.

◆ Enable users to configure their primary device.

Manually Configure a Primary User for a Device

To manually configure a primary user for a device, follow this procedure:

1. From the Configuration Manager console, choose the Assets And Compliance workspace, expand Overview, and select Devices.

2. Select a device, and click Edit Primary Users on the Home tab of the ribbon. Search for the user, as shown in Figure 9.35, select the user, and click Add and then OK to set the primary user for the device.

FIGURE 9.35
Searching for and selecting the primary user

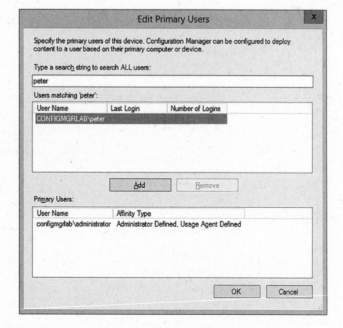

Manually Configure a Primary Device for a User

To manually configure a primary device for a user, follow these steps:

1. From the Configuration Manager console, select the Assets And Compliance workspace, expand Overview, and select Users.

2. Select a user, and click Edit Primary Devices on the Home tab of the ribbon. Search for the device, select the device, and click Add and then OK to set the primary device for the user.

Configure a Site to Automatically Create User Device Affinities

With Configuration Manager you can also create the user device affinity automatically. Creating the affinity automatically is based on thresholds configured in the client settings. You can also configure the collecting of audit account logon and audit logon events on the client by, for instance, implementing a GPO. (See https://technet.microsoft.com/en-us/library/mt629338.aspx for more information.) Configuring the client settings to create user device affinities is described here:

1. From the Configuration Manager console, choose the Administration workspace, expand Overview, and select Client Settings.

2. Select the default client settings package or create a new client device agent settings package, and click Properties on the Home tab of the ribbon.

3. Select User And Device Affinity, as shown in Figure 9.36, and configure the following options.

FIGURE 9.36
Configuring client device settings

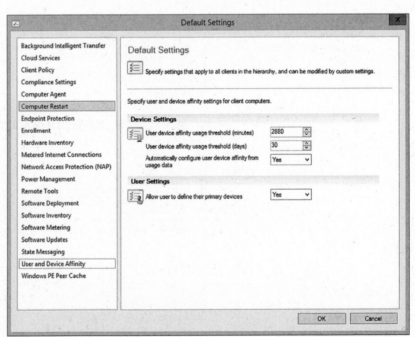

User Device Affinity Usage Threshold (Minutes)   Configure the number of minutes of usage by a user before a user device affinity is created.

User Device Affinity Usage Threshold (Days)   Configure the number of days Configuration Manager will measure the usage of the device. For example, if User Device Affinity Usage Threshold (Minutes) is configured with a value of 120 minutes and User Device Affinity Usage Threshold (Days) is set to 14 days, the user must use the device for 120 minutes over a period of 14 days before the user device affinity is created.

Automatically Configure User Device Affinity From Usage Data   Enable the feature by setting the value to Yes, or disable the feature by setting the value to No.

Import User Device Affinities

If you have the information from your client computers and primary users in a CSV file, you can import the user device affinity information to Configuration Manager.

1. From the Configuration Manager console, select the Assets And Compliance workspace, expand Overview, and select Devices or Users.

2. On the Home tab of the ribbon, select Import User Device Affinity.

3. Browse and select the CSV file containing the information that you want to import, and click Open. The format of the CSV file must be `<Domain\username>,<Device NetBIOS name>`. Select the option This File Has Column Headings For Reference Purposes if you have the following as the first line of the CSV file: `users,devices`.

4. Check in the File Preview section of the Choose Mapping page of the wizard to see if the column mapping is configured correctly, as shown in Figure 9.37, and click Next twice. Click Close after reviewing the results.

FIGURE 9.37
Checking the column mapping

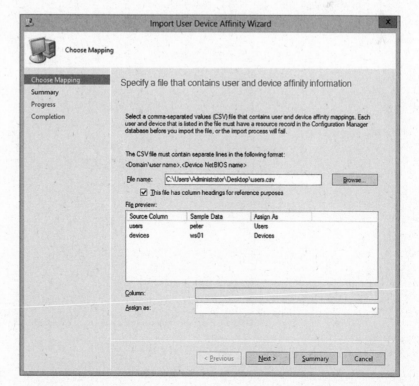

Enable Users to Configure Their Primary Device

Another option is to configure the Configuration Manager site to let the users define their own user device affinities. This is done as follows:

1. From the Configuration Manager console, select the Administration workspace, expand Overview, and select Client Settings.

2. Select the default client settings package or create a new client device user settings package. Then click Properties on the Home tab of the ribbon.

3. Select User And Device Affinity, and set the option Allow Users To Define Their Primary Devices to Yes. Setting the option to No will disable the feature.

From now on, the users can configure their user device affinity by selecting the I Regularly Use This Computer To Do My Work option in the My Devices tab of the Application Catalog website.

Pre-deploy User Applications

After configuring user device affinity for a client computer, the applications that are targeted to the primary user are pre-deployed automatically during deployment of the OS. While deploying the application to a user, set Purpose to Required, as shown in Figure 9.38. You will find more information about deploying applications in Chapter 5, "Client Installation."

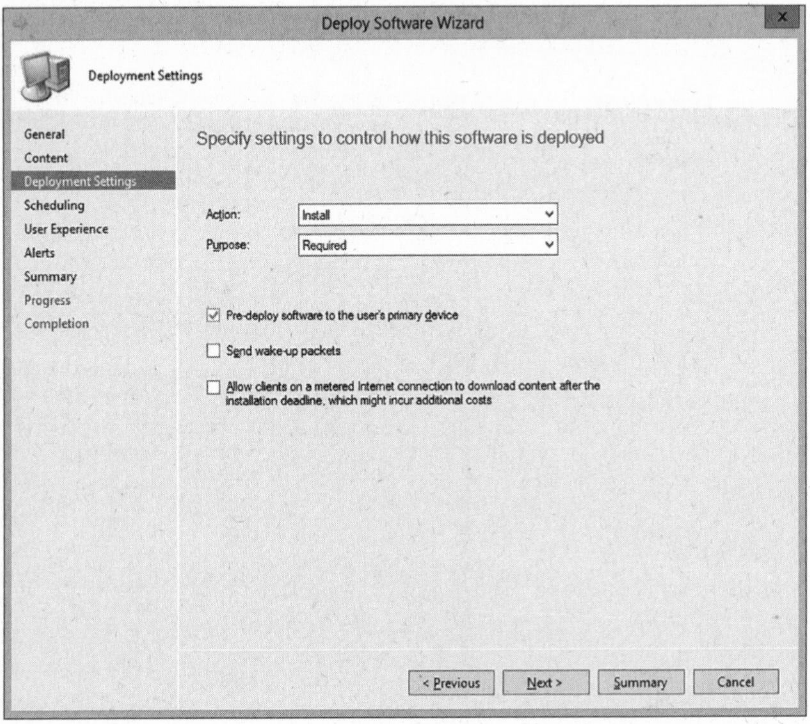

FIGURE 9.38
Configuring deployment settings

Microsoft Deployment Toolkit 2013

The Microsoft Deployment Toolkit 2013 is a solution accelerator that can be integrated with Configuration Manager. The integration gives you the ability to smooth your deployment process with the scripts that come with the MDT. Let's configure the MDT integration and see what it offers us when deploying operating systems.

The MDT includes extra deployment scenarios that are built with the Task Sequence Wizard:

Client Replace Scenario (Client Replace Task Sequence)   This scenario enables you to capture the user state from an old client computer and place it on the new client computer while deploying the new operating system.

Server Deployment Scenario (Server Task Sequence)   This scenario allows you to deploy Windows-based servers and their roles.

User-Driven Installation Scenario (User Driven Installation Replace Task Sequence)   This scenario allows your users to use the simple User Driven Installation (UDI) Wizard to initiate and customize an OS deployment on their PCs that's tailored to their individual needs.

The MDT Task Sequence wizard allows you to use the built-in MDT task sequence templates within SCCM. Using the wizard, you are also allowed to create supporting packages from MDT to use in your task MDT task sequences (and SCCM task sequences) such as MDT boot images, the MDT Toolkit package, the MDT Settings package, and the User State Migration package. This section describes the client replace scenario.

Installing Microsoft Deployment Toolkit 2013

The MDT is a free tool that you can download from the Microsoft Download site. Install the `MicrosoftDeploymentToolkit2013_x64.msi` or `MicrosoftDeploymentToolkit2013_x86.msi` file on your site system. It's a straightforward Next, Accept License Agreement, Next, Next, Next, Install, Finish installation. You need to install the MDT on every site server that you want to integrate with. Part of the integration is installing the extensions to the consoles.

Integrating the MDT

To be able to use the deployment intelligence of the MDT in Configuration Manager, you need to integrate the MDT with Configuration Manager. This is done by following these steps:

1. After installing the Microsoft Deployment Toolkit 2013 on your site system, go to the Start screen.

2. Click Configure ConfigMgr Integration to start the integration tool.

3. Configure the integration as shown in Figure 9.39. Select Install The MDT Console Extensions For Configuration Manager and Add The MDT Task Sequence Actions To A System Center Configuration Manager Server. Next, configure the Site Server Name and Site Code fields, and click Next.

4. Review the summary, and click Finish.

FIGURE 9.39
Configuring the
integration

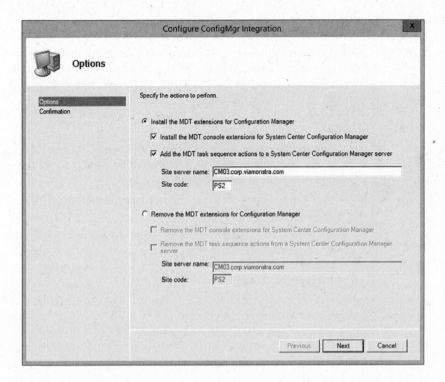

Creating a New Boot Image

This is an optional step since more and more extras of the MDT are moving to native
Configuration Manager features. Follow the next steps to re-create the MDT boot images. You
can also create a boot image with the MDT integration features while creating a new MDT task
sequence. Create a boot image for both x86 and x64 platforms.

1. From the Configuration Manager console, choose the Software Library workspace,
   expand Overview ➤ Operating Systems, and select Boot Images.

2. Click Create Boot Image Using MDT on the Home tab of the ribbon, and supply the UNC
   path to the location where you want to store the boot image; click Next.

3. Supply a name, version, and comments, and click Next.

4. Select the platform for which you are creating the boot image, select the Scratch Space
   value from the drop-down list, as shown in Figure 9.40, and click Next. Scratch Space is a
   RAM drive that is used during OSD.

5. Configure the optional languages and components like Microsoft Data Access
   Components (MDAC) support and support for Point To Point Protocol over Ethernet
   (PPPoE) support and click Next.

6. Configure the customizations, such as the pre-execution hook, custom background
   image, and command support.

FIGURE 9.40
Configure the
platform and scratch
space.

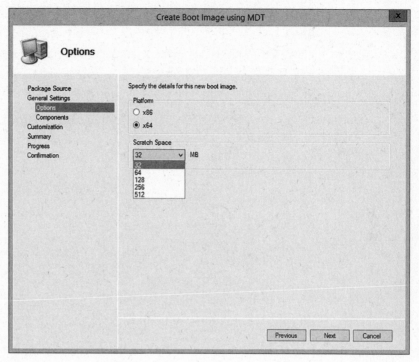

7. Click Next to review the summary.

8. Click Next after reviewing the summary, and click Finish after creating the custom boot image; this process can take a while.

9. Be sure to enable the boot image for PXE support and the deployment of the boot image to the distribution points.

Creating an MDT Task Sequence

After creating the optional MDT boot images, you need to create a task sequence that you can use to deploy the operating system. In this example we will use the client replace scenario, which consists of two task sequences: the Client Replace task sequence and one based on the new computer scenario. The new computer scenario is like the bare-metal scenario, but we also use the User State Migration Toolkit to bring back the user state.

1. From the Configuration Manager console, choose the Software Library workspace, expand Overview ➤ Operating Systems, and select Task Sequences.

2. Click Create MDT Task Sequence on the Home tab of the ribbon, and select the Client Replace Task Sequence option. Then click Next.

3. Give the task sequence a name, supply comments, and click Next.

4. Select an existing boot image, or create a new boot image using the Create A New Boot Image Package option. Click Next.

   The first time you create an MDT task sequence, you will need to create a Microsoft Deployment Toolkit Files package.

5. Select this option and supply a package source folder, as shown in Figure 9.41.

FIGURE 9.41
Create a new
Microsoft
Deployment Toolkit
Files package.

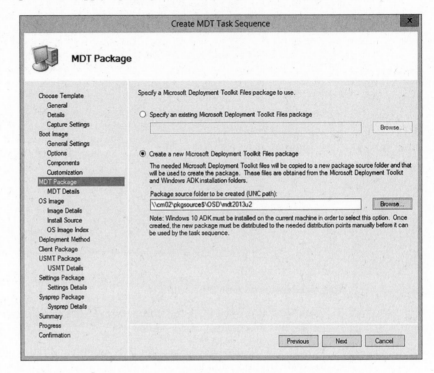

The next time you create an MDT task sequence, you can select the MDT package. This package holds a lot of useful scripts that allows you to create a Zero-Touch OSD experience.

6. Click Next.

7. Now you need to supply information about the package. Fill in the name, version language, and manufacturer, and click Next to proceed.

8. Select the User State Migration Tool package, and click Next.

9. Select Create A New Settings Package For This Operating System Deployment, supply the UNC path, and click Next. The settings package holds the customsettings.ini file. With this file you can tweak and tune the deployment of the operating system. Read more about the customsettings.ini file here: https://ref.ms/customsettings.

10. Supply information about the package. Fill in the name, version language, and manufacturer, and click Next to proceed.

11. Review the summary and click Next. Click Finish after you've finished creating the packages and the task sequence.

After creating the Client Replace task sequence, you will need to create a task sequence based on the new computer scenario.

1. From the Configuration Manager console, select the Software Library workspace, expand Overview ➤ Operating Systems, and select Task Sequences.

2. Click Create MDT Task Sequence on the Home tab of the ribbon, and select the Client Task Sequence option. Then click Next.

3. Give the task sequence a name, supply comments, and click Next.

4. Supply the domain information, the account that has permissions to join the domain, and the Windows settings, and then click Next.

5. Select This Task Sequence Will Never Be Used To Capture An Image, and click Next.

6. Select an existing boot image, or create a new boot image using the Create A New Boot Image Package option. Click Next.

7. Select the MDT package that you created earlier, and click Next.

8. Select the operating system image you want to deploy, as shown in Figure 9.42, and click Next.

FIGURE 9.42
Select or create the operating system image you want to deploy.

9. Select Perform A "Zero Touch Installation" OS Deployment, With No User Interaction, and click Next.

10. Select the Configuration Manager Client package, and click Next.

11. Select the User State Migration Tool package, and click Next.

12. Select Create A New Settings Package For This Operating System Deployment, supply the UNC path, and click Next.

13. Supply information about the package. Fill in the name, version language, and manufacturer, and click Next to proceed.

14. Select No Sysprep Package Is Required, and click Next.

15. Review the summary, and click Next.

16. After the task sequence has been created, click Finish.

Using a Replace Scenario

The next step in creating a replace scenario for a computer is creating a computer association. This way, the USMT knows where to place the user state after installing the new computer.

1. From the Configuration Manager console, select the Assets And Compliance workspace, and expand Overview ➤ Devices.

2. Click Import Computer Information on the Home tab of the ribbon.

   This will allow you to enter a single computer or import many systems from a comma-separated values (CSV) file.

3. Select the option Import Single Computer and click Next. This will bring up the Single Computer page.

   You must enter the computer name along with either the MAC address or the SMBIOS GUID. The computer name is just how the machine will appear in the collections, not what the actual computer will be named.

4. Fill in the appropriate information, and select the source computer.

   This creates an association with the old computer, and the USMT knows where to get the user state.

5. After configuring, click Next.

6. On the Data Preview page, check the information and click Next.

7. Next, you'll see the Choose Target Collection page. Here, specify which collection you want to add to this new machine.

   It is extremely valuable to put all the new computer installs into the same collection, which is used exclusively for new computer deployment.

8. Click Next.

9. After specifying the collection, you will see the Summary page. Review the information, click Next, and then click Close on the Finish page.

Next, you need to deploy the task sequences you just have created. The Client Replace task sequence must be deployed to a collection that is especially created for the old client computers.

Then you need to deploy the New Computer task sequence to the collection that was specially created for the new computers. The deployment must support booting from PXE, as you learned in the "Deploying the Task Sequence" section earlier in this chapter.

Deploying a Virtual Hard Drive

With Configuration Manager, you can deploy your images to a virtual hard drive (VHD) that can be maintained by Configuration Manager and uploaded to a System Center 2012 R2 Virtual Machine Manager library. This is another example of the fact that Configuration Manager can be used to service the datacenter.

Deploying a VHD is done in two steps:

1. Create a VHD task sequence.

2. Create a virtual hard drive.

Creating a VHD Task Sequence

To be able to install an existing reference operation system image to a VHD, you need to create a special task sequence:

1. From the Configuration Manager console, select the Software Library workspace, expand Overview ➤ Operating Systems, and select Task Sequences.

2. Click Create Task Sequence on the Home tab of the ribbon, and select the option Install An Existing Image Package To A Virtual Hard Drive in the Create Task Sequence Wizard. Click Next.

3. Supply a name and description for the task sequence, and select a boot image that will support the operating system that you want to deploy. Click Next.

4. On the Install The Windows Operating System page, select the image package by browsing to the correct image. Supply a product key and be sure to enter a local administrator password.

5. On the Configure Network page, select the domain or workgroup to join.

   If you select to join a domain, you can specify which OU to put the computer in once it joins the domain. You also will need to specify the account that has permission to join computers to a domain. The Configuration Manager Network Access account is often used to join the computer to the domain. You need to delegate this access to the user account. Verify the account by testing the connection after configuring the account.

6. Click Next to continue. On the Install Configuration Manager Client page, specify any additional installation properties. Click Browse if you do not want to use the default Configuration Manager client package.

7. Click Next to add applications to the task sequence. Click Next to review the summary.

8. After reviewing the summary, click Next and then Close to complete the creation of the task sequence. As always, be sure that all the related content is distributed to your distribution point (groups).

Creating a Virtual Hard Drive

The next step is creating the actual VHD. To do this, you need to run the Create Virtual Hard Drive Wizard from the Configuration Manager console on a machine with the Hyper-V Role and Management console installed.

1. From the Configuration Manager console, select the Software Library workspace, expand Overview ➢ Operating Systems, and select Virtual Hard Drive.

2. Click Create Virtual Hard Drive on the Home tab of the ribbon. If this option is grayed out, you do not have the Hyper-V role or administrative tools installed.

3. Supply a name, version, comments, and a path to the VHD file, as shown in Figure 9.43; then click Next.

FIGURE 9.43
Specifying general information for the VHD

4. Select the task sequence created in the previous section and click Next.

5. Select the distribution point where all packages are available and click Add. Click Next to continue.

6. Add customizations for the task sequence if necessary and click Next.

7. Review the summary and click Next to start the VDH creation process, as shown in Figure 9.44.

FIGURE 9.44
VHD creation
process

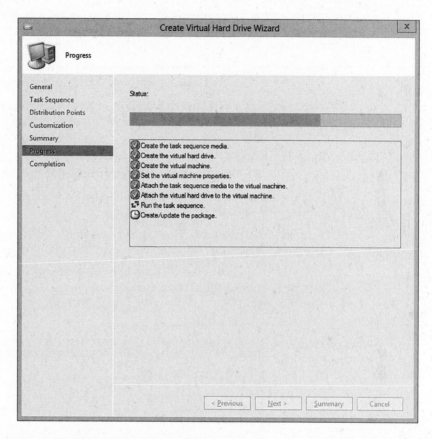

In the backend, a virtual machine with the VHD is created in Hyper-V and the task sequence is started in this virtual machine (VM). The VM that it creates has a random name, as shown in Figure 9.45.

FIGURE 9.45
The created virtual
machine in Hyper-V

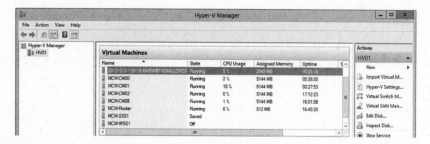

After the task sequence is finished, the VM will be deleted and the VHD file will be stored in the share that you have defined.

8. Click Close once the VHD is created.

Managing the Virtual Hard Drive

Now that you have a deployed VHD in your Configuration Manager environment, you want to do something with it. There are several options; you can use it as an existing VHD in Hyper-V when creating a virtual machine manually or upload it in the System Center 2012 R2 Virtual Machine Manager library. Uploading the VHD is done as follows:

1. From the Configuration Manager console, select the Software Library workspace, expand Overview ➤ Operating Systems, and select Virtual Hard Drive.

2. Select the created VHD and click Upload To Virtual Machine Manager in the Home tab of the ribbon. You need to install the Virtual Machine Manager (VMM) console to be able to upload the VHD.

3. Supply the VMM server name, select the VMM library share, and click Next. Review the summary, click Next, and click Close after completing the upload.

You can also modify the VHD from the Configuration Manager console. For instance, here you can change the task sequence:

1. From the Configuration Manager console, select the Software Library workspace, expand Overview ➤ Operating Systems, and select Virtual Hard Drive.

2. Select the created VHD and click Modify Virtual Hard Disk. This kicks off the same wizard for creating the VHD, but you cannot change the path and name of the VHD, as shown in Figure 9.46.

FIGURE 9.46
Modifying the VHD

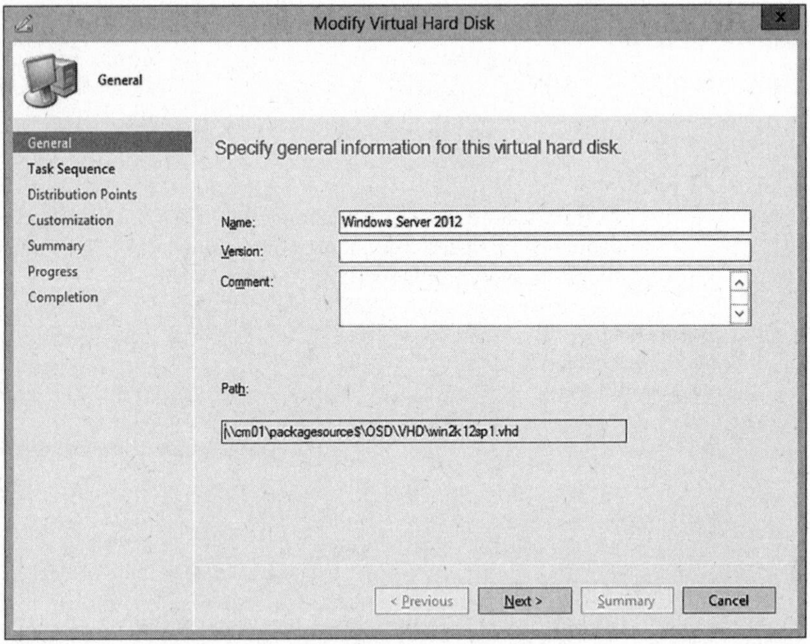

Servicing Your Operating System Images and VHDs Offline

In Configuration Manager 2007 you needed a tool called Deployment Image Servicing and Management (DISM)—a command-line tool used to maintain and update your images offline. Since Configuration Manager 2012 you have the ability to update your operating system images from the console. This feature uses the software update point and software update deployments that you configured earlier. Follow these steps if you want to update a WIM image:

1. From the Configuration Manager console, select the Software Library workspace, expand Overview ➤ Operating Systems, and select Operating System Images.

2. Select the operating system you want to update, and click Schedule Updates on the Home tab of the ribbon.

3. Select the updates that you want to install in the Windows image, as shown in Figure 9.47, and click Next.

FIGURE 9.47
Select the updates that you want to install.

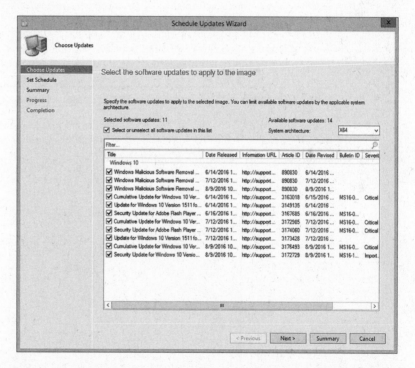

4. Select the schedule (as soon as possible or a custom schedule) for the update process, and click Next.

5. Review the summary, and click Next. Click Close when the process of scheduling the updates is finished.

The process of updating the Windows image can take a while; you can view the status of the process in the Scheduled Update Status column in the Configuration Manager console. Once the update is finished, you can see the installed updates in the console, as shown in Figure 9.48.

FIGURE 9.48
View the installed updates in the Windows image.

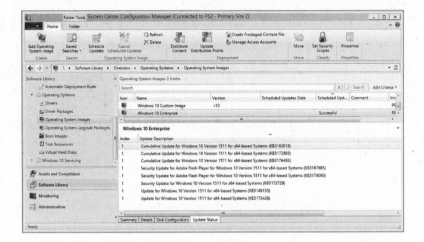

Besides installing software updates offline to operating system images, you can also schedule the installation of updates to VHDs. The Schedule Updates wizard will walk you through the process. Only updates that are deployed and downloaded can be used to service the image.

MONITORING AND TROUBLESHOOTING OFFLINE SERVICING

You can use the `OfflineServicingMgr.log` file in the logs folder of the Configuration Manager installation folder to monitor or troubleshoot while servicing your images offline.

You are also able to monitor the offline servicing by accessing the properties of the WIM image and viewing the Servicing tab, as shown in the following image. In addition, you can change the schedule if you have scheduled offline servicing.

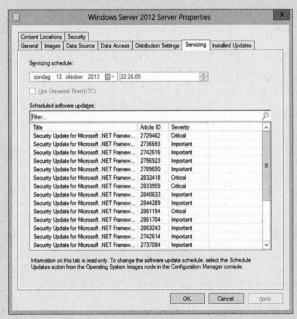

Maintaining the User State

When you browse to the User State Migration node in the Assets And Compliance workspace, as shown in Figure 9.49, you can manage computer associations. In this workspace you can create new computer associations, as mentioned earlier; see recovery information; find information about the user state migration; or specify the user accounts.

FIGURE 9.49

Managing the user state

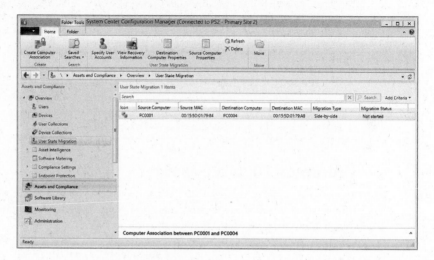

Specifying the user accounts is done as follows:

1. From the Configuration Manager console, choose the Assets And Compliance workspace and expand Overview ➤ User State Migration.

2. Select the User State Migration item, and click Specify User Accounts to add user accounts for which data needs to be migrated.

3. Click the starburst icon, and on the Add User Account screen click Browse. Search for the user and click OK twice.

4. Click OK to set the user account to migrate.

From this view you can also create computer associations when, for instance, migrating user state data from one computer to an existing computer that is being reinstalled.

 Real World Scenario

ASSIGNING MANY COMPUTERS TO THE BARE-METAL DEPLOYMENT

George T. Management sends an email to the help desk stating that his department just ordered 10 new machines with no operating system and that he wants them all configured by the end of the day with the same image that was used on his machine. The list of 10 machines was included in the email.

continues

continued

> You meet with your Configuration Manager team and decide that the best way to do this is to use Configuration Manager to push the image out using the PXE-enabled distribution point that has already been used in the environment.
>
> So, you open the Configuration Manager console, choose the Assets And Compliance workspace, expand Overview ➤ Devices, and click Import Computer Information on the Home tab of the ribbon. On the Import Computer Information page, you select Import Computers Using A File, and click Next. On the Choose Mappings page, you click Browse to browse the CSV file that Mr. Management sent you containing the list of computers on which you need to deploy the new operating system.
>
> After you import the file and assign the data mappings, you click Next. Then you verify that the data is correct on the Data Preview page and add these systems into the bare-metal collection you created earlier with the Windows 10 build already assigned. Finally, you click Finish to add the members to the collection. Configuration Manager will then deploy the new operating system when the machines are powered on and booted up in PXE boot.

Windows 10 as a Service

The release model of Windows 10 has been altered to continuously deliver upgrades and features instead of a major new version every 4 years. Microsoft is planning to release a major update more than once a year. To be able to cope with the rapid release cycle of Windows 10, Configuration Manager supports the new Windows 10 Servicing model. Read more about the Windows as a Service (WAAS) model here: `https://ref.ms/waas`.

The new Windows 10 Servicing node of the Software Library workspace in the Configuration Manager console consists of a dashboard, the All Windows 10 Updates node, and a Servicing Plan node. The dashboard shows the state of your Windows 10 versions in your environment. Figure 9.50 shows part of the dashboard. On this screen you'll find these sections:

FIGURE 9.50
Windows 10 Servicing dashboard, part 1

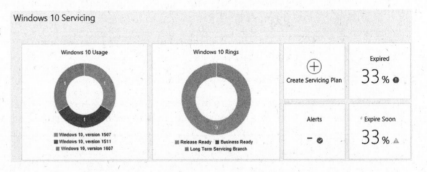

Windows 10 Usage   Shows a pie chart with the Windows 10 versions that are used and the number of devices that have those versions.

Windows 10 Rings   Shows a pie chart with the active Windows 10 Servicing Rings. The rings can be the following branches: Release Ready (Current Branch), Business Ready (Current Branch for Business), and Long-Term Servicing Branch. Read more about the branches here: `https://ref.ms/waas`.

Alerts   Shows alerts related to Windows 10 servicing.

Expired   This shows the percentage of expired Windows 10 versions that are still active in your environment.

Expire Soon   This shows the percentage of Windows 10 versions that are going to be expiring soon that are still active in your environment.

The second part of the dashboard, shown in Figure 9.51, shows the support cycle of the versions that are known and the period in which the Windows 10 versions are still supported.

FIGURE 9.51
Windows 10 Servicing
Dashboard, part 2

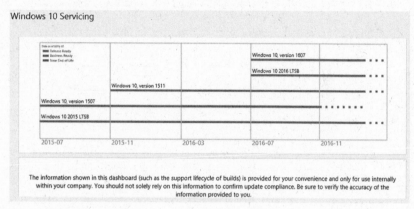

In the middle of the dashboard you can see the servicing plans that have been created. Servicing plans are automatic deployment rules that are used with the Software Updates feature, discussed in Chapter 8, "Software Updates."

Servicing Plans

The servicing plans can be used to upgrade your Windows 10 devices to the latest branch. You can create a schedule and manage the process through maintenance windows, just as you would software updates. To create a servicing plan, follow these steps:

1. From the Configuration Manager console, choose the Software Library workspace and expand Overview ➤ Windows 10 Servicing.

2. Select Servicing Plans and click Create Servicing Plan to start the Create Servicing Plan wizard.

3. Supply a name and description and click Next.

4. On the Servicing Plan page, browse to the target collection with the devices that need to be serviced. Click Next.

5. On the Deployment Ring page, specify the Windows readiness state to which the servicing plan should apply, as shown in Figure 9.52. Choose Release Ready (Current Branch) if you want to deploy the latest release of Windows 10, or choose Business Ready (Current Branch For Business) if you want to deploy a release that has been available for at least four months as the current branch.

FIGURE 9.52
Specifying the
deployment ring

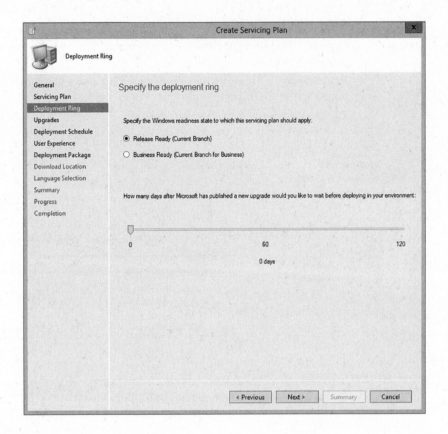

After selecting the readiness state, configure the days that need to be waited until Configuration Manager is going to deploy the released version. Click Next.

6. Configure the property filters and search criteria for this servicing plan, as shown in Figure 9.53. This way, not all versions of Windows 10 (gigabytes of data!) will be downloaded. Optionally, click Preview to see the versions that will be downloaded and deployed.

7. Click Next to configure the deployment schedule and click Next to configure the user experience.

8. Select or create a new deployment package for the servicing plan and click Next. If creating a new deployment package, assign the distribution points before specifying the download location by clicking Next.

9. Click Next to select the languages of the operating systems that need to be downloaded and click Next to review the summary.

10. Click Next to create the servicing plan and click Close to finish.

The servicing plan will now run on the configured schedule.

FIGURE 9.53
Selecting the property
filters and search
criteria

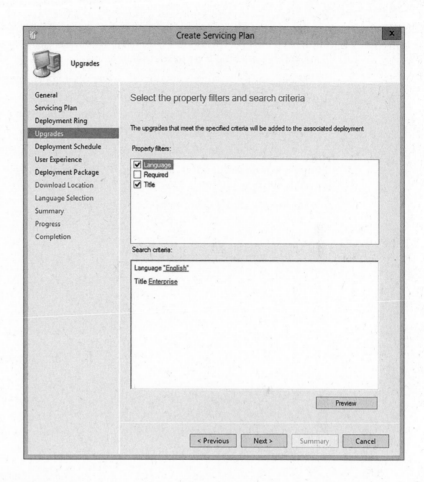

Windows 10 Updates

In addition to the Software Updates node, an All Windows 10 Updates node has been added
under the Windows 10 Servicing node. From here you can deploy individual feature updates for
Windows 10 to device collections, as described in Chapter 8.

The Bottom Line

Specify a Network Access account.   The Network Access account is the account
Configuration Manager will use to access the system while running WinPE.

Master It   How do you specify the Network Access account?

Enable PXE support.   PXE support in Configuration Manager is used to begin the operating system deployment process. The PXE feature responds to Configuration Manager clients
making PXE boot requests.

Master It   How do you set up PXE support?

Update the driver catalog package. The driver catalog allows you to add drivers to the already created packages and images you have within your organization so you are not constantly re-creating your images when you get a new machine in your environment.

Master It How do you update the driver catalog package?

Update an image from the console. In the past it was a big issue to keep your images up to date; no easy procedure existed. Configuration Manager now includes a feature called Schedule Updates that updates your Windows images.

Master It How do you easily update your Windows images?

Support Windows 10. You can support Windows 10 by using the traditional way of OSD or by using the new Windows 10 Servicing features.

Master It How can you support Windows 10?

Chapter 10

Inventory and Software Metering

The ability to provide detailed hardware and software inventory is one of the core features of Configuration Manager. Many companies rely on this data to obtain a clear understanding of the configuration of the computers in the environment. Hardware inventory gathers from your systems information such as the processor type, computer manufacturer, and amount of installed memory. Software inventory can gather lists of file types and versions that are installed on your computers. Combining this data with the extensive information in the Asset Intelligence knowledge base (covered in Chapter 11, "Asset Intelligence") provides value, so Configuration Manager becomes a valuable source of information about the computer infrastructure.

Software metering, the second major topic in this chapter, allows you to collect information on software usage to assist in managing software purchases and licensing. With this feature, you can report on the software that is being used in your environment and determine which users are running particular programs. You can also find software that is installed but isn't being used, and you can report on software license requirements and other items related to license management.

In this chapter, you will learn to

+ Configure and manage software inventory

+ Configure and manage hardware inventory

+ Configure and manage software metering

Inventory in Configuration Manager

Gathering inventory data is considered one of the most important features of any enterprise management system. The inventory data that is gathered is often used to create reports, queries, and collections. One thing that is important to know is that the inventory data is not "live" data, because it is based on the latest inventory scan and could potentially be several days or weeks old. When a Configuration Manager client performs an inventory scan and submits the data to the client's management point, the management point will verify the data, send it to a Configuration Manager site server, and then write it to the Configuration Manager database. Once the data is in the database, it can be used in many ways:

+ You can create queries that target computers based on their hardware configuration or installed software. You can use these queries to be proactive in preventing problems such as low hard disk space. Using inventory data for this proactive step may not be as important as it may have been in previous versions because you can perform checks in real time during application deployments by using global conditions.

◆ You can create queries that identify computers that do not have your organization's standard antivirus program installed. You can then use these search criteria to create a collection and then target that collection with an application deployment that will install the enterprise antivirus product.

◆ You can create reports showing hardware configuration and software installations that management can use to evaluate and improve the current computer environment.

Once the Configuration Manager client is installed, the first inventory is always a full inventory scan. Once it has been completed, all subsequent scans will send only *delta* inventory information, identifying what has changed. Delta inventory records are processed in the order in which they are received at the Configuration Manager site server. If for some reason a delta inventory is received from a client that is not in the database (such as a reimaged or new client, for example), the site server will delete the delta inventory and ask for a full inventory from that client the next time a scheduled scan is run.

Configuration Manager provides only limited support for computers that can boot up two or more operating systems. Configuration Manager clients can be discovered in multiple boot states, and the clients can be installed on each boot state. Inventory that is collected from these computers, however, will be from only the operating system that was running when the inventory scan was run.

Hardware inventory scanning will give you such information as disk space, video card type, memory installed, and much more. Configuration Manager uses Windows Management Instrumentation (WMI) to gather the needed data, and once you have learned the basics of WMI, you will find it fairly easy to modify the default hardware inventory settings.

Software inventory scanning will give you such information as the software installed, file types, and the versions of software. Unlike previous versions of Configuration Manager, the client is not configured to scan for any file types by default. The software inventory process can also collect files and store them on the primary site server, but this feature is rarely used because the collected files could create significant network usage and also consume a large amount of disk space on site servers.

Collecting Hardware Inventory

Hardware inventory collects data from clients by querying several data stores of information that are on computers, such as the registry and WMI. The Hardware Inventory Client Agent doesn't query all WMI classes; it only pulls the information that is defined in the client settings assigned to the client. As you learned in Chapter 5, "Client Installation," you can have multiple client settings and assign them to different collections. Inventory scans are done on the schedule you configure in the client settings. Unless there is a problem with the client, only delta inventories will be collected after the first inventory. This greatly decreases the network traffic required by client inventory reporting because deltas are usually only a small percentage of the size of a full inventory from a client. With every hardware inventory collection done on a client, Configuration Manager updates the site database with the current inventory while keeping a history of the previous information. You can view the current inventory identified in SQL as GS and historical inventory identified in SQL as HS information in queries, reports, and Resource Explorer.

The Hardware Inventory Client Agent will also collect certain basic information about a client's installed software. This information is gathered from the registry. By using the software inventory, however, you can get a larger amount of and much more detailed information about the software that is present on client computers.

WHAT DEFINES HARDWARE INVENTORY?

Configuration Manager gathers information about clients based on the settings defined in the client settings and the content of the `configuration.mof` (managed object format) file stored on the primary site server in the `<ConfigMgr installation directory>`\inboxes\clifiles `.src\hinv` folder.

The configuration.mof File

The `configuration.mof` file defines the data classes to be inventoried by the Hardware Inventory Client Agent. Data classes can be created to inventory existing or custom WMI repository data classes or registry keys found on clients.

This file also defines and registers the WMI providers used to access computer information during hardware inventory. Registering providers defines the type of provider to be used and the classes that the provider will support. WMI can access only registered providers, so that applies to the Hardware Inventory Client Agent as well. The `configuration.mof` file can't be used to register new providers for clients. New or custom providers must be sent to clients to be compiled manually before they can be added to hardware inventory.

When Configuration Manager clients request computer policies as part of their policy polling interval, the `configuration.mof` file is part of the policy that clients download and compile. When you add, modify, or delete data classes from the `configuration.mof` file, clients will automatically compile those changes the next time the client compiles a computer policy that it receives.

Later in the chapter you'll get hands-on practice in modifying `configuration.mof` to extend the information collected in hardware inventory.

The Client Settings

Unlike in previous versions of Configuration Manager, you now have a graphic interface in the Configuration Manager console, as shown in Figure 10.1, to edit the reporting classes used by the inventory process. In previous versions, you would modify the `sms_def.mof` file to define whether specific client data class information is reported. In Configuration Manager, you either use the default client settings or create custom client settings to enable and disable reporting classes. The reporting classes are based on the WMI data classes that are on clients by default or have been added after the `configuration.mof` file has been modified.

This reporting class information in the client settings is converted to a reporting policy that is downloaded to clients as part of their computer policy polling download. After the client has finished compiling the new reporting policy, the reporting information is stored in the client WMI repository in the `InventoryDataItem` class of the `Root\CCM\Policy\Machine` WMI namespace. Unlike the `configuration.mof` file, the inventory client settings file is never sent to clients directly. Only the policy generated by the client settings is actually compiled by Configuration Manager clients.

Later in the chapter you will see several examples of how to extend hardware inventory.

FIGURE 10.1

Default hardware
inventory settings

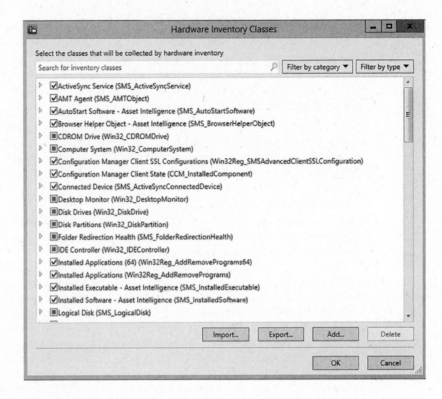

The Default Hardware Inventory Reporting Classes

The default client settings have some reporting classes enabled. These default classes might change depending on what version of Configuration Manager and which service pack you have installed and on whether you have enabled classes for Asset Intelligence. Here is an example of the hardware inventory data classes that are available in Configuration Manager with all Asset Intelligence classes available:

ActiveSync Service

AMT Agent

AutoStart Software – Asset Intelligence

Browser Helper Object – Asset Intelligence

CDROM Drive

Computer System

Configuration Manager Client SSL Configurations

Configuration Manager Client State

Connected Device

Desktop Monitor

Disk Drives

Disk Partitions

Folder Redirection Health

IDE Controller

Installed Applications (64)

Installed Applications

Installed Executable – Asset Intelligence

Installed Software – Asset Intelligence

Logical Disk

Memory

Mobile Device Client Agent Version

Mobile Device Computer System

Mobile Device Display

Mobile Device Installed Applications

Mobile Device Memory

Mobile Device OS Information

Mobile Device Password

Mobile Device Power

Mobile Device WLAN

Modem

Motherboard

NAP Client

NAP System Health Agent

Network Adapter

Network Adapter Configuration

Network Client

Operating System

Parallel Port

PC BIOS

Physical Memory

PNP Device Driver

Power Capabilities

Power Configuration

Power Insomnia Reasons

Power Management Daily Data

Power Management Exclusion Settings

Power Management Monthly Data

Power Settings

Processor

Recently Used Applications

SCSI Controller

Server Feature

Services (Note that Services is a very extensive field and can include very large amounts of data in SQL.)

Software Licensing Product – Asset Intelligence

Software Licensing Service – Asset Intelligence

Software Tag – Asset Intelligence

System Console Usage – Asset Intelligence

System Console User – Asset Intelligence

Sound Devices

System Devices

System Enclosure

Tape Drive

TS Issued License

TS License Key Pack

USB Controller

USB Device

Video Controller

Virtual Application Packages

Virtual Applications

Virtual Machine (64)

Virtual Machine

Virtual Machine Details

Windows app

Windows app User Info

Windows Update Agent Version

Each one of these reporting classes has certain criteria enabled, and these represent the actual data classes that are being collected. Some reporting classes might have all their data classes being captured or only some of them. The best way to determine what is being inventoried during the hardware inventory process is to browse through the individual classes in the Configuration Manager console.

THE ROLE OF MIF FILES IN HARDWARE INVENTORY

Management information format (MIF) files can be used to extend hardware inventory information that is collected from clients. The type of information that can be collected by MIF files can be just about anything, depending on how the MIF file is structured. During a hardware inventory cycle, the information in a MIF file is added to the client inventory report and stored in the Configuration Manager site database, where it can be used just like default client inventory data. The two types of MIF files that can be used to extend hardware inventory in this way are NOIDMIF and IDMIF.

By default, NOIDMIF and IDMIF file information is not inventoried by Configuration Manager. For this information to be added to hardware inventory, you must enable one or both file types in the hardware inventory settings. When you do, Configuration Manager creates new tables or modifies existing tables in the site database to add the properties in NOIDMIF and IDMIF files. NOIDMIF and IDMIF files are not validated, so they can be used to alter tables that you don't want altered. Doing this runs the risk that valid data could be overwritten by invalid data or large amounts of data could be imported into the Configuration Manager database, which would cause delays in all Configuration Manager functions. To lower the risk of this happening, use MIF collection only when it is absolutely necessary. Later in the chapter, you'll see how to change the location of MIF files from the default.

More on NOIDMIF Files

NOIDMIF files are the standard MIF files that are used in Configuration Manager hardware inventory. NOIDMIF files do not contain a unique identifier for the data they contain, and hardware inventory automatically associates the NOIDMIF information with the client that it was found on. NOIDMIF files are not sent to the site server during a client hardware inventory cycle, but their data is added to the client inventory report itself.

If the classes in the NOIDMIF file don't exist in the Configuration Manager database, the new inventory class tables are created in the Configuration Manager site database to store the new inventory information. As long as the NOIDMIF file is present on the client, the inventoried data from the NOIDMIF file will be updated in the Configuration Manager database. If the NOIDMIF file is removed, all the classes and properties relating to it are removed from the inventory of that client in the database. For NOIDMIF information to be pulled from a client, the NOIDMIF file must be stored here: `%windir%\ccm\inventory\Noidmifs`.

More on IDMIF Files

IDMIF files are custom MIF files that contain a unique ID and are not attached to the client that they are collected from. IDMIF files can be used to collect inventory data about devices that are not Configuration Manager clients, such as a shared network printer, an external hard drive, a copy machine, or other equipment that may not be attached to a client computer.

When you enable the IDMIF collection on your Configuration Manager site, IDMIF files are collected only if they are within the size limit that you set in the Hardware Inventory Client Agent properties. Depending on the maximum custom MIF size that you set for each site, IDMIF collection may cause increased network bandwidth usage during client inventory, which you should consider before you enable IDMIF collection.

Differences between NOIDMIF and IDMIF Files

IDMIF files are in most ways the same as NOIDMIF files. Both types have key properties that must be unique. Any class that has more than one instance must at least have one key property defined, or instances will overwrite previous instances. They differ in the following ways:

♦ IDMIF files must have a delta header that lists the architecture and a unique ID. NOIDMIF files are given a delta header automatically when processed by the client.

♦ IDMIF files must have a top-level group with the same class as the architecture being added or changed, and the class must have at least one property.

♦ Removing an IDMIF file from a client doesn't cause any data to be deleted from the Configuration Manager database.

♦ IDMIF files aren't added to a client's inventory, and the files themselves are sent across the network to be processed by a site server.

Collecting Software Inventory

When you enable Software Inventory in Configuration Manager, the software inventory process collects software inventory data directly from files by gathering data from the file's header information. Unknown files (files that don't have any detailed information in their file headers) can also be inventoried. You can also have Configuration Manager actually collect files you configure under a certain size. Both software inventory and collected file information can be viewed in Resource Explorer, which we will discuss later in the chapter.

You can also inventory encrypted and compressed files. This may cause software inventory to run more slowly because of the extra processing imposed on the client computer. When you inventory an encrypted file, an unencrypted copy of the file must be made so its information can be scanned. If antivirus software is running at the same time, it may show that the software inventory process is opening the files that are being scanned and then scanning them again to make sure they aren't infected by a virus.

Software inventory can use a considerable amount of network capacity (especially if collecting files) and also increase disk activity along with CPU usage locally on the computer while running, depending on the number of Configuration Manager clients, how frequently you schedule the software inventory process, and the size of the files you collect (if any). If you think that software inventory will cause problems with your network, schedule it to run after business hours. Figure 10.2 shows the default software inventory settings; notice that no file types are selected by default.

FIGURE 10.2
Default software
inventory settings

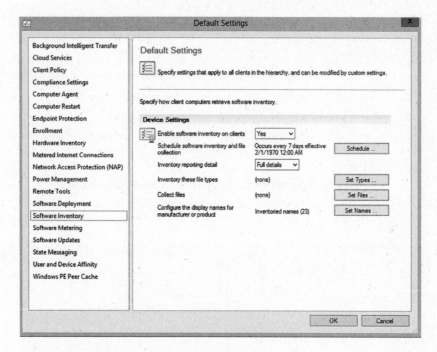

FIGURE 10.2
Default software
inventory settings

MORE ABOUT FILE COLLECTION

When a file is selected for collection, the Software Inventory Client Agent will search for that file when a software inventory scan runs on each client in the Configuration Management site. If the Software Inventory Client Agent finds a file that should be collected, then the file is attached to the inventory report and sent to the site server.

The site server keeps the five most recently changed versions of the collected files and stores them in the <Configuration Manager *installation directory*>\Inboxes\Sinv.box\Filecol directory. If a file has not changed since the last software inventory was collected, the file will not be collected again. Files larger than 20 MB are not collected by Configuration Manager software inventory file collection even if they are defined in the file collection settings.

This feature of Configuration Manager can greatly affect network bandwidth, as well as cause other problems, and is not typically utilized.

DISPLAY NAMES FOR SOFTWARE INVENTORIED PRODUCTS

During a software inventory cycle, the Configuration Manager software inventory process gets information from the file headers of files installed on clients. That information, including the names of the companies that made the files and the names of the files (or software products) themselves, is also inventoried. After the data is collected, you can view the information with Resource Explorer.

Because company and product names are retrieved from the file header information, any mismatches in the way these names are entered in the header information will also appear in the Configuration Manager database. These mismatches make it difficult to read and query against software inventory information since the data will appear to be under multiple company or software product names instead of a single name.

To help with this issue, you can set display names for inventoried products on the Inventoried Names tab of the Software Inventory Client Agent tab. For example, you can do the following:

1. Change variations of a company name to a single display name.

2. Refresh the view of software inventory in Resource Explorer.

You will see the changes. You will also see them when you make and run queries.

Doing this doesn't actually change the names in the file header information of the files installed on clients; it changes the names in the Configuration Manager site database.

Using Resource Explorer to View Inventory

When hardware and software inventory is collected from clients, it can be viewed in Resource Explorer. When you start Resource Explorer, a new console opens, as shown in Figure 10.3.

FIGURE 10.3

Resource Explorer

This displays the information collected from clients by hardware inventory and software inventory. The contents of the Resource Explorer details pane on the right will vary depending on what node is selected on the left pane in the console tree. You can use Resource Explorer to view client hardware, hardware history, and software inventory.

If a resource is a Configuration Manager client and if you are collecting hardware inventory at your site, the information displayed for that resource will be a list of the hardware installed on the client and other details. If you are collecting software inventory, then you will see a list of installed software on the client. If the resource isn't a Configuration Manager client, then no information will be displayed, since no inventory will be collected from that client.

You can start Resource Explorer to view a single client's inventory from the Configuration Manager console.

To open Resource Explorer from the Configuration Manager console, follow these steps:

1. In the Configuration Manager console, select Assets And Compliance ➤ Overview ➤ Devices.

2. Find the client that you want to view.

3. Once you have selected the client you want, click Start ➤ Resource Explorer on the ribbon.

Scheduling Inventory

The hardware inventory and software inventory processes each collect inventory according to a schedule that is set in the client settings. Table 10.1 gives a simple rundown of scheduling options for each inventory process.

TABLE 10.1:   Inventory scheduling options

TYPE	DESCRIPTION
Simple schedule	An interval between inventory cycles, such as every day
Custom schedule	A start time and an interval for inventory collection, such as every Monday or the first Tuesday of every month at a specified hour of the day

By default, both hardware and software inventory schedules are set to run every seven days. If a client is not running when an inventory is schedule to run, it will run the inventory the next time the client is started.

The simple schedule doesn't give you as much flexibility as custom scheduling does; however, the simple schedule usually causes less network traffic because the time interval between each client's inventory cycle is based on the time that the Configuration Manager client was installed and when the first policies are retrieved, for every client. When you use a custom schedule, all the clients will begin inventory cycles at exactly the same time.

Since software inventory is more resource intensive on clients than hardware inventory, you might consider not running software inventory as often as you do hardware inventory, depending on your organization's needs. For example, if your organization has locked down user rights on workstations, then the software that is installed on them should not change frequently, so you can set software inventory cycles for every few days or once a week.

When you change an inventory collection schedule on the Configuration Manager site server, this will update the client computer policies downloaded and compiled by clients according to their regular client policy polling interval. When the client inventory agent detects a change in schedule, it will make a delta inventory file. The next inventory cycle will run according to the new schedule.

Configuration Manager also keeps historical inventory records for the number of days set in the Delete Aged Inventory History site maintenance task, which has a default setting of 90 days.

SCHEDULING INVENTORY

Even if all installations are unique, it is often considered best practice to have a hardware inventory schedule of every 3–5 days and a weekly software inventory schedule. For servers it is often considered good practice to have a custom schedule for both inventory processes. That way, you can schedule when inventory will run and not put a load on the hardware during peak hours.

Configuring Inventory

Now that we have discussed the inventory process, its components, and its capabilities, you are ready to configure the inventory function to fit your company's needs.

CONFIGURING HARDWARE INVENTORY FOR A CONFIGURATION MANAGER SITE

Before you configure hardware inventory, you need to know what kind of information you are gathering. In essence you have three different scenarios, as explained in Table 10.2.

TABLE 10.2: Inventory scenarios

SCENARIO	HOW TO GATHER THE INVENTORY
Data class already exists in the default client settings.	All you have to do is enable the class in either the default client settings or custom client settings as explained later in this chapter.
Data class does not exist in the default client settings but exists locally in WMI on each client.	On the central administration site or primary site, open the default client settings. Connect to a remote host containing the data class, and import the data class.
Data class does not exist in the default client settings or on any of the local clients.	On one of the clients add the information to WMI. On the central administration site or primary site, open the default client settings. Connect to a remote host containing the data class and import the data class.

Configuring the Default Hardware Inventory Client Settings

To configure the default hardware inventory, select Client Settings in the Administration workspace. Open the default client agent settings properties, select Hardware Inventory, and click Set Classes, as shown in Figure 10.4. You can configure the following properties:

Enable Hardware Inventory On Clients Configure this to True to enable (the default) or False to disable hardware inventory. Disabling hardware inventory is not recommended.

Hardware Inventory Schedule Click Schedule and select a simple schedule or define a custom schedule:

Simple Schedule This schedules hardware inventory to run at a single, specific interval for all clients that read the client settings. By default, this option is enabled and set for 7 days. For any other setting, use the Run Every field, and enter the number and type of time units (minutes, hours, days) in the simple schedule. This setting can be from 1 to 59 minutes, from 1 to 23 hours, or from 1 to 31 days.

FIGURE 10.4
Configuring hardware
inventory

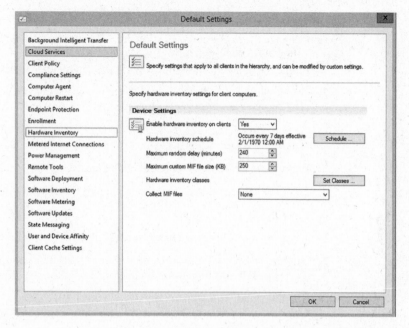

Custom Schedule   Click Customize to open the Custom Schedule dialog box and set the hardware inventory schedule. This gives you the ability to schedule the first start date and time for inventory to run on clients. Once the start time for inventory has passed, all future inventories will recur on the schedule that you set on all clients at the same time. The custom schedule can be set to run weekly, to run monthly, or to run on a custom interval, with the following criteria:

◆   Custom weekly schedules can run from 1 to 4 weeks on the day of the week you set.

◆   Custom monthly schedules can run from 1 to 12 months on either a specific day of the month from 1 to 31; the last day of each month; or the first, second, third, fourth, or last selected day of the week for each month.

◆   Custom schedules can also be set on a custom interval of either 1 to 31 days, 1 to 23 hours, or 1 to 59 minutes.

Collect MIF Files   From the drop-down box, select whether you want to collect IDMIF, NOIDMIF, both types, or none of them (default setting).

Maximum Custom MIF File Size (KB)   This is the maximum size, in kilobytes, allowed for each custom MIF file that will be collected from a client during a hardware inventory cycle. You can set the size from 1 KB to 5,120 KB; the default value is 250 KB. If a custom MIF is larger than the maximum size, the Hardware Inventory Client Agent will move the IDMIF to the \Badmifs folder, and the IDMIF file will not be sent to the site server to be processed.

Collect IDMIF files   Adds a new architecture and attributes and classes to the Configuration Manager database.

Collect NOIDMIF files   Extends the hardware inventory by adding attributes and classes to existing architectures on a client. They are used to extend, or add, new information about existing Configuration Manager clients to the site database.

Changing the Default MIF Storage Location on a Client

You can change the MIF storage location after the client is installed by modifying the registry keys for the IDMIF and MOIDMIF files.

To change the default location for IDMIF files, follow these steps:

1. On the client for which you want to change the MIF location settings, select Start ➢ Run, type **regedit**, and then press Enter to start the Registry Editor.

2. Go to the following registry key: HKEY_LOCAL_MACHINE\SOFTWARE\Microsoft\SMS\ Client\Configuration\Client Properties : IDMIF Directory.

3. Right-click IDMIF Directory, and click Modify.

4. Enter the path to which you want to change; then click OK.

5. Close the Registry Editor.

To change the default storage location for NOIDMIF files, follow these steps:

1. On the client for which you want to change the MIF location settings, select Start ➢ Run, type **regedit**, and then press Enter to start the Registry Editor.

2. Go to the following registry key: HKEY_LOCAL_MACHINE\SOFTWARE\Microsoft\SMS\ Client\Configuration\Client Properties : NOIDMIF Directory.

3. Right-click NOIDMIF Directory, and click Modify.

4. Enter the path to which you want to change; then click OK.

5. Close the Registry Editor.

Note that this procedure will change the MIF storage location on only the client that you worked on. If you want to make this a sitewide client change, you can use the remediation feature in Settings Management.

 Real World Scenario

CONFIGURE CUSTOM HARDWARE INVENTORY CHANGES FOR ALL LAPTOPS

As the Configuration Manager administrator, you have been requested to ensure that portable battery information is inventoried for all laptops.

1. Open the Configuration Manager administrative console.

2. Select the Administration workspace and browse to Client Settings.

3. On the ribbon, click Create Custom Client Device Settings.

4. Type **Hardware Settings for laptops** in the Name field.

5. From the list of custom settings, select Hardware Inventory.

6. In the left column, select Hardware Inventory and click Set Classes.

7. Find Portable Battery (Win32_Portable) and enable the data class.

8. Click OK.

9. Click OK to save the custom client settings.

10. Back in the administrative console, select the newly created custom settings and click Deploy on the ribbon.

11. Select the All Laptop device collection and click OK.

EXTENDING HARDWARE INVENTORY

As described in Table 10.2, you can also customize hardware inventory to collect information that is not reported by default or add totally new information that you want to be collected that you configure yourself.

You can extend hardware inventory by inventorying additional WMI classes, additional WMI class attributes, registry keys, and other customizations to fit your company's needs. If you need to, you can also modify the Hardware Inventory Client Agent to reduce the amount of information reported by clients.

Before you start modifying the `configuration.mof` file, you should make sure you have a good idea of what you are doing and make backups of the file before you edit it. You should also consider performing the proposed changes in a Configuration Manager test lab so that you can effectively monitor the results of the changes without impacting the production environment.

A few resources are available to help you with extending hardware inventory. For example, the article "How to Extend Hardware Inventory in Configuration Manager" discusses how to configure and extend the hardware inventory feature in Configuration Manager; see `http://technet.microsoft.com/en-us/library/gg712290.aspx`.

Providers Used in Hardware Inventory

When you extend hardware inventory that is collected by Configuration Manager clients, the `configuration.mof` file is modified to inventory client information by leveraging a registered inventory data provider. Providers used during client hardware inventory are listed at the top of the `configuration.mof` file and are registered on clients when they first get a computer policy, and then they compile the `configuration.mof` file after the Configuration Manager client is installed.

Extending Hardware Inventory Using the `configuration.mof` File

The `configuration.mof` file is used to modify data class information inventoried by clients with hardware inventory.

To modify the `configuration.mof` file, follow these steps:

1. Make a backup copy of the `configuration.mof` file, and put it in a safe location.

2. On the primary site server, go to the `<Configuration Manager install folder>/inboxes/clifiles.src/hinv` folder.

3. Using Notepad, open the `configuration.mof` file, and make any necessary changes.

   Figure 10.5 shows part of the `configuration.mof` file.

FIGURE 10.5
The configuration
.mof file

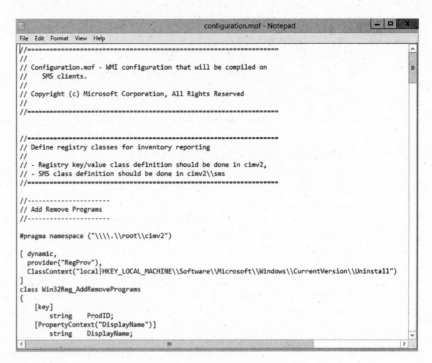

4. Close the configuration.mof file, and save the changes.

5. Copy the configuration.mof file to the same location that is listed in step 2 and to all the primary sites in your hierarchy to propagate the changes to the other sites. Note that ConfigMgr does not copy this file for you; you must copy the file to the other primary site servers in your hierarchy in order to achieve consistent inventory results from your clients.

Extending Hardware Inventory Using the Default Client Settings

The default client settings are used to modify reporting class information inventoried by clients during hardware inventory. The default client settings contain a list of classes and attributes that relate to data classes stored in the WMI repository of Configuration Manager clients.

Classes and properties that have the reporting checkmark enabled are collected, and those without a checkmark are not. You must always modify the default classes in the default client settings at the central administration site (CAS) or standalone primary site; you will not be able to enable or disable these settings in any custom client settings.

To modify the default client settings, follow these steps:

1. Navigate to the Administration workspace, under Overview select Client Settings, and open the Default Client Settings properties.

2. Select Hardware Inventory and click Set Classes.

3. Use the GUI to enable or disable any of the existing inventory data classes.

4. Choose OK to save the changes.

5. Close the Default Client Settings properties.

Configuring Software Inventory for a Configuration Manager Site

The Software Inventory option is enabled by default when you install Configuration Manager, but unlike previous versions, ConfigMgr 2012 will not inventory any files by default. In order to perform software inventory on file types, like files with an `.exe` extension, you must configure the setting:

1. Navigate to the Administration workspace, under Overview select Client Settings, and open the Default Client Settings properties.

2. Select Software Inventory.

   The first thing you will see is the default settings, as shown in Figure 10.6.

FIGURE 10.6
Default Software
Inventory settings

3. Click Set Types.

4. Click the yellow starburst New icon to create a new entry.

5. Type ***.exe**, as shown in Figure 10.7, and click OK twice.

   This will search for EXE files on the entire hard disk, excluding the Windows folder and encrypted/compressed files. If you want to, you can specify which folders to include in the scanning; likewise, you can specify a filename instead of a file type. It is worth noting that as you add file types, you will extend the amount of time that software inventory will run on the client computers.

FIGURE 10.7
Scanning for EXE files

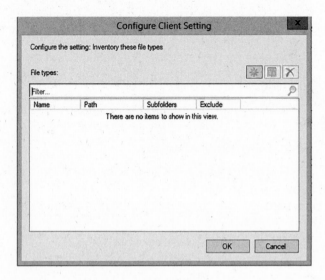

Inventory Reporting Detail is by default set to Full Details. This will ensure that you gather information about the file regardless of whether the file has a product mentioned in the file header. Selecting Product Only will not gather information from unknown files.

Collect Files allows you to copy a file from the client and store a copy on the site server. When you enable this feature, the site server will keep up to five versions of each file in <Configuration Manager *installation directory*>\Inboxes\Sinv.box\Filecol. Even though it sounds tempting to collect files, you should think twice before enabling this feature. It can generate a substantial amount of network traffic and cause your site server to run low on disk space. As shown in Figure 10.8, you can collect a single file or all files of a certain file type.

FIGURE 10.8
Collecting files

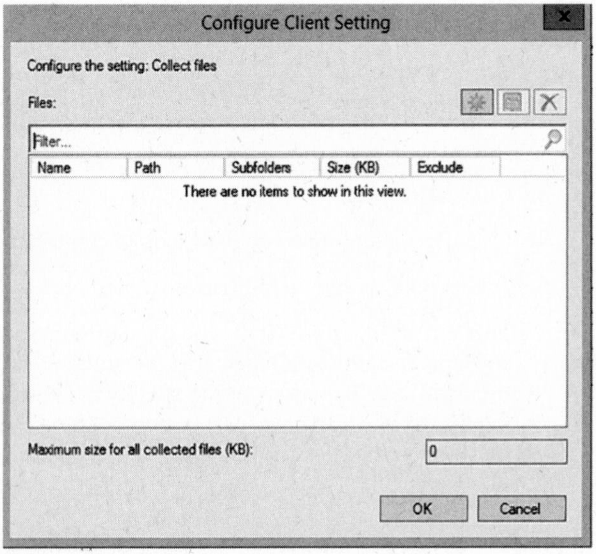

6. To specify a file, click the yellow starburst New icon, and type a filename or use a wildcard to specify a given type.

7. Click Set to narrow the search to a given location; this will speed up the process.

Figure 10.9 shows how you can search for all `*.sys` files in the `%programfiles%\MySoftware` folder.

Configuring the display names for manufacturer or product allows you to group files according to the correct vendor and application. As mentioned earlier in this chapter, the names are derived from the file header, which often contains alternative ways to spell the manufacturer's name.

FIGURE 10.9
Specifying all `*.sys` files from a folder

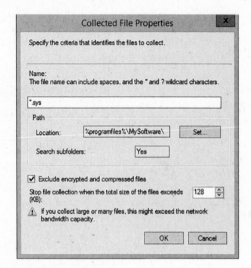

8. Click Set Names, and click the yellow starburst New icon to configure a new display name.

Figure 10.10 shows a new display name for Microsoft applications.

FIGURE 10.10
Configure a new display name.

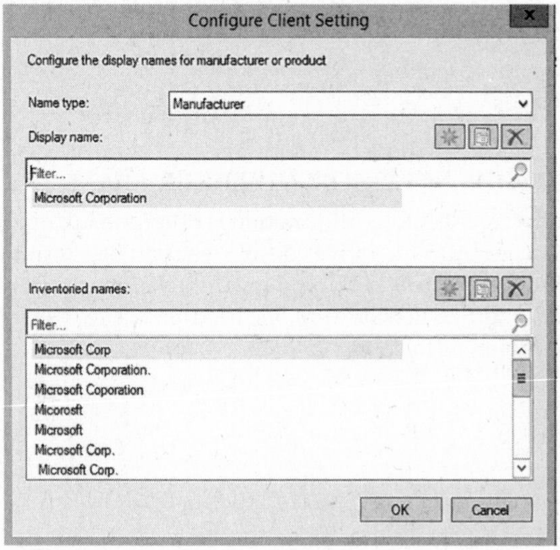

9. Once the display name is created, select the display name and click the yellow starburst New icon to the right of Inventoried Names.

When you specify an entry in the Inventoried Names section, you can use these wildcard variables:

%	Any string of zero or more characters
_ (underscore)	Any single character
[ ] (brackets)	Any single character within a range
[^]	Any single character *not* with a range

10. When you have typed a name, click OK.

Figure 10.11 shows an example where all inventory names starting with "Adobe" will be grouped below the Adobe manufacturer.

FIGURE 10.11
A custom display name

VIEWING SOFTWARE INVENTORY DATA

Software inventory information is often used in queries and reports. In the Configuration Manager administrative console, you can use Resource Explorer to view information from a single client (Figure 10.12). You will be able to read file information including File Name, File Path, File Size, File Version, and File Modified Date. The information is divided into four sections, as described in Table 10.3.

FIGURE 10.12
Software information
in Resource Explorer

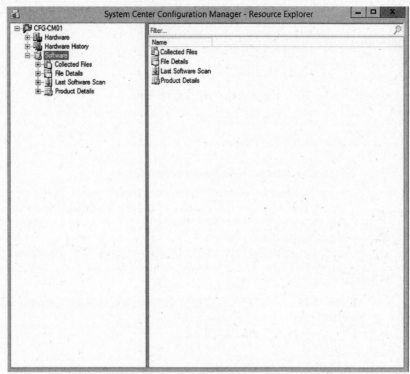

FIGURE 10.12
Software information
in Resource Explorer

TABLE 10.3: Software information in Resource Explorer

SECTION	INFORMATION AVAILABLE
Collected Files	Lists all files collected from the client.
File Details	Lists all inventoried files that are not associated with any vendor.
Last Software Scan	Lists the last file collection and software inventory scanning data.
Product Details	Lists all inventoried files that are associated with a vendor. You can modify the list of vendors by customizing the display name in the Software Inventory Client Settings.

MISCELLANEOUS INVENTORY CONFIGURATIONS AND OPTIONS

The following sections cover some configuration options for inventory that don't neatly fit into other categories.

Encrypting Client Inventory Reports

Configuration Manager can be configured to sign and encrypt data sent between the client and the management point. To enhance security for inventory, you can enable inventory encryption.

To enable inventory encryption, follow these steps:

1. In the Configuration Manager console, select the Administration workspace, then choose Overview ➤ Site Configuration ➤ Sites.

2. Right-click the site and click Properties.

3. Click the Signing And Encryption tab.

4. Select Use Encryption.

5. Click OK to finish.

Excluding Files from Software Inventory

To exclude folders or entire drives from the software inventory process, create a file called skpswi.dat and save it to the root of the area (and subfolders) you want to exclude. You can skip the entire C: partition by storing the file in C:\ or a folder (and subfolders) by saving the file in the root of the folder.

You can ensure that folders and drivers are excluded by reading the FileSystemFile.log file on the client. Figure 10.13 shows how you can verify that the skpswi.dat file is working.

FIGURE 10.13
FileSystemFile
.log

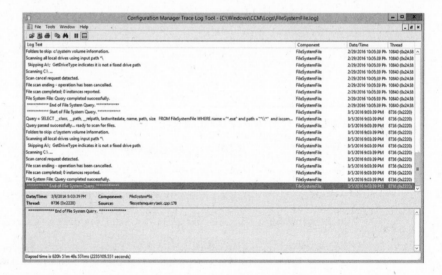

To exclude files from software inventory, follow these steps:

1. Using Notepad, make an empty file named skpswi.dat.

2. Right-click that file, and click Properties.

3. In the file properties for skpswi.dat, select the Hidden attribute.

4. Place the skpswi.dat file at the root of the drive or folder where you don't want to collect software inventory.

Monitoring the File and Size Being Sent to the Management Point

One of the questions you often hear before enabling any inventory process is, how much network utilization is generated by running this process? The Configuration Manager client will send Heartbeat Discovery data, hardware inventory data, and software inventory data on a regular basis. The three files generated by each of these processes will be temporarily stored in `%systemroot%\ccm\inventory\temp\` before being sent to the management point. After files are sent to the management point, they will automatically be deleted from the `temp` folder. You can create a file called `archive_reports.sms`, discussed next, and save it to the same folder. This will prevent the Configuration Manager client from deleting the XML files after they are sent to the management point so you can view the actual hardware inventory data the clients are sending.

Figure 10.14 shows different files generated: ones for hardware inventory, ones for software inventory, and ones for Heartbeat Discovery.

FIGURE 10.14
Files generated by the inventory and discovery processes

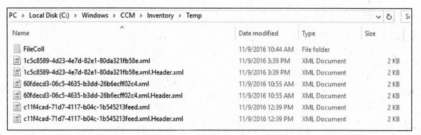

To prevent XML files from being deleted, follow these steps:

1. Using Notepad, create an empty file named `archive_reports.sms` (make sure that it's not a TXT file).

2. Save the file in the `%systemroot%\ccm\inventory\temp\` folder.

3. Initiate a hardware, software, and/or discovery inventory cycle on the client, and monitor the `%systemroot%\ccm\inventory\temp\` folder.

   You should be able to see one XML file for each process that contains data.

4. Remember to delete the `archive_reports.sms` file from the client once you have enough information to estimate the average file size for each of the three processes. Note that the first hardware and software inventories will be larger than subsequent inventory files, whereas the heartbeat discovery file should always be about the same size.

Viewing Collected Files

You can view collected files by opening the `<:\>Program Files\Microsoft Configuration Manager\inboxes\sinv.box\FileCol\` folder on the site server or through Resource Explorer. Using Resource Explorer is by far the best method because it will link the collected files and computer together. As shown in Figure 10.15, you can open and read each collected file.

FIGURE 10.15
Reading a collected
file in Resource
Explorer

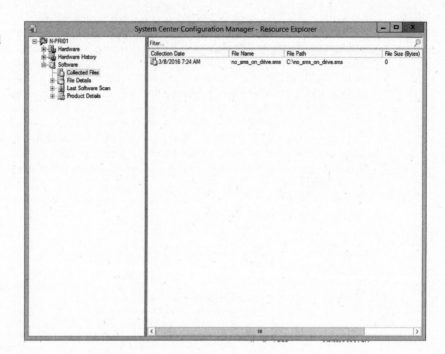

To view the collected files of a particular client, follow these steps:

1. In the Configuration Manager console, select the Assets And Compliance workspace, then choose Overview ➤ Devices.

2. In the Search area of the ribbon, type the name of the client you wish to find and click Search.

3. Once you have found the client you want, right-click it.

4. Click Start ➤ Start Resource Explorer.

5. In the left pane, select Software ➤ Collected Files.

   You will see a list of all the files that have been collected from that client in the right pane.

6. To view a file, you have two options:

   ◆ Right-click a file, and select View File.

   ◆ Right-click a file, and select Save.

Software Metering in Configuration Manager

Software metering is used to track usage of administrator-defined applications using software metering rules. It is not used to prevent users from running an application (this is a job for the Software Restriction Group Policy). By default Configuration Manager will automatically create disabled software metering rules based on the recently used inventory data. Often you will find yourself disabling the feature and creating your own software metering rules.

Overview of Software Metering

Software metering in Configuration Manager allows you to monitor and collect information about software usage on Configuration Manager clients. The information collected is based on the software metering rules that can be configured in the Configuration Manager console or created automatically based on usage data collected by inventory.

The Software Metering Client Agent on each client evaluates these rules, collects the requested data, and then reports it to the Configuration Manager database. The software metering process will continue to collect usage data even if it can't connect to its management point and will send the collected data on to the site server after it connects to the network. By default clients will send the software metering usage report every seven days.

Software metering data is held on the site server until it is summarized. The summarization schedule is defined in the Site Maintenance tasks for the site. By default the maintenance task will begin every day at 00:00.

You will be able to see the software metering data in the reports once the software metering report data has been received on the site server and summarized. By default this process can take up to eight days from client activity to seeing information in reports. This might sound like a long delay, but often you will only use the reports once a month or so when evaluating licenses. Combined with software inventory, software metering gives administrators a powerful tool to help answer questions that come up in every IT organization. Examples of these questions include the following:

- What is the relationship between how many instances of a software program are installed on clients and how many actually use that software?

- Do you need to buy more licenses when renewing your license agreement with a software vendor?

- What users are still using an obsolete program?

Configuring Software Metering

The Software Metering feature is enabled by default when you install Configuration Manager. You can enable or disable the feature by editing the default Client Agent settings or creating a custom client setting.

CONFIGURING THE SOFTWARE METERING FEATURE

Take these steps to configure the Software Metering feature:

1. Navigate to the Administration workspace; under Overview, select Client Settings; and open the Default Client Settings properties.

2. Select Software Metering, and notice the default setting, as shown in Figure 10.16.

   By default, Enable Software Metering On Clients is set to Yes.

FIGURE 10.16
Default Software
Metering settings

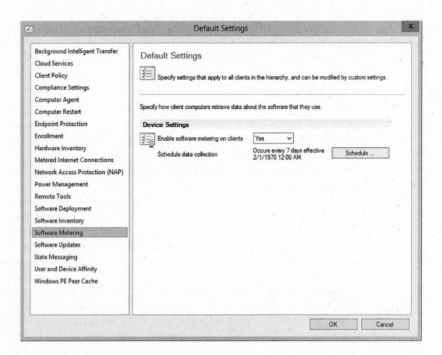

3. To disable the feature, select No in the drop-down box.

Schedule Data Collection defines how often the Configuration Manager client will send software metering data from WMI to the site server.

CONFIGURING AUTOMATIC SOFTWARE METERING RULE GENERATION

As discussed earlier in the chapter, Configuration Manager will automatically create disabled software metering rules based on recently gathered inventory data. You can configure or disable the feature from the Assets And Compliance workspace.

To configure automatic rule generation, follow these steps:

1. Navigate to the Assets And Compliance workspace; under Overview, select Software Metering; and click Software Metering Properties on the ribbon.

This opens the Software Metering Properties dialog box, as shown in Figure 10.17.

2. You can set the following options:

◆ You can specify the amount of time in Data Retention (In Days) that data generated by software rules will be held in the site database. The default setting is 90 days.

◆ You can select the Automatically Create Disabled Metering Rules From Recent Usage Inventory Data check box.

◆ You can set the percentage of computers in a Configuration Manager site that must use an executable before a software metering rule for that executable is automatically created. The default setting is 10 percent.

◆ You can set the maximum number of rules that software metering will automatically generate. The default setting is 100 rules.

FIGURE 10.17
Software Metering
Properties dialog box

3. When you have finished setting these options, click OK.

ENABLING AND DISABLING SOFTWARE METERING RULES

You don't have to delete a rule if you don't want to use it; instead, you can enable it or disable it as needed if you want to keep it.

To enable or disable a software metering rule, follow these steps. Figure 10.18 shows automatically generated software metering rules in the Configuration Manager console.

1. Navigate to the Assets And Compliance workspace, and under Overview, select Software Metering.

2. Right-click one or more rules that you want to configure, and then click either Enable or Disable.

The option that is available will depend on what state the rule is already in.

FIGURE 10.18

Software Metering node with software metering rules

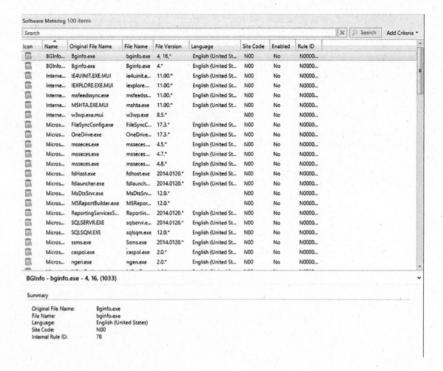

	Software Metering 100 items							
Icon	Name	Original File Name	File Name	File Version	Language	Site Code	Enabled	Rule ID
	BGInfo...	Bginfo.exe	bginfo.exe	4, 16,.*	English (United St...	N00	No	N0000...
	BGInfo...	Bginfo.exe	Bginfo.exe	4.*	English (United St...	N00	No	N0000...
	Interne...	IE4UINIT.EXE.MUI	ie4uinit.e...	11.00.*	English (United St...	N00	No	N0000...
	Interne...	IEXPLORE.EXE.MUI	iexplore...	11.00.*	English (United St...	N00	No	N0000...
	Interne...	msfeedssync.exe	msfeedss...	11.00.*	English (United St...	N00	No	N0000...
	Interne...	MSHTA.EXE.MUI	mshta.exe	11.00.*	English (United St...	N00	No	N0000...
	Interne...	w3wp.exe.mui	w3wp.exe	8.5.*		N00	No	N0000...
	Micros...	FileSyncConfig.exe	FileSyncC...	17.3.*	English (United St...	N00	No	N0000...
	Micros...	OneDrive.exe	OneDrive...	17.3.*	English (United St...	N00	No	N0000...
	Micros...	msseces.exe	msseces...	4.5.*	English (United St...	N00	No	N0000...
	Micros...	msseces.exe	msseces...	4.7.*	English (United St...	N00	No	N0000...
	Micros...	msseces.exe	msseces...	4.8.*	English (United St...	N00	No	N0000...
	Micros...	fdHost.exe	fdhost.exe	2014.0120.*	English (United St...	N00	No	N0000...
	Micros...	fdlauncher.exe	fdlaunch...	2014.0120.*	English (United St...	N00	No	N0000...
	Micros...	MsDtsSrvr.exe	MsDtsSrv...	12.0.*		N00	No	N0000...
	Micros...	MSReportBuilder.exe	MSRepor...	12.0.*		N00	No	N0000...
	Micros...	ReportingServicesS...	Reportin...	2014.0120.*	English (United St...	N00	No	N0000...
	Micros...	SQLSERVR.EXE	sqlservr.e...	2014.0120.*	English (United St...	N00	No	N0000...
	Micros...	SQLSQM.EXE	sqlsqm.exe	12.0.*	English (United St...	N00	No	N0000...
	Micros...	ssms.exe	Ssms.exe	2014.0120.*	English (United St...	N00	No	N0000...
	Micros...	caspol.exe	caspol.exe	2.0.*	English (United St...	N00	No	N0000...
	Micros...	ngen.exe	ngen.exe	2.0.*	English (United St...	N00	No	N0000...

BGInfo - bginfo.exe - 4, 16, (1033)

Summary

Original File Name:	Bginfo.exe
File Name:	bginfo.exe
Language:	English (United States)
Site Code:	N00
Internal Rule ID:	78

ADDING A SOFTWARE METERING RULE

If the automatically generated rules aren't what you need, then you can manually make your own to meet your organization's needs. To make your own software metering rules, follow these steps:

1. Navigate to the Assets And Compliance workspace, and under Overview, select Software Metering.

2. Click Create Software Metering Rule on the ribbon.

   This opens the General page of the Create Software Metering Rule Wizard, shown in Figure 10.19.

   This page has the following options:

Name   The name of the software metering rule, which should be unique. You can have rules with the same name, as long as the filenames are different. This way, you can track suites of applications like the Adobe Creative Suite or Microsoft Office.

File Name   The name of the executable file you want to meter. You can click Browse to display the Open dialog box, where you can select the file that you want to meter. You can manually type in this filename, but when you do that, no checks are made to determine whether the file exists or whether it contains the needed file header information. For the best results, always use the Browse button if possible. Wildcard characters can't be used in this field, and selecting the Original File Name field is optional.

Original File Name   The name of the executable file that you want to meter. This name is matched to the information in the file header, not the filename itself, so you still meter it if the file is renamed. Wildcard characters can't be used in this field, and selecting the File Name field is optional.

FIGURE 10.19
General page of the
Create Software
Metering Rule
Wizard

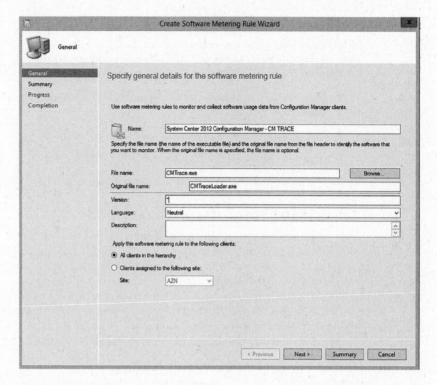

Version The version of the executable file that you want to meter. If you use the Browse button to select your file, this field will be filled out automatically from the file's header information (as shown in Figure 10.18). You can use the wildcard character (*) to represent any string of characters or the wildcard character (?) to represent any single character. If you want to meter all versions of the file, you can use the default value (*).

Language The language of the file that you want to meter. The default value is English (United States). If you use the Browse button to select your file, then this is filled out automatically from the file's header information. If you want to meter all language versions of this file, then select Any from the drop-down list.

Description A description that you want for the rule. This is an optional field.

Apply This Software Metering Rule To The Following Clients Your options are All Clients In The Hierarchy or Clients Assigned To The Following Site.

3. Fill in the information and click Next.

4. Review the information on the Summary page and click Next.

5. Click Close.

The rule is now created and will be downloaded to clients during the next machine policy cycle.

DELETING SOFTWARE METERING RULES

When you delete a software metering rule, the change will be downloaded to clients during their next policy polling interval, just like when you create rules.

To delete a software metering rule, follow these steps:

1. Navigate to the Assets And Compliance workspace, and under Overview, select Software Metering.

2. Find the metering rule that you want to delete, right-click it, and click Delete.

You will then see a Confirm Object Delete dialog box.

3. If you are sure that you want to delete this rule, then click Yes.

SOFTWARE METERING MAINTENANCE TASKS

Depending on how you configure software metering, you could end up with a lot of data collected in the Configuration Manager database. To help you manage that data, several maintenance tasks are included in the Configuration Manager console. There are four tasks in total in two categories—two tasks for deleting aged software metering data and two tasks for summarizing software metering data. All of these tasks are enabled by default.

To find them in the Configuration Manager console, navigate to the Administration workspace and under Overview choose Site Configuration ➤ Sites. From the ribbon click Site Maintenance.

Figure 10.20 shows the software metering Site Maintenance settings. To edit, just double-click the task you want to configure.

FIGURE 10.20
Software metering maintenance tasks

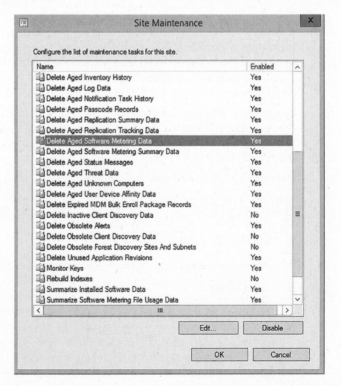

These tasks summarize software metering usage data to compress the amount that is stored in the Configuration Manager database. Summarization runs daily by default and will run only against data that is at least 12 hours old. This is required for all software metering reports to produce any meaningful data. To get an idea of what is in the most current set of summarized data, you have to know when that last summarization took place.

The Software Metering Summarization Progress report, as shown in Figure 10.21, will provide you with information about the last summarization process.

FIGURE 10.21
Software Metering
Summarization
Progress report

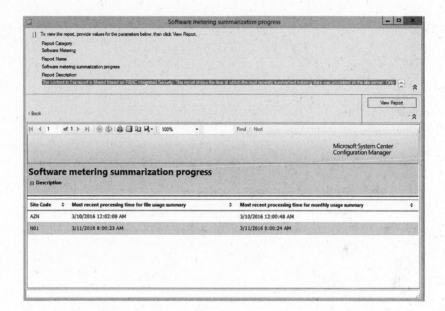

The Summarize Software Metering File Usage Data task summarizes software metering file usage data from several records into one record. This record gives information about the program name, version, language, and number of distinct users over intervals of 15 minutes to 1 hour. This process compresses and optimizes the amount of data stored in the Configuration Manager database.

For every hour and every 15-minute time frame within the hour, this task will calculate the total number of distinct user/computer combinations that are running the programs that are being metered. Within 15-minute intervals, this will give an approximate number of concurrent users of a metered program.

When software summary data is sent up the Configuration Manager hierarchy, data from each site is kept separate from the data from the other sites. When the data reaches a parent site, each record is marked with the site code of the site it came from.

The Summarize Software Metering Monthly Usage Data task summarizes detailed software metering usage data from many records into one record. This record gives information on the program name, program version, language, program running times, number of times used, last time used, username, and computer name.

The summary data also includes the number of times each matching metered piece of software was run on a specific computer by a specific user during that month. This task is set to run every day by default, and the summary is done for a period of one month.

🌐 **Real World Scenario**

MANUALLY SUMMARIZE SOFTWARE METERING DATA

As the Configuration Manager administrator, you have been requested to demonstrate the Software Metering feature. You need to ensure that all the latest data is summarized and is part of the reports. To do so, follow these steps:

1. Log on to the site server where you have the ConfigMgr 2012 Toolkit R2 or higher version installed.

2. From `(%program files(x86)% )\Configmgr 2012 Toolkit R2\ServerTools`, copy `runmetersumm.exe` to `<:>\Program Files\Microsoft Configuration Manager\bin\x64`.

3. Open a command prompt as administrator, and navigate to `<:>\Program Files\Microsoft Configuration Manager\bin\x64`.

4. Type `runmetersumm.exe CM_<Configuration Manager site code>`, for example, `runmetersumm.exe CM_S01`.

5. Press Enter, and notice the number of records that have been summarized.

MONITOR CLIENT ACTIVITY

Whenever a client runs a program, it will be registered in the `mtrmgr.log` file on the client. If the program has a matching software metering rule, the client agent will start tracking the process associated with the program, as shown in Figure 10.22.

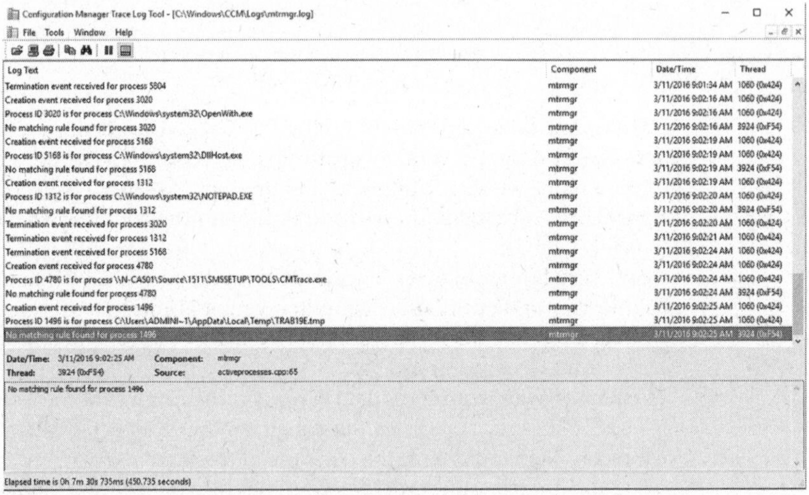

FIGURE 10.22
Reading the `mtrmgr` `.log` file on the client

Each client will generate a software metering usage report and send the report to the management point. You can initiate the action manually by running the Software Metering Usage Report Cycle action in the Configuration Manager Properties on the client, as shown in Figure 10.23.

FIGURE 10.23
Running the Software
Metering Usage Report
Cycle action on the
client

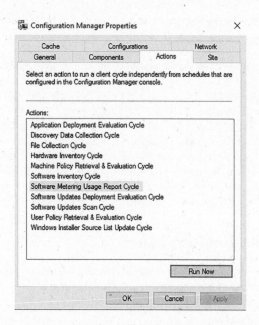

Activity from this process is written to the SWMTRReportGen.log file on the client. The data
will be sent to the site server and recorded in the swmproc.log file on the site server.

DEFAULT SOFTWARE METERING REPORTS

Configuration Manager ships with several canned software metering reports:

◆ All Software Metering Rules Applied To This Site

◆ Computers That Have A Metered Program Installed But Have Not Run The Program Since
A Specified Date

◆ Computers That Have Run A Specific Metered Software Program

◆ Concurrent Usage For All Metered Software Programs

◆ Concurrent Usage Trend Analysis Of A Specific Metered Software Program

◆ Install Base For All Metered Software Programs

◆ Time Of Day Usage Summary For A Specific Metered Software Program

◆ Total Usage For All Metered Software Programs

◆ Total Usage For All Metered Software Programs On Windows Terminal Servers

◆ Total Usage Of Specific Metered Software Product

◆ Total Usage Trend Analysis For A Specific Metered Software Program

◆ Total Usage Trend Analysis For A Specific Metered Software Program On Windows
Terminal Servers

◆ Users That Have Run A Specific Metered Software Program

◆ Software Metering Summarization Progress

One of the disadvantages of having a large number of disabled software metering rules is that all rules will be shown in the Install Base For All Metered Software Programs report. This might clutter the picture a little bit because you will see programs that you might not be interested in seeing.

By combining the values from the Install Base For All Metered Software Programs report with the Computers That Have A Metered Program Installed But Have Not Run The Program Since A Specified Date report, you can easily see how many installed instances you have and measure that against how many times the application has been used in a specific period. This will give the names of computers where you can uninstall the application and that way save money on the software budget.

The Bottom Line

Configure and manage software inventory.   Configuring software inventory has changed in Configuration Manager, although the client-processing part is almost the same as in earlier versions of Configuration Manager.

Master It   By default, Configuration Manager does not inventory for any file types. Where would you go to do that?

Configure and manage hardware inventory.   Hardware inventory provides a wealth of information on the hardware resources in your organization. That information is vital when planning for things such as updating standard business software or upgrading the standard operating system your organization uses. If the standard hardware inventory collected is not enough for your needs, then you have many options to extend the hardware inventory to get that vital information.

Master It   Where do you enable or disable data classes in hardware inventory?

Configure and manage software metering.   Keeping track of software that is installed and actually being used is a large part of being able to manage software licenses effectively. By pairing software metering in Configuration Manager with software inventory, you can get detailed information on just what software is out there and who is or is not using it. This goes a long way to help keep your software licensing in compliance.

Master It   How long do you have to wait, at the very least, after you configure software metering before you can expect to see any data returned?

Chapter 11

Asset Intelligence

System Center Configuration Manager gives organizations better control over their information technology infrastructure and assets through Asset Intelligence technologies by enabling IT professionals to see what hardware and software assets they have, who is using them, and where they are. Asset Intelligence translates inventory data into information; this gives the IT professionals the ability to build reports to understand how these assets are being used in their environment.

Configuration Manager tracks nearly all the software assets on a network, providing comprehensive details about both physical and virtual applications installed across an enterprise. Asset Intelligence lets IT professionals define, track, and proactively manage conformity to configuration standards. Metering and reporting the deployment and the use of both physical and virtual applications help organizations make better business decisions about software licensing and maintenance of licensing agreements. In this chapter we will cover the aspects of Asset Intelligence in Configuration Manager and show you how to enable it to take full advantage of this information.

In this chapter, you will learn to

◆ Enable Asset Intelligence

◆ Configure the Asset Intelligence synchronization point

◆ Import the Microsoft Volume License Statement

Requirements for Asset Intelligence

The Asset Intelligence feature in Configuration Manager has both external and internal dependencies that you will need to consider when using this feature. Those requirements include the following:

◆ Client agent requirements

◆ Site maintenance task requirements

◆ Windows event log requirements

Client Agent Prerequisites

The Asset Intelligence reports are based on information gathered through hardware and software inventory. To get the necessary information from clients for all Asset Intelligence reports, you must enable these client agents:

◆ Hardware Inventory Client Agent

◆ Software Metering Client Agent

HARDWARE INVENTORY CLIENT AGENT REQUIREMENT

To be able to collect inventory data required for Asset Intelligence reports, you must enable the Hardware Inventory Client Agent. In addition, some hardware inventory reporting classes that Asset Intelligence reports depend on must be enabled on primary site server computers. You saw how to do this in Chapter 10, "Inventory and Software Metering."

REPORTS THAT REQUIRE SOFTWARE METERING

Six reports require the Software Metering Client Agent to be enabled before they can provide any data:

Software 07A   Recently Used Executable Programs By The Count Of Computers

Software 07B   Computers That Recently Used A Specified Executable Program

Software 07C   Recently Used Executable Programs On A Specified Computer

Software 08A   Recently Used Executable Programs By The Count Of Users

Software 08B   Users That Recently Used A Specified Executable Program

Software 08C   Recently Used Executable Programs By A Specified User

Maintenance Tasks

The following maintenance tasks are associated with Asset Intelligence. By default, both maintenance tasks are enabled and configured by default.

Check Application Title With Inventory Information   This maintenance task checks to see if the software title that is reported in software inventory is reconciled with the software title in the Asset Intelligence Catalog. Basically it compares software hash from inventory to software code in the catalog to ensure accuracy and completeness. By default, this maintenance task is scheduled to run on Saturday after 12:00 a.m. and before 5:00 a.m.

Summarize Installed Software Data   This maintenance task provides the information that is displayed in the Inventoried Software node under the Asset Intelligence node in the Assets and Compliance workspace. When the task runs, Configuration Manager gathers a count of all inventoried software titles at the primary site. This task is available only on primary sites. By default, this maintenance task is scheduled to run on Saturday after 12:00 a.m. and before 5:00 a.m.

To configure these maintenance tasks, do the following:

1. In the Configuration Manager console, click Administration.

2. In the Administration workspace, expand Site Configuration, and then click Sites.

3. Select the site on which to configure the Asset Intelligence maintenance task.

4. On the Home tab of the ribbon, in the Settings group, click Site Maintenance.

   A list of all available maintenance tasks will appear, as shown in Figure 11.1.

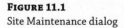

FIGURE 11.1
Site Maintenance dialog

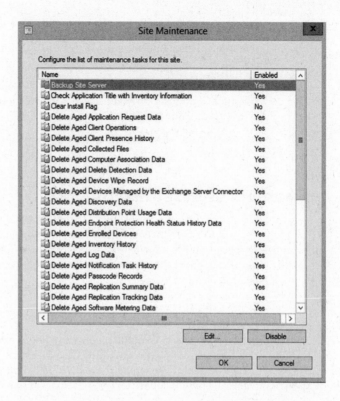

5. Choose the desired maintenance task, and then click Edit to modify the settings.

6. Enable and configure the maintenance task.

7. Click Apply to save your settings.

The task will now run according to its schedule. If you want to know more about this maintenance task, check Chapter 17, "Troubleshooting."

Windows Event Log Settings

Four Asset Intelligence reports display data gathered from the Windows security event logs on client computers. If the security event log is not set up properly, these reports will be empty even if the appropriate hardware inventory class (SMS_SystemConsoleUser) has been enabled. We will discuss configuring these settings later in the chapter. The following reports require these collected events:

Hardware 03A   Primary Computer Users

Hardware 03B   Computers For A Specific Primary Console User

Hardware 04A   Computers With Multiple Users (Shared)

Hardware 05A   Console Users On A Specific Computer

To enable auditing of success logon events, follow these steps:

1. On a domain controller computer, navigate to Administrative Tools ➤ Group Policy Management.

2. Navigate to Default Domain Policy, right-click Default Domain Policy and choose Edit ➤ Computer Configuration ➤ Policies ➤ Windows Settings ➤ Security Settings ➤ Local Policies ➤ Audit Policy.

3. In the results pane, double-click Audit Logon Events, and ensure that Success is selected.

Elements of Asset Intelligence

Asset Intelligence enhances the inventory capabilities of Configuration Manager by extending hardware and software inventory. The Asset Intelligence category now contains more than 60 reports that present this information in an easy-to-use format. Most reports link to more detailed reports that allow the administrator to query for general information and drill down to more detailed information as needed.

Asset Intelligence Catalog

The Configuration Manager Asset Intelligence Catalog is a set of tables stored in the Configuration Manager database containing categorization and identification data for more than 300,000 software titles and versions that are divided into almost 100 families and almost 2,000 specific categories. These database tables are also used to manage hardware requirements for specific software titles.

In Configuration Manager 2012 the Asset Intelligence Catalog was enhanced to allow software titles in use (both Microsoft and general software) to be manually imported. In addition, it now includes a large collection of known hardware requirements for software titles stored in the Asset Intelligence Catalog. Also, it is now possible to edit the local Asset Intelligence Catalog and to upload software title information to System Center Online (SCO) for categorization.

WHAT IS SYSTEM CENTER ONLINE?

Hosted by Microsoft, System Center Online is "software as a service," an online management service aimed at the IT community. Some of the services that will be eventually hosted are antivirus, antispyware, system monitoring, backup/restore, policy management, and, in the case of Configuration Manager, asset inventory monitoring.

Asset Intelligence Catalog updates containing newly released software and hardware definitions will be available for download periodically for bulk catalog updates, or the catalog can be dynamically updated by Microsoft Software Assurance (SA) customers using the Asset Intelligence synchronization point site system role.

SOFTWARE CATEGORIES

Administrators can view available software category information stored in the Asset Intelligence Catalog by using the Assets and Compliance ➤ Overview ➤ Asset Intelligence ➤ Catalog view in the Configuration Manager console.

These software categories are used to give broad listings of inventoried software titles and are also used as high-level groupings of more detailed software families. The Asset Intelligence Catalog has many predefined software categories, and you can create user-defined categories to continue to define inventoried software as needed. For example, the predefined E-mail And Collaboration category includes applications such as Microsoft Outlook and Outlook Express. The validation state for software categories already defined is always validated, whereas custom category information added to the Asset Intelligence Catalog is user-defined. Note that predefined software category information is read-only and can't be changed. User-defined software categories can be added, modified, or deleted by administrators. We will cover managing software categories later in the chapter in the section "Asset Intelligence Validation States."

SOFTWARE FAMILIES

Administrators can view available software family information stored in the Asset Intelligence Catalog by using the Assets and Compliance ➤ Overview ➤ Asset Intelligence ➤ Catalog view in the Configuration Manager console.

Software families in Asset Intelligence are used to define inventoried software even further within software categories. For example, the Security software family is defined by the Security and Security Threat labels. Like software categories, predefined software families always have a validation state of validated, whereas custom software family information has a state of user-defined. Also, like software categories predefined software family information can't be modified.

SOFTWARE LABELS

You can create custom software labels to even further categorize inventoried software titles that are in the Asset Intelligence Catalog. Administrators can use custom labels to create user-defined groups of software titles that share a common attribute. For example, a custom label could be called *bank software*, and that label would be used to identify inventoried bank software titles, which in turn could be used in a report to show all software that has that label. Custom labels have no validation state since they are always created locally in your Configuration Manager hierarchy.

In the Configuration Manager console, you can view all the custom labels that you or another administrator has made in the Asset Intelligence Catalog by choosing Asset Intelligence ➤ Catalog.

INVENTORIED SOFTWARE

The Inventoried Software node is located under Asset Intelligence ➤ Inventoried Software in the Configuration Manager console. Administrators can look at inventoried software title information collected from Configuration Manager clients in this node and can even create up to three custom labels per inventoried software item to further utilize user-defined categorization.

Each software title shows the following information:

◆ Name of the software title

◆ Name of the software vendor

◆ Product version

◆ Assigned software category

◆ Assigned software family

All of this information except for version can be changed via a local edit. Anything that can be changed can be reverted to the original values later.

HARDWARE REQUIREMENTS

With the Asset Intelligence ➤ Hardware Requirements node, you can manage software title hardware requirements data that is stored in the Asset Intelligence Catalog. The hardware requirements that are preloaded into the Asset Intelligence Catalog are not based on inventoried software information but are included as part of the Asset Intelligence Catalog. In addition to the default hardware requirements listed in this node, administrators can add new software title hardware requirements as needed to meet custom report requirements. The information that is displayed in this node includes the following:

◆ Name of the software title that the hardware requirement is for

◆ Validation state for the hardware requirement (System Center Online requirements are always validated; custom hardware requirements are always user-defined.)

◆ Minimum processor speed, in MHz, that the software title requires

◆ Minimum RAM, in KB, that the software title requires

◆ Minimum free disk space, in KB, that the software title requires

◆ Minimum hard disk size, in KB, that the software title requires

As in other parts of the Asset Intelligence Catalog, custom hardware requirements for software titles that aren't stored in the catalog can be modified, but the predefined information is read-only and can't be changed or deleted.

Asset Intelligence Validation States

Asset Intelligence validation states show the source and current validation status of Asset Intelligence Catalog information. They are outlined in Table 11.1, which is reproduced from the Configuration Manager documentation.

TABLE 11.1:   Asset Intelligence validation states

STATE	DEFINITION	ADMINISTRATOR ACTION	COMMENT
Validated	Catalog item has been defined by System Center Online (SCO) researchers.	None	This is the best state.
User-defined	Catalog item has not been defined by SCO researchers.	Customized the local catalog information	This state will be shown in Asset Intelligence reports.
Pending	Catalog item has not been defined by SCO researchers but has been submitted for categorization.	Requested categorization from SCO	The catalog item will remain in this state until SCO categorizes the item and the Asset Intelligence Catalog is synchronized.
Updateable	A user-defined catalog item has been categorized differently by SCO.	Customized the local Asset Intelligence Catalog to categorize an item as user-defined	The administrator can use the Software Details Conflict Resolution dialog to choose which category to use.
Uncategorized	Catalog item has not been defined by SCO; the item has not been submitted to SCO and has not been categorized by admin.	None	Request categorization or customize local catalog. This is the base state of all unknown software.

Asset Intelligence Synchronization Point

Configuration Manager has a site system role for Asset Intelligence called the Asset Intelligence synchronization point. This site system role is used to connect to System Center Online over TCP port 443 so dynamic Asset Intelligence Catalog updates can be managed.

This site role can be installed only on the Configuration Manager Central Administration Site (CAS)/stand-alone primary site, and all of your Asset Intelligence Catalog customization must be done on a Configuration Manager console that is connected to this site. You must configure all the updates at the central site, but all Asset Intelligence Catalog information is replicated to all child primary sites using the Configuration Manager data replication service. If a CAS doesn't exist in the environment, you can configure this on the stand-alone primary site server.

Using the Asset Intelligence synchronization point, Software Assurance (SA) license customers can also request on-demand catalog synchronization with System Center Online or schedule automatic catalog synchronization, and they can upload uncategorized software titles to System Center Online for identification.

The Asset Intelligence Home Page

The Configuration Manager console includes an Asset Intelligence home page and is similar to the home pages of other features, such as Software Updates.

To display the Asset Intelligence home page, do the following in the Configuration Manager console: Select Assets and Compliance ➤ Overview ➤ Asset Intelligence. Figure 11.2 shows an example of the Asset Intelligence home page.

FIGURE 11.2
Asset Intelligence home page

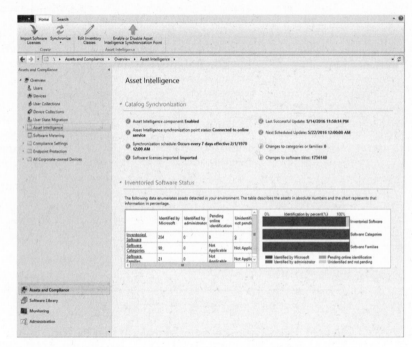

The Asset Intelligence home page is divided into the following sections:

◆ Catalog Synchronization

◆ Inventoried Software Status

ASSET INTELLIGENCE CATALOG SYNCHRONIZATION

This section displays the following information:

Asset Intelligence Component This item displays the status of the component as either Enabled or Disabled.

Asset Intelligence Synchronization Point Status This item displays the online status of the synchronization point or any failure that happened during this synchronization.

Synchronization Schedule This item matches the configured schedule of the catalog; by default, this is set for every 7 days, but you can change this on the Assets and

Compliance ➤ Asset Intelligence node. Right-click the node, choose Synchronize ➤ Schedule Synchronization, and choose the desired schedule.

Software Licenses Imported   This item shows whether the Microsoft volume license has been imported into the Configuration Manager database.

Last Successful Update   This item shows the last time Configuration Manager was able to synchronize the catalog. If it was not able to synchronize, a warning icon will show and will display a Not Applicable status.

Next Scheduled Update   This item displays the next date and time when the catalog will synchronize.

Changes To Categories Or Families   This item displays the number of changes or updates in categories that occurred on the database during the last synchronization with System Center Online.

Changes To Software Titles   This item displays the number of changes or updates in software titles that occurred during the last synchronization with System Center Online.

INVENTORIED SOFTWARE STATUS

The following data enumerates assets detected in the Configuration Manager environment. The table describes the assets in absolute numbers, and the chart represents that information in percentages.

Inventoried Software Status Table   This item displays the assets of the Asset Intelligence Catalog in summary table format with the following information:

- Inventoried Software
- Software Categories
- Software Families

Each of these is shown in one of the following states:

- Identified By Microsoft
- Identified By Administrator
- Pending Online Identification
- Unidentified And Not Pending

Identification By Percent Chart   This item displays an Asset Catalog summary in bar chart format, including the following information as percentages:

- Inventoried Software
- Software Categories
- Software Families

These in turn are shown color coded for easier identification:

- Identified By Microsoft
- Identified By Administrator

- Pending Online Identification

- Unidentified And Not Pending

Asset Intelligence Reports

To see the real power behind the Asset Intelligence feature, you have to examine the various Asset Intelligence reports that are provided with Configuration Manager right out of the box.

You can find the Asset Intelligence reports in the Configuration Manager console by choosing Monitoring ➤ Overview ➤ Reporting. Expand Reports and click Asset Intelligence. The numbers in the installed software and license information shown in Asset Intelligence reports may vary from the true number of software products installed or licenses in use on your network because of complex dependencies and limitations in inventorying software license information for software titles installed in an enterprise environment. Therefore, you should not use Asset Intelligence reports as the sole source of deciding how many software licenses to purchase for compliance.

The following are example dependencies that are involved in inventorying installed software and licenses in an enterprise using Asset Intelligence that might affect the accuracy of the data:

Client Hardware Inventory Dependency   Asset Intelligence–installed software reports are based on data collected from Configuration Manager clients by extending hardware inventory to enable Asset Intelligence reporting. Because of this, Asset Intelligence reports will report data only from Configuration Manager clients that have completed a hardware inventory scan successfully and have the required Asset Intelligence WMI reporting class enabled. Also, since hardware inventory runs on a schedule that is set by the administrator, there may be a delay in data being reported that might affect the accuracy of Asset Intelligence reports at any given time.

Software Packaging Dependencies   Because Asset Intelligence reports are based on installed software title data using standard Configuration Manager client hardware inventory processes, some of that data might not be collected properly if the software executables don't conform to standard installation processes or have been modified prior to installation.

Server Role Dependencies   When you're using CAL reporting, it is important to remember that these reports were designed to provide visibility into the specific usage of products in specific scenarios, such as a Windows server hosting only one server role. In cases where a Windows server is hosting more than one role, this might cause inaccurate Asset Intelligence reports.

Location And Usage   Remember that Asset Intelligence reports were designed to report license usage, not how many licenses have been actually bought and for what purpose they are allowed to be used.

Client Health   You should actively monitor Configuration Manager client health and ensure that your clients are healthy and able to submit inventory. This will ensure that reports based on inventory data are complete and accurate. Refer to Chapter 6, "Client Health," to learn more about the client health feature of Configuration Manager.

HARDWARE REPORTS

Asset Intelligence hardware reports provide information about hardware assets in your organization, such as a computer's age and its ability to handle a software upgrade. Some reports are based on information collected from the System Security event log, so you should clear that log if a computer is assigned to another user. The following hardware Asset Intelligence reports are available:

Hardware 01A Summary Of Computers In A Specific Collection

Hardware 03A Primary Computer Users

Hardware 03B Computers For A Specific Primary Console User

Hardware 04A Computers With Multiple Users (Shared)

Hardware 05A Console Users On A Specific Computer

Hardware 06A Computers For Which Console Users Could Not Be Determined

Hardware 07A USB Devices By Manufacturer

Hardware 07B USB Devices By Manufacturer And Description

Hardware 07C Computers With A Specific USB Device

Hardware 07D USB Devices On A Specific Computer

Hardware 08A Hardware That Is Not Ready For A Software Upgrade

Hardware 09A Search For Computers

Hardware 10A Computers In A Specified Collection That Have Changed Within A Specified Timeframe

Hardware 10B Changes On A Specified Computer Within A Specified Timeframe

 Real World Scenario

PLANNING FOR A SOFTWARE UPGRADE

You get word from your manager that the department responsible for all the company training manuals is working on updating many of the manuals because of some new federal regulations. They are making these updates with a new version of the Adobe Acrobat software, and there is a possibility that you might have to deploy Acrobat Reader X so that employees will be able to read the updated manuals properly.

The company is also in the middle of a hardware refresh, so your manager is concerned that there may be computers on the network that do not have the necessary hardware requirements to run Acrobat Reader X properly. So she wants to use Configuration Manager to generate a list of those computers if there are any.

Hearing this, you are glad that you have already enabled Asset Intelligence, because there is a specific report for just this scenario. To meet your manager's request, just go to the report Hardware 08A: Hardware That Is Not Ready for a Software Upgrade. Since you are concerned with user computers in this instance, select the desired collection in the Collection field. The Asset Intelligence knowledge base, which is part of the Configuration Manager database, already has information about Acrobat Reader X, so select that for the Product field.

After you run the report, you can provide that link to your manager so she can either print it or export it into Microsoft Excel for her own use.

SOFTWARE REPORTS

Software Asset Intelligence reports provide information about software families, categories, and specific software titles installed on computers within your organization. The following software Asset Intelligence reports are available:

Software 01A Summary Of Installed Software In A Specific Collection

Software 02A Product Families For A Specific Collection

Software 02B Product Categories For A Specific Product Family

Software 02C Software In A Specific Product Family And Category

Software 02D Computers With Specific Software Installed

Software 02E Installed Software On A Specific Computer

Software 03A Uncategorized Software

Software 04A Software Configured To Automatically Run On Computers

Software 04B Computers With Specific Software Configured To Automatically Run

Software 04C Software Configured To Automatically Run On A Specific Computer

Software 05A Browser Helper Objects

Software 05B Computers With A Specific Browser Helper Object

Software 05C Browser Helper Objects On A Specific Computer

Software 06A Search For Installed Software

Software 07A Recently Used Executable Programs By The Count Of Computers

Software 07B Computers That Recently Used A Specified Executable Program

Software 07C Recently Used Executable Programs On A Specified Computer

Software 08A Recently Used Executable Programs By The Count Of Users

Software 08B Users That Recently Used A Specified Executable Program

Software 08C Recently Used Executable Programs By A Specified User

Software 09A Infrequently Used Software

Software 09B Computers With Infrequently Used Software Installed

Software 10A Software Titles With Specific, Multiple Custom Labels Defined

Software 10B Computers With A Specific Custom-Labeled Software Title Installed

Software 11A Software Titles With A Specific Custom Label Defined

Software 12A Software Titles Without A Custom Label

LICENSE MANAGEMENT REPORTS

The following license management Asset Intelligence reports are available:

License 01A Microsoft Volume License Ledger For Microsoft License Statements

License 01B Microsoft Volume License Ledger Item By Sales Channel

License 01C   Computers With A Specific Microsoft Volume License Ledger Item And Sales Channel

License 01D   Microsoft Volume License Ledger Products On A Specific Computer

License 02A   Count Of Licenses Nearing Expiration By Time Ranges

License 02B   Computers With Licenses Nearing Expiration

License 02C   License Information On A Specific Computer

License 03A   Count Of Licenses By License Status

License 03B   Computers With A Specific License Status

License 04A   Count Of Products Managed By Software Licensing

License 04B   Computers With A Specific Product Managed By Software Licensing Service

License 05A   Computers Providing Key Management Service

License 06A   Processor Counts For Per-Processor Licensed Products

License 14A   Microsoft Volume Licensing Reconciliation Report

License 14B   List Of Microsoft Software Inventory Not Found In Mvls

License 15A   General License Reconciliation Report

License 15B   General License Reconciliation Report By Computer

Configuring Asset Intelligence

Configuration Manager Asset Intelligence is enabled by default. Depending on what data you want information on, you will have to do the following:

1. Choose the Assets And Compliance workspace in the Configuration Manager console.

2. Under Overview, right-click Asset Intelligence, and click Edit Inventory Classes.

3. Choose to enable only the desired Asset Intelligence reporting class.

4. Make sure that certain client agents are enabled, which we will go over in the following sections.

Enabling Asset Intelligence

To successfully collect data for the hardware and software reports in Asset Intelligence, you first need to enable the Hardware Inventory Client Agent.

The classes that are used for the hardware and software inventory reports include the following:

SMS_InstalledSoftware

SMS_SystemConsoleUsage

SMS_SystemConsoleUser

SMS_AutoStartSoftware

```
SMS_BrowserHelperObject

SMS_SoftwareTag

Win32_USBDevice

SMS_InstalledExecutable

SMS_SoftwareShortcut

SoftwareLicensingService

SoftwareLicensingProduct
```

To enable the classes in Configuration Manager that are required for your organization, perform the following steps:

1. Choose Assets and Compliance ➢ Overview ➢ Asset Intelligence.

2. Right-click, and choose Edit Inventory Classes. Figure 11.3 shows the dialog that opens.

FIGURE 11.3
Asset Intelligence Edit
Inventory Classes dialog

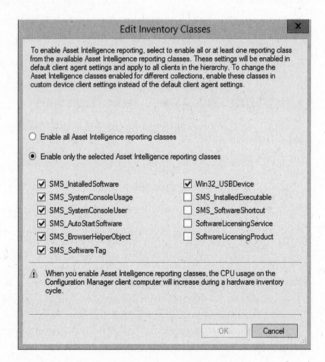

3. Choose the inventory classes that need to be enabled, and click OK.

You could also enable the Asset Intelligence hardware inventory reporting classes from the client settings properties using the default client settings or by selecting a custom client setting that you may have created. Use the Filter by category option and click Asset Intelligence Reporting Classes; then select the desired reporting classes.

After you make the change, it could take several days for the data to be reported, depending on your Configuration Manager hierarchy and how often you have the Hardware Inventory Client Agent set to collect inventory.

INSTALLING AN ASSET INTELLIGENCE SYNCHRONIZATION POINT

As discussed earlier in the chapter, the Asset Intelligence synchronization point role is used to connect Configuration Manager sites to System Center Online to synchronize Asset Intelligence Catalog information. You can install this role only on a site system located in the CAS of a Configuration Manager hierarchy, and you'll require Internet access to synchronize with System Center Online on TCP port 443. The Asset Intelligence synchronization point can also upload custom software title information to System Center Online for categorization. All information uploaded to System Center Online will be treated as public information by Microsoft, so you should be sure that your custom information does not contain any sensitive information.

To install the Asset Intelligence synchronization point and have it be secure, you can acquire an optional System Center Online authentication certificate (*.pfx), which can be acquired only by SA license customers. (For more information on Software Assurance, check out the SA website at www.microsoft.com/licensing/sa/default.mspx.) Before you begin the installation of the Asset Intelligence synchronization point, make sure that all of the following are true:

◆ You have a valid SCO authentication certificate. If you don't have one, do not put any certificate information in the field since this certificate is optional.

◆ The Asset Intelligence synchronization point will be available on a shared network folder accessible to the server where you will be running the New Site Role Wizard.

◆ The Asset Intelligence synchronization point will stay in that location until the Asset Intelligence synchronization point has done its first synchronization with System Center Online.

To install an Asset Intelligence synchronization point, follow these steps:

1. In the Configuration Manager console, select Administration ➢ Overview ➢ Site Configuration ➢ Sites.

2. Select the CAS site server name or the stand-alone primary site server name. Choose the Home tab of the ribbon, and click Add Site System Roles to start the Add Site System Roles Wizard.

3. As you have done with other Configuration Manager wizards covered in this book, verify the site system settings on the General page, and click Next.

4. On the Proxy page, enter information as needed, and click Next.

5. On the System Role Selection page, select the Asset Intelligence Synchronization Point check box, and then click Next.

6. On the Asset Intelligence Synchronization Point Settings page, you can set up an optional certificate. If you choose to do so, then set the path to the SCO authentication certificate (*.pfx) file, and click Next.

7. On the Proxy Server Settings page, configure the settings for the proxy server if needed.

8. On the Synchronization Point Schedule page, you can choose whether to set up synchronization on a simple or custom schedule, as you've seen in other Configuration Manager options.

9. On the Summary page of the wizard, review the settings you have specified to make sure they are correct. If you need to make any changes, click the Previous button. Otherwise, click Next to finish the rest of the configuration.

Import Software License into Asset Intelligence

One of the most important pieces of Asset Intelligence is the availability to import the current Microsoft Volume License Summary into the database for better reporting of this license count. Also, you can import a non-Microsoft product license count into the database by selecting the option to upload a General License Statement file.

As shown in Figure 11.4, you can now import the Microsoft Volume License Statement or General License Statement in one easy wizard. First, select the type of file you are going to import. This will be either an .xml or .csv file for the Microsoft Volume License Statement or a .csv file for the General License Statement. Once you have chosen the file you are going to upload, this information will be imported into the Configuration Manager database. On the next hardware and software inventory, the data will be analyzed, and the new imported license count will be available for the IT administrator's analysis. You can upload the license information as many times as needed to update the license or when the enterprise agreement of the Microsoft product gets updated. You'll need to follow the same process for the non-Microsoft product when you want to review the license count.

FIGURE 11.4
Import Software
Licenses Wizard

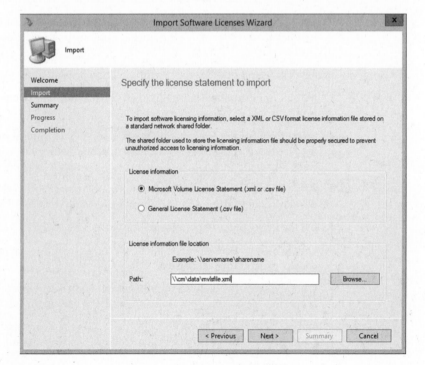

Importing Software License Information

The following sections describe the procedures necessary to import both Microsoft and general software licensing information into the Configuration Manager site database using the Import Software Licenses Wizard. When you import software licenses from license information files into the site database, the site server computer account requires Full Control NTFS permissions to the file share that will be used to import software license information. When this license information gets imported into the site, the existing software license information file used with the Import Software Licenses Wizard contains a complete list of all necessary software license information.

Follow these steps to import the software license:

1. In the Assets And Compliance workspace, click Asset Intelligence.

2. On the Home tab of the ribbon, in Create Group, click Import Software Licenses.

   The Import Software Licenses Wizard opens, as shown in Figure 11.4.

3. On the Welcome page, click Next.

4. On the Import page, specify whether you are importing a Microsoft Volume License Statement (.xml or .csv) or a General License Statement (.csv).

5. Enter the UNC path to the license information file, or click Browse to select a network shared folder and file.

6. On the Summary page, review the information you have specified to ensure that it is correct before continuing.

   If you need to make changes, click Previous to return to the Import page. Otherwise, click Next.

7. Once this is completed, click Close.

Perform the following steps for the General License Statement as well; just make sure to select this in step 4.

Creating the Microsoft Volume License Statement

Before you start the process of creating the Microsoft Volume License Statement, make sure you have access to http://licensing.microsoft.com/. If you don't have access, please talk to your Microsoft Account Manager or Microsoft Technical Account Manager and ask them to send you your License Summary. Once you have the proper access, select the License Summary from the licensing site, and export it to Excel. When you have it in Excel, make sure the following fields and values are selected, with example data shown here.

Product Pool	License Product Family	License Version	Effective Quantity	Unresolved Quantity
Applications	Access	2010	70	0

Once you have imported the Microsoft Volume License Statement, you can run any of the reports with the title "License."

Creating the General License Statement

Now let's look at an example of the General License Statement. To create this you need to manually create a .csv file with the fields you need and list the software for which you want Configuration Manager to keep track of the license count. Once you finish creating the file, follow the same steps as you did to import the software license, but now use the example shown in Figure 11.5.

FIGURE 11.5
General License
Statement import

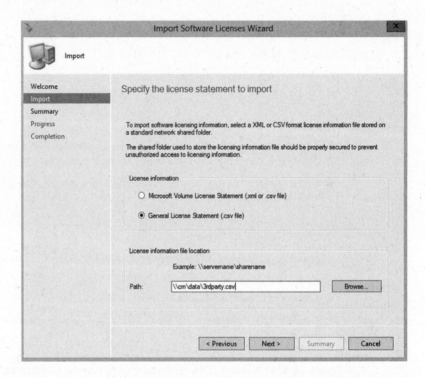

As you can see in Figure 11.6, all you need to do is create the .csv file and list the third-party software for which it needs to keep track of the license count. More information on creating the import file is available at https://technet.microsoft.com/en-us/library/gg712322.aspx.

The following is a list of reports that you can run:

License 14A   Microsoft Volume Licensing Reconciliation Report

License 14B   List Of Microsoft Software Inventory Not Found In MVLS

License 15A   General License Reconciliation Report

License 15B   General License Reconciliation Report By Computer

FIGURE 11.6
General License
Statement

Name	Publisher	Version	Language	EffectiveQuantity	PONumber	ResellerName	DateOfPurchase	SupportPurchased	SupportExpirationDate	Comments
Software Title 1	Software publisher	1.01	English	1	Purchase number	Reseller name	10/10/2010	0	10/10/2012	Comment
Software title 2	Software publisher	1.02	English	1	Purchase number	Reseller name	10/10/2010	0	10/10/2012	Comment
Software title 3	Software publisher	1.03	English	1	Purchase number	Reseller name	10/10/2010	0	10/10/2012	Comment
Software title 4	Software publisher	1.04	English	1	Purchase number	Reseller name	10/10/2010	0	10/10/2012	Comment
Software title 5	Software publisher	1.05	English	1	Purchase number	Reseller name	10/10/2010	0	10/10/2012	Comment
Software title 6	Software publisher	1.06	English	1	Purchase number	Reseller name	10/10/2010	0	10/10/2012	Comment
Software title 7	Software publisher	1.07	English	1	Purchase number	Reseller name	10/10/2010	0	10/10/2012	Comment
Software title 8	Software publisher	1.08	English	1	Purchase number	Reseller name	10/10/2010	0	10/10/2012	Comment
Software title 9	Software publisher	1.09	English	1	Purchase number	Reseller name	10/10/2010	0	10/10/2012	Comment
Software title 10	Software publisher	1.10	English	1	Purchase number	Reseller name	10/10/2010	0	10/10/2012	Comment

The Bottom Line

Enable Asset Intelligence.   If you installed Configuration Manager from scratch, you will find that Asset Intelligence is not enabled by default. Depending on the data that you want information on, you will have to select the Configuration Manager Asset Intelligence reporting classes and make sure that client agents are enabled.

Master It   Which classes in the Asset Intelligence Edit Inventory Classes dialog do you have to enable to use Asset Intelligence?

Configure the Asset Intelligence synchronization point.   The Asset Intelligence synchronization point is used to connect to System Center Online to synchronize Asset Intelligence Catalog information and get periodic updates.

Master It   What do you need to do in order to configure the Asset Intelligence synchronization point?

Import the Microsoft Volume License Statement.   In Configuration Manager you can import the Microsoft Volume License Statement and the General License Statement so that the software inventory and Asset Intelligence can count the number of licenses currently in use in the environment.

Master It   What file types does Configuration Manager support for the license statements?

Chapter 12

Reporting

Configuration Manager includes more than 450 reports that help you to gather, organize, and present information such as the following:

- Administrative security
- Inventory information
- Software update compliance data
- Migration information
- Audit information
- Power management information
- Alert information
- User data
- Mobile device
- Client health
- Compliance and settings
- Replication traffic
- Operating system deployment
- Virtual applications
- Endpoint protection

In Configuration Manager 2012, the Reporting feature changed significantly from earlier releases of the product. Configuration Manager no longer uses ASP web reports but instead utilizes SQL Server Reporting Services (SSRS) for reporting. Using SSRS gives you as an administrator several benefits compared to the classic web reports, such as these:

- Fully enabled for role-based administration
- Schedule reports to render during non-business hours
- Execute reports from a cache

- Create snapshots

- Subscribe to reports and have them mailed to you based on a schedule

- More easily modify existing reports with custom logos, text, and chart objects

- No 10,000-row limitations

- Standard reporting engine used by other Microsoft applications like SharePoint and the other Microsoft System Center applications

Another great feature of reports in Configuration Manager is that they utilize role-based access control and allow you to define what data users are able to view in the reports. With that in mind, in this chapter you will learn skills that will help you install and manage Reporting Services as well as modify and create reports.

In this chapter, you will learn to

- Install the Reporting Services point

- Manage reporting security

- Create and manage report subscriptions

- Create custom reports

Installing SQL Server Reporting Services

Prior to installing the Configuration Manager Reporting Services Point role, you need to ensure that you have installed SQL Server Reporting Services (SSRS). SSRS can be found on the SQL media you used to install SQL Server.

Before you install SSRS, you need to make sure that the server meets the minimum requirements and prerequisites. The following site provides the prerequisites for reporting in Configuration Manager:

```
https://technet.microsoft.com/en-us/library/mt488903.aspx
```

Considerations for Installing SQL Server Reporting Services

There are several considerations prior to installing SQL Server Reporting Services, such as which extra tools to install, security, where to place the site system role, and SQL instance support. This section will try to answer what are considered to be the most common considerations.

With the installation of SSRS you not only install a reporting engine, but you also install the following:

- The report server web service

- Report Builder

- Reporting Services configuration tool

- Command-line utilities, such as `rsconfig.exe`, `rs.exe`, and `rskeymgmt.exe`

Besides the core tools and services, you should consider installing these features:

Business Intelligence Development Studio   When you select to install Business Intelligence Development Studio (BIDS) using the SQL media, it will install Visual Studio and provide you with reporting and report model design tools. This tool can be useful in creating more advanced reports and report models.

SQL Server Management Studio   The client tools feature on the SQL media gives you SQL Server Management Studio, which is another tool often used in the report-creation process. SQL Server Management Studio is also used to configure SQL maintenance jobs, configure SQL security, and provide a GUI for maintaining the databases.

You also choose modes and instances:

Installation Mode   During setup you can choose between Native mode or SharePoint mode. Configuration Manager supports only Native mode.

Instance   You can install SQL Server Reporting Services in either the default instance or a named instance. Additionally, the instance you use can be shared with other System Center products as long as the other System Center products do not have restrictions for sharing the instance of SQL Server.

WHERE TO INSTALL THE REPORTING SERVICES

The reporting site system can be installed on any primary site or the Central Administration Site. It is considered a best practice to install the site system on the Central Administration Site if one exists. At the Central Administration Site you will have access to all global data and all site data. Installing the site system on a primary site will allow you to display only global data and site data that are local to the corresponding site. Installing the site system on a secondary site is not supported.

You can install the site system on the site server or on a remote server. For performance reasons you may consider using a dedicated server acting as a reporting server. However, this all depends on several factors such as hardware and number of resources and expected usage. If you implement a dedicated reporting point server, note that the SQL version being used on the primary site must match the SQL version of the dedicated SQL Reporting Services server.

SECURITY

Configuration Manager will connect to the SQL server and set the necessary permissions in Reporting Services. This eliminates the need to go into Reporting Services Configuration Manager and manually configure security. The security settings will be Credentials Stored Securely In The Report Server and Use As Windows Credentials When Connecting To The Data Source.

Installation of the Reporting Services Site System

Prior to installing the site system, you should verify that SQL Server Reporting Services is installed correctly and works as expected.

For installation and configuration information for reporting in Configuration Manager you can refer to this TechNet article: `https://technet.microsoft.com/en-us/library/mt488921.aspx`.

The account that you use to install the reporting services point role must have Read access to the database. To retrieve information about named instances, the user must also have Read access to WMI on the site system. To install a Reporting Services point, take the following steps:

1. In the Configuration Manager administrative console, select the Administration workspace and navigate to Overview ➤ Site Configuration ➤ Servers And Site System Roles.

2. Select the server where you want to install the role:

   ◆ From the ribbon click Add Site System Roles to start the Add Site System Roles Wizard.

   ◆ If you want to install the role on a new server, click Create Site System Server.

3. On the General page, click Next.

4. On the Proxy page, enter the appropriate information, and then click Next.

5. On the System Role Selection page, select Reporting Services Point from the list of available roles, and click Next.

6. On the Reporting Services Point Settings page, you must create the data source. Note that the data source includes the data source type, connection information, and authentication settings.

7. The wizard will discover the name of the site database server and the Configuration Manager database. To specify a named instance, type **_<Server Name>\<Instance Name>_**. To verify the settings in the Site Database and Database Name fields, click the Verify button.

8. The folder name will default to `ConfigMgr_<Sitecode>`; you can change the folder name if you want.

9. In the Authentication Settings area, click Set and choose an existing Configuration Manager account or select a new account. It is considered a best practice to have a specific low-rights user account for Authentication settings. The account that runs Reporting Services must belong to the domain local security group Windows Authorization Access Group, and have the Read tokenGroupsGlobalAndUniversal permission set to Allow. In addition, the account that you specify must have Log on Locally permissions on the computer hosting the Reporting Services database.

10. Once all settings are configured as shown in Figure 12.1, click Next.

11. On the Summary page, verify the settings and click Next.

12. On the Completion page, click Close.

FIGURE 12.1
Creating the data source

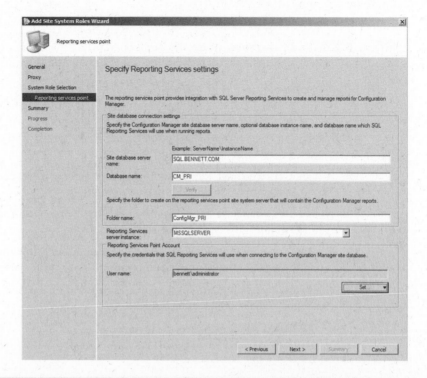

A FEW NOTES ABOUT THE DATA SOURCE AUTHENTICATION ACCOUNT

The data source authentication account is used when Reporting Services retrieves the data for reports from the site database. When you specify the account in the wizard, the installation process will take the account and do the following:

- Assign it the proper SQL permissions.

- Display it as the Configuration Manager SRS reporting point in the Administration workspace, Accounts folder.

- Store the account and password encrypted in the Reporting Services database.

WHAT HAPPENS DURING THE INSTALLATION?

When the installation begins, Configuration Manager will perform these steps:

1. Create the data source with the specified data source authentication account.

2. Create a root folder for all Configuration Manager reports.

3. Add the Configuration Manager Report Users and Configuration Manager Report Administrators security roles in Reporting Services.

4. Create subfolders and files in %programfiles%\SMS_SRSRP.

5. Deploy all reports in the `%programfiles%\SMS_SRSRP\Reports` folder.

6. Assign all user accounts in Configuration Manager the Configuration Manager Report Reader rights on root folders and the Configuration Manager folder.

7. Assign all user accounts with Site Modify rights in Configuration Manager the Configuration Manager Report Administrator rights on root folders and the Configuration Manager folder.

8. Read the current permissions in Configuration Manager, and map those to the newly created reporting folders.

9. Assign users who have Run Report permission for any object Configuration Manager Report Reader rights to the associated report folder.

10. Assign users who have Report Modify rights in Configuration Manager Report Administrator rights on the associated report folder.

11. Retrieve the mapping between report folders and Configuration Manager secured object types (those maintained in the Configuration Manager site database).

12. Configure the following rights for administrative users in Configuration Manager to specific report folders in Reporting Services:

    ◆ Add users and assign the Configuration Manager Report Users role to the associated report folder for administrative users who have Run Report Permissions for the Configuration Manager object.

    ◆ Add users and assign the Configuration Manager Report Administrators role to the associated report folder for administrative users who have Modify Report permissions for the Configuration Manager object.

Configuration Manager connects to Reporting Services and sets the permissions for users on the Configuration Manager and Reporting Services root folders and specific report folders. After the initial installation of the Reporting Services point, Configuration Manager connects to Reporting Services in a 10-minute interval to verify that the user rights configured on the report folders are the associated rights that are set for Configuration Manager users. When users are added or user rights are modified on the report folder by using Report Manager, Configuration Manager overwrites those changes by using the role-based assignments stored in the site database. Configuration Manager also removes users who do not have Reporting rights in Configuration Manager.

VERIFYING THE INSTALLATION

You can verify the Reporting Services installation by monitoring these log files:

sitecomp.log   The `sitecomp.log` file will have an entry like this:

```
Starting service <span cssStyle="font-family:monospace">SMS_SERVER_BOOTSTRAP_
Server</span> with command-line arguments
"SiteCode e:\Program Files\Microsoft Configuration Manager /install
E:\Program Files\Microsoft Configuration Manager\bin\x64\rolesetup.exe
SMSSRSRP"
```

srsrpMSI.log   srsrpMSI.log is the main log file for the installation. You can monitor this for detailed information. Most likely you will find this log file interesting only when trouble-shooting a failed installation.

srsrp.log   Once the site system is installed, you can monitor the srsrp.log file. It gives you detailed information about the folders and reports as they are published to the reporting site.

You can also monitor the folders created in %ProgramFiles%\SMS_SRSRP:

Reports   Contains all the default RDL files. The reports are imported during the original installation process. You can use the RDL files to import one or multiple reports again.

Resources   Contains various DLL files.

Style   Contains the three graphical elements used in most reports. You can replace these files with a custom company logo, for example.

The final test is to connect to the reporting site and verify that you can view all of the reports. Open a browser and type **http://reportingserver/reports**. Figure 12.2 shows the Configuration Manager reports.

FIGURE 12.2
Viewing the default reports

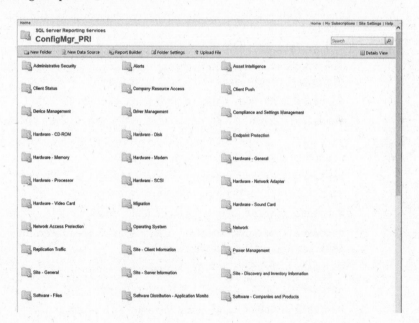

Default Reports

By default, over 470 native reports are added during the installation. The reports are organized in several different folders. You can move the reports between the folders as you like and also create new folders. The following folders are available:

Administrative Security   Contains information about role-based security, scopes, and audit information.

Alerts   Contains information about alerts, such as who closed the alerts.

Asset Intelligence   Contains inventory and software license information.

Client Push   Contains information about current and past client push installation attempts.

Client Status   Contains information about the overall client health and status of the clients installed.

Company Resource Access   Contains information about certificate issuance by the certificate registration point and devices/users with certificates about to expire.

Compliance and Settings Management   Allows administrators and others to report on Settings Management assignment for a computer or collection. Contains information about the compliance states for computers and collections along with detailed information on configuration items.

Device Management   Contains information about device information collected using the Exchange Server mobile connector and from natively managed mobile devices. Integration with Windows Intune provides asset and compliance reporting across cloud-managed PCs as well as mobile devices, including Windows RT, Windows Phone 8, iOS, and Android.

Driver Management   Contains information about drivers imported into the drivers repository.

Endpoint Protection   Provides detailed information about malware and virus activities. These reports will provide the Security department with up-to-date information about the overall security threat level in the organization.

Hardware - CD-ROM   Contains information about CD-ROMs.

Hardware - Disk   Contains physical and logical disk information.

Hardware - General   Contains a very useful hardware report along with information about the various inventory classes assigned.

Hardware - Memory   Contains memory information. You will find information for a specific computer and a count of each unique memory configuration.

Hardware - Modem   Contains modem information.

Hardware - Network Adapter   Contains network adapter information like IP address, MAC address, and adapter information.

Hardware - Processor   Contains processor information.

Hardware - SCSI   Contains SCSI information.

Hardware - Sound Card   Contains sound card information.

Hardware - Video Card   Contains video card information.

Migration   Contains information about the migration process from one Configuration Manager site to another. Includes migration jobs, migration job status, and other migration reports.

Network   Provides information about IP addresses and IP subnets. These reports will give you the number of IP subnets in the network and how many IP addresses you have in each subnet.

Network Access Protection   Provides information about NAP rules and computers that have been affected by one or more NAP policies.

Operating System   Provides information about operating systems and service packs in the organization.

Power Management   Provides power management information like computer activity, energy cost by day, and energy consumption. The information provides the organization with valuable data about the overall power consumption and also how new client power settings have lowered the environmental impact.

Replication Traffic   Provides information about database replication throughout the hierarchy.

Site - Client Information   Provides information about Configuration Manager client versions, deployments, assignments, communication settings, and out-of-band management configurations.

Site - Discovery and Inventory Information   Provides information about client discovery and inventory information. These reports can be very useful when determining the overall client health of the sites.

Site - General   Lists computers belonging to a specific Configuration Manager site, and shows when the site status was last updated.

Site - Server Information   Lists all site servers and site system roles for a specific site.

Software - Companies and Products   One of the primary folders when searching for installed software applications.

Software - Files   Provides information based on the software inventory processes.

Software Distribution - Application Monitoring   Provides basic and detailed information about application deployment. These reports will provide you with information about computers where requirements or dependencies have not been met, per asset deployment information, application usage, application infrastructure errors, and application compliance.

Software Distribution - Collections   Contains information about collections, maintenance windows, and resources belonging to specific collections.

Software Distribution - Content   Contains information about distribution points, distribution groups, content, and distribution point usage.

Software Distribution - Package and Program Deployment   Contains information about package deployments.

Software Distribution - Package and Program Deployment Status   Contains information about statuses for package deployments.

Software Metering   When software is enabled, you will use the reports as the primary information source to find information about the applications you monitor, when they were last started and by whom, and where they are installed but not used. The reports will enable you to determine which applications you can uninstall and that way cut down on the license costs.

Software Updates - A Compliance Provides overall compliance information about the software updates released from Windows Updates and also third-party software updates authored and published using the System Center Update Publisher tool.

Software Updates - B Deployment Management Provides information about the software update deployments created in the organization and updates that are required but not yet deployed. You can use the reports in this category to assist you when troubleshooting software update deployments.

Software Updates - C Deployment States This category contains some of the most used reports whenever you work with software update deployment. The single most important report (in my opinion) is States 1 - Enforcement States for a Deployment. This report can be used to track down the deployment processes of any given software update deployment along with compliance information.

Software Updates - D Scan Reports in this category provide you with information about which clients are able to perform a scan against the WSUS server. The report Scan 1 - Last scan states by collection is the very first report you should run whenever you want to troubleshoot software update problems. If clients are unable to perform a scan, they will not be able to upload compliance information or install required software updates.

Software Updates - E Troubleshooting Contains a few reports that can assist you when troubleshooting client scans and update deployments.

State Migration Provides operating system state migration information for a specific site or state migration site system point.

Status Messages Allows you to see all status messages received by the site server. Useful to determine the health of the Configuration Manager hierarchy.

Status Messages - Audit Allows you to see audit status messages for a specific site or user if using a Configuration Manager agent to remotely control devices.

Task Sequence - Deployment Status Provides you with detailed information about the status of running and historical task sequence deployments.

Task Sequence - Deployments Provides you with detailed information about running and historical task sequence deployments.

Task Sequence - Progress Provides you with detailed information about the progress of task sequences.

Task Sequence - References Provides information about the objects referenced by a specific task sequence.

Upgrade Assessment Provides you with an overview of computers that meet the system requirements for Windows 7 and Windows 8 deployment and those computers that are not capable of being upgraded.

User - Device Affinity Provides you with UDA information, such as UDA associations per collection and UDA statistics.

User Data and Profiles Health Provides you with information about users in a specific domain, a count of users, and computers used by specific users.

Users   Provides you with information about users in a specific domain, a count of users, and computers used by specific users.

Virtual Applications   Provides information about virtual applications installed in the environment and information about virtual application packages.

Volume Purchase Programs - Apple   Provides an inventory of all applications for iPhone, iPad, and iPod Touch licensed thru Apple's Volume Purchase Program.

Wake On LAN   Provides information about the Wake On LAN activity and configurations.

As you can see, Microsoft has done a good job of providing many key reports that are ready to use out of the box.

Running a Report

There are two ways to run a report. The first is to use the Configuration Manager administrative console and the second is to use the web-based Report Manager. A benefit of the web-based Report Manager is that the user does need to have the Configuration Manager administrative console installed in order to view reports.

Viewing Available Reports

You can view the list of available reports from within the Configuration Manager administrative console or through the web-based Report Manager created during the configuration of the Reporting Services site system role. Both Report Manager and Configuration Manager group reports in folders. If needed, you can always move a report from one folder to another folder or even create your own folders.

Running a Report from the Administrative Console

To run a report using the Configuration Manager administrative console, follow these simple steps:

1. Open the Configuration Manager administrative console and select the Monitoring workspace.

2. Under Overview, expand Reporting and select Reports. This will display the reports in the right pane. If you expand the Reports node, it lists out the folders, by category, that you can select and only displays the reports from that category.

3. Select the report you want to run, and click Run on the ribbon.

4. Many of the reports require that you select additional information, such as a collection, to narrow the results of the report data.

5. Click View Report.

Figure 12.3 shows the Client Push Installation Status Summary report.

FIGURE 12.3
The Client Push status report opened from the console

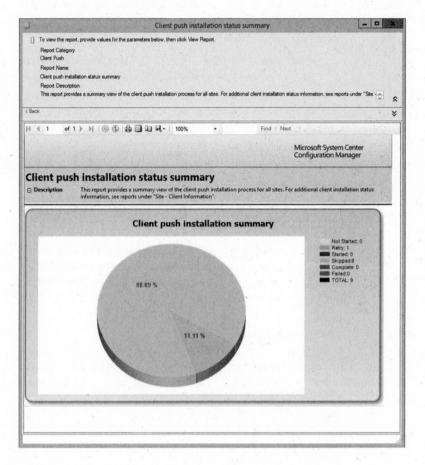

This will open the report in a new window. You can choose to print or export the report. If you choose to export the report, you can select a file format like Word, Excel, PDF, TIFF, MHTML, CSV, or XML.

Running a Report from Report Manager

To run a report using the web-based SQL Server Reporting Services, follow these simple steps:

1. Open your web browser to the URL (the default is http://ReportServer/Reports) for Report Manager.

   As described earlier in the chapter, this URL is the location you specified when setting up the reporting site system role.

2. Open the report root folder and then select the folder for the category of the report you want to run.

3. Select the report that you want to run from the list provided in the folder.

4. Many reports require that you provide values that will be used to run the report. Specify the required criteria and click View Report.

Figure 12.4 shows the All application deployments (advanced) report

FIGURE 12.4
Contents of the
All application
deployments
(advanced) report

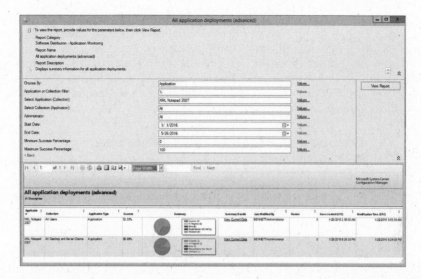

Real World Scenario

MODIFYING THE STANDARD LOGO FOR ALL REPORTS

You have been asked by your boss to make sure that the default SQL reports are branded with the company logo in the upper-right corner. In most of the default reports you will find three standard images. You decide to replace the Report_Header_Right.png file with the custom company logo. To achieve that, you'll use the Style folder and make a change in the registry.

1. Log on to the reporting server.

2. Open the %ProgramFiles%\SMS_SRSRP\style folder.

3. Make a backup of the existing Report_Header_Right.png file.

4. Copy the file of your company's logo to the Style folder and rename it **Report_Header_Right.png**.

5. Open the registry by clicking Start ➤ Run, and type **regedit**.

6. Navigate to HKEY_Local_Machine\Software\Microsoft\SMS\SRSRP\ SRSInitializeState.

7. Change the value to 0.

This will restart the deployment of the default Configuration Manager reports. It is important to note that any changes or customizations made to the reports will be overwritten. This process may take some time, and you can monitor the srsrp.log file on the site server for progress. This method could also be used if a number of the built-in reports were changed or inadvertently deleted and it's not effective to reimport the reports one by one.

Working with Reporting Security

Working with security for reports is not that different from working with security for other objects in Configuration Manager. Configuration Manager will automatically synchronize the security settings configured using the Configuration Manager administrative console to SSRS.

In theory you can configure security in both the Configuration Manager administrative console and in Report Manager. The preferred method is using the Configuration Manager administrative console because all changes applied here will automatically be synchronized to SQL Server Reporting Services. If you configure security directly in Report Manager, you will find that all your custom settings will be overwritten by the security settings in Configuration Manager. By default Configuration Manager will connect to SSRS every 10 minutes and verify that security settings are correctly configured.

Permissions Required to Run Reports

Configuration Manager will create two new Reporting security groups in SQL Server Reporting Services:

Configuration Manager Report Administrators   Offers full administrative permissions to all tasks related to working with reports.

Configuration Manager Report Users   Allows users to read reports and create subscriptions.

When you assign the Read permission to a user or group in the Configuration Manager console, that group will automatically be granted the Configuration Manager Report Users role in SQL Server Reporting Services.

Most, but not all, objects will be assigned either Run Report or Modify Report or both, as shown in Figure 12.5, for the Asset Manager. To read reports not associated with a specific role, you must have Read permission to the site. When security is granted, Configuration Manager will automatically assign the appropriate group or user permissions to the reports.

FIGURE 12.5
Report options for
built-in security roles

> ### 🌐 Real World Scenario
>
> #### ASSIGN A GROUP PERMISSION TO VIEW ALL REPORTS
>
> In your organization you have an Active Directory group named CM_Reporting_Viewers that requires read access to all reports in Configuration Manager. As a Configuration Manager administrator you have been given the task of assigning the appropriate permissions using the least administrative effort possible. Follow these steps to accomplish this task:
>
> 1. Open the Configuration Manager administrative console.
>
> 2. Navigate to the Administration workspace, and in Overview select Security ➢ Administrative Users.
>
> 3. From the ribbon click Add User Or Group.
>
>   This will launch the Add User Or Group dialog.
>
> 4. In User Or Group Name field, click Browse, type **CM_Reporting_Viewers**, and click OK.
>
> 5. In the Associated Security Roles dialog, click Add, select the Read-only Analyst security role, and click OK.
>
> 6. Click OK to close the Add User Or Group dialog.

Managing Reports

One of the main benefits of using SQL Server Reporting Services is the ability to manage reports. Once a report is published, you will be able to use the Report Manager to modify some of the reporting properties. The properties control security, parameter values, the data source, when the report runs (scheduled or on demand), caching options, and more.

To manage the properties for a report, follow these simple steps:

1. Open your web browser to the URL (the default is http://ReportServer/Reports) for the Report Viewer.

2. Open the root report folder and then the folder for the category of the report you want to manage, for example, Software Distribution – Application.

3. Click the drop-down arrow for the report you want to manage.

4. From the list of options, click Manage.

The first properties you will see are the General properties for the report. You will find a list of report properties in Tables 12.1 through 12.9. Table 12.1 lists the General properties.

TABLE 12.1:   General properties

PROPERTY	DESCRIPTION
Delete	Allows you to delete the report.
Move	Allows you to move the report to another folder. This is especially useful if you want to create your own folder with a mix of canned reports from different folders. You should always consider creating custom folders like Servicedesk, Software, or License and move the reports you use the most to those folders.

TABLE 12.1: General properties *(continued)*

PROPERTY	DESCRIPTION
Create Linked Report	Allows you to create a link to another report. You will find more information on this property later in this chapter.
Download	Allows you to save the report as an RDL file.
Replace	Allows you to import a new version of the report.
Name	Lets you specify the name of the report.
Description	Lets you provide the report description.
Hide In Tile View	Enable this to hide the report from the Report Manager tile view mode. Tile view mode is the default view when users browse for reports.

SHOWING HIDDEN REPORTS IN REPORT MANAGER

To view a report that is configured to be hidden in List view, do the following:

1. Open the Report Manager website.
2. Click Details View.
3. Open the folder containing the report you want to view.
4. In Details view all reports and data sources are visible. You can now open the specific report's properties and remove the check mark from Hide In Tile View on the General properties page.

 Real World Scenario

REIMPORT A DEFAULT REPORT

As you start working with reports, you may find yourself modifying the default reports and later regretting it. All default reports that are installed with Configuration Manager are located in a folder on the reporting site system. In this example we will reimport the Client Status Summary report from the Client Health folder. To manually import this report, do the following.

1. Open the Report Manager website.
2. Open the Client Health folder.
3. Open the Client Summary report properties, and make sure you are on the General properties page.
4. Click Replace.
5. Click Browse and navigate to E:\Program Files\SMS_SRSRP\Reports\Client_Health, where E:\ is the disk volume where you have installed the reporting site system role.
6. Select CH_Report_ClientSummaryCurrent.rdl and click Open.
7. Back in Report Manager, click OK.
8. Click Apply and close the report properties.

Using prompts (or parameters) in reports is very common. It is an easy way for the report user to specify what data to view without having to have deep knowledge of the underlying dataset or SQL reporting skills. You as the administrator can customize the parameters and configure settings such as the default parameter values described in Table 12.2.

TABLE 12.2:   Parameter properties

PROPERTY	DESCRIPTION
Parameter Name	The name of the parameter.
Data Type	Specification of the data type.
Has Default	Allows you to specify a default value, thus saving time whenever you run the report. With this selected you can specify the value in Default Value and/or use the Null property.
Default Value	A default value can originate from the report definition, can be query based, or can be a value you type in. The value you enter must adhere to the data type; the use of wildcards is also determined in the report itself.
Null	Allows you to specify that the report will run even if the user does not select any prompted value. This does require that the report allows the use of Null values.
Hide	Allows you to hide the parameters in the Report Manager from users when they run a report. The parameter value will still be visible if the user starts the subscription wizard.
Prompt User	With this selected, users will be prompted for a parameter. Deselect the check box if you want to control the parameters to be used in the report.
Display Text	Text that will be displayed with the parameter value.

As part of the SQL Server Reporting Services point installation, a shared data source is created. The data source is used to specify what data to access and which security credentials to use. Table 12.3 describes the values you can specify for the created data source. Notice that it is highly unlikely that you will need to change the data source from the Report Manager.

TABLE 12.3:   Data Source properties

PROPERTY	DESCRIPTION
A Shared Data Source	Specifies the shared data source.
A Custom Data Source	Allows you to specify a custom data source.
Connection String	Specifies the connection string used to connect to the data source.

TABLE 12.3: Data Source properties *(continued)*

PROPERTY	DESCRIPTION
Connect Using	Defines how you connect to the data source. For all the canned reports, the connection settings are already defined in the connection string.
Connect Using Credentials Supplied By The User Running The Report	Defines that each user must provide a username and password.
Use As Windows Credentials When Connecting To The Data Source	Configure this option if the credentials supplied by the user are Windows Authentication credentials.
Credentials Stored Securely In The Report Server	Encrypts and stores the credentials in the report server. This will allow you to run a report unattended, which is a requirement for scheduled reports.
Impersonate The Authenticated User After A Connection Has Been Made To The Data Source	Used only on rare occasions to allow delegation of credentials if supported by the data source.
Windows Integrated Security	Uses the credentials of the logged-on user to access the data source.
Credentials Are Not Required	Does not prompt for credentials when running the report. This works only if the data source does not require a user logon.
Test Connection	Performs a test to the data source using the supplied credentials.

One of the advantages of using SQL Server Reporting Services is that you can configure automatic delivery of specified reports by either email or storing the report to a file share. You can create subscriptions in the Report Manager or by using the Create Subscription Wizard in the Configuration Manager administrative console. Table 12.4 explains the subscription options available when you are using the Report Manager.

TABLE 12.4: Subscription options

PROPERTY	DESCRIPTION
New Subscription	Allows you to create a new report subscription.
Delete	Lets you delete the selected subscription.
Edit	Allows you to edit the subscription properties.
Report Delivery Options (Email Selected)	Can be delivered by email or can be file based. The following are the properties for an email-based subscription.
To	Fill in the recipient email address; it can be a group or a list of individual email addresses separated by a semicolon (;). Note that the reporting server will not validate any of the email addresses.

TABLE 12.4:   Subscription options   *(continued)*

PROPERTY	DESCRIPTION
Cc	Fill in the email address of any recipients who will receive the email as Cc. Can be a group or a list of individual email addresses separated by a semicolon.
Bcc	Fill in the email address of any recipients who will receive the email as Bcc. Can be a group or a list of individual email addresses separated by a semicolon.
Reply-To	Fill in the Reply To email address.
Subject	The email subject; you can use these variables combined with custom text: *@ExecutionTime*—The runtime for the report *@ReportName*—The name of the report
Include Report	Includes the report in the email as an attachment.
Render Format	Reports can be delivered in different formats: XML CSV (comma delimited) Data Feed PDF HTML 4.0 MHTML (MIME HTML) Excel RPL Renderer (RPL) TIFF File Word
Include Link	Includes a URL in the email body.
Priority	Choose from these email priorities: Low Medium High
Comment	Text entered in the comment will be added to the email body.
Report Delivery Options (Windows File Share)	The following are the properties for Windows file share subscription.
File Name	Type in the filename of the report.
Add A File Extension When The File Is Created	By default the file type will not be appended to the filename unless you enable this setting.
Path	A UNC to an existing folder on the network. The specified user account must have Write permissions to the share.

TABLE 12.4:   Subscription options   *(continued)*

PROPERTY	DESCRIPTION
Render Format	Same as the email rendering formats.
Credentials Used To Access The File Share	Specify the user account that will be used to save the file.
Overwrite Options	Choose from these options:
	Overwrite An Existing File With A Newer Version.
	Do Not Overwrite An Existing File.
	Increment File Names As Newer Versions Are Added. This will place a number at the end of the filename and increment the number as new reports are saved.

When reports are executed, they will be transformed from the reporting database into a viewable format. The defined query in the dataset will be executed and will return data to the reporting server, where the selected rendering extension will create the report. The performance impact of running a report depends very much on the amount of data retrieved and the rendering format selected. By default when users run a report, that report is generated on demand. Most of the data in Configuration Manager is either inventory data or state messages, which are very rarely real-time data. By knowing the processing options described in Table 12.5 and the report content, you will quickly learn how to speed up the processing for reports.

TABLE 12.5:   Processing options

PROPERTY	DESCRIPTION
Always Run This Report With The Most Recent Data	Always shows the latest data in the report.
Cache A Temporary Copy Of The Report. Expire Copy Of Report After A Number Of Minutes.	Specifies the number of minutes the intermediate format will be available in the cache.
Cache A Temporary Copy Of The Report. Expire Copy Of Report On The Following Schedule	You can specify when the intermediate format will be removed from the cache based on a custom specific schedule or by using a shared schedule.
Render This Report From A Snapshot	This option allows you to create the intermediate format prior to running the report the first time. The intermediate format can be created on a custom specific schedule or by using a shared schedule. Note that cached reports will be added as permanent storage to the ReportServer database, unlike cached reports, which will be removed. This feature is closely related to the values you specify on the Snapshot Options page.

TABLE 12.5:   Processing options   *(continued)*

PROPERTY	DESCRIPTION
Create A Report Snapshot When You Click The Apply Button On This Page	Creates a snapshot of the report as soon as possible without using the specified schedule.
Report Timeout	Controls the report processing timeout value. The default timeout value is specified in the Site Settings page.

When you cache a report, the first time the report is executed the process is similar to running an on-demand report. However, the intermediate format is stored in ReportServerTempDB (cache) for a configured period. If any other users request the same data, the server will take the intermediate format and render the report much more quickly.

You can preload the cache with temporary copies of the report by creating a refresh plan with the parameters described in Table 12.6. Creating a cache refresh plan requires that the cache options have been defined.

TABLE 12.6:   Cache Refresh options

PROPERTY	DESCRIPTION
New Cache Refresh Plan	Lets you create a new plan.
Description	You can provide a meaningful description for the plan.
Refresh The Cache According To The Following Schedule	The cache can be refreshed on a custom specific schedule or by using a shared schedule.

As snapshots are generated, you will be able to view the reports in the Report History page. On this page you can also create a manual snapshot of the report. The options are shown in Table 12.7.

TABLE 12.7:   Report History options

PROPERTY	DESCRIPTION
Delete	Deletes the selected report snapshot.
New Snapshot	Creates a new snapshot. This option is available only if Allow Report History To Be Created Manually has been selected on the Snapshot Options page.

Report history is stored in the Report Server database. The Snapshot options, shown in Table 12.8, will assist you in controlling how many items are stored and when the snapshot is generated.

TABLE 12.8:   Snapshot options

PROPERTY	DESCRIPTION
Allow Report History To Be Created Manually	Enables the New Snapshot button on the Report History page.
Store All Report Execution Snapshots In Report History	With this feature, reports that are created based on the execution settings on the Processing Options page will be added to the Report History page.
Select The Number Of Snapshots To Keep	Controls how many snapshots are added to the history. You can select from three different values: Use Default Unlimited Snapshots Limit To A Specific Number

As described earlier in this chapter, Configuration Manager will apply default security settings when the Reporting Services point is installed and will check those security settings every 10 minutes. Table 12.9 describes the Security setting applied to a report.

TABLE 12.9:   Security option

PROPERTY	DESCRIPTION
Edit Item Security	Allows you to customize the default Security settings. Notice that Configuration Manager will overwrite any custom settings you configure.

CREATING A SHARED SCHEDULE

To lower the performance requirements on the server when running reports, you have been asked to control when reports are rendered. Prior to configuring the execution options, you decide to create a shared schedule that can be selected for all reports. You follow these steps to create a shared schedule:

1. Open the Report Manager website.
2. Click Site Settings.
3. Click the Schedules link.
4. Click New Schedule.
5. Type in a schedule name and configure the schedule details.
6. Click OK to save the shared schedule.

Working with Subscriptions

One of the many powerful features of using SQL Server Reporting Services is the ability to create subscriptions to reports. You can subscribe to reports and have them delivered via mail or as a file on a network share. A standard user can create and customize their own subscriptions with the options described in Table 12.4. You can create a subscription in Report Manager or use the Create Subscription Wizard in the Configuration Manager administrative console.

CREATING A FILE-BASED REPORT SUBSCRIPTION

Prior to creating a file-based subscription, you need to ensure that you have an account with write permissions to a predefined server share. In this example we'll create a subscription for the Client Push Status Summary report.

To create a file-based report subscription using the Configuration Manager administrative console, follow these steps:

1. Open the Configuration Manager console and select the Monitoring workspace.

2. Inside Overview, click Reporting, and select the report from the Reports folder.

3. With the report selected, click Create Subscription on the ribbon.

4. In the Report Delivered By field, ensure that Windows File Share is selected.

5. In File Name field, type in the name of the file without any extension—for example, **ClientPushSummary**.

6. Enable the Add File Extension When Created check box.

7. In the Path field, type in the UNC to an existing share.

8. Select the rendering format; in the example we have selected Acrobat (PDF) File.

9. In the User Name field, specify an account with Read access to the report and Write permissions to the specified UNC.

10. Configure the needed Overwrite Option, and click Next.

Figure 12.6 shows how the delivery options can be specified.

FIGURE 12.6
Creating a Windows file-based report subscription

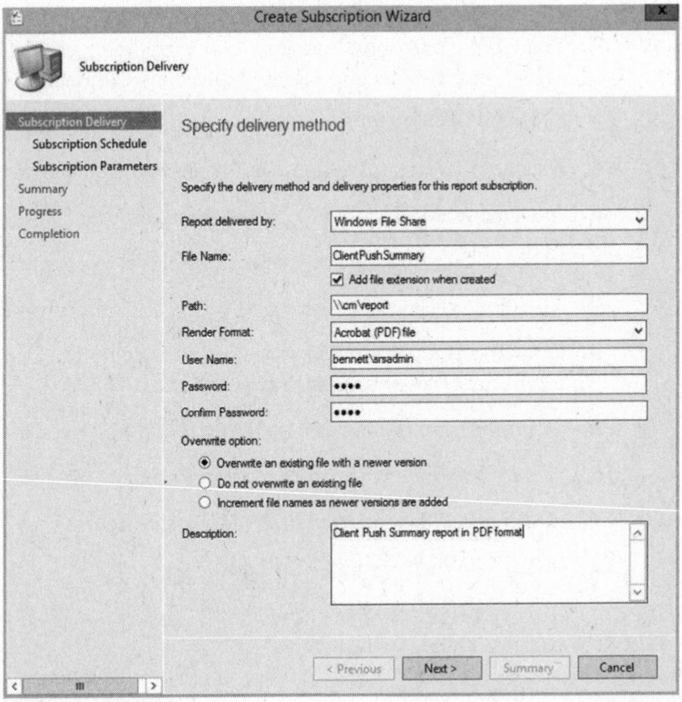

11. On the Subscription Schedule page, select a shared schedule or create a new schedule, and click Next.

    This report is a prompted report, and it requires that you select the prompted value. In this example you must click Values and select the number of days.

12. Select All, click OK, and click Next.

13. Read the summary information, and click Next.

14. Click Close; the subscription is now created.

You can view information and edit the scheduled report by clicking Reporting ➤ Subscriptions in the Monitoring workspace. You can also open the Report Manager and open the properties for the report. Select Subscriptions; here you will find detailed information about when the subscription is about to run or when it was executed the last time.

CREATING AN EMAIL-BASED REPORT SUBSCRIPTION

You learned that you can create a report subscription that creates a document in a specified share on a defined schedule and that you can also create an email-based subscription that will deliver the report via email. Prior to creating an email-based subscription, you need to configure the email options in the Reporting Services Configuration Manager. In this example, you will configure the required mail options and use Report Manager to create a subscription for the Client Push Status Summary report.

To configure email support in the Reporting Services Configuration Manager and create an email-based subscription in Report Manager, follow these steps:

1. From the Start menu, choose All Programs ➤ Microsoft SQL Server ➤ Configuration Tools ➤ Reporting Services Configuration Manager.

2. You will be prompted to connect to a reporting server. Make sure the correct reporting server and instance are selected and click Connect.

3. Click E-Mail Settings.

4. In Sender Address, type the email address that will be used to send the mail.

5. In Current SMTP Delivery Method, ensure that Use SMTP Server is selected.

6. In SMTP Server, type the name of the SMTP server and click Apply to store the settings.

7. Click Exit to close the Reporting Services Configuration Manager.

8. Open the SQL Report Manager and connect to the Configuration Manager report by typing `http://reportingserver/reports`.

9. Open the `Configuration Manager` folder and the `Client Push` folder.

10. Hover the pointer over the report, and select Subscribe from the drop-down list.

11. In Delivered By, ensure that E-Mail is selected.

12. In To, type the recipient email addresses.

Note that there will be no validation of the addresses; you need to make sure that what you type is correct. You can type multiple addresses by separating them with a semicolon (;).

13. Fill in any other CC, BCC, and Reply-To email addresses.

14. Type a subject using the variables explained in Table 12.4.

15. Choose from among the following options:

♦   Send A Link

♦   Include The Report As Attachment

♦   Embed The Report In The Mail

If the recipients support HTML 4.0 and MHTML 5.0, you can select the Render format MHTML; this will embed the report in the mail.

16. In the Comment field, type in any information that you want to include in the mail body.

17. Configure the processing options, and click OK to create the subscription.

You can create the subscription in Report Manager as explained previously or in the Configuration Manager administrative console as explained for file-based subscription. The difference between the two methods is that subscriptions created in the administrative console will be listed in the administrative console as well as in Report Manager, unlike subscriptions created in Report Manager, which will be listed only in Report Manager.

Creating Reports

Configuration Manager includes over 470 default reports that meet many common reporting requirements. However, it's possible that you may need to modify an existing report or create a new one to meet a specific reporting requirement. Creating reports requires at least a basic understanding of the Transact-SQL (T-SQL) query language, requires you to have some knowledge of the data and the views that are contained in the Configuration Manager database, and requires you to be familiar with the various tools available to create and customize reports.

You can create a new Configuration Manager report in the following ways:

♦   By copying an existing Configuration Manager report and modifying the copy

♦   By creating a new Configuration Manager report based on a report model

♦   By creating the report from scratch using Report Builder or BIDS (Business Intelligence Development Studio)

Functions vs. Views

The native reports in Configuration Manager are based on the role-based access control (RBAC) model. As a result, users will see only the report data that they are allowed to see when they run the default Configuration Manager reports. These RBAC-enabled reports use table-based functions in the Configuration Manager database as well as identifiers for the user running the report to present only the report data that the user is allowed to view. An example of a table-based function for installed software inventory information is fn_rbac_GS_INSTALLED_ SOFTWARE. Configuration Manager users can also create and run reports that do not follow the RBAC model; these reports are based on the SQL views in the database. An example of a view for installed software inventory information is v_GS_INSTALLED_SOFTWARE.

When you create reports for your organization, you will need to determine if RBAC is necessary for the new reports. There is no question that RBAC security is important when users interact with the Configuration Manager console because it limits what actions the user is able to perform on the site. However, it's possible that, for your organization, security is not as important for Configuration Manager report data. If Configuration Manager report security is an essential requirement for your organization, then you will use the table-based functions when you create the queries that will be used in your custom reports. If report security is a not a critical concern for your organization, then you may find it easier to create reports that use SQL views in the queries for your custom reports. It is worth noting that many customers decide that RBAC in the reports is not critical and will build reports based on SQL views. Also, many of the sample reports you may download from blogs and Configuration Manager–related websites will be based on SQL views, not the RBAC-based functions. This chapter assumes that report security is not a critical concern for the organization and uses SQL views when creating queries that will be used in reports.

Basic SQL Commands

As previously discussed, Configuration Manager provides the ability to create reports based on queries that use SQL views to retrieve data from the database. The SQL views are essentially virtual tables that do not contain data but are based on tables that contain data. The data is dynamically compiled from source tables when the view is referenced. We do not recommend that you create reports that access the database tables directly because the table names may change in future versions of Configuration Manager and the reports will no longer work.

To create a Configuration Manager report, you need to create a SQL query based on views that retrieves the desired data from Configuration Manager.

NOTE Numerous tools are available for creating SQL queries. You can create the query directly in the Report Builder application, or you can create the query in another tool, like SQL Server Management Studio, and then copy the query into the Report Builder query design window. Feel free to use whichever approach is easier for you to use.

An in-depth study on how to create SQL queries is beyond the scope of this book, but some general knowledge may be helpful. As you examine the views in the Configuration Manager database, you may notice some standardized naming of the views. Some examples are:

◆ V_GS_*Name*—Contains current inventory data

◆ V_HS_*Name*—Contains historical inventory data

◆ V_R_*Name*—Contains discovery data

◆ V_RA_*Name*—Contains array (multivalue) discovery data

There are many commands and clauses in the T-SQL query language. Some of the more common ones you may use are SELECT, ORDER BY, and WHERE.

Consider the following query:

```
SELECT * FROM v_GS_COMPUTER_SYSTEM
```

This query would return all the rows from the Configuration Manager database for the view v_GS_COMPUTER_SYSTEM. If you wanted the query to return data for only computers that are virtual machines, you could add a WHERE statement:

```
SELECT * FROM v_GS_COMPUTER_SYSTEM
WHERE (MODEL0 = 'Virtual Machine')
```

If you wanted to sort the results by computer name, you could add an ORDER BY clause and then specify whether the list should be in ascending or descending order. The following query would sort the results by computer name in ascending order:

```
SELECT * FROM v_GS_COMPUTER_SYSTEM
WHERE (MODEL0 = 'Virtual Machine')
ORDER BY NAME0 ASC
```

It's likely that the report you are creating should only include certain fields, not every possible field from the view. For example, if we only wanted to include the fields for computer name, computer manufacturer, and model, we could use the following query:

```
SELECT NAME0, MANUFACTURER0, MODEL0
FROM V_GS_COMPUTER_SYSTEM
WHERE (MODEL0 = 'Virtual Machine')
ORDER BY NAME0 ASC
```

The results for this query would be

```
NAME0   MANUFACTURER0                   MODEL0
CM      Microsoft Corporation           Virtual Machine
CMSEC   Microsoft Corporation           Virtual Machine
DC      Microsoft Corporation           Virtual Machine
OM      Microsoft Corporation           Virtual Machine
SCORCH  Microsoft Corporation           Virtual Machine
SQL     Microsoft Corporation           Virtual Machine
WIN101  Microsoft Corporation           Virtual Machine
WIN102  Microsoft Corporation           Virtual Machine
WIN103  Microsoft Corporation           Virtual Machine
```

And you will likely want to change the column headings to more user-friendly names. You can rename the headers when you create the report in Report Builder (or BIDS), or you can rename them via the AS command in the SQL query.

```
SELECT NAME0 AS 'Computer Name', MANUFACTURER0
AS 'Computer Manufacturer', MODEL0 AS 'Computer Model'
FROM V_GS_COMPUTER_SYSTEM
WHERE (MODEL0 = 'Virtual Machine')
ORDER BY NAME0 ASC
```

The results for this query would be

```
Computer Name Computer Manufacturer       Computer Model
CM              Microsoft Corporation     Virtual Machine
CMSEC           Microsoft Corporation     Virtual Machine
DC              Microsoft Corporation     Virtual Machine
OM              Microsoft Corporation     Virtual Machine
```

```
SCORCH          Microsoft Corporation      Virtual Machine
SQL             Microsoft Corporation      Virtual Machine
WIN101          Microsoft Corporation      Virtual Machine
WIN102          Microsoft Corporation      Virtual Machine
WIN103          Microsoft Corporation      Virtual Machine
```

Obviously these are very simple queries but they may be useful as you begin learning how to create powerful queries that you will implement in your custom Configuration Manager reports.

Report Models

A report model contains predefined views and fields logically grouped together. By using report models, you can assist users in building reports that expose only the needed views and fields. This shortens the learning curve for building reports and also speeds up the process because only the selected views and fields will be presented to Report Builder. In the next section you will learn how to build your own report model and create reports based on the included Configuration Manager report models. Some of the benefits of using report models are as follows:

◆ You can assign reporting model logical names.

◆ The underlying database structure can be hidden from the person creating the report.

◆ The report model can contain multiple tables and views yet still list the model as a single object.

◆ Time saved is money saved. When reporting models are created, not every person creating reports needs to have deep SQL knowledge.

Creating a Report Using Report Builder

Configuration Manager uses Microsoft SQL Server Reporting Services Report Builder 3.0 as the authoring and editing tool for both model and SQL-based reports. Report Builder will automatically be installed on your computer when you create or modify a report for the first time. With Report Builder, you are able to

◆ Develop one report at a time in a Microsoft Office lookalike environment

◆ Create charts and gauges

◆ Create rich SQL

◆ Use rich formatting capabilities

◆ Export to reports in other formats

We will now go through the process of creating a new report using Report Builder. The report will be created in the report folder Hardware - General. Use the following steps to create a basic SQL report that will show and count all the different hardware models you have in the database.

1. Open the Configuration Manager console and select the Monitoring workspace.

2. In Overview, expand Reporting and right-click Reports.

3. From the drop-down menu, select Create Report.

4. Select SQL-Based Report.

5. In the Name field, type **Count Hardware Models**.

6. In the Description field, type **Group and count all hardware models**.

7. In the Path field, click Browse, select the Hardware - General folder, and click OK.

8. Click Next.

9. On the Summary page, click Next (this will create the report).

10. Click Close.

   Report Builder will launch automatically and allow you to finish creating the report. If this is the first time you launched the wizard, you will be prompted to install Report Builder.

11. In Report Builder, click Table Or Matrix.

   This will launch the New Table Or Matrix Wizard.

12. Click Create A Dataset and click Next.

13. In Data Source Connections, verify that the Configuration Manager data source is selected, and click Next. If you want to verify that the connection is correct, use the Test Connection option at the bottom-right corner of the New Table Or Matrix window.

14. Expand dbo ➤ Views ➤ v_GS_COMPUTER_SYSTEM.

15. Select Manufacturer0 and Model0, as shown in Figure 12.7, and click Next.

FIGURE 12.7
Creating a report using Report Builder 3.0

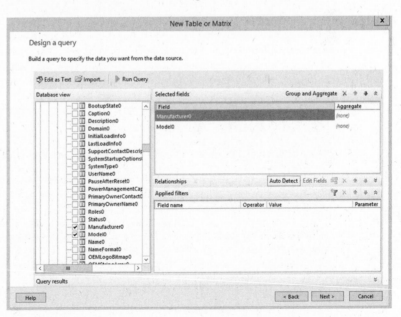

16. Drag Manufacturer0 and Model0 to Row Groups and Model0 to Values.

17. In Values, right-click Model0 and select Count; click Next when finished.

18. In Choose The Layout, select Stepped Subtotals Above, and click Next.

19. Select a style and click Finish.

The report is now open in Design view, allowing you to customize colors, fonts, and much more.

20. To view the report, click Run in the ribbon.

21. If you want to make additional changes to the format of the report, click Design in the ribbon.

22. Once the report is formatted properly and ready to be published, click Save to save the report.

23. Exit Report Builder.

24. When prompted to publish the report, click Yes.

BUSINESS INTELLIGENCE DEVELOPMENT STUDIO

You can also use BIDS to create reports. BIDS is fairly commonly used by developers and is a component that ships with SQL Server. BIDS is in essence Microsoft Visual Studio 2008 with prebuilt project types used in SQL-like reporting services. More information on creating reports with BIDS is available here:

https://technet.microsoft.com/en-us/library/cc281300(v=sql.105).aspx

---

Linked Reports

A linked report is something you can create when you want to have several versions of the same report with different data. You can look at linked reports as you would cloning an existing report, with the exception that a linked report inherits the layout and data source properties of the original report. Properties like parameters, subscriptions, and schedules can be changed in the linked report.

 Real World Scenario

PROVIDING DIFFERENT TEAMS WITH THE SAME REPORT BUT DIFFERENT DATA

You need to provide managers from the desktop and server team with a monthly third-party software license reconciliation report in their mailbox. The managers need the same report but with data from different collections. From time to time, you have modified the layout of the report, and you do not want to do that on multiple reports. To meet the challenge, you decide to create two linked reports derived from the canned report License 15A - General License Reconciliation Report. Here's how you create the first linked report:

1. Open a browser and connect to http://reportingserver/reports.

2. Open the Asset Intelligence folder.

3. Click the drop-down arrow for the report License 15A - General License Reconciliation.

4. Select Create Linked Report; notice that you can also do the same thing by opening the report properties.

5. Type a descriptive name for the linked report like `License 15A - Server License Reconciliation Report`.

6. Click OK.

7. Open the properties for the new linked report (notice that by default you still have the properties for the original report open).

8. Select Parameters.

9. Check Has Default, and type the Collection ID in the Default Value field. You can find the Collection ID by viewing the collection properties in the Configuration Manager administrative console.

10. Check Hide, and remove the check mark from Prompt User.

11. Click Apply, and run the report.

Importing and Exporting Reports

One of the fastest and easiest ways to build reports in your Configuration Manager console is to import them from others who have already created the report you want. This technique allows administrators to share reports quickly and easily. Here is a list of some popular sites where you can download examples:

`http://blog.coretech.dk/category/confmgr/config-mgr-inventory-and-reporting/`   Contains ready-made reports to download and import. Offers step-by-step descriptions of how to create and modify reports.

`http://myitforum.com/myitforumwp/`   Large online System Center community where you will find several community leaders and contributors posting reporting solutions.

Please see the Microsoft TechNet Library article detailing how to create custom reports by using SQL Server views in System Center 2012 Configuration Manager at `http://technet.microsoft.com/en-us/library/dn581954.aspx`.

Note that there are many other community websites that contribute to the SQL reporting knowledge base, and the previous list provides just a base reference.

Importing Reports

Unlike in previous versions of Configuration Manager, you will not be able to import reports using the Configuration Manager console. Instead you will use Report Manager and upload a Report Definition Language (RDL) file as described here:

1. Open a browser and connect to `http://reportingserver/reports`.

2. Open the `ConfigMgr_<SITECODE>` folder.

3. Click New Folder, and enter a name like **Mastering Configuration Manager**. Click OK when finished.

4. Open the newly created folder and click Upload File.

5. Click Browse, select the report file, and click Open.

6. You can type a new name for the report; click OK when finished.

   It is very likely that the data source specified in the report is not valid and needs to be changed after the import.

7. Hover the pointer over the right side of the report to access the drop-down arrow, and select Manage.

8. Select Data Sources.

9. Select A Shared Data Source and click Browse.

10. Navigate to the Configuration Manager site folder, and select the data source.

11. Click OK.

12. Back in Data Sources, click Apply.

The newly imported report is now ready for use and will also be imported into the Configuration Manager administrative console.

Exporting Reports

Exporting reports also requires that you use Report Manager and download the report as described here:

1. Open a browser and connect to http://reportingserver/reports.

2. Open the Configuration Manager folder.

3. Navigate to the report you want to export.

4. Open the report properties as explained previously in this chapter.

5. Select Properties and click Download.

6. Click Save, and save the RDL file to a location of your choice.

The Bottom Line

Install the Reporting Services point. Installing a Reporting Services site system within Configuration Manager allows not only administrators but everyone to view reports in some fashion via either different file formats or a direct link within the Report Manager Website.

Master It What is the procedure to enable Reporting with Configuration Manager?

Manage reporting security. Reporting security is an integrated part of the built-in security. You provide users with access to reports by adding them to a predefined security role or by creating a custom role with permissions to run or modify reports.

Master It Add users to a security role that is able to view reports.

Create and manage report subscriptions. Creating subscriptions can be very helpful in many scenarios. You can configure subscriptions from Report Manager or in the Configuration Manager console.

Master It Create an email-based subscription.

Create custom reports. You may find some scenarios where the included reports in Configuration Manager may not meet your reporting needs and you need to create a custom report.

Master It Create a custom report. Determine whether the query in the report should use table functions or views.

Chapter 13

Compliance Settings

The Compliance Settings feature in System Center Configuration Manager allows you to assess the compliance of client devices with regard to a number of configurations, such as whether the correct operating system version is installed and configured appropriately, whether all required applications are installed and configured correctly, whether optional applications are configured appropriately, and whether prohibited applications are installed on your clients. Additionally, you can check for compliance with software updates, security settings, and mobile devices. Configuration item settings for the Windows Management Instrumentation (WMI), the registry, and scripts in Configuration Manager allow you to automatically remediate noncompliant settings when they are found.

In this chapter, you will learn to

◆ Enable the client settings

◆ Create configuration items

◆ Define a configuration baseline

Overview of Compliance Settings

Compliance settings are evaluated by defining a configuration baseline that contains the configuration items you want to monitor and rules that define the required compliance.

After a configuration baseline is defined, it can be deployed to devices through collections and evaluated on a schedule. Client devices can have multiple configuration baselines assigned to them, which provide the administrator with a high level of control.

Client devices evaluate their compliance against each configuration baseline they are assigned and immediately report back the results to the site using state messages and status messages. If a client is not currently connected to the network but has downloaded the configuration items referenced in its assigned configuration baselines, the compliance information will be sent upon reconnection.

You can monitor the results of the configuration baseline evaluation compliance from the Deployments node of the Monitoring workspace in the Configuration Manager console. You can also run a number of compliance settings reports to drill down into details, such as which devices are compliant or noncompliant and which element of the configuration baseline is causing a computer to be noncompliant. You can also view compliance evaluation results from Windows clients on the Configurations tab of Configuration Manager in the Windows Control Panel.

What's New in Configuration Manager?

The following Compliance Settings features are new or have been changed since Configuration Manager 2012 (see Figure 13.1).

◆   Compliance Policies

◆   Conditional Access

◆   Company Resource Access

◆   Terms and Conditions

◆   Windows 10 Edition Upgrade

FIGURE 13.1
Compliance Settings main page

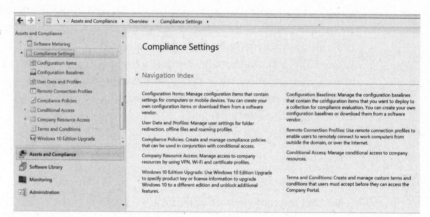

What Can You Do with Compliance Settings?

The best answer is that with Compliance Settings you can automatically check the compliance of your Configuration Manager clients against standards that you choose. Those standards can be company policies regarding how a computer is configured, policies for compliance with regulations such as Sarbanes–Oxley (SOX), or best practices defined by a vendor or based on your internal IT department's experience. For example, they can be settings that a department manager has decided all the computers within the department must meet or a means to identify computers that need more memory as defined by the IT manager in charge of desktops.

Given that range of potential applications, the next question is, what settings can you check with Compliance Settings? This seems like an easy question to answer, but of course it isn't. So, let's explore what you can and cannot do with Compliance Settings.

Let's examine this from a different perspective, and then it will be clear what exactly you can and cannot check for using Compliance Settings.

Configuration Items

Configuration items (CIs) are the smallest single settings or standards that you assemble with other CIs to create a configuration baseline. That baseline is then applied to devices on which you have installed Configuration Manager client software, to mobile devices that are managed with Microsoft Intune, or to mobile devices managed with Configuration Manager on-premises device management. You can choose from specific types of configuration items to create these checks:

- Windows 10 CIs
- Mac OS X CIs
- Windows Desktops and Servers CIs
- Application settings CIs
- Software update CIs
- Mobile device CIs

These checks are keys to understanding the limits of what you can do with Compliance Settings. When you choose the type of configuration items using the wizard in the Configuration Manager console, it will determine what types of checks you are allowed to include as part of a CI. Table 13.1 summarizes the main CI types.

TABLE 13.1:   Configuration item types

TYPE	DEFINITION	EXAMPLE
Application settings	Used to check an application's settings for compliance	Checking Microsoft Office Word for the latest Normal.dot file
Windows Desktops and Servers (custom)	Used to check a particular operating system's version or settings for compliance	Checking to ensure that Configuration Manager clients have the latest cumulative update for Microsoft Windows 10 installed
Windows 10	Used to check settings specific to Windows 10 for compliance	Checking to ensure that file encryption device is On and User Account Control is configured and Smart Screen is Enabled
Windows Desktops and Servers (custom)	Windows Version, Objects, Settings, Security	Detection Method, Applicable
Software update	General, Security	Windows Version, Objects, Settings, Detection Method, Applicable

As you would expect, not all of these configuration item types offer the same properties. For example, the Windows Desktops and Servers type contains a property to check for the exact build of the operating system that is running on the Configuration Manager client being evaluated; this option is not available in the other configuration types. As mentioned earlier, a configuration baseline can (and almost always will) contain multiple configuration items of all configuration types. The properties available to each configuration item type are listed in Table 13.2.

TABLE 13.2: Properties of configuration item types

TYPE	AVAILABLE	NOT AVAILABLE
Software update	Used to check Configuration Manager clients for software update compliance	Checking the status of approved software updates on Configuration Manager clients
Mobile device	Used to check and enforce settings on supported mobile devices	Checking to ensure an unlock PIN setting is enforced to secure the device
Mac OS X	Used to check settings for compliance on supported Mac OS X devices	Checking a preference list to ensure corporate settings are configured
Windows Desktops and Servers (custom)	Used to check settings of objects in Windows	Checking the hosts file to ensure that spyware has not modified the file or that the system has the latest hosts file installed

The reason for restricting configuration item types to specific properties, instead of having a single type with all properties available, is to keep the configuration items as small as possible. Defining configuration items as specific types allows you to reuse them when you create configuration baselines. For example, you can create an operating system configuration item that checks for Microsoft Windows 8.1.

Additional objects and settings are available when you create this configuration item type. You can also check for the presence of a specific file and its attributes. You can run validation against an assembly that is present, and you can even check the string value of a registry key and report on noncompliance for any of these objects or settings, all within the same configuration item. But if you design your configuration items with the idea of being able to reuse them in multiple configuration baselines, they should be as lean and specific as possible. If you need the configuration item to validate something else for a particular scenario, you can simply create a child configuration item. This configuration item will inherit all the original settings of the configuration item and allow you to add additional validations, leaving the original configuration item intact and not affecting any of the configuration baselines that are using that configuration item.

Configuring Compliance Settings Client Settings

Configuring the Compliance Settings client settings is as easy as selecting Yes or No for the Enable Compliance Evaluation On Clients option and determining the appropriate schedule for clients to evaluate their compliance. This setting is located in the Administration workspace under Overview ➤ Client Settings ➤ Default Client Agent Settings. Then right-click and select Properties. This will open the properties window for the client settings (see Figure 13.2). By setting the Enable Compliance Evaluation On Clients option to Yes, you enable this option in the default settings. The default schedule for evaluation is every seven days. You can adjust this schedule as necessary for your environment, including using a custom schedule that will allow you more control over when it runs, but the default schedule will typically be adequate for most environments. You can also modify the default client settings, create new custom client settings, or modify existing custom client settings. You can create or modify custom client settings when you want to apply a group of client settings to specific collections.

FIGURE 13.2

The default client settings

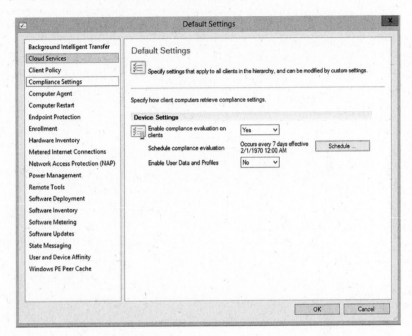

Creating Configuration Items

Configuration items are pieces of the configuration baseline that, when assembled, will allow you to monitor configuration drift from what you have specified. To demonstrate the processes of creating configuration items and a configuration baseline, we'll use a utility called Microsoft Mathematics, described in the accompanying sidebar. Because there are so many ways to configure this product and use it, we'll demonstrate its use throughout this chapter so you can gain a better understanding of Compliance Settings. You can then take these examples and apply them to any product you choose.

MICROSOFT MATHEMATICS

This application provides a graphic calculator that plots in 2D and 3D, step-by-step equation solving, and useful tools to help students with math and science studies. This is a very small application, which is why we selected it to use in this example.

To download this application, go to

`https://www.microsoft.com/en-us/download/details.aspx?id=15702`

You will need to install this application on your Configuration Manager client.

Start by opening the Configuration Manager console, if necessary. From the Assets and Compliance workspace, expand Overview; then expand Compliance Settings, right-click Configuration Items, and click Create Configuration Item. You should be on the General page of the Create Configuration Item Wizard, as shown in Figure 13.3.

FIGURE 13.3
The Create Configuration Item Wizard, General page

To create a new configuration item, follow the instructions in the wizard. As part of this chapter you will be guided through the steps to create your first configuration item and apply this to any collection for evaluation. In this example we will validate that Microsoft Mathematics is installed. You could also use any of the applications discussed in Chapter 7, "Application Deployment."

Name, Description, and Category

In the Create Configuration Item Wizard, you begin on the General tab. Fill in the Name and Description fields and then create a category before moving to the next tab:

1. In the Name field, type **Microsoft Mathematics - Installed**.

2. In the Description field, type **This configuration item validates that the Microsoft Calculator is installed**.

3. Then, still in the Description field, press Ctrl+Enter to simulate a carriage return and add something descriptive stating when and by whom this item was created or changed.

   You could use your initials or the current date or a combination; it just needs to be something that will help you later know who created or changed the item and when, so that if anyone has a question about your configuration item, they know who to contact.

4. Click the Categories button to open the categories list.

The list is populated with a few default categories, and the top section allows you to add your own custom categories.

 Real World Scenario

WHAT IS A GOOD CATEGORY?

This will depend on your own administration style to a certain degree as well as the number of configuration items you will be creating. If you plan to check only Exchange servers for configuration drift, then you may not need any additional categories (or just a few more). If you plan to check clients for application settings, Internet Explorer for configuration drift, different operating systems files for the correct security settings, and so on, you would probably be wise to set up a standard for determining when new category types are needed and when you can use existing ones.

We have seen administrators who set up categories for every possible difference and others who set up none. If you are going to use the categories and build a large number of configuration items and baselines, then you should set up custom categories, but don't go overboard. Remember that categories are used to sort and search, so if you have too many, you get little or no benefit; too few is the same as none. It's best to use simple rules to create a standard: Does this configuration item fit into a category that exists already? Does that category generally and easily define this configuration item's purpose? If the answer is no to either, then you probably need a new category.

For this example, we are going to create a new category.

5. In the Manage Administrative Category section, select the Create button, then type **Microsoft** and click the OK button.

This should add it to the Administrative Categories section and select it.

6. Before you click OK, verify that your categories look like those in Figure 13.4.

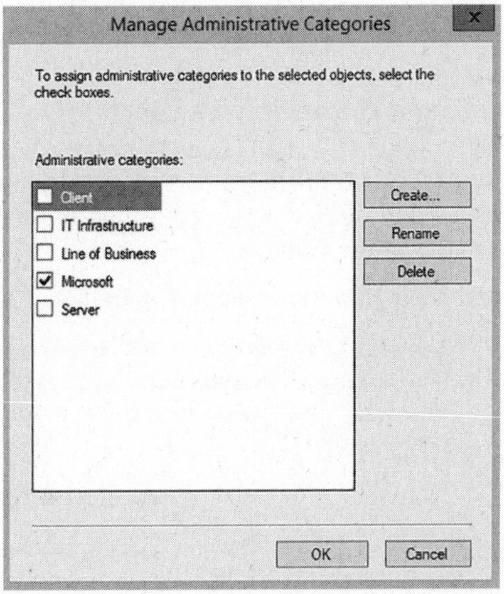

FIGURE 13.4
The Create Configuration Item Wizard's Manage Administrative Categories dialog box

7. Click OK to return to the General tab in the Create Configuration Item Wizard, which should now contain the item's name, a description, and your newly created category.

8. Verify that your dialog looks the same as Figure 13.5, and then select the check box "This configuration item contains application settings," and then click Next.

FIGURE 13.5
Create Configuration
Item Wizard, General
page completed

Choosing a Detection Method

The next tab in the wizard is Detection Methods, which is unique to the application configuration item type; it is not offered with the other types. The purpose of this tab is to specify the method used to verify that the application being checked for is installed on the client.

Four options are available:

◆ The first is Always Assume Application Is Installed.

This will skip any verification check, which sounds great; you're essentially telling the system to check the application for just the settings you're about to specify. But if you do this while using certain rules in creating your configuration baseline, you will run into problems.

BASELINE RULES

Which baseline rules cause problems? You will need to decide which if any of the following are problematic: if these optional application configuration items are detected, they must be properly configured.

These application configuration items must not be present. If another baseline is dependent on these configuration items, it may invalidate your dependency.

◆ The second option, Use Windows Installer Detection, is used to verify the product code the application vendor included with the MSI installer and the version.

◆ The third option is "Detect a specific application and deployment type"; you can select an existing application and deployment type that has been previously created.

◆ The final option is "Use a custom script to detect this application"; you can use VBScript, JScript, or PowerShell.

In the following procedure, you'll use the second option:

1. Select the Use Windows Installer detection radio button.

   This will require you to have access to the MSI installation file; after you download the 64-bit version of Microsoft Mathematics application from the Microsoft Downloads site, extract its content to `C:\temp`, using the command `MSetup_x64.exe /C`.

2. Assuming you have the Microsoft Mathematics files downloaded and extracted, click the Open button on the Detection Methods page, and browse to the `C:\temp` folder where you saved the MSI file.

3. Find and double-click the `MSMath_x64.msi` file, and it will populate the Product Code and Version fields on the Detection Methods page.

   If this application is installed on a per-user basis, you may also need to check the corresponding box for it to be properly detected. If it was installed for all users, that is not necessary.

4. Before moving on to the next step, creating and validating an object, verify that your wizard settings look similar to those in Figure 13.6. (Your product code and version number may be different.)

5. If everything is in order, click Next to proceed to the Settings tab.

Creating and Validating a Setting

On the Settings page, you tell the Create Configuration Item Wizard what type of setting to look for and where that setting is found.

FIGURE 13.6
CI application
Detection Methods
page

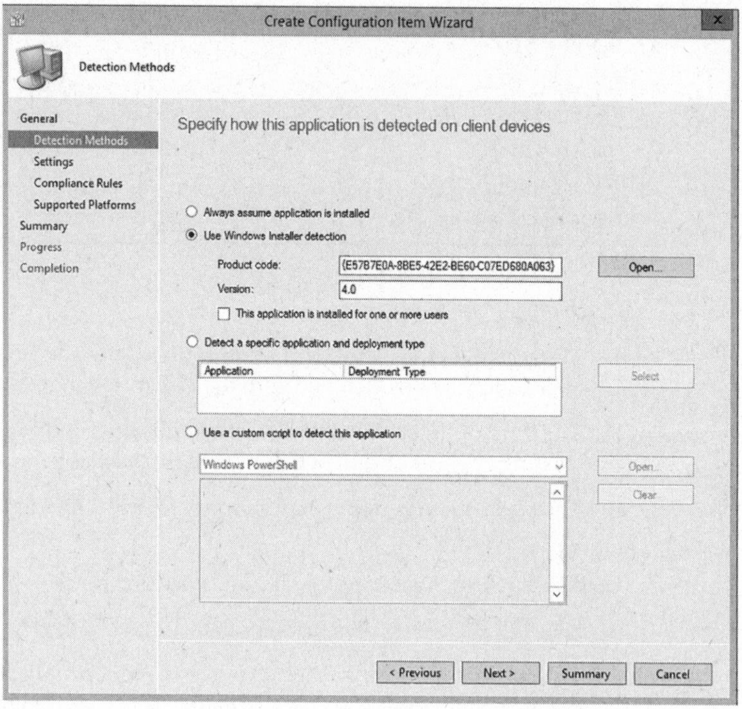

CREATING A SETTING

In the empty window there are four columns—Name, Setting Type, Inherited, and User Setting—and a New button.

1. Click New (see Figure 13.7); a Create Setting window will appear, as shown in Figure 13.8.

   The General tab of the Create Setting window has several fields and drop-down menus. The red circles with exclamation points indicate that the blank fields require input before you can create the configuration item. In the Name field, enter **MathApp version.**

2. From the Setting Type drop-down menu, select File System.

3. In the Path field, enter **C:\Program Files\Microsoft Mathematics**, and in the File Or Folder Name field, enter **MathApp.exe.**

WILDCARDS AND ENVIRONMENT VARIABLES WITH COMPLIANCE SETTINGS

The use of wildcards is allowed and actually required for the Specify File Or Folder To Assess For Compliance On The Computer section in the Path field. The ? and * characters are the permitted wildcards, but you should carefully consider whether to use them. Using wildcards can produce additional overhead when you're trying to find a file or folder, because the search will work exactly as instructed. Specifying the Windows directory, for example, and then telling it to search all subdirectories is not ideal. You can also make use of environment variables such as %ProgramFiles% or %AllUsersProfile%. The result may be that you get more than one result if the users all have the file or folder you are looking for in the search path.

FIGURE 13.7
CI application Settings
page

FIGURE 13.8
Create Setting dialog

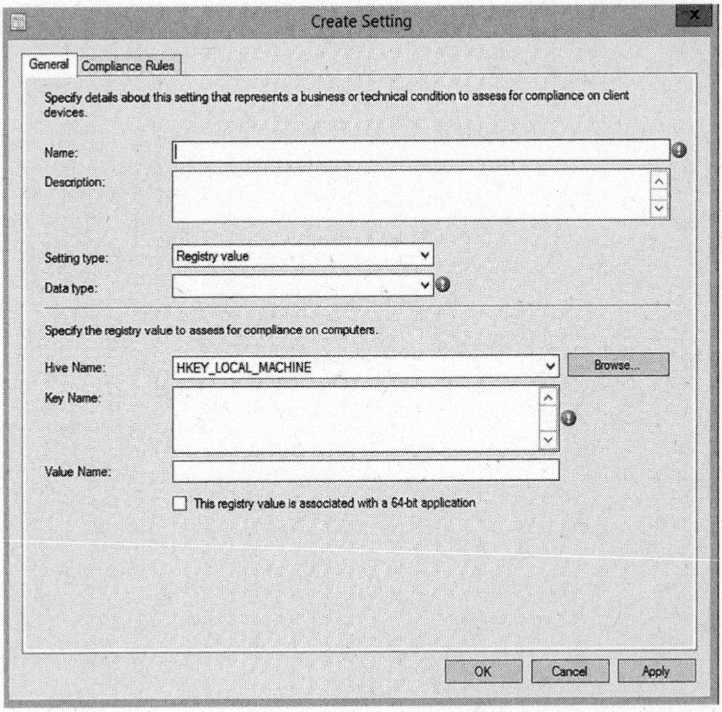

4. In the Description field, enter **This configuration item locates the file MathApp.exe and validates that it is the latest version of this file**.

5. Select the check box "This file or folder is associated with a 64-bit application."

64-BIT APPLICATIONS AND THE REGISTRY

Readers who have 64-bit applications should be aware of a possible issue with the registry and configuration baselines. Because of the registry reflector that mirrors certain registry keys for interpretability, it is possible that you could detect the presence of two registry keys with a single configuration baseline. If you are running 64-bit applications, you will need to check for this before deploying a configuration baseline containing a configuration item that involves checking for a registry key associated with a 64-bit application.

You have finished creating the object's details by telling Compliance Settings what you are looking for and where to look for it. The next step is to validate the setting by telling Compliance Settings the specifics of the setting to validate.

6. Make sure your General page looks like the one in Figure 13.9 and then click the Compliance Rules tab.

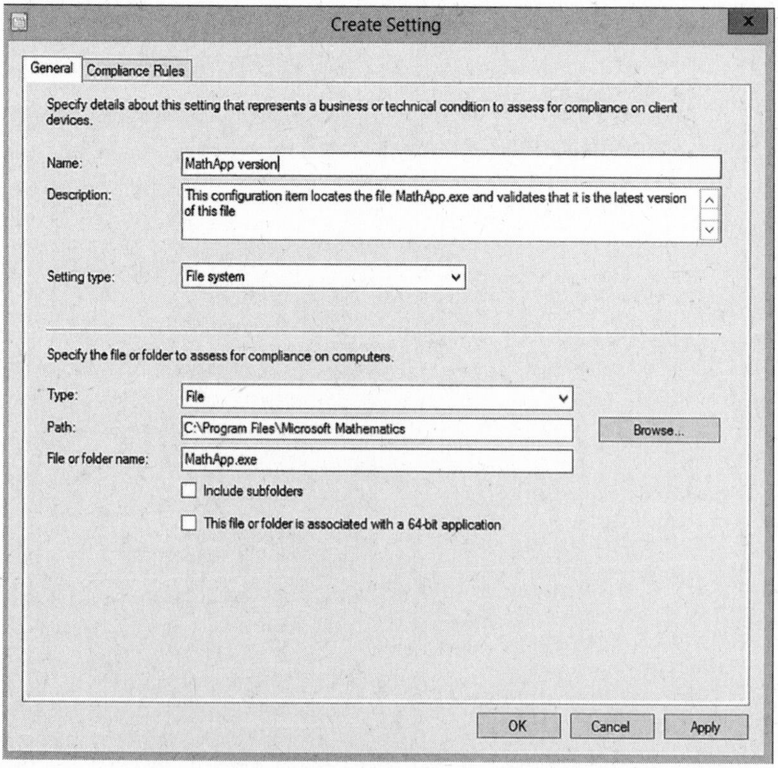

FIGURE 13.9
General page of the Create Setting dialog box completed

VALIDATING A SETTING

Now that you have created your setting, you need to tell Compliance Settings how you want this CI to validate the file.

1. As you did when creating a new setting, click the New button, shown in Figure 13.10, to get started.

FIGURE 13.10

The Compliance Rules page

The top field of the Create Rule dialog box contains the name of the compliance rule. This is a required field, and a value will be supplied by default.

2. In the Name field, enter a rule name of **File_MathApp.exe_Date_Modified**.

3. In the Description text box, enter the following or something similar, but make sure you also put your initials and the date in the event someone else reviewing this rule has questions: **Validates that the MathApp.exe file in the Microsoft Mathematics folder has the latest version of the file approved and distributed by IT. 12/06/2016.**

In the Create Rule dialog box, you tell Compliance Settings exactly how to validate this file. The Setting Must Comply With The Following Rule field in the middle of the page is grayed out and unavailable because you have already selected the type of setting you are going to validate against. Next to that is a drop-down menu, where you have nine operators to choose from:

- Equals
- Not Equal To
- Greater Than
- Less Than
- Between
- Greater Than Or Equal To
- Less Than Or Equal To
- One Of
- None Of

If you choose Between as the operator, you get the option to specify a range.

4. In this example, choose the Equals operator, and in The Following Values field, enter the date and time for which you want the rule to be applied.

   Obviously, because you are going to use this as a test, you should use a date that is not its original date, or input your validation date and time.

   In the bottom section of the Create Rule dialog, choose the level of Noncompliance Severity For Reports should this check fail on one of your Configuration Manager clients. There are five levels to choose from:

   - None
   - Information
   - Warning
   - Critical
   - Critical With Event

   The Information, Warning, Critical, and Critical With Event levels report back to Configuration Manager, but None does not write an event to the application event log in Windows as the last one does. This was made an option to prevent Compliance Settings rules from filling up the event logs on clients if a check comes back as invalid too many times. This might happen if, for example, you input the wrong validation data or if something out of your control occurs, such as an upgrade or service pack installation.

5. In this exercise, select None if you don't already have it selected, and then verify that your window looks like Figure 13.11 before clicking OK to continue.

FIGURE 13.11
The Compliance Rules,
Create Rule dialog box

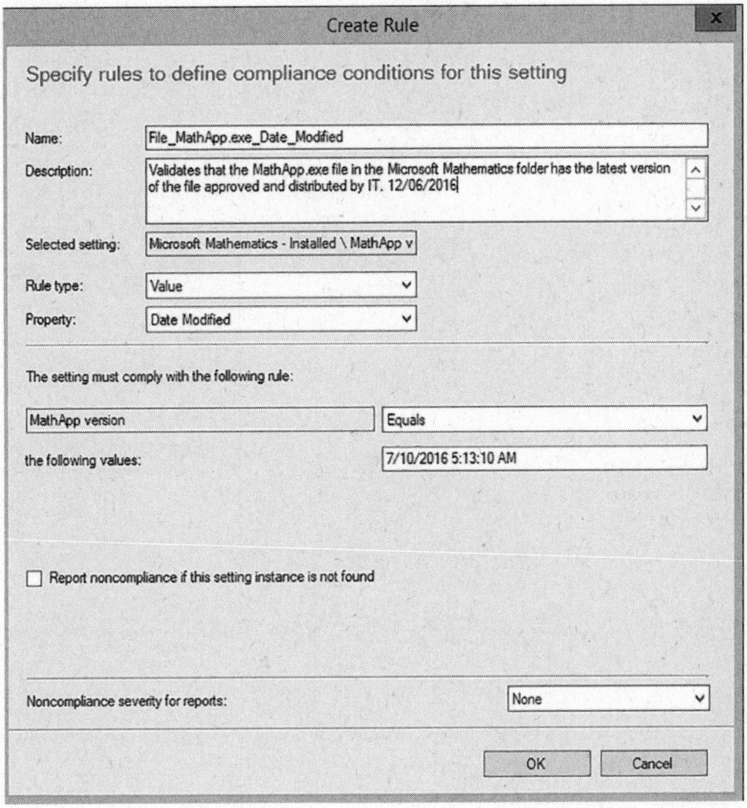

6. Return to the Compliance Rules window, where in the formerly empty section you'll now see the new compliance rules for this file.

   You now have to tell Compliance Settings if you want it to report on a noncompliant event and, if so, the details of when and how it should report.

   Select the File_MathApp.exe_Date_Modified rule you just created, and click Edit. Check the "Report noncompliance if this setting instance is not found" check box so that it is enabled.

   This option turns on and off the reporting of a noncompliant client and allows you to set the severity of noncompliance as well as at what point it should report. Click OK twice.

7. You have now created your first compliance item. After reviewing all information and verifying that it is correct, click Next twice to validate the supported operating systems.

   This is the only object you are going to create in this first example, but we'll cover other tabs and their options in the following examples or in later examples.

8. Because you are not going to make changes to this configuration item, you can click through to the end using the Next button at the bottom of the window.

   Eventually you should reach the Summary tab, shown in Figure 13.12, which will give you a list of all the options and settings selected while creating this configuration item.

FIGURE 13.12
Application CI
Summary page

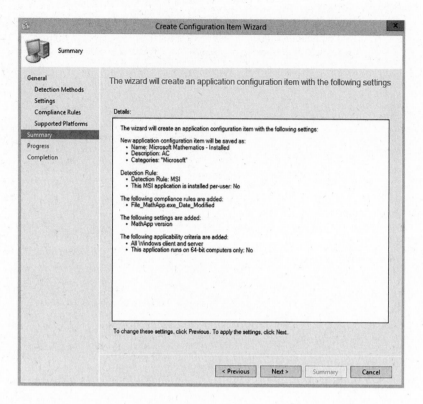

9. Verify that the settings are as you expect them to be; if any are not, use the Previous button or the tabs to make any modifications.

10. Once you have checked to ensure that everything is in order, click the Next button or the Progress tab to start the process of building the configuration item.

   After a short period, the progress indicator and window should disappear and you should see the Completion window, which says

   ```
   Success: The Create Configuration Item Wizard completed successfully.
   ```

   It also shows a list of the settings you chose. Verify again that everything is listed as expected. You can now click the Close button to complete the wizard and return to the Configuration Manager console.

Building a Configuration Baseline

You have built a configuration item to make your configuration baseline, which is what you assign to your clients to check for drift.

Briefly, you have a configuration item that validates that your Microsoft Mathematics application is installed and the file is the latest file you deployed. In order to deploy this compliance setting and rule, you need to create a baseline and apply this baseline to a specific collection to validate its compliance.

Configuration baselines in System Center Configuration Manager contain configuration items and optionally other configuration baselines. After a configuration baseline is created, you can deploy it to a collection so that devices in that collection will download the configuration baseline and assess their compliance with it.

Configuration baselines in System Center Configuration Manager can contain specific revisions of configuration items or can be configured to always use the latest version of a configuration item.

Creating the Initial Baseline

As it does with most tasks, Configuration Manager provides a wizard to guide you in creating a configuration baseline.

1. In the Configuration Manager console, choose the Assets and Compliance workspace, select Overview ➤ Compliance Settings ➤ Configuration Baselines, and right-click Create Configuration Baseline.

   You should now see the Create Configuration Baseline Wizard, shown in Figure 13.13. Here you select the categories and input the name, description, and configuration data.

FIGURE 13.13
Create Configuration
Baseline Wizard,
Create Configuration
Baseline dialog

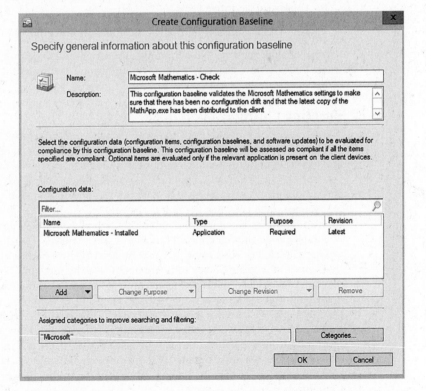

2. Fill in the following details:

   Name: **Microsoft Mathematics - Check**

   Description: **This configuration baseline validates the Microsoft Mathematics settings to make sure that there has been no configuration drift and that the latest copy of the MathApp.exe has been distributed to the client.**

3. To select Microsoft as the category, click the Categories button to display a list. This section is at the bottom of the window.

   The Configuration Data list displays all the configuration items or configuration baselines that are included in the configuration baseline.

4. Click Add to add a new item to the list. You can choose from the following:

   Configuration items

   Software updates

   Configuration baselines

5. In the Add Configuration Items window, choose the item Microsoft Mathematics - Installed.

6. Click Add, and then click OK.

7. Verify that your settings match those shown in Figure 13.13 and click OK.

You can now click the Close button and return to the Configuration Manager console, where you will next assign your new configuration baseline to clients that will be evaluated for compliance.

Baseline Configuration Data

The process of creating rules is similar to the way you build rules in Outlook. Or you can think of it as telling Compliance Settings a story or writing a recipe to build your baseline. The available baseline configuration data options include those that reference which operating system you want to check for; in this option you will be able to see all the different operating systems and service pack levels. If you have not built a configuration item to check for a specific operating system, when you click the link in the rule there will be no configuration items to choose from and nothing to put into this rule. Although our example doesn't include them, Figure 13.14 illustrates the additional selections available when you have created one or more CIs.

One available rule is Checking For Software Updates. Earlier in the chapter we mentioned that you cannot create CIs for software updates in the same location as the other CI types and you must specify the updates when creating your configuration baseline; this is exactly where you would specify the software updates to check for. If you select the software updates option, the Add Software Updates window will open. This window will show a similar display for the software updates node in the Configuration Manager console, where you can select the updates you wish to add to your baseline (see Figure 13.15). It is important to understand that you will not see software updates that you have already added to the baseline. You can see the software updates that are included in the configuration baseline by viewing its properties in the Configuration Manager console.

FIGURE 13.14
Add Configuration
Items

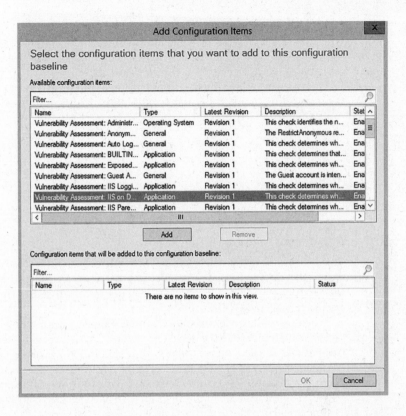

FIGURE 13.15
Add Software Updates
window

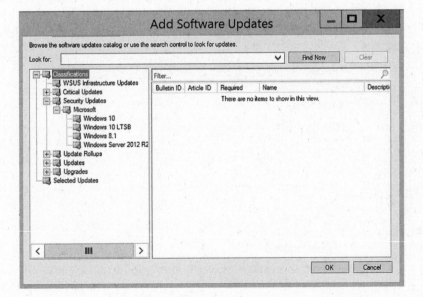

Another option that you can use is Configuration Baselines. This is how you would reuse other configuration baselines that you have created and thus save quite a few steps. Clicking this option opens another window that lists the configuration baselines previously created and available to select, much like in Figure 13.14.

We have saved the other three options for last because they are all related to application CI types, differing in the way that they build the rules for your baseline. An application-type CI can be marked in one of three ways:

◆ Required

◆ Optional

◆ Prohibited

Let's consider how each of these might be used when building a configuration baseline.

REQUIRED

This rule means that if you select an application CI, it will use the detection method specified to ensure that the application is installed. We used two different detection methods when we built the application CIs for Microsoft Mathematics. For the first one, we pointed it at the MSI file and got the version and GUID.

When you build an application CI and use the "always assume installed" detection method, you are simply skipping the detection method. Thus, there is no chance that the detection method will fail, and the next step in your application CI will do its check. Once a CI fails a check, the remainder of the CI checks to see if settings or objects are not validated against the client. The actual status returned can vary depending on these settings as well; if the detection method is specified and it fails, it will return Not Detected compliance.

You would use this to add general CIs to your list of rules but also for applications that you want to ensure are installed, or at least to detect that they are installed and that they are configured correctly. Going back to the CIs we created for Microsoft Mathematics, if we specified the CIs that detect if the latest `MathApp.exe` file is on the client, the CI for Microsoft Mathematics would first have to pass the detection method we specified. So if the version or GUID returned Non-compliant, then the rest of the CI validation would be skipped and we would get a status message indicating that the application was not detected.

OPTIONAL

The rule that if optional application CIs are detected, they must be properly configured means that if you make application CIs part of the baseline and they fail to be detected, then the validation checks that are part of that CI will be skipped; if the application is detected, it will then validate the objects or settings specified in the CI and report compliance or noncompliance. A typical use for this type of rule might be a situation in which you are not sure an application is installed on the client, but in the event that it is, you want to make sure that the application is configured correctly.

PROHIBITED

The last application CI rule specifies that selected application CIs must *not* be present. This type of rule could be used to make sure that an application is not present on a system. For instance, if you are checking the configuration of Microsoft Mathematics 4.*x*, you might want to make sure that Microsoft Mathematics 3.*x* was properly removed. Assuming you had a baseline that you used to check the configuration of Microsoft Mathematics 3.*x*, you could select one of these rules and run it to validate that the application had been previously uninstalled.

Assigning the Configuration Baseline to Clients

Now that you have all the baselines configured, you need to assign them to the clients or all your hard work will be in vain. Assigning the configuration baselines to the clients will allow Configuration Manager to monitor the clients and ensure the baselines are met.

1. Back in the Configuration Manager console, you should still see the configuration baselines. If you highlight the newly created baseline, you will see its details at the bottom of your console.

2. To assign this configuration baseline to clients for validation, right-click the baseline and choose Deploy.

   This will start the Deploy Configuration Baselines Wizard, shown in Figure 13.16.

FIGURE 13.16
Deploy Configuration
Baselines Wizard

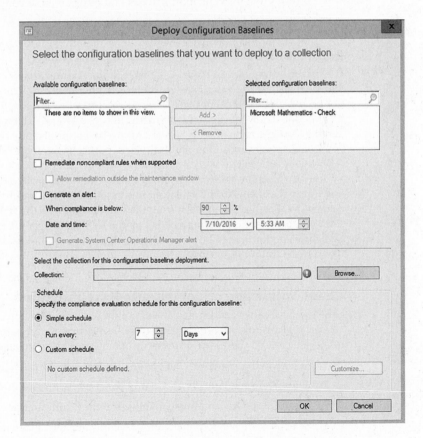

This should prepopulate with the configuration baseline that you used to launch the wizard; as you can see, you can add or remove configuration baselines by clicking the Add or Remove button on the center.

3. At this time if you see the correct configuration baseline in the available list, select the baseline and click Add to move it to the list on the right.

4. In the Select The Collection For This Configuration Baseline Deployment section, indicate the collection you are going to assign this baseline to by clicking the Browse button.

   Be sure to select a collection that includes the clients where you have installed and configured the Microsoft Mathematics software.

5. After you have selected the appropriate collection, click OK to go back to the deployment baseline window.

   Next, you set the compliance evaluation schedule, much as you do with a deployment. You can create a simple schedule such as Run Every 7 Days or create a custom schedule for more flexibility.

6. For the example, choose Custom Schedule and set it to reoccur every four hours; this ensures that the validation will run and return data so you can examine the reports.

7. After reviewing the settings, proceed to assigning the baseline by clicking OK.

Additional Configuration Baseline Options

Within the Configuration Manager console, some additional options are available when you view the configuration baseline folder. On the ribbon, there is an option called Import Configuration Data. This option allows you to import a CAB file that could have been created by a vendor, using an external tool such as Silect Software's CP Studio, or it could come from another Configuration Manager. If you have a baseline currently selected, you should see some additional options, including the ability to export configuration data. This will allow you to export your data so that you can import it to another site or edit it with an external tool.

You also have the ability to enable or disable the baseline; if you select the Disable option, it will stop the clients from evaluating this baseline. Once a baseline is disabled, the option changes to allow you to enable it from the same location on the ribbon. You can also view the XML that defines this baseline by clicking the View XML Definition button of the ribbon. The Categorize option should be self-evident at this point; you can add or remove categories from the baseline using this button.

Client Validation of Compliance Baseline Rules

Once you have deployed the compliance baseline to a collection, you should log on to a client and validate that this rule has been applied and what its current state is; this will help you to understand better if the rule has been applied correctly or not and if the compliance state is the desired one.

1. Log on to the Windows client or any resource on the collection deployed.

2. Choose Control Panel ➢ All Control Panel Items, and locate Configuration Manager.

3. Open Configuration Manager and select the Configurations tab.

4. Select the Microsoft Mathematics baseline and click Evaluate. Note that if the client has not polled for machine policy from the Configuration Manager site server, you might also need to first request the machine policy update action.

As shown in Figure 13.17, the Compliance State field now shows Non-Compliant.

FIGURE 13.17
Configuration Manager
client configurations

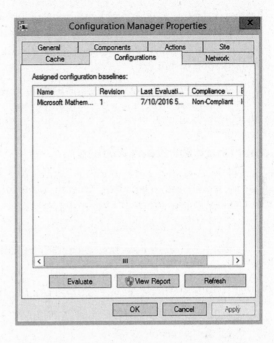

5. Now click View Report and wait for Internet Explorer to show the results (see Figure 13.18).

FIGURE 13.18
Compliance
report

Setting Name	Setting Type	Setting Description	Rule Name	Rule Description	Severity	Instance Data				
						Expression	Current Value	Instance Source	Rule Type	
MathApp version	File	This configuration item locates the file MathApp.exe and validates that it is the latest version of this file	File_MathApp.exe_Date_Modified	Validates that the MathApp.exe file in the Microsoft Mathematics folder has the latest version of the file approved and distributed by IT. 12/06/2016	None	Equals 2016-07-10T11:13:10Z	2010-11-10T19:14:42Z	Location = c:\program files\microsoft mathematics\MathApp.exe, Property = DateModified	Value	

REVISION: 1
COMPLIANCE STATE: Non-Compliant
NON-COMPLIANCE SEVERITY: None
DESCRIPTION: This configuration baseline validates the Microsoft Mathematics settings to make sure that there has been no configuration drift and that the latest copy of the MathApp.exe has been distributed to the client

NAME: Microsoft Mathematics - Installed
TYPE: Application Configuration
REVISION: 1
COMPLIANCE STATE: Non-Compliant
NON-COMPLIANCE SEVERITY: None
DESCRIPTION: AC

Non-Compliant Rules:

Once you have finished reviewing the compliance setting results, you can also look at the client log files to see more details about the compliance state; two of these log files are as follows:

dcmagent.log   Provides high-level information about the evaluation of assigned configuration baselines and desired configuration management processes

ciagent.log   Provides information about downloading, storing, and accessing assigned configuration baselines

Open these log files using CMTrace.exe and you will see more details. Now that you have been able to successfully apply a configuration baseline, you may want to try this again using a production application for which you may need to confirm its compliance state.

COMPLIANCE SETTINGS ALERTS

As part of the new alert and notification system, once the compliance baseline is deployed you can decide if you need to get alerts when the compliance check falls below a specific percentage. To do this you must perform the following task:

1. In the Configuration Manager console, choose the Assets And Compliance workspace.

2. Under the Overview section, expand Compliance Settings.

3. Select Configuration Baselines.

4. In the right section select Microsoft Mathematics - Check; right-click and select Properties.

5. Click the Deployment tab.

6. Select the deployed collection and click Properties.

7. Click Generate An Alert, as shown previously in Figure 13.16.

8. Set the compliance percentage to 95.

9. Click OK twice.

This will generate the alert configuration on the Monitoring workspace should less than 95 percent of the systems in the targeted collection be noncompliant.

Compliance Settings Reporting

After a short period of time you should be able to run several of the reports included with Configuration Manager for compliance and settings management. These reports can be customized to suit your needs, or you can build your own reports if they don't provide the level of detail you require. Reports are located in the Monitoring workspace, under Overview ➢ Reporting ➢ Reports; in the search criteria look for Compliance And Settings Management. The current list of reports is as follows:

◆ Compliance history of a configuration baseline

◆ Compliance history of a configuration item

◆ Details of compliant rules of configuration items in a configuration baseline for an asset

- Details of conflicting rules of configuration items in a configuration baseline for an asset
- Details of errors of configuration items in a configuration baseline for an asset
- Details of noncompliant rules of configuration items in a configuration baseline for an asset
- Details of remediated rules of configuration items in a configuration baseline for an asset
- List of assets by compliance state for a configuration baseline
- List of assets by compliance state for a configuration item in a configuration baseline
- List of noncompliant apps and devices for a specified user
- List of rules conflicting with a specified rule for an asset
- List of unknown assets for a configuration baseline
- List of unknown assets for a configuration item
- Rules and errors summary of configuration items in a configuration baseline for an asset
- Summary compliance by configuration baseline
- Summary compliance by configuration items for a configuration baseline
- Summary compliance by configuration policies
- Summary compliance of a configuration baseline for a collection
- Summary of users who have noncompliant apps
- Terms and conditions acceptance

Configuring Windows Information Protection

Starting with version 1606, it is possible to configure a new feature of Windows 10 1607 called Windows Information Protection (WIP). Similar to Mobile Application Management for Android and iOS, Windows Information Protection (formerly known as Enterprise Data Protection) allows you to configure restrictions and settings to protect your enterprise data. With WIP, for example, you can block, "allow override," or simply audit how users share data and you can decide which application can be used to open files that belong to your company.

The configuration steps are very similar to the ones for configuring a traditional CI.

This is how you could configure a basic WIP policy:

1. In the Configuration Manager console, choose the Assets And Compliance workspace.

2. Under the Overview section, expand Compliance Settings.

3. Select Configuration Item and then right-click to open the Create Configuration Item wizard.

4. On the General page, under Settings For Devices Managed With The Configuration Manager Client, select Windows 10 (as shown in Figure 13.19), and then click Next.

FIGURE 13.19
Windows 10
Configuration Item

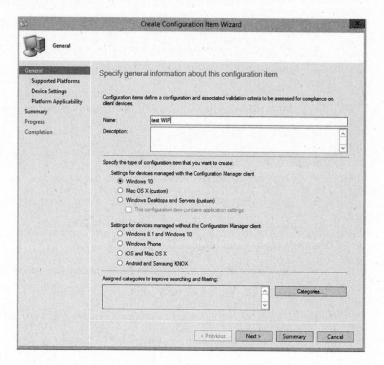

5. On the Supported Platform page, select Windows 10 and click Next.

6. On the Device Settings page, select Windows Information Protection, as shown in Figure 13.20, and click Next.

FIGURE 13.20
Selecting Windows
Information Protection

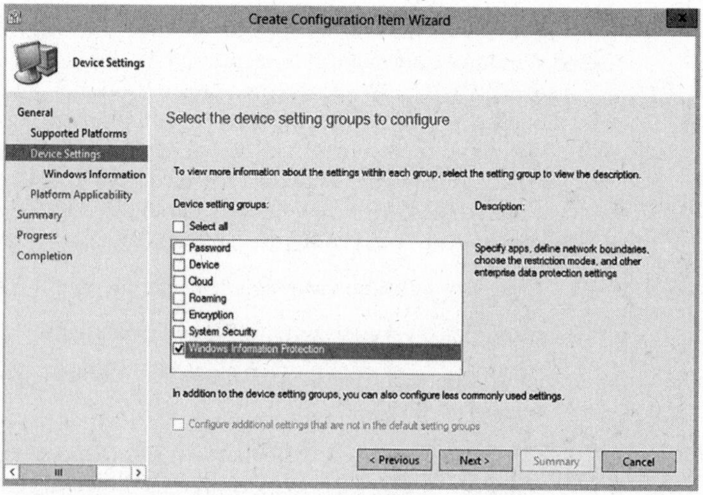

7. On the Windows Information Protection page, note that there is already a default rule for Configuration Manager settings, as shown in Figure 13.21. This rule is needed for the correct operation of the Configuration Manager agent and the Windows client, and should not be modified.

FIGURE 13.21
Windows Information
Protection Default
allow rule

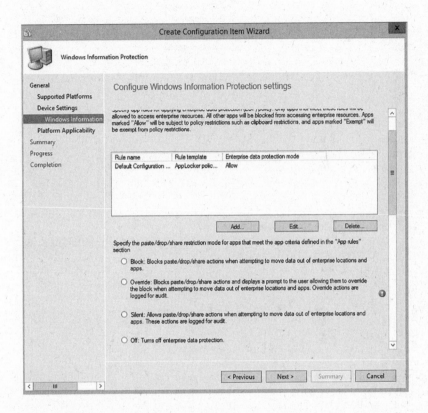

8. To create your own rule(s), click Add (see Figure 13.21) and change the Rule Template field to AppLocker Policy File, as shown in Figure 13.22. It is much easier to create rules based on AppLocker Policy files so that you don't have to worry about putting the correct publisher, product name, binary name, and version manually in the wizard (see Figure 13.23). All you need is a computer with Windows 10 version 1607, and to run secpol.msc there. Then, select Application Control Policies ➤ AppLocker, right-click Executable Rules (to create a rule for a "traditional" desktop app), or right-click Packaged App Rules (to create a rule for a "modern" store app). When you are happy with all the rules you have created, right-click AppLocker to export them in one XML file (see Figure 13.24). This is the AppLocker policy file needed in the Configuration Manager console.

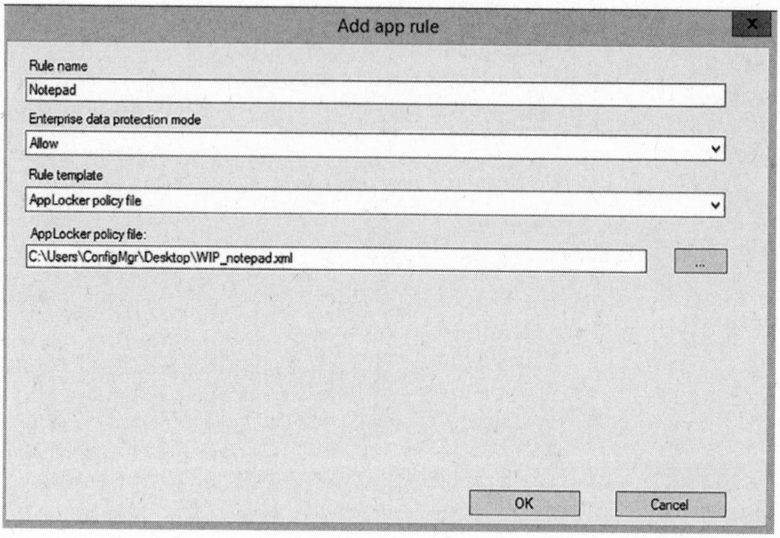

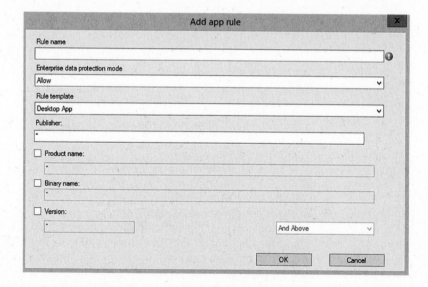

FIGURE 13.22
Creating a WIP rule based on AppLocker Policy files

FIGURE 13.23
Create a WIP rule by publisher, product name, binary name, and version

9. Enter a name in the Rule Name field, and select Allow As Enterprise Data Protection Mode. Click the ellipsis (...) to select your pre-created AppLocker Policy file; then go back to the wizard by clicking OK. The result should be similar to Figure 13.25.

10. Under "Specify the paste/drop/share restriction mode for apps that meet the app criteria defined in the 'App rules' section," select "Override: Blocks paste/drop/share actions and displays a prompt to the user..."

FIGURE 13.24
Create an AppLocker
policy file (XML)

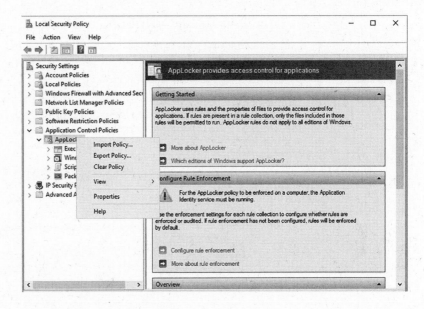

FIGURE 13.25
Configure Windows
Information Protection
Settings, part 1

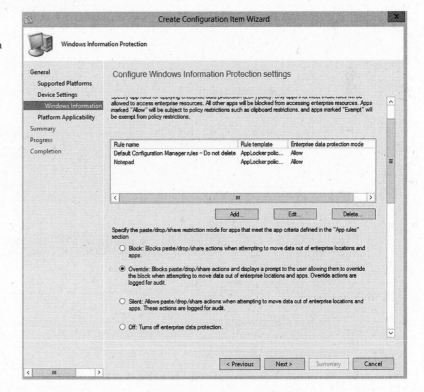

11. As shown in Figure 13.26, fill in all the required fields:

   ◆ Corporate Identity: This is the label that will show up in the managed app if you click the briefcase icon overlay (see Figure 13.27).

   ◆ Corporate Network Definition: Here you have to specify at least one Enterprise Network domain name and one IPv4 range. This is the boundary that will be used to define which documents are considered enterprise data; documents created outside this boundary are considered personal data.

FIGURE 13.26
Configure Windows
Information Protection
Settings, part 2

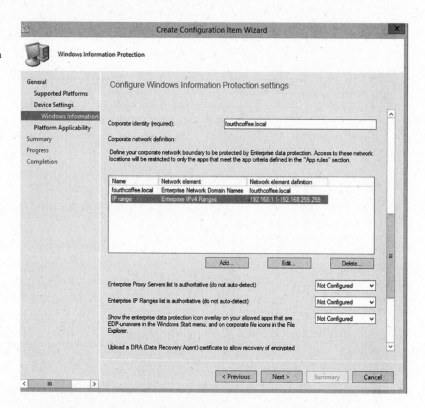

FIGURE 13.27
Enterprise Data
Protection icon overlay
(briefcase)

12. For the option "Show the enterprise data protection icon overlay on your allowed apps that are EDP-Unaware in the Windows Star Menu and on corporate file icons in File Explorer," select Yes.

13. Click Browse to upload a Data Recovery Agent certificate.

> ### WHAT IS THE DATA RECOVERY AGENT (DRA) CERTIFICATE? HOW DO I GET ONE?
>
> When WIP is used, all enterprise data on the user's device is encrypted using Encrypting File System (EFS): users can only decrypt documents that they have created or copied to their PC. If a user leaves the company or the user certificate gets revoked in error and the protected data needs to be available, the private key of the DRA certificate can also be used to decrypt that data. This is possible because when the WIP policy is provisioned to a device, the public key of the DRA certificate is also provisioned to the device, so the file is actually encrypted with both the user public key and the DRA public key.
>
> The DRA certificate can be created either using your existing PKI Infrastructure, or as a self-signed certificate, using the command `cipher /r:DRA_filename`. The following article
>
> https://technet.microsoft.com/en-us/library/cc512680.aspx
>
> contains all the information you need to know on how to create, export, and use a Data Recovery Agent certificate.

14. Confirm that the end result looks like Figure 13.28; then click Next to go to the Platform Applicability page.

FIGURE 13.28
Configure Windows Information Protection Settings, part 3

15. Click Next to go to the Summary page, and review the settings.

16. Lastly, click Next and Close to complete the creation of the WIP CI.

As with any other CI, you will need to add it to a configuration baseline and deploy it to a collection.

It is important to note that when you deploy a WIP baseline, you will also have to select Remediate Noncompliant Rules When Supported, as shown in Figure 13.29, so the app restrictions will be applied correctly.

FIGURE 13.29
Deploying a WIP policy with the remediate noncompliant rule

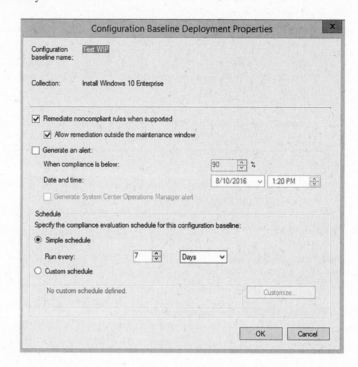

After you have created your first WIP baseline, you could test it by trying to copy and paste some text from a managed application to an unmanaged application. You should get a pop-up message asking "Change this content to personal?" (see Figure 13.30). This is because you have selected Override in the Windows Information Protection policy.

FIGURE 13.30
Overriding the behavior of WIP

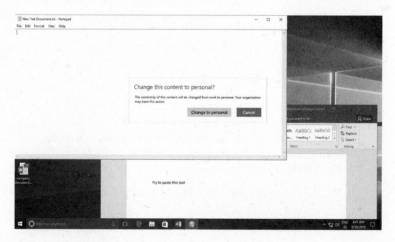

If you create a new policy, and you select Block in the restriction mode, when you copy and paste from a managed to an unmanaged application you will get a "This is work content only" pop-up, as shown in Figure 13.31.

FIGURE 13.31
Blocking the behavior
of WIP

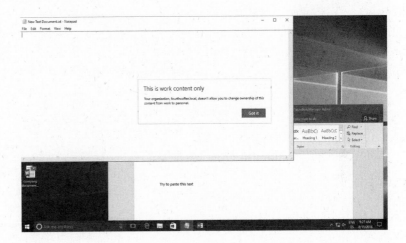

WIP events are visible with the Event Viewer, under Application And Services Logs ➤ Microsoft ➤ Windows ➤ EDP-audit-regular.

Importing Configuration Packs

In this section you will learn how to implement a configuration pack from the Security Compliance Manager tool. This tool has different baselines, and each of the baselines can be exported to Configuration Manager and later or imported as Compliance Settings data.

WHAT IS SECURITY COMPLIANCE MANAGER?

Microsoft Security Compliance Manager 4.0 provides security configuration recommendations from Microsoft, centralized security baseline management features, a baseline portfolio, customization capabilities, and security baseline export flexibility to accelerate your organization's ability to efficiently manage the security and compliance process for the most widely used Microsoft products.

To download this tool, go to

https://www.microsoft.com/en-us/download/details.aspx?id=53353

To learn more about this tool, go to

http://technet.microsoft.com/en-us/library/cc677002.aspx

Figure 13.32 shows the Security Compliance Manager console focused on Internet Explorer 11 Computer Security Compliance. As an example, to import the Internet Explorer 11 configuration pack, perform the following steps:

FIGURE 13.32
Microsoft
Security
Compliance
Manager

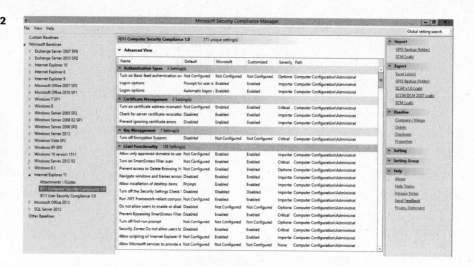

1. Download Security Compliance Manager from the Microsoft Download site.

2. Install Security Compliance Manager (SCM).

   Note that SCM requires a SQL instance; the instance can be SQL Express (at a minimum, SQL Express 2008 with Service Pack 4), or Windows Internal Database (WID).

3. Confirm that the product has been installed and all the latest baselines have been downloaded.

4. Launch the Security Compliance Manager tool.

5. For the Microsoft baseline, select Internet Explorer 11.

6. For Internet Explorer 11, select IE 11 Computer Security Compliance 1.0.

7. In the right section, the Export option will be enabled; click SCCM DCM 2007 (.cab).

   The Export To SCCM DCM 2007 dialog box will open. Note that even though it says SCCM DCM 2007, this works great with any version of Configuration Manager.

8. Save the CAB file to a known location.

9. Open the Configuration Manager console.

10. Choose the Assets And Compliance workspace.

11. In the navigation pane, expand Compliance Settings, and then right-click Configuration Baselines.

12. Choose Import Configuration Data.

    The Import Configuration Data Wizard will appear, as shown in Figure 13.33.

FIGURE 13.33
Import Configuration
Data Wizard, Select
Files page

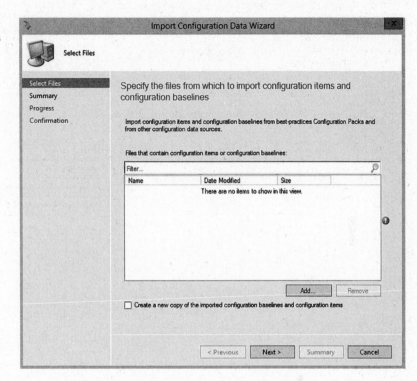

13. Click Add.

14. The Open dialog box will appear; locate the file saved in Step 8 and click Open. Confirm (by selecting Yes) that you want to import a CAB file that could not be verified.

15. Click Next. The import will analyze the CAB file.

The Import Configuration Data Wizard Summary page will list one configuration baseline and five configuration items.

16. Click Next.

The Import Configuration Data Wizard will complete at this point. Your Confirmation screen should look like the one in Figure 13.34. You can close the wizard.

Now that you have imported the configuration data to Configuration Manager's Compliance Settings, you can deploy this baseline to any collection and evaluate the current compliance state for Internet Explorer 11. This will also give you a better idea of how to use Compliance Settings and the configuration items.

FIGURE 13.34
Import Configuration
Data Wizard,
Confirmation page

VULNERABILITY ASSESSMENT CONFIGURATION PACK

If you are interested in trying more ready-made baselines, you could also implement the Vulnerability Assessment Configuration Pack that has been created to help identify missing security updates and misconfigurations in an environment. The CAB file with the baselines and instructions are available for download from

https://www.microsoft.com/en-us/download/details.aspx?id=51948

User Data and Profiles

User data and profiles configuration items contain settings that control how users in your hierarchy manage folder redirection, offline files, and roaming profiles on computers that run Windows 8 and later versions. You can deploy them to a collection of users and then monitor their compliance from the Monitoring node of the Configuration Manager console.

The following are examples of user data and profiles configuration items you can manage in Configuration Manager:

◆ Redirect a user's Documents folder to a network share

◆ Ensure that specified files stored on the network are available on a user's computer when the network connection is unavailable

◆ Configure which files in a user's roaming profile are synchronized with a network share when the users log on and off

Use the following steps to create a user data and profiles configuration item in Configuration Manager:

1. Open the Configuration Manager console and select Assets And Compliance ➤ Overview.

2. Choose Compliance Settings ➤ Users Data And Profiles. Right-click and select Create User Data And Profiles Configuration Item.

3. In the wizard, as shown in Figure 13.35, enter the information requested and select the appropriate check boxes:

   a. Name: Enter the name of this configuration item.

   b. Description: Enter details about this CI.

   c. Folder Redirection: Enable this check box if you are going to configure it as folder redirection.

   d. Offline Files: Enable this check box if you plan to configure offline files.

   e. Roaming User Profiles: Enable this check box if you want to configure roaming user profiles.

FIGURE 13.35
Create User Data And Profiles Configuration Item Wizard

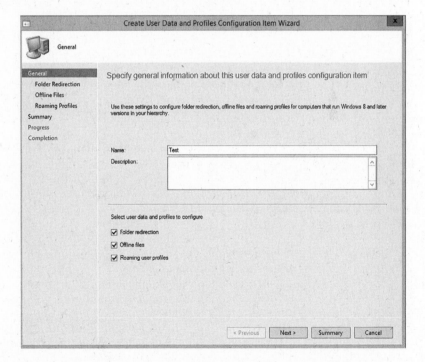

4. Click Next to go to the Folder Redirection step, shown in Figure 13.36. Specify how you want the client computers of users who receive this configuration item to manage folder redirection. You can configure settings for any device the user logs onto or for only the user's primary devices. This section will be available only if you checked the Folder Redirection box on the previous screen.

FIGURE 13.36
Create User Data And Profiles Configuration Item Wizard, Folder Redirection screen

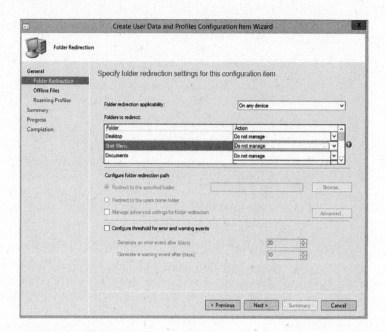

5. Click Next to go to the Offline Files page, shown in Figure 13.37. You can enable or disable the use of offline files for users who receive this configuration item and configure settings for the behavior of the offline files. This section will appear only if you checked the Offline Files box on the initial screen shown in Figure 13.35.

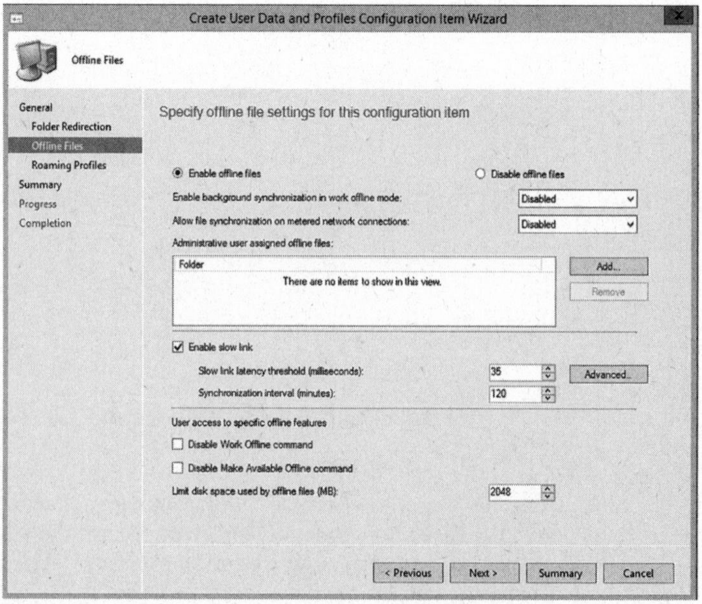

FIGURE 13.37
Create User Data And Profiles Configuration Item Wizard, Offline Files screen

6. Click Next to go to the Roaming Profiles page, shown in Figure 13.38. You can configure whether roaming profiles are available on computers that the users log onto and also configure further information about how these profiles behave. This section will appear only if you checked the Roaming Profiles box shown in Figure 13.35.

FIGURE 13.38

Create User Data And Profiles Configuration Item Wizard, Roaming Profiles screen

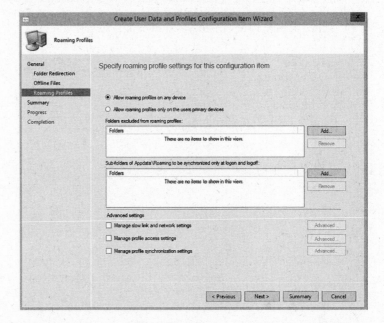

7. Click Next to go to the Summary page, as shown in Figure 13.39. On this screen you can review the actions that are going to be taken and then click Next to create the configuration item.

FIGURE 13.39

Create User Data And Profiles Configuration Item Wizard, Summary screen

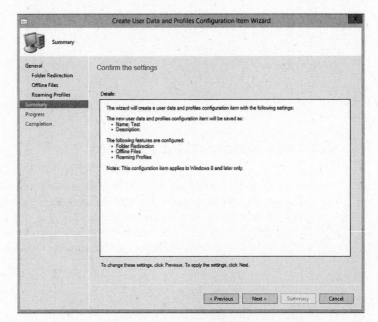

8. Once you have completed the wizard, the New User Data And Profiles configuration item is shown in the User Data and Profiles node of the Assets And Compliance workspace. From here you can just deploy it to the desired collection.

Unlike with other configuration items, you do not add these to configuration baselines before you deploy them. You can deploy them directly with the Deploy User Data And Profiles Configuration Policy dialog, as shown in Figure 13.40.

FIGURE 13.40
Deploy User Data And Profiles Configuration Policy dialog

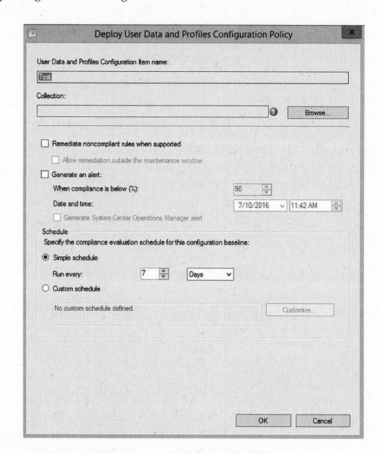

Remote Connection Profiles

Remote connection profiles in System Center Configuration Manager provide a set of tools and resources to help you create, deploy, and monitor remote connection settings to devices in your organization. By deploying these settings, you minimize the effort that end users require to connect to their computers on the corporate network. You can use remote connection profiles in Configuration Manager to allow users to remotely connect to work computers when they are not connected to the domain or if their personal computers are connected over the Internet.

Remote connection profiles let you deploy Remote Desktop Connection settings to users in the Configuration Manager hierarchy. Users can then use the company portal to access any of their primary work computers by using the Remote Desktop Connection settings provided by the company portal. Microsoft Intune is required if you want users to connect to their work PCs by using the company portal.

To configure remote connection profiles:

1. In the Configuration Manager console, select the Assets and Compliance workspace.

2. Expand Compliance Settings.

3. Right-click Remote Connection Profiles and click Create Remote Connection Profile. The Create Remote Connection Profile Wizard will start, as shown in Figure 13.41.

FIGURE 13.41
Create Remote Connection Profile Wizard, General page

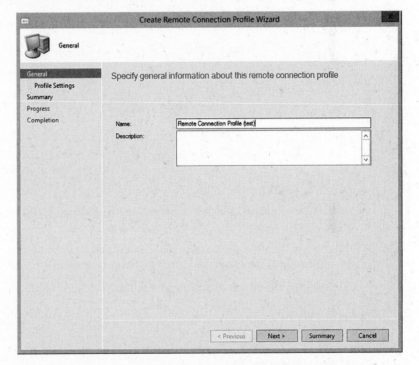

4. Once you're in the Create Remote Connection Profile Wizard, enter the name of the remote connection profile and click Next.

5. On the Profile Settings screen, you will need to provide the full name and port of the Remote Desktop Gateway server, as shown in Figure 13.42.

When do you need a Remote Desktop Gateway server?

The Remote Desktop Gateway server is required only if the connection is over the Internet, as explained in the following TechNet article:

https://technet.microsoft.com/en-us/library/mt595721.aspx

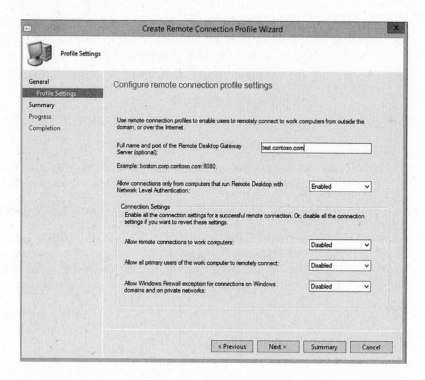

FIGURE 13.42
Create Remote
Connection Profile
Wizard, Profile
Settings page

6. Select Enabled or Disabled for each of the connection settings as required by your company policies.

Note that all three items under Connection Settings must be set to either Enabled or Disabled. They must all match, regardless of which setting you choose.

7. When all settings are configured, click Next.

8. The Summary page will be displayed. Click Next to create the remote connection profile and then click Close to complete the Create Remote Connection Profile Wizard.

Compliance Policies

The Compliance Policies feature allows you to monitor and remediate compliance issues on devices. When used in conjunction with Conditional Access, it allows you to define what rules and settings a device must have in order to access corporate email and other services. For example, you could easily prevent a rooted or jailbroken device from being used to connect to your Exchange Online, or you can request users to turn on encryption if they want to access their email.

Basically, with compliance policies you can set a minimum threshold of security for any user who wants to access your corporate data.

There are two separate sets of rules, depending on whether you like to create policies for devices managed with or without the Configuration Manager client.

For devices managed with the Configuration Manager client (Windows 7, 8.1, and 10), the possible rules are as follows:

♦ Network Firewall On

♦ Require Registration In Azure Active Directory

♦ All Required Updates Installed With A Deadline Older Than X Days

♦ Require BitLocker Drive Encryption

♦ Require Antimalware

> **Enabling Compliance Policies for PCs**
>
> In Configuration Manager version 1606, Conditional Access For Managed PCs is still in pre-release. If you want to create a compliance policy for PCs, you should first consent to use pre-release features under Administration ➢ Overview ➢ Site Configuration ➢ Sites ➢ Hierarchy Settings. Then you will have to select Pre-release - Conditional Access For Managed PCs under Administration ➢ Overview ➢ Cloud Services ➢ Updates and Servicing ➢ Features.

For devices managed without the Configuration Manager client (Android, iOS, Windows 10, Windows 10 Mobile, Windows Phone), the rules are as follows:

♦ Require Password Settings On Mobile Devices

♦ Minutes Of Inactivity Before A Password Is Required

♦ Require A Password To Unlock An Idle Device

♦ Minimum Classification Of Required Updates (only for Windows 10)

♦ Minimum Password Length

♦ Allow Simple Password

♦ File Encryption On Mobile Devices

♦ Device Is Jailbroken Or Rooted (only for Android and iOS)

♦ Email Profile Must Be Managed By Intune (only for iOS)

♦ Minimum Operating System Version

♦ Reported As Healthy By Health Attestation Service (only for Windows 10)

To create a compliance policy, follow these steps:

1. Open the Configuration Manager console and select Assets And Compliance ➢ Overview.

2. Choose Compliance Settings ➢ Compliance Policies. Right-click and select Create Compliance Policy.

3. Enter the name of the compliance policy.

4. Under "Specify the type of compliance rule that you want to create," select "Compliance rules for devices managed without the Configuration Manager client," as shown in Figure 13.43, and click Next.

FIGURE 13.43
Create Compliance Policy Wizard, General page

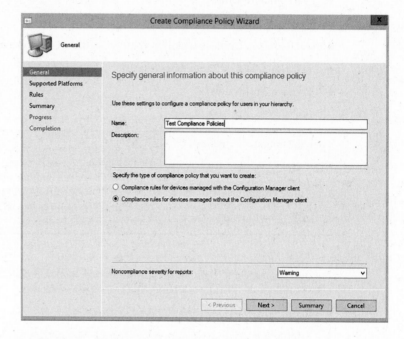

5. On the Supported Platforms page, select the specific version of the OS you want to configure, as shown in Figure 13.44, then click Next.

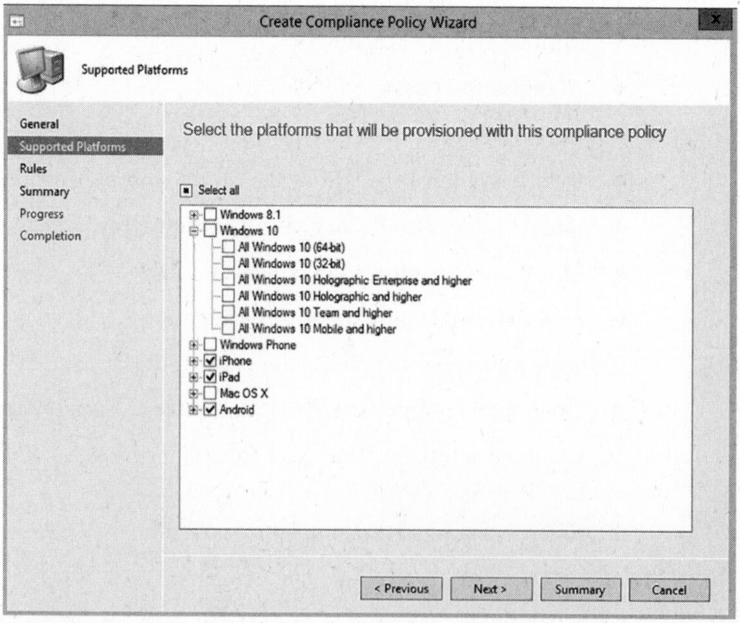

FIGURE 13.44
Create Compliance Policy Wizard, Supported Platforms page

6. On the Rules page, configure the following set of rules:

◆ Allow Simple Passwords: False

◆ Device Is Jailbroken Or Rooted: False

◆ Minimum Password Length: 6

◆ Minutes Of Inactivity Before Password Is Required: 15 Minutes

◆ Require Password Settings On Mobile Devices: True

Confirm that the rules you have created look like the ones shown in Figure 13.45 and click Next.

FIGURE 13.45
Create Compliance Policy Wizard, Rules page

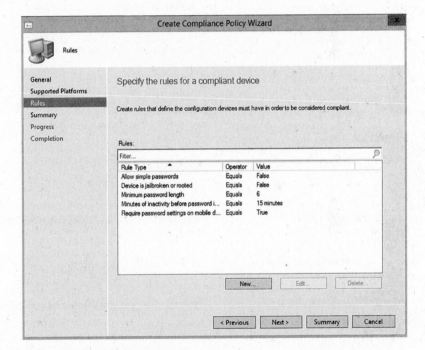

7. On the Summary page, click Next and then Close, and your policies are ready to be deployed to a user collection of your choice.

Conditional Access

Now that you have learned how to create compliance policies, you can select Conditional Access in the Configuration Manager console and configure Exchange Online and SharePoint Online access policies, or you can create policies for clients that are using Exchange On-Premises.

By configuring conditional access, you are allowing only compliant devices to use your corporate resources.

An Intune subscription is required when you configure conditional access for Exchange Online or SharePoint Online, whereas if you want to set up conditional access for Exchange On-Premises, you must have previously configured an Exchange Server connector.

For example, if you enable this feature for Exchange Online, any user with a noncompliant device will receive an email (see Figure 13.46 and Figure 13.47) that will explain the steps needed to make the device compliant (such as enrolling the device first). Once the device is found to be compliant, email will start working on the device.

FIGURE 13.46
Exchange Online action required message for noncompliant Android device

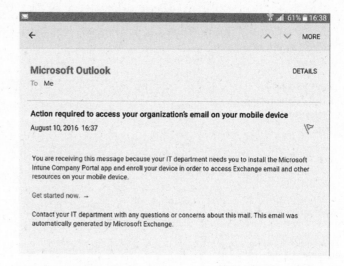

FIGURE 13.47
Exchange Online action required message for noncompliant iOS device

Follow these steps to set up conditional access for Exchange Online:

1. Open the Configuration Manager console and select Assets And Compliance ➢ Overview.

2. Choose Compliance Settings ➢ Conditional Access ➢ Exchange Online (see Figure 13.48).

FIGURE 13.48
Configuring conditional access for Exchange Online

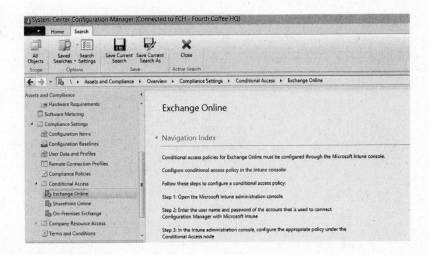

3. Right-click Configure Conditional Access Policies In The Intune Console, which will open `https://manage.microsoft.com`. Here you will have to enter your global admin credential for the Microsoft Intune management portal.

   In the Microsoft Intune admin console, you will be automatically directed to Policy ➤ Conditional Access ➤ Exchange Online Policy.

4. Select Enable Conditional Access Policy.

5. The first section is specific to Outlook or other apps that use modern authentication. Here you can configure which platform is allowed access. At present you can choose

   ◆ iOS

   ◆ Android

6. In the second section, you can configure Outlook Web Access (OWA) and whether you want to block noncompliant devices.

7. The third part of the policy is specific to access via Exchange Active Sync and Basic Authentication. Here you can

   ◆ Block any device that is not compliant and is using a platform supported by Microsoft Intune

   ◆ Block any other device that is using a platform not supported by Microsoft Intune

8. The fourth section is about Policy Deployment. Here you can specify the groups of users that will be targeted by conditional access as well as the groups of exempt users.

9. Confirm that the Exchange Online policy looks like the one shown in Figure 13.49, then click Save and go back to the Configuration Manager console.

FIGURE 13.49
Exchange Online policy

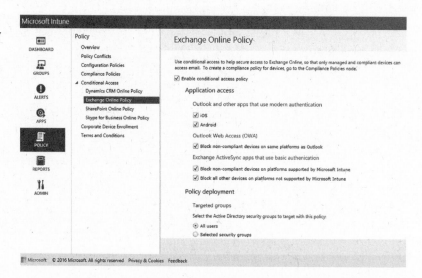

The policy is created and the access to Exchange Online is restricted to compliant devices only. If users want to configure the email but they do not have the company portal installed or they are using a noncompliant device, they will get an "action required" message first. By clicking on Get Started Now, they will be redirected to the store so they can install the latest version of the Company Portal app (see Figure 13.50 and Figure 13.51).

FIGURE 13.50
Web redirect to install the Company Portal app on iOS

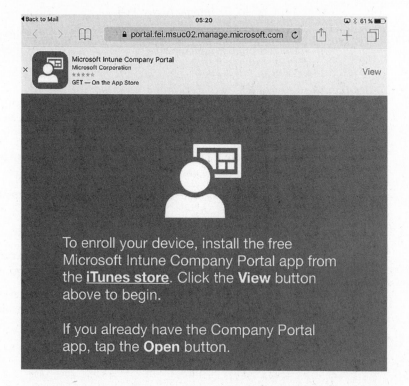

FIGURE 13.51
Web redirect to install
the Company Portal
app on Android

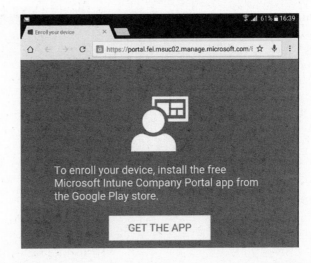

Once the Company Portal app is installed, users will be able to enroll the device into Configuration Manager via Microsoft Intune, as shown in Figure 13.52 and Figure 13.53.

FIGURE 13.52
Company Access Setup
on iOS

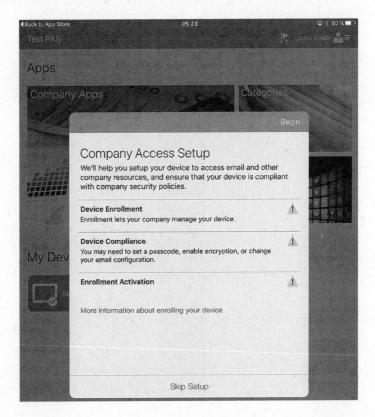

FIGURE 13.53
Company Access Setup
on Android

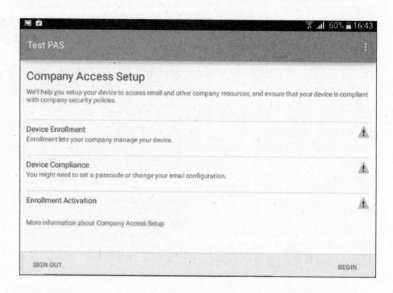

After the device is enrolled, it will be checked for compliance. When found compliant, as in Figure 13.54 and Figure 13.55, Exchange Online will allow the device to send and receive corporate email.

FIGURE 13.54
Policy Compliance
Status: In Compliance
(iOS)

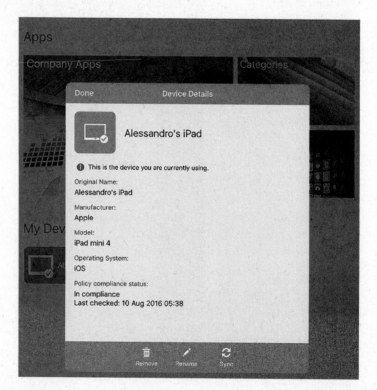

FIGURE 13.55
Policy Compliance
Status: In Compliance
(Android)

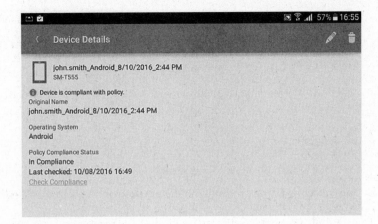

Company Resource Access

The Company Resource Access feature of System Center Configuration Manager provides a set of tools and resources that enable you to give users in your organization access to data and applications from remote locations. This new feature allows you to create certificate, email, VPN, and Wi-Fi profiles in Configuration Manager and deploy them to users or device collections. To create each of these profiles, you need to access the Compliance Settings section of the console, as shown in Figure 13.56.

FIGURE 13.56
Compliance
Settings,
Company
Resource Access

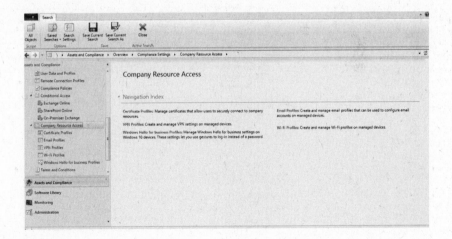

Certificate Profiles

Certificate profiles provide a set of tools and resources to help provision computers in your organization with the certificates that users require to connect to various company resources. Certificate profiles in Configuration Manager work with Active Directory Certificate Services and the Network Device Enrollment service role to provision authentication certificates for managed devices so that users can seamlessly access company resources. This setting is available on the Company Resource Access area of Compliance Settings.

Certificates profiles provide the following management capabilities:

◆ Certificate enrollment and renewals from an enterprise certification authority for devices that run iOS, Windows 8.1/RT 8.1/10, Windows Phone 8.1, Windows 10 Mobile, and Android 4.x and 5. These certificates can then be used for Wi-Fi and VPN connections.

◆ Deployment of trusted root CA certificates and intermediate CA certificates to configure a chain of trust on devices for VPN and Wi-Fi connections when server authentication is required.

◆ Deployment of Personal Information Exchange - PKCS #12 (PFX) settings.

◆ The ability to monitor and report on the installed certificates.

Now that you understand the purpose of certificate profiles, let's configure a certificate profile and deploy it to users or device collections.

To create the certificate profile, follow these steps:

1. In the Configuration Manager console, navigate to the Assets And Compliance workspace.

2. Expand Compliance Settings ➤ Company Resource Access.

3. Right-click Certificate Profiles and select Create Certificate Profile.

The Create Certificate Profile Wizard will be displayed, as shown in Figure 13.57.

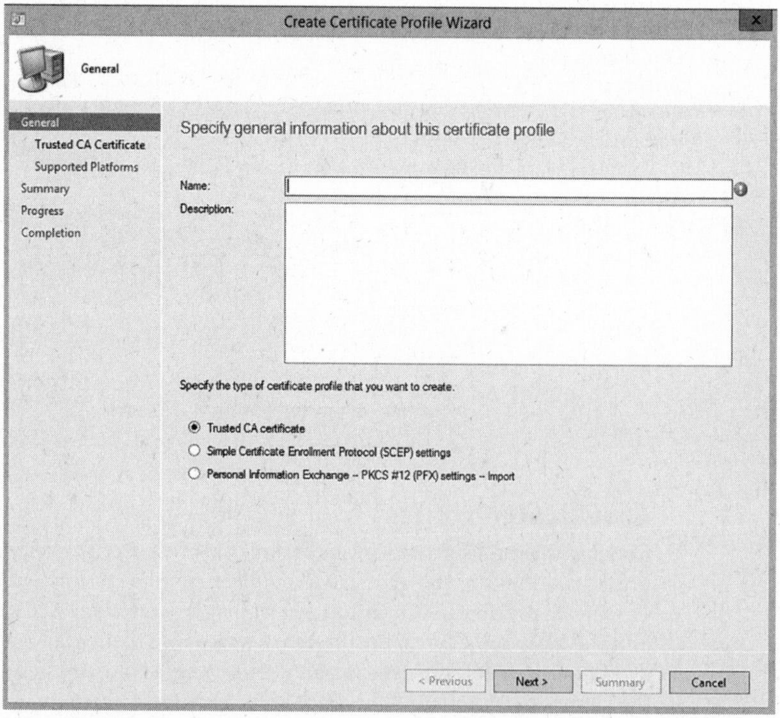

FIGURE 13.57
Create Certificate
Profile Wizard, General
page

4. Enter the name of the certificate profile.

5. Select the Trusted CA Certificate.

6. Click Next to continue the wizard.

7. Click Import, as shown in Figure 13.58, and select the certificate that you want to deploy.

FIGURE 13.58

Create Certificate
Profile Wizard, Trusted
CA Certificate page

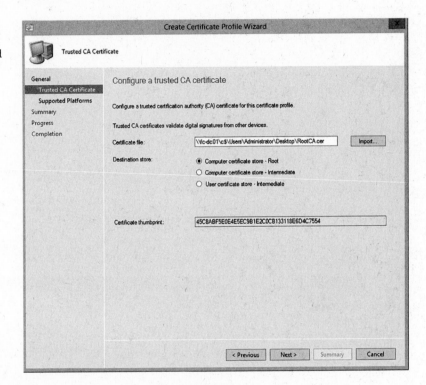

8. Click Next to go to the Supported Platforms page, as shown in Figure 13.59.

9. Select all the OS versions that you need for the certificate, and then click Next.

10. Review the Summary page, and click Next.

11. When the configuration is complete, review the Completion screen, as shown in Figure 13.60; then click Close to complete the Create Certificate Profile Wizard.

Your certificate profile should now be visible on the system.

Once the certificate profile is created, you can deploy it to a user or a device collection of your choosing.

FIGURE 13.59
Create Certificate
Profile Wizard,
Supported Platforms
page

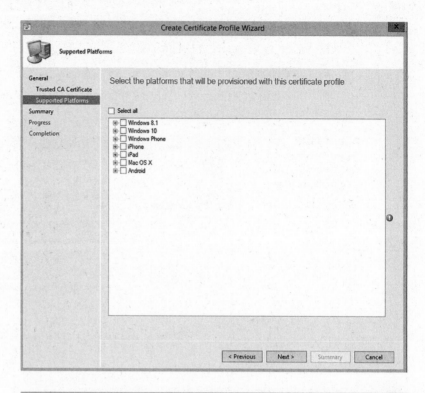

FIGURE 13.60
Create Certificate
Profile Wizard,
Completion page

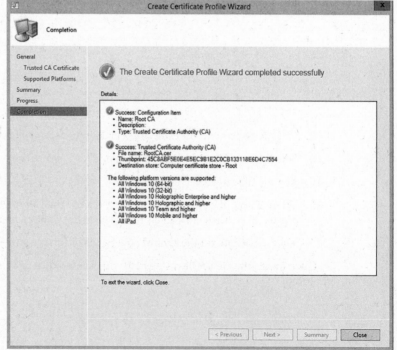

Email Profiles

You can use email profiles to create Exchange Active Sync profiles that can be deployed to users in your organization. The supported platforms are Windows 8.1, Windows RT, Windows 10, Windows Phone 8.x, Windows 10 Mobile, iOS, and Android with Samsung KNOX only.

To create an email profile, follow these steps:

1. Open the Configuration Manager console and choose the Assets And Compliance workspace.

2. Expand Compliance Settings ➢ Company Resource Access.

3. Right-click Email Profiles and click Create Exchange ActiveSync Profile to open the wizard shown in Figure 13.61.

FIGURE 13.61

Create Exchange ActiveSync Email Profile Wizard, Exchange ActiveSync page

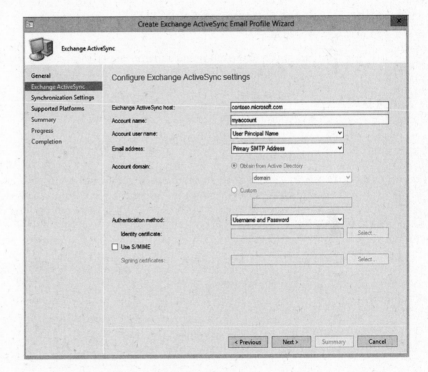

4. Enter the name and a description for the Exchange ActiveSync profile and click Next.

5. On the Exchange ActiveSync page, enter the Exchange ActiveSync hostname and the account name.

6. Choose how the email account user name is configured on client devices from the following list:

   ◆ User Principal Name

   ◆ sAMAccountName (this is the logon name used to support clients and servers running earlier versions of the operating system, such as Windows NT 4.0, Windows 95, Windows 98, and LAN Manager)

   ◆ Primary SMTP Address

7. Choose how the email address for the user on each client device is generated, selecting an option from the following list:

   ◆ Primary SMTP Address

   ◆ User Principal Name

   Note that if you want to generate the user's email address in an email profile by using the user's primary SMTP address, User Discovery must be configured to discover the mail attribute from Active Directory (and the mail attribute must exist for the user).

8. If you have selected sAMAccountName as the account username, you need to choose how to obtain the account domain:

   ◆ Obtain From Active Directory

   ◆ Custom

9. Select one of the following authentication methods that will be used to authenticate the connection to Exchange ActiveSync:

   ◆ Certificates

   ◆ Username and Password

10. If you have selected Certificate, you also need to click Select and choose the certificate to use for identity.

11. If you are creating an email profile for an iOS device, you can also configure it to use S/MIME, and then select the appropriate Encryption and Signing certificates.

12. Click Next to go to the Synchronization Settings page (see Figure 13.62).

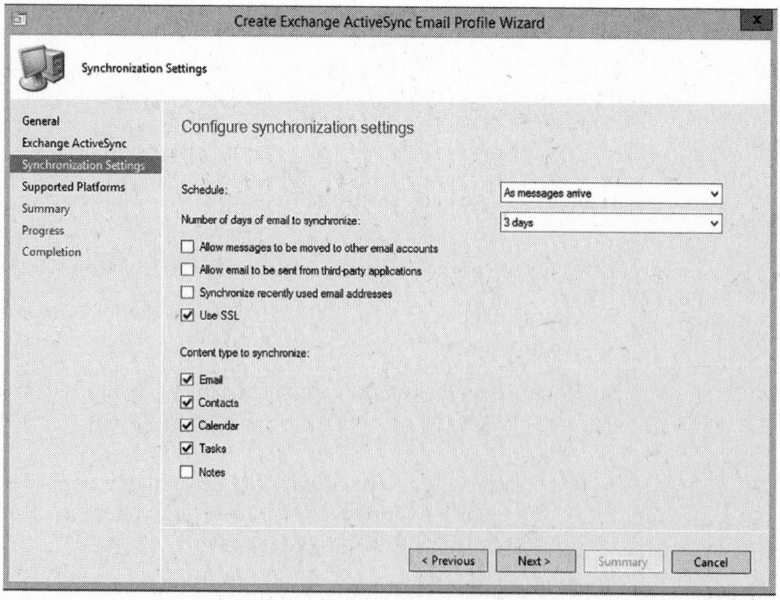

FIGURE 13.62
Create Exchange
ActiveSync Email
Profile Wizard,
Synchronization
Settings page

13. Select the schedule for your synchronization, choosing one of these options:

    ◆ As Messages Arrive

    ◆ 15 Minutes

    ◆ 30 Minutes

    ◆ 60 Minutes

    ◆ Manual Synchronization

14. Then you can specify the number of days of email to synchronize, selecting one of these following options:

    ◆ Not Configured

    ◆ Unlimited

    ◆ 1 Day

    ◆ Days

    ◆ 1 Week

    ◆ Weeks

    ◆ 1 Month

    Other optional settings that you can configure are

    ◆ Allow Messages To Be Moved To Other Email Accounts

    ◆ Allow Email To Be Sent From Third-Party Applications

    ◆ Synchronize Recently Used Email Addresses

    ◆ Use SSL (Selected By Default)

15. Finally, you can also specify what content type you want to synchronize:

    ◆ Email (selected by default)

    ◆ Contacts

    ◆ Calendar

    ◆ Tasks

    ◆ Notes

16. On the Supported Platforms page, select the devices required for your environment or just click Select All, and then click Next.

17. On the Summary page, review the information; make sure to validate the configuration before you deploy this profile.

Email profiles are easy to implement, and by deploying these settings, you allow users to access corporate email on their personal devices without any required configuration on their end. At present, only native device email apps can be configured with email profiles; this does not include the Outlook App for iOS and Android.

VPN Profiles

You use VPN profiles in Configuration Manager to deploy VPN settings to users in your organization. By deploying these settings, you can minimize the effort required to connect to the resources of the company network. With a new VPN profile, you can easily configure any devices on your organization that may need this setting to connect to the network. You can create this profile to support Windows 8.1, Windows RT, Windows 10, Windows Phone 8.1, Windows 10 Mobile and iOS, and Android 4.x and 5.

A VPN profile can include a wide range of security settings, including certificates for server validation and client authentication that have been provisioned by Configuration Manager certificate profiles.

To create a VPN profile, follow these steps:

1. Open the Configuration Manager console and choose the Assets And Compliance workspace.

2. Expand Compliance Settings ➤ Company Resource Access.

3. Right-click VPN Profiles and click Create VPN Profiles.

4. The Create VPN Profile Wizard will appear, as shown in Figure 13.63.

FIGURE 13.63
Create VPN Profile
Wizard, General page

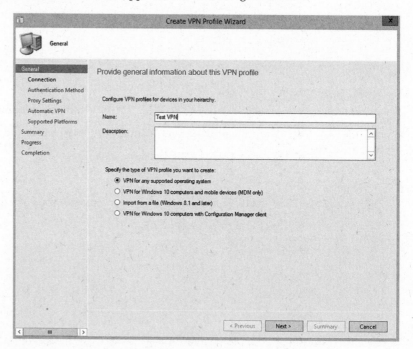

5. Enter the name and a description for the VPN profile.

6. Check Import An Existing VPN Profile From A File, if you already have these details saved. Otherwise, click Next.

7. On the Connection page, as shown in Figure 13.64, select the right connection type and server list for your environment.

FIGURE 13.64
Create VPN Profile
Wizard, Connection
page

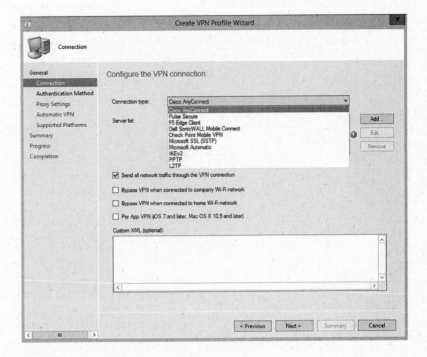

8. Click Add to specify a VPN server. Enter a friendly name and the IP address of the server or FQDN. Once you've entered all the information, click Next.

9. Select the authentication method that you are going to use for this VPN connection, as shown in Figure 13.65.

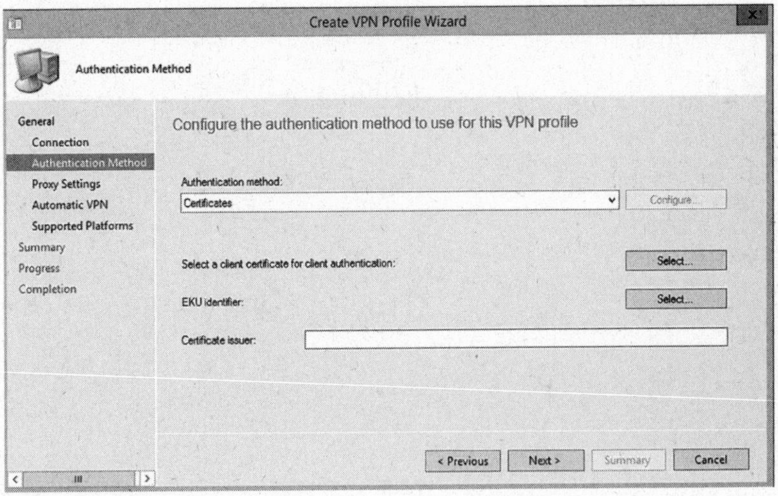

FIGURE 13.65
Create VPN Profile
Wizard, Authentication
Method page

10. Click Next once you've configured the authentication method.

11. Configure the proxy setting that is needed for this VPN profile, as shown in Figure 13.66.

FIGURE 13.66
Create VPN Profile
Wizard, Proxy Settings
page

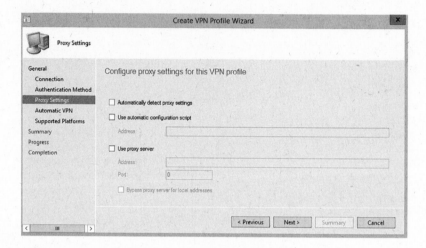

12. Click Next once you've configured the proxy settings appropriately.

13. On the Automatic VPN page, shown in Figure 13.67, you need to indicate which requests you wish to trigger a VPN connection to. Check Enable VPN On-Demand, and then enter the VPN suffixes in order to trigger an automatic VPN connection. All settings on this page are optional. Click Next to move to the next page in the wizard.

FIGURE 13.67
Create VPN Profile
Wizard, Automatic
VPN page

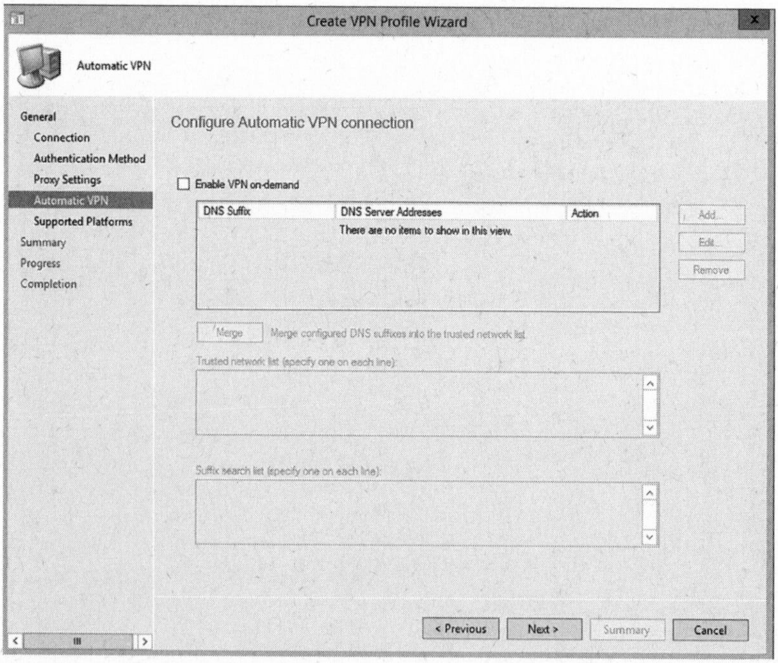

14. Select the supported platforms for this VPN profile, as shown in Figure 13.68, and then click Next.

FIGURE 13.68
Create VPN Profile
Wizard, Supported
Platforms page

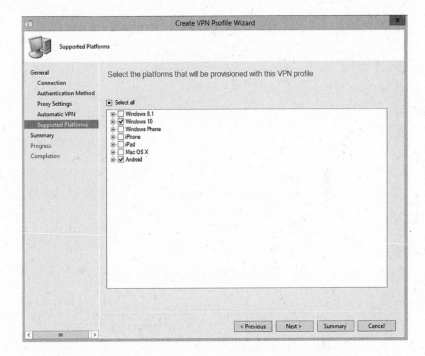

15. On the Summary screen, review all settings to ensure every configuration you wanted is set up; then click Next.

16. Click Close to complete the configuration of your VPN profile.

VPN profiles can save your users lots of time. Make sure you configure all the settings that are needed for the VPN profile before deploying it to your production devices.

Wi-Fi Profiles

In Configuration Manager you can configure Wi-Fi profiles and deploy them to your users and device collections to ensure the Wi-Fi settings are correct. This will help you minimize the end-user effort required to connect to the corporate wireless network.

If you install a new Wi-Fi network and you want to provision it to all the devices in your organization, you can create a Wi-Fi profile containing the settings necessary to connect to the new Wi-Fi network. Then you can deploy this profile to all users or devices. The new Wi-Fi profile supports the following device types: Windows 8.1, Windows 10 and RT, Windows Phone 8.1, Windows 10 Mobile, and iOS, as well as Android devices that run versions 4.x and 5.

Follow these steps to configure a Wi-Fi profile:

1. Open the Configuration Manager console and choose the Assets And Compliance workspace.

2. Expand Compliance Settings ➢ Company Resource Access.

3. Right-click Wi-Fi Profiles and select Create Wi-Fi Profiles.

4. The Create Wi-Fi Profile Wizard will appear, as shown in Figure 13.69.

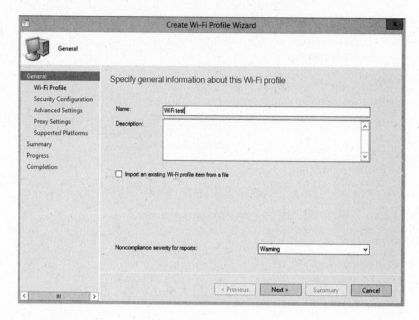

5. Enter the name and a description for the Wi-Fi profile. If you have an existing Wi-Fi profile in a file, you can select to import it and click Next.

6. As shown in Figure 13.70, enter the network name and SSID. Select Connect Automatically When This Network Is In Range if you need this to be the default Wi-Fi profile; otherwise leave all boxes unchecked and click Next.

FIGURE 13.70
Create Wi-Fi Profile
Wizard, Wi-Fi Profile
page

7. On the Security Configuration page, select a security type, as shown in Figure 13.71. Click Next once you finish configuring the proper security for the Wi-Fi profile.

FIGURE 13.71
Create Wi-Fi Profile Wizard, Security Configuration page

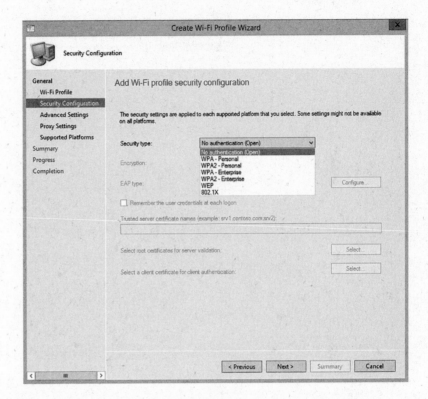

8. On the Advanced Settings page, configure additional options for the WiFi profile, as shown in Figure 13.72, and then click Next.

9. On the Proxy Settings page, enter the proxy information for this Wi-Fi profile if needed. No settings are required, as shown in Figure 13.73. Click Next to continue.

10. On the Supported Platforms page, select the devices required for your environment or just click Select All, and then click Next.

11. On the Summary page, review the information; be sure to validate the configuration before you deploy this profile.

As you have seen, using the Wi-Fi Profiles feature makes it very easy to configure and manage the process of deploying Wi-Fi profiles to Configuration Manager users and devices.

FIGURE 13.72
Create Wi-Fi Profile
Wizard, Advanced
Settings page

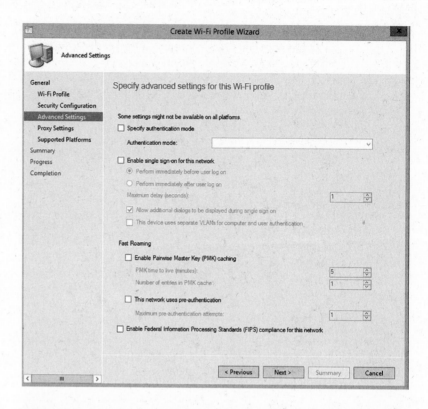

FIGURE 13.73
Create Wi-Fi Profile
Wizard, Proxy Settings
page

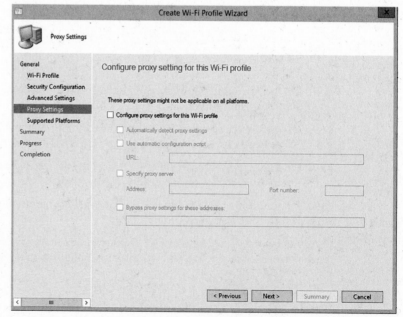

Windows Hello for Business Profiles

The feature formerly known as Microsoft Passport for Work has been renamed to Windows Hello for Business in Windows 10 version 1607, and it is used to manage strong two-factor authentication on PC and mobile devices. With Configuration Manager, starting with version 1606, you are now able to configure it like any other Company Resource policy:

1. Open the Configuration Manager console and choose the Assets and Compliance workspace.

2. Expand Compliance Settings ➢ Company Resource Access.

3. Right-click Windows Hello For Business Profiles and select Create Windows Hello For Business Profile.

4. On the General page, enter a name for the profile and click Next.

5. On the Supported platform page, select Windows 10 and click Next.

6. On the Settings page (see Figure 13.74), configure the minimum PIN length to 6 and click Next.

7. On the Summary page, click Next and then Close.

FIGURE 13.74
Windows Hello For
Business Wizard,
Settings page

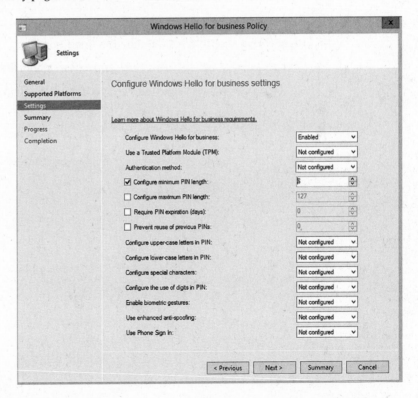

You can now deploy the newly created policy to a collection and configure a Windows Hello for Business profile for your Windows 10 users.

> **IMPLEMENTING WINDOWS HELLO FOR BUSINESS AT MICROSOFT IT**
>
> If you want to learn how Microsoft IT implemented Windows Hello for Business, have a look at this case study article:
>
> https://www.microsoft.com/itshowcase/Article/Content/756/Implementing-strong-user-authentication-with-Windows-Hello-for-Business

Terms and Conditions

Starting with Configuration Manager version 1511, you can create and deploy custom terms and conditions for mobile devices to end users. The idea is to explain how device enrollment, access to work resources, and use of the company portal affects end users and their devices. Users must accept custom terms and conditions before they can use the company portal to enroll their devices. When terms and conditions are deployed to users, they need to accept them only once, unless specifically configured in an updated version of the custom terms and conditions.

To configure custom terms and conditions:

1. Open the Configuration Manager console and choose the Assets And Compliance workspace.

2. Expand Compliance And Settings, then select Terms And Conditions.

3. Right-click and select Create Terms And Conditions.

4. On the General page, specify a name and a description, then click Next.

5. On the Terms page (see Figure 13.75), specify a Title, a Text for terms, and a Text to explain what it means if the user accepts, then click Next.

6. Review the Summary page and click Next.

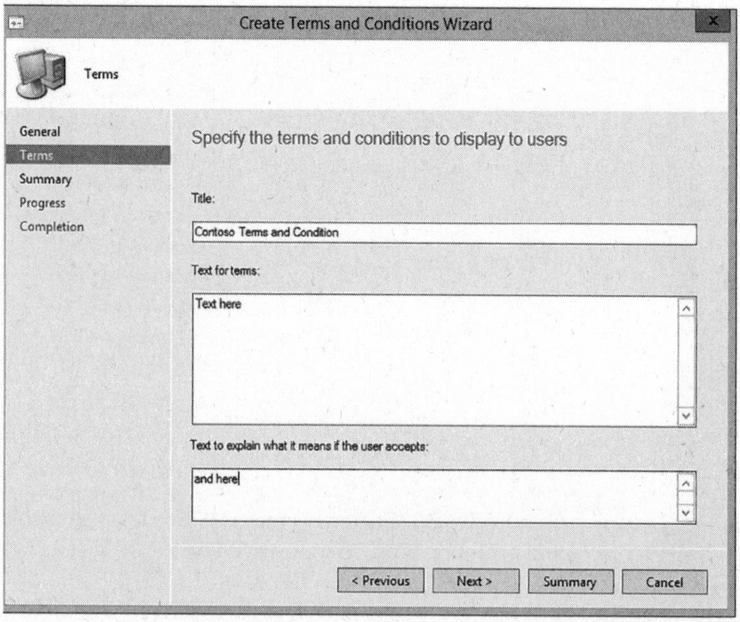

FIGURE 13.75
Create Terms And Conditions Wizard, Terms page

You have now created a new Terms and Conditions policy that can be deployed to a users collection and that will be displayed in the company portal before the enrollment starts.

Windows 10 Edition Upgrade

The Windows 10 Edition Upgrade policy allows you to specify a product key or license information used to upgrade devices enrolled via Mobile Device Management.

To configure a Windows 10 Edition Upgrade Policy:

1. Open the Configuration Manager console and choose the Assets And Compliance workspace.

2. Expand Compliance And Settings; then select Windows 10 Edition Upgrade.

3. Right-click and select Create An Edition Upgrade Policy.

4. Specify a name and a description and select the SKU to upgrade the device to (as shown in Figure 13.76).

5. Select the Product key choosing one of these two options, then click Next:

   ◆ Product Key

   ◆ License File (XML)

6. Review the Summary page, and then click Next.

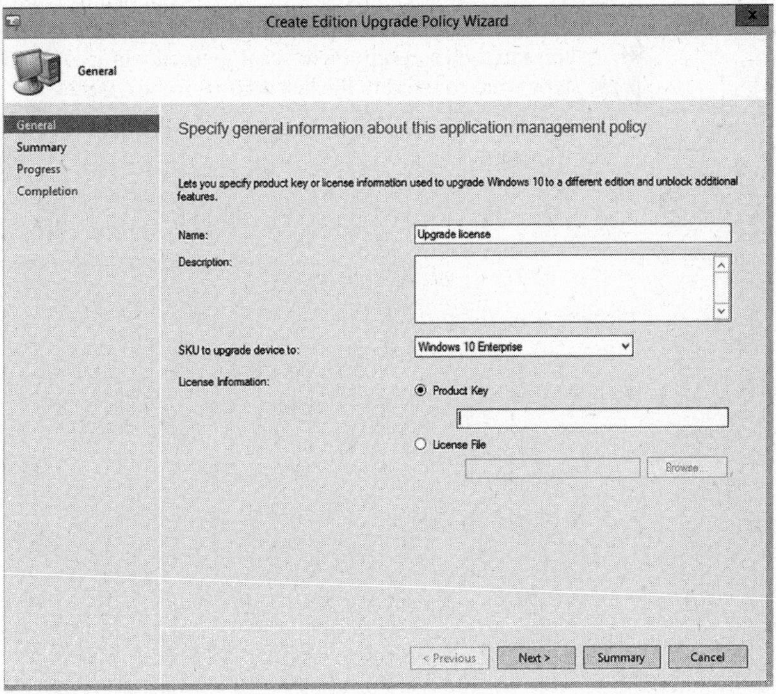

FIGURE 13.76
Create Edition
Upgrade Policy
Wizard, General page

You are now ready to deploy the policy to a collection. Please remember that devices targeted by this policy must be enrolled in Microsoft Intune. This feature is not currently compatible with PCs that run the Configuration Manager client software, or PCs that are managed by on-premises MDM.

The Bottom Line

Enable the client settings.   Until the client settings are enabled for your Configuration Manager clients, your clients will not evaluate any of the configuration baselines. This is the first step in using Compliance Settings to validate client settings.

Master It   Enable Compliance Settings for the Configuration Manager clients.

Create configuration items.   Configuration items are the pieces that make up a configuration baseline. There are a number of different configuration item types in Configuration Manager, and depending on the type you choose to create, you are presented with certain options when creating your configuration item. The steps to create configuration items were covered in the first part of this chapter, and they included several examples of how to create the different types of configuration items.

Master It   Create a configuration item for an application that checks a registry string value.

Define a configuration baseline.   This is where you take one or more of the CIs and put them into a package that the Configuration Manager client downloads and at the scheduled time validates by checking the CIs against the computer. The Configuration Manager client then reports the outcome of those checks back to Configuration Manager, where you can then run reports to see if your clients are within the specified configuration. These steps were covered in the last section of the chapter.

Master It   Assemble a configuration baseline with one or more configuration items you have created.

Chapter 14

Endpoint Protection

Endpoint Protection is integrated in System Center Configuration Manager and allows you to easily manage antimalware policies and automatically download and deploy the latest antimalware definition files to your Configuration Manager hierarchy. Endpoint Protection also provides detailed reporting and monitoring abilities so you can rest assured that you will know immediately if any malware events occur in your managed hierarchy.

In this chapter, you will learn to

◆ Deploy and configure the Endpoint Protection site system and client

◆ Create and assign an Endpoint Protection policy

Benefits of Endpoint Protection

In this section we will review some of the benefits and features of Endpoint Protection. Note that this feature of Configuration Manager is sometimes referred to as *Endpoint Protection in System Center Configuration Manager* and you also may see it referred to as *System Center Endpoint Protection*. Both terms refer to the same feature within Configuration Manager.

Deployment

The configuration and deployment of Endpoint Protection is managed in the Configuration Manager console. Because of the tight integration with Configuration Manager, Endpoint Protection is easily deployable to environments of any size. The Configuration Manager administrator enables Endpoint Protection in Configuration Manager by deploying the Endpoint Protection site system role, enabling the Endpoint Protection client (for Windows 8.1 and earlier computers—more on this later), and then configuring the antimalware policies. Endpoint Protection includes several policy templates that provide recommended antimalware configurations for standard workloads. These templates are generally ready to deploy but can be customized to meet the specific needs of the organization if needed. You can also export policies that may have been created in Forefront Endpoint Protection 2010 or the Endpoint Protection feature that was included in Configuration Manager 2012 and import them into Endpoint Protection with Configuration Manager.

WHAT IS MALWARE?

We will use the term *malware* a great deal in this chapter, so it's probably a good idea to define that word.

Malware is short for *malicious software*, which is basically software, code, or scripts that are typically designed to perform invasive, destructive actions on a computer. Some malware attempts to delete files or corrupt the operating system, whereas others may attempt to steal personal or corporate data. Malware includes items such as computer viruses, worms, Trojan horses, adware, and some rootkits. Antimalware software (such as Microsoft's Endpoint Protection) is software designed to detect, block, and remove malware.

Protection

Endpoint Protection provides Configuration Manager administrators with the ability to ensure that their computer infrastructure is safe and secure from malware attacks. The Endpoint Protection feature of Configuration Manager protects the computer infrastructure by detecting and blocking malware and also by providing management of Windows Firewall. Endpoint Protection ensures that the computers are protected from many known exploits and vulnerabilities, and it is backed by the Microsoft Security Response Center. For more information on the Microsoft Security Response Center, visit

```
www.microsoft.com/security/msrc
```

Monitoring

Configuration Manager provides extensive monitoring and reporting of the health and status of the environment. This is especially true for the Endpoint Protection feature of Configuration Manager. Configuration Manager utilizes a client communication channel that uses state messages to deliver malware activity information from the client to the site server in near real time. As a result, the Configuration Manager administrator will typically become aware of malware activity within just a few minutes of it taking place. Configuration Manager uses this channel for all endpoint-related operations as well as other client actions. You will learn more about the fast channel later in the Client Notification section of this chapter.

Security

The role-based access security model in Configuration Manager greatly simplifies the process of defining access for administrative users. The Configuration Manager security role that is related to the Endpoint Protection feature is the Endpoint Protection Manager. This security role provides the administrative user with the ability to create, modify, and delete security policies. Administrative users with this security role can also manage the security policies that are assigned to collections, monitor the status of Endpoint Protection, and execute remediation tasks on managed computers.

One possible use of this role is to assign it to the corporate IT security department and allow them to manage the configuration of Endpoint Protection without giving them access to other areas of Configuration Manager.

Now that you understand some of the benefits of Endpoint Protection, let's take a closer look at the feature.

Endpoint Protection Point Site System Role

The Endpoint Protection Point site system role is a critical component for the Endpoint Protection feature of Configuration Manager and must be installed and configured before you can use the feature. The role must be installed at the top of the Configuration Manager hierarchy. If the hierarchy includes a central administration site (CAS), the role should be installed there.

THE ENDPOINT PROTECTION CLIENT LICENSE

Note that you must accept the license agreement in order to install the Endpoint Protection Point role. The Endpoint Protection client license is part of the Microsoft core Client Access License (CAL). However, the license for the Endpoint Protection site server may not be part of the core CAL and may have specific licensing requirements. Contact your Microsoft account team or software reseller for additional information on the licensing requirements for Endpoint Protection.

The installation and configuration of the Endpoint Protection role is fairly straightforward:

1. In the Configuration Manager console, select Administration ➢ Overview ➢ Site Configuration ➢ Servers And Site System Roles.

2. Select the CAS (or the standalone primary site server), right-click, and select Add Site System Roles. The Add Site System Roles Wizard opens.

3. On the General page, specify the settings for the site system server. Click Next.

4. Select the proxy settings and configure them if needed; then click Next.

5. On the next screen, select Endpoint Protection Point from the list of available roles and click Next. See Figure 14.1.

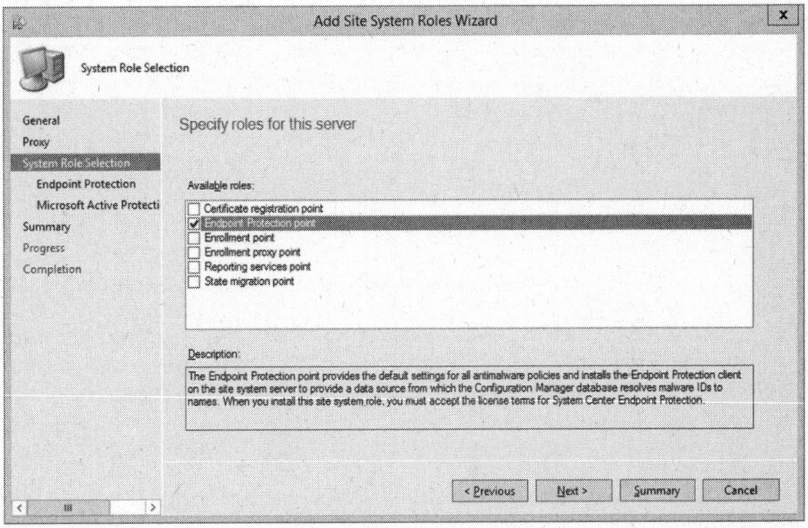

FIGURE 14.1
Selecting the Endpoint Protection Point role

6. On the Endpoint Protection License Terms Page, review the license terms and privacy statement if needed and then check the box to acknowledge that you accept the terms. Click Next.

7. On the Specify Microsoft Active Protection Service membership type window, choose the membership option you require for your environment and click Next.

WHAT IS MAPS?

Before moving on, we should discuss the Microsoft Active Protection Service (MAPS).

MAPS is a cloud-based service that allows the endpoint client on a computer to report data about programs that exhibit suspicious behavior to the Microsoft Malware Protection Center (MMPC). Once the data is submitted to the MMPC, it can be analyzed and researched by engineers. Once the data has been analyzed, information about the behavior can be included in new definition updates and deployed to computers around the world via Endpoint Protection. This feature is sometimes referred to as the Dynamic Signature Service.

When you configure the Endpoint Protection site system, you will need to define how MAPS should be configured for your environment.

As you can see in the following illustration, there are three available choices for the Microsoft Active Protection Service:

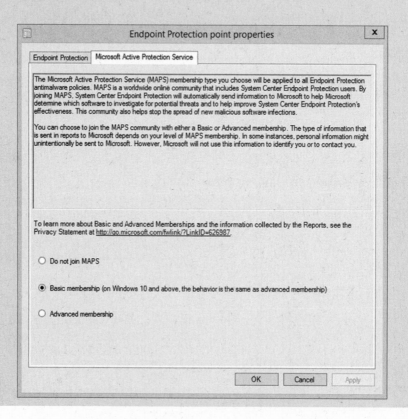

◆ Do Not Join MAPS

If you choose this option, it means that information will not be sent from the managed computers to Microsoft.

◆ Basic Membership

If you choose the Basic Membership option, Endpoint Protection will submit information to Microsoft about potentially unsafe software or software that has not yet been analyzed for risks. Note that for Windows 10 and above, the behavior is the same as for advanced membership.

◆ Advanced Membership

If you choose the Advanced Membership option, Endpoint Protection may submit more detailed information about detected software. This may include the location of the software, filenames, and other data.

You can change the membership setting at any time by making the change in the Endpoint Protection site system properties. You can also override this sitewide setting with a custom antimalware policy if needed.

You can read more about the information that is submitted in the System Center Configuration Manager Privacy Statement Overview: `http://aka.ms/cmprivacy`.

8. On the Confirm Settings page, click Next and then click Close once the role has been successfully installed.

9. You can monitor the status of the installation of the role in the `EPMgr.log` and `EPSetup.log` files on the site server.

SHOW ME THE LOGS!

Configuration Manager has many detailed, informative site server and client logs. The relevant logs for Endpoint Protection are discussed here:

ON THE ENDPOINT PROTECTION SITE SYSTEM

The Endpoint Protection site system log files are in the standard location for Configuration Manager site server logs (`\Program Files\Microsoft Configuration Manager\Logs`), and there are three logs related to Endpoint Protection:

◆ `EPCtrlMgr.log` records information about the sync of malware threat data from the Endpoint Protection site system role to the Configuration Manager database.

◆ `EPMgr.log` monitors the status of the Endpoint Protection role.

◆ `EPSetup.log` records information about the installation of the Endpoint Protection role on the site server.

ON THE ENDPOINT PROTECTION CLIENTS

The Endpoint Protection client log files are located in `\Program Files\SMS_CCM\Logs` on the Configuration Manager site servers and in `\Windows\CCM\Logs` for Configuration Manager clients. There is one log related specifically to Endpoint Protection: `EndpointProtectionAgent.log`. This logs details the installation of the Endpoint Protection client and the application of antimalware policy.

Endpoint Protection Client Agent

Once the Endpoint Protection Point site system role has been enabled and configured, the next step is to configure the System Center Endpoint Protection client agent. The Endpoint Protection client cannot be enabled until the Endpoint Protection site system role is enabled. The installation media for the Endpoint Protection client is distributed to the managed devices as part of the Configuration Manager client install media. The name of the file is SCEPInstall.exe, and it can be found in the CCMSETUP folder (C:\Windows\CCMSETUP) on the client. Although the Endpoint Protection client install media is copied to the CCMSETUP folder during the Configuration Manager client install, the Endpoint Protection client won't actually be installed until the Endpoint Protection client is enabled and configured in an assigned client settings policy.

If the client is running Windows 10, then the Endpoint Protection antimalware policies will manage the Windows Defender agent that is already included in Windows 10. In this scenario, the Endpoint Protection agent will install an additional management layer on the Windows Defender agent and will use that integration to manage the Windows Defender agent. As shown in Figure 14.2, you will still see the Endpoint Protection agent listed in the Programs and Features list on a Windows 10 computer but Windows Defender is protecting the Windows 10 client.

FIGURE 14.2
Endpoint Protection listed in Programs and Features

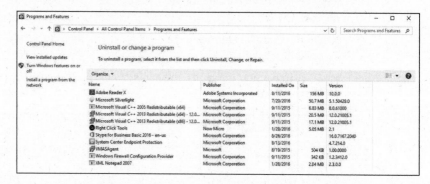

As with the other client agent settings, either you can configure the Endpoint Protection client policies in the default client settings or you can create a custom device client settings policy and use it to configure Endpoint Protection on the client. A general recommendation is to create a custom device client settings policy when enabling and configuring Endpoint Protection.

Use the following steps to create a separate client settings policy for Endpoint Protection:

1. Open the Configuration Manager console and choose Administration ➢ Overview ➢ Client Settings.

2. Click Create Custom Client Device Settings in the ribbon.

3. Give the custom device settings a name and description.

4. Select Endpoint Protection as the custom setting to be enforced on the client devices. See Figure 14.3.

5. Click the Endpoint Protection option on the left side of the window. This will open the Endpoint Protection configuration settings. See Figure 14.4.

FIGURE 14.3
Selecting the
Endpoint Protection
custom setting

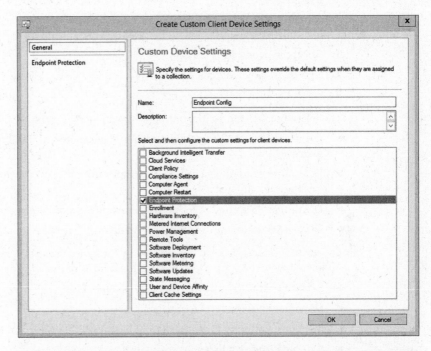

FIGURE 14.4
Configuring
Endpoint Protection
settings

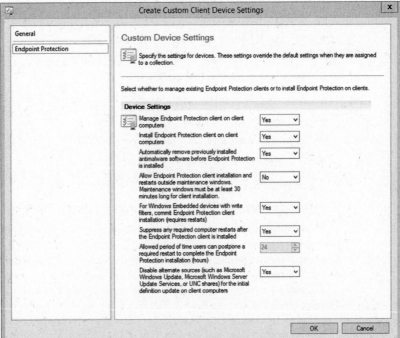

6. Set the required configuration settings, and click OK.

After creating the client settings policy for Endpoint Protection, you will need to assign the policy to a collection:

1. Select the policy you created.

2. Choose Deploy from the ribbon.

3. Select the appropriate collection.

The following are some of the options that can be configured:

◆ Define whether the Endpoint Protection client should be installed and whether it should be managed.

◆ Determine if previously installed antimalware software should be automatically removed (see the following list).

◆ Define if any required reboots after enabling Endpoint Protection will be suppressed.

◆ Disable alternate sources for the initial definition update.

The list of products that can be replaced by Endpoint Protection may change somewhat, but the following were the supported titles for removal as of this writing:

◆ Symantec AntiVirus Corporate Edition version 10

◆ Symantec Endpoint Protection version 11

◆ Symantec Endpoint Protection Small Business Edition version 12

◆ McAfee VirusScan Enterprise version 8

◆ Trend Micro OfficeScan

◆ Microsoft Forefront Codename Stirling Beta 2

◆ Microsoft Forefront Codename Stirling Beta 3

◆ Microsoft Forefront Client Security v1

◆ Microsoft Security Essentials v1

◆ Microsoft Security Essentials 2010

◆ Microsoft Forefront Endpoint Protection 2010

◆ Microsoft Security Center Online v1

Use this website to obtain an updated list of products that can be removed:

`http://technet.microsoft.com/en-us/library/gg682067.aspx`

If you have an antimalware product installed in the environment that is not on this list, you will need to deploy a removal package for that product. In that scenario, make sure you coordinate the removal of the old product and the enabling and deployment of the Endpoint Protection client in order to minimize the amount of time that the computer is not protected by antimalware software.

Endpoint Protection also supports Mac-based clients as well as Linux/Unix-based clients. The Endpoint Protection client installation files for these platforms are not supplied with the Configuration Manager client setup media; they can only be obtained from the Microsoft Volume Licensing website: `www.microsoft.com/Licensing/`. Also, the configuration of the Linux/ Unix-based and Mac clients is different from the Windows devices. For Windows devices, these settings are received from the client settings and antimalware policies via the Configuration Manager client. For Linux/Unix and Mac, it is a manual process. For Linux/Mac, you must create a `scep.cfg` file and copy and deploy it to each Linux/Unix machine in order to configure the Endpoint Protection agent. For Mac devices, you can configure the Endpoint Protection agent on a Mac device, export the configuration, and then deploy this to other Mac devices.

Endpoint Protection Policies

Endpoint Protection has two policy types:

Antimalware   The antimalware policy is used to define the antimalware settings that will be applied to the endpoint client.

Windows Firewall   The Windows Firewall policy can be used to control the configuration of Windows Firewall on managed computers.

Both types of Endpoint Protection policies can be created and modified in the Configuration Manager console.

Antimalware Policy

Configuration Manager includes a default antimalware policy (Default Client Malware Policy) that can be modified. However, you should understand that changes made to that policy will be applied to all managed computers in the environment. Instead, the Configuration Manager administrator may decide to create a custom policy (or policies), and use those policy settings to override the default client policy.

The following configuration changes can be made in the antimalware policy:

Scheduled Scans   This option defines various information about the antimalware scan, including when the scan should occur, when the definition files should be updated, and if CPU usage should be limited. See Figure 14.5.

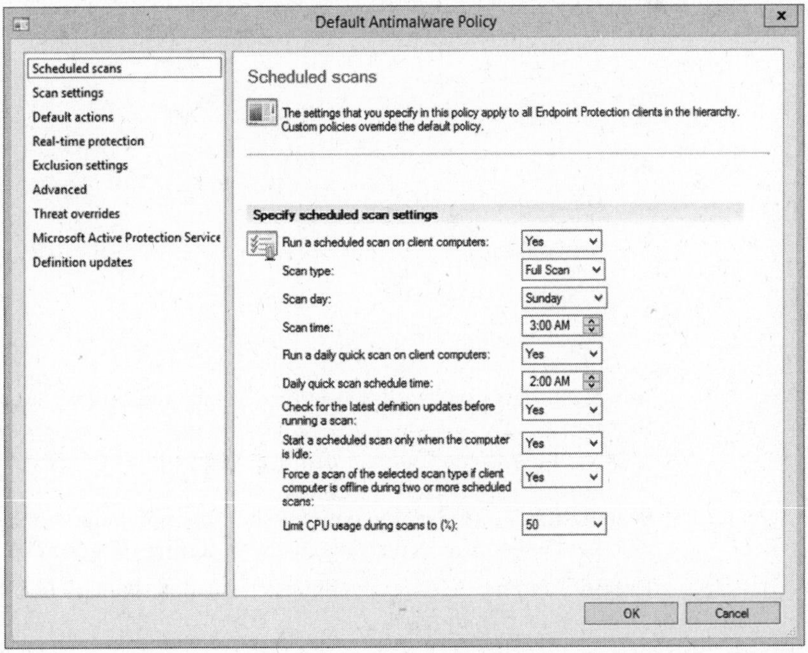

FIGURE 14.5
Configuring the Scheduled Scans settings

QUICK SCAN OR FULL SCAN?

The Scheduled Scans option allows you to configure when quick and full scans occur. But what is the difference between a quick scan and a full scan?

A quick scan does a check on locations where malware likes to hide in memory and on the hard drive. A quick scan should take only a few minutes, and performing the quick scan daily is a good practice.

A full scan checks all of the files on the hard disk and also checks memory and all programs that are currently active. This scan is more intensive and uses more resources on the computer, so performance on the computer may be impacted somewhat. This scan should typically be performed weekly and at a time when the computer will be on but not in use.

In the event of an active malware outbreak, you can trigger a quick or a full scan or a definition file download from the Configuration Manager console. The specified action will utilize the client communication channel and should take place immediately if the client is accessible. To trigger the scan or definition file download action against a collection, follow these steps:

1. Select Assets And Compliance ➢ Overview ➢ Device Collections.

2. Right-click the appropriate collection.

3. Select Endpoint Protection, and choose the appropriate action (Full Scan, Quick Scan, or Download Definition), as shown in the following illustration.

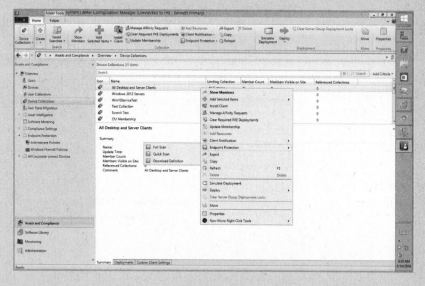

This will initiate an antimalware scan or definition download against the member computers of the collection.

Scan Settings This option defines what types of items should be scanned and also defines whether the end user can change the scan settings (Figure 14.6).

Default Actions This option defines the action that will be taken on threats based on their classification (Figure 14.7).

FIGURE 14.6
Configuring the
Scan Settings

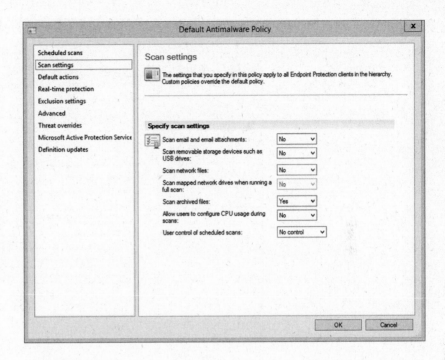

FIGURE 14.7
Configuring the
Default Actions
settings

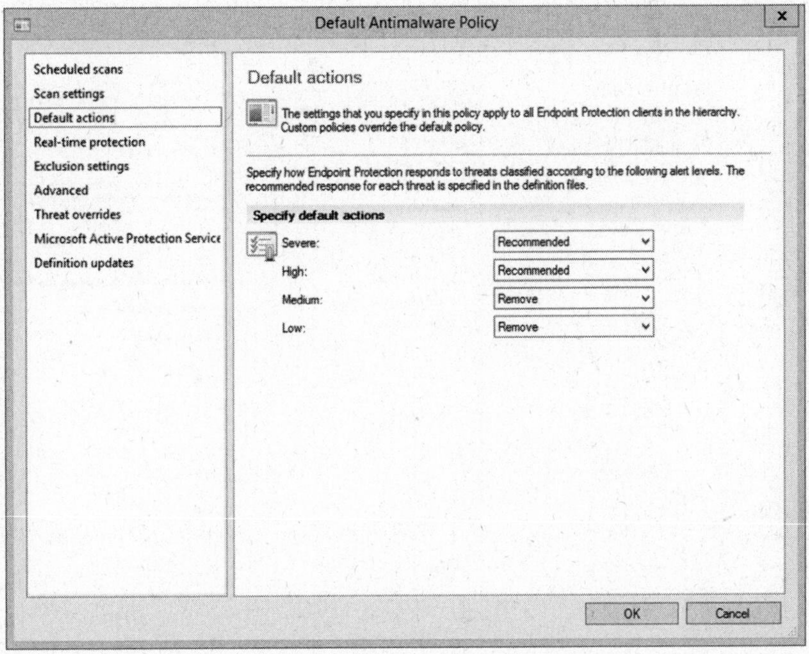

Real-Time Protection   This option defines the configuration of real-time protection and scanning (Figure 14.8).

FIGURE 14.8
Configuring the
Real-Time Protection
settings

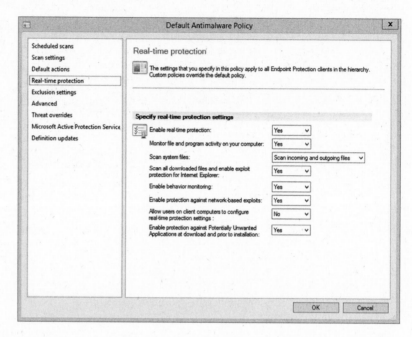

Exclusion Settings   This option defines any files, folders, file types, or processes that should be excluded from malware scanning (Figure 14.9). Note that excluding items may increase the risk of malware not being detected on a computer.

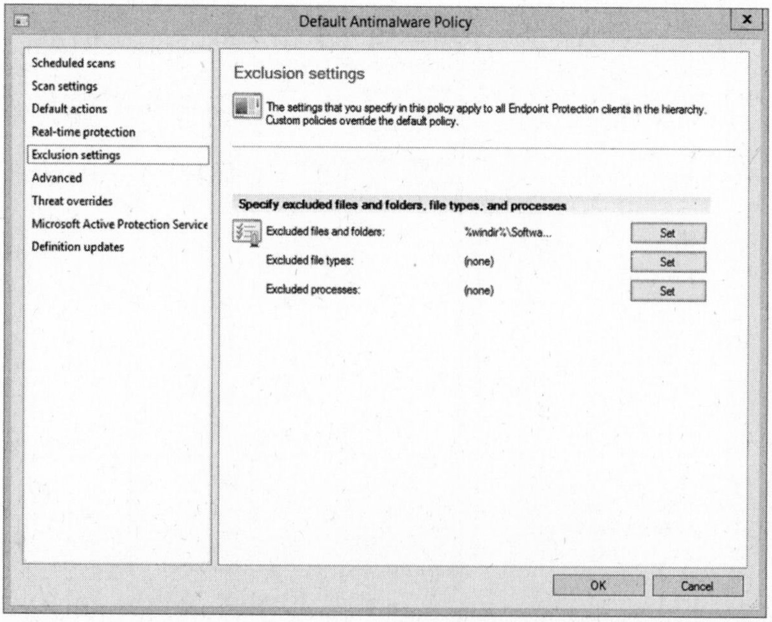

FIGURE 14.9
Configuring the
Exclusion Settings

Advanced This option provides the ability to customize advanced settings, including interaction with users, how long quarantined files should be retained, and so on (Figure 14.10).

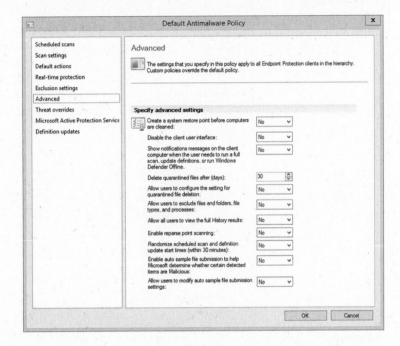

Threat Overrides This option allows you to add threat names to the threat list (Figure 14.11).

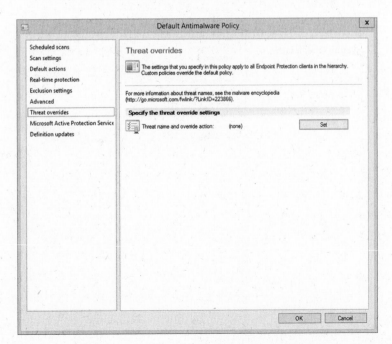

Microsoft Active Protection Service   This option allows you to configure MAPS (Figure 14.12).

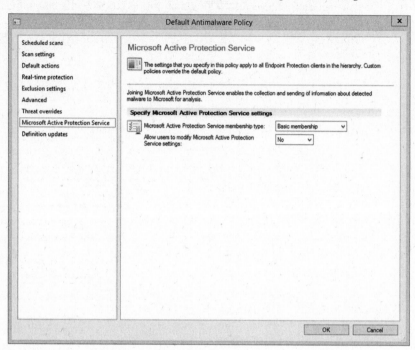

Definition Updates   This option allows you to configure how Endpoint Protection clients
will receive definition updates (Figure 14.13).

Configuration Manager includes several predefined antimalware policy templates:

SCEP_Default_CfgMgr
SCEP_High_Security
SCEP_Performance_Optimized
SCEP_Standard_Desktop

These policies apply settings that are optimized for a particular product or feature and can easily be imported and used in the environment. You can also import antimalware policies that were created in Forefront Endpoint Protection (FEP) 2010 if you were previously using it in earlier versions of Configuration Manager.

To import one of the predefined antimalware policy templates:

1. Open the Configuration Manager console and choose Assets And Compliance ➢ Overview ➢ Endpoint Protection ➢ Antimalware Policies.

2. Right-click on Antimalware Policies and select Import.

3. Select the desired policy template and click Open.

4. Make any adjustments to the imported template that may be required for your environment and click OK.

5. Deploy the template to a collection.

In Configuration Manager you can also merge policies by taking a default policy and merging it with another policy. This scenario may be useful if you want to use the default client policy but apply some specific file or folder exclusions that were included in one of the policies that was imported.

Windows Firewall Policy

The Endpoint Protection feature of Configuration Manager can also be used to manage the Windows Firewall policies for managed computers. Configuration Manager does not include a default Windows Firewall policy, and there is no ability to import or export a policy, but you can easily create a new policy in the Configuration Manager console.

As you can see in Figure 14.14, the Windows Firewall policy configuration is straightforward. You can create a new Windows Firewall policy in the Configuration Manager console and configure the policy to enable/disable the firewall, to block incoming connections, and also to define user communication. Once you have configured the policy, you can then deploy it to a collection.

The Windows Firewall policy includes three profile types: domain, public, and private. These profiles are related to the network that the user or computer is connected to.

Domain   The domain profile will be applied if the connection is authenticated to a domain controller for the domain of which the user or computer is a member. By default, all other network connections are initially classified as public networks, and Windows asks the user to identify the network as either public or private.

Public   The public profile is intended for use in public locations (such as airports and coffee shops).

Private   The private network location is typically intended for use in a home or office.

FIGURE 14.14
Configuring Windows
Firewall policy

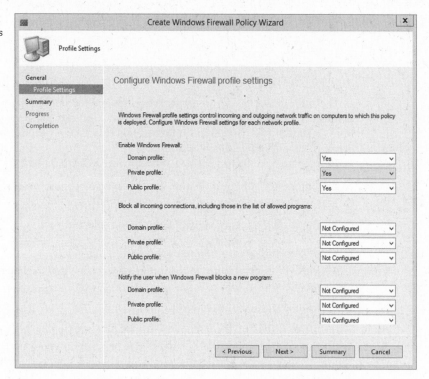

Assigning Policy

The Default Client Malware Policy is automatically applied to all of the computers managed by Configuration Manager. If you create a custom policy and assign it to a collection, the settings in the custom policy will override the settings that are defined in the default policy.

Use the following steps to assign a custom antimalware policy to a collection:

1. Open the Configuration Manager console and choose Assets And Compliance ➤ Overview ➤ Endpoint Protection ➤ Antimalware Policies.

2. Select the custom policy and choose Deploy from the ribbon.

3. Select the collection, and click OK.

The next time the Configuration Manager clients in the targeted collection retrieve policy (every 60 minutes by default), they will apply the Endpoint Protection client settings that were established in the policy. If two custom policies have different values configured for the same settings, the policy with the highest order value will be applied. You can adjust the order in the Configuration Manager console by right-clicking the custom policy and selecting Increase Priority or Decrease Priority. See Figure 14.15.

FIGURE 14.15
Increasing policy
priority

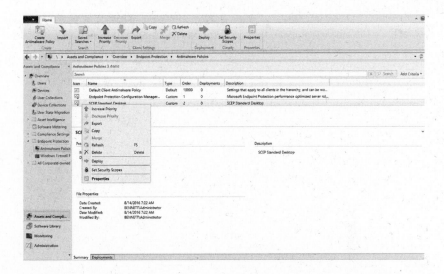

DEFAULT ORDER VALUE

The order for the Default Client Malware Policy has a default value of 10,000 and cannot be changed.

Definition Files

As discussed in Chapter 8, "Software Updates," Configuration Manager provides the ability to automatically download and deploy security updates to managed computers using a feature called Automatic Deployment Rules (ADR). These rules can be used for monthly security updates (Patch Tuesday, for example), and they can also be used for Endpoint Protection definition file updates. The Endpoint Protection definition files are updated several times a day, and an automated deployment solution like an ADR is quite useful in ensuring that your Configuration Manager clients received updated definition files as they become available. For more information on how to create automatic deployment rules, refer to Chapter 8. Note that if you are managing Windows 10 devices, those clients will utilize Windows Defender as the antimalware agent, not the Endpoint Protection agent, so you will need to ensure that your ADR retrieves the definition files for both FEP 2010 and Windows Defender.

Once the automatic deployment rules for Endpoint Protection have been configured, you may want to verify that the automatic deployment rules are working properly for the Endpoint Protection definition updates. The following process will help verify that the clients have the latest definition files.

The first question you may be wondering is, what is the latest version of the Endpoint Protection definition files? Checking the Microsoft Malware Protection Center website

```
https://www.microsoft.com/en-us/security/portal/definitions/whatsnew.aspx
```

is one quick method to provide that answer.

As you can see in Figure 14.16, the latest definition update that was available at the time this image was captured is 1.225.3909.0. So you now know how to tell which version of the definition file the Configuration Manager environment should be using.

FIGURE 14.16
Obtaining the definition update version

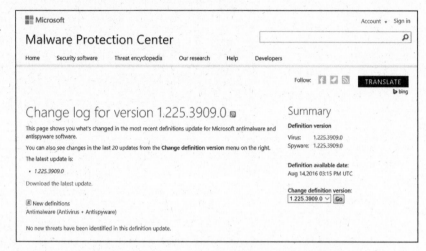

If you open the Configuration Manager console and choose Software Library ➤ Overview ➤ Software Updates ➤ All Software Updates, you can view the list of software updates in the catalog in your Configuration Manager environment. If you search for "definition update," you can look for software updates that have a matching title and focus on the Endpoint Protection definition files.

Expect to see several definition files listed, but only one should typically be current and active (the black arrow in the image highlights the current definition file). As you can see in Figure 14.17, the version of that file is 1.225.3909.0, so all of your clients should be using that version of the definition file. Note that in the console the current updates have a green arrow, superseded updates have yellow arrows, and the expired definition files have a black X.

FIGURE 14.17
Definition update status

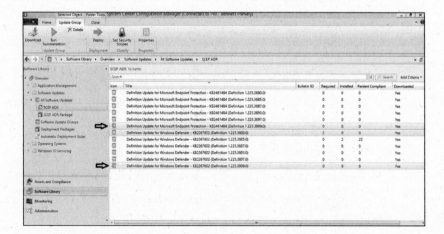

You now know that the endpoint clients should be using version 1.225.3909.0 of the definition file. If you open the Endpoint Protection client on a managed workstation, you can check the definition file that is currently being used by the client. See Figure 14.18.

FIGURE 14.18
Verifying the
Endpoint Protection
client definition
version

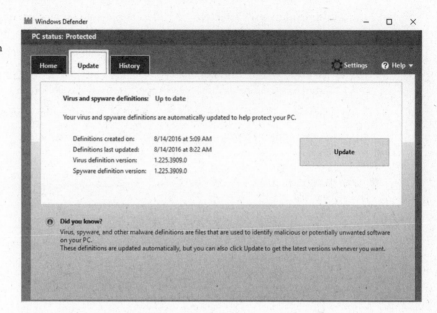

As you can see, this client is using the correct version of the definition file. If you find in your environment that the definition file is an older version, it's possible that the client hasn't triggered the process yet to get the latest definition file. You could click Update and force the client to obtain the latest file. If the client still does not have the latest definition file, then you may need to troubleshoot the issue further and determine why the client is unable to retrieve the updated content.

Alerts

The ability to create alerts is a very useful feature in Configuration Manager. Alerts can be used to notify a Configuration Manager administrative user when specific events (such as a malware outbreak) have occurred in the environment. The administrator can view alerts in the Configuration Manager console, in reports, and via email subscriptions. The ability to display alerts in the console or via email is especially important for Endpoint Protection–related events because it allows the administrator to quickly become aware of a malware event.

Endpoint Protection alerts are configured in the device collection properties. You cannot configure user collections for alerts. Configuration Manager has alerts for various issues and conditions and includes four alerts related specifically to malware:

Malware Detection   An alert is generated if a managed computer in the specified collection has malware.

Malware Outbreak An alert is generated when a certain percentage of managed computers in the specified collection have malware detected.

Repeated Malware Detection An alert is generated if specific malware is detected more than a certain number of times over a certain number of hours in a specified collection.

Multiple Malware Detection An alert is generated if more than a specified number of malware types are detected over a given period for a specified collection.

To receive alerts, you must enable a device collection to send alerts. Here is the process:

1. In the Configuration Manager console, select the device collection that should be configured to send alerts, and select Properties from the ribbon.

   In this example, we will select a collection named Dallas Computers.

2. In the collection properties window, select the Alerts tab. See Figure 14.19.

FIGURE 14.19
Alerts tab in the collection properties

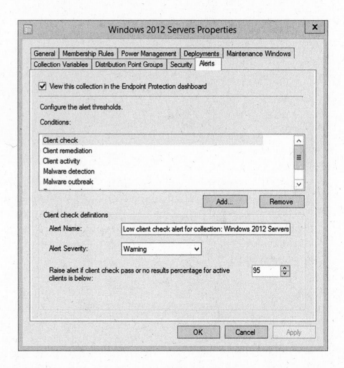

3. Enable the View This Collection In The Endpoint Protection Dashboard option, and click Add to specify alert thresholds.

   When you click Add to specify alert thresholds, the Add New Collection Alerts window will appear, and all of the items will be unchecked by default. You can make the necessary changes that meet your requirements and click OK to apply the change.

At this point, you have configured the devices in a collection to generate alerts if the alert conditions are met. Those alerts can be viewed in the console, viewed in reports, and sent via email subscriptions.

CONFIGURATION MANAGER CAN SEND YOU EMAIL

In Configuration Manager you can configure an SMTP server that will be used to email Endpoint Protection alerts to administrative users. Follow these steps:

1. In the Configuration Manager console, choose Administration ➤ Overview ➤ Site Configuration ➤ Sites.

2. Select the CAS (or standalone primary site server) and click Settings ➤ Configure Site Components ➤ Email Notification.

3. Enable the email notification option, enter the required email settings for your environment, and click Apply.

   You also have the option to test the SMTP server and verify that the configuration is set properly.

4. Configure alert email subscriptions in the Monitoring workspace by choosing Monitoring ➤ Overview ➤ Alerts ➤ Subscriptions and selecting Create Subscription in the ribbon.

Reporting

Configuration Manager has several reports related to the Endpoint Protection products. There are currently six reports in the Endpoint Protection category:

Antimalware Activity Report This report shows an overview of antimalware activity and is shown in Figure 14.20.

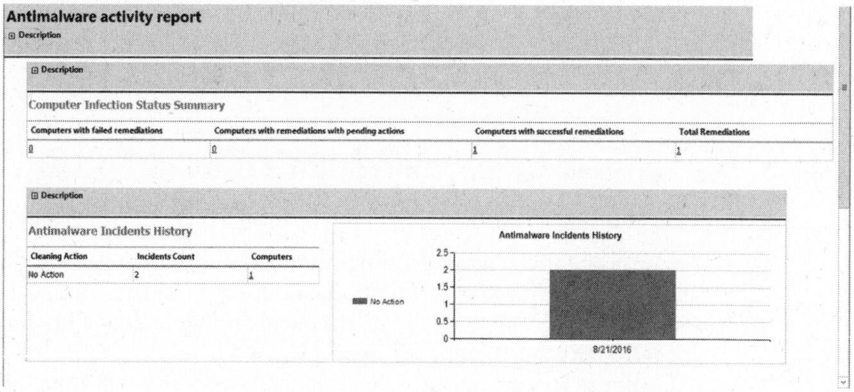

FIGURE 14.20
Antimalware
Activity Report

Antimalware Overall Status And History This report shows an overall status of antimalware activity over a specified period.

Computer Malware Details This report shows the endpoint client status and antimalware activity.

Infected Computers This report shows a list of computers with a particular threat detected.

Top Users By Threats This report lists the users with the highest number of detected threats.

User Threat List This report shows the list of threats found under a particular user account.

Client Notifications

Many activities in Configuration Manager are pull-based and use polling intervals and scheduled intervals to define when processes take place. This is acceptable for many features in Configuration Manager, but in the case of an outbreak of malware in an environment, an administrator may need to take immediate action on the managed clients and not wait for a policy cycle to occur. Configuration Manager accomplishes this expedited communication process by creating a client notification channel between the site server and the managed clients. This "fast" channel is used for all endpoint-related activities as well as other client actions, including triggering the retrieval of computer or user policies and initiating a hardware or software inventory cycle. This client notification channel is a push-based communication process and allows a Configuration Manager administrator to take immediate action against clients, like forcing clients to perform a scan to look for malware. The client notification channel is supported only on Windows devices.

The client notification process consists of several parts. The Notification Manager component exists on the Configuration Manager site server and the notification server exists on the management points. The notification agent is part of the Configuration Manager client. The notification agent on the client initiates a persistent connection with the notification server and will attempt to use TCP mode first and then fall back to HTTP if TCP mode fails. Once the connection is established, the notification agent will send a keep-alive message every 15 minutes to maintain the connection with the notification server. The default TCP port is 10123.

The following are the related Configuration Manager logs for the client notification channel components:

◆ Notification Manager: `..\Microsoft Configuration Manager\Logs\bgbmgr.log`

◆ Notification Server: `..\Microsoft Configuration Manager\Logs\BgbServer.log`

◆ Notification Agent: `C:\Windows\ccm\logs\CcmNotificationAgent.log`

For example, if you use the Configuration Manager console to trigger a quick malware scan against a client computer, you can monitor the client communication channel request via `CcmNotificationAgent.log` on the client and the status of the endpoint scan via `EndpointProtectionAgent.log`. See Figure 14.21.

We will use the remainder of this chapter to work through a real-world scenario and show Endpoint Protection in action.

FIGURE 14.21
Notification Agent
log and Endpoint
Protection log

Log Text	Component	Date/Time	Thread
EP version 4.7.214.0 is already installed.	EndpointProtectionAgent	8/21/2016 2:05:00 PM	212 (0xD4)
Expected Version 4.7.214.0 is exactly same with installed version 4.7.214.0.	EndpointProtectionAgent	8/21/2016 2:05:00 PM	212 (0xD4)
Re-apply EP AM policy.	EndpointProtectionAgent	8/21/2016 2:05:00 PM	212 (0xD4)
Apply AM Policy.	EndpointProtectionAgent	8/21/2016 2:05:00 PM	212 (0xD4)
Create Process Command line: "c:\Program Files\Windows Defender\\ConfigSecurityP...	EndpointProtectionAgent	8/21/2016 2:05:00 PM	212 (0xD4)
Applied the C:\Windows\CCM\EPAMPolicy.xml with ConfigSecurityPolicy.exe successf...	EndpointProtectionAgent	8/21/2016 2:05:04 PM	212 (0xD4)
Save new policy state 1 to registry SOFTWARE\Microsoft\CCM\EPAgent\PolicyApplicat...	EndpointProtectionAgent	8/21/2016 2:05:04 PM	212 (0xD4)
State 1 and ErrorCode 0 and ErrorMsg and PolicyName Default Client Antimalware Poli...	EndpointProtectionAgent	8/21/2016 2:05:04 PM	212 (0xD4)
Skip sending state message due to same state message already exists.	EndpointProtectionAgent	8/21/2016 2:05:04 PM	212 (0xD4)
Firewall provider is installed.	EndpointProtectionAgent	8/21/2016 2:05:06 PM	212 (0xD4)
Installed firewall provider meet the requirements.	EndpointProtectionAgent	8/21/2016 2:05:07 PM	212 (0xD4)
Endpoint is triggered by message.	EndpointProtectionAgent	8/21/2016 3:22:00 PM	4940 (0x134C)
File C:\Windows\ccmsetup\SCEPInstall.exe version is 4.7.214.0.	EndpointProtectionAgent	8/21/2016 3:22:00 PM	4940 (0x134C)
EP version 4.7.214.0 is already installed.	EndpointProtectionAgent	8/21/2016 3:22:00 PM	4940 (0x134C)
Expected Version 4.7.214.0 is exactly same with installed version 4.7.214.0.	EndpointProtectionAgent	8/21/2016 3:22:00 PM	4940 (0x134C)
Check and enforce EP Deployment state.	EndpointProtectionAgent	8/21/2016 3:22:00 PM	4940 (0x134C)
EP Client is already installed, will NOT trigger reinstallation.	EndpointProtectionAgent	8/21/2016 3:22:00 PM	4940 (0x134C)
Sending message to external event agent to test and enable notification	EndpointProtectionAgent	8/21/2016 3:22:00 PM	4940 (0x134C)
Sending message to endpoint ExternalEventAgent	EndpointProtectionAgent	8/21/2016 3:22:00 PM	4940 (0x134C)
EP Policy Default Client Antimalware Policy is already applied.	EndpointProtectionAgent	8/21/2016 3:22:00 PM	4940 (0x134C)
Firewall provider is installed.	EndpointProtectionAgent	8/21/2016 3:22:01 PM	4940 (0x134C)
Installed firewall provider meet the requirements.	EndpointProtectionAgent	8/21/2016 3:22:01 PM	4940 (0x134C)
start to send State Message with topic type = 2001, state id = 3, and error code = 0x0000...	EndpointProtectionAgent	8/21/2016 3:22:01 PM	4940 (0x134C)
Skip sending state message due to same state message already exists.	EndpointProtectionAgent	8/21/2016 3:22:01 PM	4940 (0x134C)
Endpoint is triggered by message.	EndpointProtectionAgent	8/21/2016 5:25:30 PM	5316 (0x14C4)
File C:\Windows\ccmsetup\SCEPInstall.exe version is 4.7.214.0.	EndpointProtectionAgent	8/21/2016 5:25:30 PM	5316 (0x14C4)
EP version 4.7.214.0 is already installed.	EndpointProtectionAgent	8/21/2016 5:25:30 PM	5316 (0x14C4)
Expected Version 4.7.214.0 is exactly same with installed version 4.7.214.0.	EndpointProtectionAgent	8/21/2016 5:25:30 PM	5316 (0x14C4)
Starting quick scan action...	EndpointProtectionAgent	8/21/2016 5:25:30 PM	5316 (0x14C4)
Create Process Command line: "c:\Program Files\Windows Defender\MpCmdRun.exe" ...	EndpointProtectionAgent	8/21/2016 5:25:30 PM	5316 (0x14C4)
Trigger the application c:\Program Files\Windows Defender\MpCmdRun.exe starting s...	EndpointProtectionAgent	8/21/2016 5:25:30 PM	5316 (0x14C4)
Send State Message with topic type = 2003, state id = 3, and message = <INSTANCE><...	EndpointProtectionAgent	8/21/2016 5:25:30 PM	5316 (0x14C4)

C:\Windows\CCM\Logs\CcmNotificationAgent.log

Log Text	Component	Date/Time	Thread
Successfully sent keep-alive message.	BgbAgent	8/21/2016 4:22:21 PM	4516 (0x11A4)
Successfully sent keep-alive message.	BgbAgent	8/21/2016 4:37:21 PM	4516 (0x11A4)
Successfully sent keep-alive message.	BgbAgent	8/21/2016 4:52:21 PM	4516 (0x11A4)
Successfully sent keep-alive message.	BgbAgent	8/21/2016 5:07:21 PM	4516 (0x11A4)
Successfully sent keep-alive message.	BgbAgent	8/21/2016 5:22:22 PM	4516 (0x11A4)
Receive task from server with pushid= 70, taskid=69, taskguid= 1F6F8EF5-952B-4A80-9B...	BgbAgent	8/21/2016 5:25:30 PM	4516 (0x11A4)

 Real World Scenario

LET'S INSTALL SOME MALWARE!

You are the Configuration Manager administrator at a company, and you have been telling your fellow IT department personnel about all of the great features that Configuration Manager offers. You are especially excited about the Endpoint Protection feature and the security against malware that it provides.

Your manager has asked you to demonstrate to the team how the Endpoint Protection feature works. You decide it would be a great demo to actually deploy malware to the environment and have Configuration Manager identify the outbreak and remediate it. Seems a bit risky, right? And where do you get a virus so that you can prove Endpoint Protection works? Download some questionable files from the Internet or click on that email attachment from an unknown person? Not likely. It would be much safer to use a test virus, a piece of software that *looks* like malware but doesn't actually cause any damage.

continues

continued

One option is to use the antimalware test file that was created by the IT security research organization called EICAR (you can read more about them at www.eicar.org). The EICAR test file that they provide on their website looks like a virus or malware to antimalware software, but it is completely safe and benign. The test file simulates a malware attack but does not harm the computer in any way. However, just to be safe, you decide to perform this demo in your Configuration Manager test environment that is separate from the production network.

Using the EICAR antimalware test file, in a *test* Configuration Manager environment that is *not* connected to the production network, you can safely simulate the occurrence of a malware event on a managed computer without actually damaging the computer or causing a malware outbreak panic.

Note: Before using this tool, visit the EICAR website and make sure you read through all of the documentation and disclaimers for the use of the tool.

RUN THE TEST!

You are now ready to run the demo for your team.

1. Log on to the Windows computer that will become your "infected" workstation, launch the EICAR malware test file from the EICAR website, and then monitor the results.

   First, you see by the status window that Windows Defender (for Windows 10) or Endpoint Protection on the Windows computer detected malware and is taking action to remove it.

2. Look at the Windows Defender or Endpoint Protection client on the computer, choose the History tab, and see the malware activity. You can view the name of the detected malware item, the alert level, the date and time the event occurred, and the action that was taken.

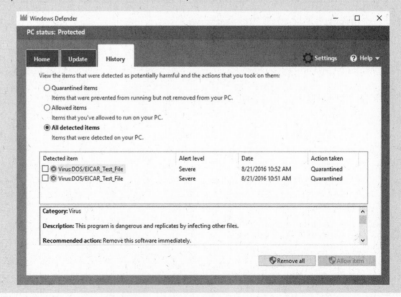

BUT WHAT HAPPENED ON THE SITE SERVER?

You saw Endpoint Protection on the Windows computer flag the EICAR test file as malware and immediately quarantine the malware. But what would you see at the site server level? How would the built-in monitoring make you aware of the issue? Follow these steps to find out:

1. Open System Center Endpoint Protection Status in the Configuration Manager console (Monitoring ➤ Overview ➤ Security ➤ Endpoint Protection Status ➤ System Center Endpoint Protection Status).

2. Select the collection to see the overall status for the environment, including the number and percentage of clients that were affected by malware (one computer in this test). You can also view the top five malware by number of computers and the status of the definition files on managed computers in this window.

3. You could open the Alerts section of the Monitoring workspace to view the alerts that were generated as a result of the EICAR malware test being executed on the client, and if you have configured email subscriptions, you would have received those alerts as emails.

4. You can also use the endpoint reports to view the status of the environment. Select the Antimalware Activity Report to view the overall status. You can clearly see the total number of remediation activities, the number of antimalware incidents, and so on.

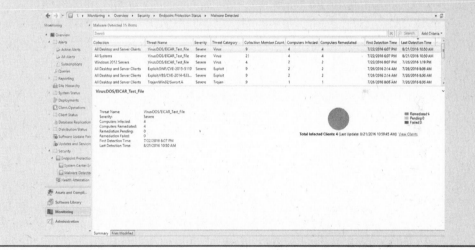

The Bottom Line

Deploy and configure the Endpoint Protection site system and client. The three main components of enabling Endpoint Protection are as follows:

- Install and configure the Endpoint Protection site system.

- Enable and configure the Endpoint Protection client.

- Configure the antimalware policies.

Master It Do you need to create a package or application to deploy the Endpoint Protection client? Do Windows 10 computers use the Endpoint Protection agent?

Create and assign an Endpoint Protection policy. Endpoint Protection has two types of policy:

◆ Antimalware

◆ Windows Firewall

The antimalware policy is used to define the antimalware settings, whereas the Windows Firewall policy can be used to control the configuration of Windows Firewall on managed computers. Both types of Endpoint Protection policies are created and modified in the Configuration Manager console.

Master It If you modify the default client antimalware policy and also create a custom antimalware policy with different values for the settings and apply it to a collection, which settings will be applied?

Chapter 15

Role-Based Administration

Ask a System Center Configuration Manager administrator about one of the more challenging aspects of administering Configuration Manager in their environment, and they might answer, "Security!"

System Center Framework introduced the concept of role-based security administration. Under the role-based access control (RBAC) model, administrators are able to use security roles and security scopes to define access to resources for the administrative users in the environment. System Center Configuration Manager adopts the RBAC security model and, as a result, greatly simplifies the administration of security in Configuration Manager.

In this chapter, you will learn to

◆ Understand the role-based administration model in Configuration Manager

◆ Distinguish security roles from security scopes

◆ Understand which objects in Configuration Manager define an administrative user

◆ Understand how to simulate permissions in the Configuration Manager console

Overview of Role-Based Administration

Configuration Manager uses the RBAC model to define access to its features and functions. Under this model, the Configuration Manager administrator uses security roles, security scopes, and collections to define the administrative scope for the Configuration Manager administrative users. This provides the administrator with the ability to define the security configuration for an administrative user in such a way that the only features that the user is able to view and interact with in the console are those that are part of their responsibility. All other items are essentially hidden and not available to the administrative user. This behavior is sometimes referred to as "Show me" behavior.

For example, consider a help desk analyst who needs the ability to deploy an application to computers in one geographic location but should not have the ability to deploy applications to computers in any other locations. Using the RBAC model, the administrator could easily create security roles, security scopes, and collections to satisfy those requirements. We will look at a sample scenario later.

One important new feature in Configuration Manager is that reports can now utilize the RBAC model. The data that is returned by all of the reports will be filtered based on the permissions of the administrative user who is running the report. This greatly simplifies the process of securing access to report data.

Using Security Roles and Security Scopes

Security roles are used to define tasks or functions, while security scopes are used to define access to objects. Configuration Manager provides some default roles and scopes, and administrators can also create their own to meet specific business needs. By using combinations of security roles, security scopes, and collections, administrators can easily control access to the environment and define what the administrative users can view and manage.

As stated previously, this is sometimes referred to as "Show me" behavior and basically means that administrative users will see only what is relevant to them and what they have access to in the Configuration Manager console. This is also known as *access-based enumeration*. Console objects that the administrative user has access to are visible in the console, whereas all others are hidden. This greatly simplifies the console experience for the administrative user and helps reduce confusion.

Managing with Flat Hierarchies

One of the design goals for Configuration Manager is that organizations should have flat hierarchies. In fact, many companies may find they need only a single Configuration Manager primary site. One common reason for multiple SMS or Configuration Manager sites in previous versions of the product was to completely segregate the environment based on roles or functions. For example, one primary site may have been used to manage only desktops and laptops, and another primary site used to manage only servers. Separating the sites completely ensured that the administrators for the desktop and laptop site could not manage the servers in any way, and vice versa.

With the ability to designate control based on security roles, security scopes, and collections in Configuration Manager, segregating the environment through the use of multiple primary sites is unnecessary. The administrator could have all devices report to a single primary site and then use role-based security to define the required access for the administrative users. The desktop support team could be configured to see and manage only desktop computers, and the server team could be configured to see and manage only servers.

Another benefit of the new security model in Configuration Manager is that the administrative objects (security roles, security scopes, and collections) need to be created only once in a Configuration Manager hierarchy with a CAS and child primary sites because that information is sent throughout the hierarchy as globally replicated data.

Security Roles

Configuration Manager uses security roles to define access to resources for administrative users. Security roles can be configured to provide administrative users with as much or as little access as they need to perform their job.

Configuration Manager includes several built-in security roles that handle many common administrative task scenarios. Figure 15.1 shows the security roles that are included. The following list provides a brief description of the built-in roles:

Application Administrator This role provides the permissions to perform both the application Deployment Manager role and the Application Author role. This role also provides the ability to manage queries, view site settings, manage collections, and edit settings for user device affinity.

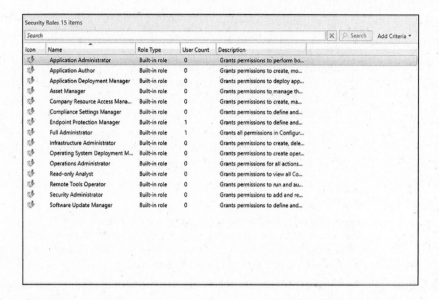

FIGURE 15.1
Built-in security roles

Application Author This role provides the ability to create, modify, and delete applications. This role also provides the ability to manage packages and programs, manage alerts, and view status messages.

Application Deployment Manager This role provides the ability to deploy applications. Application deployment managers can view the list of applications and can manage other items related to applications, including alerts, templates, packages, and programs. They can view collections and collection membership and can also view status messages, queries, and conditional delivery rules.

Asset Manager This role provides the ability to manage the Asset Intelligence synchronization point, the Asset Intelligence reporting classes, hardware and software inventory, and software metering settings.

Compliance Resource Access Manager This role provides permissions to create, manage, and deploy the company resource access profiles. These include Wi-Fi, VPN, and certificate profiles to users and devices.

Compliance Settings Manager This role provides permissions to manage the Compliance Settings feature. Compliance Settings managers can create, modify, and delete configuration items and baselines. They can also deploy configuration baselines to collections, initiate compliance evaluation, and initiate remediation for noncompliant computers.

Endpoint Protection Manager This role provides the ability to manage and monitor Endpoint Protection security policies. Administrative users with this role can create, modify, and delete Endpoint Protection policies. They can also deploy Endpoint Protection policies to collections, create and modify alerts, and monitor Endpoint Protection status.

Full Administrator This role provides access to all objects. The administrator who installs Configuration Manager is automatically granted this security role.

Infrastructure Administrator This role allows the administrative user to create, delete, and modify the Configuration Manager Server infrastructure and also provides access to the site migration tasks.

Operating System Deployment Manager This role provides the ability to create operating system images and to deploy them to computers. Administrative users with this role can manage many aspects of the OSD process, including the operating system upgrade packages and images, task sequences, drivers, boot images, and state migration settings.

Operations Administrator This role provides permissions for all actions in Configuration Manager except for the ability to manage security (managing administrative users, security roles, collections, and security scopes).

Read-Only Analyst This role provides the ability to only read all objects in Configuration Manager.

Remote Tools Operator This role grants permissions to run and audit the remote administration tools. Administrative users with this role can use the Configuration Manager console to run the out-of-band management console and can use remote control, Windows Remote Assistance, and Remote Desktop Services.

Security Administrator This role provides the ability to add and remove administrative users and to associate administrative users with security roles, collections, and security scopes.

Software Update Manager This role provides the ability to define and deploy software updates. Administrative users with this role can create collections, software update groups, deployments, and templates and can enable software updates for Network Access Protection.

FULL ADMINISTRATOR? OH MY!

As shown in the list, the Full Administrator role in Configuration Manager provides access to all objects in the environment. Users (or groups) who are assigned to this security role hold all the keys to all of the castles in the Configuration Manager environment. As a result, the number of users or groups who have this security role should be very limited. Because of the power that this role holds, the fewer the administrative users who have this role the better! Also, the organization should periodically review the access requirements for administrative users who hold this role and determine if they can be provided with a less powerful security role.

As you can see in the preceding list, each security role provides specific permissions for various object types. If you want to see the permissions that a specific security role holds, you can view that information in the Configuration Manager console. For example, if you wanted to examine the permissions for the Application Administrator role, you would perform the following steps:

1. In the Configuration Manager administrative console, select Administration ➤ Overview ➤ Security ➤ Security Roles.

2. Select the role that you want to inspect. In this case, it is the Application Administrator role.

3. Click Properties in the Home tab of the ribbon.

   This will open the Application Administrator Properties window.

4. Select the Permissions tab.

5. Now you can view the permissions for the role (Figure 15.2).

FIGURE 15.2
Application
Administrator
Properties

It is worth noting that you cannot change the permissions for the built-in security roles. You also cannot delete the built-in roles or export them. If you need to customize a built-in security role, then you should choose an existing role that is similar to the new role and make a copy of it. You will then have the ability to modify or delete the copied role. You can also export and import copied security roles. This import/export ability may be useful in a test or pilot Configuration Manager environment and would provide you with the ability to fine-tune the required security roles and permissions in the test site before deploying them to the production Configuration Manager site.

Also, if administrative users will perform multiple functions in Configuration Manager (such as deploy applications *and* use remote tools), the administrator should assign multiple security roles to the administrative user instead of creating a new security role that combines a variety of tasks into a single role.

Security Scopes

Configuration Manager uses security scopes (Figure 15.3) to provide administrative users with access to secured objects. All secured objects must be assigned to at least one security scope. The association between the object and the security scope is managed from the object itself, not from the security scope.

FIGURE 15.3

Security scopes

As shown in Figure 15.3, Configuration Manager includes two built-in security scopes: All and Default.

All   The All security scope grants access to all scopes. Objects cannot be assigned to this security scope.

Default   All objects are assigned to the All security scope when Configuration Manager is installed. As new objects are added to Configuration Manager, they are also automatically added to the Default scope.

The administrator can also create custom security scopes that are based on the needs of the environment and add the objects to the custom scopes.

Creating a Custom Security Scope

The following are the steps to create a custom security scope:

1. In the Configuration Manager administrative console, select the Administration work-space and then choose Overview ➤ Security ➤ Security Scopes.

2. In the ribbon select Create Security Scope.

3. Provide a descriptive name for the security scope in the security scope Name field. In this case, name the new scope **Mastering**.

   You can add a description and make changes to the administrative assignments if needed.

4. Once the changes have been completed, click OK.

The new security scope should now be visible in the console, as shown in Figure 15.4.

FIGURE 15.4
New security scope

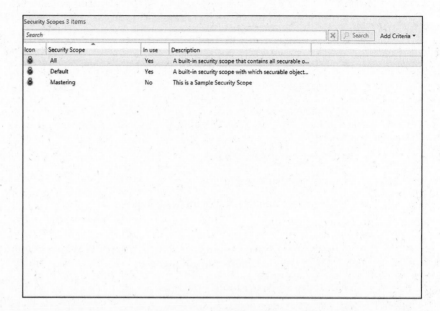

Security scopes can contain one or more object types, which include the following:

- Alert subscriptions
- Antimalware policies
- Applications
- Boot images
- Boundary groups
- Collections
- Configuration items
- Custom client settings
- Distribution points and distribution point groups
- Driver packages
- Global conditions

◆ Migration jobs

◆ Operating system images

◆ Operating system installation packages

◆ Packages

◆ Queries

◆ Sites

◆ Software metering rules

◆ Software update groups

◆ Software updates deployment packages

◆ Task sequences

Several object types cannot be included in security scopes and must be secured via security roles. These objects include the following:

◆ Active Directory forests

◆ Administrative users

◆ Alerts

◆ Boundaries

◆ Computer associations

◆ Default client settings

◆ Deployment templates

◆ Device drivers

◆ Exchange Server connectors

◆ Migration site-to-site mappings

◆ Mobile device enrollment profiles

◆ Security roles

◆ Security scopes

◆ Site addresses

◆ Site system servers and roles

◆ Software titles

◆ Software updates

◆ Status messages

◆ User device affinities

Assigning Resources to a Security Scope

Now that you understand how to create a security scope and you know which object types can be included, you will assign a resource to the new security scope you just created.

1. In the Configuration Manager administrative console, select the resource that will be added to the Custom Security Scope you created previously.

   Remember that only certain types of objects can be added to security scopes.

2. For this example we will select an application called XML Notepad, which was previously configured by another administrator.

3. Select Software Library ➤ Overview ➤ Application Management ➤ Applications in the Configuration Manager console, and choose the application that you want to manage.

4. Now choose the Classify section in the ribbon and then select Set Security Scopes.

   You could also right-click the application and select Set Security Scopes there.

5. In the Set Security Scopes window, select the desired scope or scopes for this object and click OK.

   For this scenario select the new security scope Mastering. It should now be visible in the console (Figure 15.5).

FIGURE 15.5
New security scope
and application

6. Once the setting is applied, view the security scope and see that the In Use value is now set to Yes, as shown in Figure 15.6.

FIGURE 15.6

New security scope

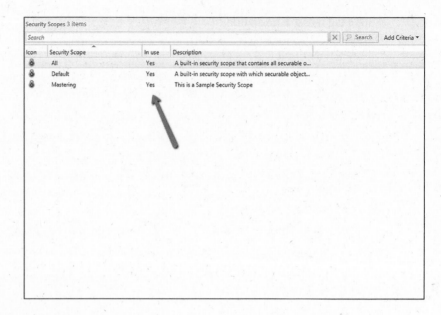

Viewing Security Scope Objects

If you want to view all the objects that are associated with a given security scope, a built-in report in Configuration Manager will provide that information.

1. In the Configuration Manager administrative console, choose Monitoring ➤ Overview ➤ Reporting ➤ Reports.

   There are a few reports related to security scopes. The report you will run is titled Objects Secured By A Single Security Scope.

2. Right-click the report and select Run.

   For this example use Application <all values> for the Object Type field, and in the Security Scope field specify the scope you created earlier. You can either enter the scope name in the field or select the Values option to list all known values for that particular field.

3. For this scenario use **Mastering** because this was the name you gave the security scope when it was created.

4. Once the values have been set, click View Report (Figure 15.7).

This report is designed to show objects that are secured by only the specified security scope, which is Custom Security Scope in this scenario. If an object is secured by two or more security scopes (the Custom Security Scope and the default security scope, for example), then the object will not be displayed in this report.

FIGURE 15.7
Objects Secured By A
Single Security Scope
report

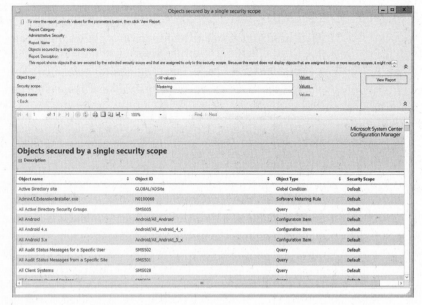

Collections

We have discussed how security roles and security scopes are used in the role-based administration model in Configuration Manager. In order for an administrative user to perform functions (for example, deploy an application) on a resource, the user must have access to a collection that contains the resource. You can use collections, along with security roles and security scopes, to tightly control what objects in the Configuration Manager console an administrative user can access.

Collections are probably not a new concept to the SMS and Configuration Manager veterans reading this book, but there are some changes to how collections work in Configuration Manager. This chapter does not perform an exhaustive examination of those changes, but it does highlight some of the changes and differences.

Using Collections

As a bit of background, collections are a way to logically group resources, such as devices or users, and collections can be created to meet various manageability and targeting requirements. The following are just a few examples:

◆ Use collections to separate servers from workstations or laptops.

◆ Use collections to separate pilot users or devices from production resources.

◆ Use collections based on departments, business units, or geographical location for targeting or administrative purposes.

Once the requirements for the collection have been defined and the collection has been created, the collection can be assigned to a Configuration Manager administrative user.

Collections in Configuration Manager contain one or more rules that control the membership of the collection. There are four rule types:

Direct Rule This rule type allows the administrator to explicitly define the users or computers that should be members of the collection. The membership of this collection does not change unless the administrator removes the explicit entry in the collection properties or the resource is removed from Configuration Manager. You might think of this approach as hard-coding machine names into the collection membership properties.

Query Rule This rule type dynamically updates the membership of the collection based on a query that is run on a schedule by Configuration Manager. Configuration Manager uses query-based collections for the built-in collections. Query-based collections are useful because they routinely evaluate the specified criteria and identify matching devices or users.

Include Collections Rule This new rule type allows the administrator to include members of another collection in a Configuration Manager collection. The membership of the current collection will be updated on a schedule when members of the included collection change.

Exclude Collections Rule This is another new rule type, and it allows the administrator to exclude the members of another collection from a Configuration Manager collection. The membership of the current collection will be updated on a schedule when members of the collection change.

Understanding the Default Collections

Configuration Manager includes a number of default collections. None of the default collections can be modified or deleted. The following are the default collections:

All User Groups Contains user groups discovered during Active Directory Security Group Discovery.

All Users Contains users discovered during Active Directory User Discovery.

All Users And User Groups Contains the All Users and the All User Groups collections. This collection cannot be modified and contains the largest scope of user resources.

All Desktop And Server Clients Contains server and desktop devices that have the Configuration Manager client installed. Membership is determined by Heartbeat Discovery.

All Mobile Devices Contains mobile devices that are managed by Configuration Manager. Membership is restricted to mobile devices that are successfully assigned to a site or discovered by the Exchange Server connector.

All Systems Contains the All Desktop And Server Clients, the All Mobile Devices, and All Unknown Computers collections. This collection cannot be modified and contains the largest scope of device resources.

All Unknown Computers Contains generic computer records for multiple computer platforms. It's typically used to deploy an operating system via PXE boot, bootable media, or prestaged media.

For more information about collections, see https://technet.microsoft.com/en-us/library/mt629314.aspx.

Administrative Users

An *administrative user* is an individual or group who will manage resources in the Configuration Manager infrastructure. The administrative user may have very limited access to resources in the environment (for example, a help desk analyst who can only deploy Adobe Reader DC to computers in a specific office location) or may have complete access to all objects in the Configuration Manager environment (the Configuration Manager administrator).

The administrative user consists of a Windows user account (or a group) and at least one security role and one security scope. If needed, a collection could be used to limit the administrative scope of the administrative user (Figure 15.8). These items are configured when the administrative user is created and can be changed later if need be.

FIGURE 15.8
Assigned security
scopes and collections

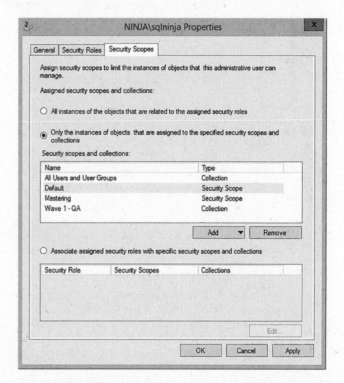

"ASSIGNED SECURITY SCOPES AND COLLECTIONS"—WHAT DOES THAT MEAN?

One issue that comes up during the administrative user creation process requires a bit more explanation. When you create a new administrative user, two options appear when you define the assigned security scope and collection for the user (see Figure 15.8).

The first choice is All Instances Of The Objects That Are Related To The Assigned Security Roles. If this option is selected, the administrative user will be associated with the All security scope and all collections.

continues

continued

The second choice is Only The Instances Of Objects That Are Assigned To The Specified Security Scopes Or Collections. This option allows the Configuration Manager administrator to add or remove security scopes and/or collections in order to provide a customized administrative scope for the user.

If you modify an administrative user, a third option is available called Associate Assigned Security Roles With Specific Security Scopes And Collections. As the wording of the option implies, this option allows the administrator to create associations between security roles, security scopes, and collections for the user. For example, if you have a Help Desk Group whose security role cannot be changed, and you just want to focus on their scopes and collection, you should be able to use this method to make the necessary changes to the administrative user without having to change their role.

We will now apply what you have learned and walk through a real-world scenario.

 Real World Scenario

HELPING THE HELP DESK ANALYST

You are the Configuration Manager administrator and have been asked to provide Configuration Manager access to an administrative user. A help desk analyst needs the ability to deploy Adobe Reader to all computers in the Tampa location. The analyst should also have the ability to use remote tools on the computers in the Tampa location. The analyst should not be able to deploy any other software to or interact in any way with the other computers in the infrastructure.

WHICH SECURITY ROLE(S) TO USE

As the Configuration Manager administrator, you first need to identify whether any of the existing security roles meet the needs of the scenario. In the Configuration Manager console, select Administration ➤ Overview ➤ Security ➤ Security Roles to view the roles that have been defined. The built-in Application Deployment Manager role appears to meet the requirements for the application delivery portion of the requirements. The built-in Remote Tools Operator role appears to meet the requirements for the remote tools functionality. So, you appear to have two existing security roles that will meet your needs. Later in this chapter you will learn how to use the RBA Viewer application to create custom security roles.

YOU NEED A SECURITY SCOPE

The next step is to define the required security scope for the help desk analyst. The requirements stated that this user should only be able to deploy Adobe Reader, so you need to create a security scope. You will use the process defined earlier in this chapter to create the security scope, and you will call the security scope **Apps Help Desk Can Deploy**. (See Figure 15.9.)

Remember that the In Use column value will be No until the security scope is associated with at least one object.

FIGURE 15.9
Create
Security
Scopes

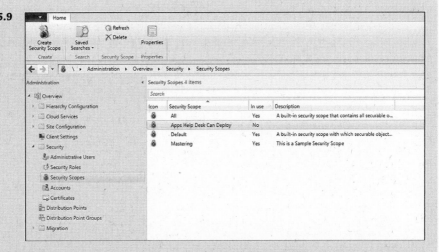

You may remember that the association between an object and the security scope is managed from the object, not from the security scope. So, you need to associate the security scope you just created with the Adobe Reader DC application by performing the following steps:

1. In the Configuration Manager console, select the Adobe Reader DC application in the Software Library workspace (Software Library ➢ Overview ➢ Application Management ➢ Applications).

   For the purposes of this scenario, assume that an administrator has already created and configured the Adobe Reader DC application installation in Configuration Manager and it is ready for deployment.

2. Right-click the Adobe Reader DC application and select Set Security Scopes.

3. Uncheck the Default security scope, and check the Apps Help Desk Can Deploy security scope.

4. Click OK. (See Figure 15.10.)

FIGURE 15.10
Set Security
Scopes

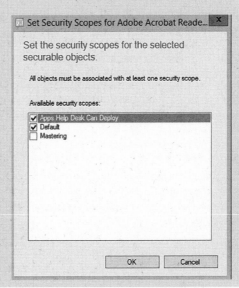

continues

continued

You may also need to include a distribution point or a distribution point group in the security scope in order for the Deploy Software Wizard to complete when executed under the administrative user's credentials.

If you go back and view the status of the Apps Help Desk Can Deploy security scope in the Configuration Manager console, it should now show a value of Yes in the In Use column. See Figure 15.11.

FIGURE 15.11
Security Scope
List, In Use

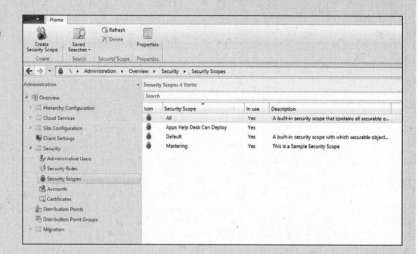

AND NOW YOU NEED A COLLECTION

There are several ways to create the collection for this scenario. In fact, someone else may have already built a collection that includes the Tampa computer devices, and you could use that collection for your scenario.

However, let's assume you don't already have a collection that meets your needs and you need to create one. You may already know the names of the computers in the Tampa location and you could simply create a direct membership collection and directly add the computer names to the collection. Or you could create a query-based collection and use data that is unique to the Tampa site to find computers that match the criteria. Examples of the data could be an Active Directory site, an Active Directory Organizational Unit, certain TCP/IP subnet ranges, a certain naming standard in the computer names, and so on. For now, assume that you were provided a list of computers in Tampa, and you're going to add them to a direct-membership device collection called Tampa Computers.

FINALLY: CREATING THE ADMINISTRATIVE USER

You have gone through several steps to prepare the required access in Configuration Manager. This may seem rather labor intensive at first, but you created several items that may be used multiple times in future security configuration requests. Let's take a moment to review what you will be using to create the administrative user.

You are going to use two built-in security roles for this scenario: Application Deployment Manager (so the analyst can deploy Adobe Reader DC to the Wave 1 QA Collection) and Remote Tools Operator (so the analyst can use remote tools on the Wave 1 QA Collection).

You created a security scope called Apps Help Desk Can Deploy and associated the scope with the Adobe Reader DC application. This limits the help desk analyst to the Adobe Reader DC application.

You created a direct-membership collection that contains the computers in the Wave 1 QA Collection.

The next step is to create the actual administrative user:

1. In the Configuration Manager console, select Administration ➤ Overview ➤ Security ➤ Administrative Users.

2. Either select the Add User Or Group option in the ribbon or right-click the Administrative Users option and select Add User Or Group.

   You need to designate the user or group that is being configured as an administrative user. In this scenario you are managing a single user.

3. Select the user's domain account (named ConfigNinja in this example). It is not part of the username.

4. In the Assigned Security Roles section, use the Add option to select the security roles that you decided to use for this scenario: Application Deployment Manager and Remote Tools Operator.

5. In the Assigned Security Scopes And Collections section, select the Add option to choose the predefined collection and security scope that will limit what the help desk analyst has access to in the console. (See Figure 15.12.)

FIGURE 15.12
Add Scope to
User

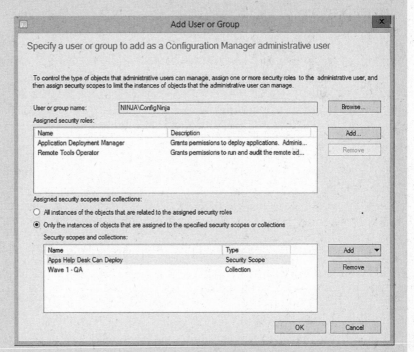

6. After adding the entries, click OK.

continues

continued

If there were several help desk analysts who needed the same configuration, you would probably create a group in Active Directory, add the users to that group, and then configure that group as an administrative user and avoid having to repeat these steps for each user individually.

At this point you have completed your work and are ready for the help desk analyst to test their Configuration Manager console with their logon credentials and make sure they can perform the required functions.

If you performed the configuration properly, then the administrative user ConfigNinja should be able to open the Configuration Manager console and do the following:

◆ View only the Wave 1 QA Computers collection in the Assets And Compliance ➢ Overview ➢ Device Collections view. (See Figure 15.13.)

FIGURE 15.13
User with RBA
Rights Console
View

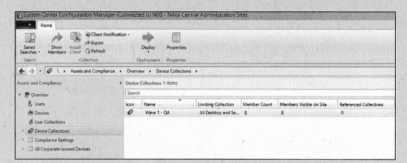

◆ See only the Wave 1 QA devices in the Assets And Compliance ➢ Overview ➢ Devices view. Also since the user can see only the Wave 1 QAdevices, they can also use only remote tools against those computers. (See Figure 15.14.)

FIGURE 15.14
User with RBA
Rights Devices
View

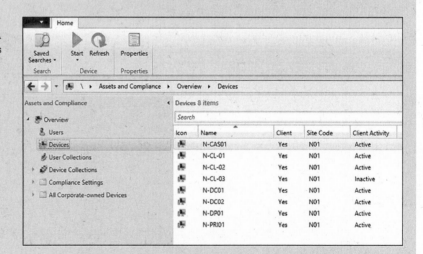

◆ View only the Adobe Reader DC application in Software Library ➢ Overview ➢ Application Manager ➢ Applications, and when they deploy it, they should only be able to select the Tampa Computers collection. (See Figure 15.15 and Figure 15.16.)

FIGURE 15.15
User with
RBA Rights
Applications
View

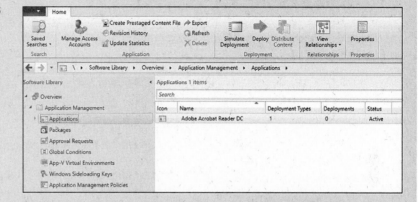

FIGURE 15.16
User with
RBA Rights
Deployments
View

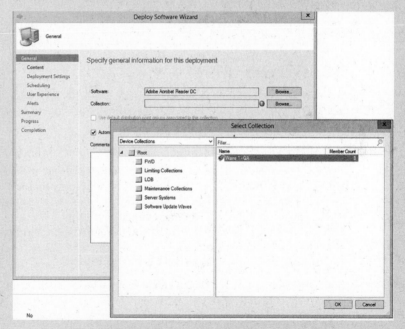

Also, as you learned earlier, Configuration Manager uses the role-based administration model for reporting data as well. The ConfigNinja user should only be able to view report data about objects that the user has access to. If you open the reporting site and select the report titled All Resources In A Specific Collection, the user can only select the Wave 1 QA Computers collection and view data about the computers in the collection. (See Figure 15.17.)

continues

continued

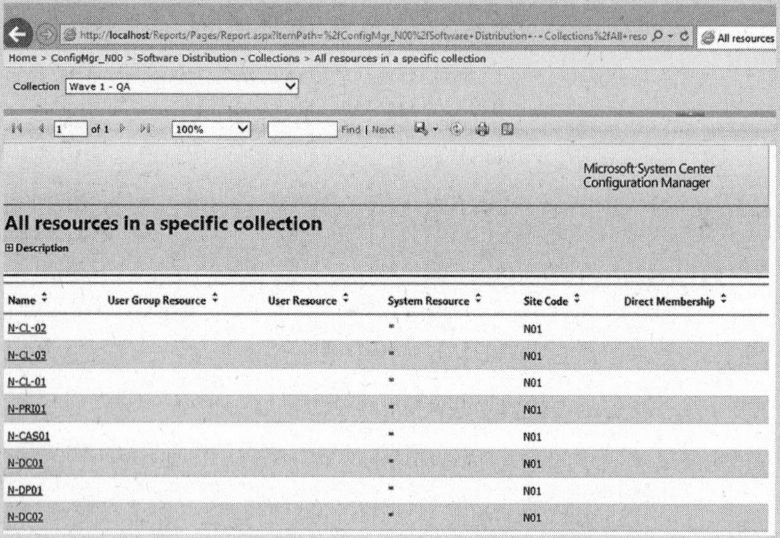

FIGURE 15.17
User with RBA
Rights Reports
View

RBA Viewer

You may already be familiar with the System Center 2012 Configuration Manager toolkit. It includes many useful utilities and tools that will help you manage your Configuration Manager environment and is available here:

```
https://www.microsoft.com/en-us/download/details.aspx?id=50012
```

One of the tools included in the toolkit is officially titled the Role-Based Administration Modeling and Auditing Tool, but the utility is commonly referred to as RBA Viewer. The RBA Viewer application allows you to model security roles with a specific set of permissions and also allows you to audit the security scopes and security roles of other Configuration Manager users. RBA Viewer should be very helpful as you develop the Configuration Manager security configuration for your environment.

The RBA Viewer application has a few requirements:

◆ The Configuration Manager console must be installed on the same computer as the RBA Viewer application.

◆ The user running the RBA Viewer application must be a member of the Full Administrator, Read-Only Analyst, or Security Administrator role.

◆ The user running RBA Viewer must be assigned to all security scopes and all collections.

◆ To analyze report folder security, the user must have SQL access and the RBA Viewer application must run on the site that has the Reporting Services point installed.

We will use a case study to demonstrate how to use RBA Viewer to create a new security role and verify that it will meet your needs.

Real World Scenario

CREATING AN ADMINISTRATIVE USER

You are the Configuration Manager administrator and have been asked to provide Configuration Manager access to an administrative user. The user will need the access provided by the Application Administrator security role but also will need the added ability to create and modify software metering rules. You will use the RBA Viewer to define the new security role, verify that it meets the requirements, and then export it from RBA Viewer so that it can imported into the Configuration Manager console. Click Start ➤ Configuration Manager Toolkit and select RBA Viewer to open the RBA Viewer application.

1. In RBA Viewer you have the option to select a default security role and use that as a starting point for the required permissions, or you can start with an empty list of permissions. For this scenario you are adding additional permissions to the Application Administrator role, so select the Application Administrator role from the list in RBA Viewer.

2. Verify that the Show Roles option is selected by clicking the icon in the top right of the RBA Viewer application; then select Application Administrator from the list of available security roles in the drop-down. See Figure 15.18.

FIGURE 15.18
RBA Viewer
Roles
Similarity

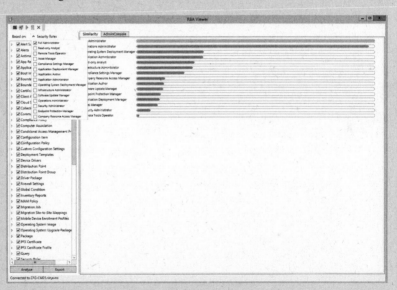

3. In this example you are adding the ability to create and modify software metering rules to the permissions provided by the Application Administrator role. Scroll down the list of available items and select Software Metering Rule Under Software Metering Rule, Read, Modify, Delete, and Create.

4. Once the required permissions have been configured, click Analyze. RBA Viewer will identify any existing security roles that are similar to the permissions that have been configured in the tool.

continues

continued

5. Select the AdminConsole tab in RBA Viewer to verify that the user with this security role has the proper access. With this custom security role, you should have the access provided by the Application Administrator role as well as the ability to manage software metering rules. You can also use the AdminConsole feature in RBA Viewer to verify that the security role cannot access or view other settings.

6. Once the permissions have been properly configured, click the Export button. This will save the security role configuration to an XML file, which you can then import into the Configuration Manager console.

7. Open the Configuration Manager console and select the Administration workspace. See Figure 15.19.

FIGURE 15.19
RBA Viewer
Console
Review

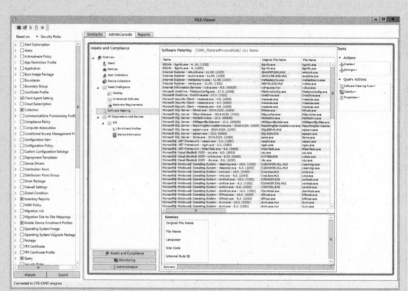

8. Select Overview ➤ Security ➤ Security Roles and choose the Import Security Role option from the ribbon.

9. At the Import Security Role window, select the XML file that you exported from RBA Viewer and click Open.

10. Configuration Manager will import the information from the XML file and create the security role. The security will use the name of the import file as the name of the new security role, but you can change the name if needed in the Configuration Manager console. You can also open the role and use the Permissions tab in the properties to ensure the correct permissions have been created for the role.

Collection Best Practice for RBA

Collections in Configuration Manager provide the means to organize resources into manageable units, very similar to how you will structure Active Directory. With role-based administration, it is very important to understand collections and how to work with them. Collections are also used to perform Configuration Manager operations on multiple system resources or users at one time.

LIMITING COLLECTIONS

Whenever a collection is created, it must be limited to a collection, since they are limited to either a custom collection or a default one. It is very important to understand the effects on security that this may have on the user, to whom you are giving a specific collection. For example, if you give a user a collection name of Wave 1 QA that is limited to All Systems, this will give the user access not just to the collection Wave 1 QA but also to All Systems. It is very important to understand the collection structure and how it will impact the user.

One of the default collections, All Desktop And Server Clients, contains only valid clients. Normally you would split this collection into two and then limit the same to All Desktop And Server Clients. See Figure 15.20.

FIGURE 15.20
Collection limiting

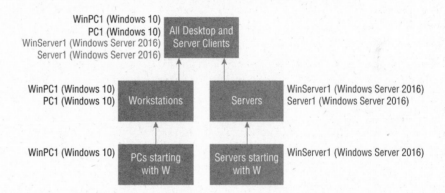

The Workstations and Servers collections are limited to All Desktop And Server Clients and contain relevant objects. There is a collection called PCs starting with W, which is limited to Workstations, and a collection called Servers starting with W, which is limited to Servers. The query of each collection is *Resource name starts with W*. In this instance, even though the query for the Servers starting with W would find WinPC1, WinPC1 does not become a member of the collection because it is not a member of the limiting collection Servers.

The Bottom Line

Understand the role-based administration model in Configuration Manager. SMS and Configuration Manager 2007 used a class and instance security model, which could be confusing at times. Configuration Manager now adopts the RBAC model, thereby making the administration of security in Configuration Manager a less-daunting task.

Master It What does RBAC stand for? And what does role-based administration mean?

Distinguish security roles from security scopes. Security roles and security scopes are important components of the role-based security model in Configuration Manager.

Master It Can you identify the key differences between a security role and a security scope?

Understand which objects in Configuration Manager define an administrative user. The administrative user consists of the security role, the security scope, and collections. In this chapter you learned the differences between a security role and a security scope, and you know that collections can be used to control the objects that an administrative user can access.

Master It   As the Configuration Manager administrator, do you need to create a custom Configuration Manager console so that the administrative user can see only what you want them to see?

Understand how to simulate permissions in the Configuration Manager console.   The RBAC model in Configuration Manager greatly simplifies the process for creating administrative users and defining what objects in Configuration Manager they can access.

Master It   Besides the Configuration Manager console itself, what other tool can you use to simulate Configuration Manager user security and verify that the security model will provide the desired level of access?

Chapter 16

Disaster Recovery

Configuration Manager supports several site backup options that can be used to ensure that your site can be recovered in the event of a server crash, corrupted site, or some other unexpected Configuration Manager outage. You can evaluate the available site backup methods and choose the option that best meets your needs and requirements.

One option is the Backup Site Server maintenance task that is included in Configuration Manager. This maintenance task is created as part of the Configuration Manager site installation process but is disabled by default. This task, if enabled, will create a site backup that includes the files and information you would need to successfully recover your site server. Other supported Configuration Manager site backup options include performing a full backup of the Configuration Manager database as part of a Microsoft SQL Server maintenance plan or using System Center Data Protection Manager to perform the Configuration Manager site backup. It is worth noting that Configuration Manager does not support using third-party tools to back up the site; neither does it support using the server snapshot abilities that are included in virtual server products to recover a site server. The Configuration Manager Backup Site Server maintenance task is the most commonly used option in many environments and will be the primary focus of this chapter. In this chapter, you will learn to

◆ Configure backups for Configuration Manager sites

◆ Archive backup snapshots to another location

◆ Reinstall the site components and reset file and registry permissions to their default settings

Planning for Disaster Recovery

The Backup Site Server maintenance task in Configuration Manager runs on a schedule and backs up the site database, specific registry keys, and specific files and folders. This task is created as part of the site installation process but is disabled by default. The backup task uses the Volume Shadow Copy Service (VSS) and the SMS Writer service to perform the backup. VSS is a component of the Windows Server operating system and is used to create the backup snapshot during the backup process. SMS Writer is a Configuration Manager service that interacts with VSS during the backup process. The SMS Writer service must be running when VSS initiates a backup or a restore process in Configuration Manager.

A complete backup of a Configuration Manager site server includes the following:

- The Configuration Manager site database
- The Configuration Manager site database transaction log
- The <ConfigurationManager installation dir>\Bin folder
- The <ConfigurationManager installation dir>\Inboxes folder
- The <ConfigurationManager installation dir>\Logs folder
- The <ConfigurationManager installation dir>\Data folder
- The <ConfigurationManager installation dir>\srvacct folder
- The <ConfigurationManager installation dir>\CD.Latest folder
- <ConfigurationManager installation dir>\install.map
- HKLM\Software\Microsoft\SMS registry key on the site server

---

WHAT IS THE *CD.LATEST* FOLDER?

Configuration Manager includes a new update process for delivering product updates via the Configuration Manager console. This is accomplished by storing a copy of the updated Configuration Manager installation files in the CD.Latest folder. The content in this folder is created or updated when you install an update or hotfix from the Configuration Manager console or when you run the built-in Configuration Manager backup task. The source files in the CD.Latest folder are used when you need to reinstall your site as part of a site recovery, when you install a child primary site below a central administration site (CAS), or when you expand a standalone primary site to join a CAS. The setup files in the CD.Latest folder are not supported for installing a new site for a new hierarchy or for upgrading a Configuration Manager 2012 site to Configuration Manager Current Branch.

The following TechNet link discusses the CD.Latest folder in more detail and scenarios where it can be used:

https://technet.microsoft.com/en-us/library/mt703293.aspx

What Is Not Included in the Backup

You now have an idea of what data is backed up as part of the site backup task in Configuration Manager, but it's also important to know what is *not* backed up. You should consider incorporating the backup of these other Configuration Manager–related components, such as the content library and source files, in your enterprise backup solution.

THE CONTENT LIBRARY

The content library contains all of the applications, packages, software updates, and operating system images that are available to your clients. The content library exists on the site server and the distribution points, and you should consider adding the content library to your enterprise backup solution. During a site server restore process, you may need to add several hours to the restore process if there is no backup of the content library and the content must be processed from the original source folders and inserted into the content library. Also consider where the source files for the content are located and ensure that these files are being backed up as part of your enterprise backup solution.

CONFIGURATION MANAGER LOGS

The Backup Site Server maintenance task will back up the site server log files located in the Logs folder (`ConfigMgrInstallationPath`>\Logs), but some Configuration Manager site system roles or related functions may write log files to other locations on the site server and will not be backed up. One example is the Configuration Manager site server setup logs, which are located on the root of the C: drive on the site server by default. If any of these additional log files should be backed up, you should include them in your enterprise backup solution.

SQL REPORTING SERVICES

SQL Reporting Services and its related components are not backed up as part of the Configuration Manager site backup task. When planning for a backup solution for SQL Reporting Services, consider the following:

◆ Use the full recovery model in a SQL database backup to back up the reportserver database.

◆ Use the simple recovery model in a SQL database backup to back up the reportserver-tempdb database.

◆ Back up the encryption keys by using the rskeymgmt utility or the Reporting Services Configuration Manager utility.

◆ Back up these configuration files:

  ◆ `Rsreportserver.config`

  ◆ `Rssvrpolicy.config`

  ◆ `Rsmgrpolicy.config`

  ◆ `Reportingservicesservice.exe.config`

  ◆ `Web.config` for both the Report Server and Report Manager ASP.NET applications

  ◆ `Machine.config` for ASP.NET

Also verify that any custom reports, report models, and custom projects are being backed up. Note that the Configuration Manager reports are not backed up as part of the site backup task. Any customizations that have been made to the default reports, and any custom reports that have been created, will be lost in the event of a site server failure. The default Configuration Manager reports will be installed when the site is recovered and you will need to restore any customized reports that have been created or default reports that have been modified.

For more detailed information about backing up SQL Reporting Services, see

`http://msdn.microsoft.com/en-us/library/ms155814.aspx`

WSUS Database

Windows Server Update Services (WSUS) is not included in the Configuration Manager site backup task. You should consider including the WSUS backup in your enterprise backup solution. You'll find additional guidance on backing up WSUS data in this article:

```
https://technet.microsoft.com/en-us/library/dd939904(v=ws.10).aspx
```

System Center Updates Publisher

System Center Updates Publisher (SCUP) is a standalone product installed with a single database that is typically stored in the user profile and is not backed up as part of the site backup task. Again, you should consider backing up the database in your enterprise backup solution. The location of the database will depend on how SCUP is configured. Each user who runs SCUP will have their own database file and it will be located in the user's profile folder. If you have configured SCUP to use a database on a shared network location, you should include that location in your enterprise backup solution.

Microsoft Deployment Toolkit

Microsoft Deployment Toolkit (MDT) is a free standalone image deployment tool from Microsoft that is often integrated with Configuration Manager to provide additional options and features during the operating system deployment process. Depending on how MDT is being used, it may contain a database, and that database should be included in your enterprise backup solution. Also ensure that you are backing up the entire deployment share, including any custom scripts that have been implemented.

User State Migration Data

As part of the operating system deployment feature in Configuration Manager, you can configure the task sequences to capture and restore the user state data. The files and folders that are used to store user state data on the Configuration Manager state migration point are not backed up as part of the site backup task. You should determine if these folders and files should be backed up and included in your enterprise backup solution.

Backing Up Configuration Manager

When you enable and configure the Backup Site Server maintenance task in Configuration Manager, part of the configuration process requires you to schedule when the backup process should start. At the scheduled day of the week and the time of day, the Configuration Manager backup service (SMS_SITE_BACKUP) will start and uses the backup instructions that are included in the site backup control file to perform the backup. This file is created automatically by the site server; it is named SMSBKUP.CTL and is located in the \Inboxes\SMSBKUP.BOX folder. It is typically not necessary to modify this file, but you can make customizations if needed. If you modify the file, take care not to modify any of the default settings and you should only add custom entries in the section of the file that says "Editing Allowed." Examples of some custom entries that may be useful are adding commands to back up certain registry keys or to back up certain files or folders that exist on the site server.

Once the site backup process starts, the smsbkup.log file is updated. This log can be very useful in verifying that the backup task is completing successfully and for researching any site backup issues. The smsbkup.log file is located in the default location for the site server logs.

Backup Considerations for the Central Administration Site

The process of backing up and recovering a CAS is similar to the process used for a primary site server, but there are a few considerations to keep in mind. The CAS is typically the busiest site in a hierarchy, and you may need to determine the optimal time of the day to perform the backup. For many customers, this is either very late at night or very early in the morning. Also, the CAS will have the largest amount of data in the hierarchy because it contains the global data and site data, and it will take longer for the backup process to complete.

A general recommendation is to configure the site backup task to occur every day of the week, including weekends, on the CAS and the primary sites. This will help ensure a minimal loss of data in the event of a site server failure. You could argue that since the data is replicated across the hierarchy in a CAS/primary environment, a daily backup of a primary site may not be necessary. However, restoring a primary site from an older backup may generate a significant amount of data across the wide area network as the restored primary is brought up-to-date with the rest of the hierarchy. This is discussed in more detail later in this chapter.

Copying Site Backups to Another Location

When the Backup Site Server maintenance task runs, it stores the backup files to the location specified when the task was configured. The next time that the backup runs, it creates a new backup snapshot and will override the files that were stored in the backup location in the previous backup. This may pose a problem if the current backup snapshot becomes corrupted and has overwritten what may have been a valid backup from the previous backup. For this reason, also consider adding the backup location to your enterprise backup solution so that it can be retrieved later if needed. You can also archive the backup files to a remote location, using the process defined in the next section.

Archiving the Backup Snapshot to Another Server with *AfterBackup.bat*

Near the end of the Configuration Manager site backup maintenance task, the backup process looks for an optional file named AfterBackup.bat in the \Microsoft Configuration Manager\inboxes\smsbkup.box folder on the site server. If the file exists, the commands in the batch file are executed. If the file does not exist, the backup proceeds normally. Note that this file does not exist by default; it must be created by the Configuration Manager administrator and placed in the smsbkup.box folder. The batch file should include the commands that the administrator wants to be carried out. One common use of the AfterBackup.bat file is to run commands that will copy the site backup files from the site server to a remote site server. This would help ensure that the backup files are available on another location if the drives on the primary site crashed and the site needed to be restored.

There are several methods you could use to copy the site backup files from the local server to a remote server, ranging from simple DOS commands to Robocopy to PowerShell. Figure 16.1 provides a sample AfterBackup.bat file and a PowerShell script that can be used to perform the copy process. Note that in this example the AfterBackup.bat file is being used to launch the PowerShell script that is performing the file copy. The script is also configured to create a folder based on the day of the week that the script is running and then copy the files to that folder. With this approach, you would have up to 7 days of backups in the remote location. You should note that this approach may require significant available disk space on the remote server share because you will be storing the entire site backup data set, which may be many gigabytes of data, up to seven times on the remote server. If you just wanted to keep one day of archived backups on the remote server, you would remove the date logic from the script.

FIGURE 16.1

A sample AfterBackup.bat file calling a PowerShell script

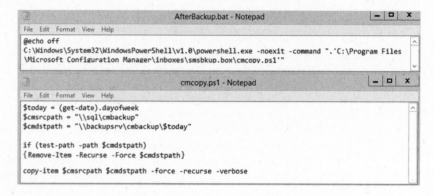

To create the AfterBackup.bat file, follow these steps:

1. Open Windows Explorer and navigate to \Microsoft ConfigMgr\inboxes\smsbkup.box.

2. Using Notepad, create a new ASCII batch file and name it **AfterBackup.bat**.

3. Add the following commands to the AfterBackup.bat file:

   ```
   @ECHO OFF
   C:\Windows\System32\WindowsPowerShell\v1.0\powershell.exe -noexit -command ".
   'C:\Program Files\Microsoft

   Configuration Manager\inboxes\smsbkup.box\cmcopy.ps1'"
   ```

4. Save and close the file.

5. Using Notepad, create another new ASCII batch file in the smsbkup.box folder and name it CMCOPY.PS1.

6. Add the following lines to the CMCOPY.PS1 file and replace \\sql\cmbackup with the correct name and share path for the site server backup files. Then replace \\backupsrv\cmbackup with the correct name and share path for the remote server that will host the archives of the backup files.

   ```
   $today = (get-date).dayofweek
   $cmsrcpath = "\\sql\cmbackup"
   $cmdstpath = "\\backupsrv\cmbackup\$today"

   if (test-path -path $cmdstpath)
   {Remove-Item -Recurse -Force $cmdstpath}

   copy-item $cmsrcpath $cmdstpath -force -recurse -verbose
   ```

7. Save and close the file.

Another possible concern with copying the site backup files from the site server to a remote share is the amount of data that will be transmitted across the network to the remote file share. The total size of the backup set being copied will vary by environment, but it could easily be 10 GB of data, perhaps much more in a larger environment. If the remote file share is across the wide area network from the source server, it may negatively impact the network until the copy is finished. If this is a concern, you may consider adding some compression logic to the commands. For example, consider using a file compression option to compress the files before they are transmitted and then uncompress them at the remote location once the file copy has been completed.

Windows Application Log Entries Created by the Backup Process

The Backup Site Server task will write backup status messages to the Application log in the Windows Event Viewer on the site server. Table 16.1 provides a list of the events and their event IDs that are written to the Application log. It may be useful to use a monitoring product such as System Center Operations Manager to monitor for these events and alert you if specified event IDs occur.

TABLE 16.1:   Configuration Manager backup Application log entries

EVENT ID NUMBER	MESSAGE
3197	I/O is frozen on database CM_SiteCode. No user action is required. However, if I/O is not resumed promptly, you could cancel the backup.
3198	I/O was resumed on database CM_SiteCode. No user action is required.
5040	This event is used to indicate that the AfterBackup.bat file was successfully started.
5055	Component SMS_SITE_BACKUP on computer site server reported: Site Backup task is starting. This task will interact with the Windows VSS services and the appropriate writers to create a volume snapshot and then back up the required files to the specified destination.
5056	Component SMS_SITE_BACKUP on computer site server reported: Site Backup is starting to copy the files from the snapshot.
5057	Component SMS_SITE_BACKUP on computer site server reported: Site Backup has successfully completed copying the files from the snapshot.
6829	Component SMS_SITE_VSS_WRITER on computer site server reported: SMS Writer is about to stop the Configuration Manager Services as part of the preparation for the site backup.
6830	Component SMS_SITE_VSS_WRITER on computer site server reported: The snapshots of the volumes required for the site backup have been successfully created.
6831	Component SMS_SITE_VSS_WRITER on computer site server reported: SMS Writer has started the Configuration Manager Services successfully.

TABLE 16.1:   Configuration Manager backup Application log entries   *(continued)*

EVENT ID NUMBER	MESSAGE
6833	Component SMS_SITE_BACKUP on computer site server reported: Site Backup has successfully completed copying the files from the snapshot.
18265	Database backed up.

Configuring the Backup Configuration Manager Site Server Maintenance Task

As you have learned, the Backup Site Server maintenance task performs a backup of the key information needed to restore the site and the Backup Site Server maintenance task is not enabled by default. The following section will discuss how to enable and configure the Backup Site Server task. The task is available on both a CAS and a primary site.

BACKING UP A SITE SERVER

To configure the Backup Site Server maintenance task in Configuration Manager, perform the following steps:

1. In the Configuration Manager console, navigate to the Administration workspace, and then select Overview ➤ Site Configuration ➤ Sites.

2. Select the site and choose Settings ➤ Site Maintenance from the ribbon.

3. Select the Backup Site Server task, and click Edit.

4. Select Enable This Task.

5. Click Set Paths and type the path for the backup folder.

   Depending on the location of the SQL database, you will be given three choices for where to save the database and the site backup files:

   ◆ Local Drive On Site Server

      This option is available if the SQL database is hosted locally on the site server.

   ◆ Network Path (UNC Name) For Site Data And Database

      This option will allow you to specify a network share to store the backup files.

   ◆ Different Paths For Site Backup And Database Backup

      This option is available only if you have SQL running on a remote server. This option allows you to back up the Configuration Manager site data to one location and back up the Configuration Manager SQL database to another location.

      Regardless of what location you select, you need to ensure that the site server computer account has write access to the target folder and share that is used to store the backup files. We recommend that you create the target folder before running the backup task.

6. You can adjust the Start After and Latest Start Time settings if the default schedule interferes with other maintenance routines.

7. Configure the days of the week that the backup should be executed. Our general recommendation is to perform a backup every day of the week in order to minimize the amount of data lost in the event of a site server failure.

8. Select Enable Alerts For Backup Task Failures and click OK.

Figure 16.2 shows the configured Backup Site Server maintenance task.

FIGURE 16.2
The Backup Site Server
properties

TESTING THE SITE BACKUP

Once you configure the Backup Site Server task, you may want to test the site backup and verify that it is working properly. This may impact any active Configuration Manager processes and should only be done during your testing phases or during a scheduled maintenance window. To initiate the backup, perform the following steps:

1. Log on to the Configuration Manager site server.

2. Open a command prompt as an administrator.

3. Type **net start sms_site_backup** and press Enter. This will start the Configuration Manager site backup service and perform the site backup. You could also open the Services application on the site server and start the SMS_SITE_BACKUP service by right-clicking the service and selecting Start to manually initiate the site backup.

4. If you want to monitor the status of the backup task, you can use the Configuration Manager Trace Log Tool to open the smsbkup.log file from the Logs folder on the site server. The backup log file will give you valuable information about the backup process, including identifying any errors that may occur during the backup process and also ensuring that the AfterBackup.bat file was executed successfully if it has been configured.

WHAT ABOUT SECONDARY SITES?

There is no backup task for Configuration Manager secondary sites. If you need to recover a secondary site, you can select the site in the Configuration Manager console and initiate the recovery process. The secondary site will be reinstalled and the necessary data will be replicated from the primary site. This will be discussed in more detail later in the chapter.

Restoring Configuration Manager

Configuration Manager includes a site maintenance task that will back up the site database and other key files and settings that can be used to restore the CAS or primary site server in the event of a site server failure. This section will discuss how to use the site backup data to restore Configuration Manager functionality.

Understanding the Effects of a Site Failure

A Configuration Manager hierarchy consists of several site servers, site roles, and components. If any of these items fail, then the services provided by Configuration Manager will be impacted. The level of impact, and the work required to regain functionality, will depend on the components that have failed. Table 16.2 lists various scenarios of site component outages and the related impact.

TABLE 16.2: Results of Configuration Manager site failure

SITE SERVER	SITE DATABASE *	MANAGEMENT POINT *	DISTRIBUTION POINT *	RESULT
Offline	Online	Online	Online	No site administration will be possible, including creation of new deployments. The management point will collect client information and cache it until the site server is back online. Existing deployments will run and clients can find distribution points.

TABLE 16.2:   Results of Configuration Manager site failure   *(continued)*

SITE SERVER	SITE DATABASE *	MANAGEMENT POINT *	DISTRIBUTION POINT *	RESULT
Online	Offline	Online	Online	No site administration will be possible, including creation of new deployments. If the Configuration Manager client already has a policy assignment with new policies and if the management point has cached the policy body, the client can make a policy body request and receive the policy body reply. No new policy assignment requests can be serviced. Clients will be able to run deployments only if they have already been detected and the associated source files are already cached locally at the client.
Online	Online	Offline	Online	Although new deployments can be created, the clients will not receive them until a management point is online again. Clients will still collect inventory, software metering, and status information and store it locally until the management point is available. Clients will be able to run deployments only if they have already been detected and the associated source files are already cached locally at the client.
Online	Online	Online	Offline	Configuration Manager clients will be able to run deployments only if the associated source files have already been downloaded locally.

Note that you can configure multiple management points and distribution points and cluster the SQL database. This may help minimize the risk of Configuration Manager functionality being impacted in the event a site server is unavailable.

Overview of the Recovery Options

Previous versions of System Management Server and Configuration Manager provided a Site Repair Wizard that was specifically used to perform a site server restore or a site reset. Now the site restore or site reset process is initiated via the Configuration Manager Setup Wizard, as shown in Figure 16.3.

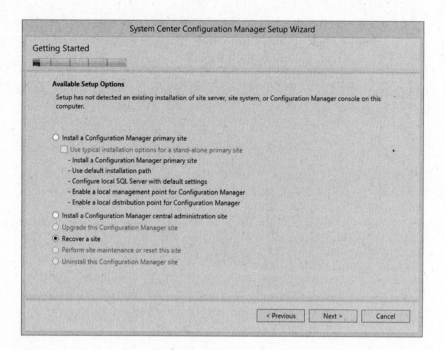

The site reset option may be useful if a Configuration Manager site has become corrupted or is experiencing issues and a site reset has been identified as the recommended solution. If the site server crashed and the site server is no longer available, you will likely need to perform a site server restore. The Setup Wizard provides the available recovery options based on the status of the site server at that time. Note that if you launch the Configuration Manager Setup from the Start menu, the Recover A Site option will not be available. To recover a site, you must run Setup Wizard from the installation media. This process is discussed later in the chapter. You can also perform an unattended site recovery; this will be discussed later in the chapter as well.

RECOVERING WHILE CONFIGURATION MANAGER IS STILL INSTALLED

It is worth noting that if you are attempting to recover a Configuration Manager site that is not completely uninstalled, or the previous site recovery failed, then you must select Uninstall This Configuration Manager Site from the Setup Wizard before you will have the option available to recover the site. If the failed site has child sites and you need to uninstall the site, you must manually delete the site database from the failed site before you select the Uninstall This Configuration Manager Site option or the uninstall process will fail.

Figure 16.4 shows the database options that are available during the recovery, and Table 16.3 provides additional information on those options.

FIGURE 16.4
Site Server
And Database
Recovery Options

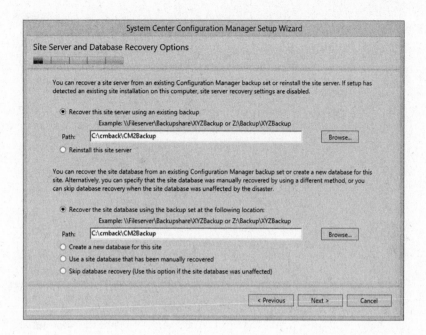

TABLE 16.3: Recovery options

OPTION	USED WHEN
Recover This Site Server Using An Existing Backup	You have the backup files created using Configuration Manager. This offers you a complete recovery scenario, as described later in this chapter.
Reinstall The Site Server	You do not have a backup of the site server. All site settings will be lost, and you will have to manually reconfigure the site.
Recover The Site Database Using The Backup Set At The Following Location	You have a backup of the Configuration Manager site database. This offers you a complete recovery scenario, as described later in this chapter.
Create A New Database For This Site	You are recovering a site that is part of a hierarchy, and you want to replicate data from the CAS or from another reference site. Note that this option is available only in multisite environments. Depending on the size of the site database, this recovery option may generate a significant amount of traffic across the network.
Use A Site Database That Has Been Manually Recovered	You have recovered the site database from another supported site backup solution (like a SQL database dump or a Data Protection Manager backup).
Skip Database Recovery	You haven't experienced any data loss and the existing database is intact.

Recovering Configuration Manager

The following section will discuss how to restore a Configuration Manager site server.

How to Start the Recovery Process

The site recovery process is designed to make recovering a Configuration Manager site easy and straightforward. Before you start the recovery process, ensure that you have the following:

◆ SQL server installation media

◆ Configuration Manager prerequisites

◆ Configuration Manager installation media

◆ Access to the Configuration Manager site backup files

Furthermore, if you are rebuilding a Configuration Manager site server as a result of a site server crash, there are some configuration items on the rebuilt server that must match those of the original server:

◆ The computer name of the site server must be the same as before.

◆ The computer name of the SQL Server must be the same and must be the same version and edition of SQL as before.

◆ You must use the same Configuration Manager site code as before.

◆ You must use the same Configuration Manager database name as before.

◆ You must use the same Configuration Manager major version as before.

Change Tracking Retention

Changing tracking is enabled for the site database by default and allows Configuration Manager to query for information about changes that have been made to the database tables after a certain point in time. The retention period specifies how long the change tracking information is retained, and this is set to 5 days by default. This retention period is important when recovering a CAS or a primary site in a CAS hierarchy; the recovery process that occurs will depend on whether the database backup is inside or outside the retention period. For example, if the site backup has been failing, or was never configured to occur, then the database that is being restored is outside the retention period and the recovery process will perform differently than if the backup was recently performed and within the retention period. After a site database is restored from a backup in a CAS/primary hierarchy, Configuration Manager attempts to restore the changes in site and global data after the last database backup. Table 16.4 provides the actions that Configuration Manager will start after a site database is restored from backup and the change tracking retention period is evaluated by Configuration Manager.

TABLE 16.4: Change tracking retention period impact on site recovery

RECOVERED SITE	DATABASE BACKUP WITHIN CHANGE TRACKING RETENTION PERIOD		DATABASE BACKUP OLDER THAN CHANGE TRACKING RETENTION PERIOD	
	GLOBAL DATA	SITE DATA	GLOBAL DATA	SITE DATA
Primary site	The changes in global data after the backup are replicated from the CAS.	The CAS reinitializes the site data from the primary site. Changes after the backup are lost, but most data is regenerated by clients that send information to the primary site.	The primary site reinitializes the global data from the central administration site.	The CAS reinitializes the site data from the primary site. Changes after the backup are lost, but most data is regenerated by clients that send information to the primary site.
Central administration site	The changes in global data after the backup are replicated from all primary sites.	The changes in site data after the backup are replicated from all primary sites.	The CAS reinitializes the global data from the reference primary site, if you specify it. Then all other primary sites reinitialize the global data from the CAS. If no reference site is specified, all primary sites reinitialize the global data from the CAS (the data that was restored from backup).	The CAS reinitializes the site data from each primary site.

Recovering a Central Administration Site

You can restore the site through the Setup Wizard, which will step you through the entire process, or you can automate the recovery process by using an unattended site recovery script. We will focus on using the Setup Wizard approach first.

To restore the CAS, do the following:

1. On the CAS site server, open a command prompt with administrative privileges.

2. Navigate to .\SMSSetup\BIN\X64\ in the Configuration Manager installation source and run Setup.exe.

3. Click Next on the Before You Begin page.

4. Select Recover A Site.

5. On the Site Server And Database Recovery Options page, click Browse, and select the location of the Configuration Manager site backup files.

6. Select Recover This Site Server Using An Existing Backup.

7. Click Browse, and navigate to the location of the site backup folder.

8. In the site database option, select Recover The Site Database Using The Backup Set At The Following Location.

9. Click Browse and navigate to the location of the site backup folder.

10. Once you have selected the recovery options for the site and the database, click Next.

11. On the Site Recovery Information page, shown in Figure 16.5, type the name of the site to reference and click Next.

FIGURE 16.5
The Site Recovery
Information page

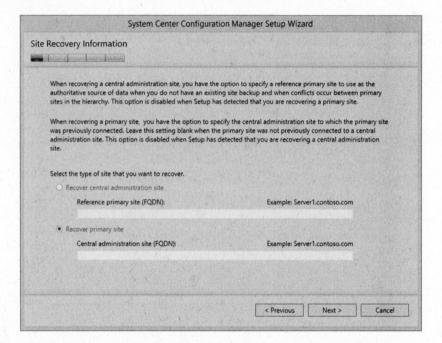

The reference site can be used as the authoritative source in case there is no site backup data. Any data changes from other nonreference primary sites will be lost. If you are recovering a standalone primary site there is no reference site, so leave the setting blank.

12. Enter the product key for Configuration Manager and click Next

13. Accept the license terms and click Next.

14. On the Prerequisite Downloads page, shown in Figure 16.6, select Use Previously Downloaded Files if you have access to the files and browse to the location where they are stored. Otherwise, choose the option to download the required file again and specify the path to use to store them

FIGURE 16.6
The Prerequisite
Downloads page

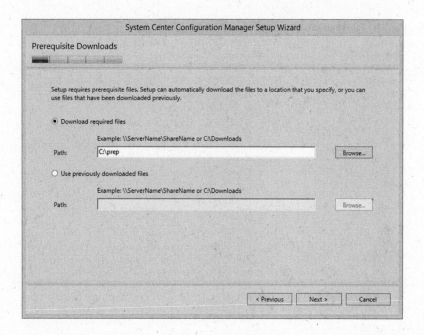

FIGURE 16.6
The Prerequisite
Downloads page

15. On the Site And Installation Settings page, shown in Figure 16.7, specify the installation folder that should be used to install Configuration Manager, and click Next.

FIGURE 16.7
Site And Installation
Settings page

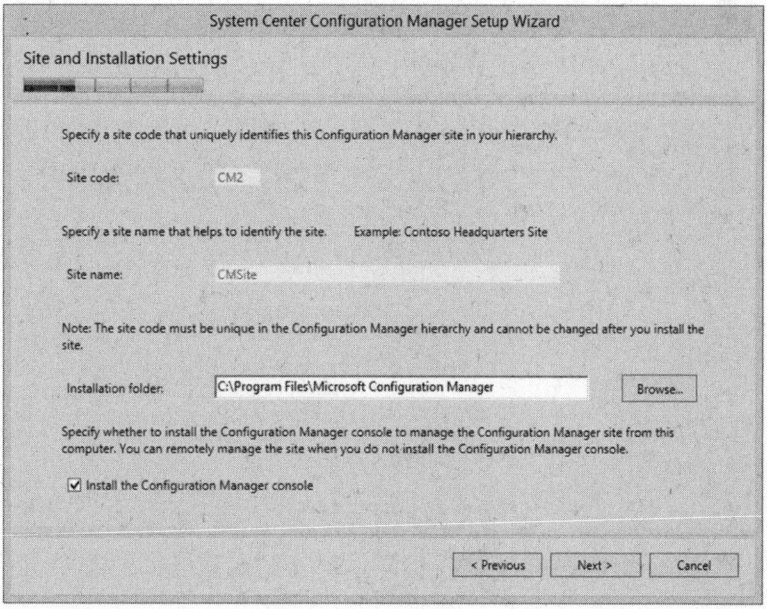

16. On the Database Information page, shown in Figure 16.8, verify that the SQL Server Service Broker Port is correct, and click Next.

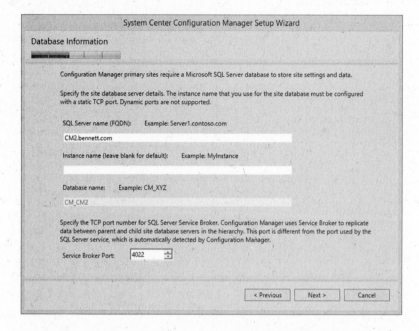

17. On the next Database Information page, shown in Figure 16.9, review the information, make any required changes, and click Next.

FIGURE 16.9
Database Information page

18. Review the Usage Data screen and click Next

19. On the Settings Summary screen, review the configuration settings and click Next if the data is correct.

20. On the Prerequisite Check page, shown in Figure 16.10, ensure that all the prerequisites are met, and click Begin Install.

FIGURE 16.10
Prerequisite Check page

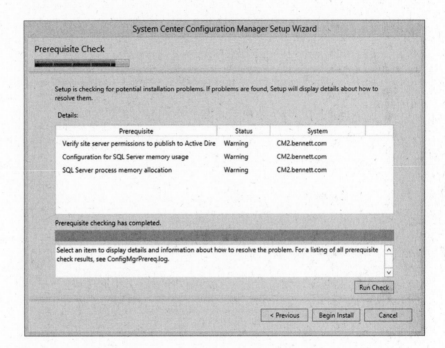

The installation and recovery process will require some time to finish. Once the process is finished, you will see the Install page with the status of Core Setup Has Completed, as shown in Figure 16.11.

21. Review the page, and click Next.

22. The Finished page, shown in Figure 16.12, is the last page and explains the postrecovery tasks that you must perform. Read the information, note any postrecovery actions that must be completed, and click Close. You can also review this information in the `ConfigMgrPostRecoveryActions.html` file located in the root of the `C:` drive on the site server.

After the recovery process and the global data has been replicated from the reference site, the CAS will perform some additional steps automatically, such as initiating a site reset to reinstall site components and generating public keys for the child sites.

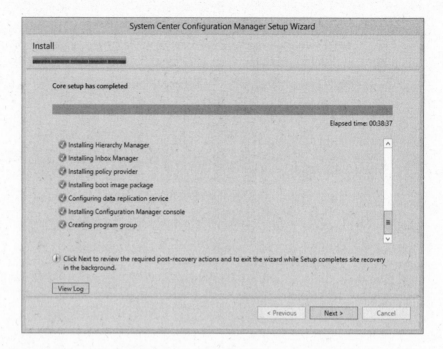

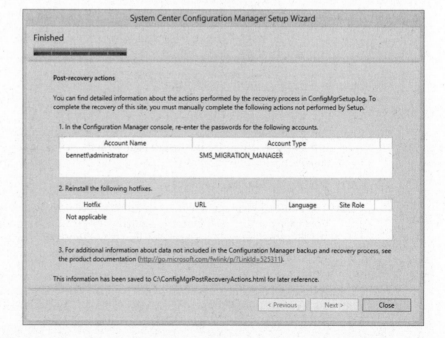

MONITORING THE RECOVERY PROCESS

You can monitor the recovery process by viewing the `ConfigMgrSetupWizard.log` and `ConfigMgrSetup.log` files for additional insight into the progress of the recovery process, as shown in Figure 16.13.

FIGURE 16.13
Viewing
`ConfigMgrSetup`
`.log`

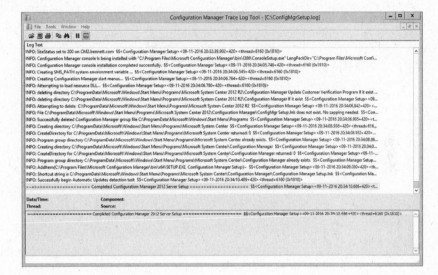

Recovering a Primary Child Site

Recovering a Configuration Manager primary site that is a child site of a CAS is a similar process to recovering the CAS itself except that the setup wizard will automatically configure the CAS as the reference site. The steps provided in the previous section will walk you through the remainder of the process.

Recovering a Primary Standalone Site

Recovering a primary standalone site is almost identical to recovering a CAS except that the Setup Wizard will not allow you to configure a reference site since there is no reference site in a standalone primary site server hierarchy. The steps provided in the previous section will walk you through the remainder of the process.

Recovering a Secondary Site

Configuration Manager does not support the backup of a secondary site. If the secondary site fails, you will have to recover the site by using the Recover Secondary Site option in the Sites node of the Configuration Manager console and the secondary site will be reinstalled. If you have to rebuild the secondary site server due to a server crash, the rebuilt server must match the configuration of the previous server, including the same computer name, the same installation path for Configuration Manager, and the same version and same instance of SQL Server (SQL Server Express or SQL Server) that was used previously. Also, during a secondary site recovery, SQL Server Express is not automatically installed by Configuration Manager; you will need to manually install SQL Server Express on the server.

During the secondary site recovery process, if the content library still exists on the secondary site, then Configuration Manager will verify that the content library is valid and then USE it. If the content library does not exist or has become corrupted, you will need to redistribute the content to the secondary site or use the prestage content option to deploy the content via that method. Additional information on the prestage content option is available here: `https://technet.microsoft.com/en-us/library/gg712694.aspx#BKMK_PrestageContent`.

Unattended Recovery of a Site

As discussed, Configuration Manager supports recovering a CAS and a primary site via the Setup Wizard. You can also recover these sites via an unattended site initialization file.

In order to use the unattended recovery solution, you will need to create the initialization file that will be used with the `Setup.exe` application in the installation media to initiate the site recovery process. You choose how to name the initialization file but the file extension must be `.ini`. You will use the `/script` setup command-line option to specify the initialization file that will be used.

For example, if you named the initialization file `sitesetup.ini` and it is located on the site server `C:` drive in the `CMRECOVER` folder the command would be:

```
Setup.exe /script C:\CMRECOVER\sitesetup.ini
```

The account that is used to execute the command must have administrator rights on the right server. You also should open a command prompt as administrator and run the command from there.

The INI file that you create will provide the same information that would be provided if you performed the site recovery via the Setup Wizard. One key difference is that in the unattended recovery no default settings are applied, and as a result, every value for the recovery process must be specified in the INI file.

The information that is required in the INI file will depend on the recovery scenario. Also, the keys in the file are not case sensitive, and when you provide values for keys you must use an equals sign to separate the key from the value. The TechNet article Backup and Recovery in Configuration Manager documents the available keys that can be used in the INI file in the "Unattended Site Recovery Script File Keys" section of the article

`https://technet.microsoft.com/en-us/library/gg712697.aspx`.

Other Site Maintenance Options

Besides doing a full site recovery, you can use the Setup Wizard to initiate other site maintenance options. As shown in Figure 16.14, you can select the Perform Site Maintenance Or Reset This Site option to initiate the site maintenance and reset processes.

Figure 16.15 shows the options that are available in the Site Maintenance process. These options are discussed in Table 16.5.

FIGURE 16.14
Selecting the Perform
Site Maintenance Or
Reset This Site option

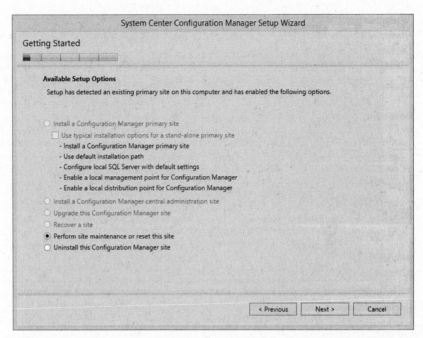

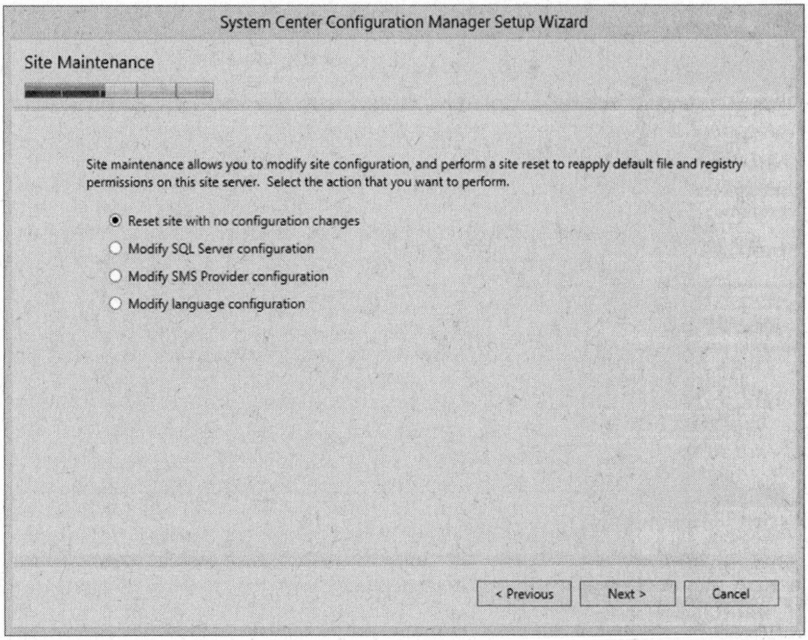

FIGURE 16.15
Available Site
Maintenance options

TABLE 16.5: Site reset and maintenance options

OPTION	USED WHEN
Reset Site With No Configuration Changes	This performs a site reset. During the site reset, all site components are reinstalled, and permissions and registry keys are restored to their default settings.
Modify SQL Server Configuration	Use this to move the site database to another SQL Server. Note that this process requires that you have already copied the SQL database to the new SQL Server. The process will not detach the database from the old location or attach it to the new server. The process also allows you to modify the SQL Service broker port.
Modify SMS Provider Information	Use this to install the SMS provider on another server.
Modify Language Configurations	Use this to add new server and client languages to the installation.

The Hierarchy Maintenance Tool

The Hierarchy Maintenance tool (preinst.exe) is a command-line tool that can be used to diagnose problems with a site system, help repair a site, shut down site systems, or perform other maintenance tasks that may not be available in the Configuration Manager console. This tool must be run locally on the site server.

To use the Hierarchy Maintenance tool, do the following:

1. Open a command prompt window with administrative privileges.

2. Navigate to the location of preinst.exe, which by default is

   ```
   <drive where Configuration Manager is installed>\Microsoft Configuration
   Manager\bin\x64\<language code>
   ```

   The language code for English is 00000409.

3. Once you are there, just type **preinst.exe** to get a list of command-line options.

4. Use preinst.exe with its command-line options, listed in Table 16.6 (adapted from Microsoft documentation), to complete your task.

TABLE 16.6: Hierarchy Maintenance tool syntax

COMMAND	DESCRIPTION
/dump <site code>	This command writes site control images to the root of the folder of the drive where the site is installed. /dump <site code> writes the site control file of only the site specified. /dump writes the site control files for all sites.

TABLE 16.6: Hierarchy Maintenance tool syntax *(continued)*

COMMAND	DESCRIPTION
/deljob <*site code*>	This command deletes all jobs targeted to the site you specify in the command line.
/delsite <*site code*>	This command deletes child sites that were not previously removed successfully from the site database of its parent site. This command does not uninstall the site server components on the designated site server.
/stopsite	This command shuts down the Configuration Manager Site Component Manager service, which will partially reset the site. When this shutdown is finished, Configuration Manager Services on a site server and its remote systems are stopped. These services are flagged for reinstall, and some passwords are automatically changed when these services are reinstalled. When the shutdown cycle is started, it automatically runs and skips any computers or components that are not responding. If the Site Component Manager service can't access a remote site system during this process, the components on the remote site system will be reinstalled when the Site Component Manager service is restarted. This will continue until Site Component Manager succeeds in reinstalling all services that are marked for reinstallation. You can restart the Site Component Manager service using Service Manager just like other Windows services. After you use the /stopsite command to start a shutdown cycle, there is nothing you can do to stop the subsequent reinstall cycles when the Site Component Manager service is restarted. You can monitor the effect of the process by reading the sitecomp.log file on the site server.
/keyforparent	This command is run on sites that you are trying to recover after failure and is used to distribute the new public key to a parent site of the failed site. The /keyforparent command places the public key of the failed site in the file <*site code*>.CT4 at the root of the drive from where the command is run. After the file is made, you will have to manually copy it to the parent site's hman.box inbox (not in the pubkey folder).
/keyforchild	This command is run on sites that you are trying to recover after failure and is used to distribute the new public key to a child site of the failed site. The /keyforchild command places the public key of the failed site in the file <*site code*>.CT6 at the root of the drive from where the command is run. After the file is made, you will have to manually copy it to the child site's hman.box inbox (not in the pubkey folder).
/childkeys	This command is run on the recovering site's child sites and is used to distribute public keys from all child sites to the recovering site. The /childkeys command places this and all child site public keys into the file <*site code*>.CT6 at the root of the drive from where the command is run. After the file is made, you will have to manually copy it to the parent site's hman.box inbox.
/parentkeys	This command is run on the recovering site's parent site and is used to distribute public keys from all parent sites to the recovering site. The /parentkeys command places this and all parent site public keys into the file <*site code*>.CT7 at the root of the drive from where the command is run. After the file is made, you will have to manually copy it to the child site's hman.box inbox.

Postrecovery Tasks

After you recover a site, there are postrecovery tasks that you will need to complete in order to regain the full functionality of Configuration Manager. Many of the actions are listed here and the full details are available in the "Post-Recovery Tasks" section of the article at https://technet.microsoft.com/en-us/library/gg712697.aspx.

- ◆ Monitor site processes.

- ◆ Verify site setting configuration.

- ◆ Reenter user account passwords.

  All of the user account passwords will be reset during the recovery process. You can find a list of affected user accounts in the C:\ConfigMgrPostRecoveryActions.html file.

- ◆ Reinstall previously applied hotfixes.

  You can find a list of installed hotfixes in the C:\ConfigMgrPostRecoveryActions.html file.

- ◆ Reenter Windows sideloading keys if they were being used for mobile device management in the site. Also re-create the Microsoft Intune subscription.

- ◆ Verify that the content library is fully rebuilt from the original data sources. If you need to determine the package source location, you can run the SQL query SELECT * FROM V_ PACKAGE command against the Configuration Manager database in Microsoft SQL Server to list the package properties.

- ◆ Recover any custom reports.

- ◆ Recover the SCUP database if it was affected.

- ◆ If the IIS server was configured to use HTTPS, you will need to reconfigure IIS to use the web server certificate.

- ◆ Reprovision previously provisioned Intel AMT computers.

- ◆ Recover the MDT database.

- ◆ The content stored in the user state migration data folders is not backed up by Configuration Manager and should be restored from your enterprise backup process.

- ◆ If cloud distribution points are being used, you will need to update the certificate.

The Bottom Line

Configure backups for Configuration Manager sites.   Backing up Configuration Manager sites can be automated by scheduling the Backup Site Server maintenance task. When the Configuration Manager backup service (SMS_SITE_BACKUP) starts, it uses instructions in the backup control file, located at

```
ConfigMgr Install Location]Microsoft Configuration Manager\Inboxes\smsbkup.box\
smsbkup.ctl
```

Master It   Recovering a complete Configuration Manager site is only supported with site backups from what source?

Archive backup snapshots to another location.   The Backup Site Server task creates a backup snapshot and can be used to recover a Configuration Manager site system if it fails. The next time the backup task runs, it makes a new backup snapshot that will overwrite the one that was made during the last snapshot. This could be a problem if the current backup snapshot becomes corrupted for some reason, because there is no other backup to restore from.

> **Master It**   What process could you use to copy backup snapshots from the site server to a new location?

Reinstall the site components and reset file and registry permissions to their default settings.   It's possible that at some point the site will have issues or become corrupted. Or maybe the Configuration Manager folder permissions were modified and are impacting the functionality of the site.

> **Master It**   How can you restore the file and registry permissions without performing a complete restore?

Chapter 17

Troubleshooting

So far you have read about various aspects of Configuration Manager, and in each chapter we have explained different aspects of the product and have assumed that every component will work correctly. However, everyone knows that situations may occur with the product that require troubleshooting, and every IT professional needs to know how to identify the problem and find a possible solution. Many resources are available online that can assist you in this process; some of these places are Microsoft TechNet, Bing, and MVP blogs.

In this chapter, we will cover the basics of troubleshooting a Configuration Manager infrastructure and determining which log file you should look at first when a problem arises.

In this chapter, you will learn to

- ◆ Create a basic maintenance plan

- ◆ View log files using CMTrace

- ◆ Troubleshoot DRS replication

- ◆ Master the troubleshooting steps

Creating the Maintenance Plan

The best way to prevent issues from arising in Configuration Manager is to create and follow a standard maintenance plan. A well-executed maintenance plan allows administrators to be actively aware of their Configuration Manager hierarchy, offering a better chance of finding possible concerns before they become issues. Proactively watching the environment can reduce the number of major issues and thus keep your environment healthier.

Configuration Manager has some predefined site maintenance tasks that are enabled by default and some that need to be enabled. To view and modify the site maintenance tasks, take the following steps:

1. Open the Configuration Manager console, and choose the Administration workspace.

2. Expand Overview ➤ Site Configuration ➤ Sites, and select Site Name.

3. Right-click, browse to Site Maintenance, and click it to open the Site Maintenance window, shown in Figure 17.1.

   By default, Microsoft has 15 predefined tasks for the CAS server and 37 predefined tasks for primary sites. Secondary sites have only 4 predefined tasks. Some of these predefined tasks are enabled, whereas others are disabled by default.

FIGURE 17.1
Enabling the Backup
Site Server task

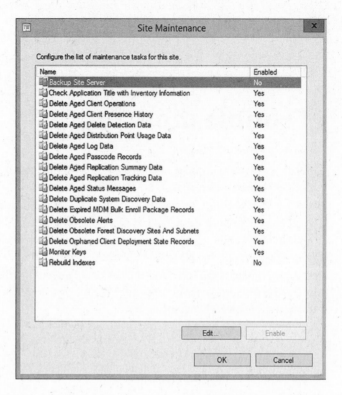

4. To enable a task, select its name and click Edit to display the task's Site Maintenance dialog box.

5. Select Enable This Task.

SECONDARY SITES

You can back up a CAS and a primary site, but there is no backup support for secondary sites or site system servers.

To ensure the proper health of the site, you should enable some of the predefined site maintenance tasks provided by Microsoft, and you'll need to modify the schedule of other tasks. Table 17.1 lists how the tasks should be configured in a typical maintenance plan; this might not be appropriate for all environments, but you can use the table as a guide.

TABLE 17.1:   Site maintenance tasks

TASK NAME	ENABLED BY DEFAULT?	SCHEDULE	SITE LEVEL
Backup Site Server	No	Daily	CAS/Primary
Check Application Title with Inventory Information	Yes	Weekly	CAS

TABLE 17.1: Site maintenance tasks *(continued)*

Task name	Enabled by default?	Schedule	Site level
Clear Install Flag	No	Weekly	Primary
Delete Aged Application Request Data	Yes	Daily	Primary
Delete Aged Client Operations	Yes	Daily	CAS/Primary
Delete Aged Client Presence History	Yes	Daily	CAS/Primary
Delete Aged Collected Files	Yes	Weekly	Primary
Delete Aged Computer Association Data	Yes	Weekly	Primary
Delete Aged Delete Detection Data	Yes	Daily	CAS/Primary
Delete Aged Device Wipe Record	Yes	Weekly	Primary
Delete Aged Devices Managed by the Exchange Server Connector	Yes	Weekly	Primary
Delete Aged Discovery Data	Yes	Weekly	Primary
Delete Aged Distribution Point Usage Data	Yes	Daily	CAS/Primary
Delete Aged Endpoint Protection Health Status History Data	Yes	Weekly	Primary
Delete Aged Enrolled Devices	Yes	Weekly	Primary
Delete Aged Inventory History	Yes	Weekly	Primary
Delete Aged Log Data	Yes	Daily	CAS/Primary/ Secondary
Delete Aged Notification Task History	Yes	Daily	Primary
Delete Aged Replication Summary Data	Yes	Daily	CAS/Primary/ Secondary
Delete Aged Passcode Records	Yes	Daily	CAS/Primary/ Secondary
Delete Aged Replication Tracking Data	Yes	Daily	CAS/Primary/ Secondary
Delete Aged Software Metering Data	Yes	Daily	Primary
Delete Aged Software Metering Summary Data	Yes	Weekly	Primary
Delete Aged Status Messages	Yes	Daily	CAS/Primary

TABLE 17.1: Site maintenance tasks *(continued)*

TASK NAME	ENABLED BY DEFAULT?	SCHEDULE	SITE LEVEL
Delete Aged Threat Data	Yes	Weekly	Primary
Delete Aged Unknown Computers	Yes	Weekly	Primary
Delete Aged User Device Affinity Data	Yes	Weekly	Primary
Delete Inactive Client Discovery Data	Yes	Weekly	Primary
Delete Obsolete Alerts	Yes	Daily	CAS/Primary
Delete Obsolete Client Discovery Data	Yes	Weekly	Primary
Delete Obsolete Forest Discovery Sites and Subnets	Yes	Weekly	CAS/Primary
Delete Unused Applications Revisions	Yes	Daily	Primary
Evaluate Collection Members	Yes	Weekly	Primary
Monitor Keys	Yes	Weekly	CAS/Primary
Rebuild Indexes	No	Weekly	CAS/Primary/Secondary
Summarize Installed Software Data	Yes	Weekly	Primary
Summarize Software Metering File Usage Data	Yes	Daily	Primary
Summarize Software Metering Monthly Usage Data	Yes	Daily	Primary
Update Application Available Targeting	Yes	Daily	Primary
Update Application Catalog Tables	Yes	Intervals	Primary

Some tasks do not need to be performed as frequently as others, but it's important to develop a maintenance plan for them to ensure the proper health of the site.

Table 17.2 summarizes what a typical maintenance plan should be for Configuration Manager. Again, these recommendations might not be appropriate for organizations of all sizes; the table is meant to be used only as a guide.

TABLE 17.2: Maintenance plan

TASK	INTERVAL	COMMENTS
Check status messages.	Daily	Check for warnings and errors. They are available in either a web report or within the administrative console.

TABLE 17.2:   Maintenance plan *(continued)*

TASK	INTERVAL	COMMENTS
Check event log on site server for warnings or errors.	Daily	This is the Windows event log.
Check log folders for crash dumps.	Daily	This will help you know whether the site system failed.
Monitor site system's inbox folder(s).	Daily	Check this for possible backlogs of files.
Clean out old machines and user accounts.	Daily	Remove old resources.
Check client status.	Daily	
Back up site server to removable media.	Daily	Ensure that the copy of the site backup is moved to removable media such as tape.
Delete unnecessary objects.	Weekly	Remove unneeded collections, packages, programs, advertisements, and queries.
Delete unnecessary files from site systems.	Weekly	Delete unneeded files.
Check disk space on all site systems.	Weekly	
Defragment all site systems.	Monthly	This can improve site performance.
Review site boundaries.	Quarterly	Ensure that your site boundaries are still valid.
Perform DR test.	Biannually	Ensure that backups actually work.
Review documentation.	Biannually	Confirm that documentation is updated and complete.
Review maintenance plan.	Biannually	Modify the maintenance plan if anything has changed or needs to be added or removed.

Getting an approved maintenance plan for your hierarchy is your first step to developing a solid Configuration Manager infrastructure. The next step is to automate as many of the tasks as possible so they can be done in the most efficient manner without sacrificing the results. A maintenance plan is only as strong as the people implementing the plan.

Using Troubleshooting Tools

The most important troubleshooting tools are log files and status messages. Getting to know the most common log files for Configuration Manager is the first step in identifying a potential situation on your site servers; you can also use this to monitor your site server activity and to know what is being processed in your environment. That being said, let's take a look at the most common log files.

Log Files

For the majority of troubleshooting, administrators will focus on the log (.log) files on either the client or the server and in some cases both. The client stores the log files in the folder C:\Windows\ccm\logs, whereas the site server stores the log files in the folder <*installation Directory*>\Microsoft Configuration Manager\Logs. Table 17.3 lists site server log files, Table 17.4 lists management point log files, and Table 17.5 lists client log files.

The default location for the management point log files is Program Files\SMS_CCM\Logs on the management point.

TABLE 17.3: Site server and site system server log files

LOG FILE	PURPOSE
Ccm	Records client Configuration Manager tasks
Cidm	Records changes to the client settings by the Client Install Data Manager (CIDM)
Colleval	Logs when collections are created, changed, and deleted by the Collection Evaluator
Compsumm	Records Component Status Summarizer tasks
Dataldr	Processes management information format (MIF) files and hardware inventory in the Configuration Manager database
Ddm	Saves Discovery Data Record (DDR) information to the Configuration Manager database by the Discovery Data Manager
Despool	Records incoming site-to-site communication transfers
Distmgr	Records package creation, compression, delta replication, and information updates
Hman	Records site configuration changes and publishes site information in Active Directory Domain Services
Inboxast	Records files that are moved from the management point to the corresponding INBOXES folder
Inboxmgr	Records file maintenance
Invproc	Records the processing of delta MIF files for the Dataloader component for client inventory files
Mpcontrol	Records the registration of the management point with WINS and records the availability of the management point every 10 minutes
Mpfdm	Management point component that moves client files to the corresponding INBOXES folder
Mpmsi	Management point MSI installation log
Mpsetup	Records the management point installation wrapper process

TABLE 17.3:   Site server and site system server log files   *(continued)*

LOG FILE	PURPOSE
Offermgr	Records advertisement updates
Offersum	Records summarization of advertisement status messages
Policypv	Records updates to the client policies to reflect changes to client settings or advertisements
Replmgr	Records the replication of files between the site server components and the scheduler component
Schedule	Records details about site-to-site job and file replication
Sender	Records the files that transfer by file-based replication between sites
Sinvproc	Records client software inventory data processing to the site database in Microsoft SQL Server
Sitecomp	Records maintenance of the installed site components
Sitectrl	Records site setting changes to the Sitectrl.ct0 file
Sitestat	Records the monitoring process of all site systems
Smsdbmon	Records database changes
Smsexec	Records processing of all site server component threads
Smsprov	Records WMI provider access to the site database
Statmgr	Writes all status messages to the database
Swmproc	Processes metering files and maintains settings
Adctr	Records enrollment processing activity
ADForestDisc	Records Active Directory Forest Discovery actions
ADService	Records account creating and security group detail in Active Directory
Adsgdis	Records Active Directory Security Group Discovery actions
Adsysdis	Records Active Directory System Discovery actions
Adusrdis	Records Active Directory User Discovery actions
CertMgr	Records the certificate activities for intra-site communications
Chmgr	Records activities of the Client health manager

TABLE 17.3: Site server and site system server log files *(continued)*

LOG FILE	PURPOSE
Compmon	Records the status of component threads monitored for the site server
ComReqSetup	Records the initial installation of COM registration results for a site server
ConfigMgrPrereq	Records prerequisite component evaluation and installation activities
EPCtrlMgr	Records information about the synchronization of malware threat information from the endpoint protection site system role into the Configuration Manager database
EPMgr	Records the status of the endpoint protection site system role
EnrollSrv	Records activities of the enrollment service process
EnrollWeb	Records activities of the enrollment website process
Migmctrl	Records information for migration actions involving migration jobs, shared distribution points, and distribution point upgrades

TABLE 17.4: Management point log files

MANAGEMENT POINT LOG FILE	PURPOSE
MP_Ddr	Records the conversion of XML .ddr records from clients and copies them to the site server
MP_GetAuth	Records the status of the site management points
MP_GetPolicy	Records policy information
MP_Hinv	Converts XML hardware inventory records from clients and copies the files to the site server
MP_Location	Records Location Manager tasks
MP_Policy	Records policy communication
MP_Relay	Copies files that are collected from the client
MP_Retry	Records the hardware inventory retry processes
MP_Sinv	Converts XML hardware inventory records from clients and copies them to the site server
MP_Status	Converts XML .svf status message files from clients and copies them to the site server

TABLE 17.4: Management point log files *(continued)*

MANAGEMENT POINT LOG FILE	PURPOSE
MP_CliReq	Records the client registration activity processed by the management point
MP_Framework	Records the activities of the core management point and client framework components
MP_OOBMgr	Records the management point activities related to receiving
MP_SinvCollFile	Records details about file collection

TABLE 17.5: Client log files

CLIENT LOG FILE	PURPOSE
CAS	Content Access Service for the local machine's package cache
CcmExec	Tracks the client's activities and SMS agent host service information
CertificateMaintenance	Records Active Directory certificates for the directory service and management points
ClientIDManagerStartup	Used for the maintenance of the resource's GUID and Client Registration Certificate
ClientLocation	Tracks the resource's site assignments
ContentTransferManager	Records scheduling information for the Background Intelligence Transfer Service (BITS) or Server Message Block (SMB) to download or to access Configuration Manager packages
DataTransferService	Records all BITS communication for policy or package access
Execmgr	Records advertisement information as advertisements execute
FileBITS	Records SMB package access tasks
InventoryAgent	Creates DDRs and hardware and software inventory records
LocationServices	Identifies located management points and distribution points
MIFProvider	Identifies the MIF WMI provider
Mtrmgr	Tracks software-metering processes
PolicyAgent	Requests policies by using the data transfer service

TABLE 17.5: Client log files *(continued)*

CLIENT LOG FILE	PURPOSE
PolicyAgentProvider	Records any policy changes
PolicyEvaluator	Records any new policy settings
Scheduler	Records schedule tasks for all client operations
SMSCliui	Records usage of the Systems Management tool in Control Panel
StatusAgent	Logs status messages that are created by the client components
SWMTRReportGen	Generates a usage data report that is collected by the metering agent
EndpointProtectionAgent	Records details about the installation of the Endpoint Protection client and the application of antimalware policy to that client

There are also log files outside Configuration Manager that you will need to be aware of when troubleshooting issues within Configuration Manager; Table 17.6 lists them.

TABLE 17.6: Additional log files

NAME OR CATEGORY	LOCATION	DESCRIPTION
IIS log files	%windir%\system32\Logsfiles	Log file for Internet Information Services (IIS). Logs HTTP transactions.
SQL log files	SQL Enterprise Manager	Logs SQL activities.
WMI	%windir%\system32\wbem\logs	The WMI repository is the key to the hardware inventory of the clients. Become very familiar with these logs.

There are many more log files for each Configuration Manager component. To learn more about the rest of the log files, you can check out the Configuration Manager Library at https://technet.microsoft.com/en-us/library/mt622755.aspx. Here you can find such details as the log file location and descriptions. Since Configuration Manager has many log files, we point out only the most common ones in this chapter.

The best tool for reading log files we have seen is CMTrace, a log viewer that constantly monitors the opened file for updates. You can find CMTrace in the SMSSETUP\Tools folder on the Configuration Manager source media or *Installation Path*\tools. It provides real-time updates of any log file, allowing administrators to see exactly what is happening on a client or site system. If that isn't enough to win you over, CMTrace includes the capability to highlight and filter features to allow at-a-glance log viewing. Finally, the tool includes an error code dictionary, shown in Figure 17.2, so that you can quickly translate most of Microsoft's decimal error codes into useful information right within the tool. For example, entering 5 in the Error Lookup window returns "Access Denied." This feature is available by selecting Tools ➢ Lookup in the CMTrace utility. CMTrace will highlight errors, as shown in Figure 17.3, so they stand out.

FIGURE 17.2
CMTrace Error
Lookup window

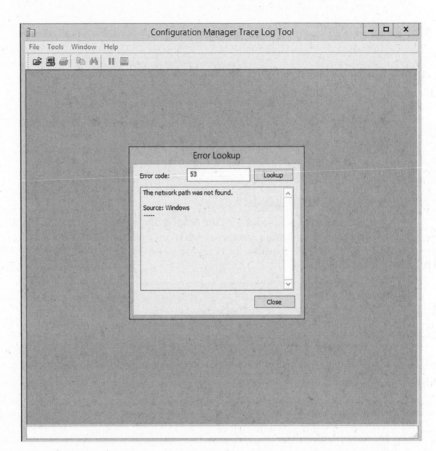

The other tool you need is a reference to all the log files. We covered the log files and their locations earlier in this chapter, and this information is a great reference. So now you are well equipped to troubleshoot a Configuration Manager (Current Branch) site using the log files from the client or site systems, using the status messages in Configuration Manager, or using the web reporting feature of Configuration Manager.

FIGURE 17.3

Highlighted error in CMTrace

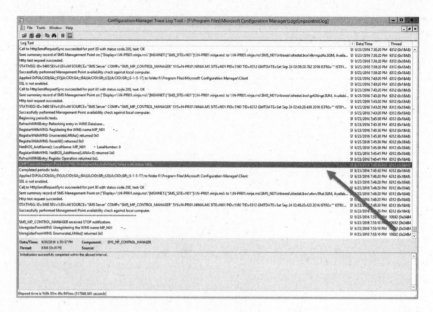

Status Messages

Now that you have seen where the log files reside on both the client and servers, we will cover the troubleshooting components in the Configuration Manager (Current Branch) console. Microsoft has continued to provide status messages within the console.

LIMITATIONS OF STATUS MESSAGES

Status messages do have some limitations. The first limitation is that site systems must be able to communicate in order for status messages to be transferred back; if a site system component cannot report back because of a failed network connection, it might still be showing that it is available. Another limitation is that most client messages are transferred as low priority by default, and during high utilizations these messages might be delayed.

Although status messages have some limitations, they can still be vital weapons in the troubleshooting arsenal of a Configuration Manager administrator. They just shouldn't be the only source for troubleshooting, however.

Status messages reside in one location, which is why they provide some benefit when troubleshooting. They are arranged in one place so you can quickly see the health of the site at a glance. To view the site status, in the Configuration Manager console choose Monitoring ➤ Overview ➤ System Status ➤ Site Status.

The System Status dashboard is a summarized collection of the status of all the reported sites for easy viewing, and it has drill-down capability for each message. The System Status dashboard is organized into two categories, Component Status and Site Status, as shown in Figure 17.4.

FIGURE 17.4

The Site Status
dashboard

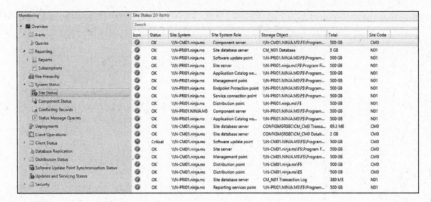

To dig deeper into a Component Status message to see details about a problem, follow these steps:

1. In the Configuration Manager console, choose Monitoring ➤ Overview ➤ System Status ➤ Component Status.

2. Select the component you want to investigate. For this example, select SMS_DATABASE_NOTIFICATION_MONITOR.

3. Right-click the component, and select Show Messages ➤ All, as shown in Figure 17.5.

FIGURE 17.5

The Show Messages
menu

This opens the Configuration Manager Status Message Viewer for *<Site Code> <Site Name>* window, as shown in Figure 17.6.

FIGURE 17.6

The Configuration
Manager Status
Message Viewer
window

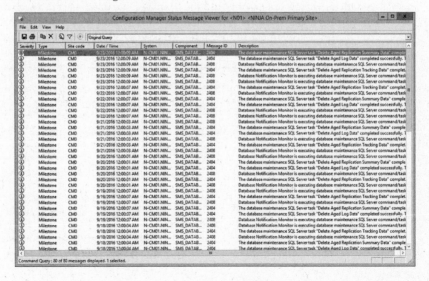

Note that you can filter the returned messages by selecting All, Info, Warning, or Error messages.

4. Within the Configuration Manager Status Message Viewer window, double-click any of the messages to get a detailed view of the message, as shown in Figure 17.7.

FIGURE 17.7
The Status Message
Details dialog

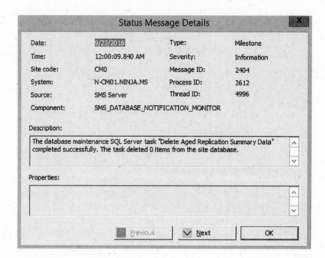

USING WEB REPORTS TO VIEW STATUS MESSAGES

You can view status messages from the Web Reports tool within Configuration Manager (Current Branch). This is beneficial in case you are not able to access the Configuration Manager console or you have limited access to it. In either case, you can browse to your reporting point web console and view the status messages within a browser.

As discussed in Chapter 12, "Reporting," web reports allow administrators to provide focused views of a Configuration Manager site database via a web browser and can be set up within a dashboard to give managers an at-a-glance overview of the hierarchy. Table 17.7 lists the reports available in the Status Messages category.

TABLE 17.7:   Status Messages reports

NAME	DESCRIPTION
All Messages for a Specific Message ID	Lists the messages with a single message ID
Clients Reporting Errors in the Last 12 Hours for a Specific Site	Lists the computers and components reporting errors in the last 12 hours and the number of errors reported
Component Messages for the Last 12 Hours	Lists the component messages for the last 12 hours for a specific site code, computer, and component
Component Messages for the Last Hour (for a Specific Site)	Lists the status messages created in the last hour by a specified component on a specified computer in a specified SMS site

TABLE 17.7: Status Messages reports *(continued)*

NAME	DESCRIPTION
Count Component Messages for the Last Hour for a Specific Site	Displays the number of status messages by component and severity reported in the last hour at a single specified site
Count Errors in the Last 12 Hours	Displays the number of server component error status messages in the last 12 hours
Fatal Errors (by Component)	Lists the computers reporting fatal errors by component
Fatal Errors (by Computer Name)	Lists the computers reporting fatal errors by computer name
Last 1000 Messages for a Specific Computer (Errors and Warnings)	Summarizes the last 1,000 error and warning component status messages for a single specified computer
Last 1000 Messages for a Specific Computer (Errors)	Summarizes the last 1,000 error server component status messages for a single specified computer
Last 1000 Messages for a Specific Computer (Errors, Warnings, and Information)	Summarizes the last 1,000 error, warning, and informational component status messages for a single specified computer
Last 1000 Messages for a Specific Server Component	Summarizes the most recent 1,000 status messages for a single specified server component

As you can see, Microsoft has provided some nice reports out of the box for status messages. Of course, you can create your own report or modify any of the existing reports to fit your needs.

DEPLOYMENT STATUS

Configuration Manager offers deployment status via the Monitoring workspace in the Configuration Manager console; you can monitor the deployment of all software (software updates, compliance settings, applications, task sequences, packages, and programs). To view this section of the console, do the following:

1. In the Configuration Manager console, choose the Monitoring workspace.

2. In Overview, choose Deployments.

3. To review general status information about an application deployment, select a deployment, and then choose the Summary tab of the Selected Deployment window.

4. To review deployment details for a compliance state and the devices in that state, select a deployment, and then, at the bottom of the screen in the Compliance Statistics section, click View Status.

5. To review information about the application's deployment type, select a deployment, and then click the Deployment Types tab of the Selected Deployment window.

Applications in Configuration Manager support state-based monitoring, which allows you to track the last application deployment state for users and devices. These state messages display information about individual devices. As you can see in Table 17.8, you can review the different states within the deployment.

TABLE 17.8: Application deployment state

COLUMN NAME	DESCRIPTION
Success	The application deployment succeeded.
In Progress	The application deployment is in progress.
Unknown	The state of the application deployment could not be determined; by default all deployments will be on this state.
Requirements Not Met	The application was not deployed because it was not compliant with a dependency or a requirement rule.
Error	The application failed to deploy because of an error.

You can view additional information for each compliance state, which includes subcategories within the compliance state and the number of users and devices in this category. For example, the Error compliance state contains three subcategories:

◆ Error Evaluating Policy

◆ Content Related Errors

◆ Installation Errors

When more than one compliance state applies for an application deployment to a user who has more than one device, you will see the aggregate state that represents the lowest compliance. For example, if a user logs into two devices, and the application is successfully installed on one device but fails to install on the second device, the aggregate deployment state of the application for that user is Error.

Use these subcategories to help you to quickly identify any important issues with an application deployment. You can also view additional information about which devices fall into a particular subcategory of a compliance state.

DISTRIBUTION STATUS

The Configuration Manager console provides improved content monitoring, including the status for all package types in relation to the associated distribution points, including the content validation status for the content in the package, the status of content assigned to a specific distribution point group, the state of content assigned to a distribution point, and the status of optional features for each distribution point.

The console provides a Content Status node in the Monitoring workspace (see Table 17.9). Inside this workspace you can review the information of the different packages and how many distribution points have been targeted. This is very similar to the old package status on Configuration Manager 2007. To monitor the content status and view the status, follow these steps:

1. In the Configuration Manager console, choose Monitoring.

2. In the Monitoring workspace, under Overview, expand Distribution Status, and then choose Content Status. The packages are displayed.

3. Select the package for which you want detailed status information.

4. At the bottom of the screen, in the Completion Statistics area, click View Status. Detailed status information for the package is displayed.

TABLE 17.9:   Content status monitoring

COLUMN NAME	DESCRIPTION
Software	Displays the name of the package
Type	Displays the type of content
Source Version	Displays the version number of the source files
Date Created	Displays the time and date the package was last changed
Targeted	Displays the total number of distribution points that have a copy of this package
Installed	Displays the total number of distribution points that have a copy of the current version
Pending	Displays the total number of distribution points that have had a failure in copying the package but have not exceeded the number of retries allowed and are currently retrying to copy the package or are in the state of removing the old package
Failed	Displays the total number of distribution points that have exceeded the number of retries and were unsuccessful at copying the package
Size	Displays the size of the package source folder
Source Site	Displays the site code of the site where the content was created
Package ID	Displays the package ID

DISTRIBUTION POINT GROUP STATUS

This view can be found in the Monitoring workspace in the Configuration Manager console; here you can review information such as the distribution point group name, description, how many distribution points are members of the distribution point group, how many packages have been assigned to the group, distribution point group status, and compliance rate. You can also identify errors for the distribution point group, how many distributions are in progress, and how many have been successfully distributed. To perform this action, take the following steps:

1. In the Configuration Manager console, choose Monitoring.

2. In the Monitoring workspace, under the Overview, expand Distribution Status, and then choose Distribution Point Group Status. The distribution point groups are displayed.

3. Select the distribution point group for which you want detailed status information.

4. In the bottom section, in the Distribution Statistics area, click View Status.

   Detailed status information for the distribution point group is displayed.

DISTRIBUTION POINT CONFIGURATION STATUS

On this node you can review what attributes are enabled for the distribution point, such as PXE, multicast, and content validation, as well as the distribution status for the distribution point. To view this information, perform the following steps:

1. In the Configuration Manager console, choose Monitoring.

2. In the Monitoring workspace, under the Overview, expand Distribution Status, and then choose Distribution Point Configuration Status. The distribution points are displayed.

3. Select the distribution point for which you want distribution point status information.

4. In the results pane, click the Details tab.

   Status information for the distribution point is displayed.

SYSTEM STATUS

The System Status home page will highlight all the site systems within your Configuration Manager infrastructure and show a summary of the systems. Table 17.10 displays the information shown when you browse to the System Status home page by choosing the Monitoring workspace ➤ Overview ➤ System Status in the Configuration Manager console.

TABLE 17.10:   System status

COLUMN NAME	DESCRIPTION
Status	Displays the status of the Configuration Manager site and any child site. The status will be OK, Warning, or Critical.
Site System	Displays the NetBIOS name of the site system.
Site System Role	Displays the role assigned to the site system.
Storage Object	Displays the name and location of the storage unit.
Total	Displays the total available disk space.
Free	Displays the total available free space.

TABLE 17.10: System status *(continued)*

COLUMN NAME	DESCRIPTION
Free Disk (%)	Displays the percentage of available free space.
Down Since (Time)	Displays the time when the site system could not be contacted.
Availability	Displays whether the site system is currently online or offline.

Because of the comparatively slower replication speed of status messages, most Configuration Manager administrators will focus on the log files of the client, the server, and often a combination of both. Because there are so many log files, to keep track of which log file contains the information needed for troubleshooting every Configuration Manager administrator needs two tools:

CMTrace   With this tool you can view the log file in real time.

Flowcharts   These usually explain how each process works and its flow.

ADDITIONAL TOOLS

One other set of tools available to you for troubleshooting is the System Center Configuration Manager Toolkit, available at `https://www.microsoft.com/en-us/download/details .aspx?id=50012`. This toolkit contains 15 tools to help you manage and troubleshoot Configuration Manager (Current Branch). We cover the tools next, divided into server-based tools and client-based tools.

Server-Based Tools

Distribution Point Job Queue Manager (DPJobManager) helps you troubleshoot and manage ongoing content distribution jobs to Configuration Manager distribution points, as shown in Figure 17.8.

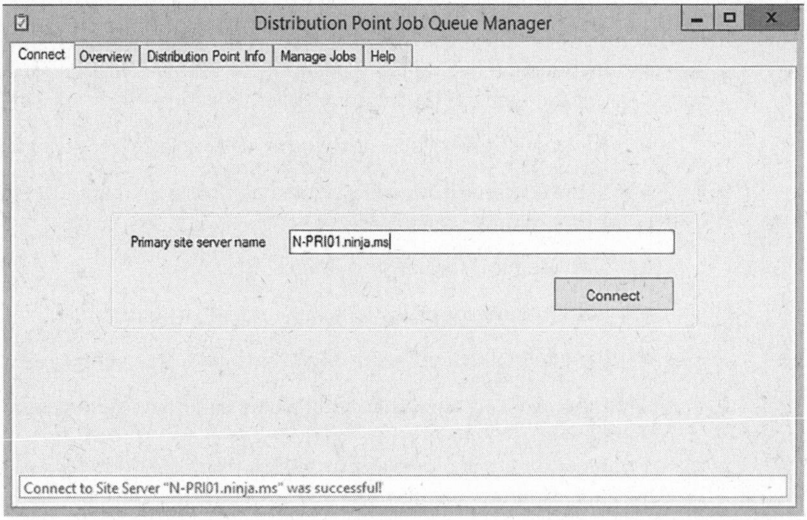

FIGURE 17.8
Distribution Point
Job Queue Manager

With DPJobManager open, you enter the name of the primary site server where those distribution points are connected. You can then choose the Overview, Distribution Point Info, Manage Jobs, or Help tabs to get additional details about the queues.

Collection Evaluation Viewer (CEViewer) assists you in troubleshooting collection evaluation–related issues by viewing collection evaluation details, as shown in Figure 17.9.

FIGURE 17.9
Collection
Evaluation Viewer

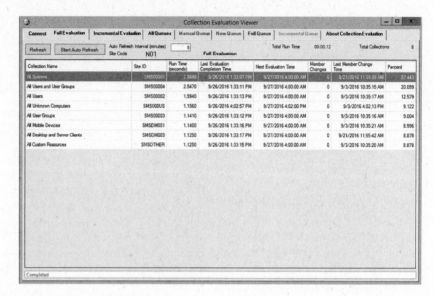

Once you're connected to the primary site, you will be able to review the current collections. For example, as you can see in Figure 17.9, from the current collections that are performing a full evaluation in this list you can determine the collection name, site ID, runtime, last evaluation time, next evaluation time, member changes, last member change time, and percent of members. All this information is useful when troubleshooting collections. Besides the full evaluation, there are other tabs that will help on this troubleshooting. Here are more details about each tab.

◆ Incremental Evaluation will show you all the collections that have been marked with the Use Incremental Updates For This Collection.

◆ All Queues gives you a dashboard of what is currently running on all the queues.

◆ Manual Queue is for collections that have been manually selected for evaluation from the administrative console UI.

◆ New Queue is for newly created collections.

◆ Full Queue is for collections due for full evaluation.

◆ Incremental Queue is for collections with incremental evaluation.

This is a very good tool that will help you address the question of why a collection has not updated.

Content Library Explorer assists you in troubleshooting issues with and viewing the contents of the content library, as shown in Figure 17.10.

FIGURE 17.10
Content Library
Explorer

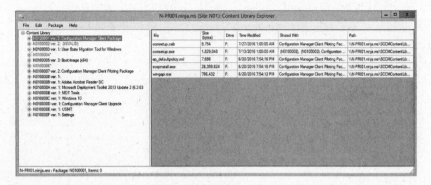

Once you open Content Library Explorer, it will ask you to connect to the distribution point by entering its FQDN. Once you're connected to the distribution point, you will be able to browse the Content Library and select the package ID you are trying to troubleshoot.

You can use the Security Configuration Wizard Template for System Center (Current Branch) Configuration Manager to help secure the site server. The wizard is an attack-surface reduction tool for the Microsoft Windows Server 2008 R2 operating system. Security Configuration Wizard determines the minimum functionality required for a server's role or roles and disables the functionality that is not required. An example of this is shown in Figure 17.11. With this file you can then use the Security Configuration Wizard (SCW) to apply the XML file to the site server by running the following command line:

```
scwcmd register /kbname:"Configuration Manager" /kbfile:"C:\Program Files
(x86)\ConfigMgr 2012 Toolkit R2\ServerTools\ConfigMgr2012SCW.xml"
```

FIGURE 17.11
Security Configuration
Wizard Template XML
file

```xml
<?xml version="1.0" encoding="UTF-8"?>
<SCWKBRegistrationInfo ServicePackMinorVersion="0" ServicePackMajorVersion="1" OSMinorVersion="1" OSMajorVersion="6">
  <SCWKnowledgeBase>
    <Roles>
      <!-- ***************************************************** -->
      <!-- Central Administration Site -->
      <!-- ***************************************************** -->
      <Role Name="SMSCentralSite" Type="Server" Status="Enabled">
        <Satisfiable DLLPath="%windir%\security\msscw\bin\configmgrscwhelper.dll" FunctionName="IsSCCMCentralSite"/>
        <Selected Value="TRUE"/>
        <Services>
          <Service Name="SMS_EXECUTIVE"/>
          <Service Name="SMS_SITE_COMPONENT_MANAGER"/>
          <Service Name="SMS_SITE_VSS_WRITER"/>
          <Service Name="SMS_SITE_SQL_BACKUP"/>
          <Service Name="MSIServer"/>
          <Service Name="Winmgmt"/>
          <Service Name="RemoteRegistry"/>
          <Service Name="lanmanserver"/>
          <Service Name="lanmanworkstation"/>
        </Services>
        <Firewall>
          <FirewallRule Id="sccm-rpcepm-135-in"/>
          <FirewallRule Id="sccm-rpcepm-135-out"/>
          <FirewallRule Id="sccm-smb-445-in"/>
          <FirewallRule Id="sccm-smb-445-out"/>
          <FirewallRule Id="sccm-SQL-1433"/>
          <FirewallRule Id="sccm-SQL-4022"/>
          <FirewallRule Id="sccm-wmi-winmgmt-in-tcp"/>
        </Firewall>
      </Role>
      <!-- ***************************************************** -->
      <!-- Primary Site Server -->
      <!-- ***************************************************** -->
      <Role Name="SMSPrimarySite" Type="Server" Status="Enabled">
        <Satisfiable DLLPath="%windir%\security\msscw\bin\configmgrscwhelper.dll" FunctionName="IsSCCMPrimarySite"/>
        <Selected Value="TRUE"/>
        <Services>
          <Service Name="SMS_EXECUTIVE"/>
          <Service Name="SMS_SITE_COMPONENT_MANAGER"/>
          <Service Name="SMS_SITE_VSS_WRITER"/>
          <Service Name="SMS_SITE_SQL_BACKUP"/>
          <Service Name="MSIServer"/>
          <Service Name="Winmgmt"/>
          <Service Name="RemoteRegistry"/>
          <Service Name="lanmanserver"/>
          <Service Name="lanmanworkstation"/>
        </Services>
        <Firewall>
          <FirewallRule Id="sccm-rpcepm-135-in"/>
          <FirewallRule Id="sccm-rpcepm-135-out"/>
          <FirewallRule Id="sccm-smb-445-in"/>
```

Content Library Transfer is a tool that transfers content from one disk drive to another, as you can see in Figure 17.12.

FIGURE 17.12
Content Library
Transfer

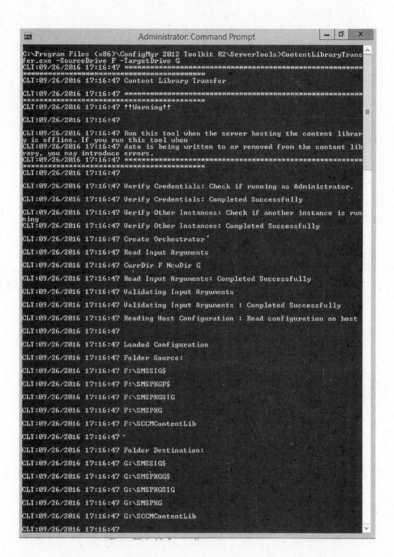

You can imagine a distribution point whose drive is filling up quickly, and you need to move the content from one drive to another but don't want to rebuild the distribution point. Instead, you can move the content from one drive to another by entering the following command: `ContentLibraryTransfer.exe -SourceDrive X: -TargetDrive Y`. Once the command finishes, the content library will be located on the new drive.

The Content Ownership Tool changes the ownership of orphaned packages (packages without an owner site server), as shown in Figure 17.13.

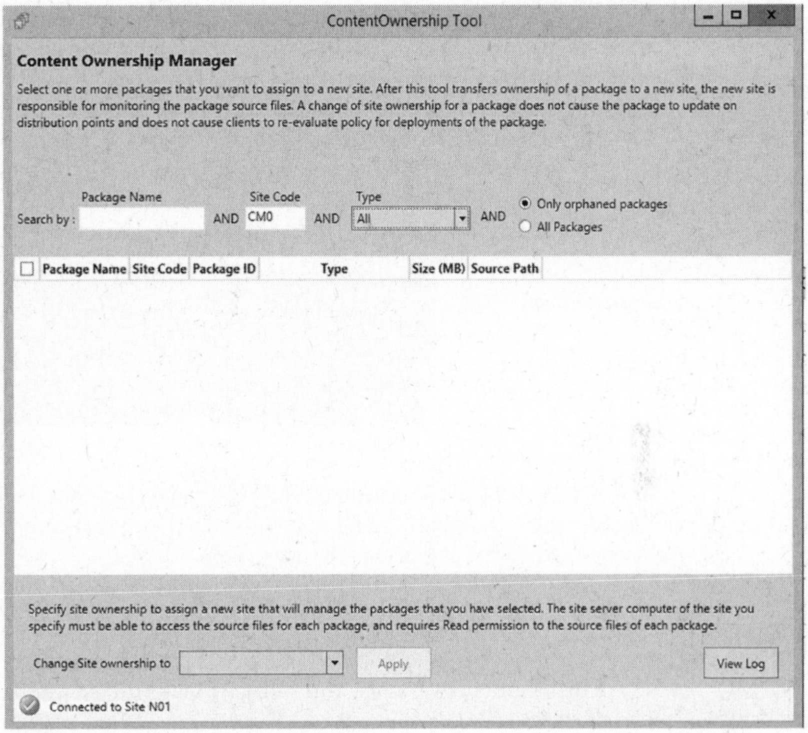

FIGURE 17.13
Content Ownership
Tool

If you select Only Orphaned Packages, all orphaned packages will be displayed in the list. You can also choose All Packages to see all the package names. Once you find an orphaned package, you can click Change Site Ownership To and specify the new site; then click Apply.

The Role-Based Administration Modeling and Auditing Tool (RBA Viewer) helps administrators model and audit RBA configurations, as shown in Figure 17.14.

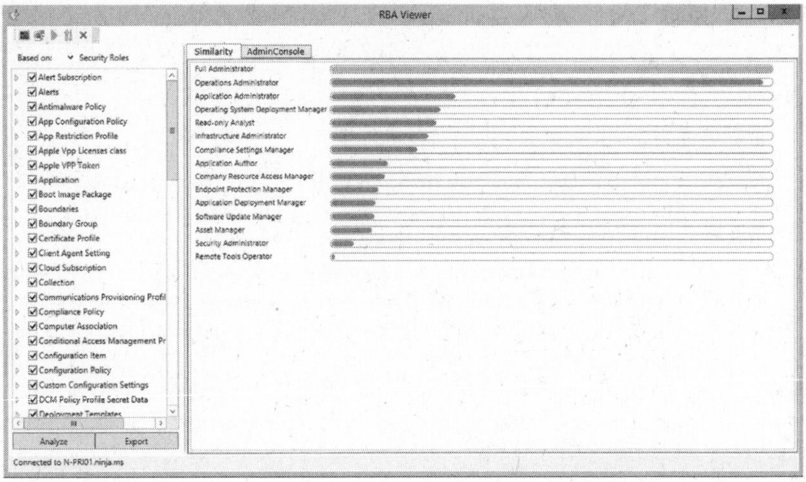

FIGURE 17.14
RBA Viewer

RBA Viewer is a great tool to use to model the security role; more importantly, you can audit a user by clicking the green play button at the top of the screen. Then all you need to do is enter the user information and click Check. This will display the current assignments and console view.

The Run Metering Summarization Tool (runmetersumm) runs the metering summarization task to analyze raw metering data, as shown in Figure 17.15.

FIGURE 17.15
Run Metering
Summarization Tool

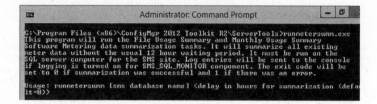

You can use this tool to update the software metering data. This needs to run at the primary site server where the data is going to be inserted. Once that's completed, you will be able to run the software metering reports with no problem.

Client-Based Tools

Client Troubleshooting Tool (CliSpy) is a tool that helps you troubleshoot issues related to software distribution, inventory, and software metering on Configuration Manager clients, as shown in Figure 17.16.

FIGURE 17.16
Client Troubleshooting
Tool (CliSpy)

To use this tool, you must click Tools and connect to the client you are currently trouble-shooting. Once you're connected, you will have the option to review each tab and identify the potential problem on the client.

Configuration Manager Trace Log Viewer (CMTrace) is a tool used to view log files created by Configuration Manager components and agents. This tool was covered earlier in this chapter and is shown in Figure 17.3; it is the day-to-day tool of every Configuration Manager administrator.

The Deployment Monitoring Tool is a graphical user interface designed to help troubleshoot applications, updates, and baseline deployments on Configuration Manager clients, as shown in Figure 17.17.

FIGURE 17.17
Deployment
Monitoring Tool

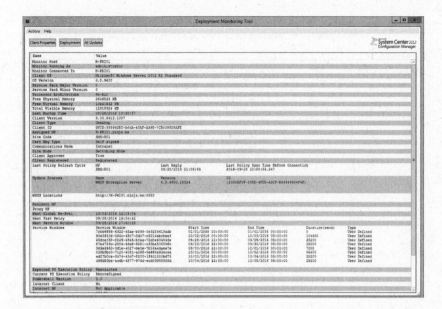

Once open, it will connect by default to the current computer. To connect to another computer, you must click Actions and then click Connect To Remote Machine. Once you have chosen the computer to troubleshoot, you can click Client Properties to review the information of the client. You can click Deployments to validate what deployments have been completed on the machine or are optional to the machine. This will also include baseline deployments, as mentioned earlier. You can also click All Updates; this status will display all the current installed or missing.

PolicySpy is a policy viewer that helps you review and troubleshoot the policy system on Configuration Manager clients, as shown in Figure 17.18.

FIGURE 17.18
PolicySpy

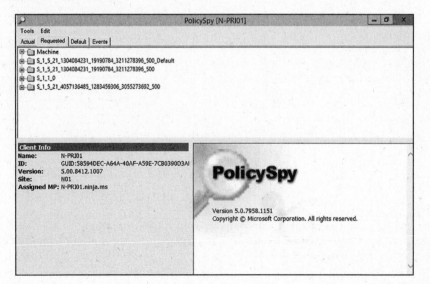

You can use the Power Viewer Tool to view the status of the power-management feature on Configuration Manager clients, as shown in Figure 17.19.

FIGURE 17.19
Power Viewer

The Send Schedule Tool is used to trigger a schedule on a client or trigger the evaluation of a specified DCM baseline. You can trigger a schedule either locally or remotely, as shown in Figure 17.20.

FIGURE 17.20
Send Schedule Tool

WakeupSpy is a tool that provides a view of the power state of Configuration Manager client computers, as shown in Figure 17.21.

FIGURE 17.21
WakeupSpy

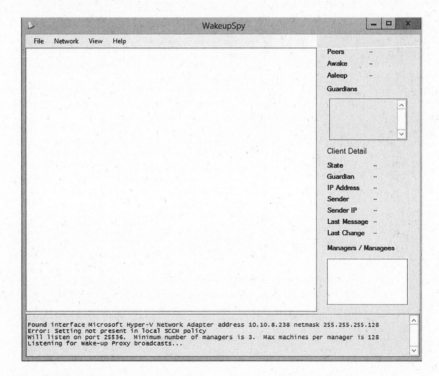

System Center Support Center

System Center Support Center (see Figure 17.22) helps you gather information about Configuration Manager clients so that you can address issues with those clients when working with product support. Configuration Manager Support Center lets you gather log files and includes a feature that is used by product support to examine log files and other client data for in-depth analysis of issues. You can download System Center Support Center from http://go.microsoft.com/fwlink/?LinkId=397734.

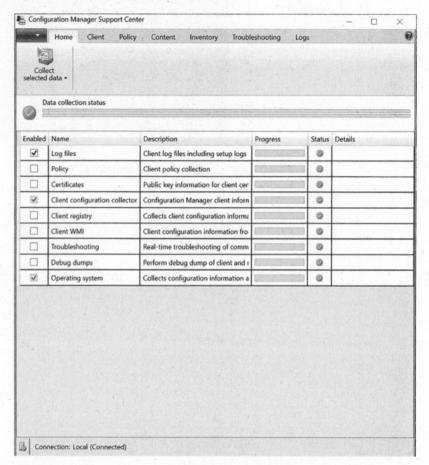

Once you have downloaded System Center Support Center, you will be able to connect to clients by using the menu section of the tool and perform different troubleshooting. Keep in mind the various steps of troubleshooting when using the tool so you can find the solution to the problem you are currently working on. If you want to learn more about the tool, check out the User Guide: https://technet.microsoft.com/en-us/library/dn688621.aspx.

Troubleshooting a Configuration Manager Site Installation

We've validated the hierarchy installation, but that doesn't guarantee the site is working properly. Configuration Manager has many moving parts, and at times problems will surface. Understanding how to troubleshoot those problems is important to maintaining a healthy

Configuration Manager hierarchy. So where should you look to troubleshoot issues with a site? Fortunately, Configuration Manager is not lacking in information to help administrators check for problems and ascertain the nature of the problems. As with validation, this brief trouble-shooting discussion will focus on the primary site that was installed.

The key component in place at a site, whether that site is the CAS, a primary site, or a second-ary site, is the SMS_Executive component. This one service orchestrates most every activity at a site, and the list of SMS_Executive threads is extensive. Figure 17.23 shows the various threads that run as part of the SMS_Executive component.

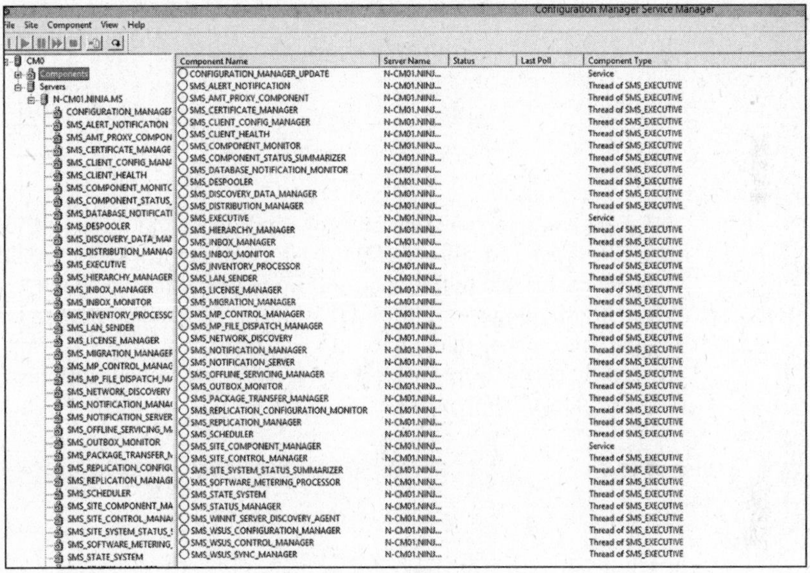

FIGURE 17.23
SMS_Executive threads

Since this is such a key service for all sites, it's a good idea to check the status of the Executive service in general to make sure all is well. Details on the various threads of the SMS_Executive component will mostly be left for later on this chapter.

There are several ways to view details on the status of SMS_Executive. First, Configuration Manager provides a robust status message system so administrators can tell at a glance if all is good with a particular component. Take a look at the Monitoring ➢ System Status ➢ Component Status node of the administrative console; the SMS_Executive component, along with all of the other threads, is visible. A quick look shows that the status of this thread is OK, as shown in Figure 17.24. Note that the SMS_Executive component from all three sites is dis-played here.

Status messages are not shown in real time, and there may be some short lag in reporting an error condition or reverting to an OK condition if a component is again running healthy.

If the status is not OK or you need more details about this component, you can see them by right-clicking, selecting Show Messages, and selecting what kind of messages are of interest. On the context menu is also the Reset Counts option, which will reset to 0 any error counts being held for the various types of messages, errors, and warnings. You can take this action after resolving an issue and to restart tracking of a component.

FIGURE 17.24
SMS_Executive
component status

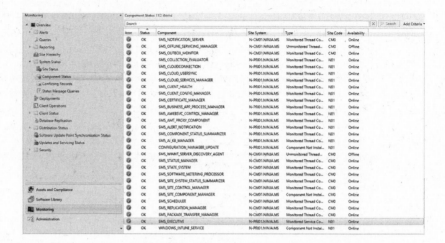

Another way to view the status of a component, and the method preferred by many administrators, is to take advantage of the extensive logging system provided in Configuration Manager. The logs are located in the Microsoft Configuration Manager ➢ Logs directory on the site server. Just as the status system showed the various components, there are logs representing them as well. The names aren't identical to the component names, but they are similar and generally easy to correlate. In the case of the SMS_Executive component, the corresponding log is smsexec.log, as shown in Figure 17.25.

FIGURE 17.25
smsexec.log file

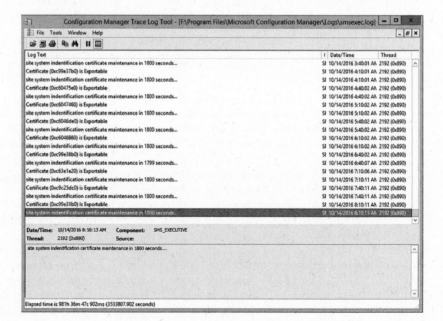

These log files can be viewed directly in Notepad, but the native CMTrace log viewer utility is preferred because it formats the logs nicely and also allows monitoring logs in real time as they are written.

Another critical component of the site is the site server database. Without the database, the site fails to function. To that end, you must understand how to at least begin an investigation of the database should problems arise. The database status can be seen in the Monitoring node of the Configuration Manager console as well. In terms of the database, isolating specific components to troubleshoot is difficult because it depends on the problem at hand. However, two components are fairly important for interaction with the database: the SMS Database Monitor and the SMS Provider.

SMS Database Monitor   The SMS Database Monitor, represented in the Monitoring node as SMS_Database_Notification_Monitor and in the logs as smsdbmon.log, is responsible for monitoring actions that are taken by the administrator in the console and for taking steps to implement those changes by notifying the various components of the SMS_Executive component that work is waiting to be done.

SMS Provider   The SMS Provider is important because it is the conduit between most console actions and making those actions effective in the database. As an example, when an administrator selects a site to view in the console or makes changes to a console setting, the SMS Provider interacts with the SMS database via WMI to retrieve needed data or make changes to data. Without the SMS Provider, the site cannot function.

Another useful location for quickly checking the status of the database and more is again in the Monitoring node but this time under Site Status. In this node it's quick to see the amount of disk space available for various components that make up a site.

TROUBLESHOOTING A CONFIGURATION MANAGER COMPONENT SERVER

This role manages the threads of the SMS_Executive service. It maintains which roles are local and remote for a given site. The overall health of the site server role can be reviewed in the Monitoring node. You can review the following logs to gain insight into the component server health:

sitecomp.log   This log shows all the site roles and where they're configured to be running.

compmon.log   This log records the status of all the threads of the SMS_Executive service and writes that status to the system registry under HKEY_LOCAL_MACHINE\SOFTWARE\Microsoft\SMS\Operations Management. This information is used to keep track of component status and is also used as a resource for System Center Operations Manager in monitoring the status of Configuration Manager.

TROUBLESHOOTING A CONFIGURATION MANAGER DISTRIBUTION POINT

Without the packages being staged on the distribution points, content deployment (packages, applications, operating systems, and software updates) in the environment cannot be completed. Providing insight into the process and health of the hierarchy distribution points, status messages and log files can be an administrator's best friend.

The Distribution Point Configuration Status, in the Distribution Status node of the Monitoring workspace shown in Figure 17.26, will give insight into the health of the distribution points.

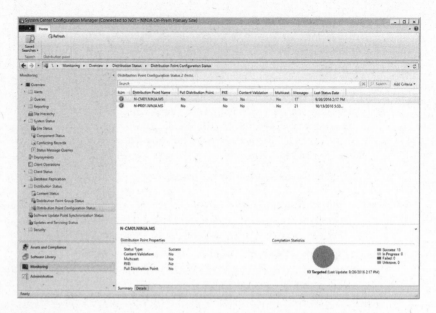

There is a specific folder for the distribution points, called `Distribution Status`, that provides insight into the status of content, distribution groups, and distribution point configuration. There is also the `Component Status` folder, where you can review the health of SMS_DISTRIBUTION_MANAGER, the key component for deploying content to distribution points.

In addition to status messages, `distmgr.log` provides insight into the distribution points for troubleshooting purposes. It tracks the different packages by package ID, size, and location where they are to be stored.

TROUBLESHOOTING A CONFIGURATION MANAGER MANAGEMENT POINT

The Configuration Manager management point (MP) is the entry point into a Configuration Manager hierarchy from a client perspective. The client receives its Configuration Manager policies and advertisements from the MP and places its inventories and status there. As with all components, administrators have a choice of using status messages and/or log files to verify management point function.

You can view management point status in the Monitoring node of the console by checking components such as SMS_MP_CONTROL_MANAGER or SMS_MP_FILE_DISPATCH_MANAGER. If you prefer using logs, then the following logs are important for verifying proper management point installation and function:

mpMSI.log This is the Microsoft Installer (MSI) log for the management point installation.

mpSetup.log This is the site-specific management point log, which shows which site and server the management point is configured to use.

mpcontrol.log This log maintains the management point by reviewing and checking the management point availability and status.

TROUBLESHOOTING A CONFIGURATION MANAGER SITE DATABASE SERVER

This is the database server that hosts the Microsoft SQL Server database. There is one database that holds all information about inventory, packages, status, and all the other pertinent data of System Center Configuration Manager. The following logs provide insight into the health of the database server:

smsdbmon.log This log shows all activities such as inserts, updates, drops, and deletes from the Configuration Manager database.

smsprov.log This log shows the SQL transaction calls made from the Configuration Manager console or automation scripts via the SDK.

TROUBLESHOOTING A CONFIGURATION MANAGER STATE MIGRATION POINT

This role is leveraged during the operating system deployment. In particular, it is used to store user data for migration back onto their machine that was just reimaged or replaced. The health of the state migration point is visible in the Monitoring node of the console and also by reviewing the following logs:

smssmpsetup.log This log documents the appropriate prerequisites and logs the initialization of the smp.msi file and installation completion.

smpmsi.log This log documents the installation setup progress of the smp.msi file.

TROUBLESHOOTING THE FALLBACK STATUS POINT

The fallback status point is meant for clients that are having difficulties communicating with a Configuration Manager hierarchy. To provide insights into the proper configuration of this role, the component status is available in the Monitoring node of the console and also by reviewing the following logs:

SMSFSPSetup.log This log documents the prerequisites and kicks off the fsp.msi installation.

fspMSI.log This log provides the installation status of the fallback status point role.

TROUBLESHOOTING THE REPORTING SERVICES POINT

The Reporting Services point is the reporting engine for Configuration Manager and is an important role for most users. Ensuring that this role installs and functions correctly is also critical. To provide insight into the proper configuration for this role, the component status is available in the Monitoring node of the console and also by reviewing associated log files.

srsrpsetup.log This log tracks the setup status of the reporting point.

srsrpMSI This log provides detail status of the reporting point setup process.

srsrp.log This log tracks ongoing operational health of the reporting point.

TROUBLESHOOTING THE APPLICATION CATALOG WEBSITE POINT AND APPLICATION CATALOG WEB SERVICE POINT

The Application Catalog roles are key interfaces to enable user self-provisioning of content. Thus, ensuring that these roles are functional is critical. As with all roles, the Monitoring node of the console can provide insight into overall health. Log files are useful to track ongoing operation as well:

smsawebsvcsetup.log   This log tracks the installation of the application web service.

smsportwebsetup.log   This log tracks installation of the application web portal.

awebsvcMSI.log   This is a detailed MSI log to track installation of the application web service.

portalwebMSI.log   This is a detailed MSI log to track installation of the application web portal.

awebsctrl.log   This log tracks the ongoing operation of the application web service.

portlctl.log   This log tracks the ongoing operation of the application web portal.

TROUBLESHOOTING THE ENROLLMENT PROXY POINT AND ENROLLMENT POINT

Enrollment points are the key roles to enable mobile devices and MAC Management to enter into the Configuration Manager world. To provide insights into the proper configuration of this role, the component status is available in the Monitoring node of the console and also by reviewing the following logs:

smsenrollwebsetup.log   This log tracks the installation of the enrollment web proxy point.

smsenrollsrvsetup.log   This log tracks the installation of the enrollment web point.

enrollwebmsi.log   This log tracks the installation of the enrollment web proxy point in detail.

enrollsrvmsi.log   This log tracks the installation of the enrollment web service point in detail.

enrollweb.log   This log tracks the ongoing operation of the enrollment web point.

enrollsvc.log   This log tracks the ongoing operation of the enrollment web proxy point.

TROUBLESHOOTING THE ENDPOINT PROTECTION POINT

Proper installation of the Endpoint Protection point is necessary for managing malware and firewall settings through Configuration Manager in your environment. To provide insights into the proper configuration of this role, the component status is available in the Monitoring node of the console and also by reviewing the following logs:

EPsetup.log   This log tracks the installation of the Endpoint Protection point.

EPCtrlmgr.log   This log details the synchronization of malware threat information from the Endpoint Protection role server to the Configuration Manager database.

EPMgr.log   This log monitors the status of the Endpoint Protection site system role.

TROUBLESHOOTING THE ASSET INTELLIGENCE SYNCHRONIZATION POINT

The proper installation of the Asset Intelligence synchronization point is important for keeping your Asset Intelligence catalog up to date for use in Configuration Manager. This is also critical for communicating your requested updates to the catalog to Microsoft. To provide insights into the proper configuration of this role, the component status is available in the Monitoring node of the console and also by reviewing the following logs:

AIUSsetup.log   This log tracks the installation of the Asset Intelligence synchronization point.

AIUSMSI.log This log tracks the specific MSI installation process detail for the Asset Intelligence synchronization point.

AIUpdateSvc.log This log tracks the ongoing operation of the Asset Intelligence synchronization point.

Troubleshooting Configuration Manager Deployment

If you experience issues deploying Configuration Manager, you should first look into the following areas to see whether the issue is related to permissions, disk space, network connectivity, or timing:

Permissions Permissions are extremely important to Configuration Manager deployment. If Configuration Manager does not have appropriate rights to make the connection, then the operation will fail. Admins using the Configuration Manager console will need the appropriate permissions for WMI, for DCOM, for NTFS, and within Configuration Manager itself.

Disk Space Disk space is used to store the site database, packages, software updates, inventory, and collected files; all of these can use up a lot of disk space. How much space is used depends on your environment, but you should always verify that you have sufficient disk space to store all the data within Configuration Manager.

Network Connectivity Network connectivity is a key requirement of Configuration Manager. The site system must be able to communicate with other site systems and clients. As stated earlier, sometimes the network connectivity might be down but the status messages have not updated, so you need to ensure the clients and servers can connect to each other.

Timing Patience is not always a trait of Configuration Manager administrators, but it is an important one to develop. Some tasks within Configuration Manager, Active Directory, and Windows in general take some time to complete. That is why examining the log files is so important.

Troubleshooting Configuration Manager Database Replication

Database Replication in Configuration Manager (Current Branch) (shown in Figure 17.27) is based on the Data Replication Service (DRS). This depends on two SQL features: SQL Server Service Broker and Change Tracking; these have nothing to do with transactional replication. This replication is very important in Configuration Manager, and for this reason you need to ensure that this replication is working at all times. SQL Server Service Broker manages internal and external processes that can send and receive guaranteed async messages by using a data manipulation language. Messages can be sent to a queue in the same database as the sender, to another database in the same SQL instance, or to another SQL instance on a remote server. To better understand this concept, visit the following site: https://docs.microsoft.com/en-us/sccm/core/servers/manage/monitor-hierarchy-and-replication-infrastructure.

To look at the status of the current database replication, in the Monitoring workspace Overview ➤ Database Replication.

A SQL communication link is a logical entity that is used to reflect the overall status of SQL communication between two sites. The link reflects the overall status of global and site data being replicated between two sites.

FIGURE 17.27
The Database
Replication node

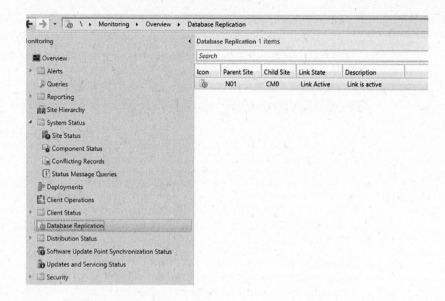

Each global and site data replication link will have one of the following states:

Link Active   This state implies that data is being replicated as per schedule.

Link Failed   This state implies that data is not being replicated because of errors. This state can also be caused when communication does not occur for more than 25 minutes.

Link Degraded   This state implies that no communication has occurred for approximately 15 minutes. Regular replication intervals are approximately every 2 minutes, so a 15-minute delay in communication could indicate a degraded link.

Link Error   This state implies that the replication data has synced but with errors; these errors could be due to failed data validation or conflicts.

Data Types

There are various data types in Configuration Manager. Objects that will be replicated in Configuration Manager are based on these types.

The type of data generated at the Central Administration Site and primary sites and replicated across the hierarchy is called *global data*. Since this data is globally available, it can be modified or deleted from the Central Administration Site or any primary site, regardless of where it was created, provided proper role-based access control (RBAC) permissions are configured.

The following elements are part of global data:

◆   Collections

◆   Packages

◆   Programs

- Deployments
- Configuration items
- Software updates
- Task sequences
- OS images (boot images, driver packages, and the like)
- Site control file
- System resource list (site servers)
- Site security objects (roles, scopes, and so on)
- Client authentication
- Client discovery

Global data replication is built on the Service Broker infrastructure provided by SQL Server.

Primary sites generate *site data*; it is potentially replicated to the CAS but never replicated between primary sites. Since this data is visible only at the CAS and the primary site where the data originated, it cannot be modified or deleted from other primary sites. If the data needs to be modified, it can be modified only at the originating site.

The following elements are part of site data:

- Collection membership
- Alerts
- Hardware inventory
- Software inventory and metering
- Status messages
- General site data
- Asset Intelligence CAL Client Access License track data
- Software distribution status details
- Software updates replicated site data
- Software updates non-replicated site data
- Status summary data
- Component and site status summarizers
- Client health data
- Client health history
- Wake On LAN
- Quarantine client restriction history

DRS Initialization

The process of DRS initialization is as follows:

1. A receiving site sends an `init` request to the sending site for the required replication group.

2. The sending site uses `bcp` (Bulk Copy Program) to export all the data from the tables in the replication group. During this phase, you can open the `RCMCtrl.log` file, as shown in Figure 17.28.

FIGURE 17.28
RCMCtrl.log
viewed in
CMTrace.exe

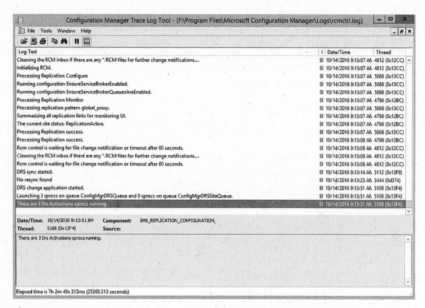

3. Hierarchy replication copies the BCP files and sends a count of each row for each table to the receiving site inbox via the senders.

By default Configuration Manager starts with the Replication Configuration Data group, which contains the data about other groups to be replicated.

To evaluate this process, you can then open the `RCMCtrl.log` at the primary site or CAS.

You can also open SQL Server Management Studio and expand the Configuration Manager database ➤ Programmability and locate the `spDiagDRS` stored procedure. Executing this stored procedure will show the different statuses of the data types and the link status between sites.

 **Real World Scenario**

TROUBLESHOOTING CONTOSO

In this scenario you have been asked to go onsite to troubleshoot a problem with a Contoso hierarchy. Contoso is a financial institution that has a Tier 2 Configuration Manager hierarchy, with a CAS and two primary sites. As an engineer, you will review Contoso's environment for potential issues.

THE SITUATION

The hierarchy is not replicating changes about a package to a specific site.

TROUBLESHOOTING STEPS

The first thing you have to do is understand Contoso's issues and goals. It's important to follow a process to resolve the problem. Here are the seven steps of problem solving:

1. Define and identify the problem.
2. Analyze the situation.
3. Identify possible solutions.
4. Select the best solution.
5. Evaluate the solution.
6. Develop an action plan.
7. Implement the solution.

If you follow these steps, you will be able to resolve most Configuration Manager issues or any problems that may arise.

1. Define and identify the problem.

   One package is not replicating to a primary site.

2. Analyze the situation.

   Find this package on the Configuration Manager console and note the Package ID. Then validate the current state of the database replication. In the Monitoring workspace, you can validate the content by using Content Monitoring.

   At this point you know the package ID, the distribution points this package is currently deployed to, and the potential issues this package may have. But the problem is still not fixed because you have only identified potential issues.

3. Identify possible solutions.

   During the review of database replication, you found that the current state is Link Degraded. Earlier in this chapter you learned that this state indicates that SQL has not been able to communicate with the server in the past 15 minutes. To continue troubleshooting this issue, you must open `RCMCtrl.log` using `CMTrace.exe` and find out the last time the package was replicated to this site. If the replication hasn't occurred in the past 15 minutes, you must try to resolve other potential issues related to communication.

4. Select the best solution.

   You have determined that the issue identified in step 3 is related to communication with the primary site. You contact the network administrator and explain the communication problems you are having on the site. The administrator promises to resolve the issue within a couple of hours. To solve the problem, you decide you will reinitiate database replication, resend the package to the primary site, and review the log files for confirmation that the package has replicated.

continues

continued

5. Evaluate the solution.

The solution provided in step 4 was to reinitiate database replication. If this solution is the one that makes the most sense to implement in this environment, then it is the one you will execute. It's very important to evaluate the solution in detail before implementing it.

6. Develop an action plan.

To be able to accomplish this, you need to understand what you must do to solve this problem:

◆ You need to determine which people need to be involved and what tasks they need to perform.

◆ Since the solution provided is related to communication, you must explain your action plan to the network administrator, who will evaluate the communication.

◆ You will execute a new database replication on the Configuration Manager environment; it's a good idea to have the database administrator involved just in case you need to back out your plan or have them help you understand the process involved in resolving the situation.

◆ Once all the tasks are outlined and everyone understands what is needed to solve the problem on the site, you can execute the plan on the environment.

You should always have a back-out plan just in case your solution doesn't solve the problem. If that happens, you'll need to go back to step 1.

7. Implement the solution.

Now that you have all the tasks figured out, go ahead and execute the plan to solve this problem:

a. Get the database replication in place again.

b. Resend the package to the distribution point.

c. Evaluate the log files to confirm the package was sent out to the distribution point.

d. Validate that the content is on the primary site where you were having the problem.

After executing each task, the problem on the primary site should be solved and the package should be replicated. If the problem is still not fixed at this point, go back to steps 5 and 6, and make sure you understand the situation correctly.

Solving a problem can take from minutes to hours in a Configuration Manager environment; it will depend on the complexity of the hierarchy you are working on and the type of problem. This was a quick guide to resolving issues in a structured way. Always make sure you understand the problem correctly before attempting to solve it.

Understanding these processes is key to troubleshooting DRS replication in Configuration Manager. Be sure to review this process and learn how the DRS and stored procedures are executed in this process for a successful replication.

REPLICATION LINK ANALYZER

If a Configuration Manager hierarchy is experiencing replication link failures, one important tool for identifying and remediating the failure is the Replication Link Analyzer (RLA). This tool can be initiated from the Configuration Manager console under the Database Replication node in the Monitoring workspace, as shown in Figure 17.29.

FIGURE 17.29
Replication Link
Analyzer

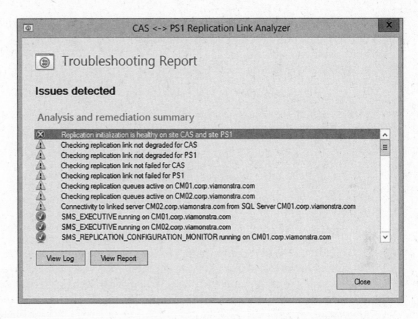

FIGURE 17.29
Replication Link
Analyzer

You can also run the RLA tool from a command prompt. Navigate to the installation path
for the Configuration Manager console and go the `%path%\AdminConsole\bin` folder. From
the folder run `Microsoft.ConfigurationManager.ReplicationLinkAnalyzer.Wizard.exe`
and specify the fully qualified domain name (FQDN) of the source Configuration Manager site
server and the destination Configuration Manager site server. For example, to initiate the RLA
against the link between a CAS with the computer name CAS.CONTOSO.COM and a child primary site with the computer name PRI1.CONTOSO.COM, you would issue this command:

```
Microsoft.ConfigurationManager.ReplicationLinkAnalyzer.Wizard.exe
CAS.CONTOSO.COM PRI1.CONTOSO.COM
```

The Replication Link Analyzer tool will attempt to verify and resolve a variety of issues, including ensuring that the Configuration Manager–related services are running, that the network is
available between the two servers, and that SQL Server is working and configured properly.

Once RLA has finished, it saves the results in an XML-based report named
`ReplicationAnalysis.xml`. It also creates a log file named `ReplicationLinkAnalysis.log`
on the desktop of the user who ran the tool. To run the RLA tool, the Configuration Manager
administrator must have local administrator rights on the source and target site server as well
as sysadmin rights on each of the SQL server databases that are involved in the replication
link. Note that when the RLA tool is used, it may stop and start the SMS_SITE_COMPONENT_
MANAGER and SMS_EXECUTIVE services. If the RLA tool fails to complete the remediation,
you should ensure that these services are started if they were not automatically restarted.

VLOGS

Earlier in this chapter you learned about `rcmctrl.log` and how this log shows an overview of
the site sync status. If you wanted to perform more detailed troubleshooting, you may find it
necessary to run SQL Server queries in SQL Server Management Studio against the vLogs view
in the Configuration Manager database.

Note that this particular view may contain hundreds of thousands of rows, so you may want to add some limiting criteria to any queries that you execute against the vLogs view. For example, if you only wanted to see the top one thousand rows from the database and sort them by the date and time, you could use the following query:

```
select top 1000 * from vlogs order by logtime desc
```

If you wanted to view the records that have been recorded in the past day, you could use the GETDATE command in the query and specify the number of days, which in this case would be 1:

```
select * from vlogs where logtime >GETDATE()-1
```

If you wanted to go back one week, change the value to **7**:

```
select * from vlogs where logtime >GETDATE()-7
```

SPDiagDRS

SPDiagDRS is a stored procedure in SQL Server that you can execute manually. It provides an overview of the state of the Data Replication Service (DRS) at the site. This stored procedure returns a large amount of data, including the current status, the messages that are in the queue, the current link status, the last sync for each replication group, and much more.

To run the SPDiagDRS stored procedure, open SQL Server Management Studio, connect to the databases for the two Configuration Manager site servers that you are investigating, and run the command Exec SPDiagDRS on both Configuration Manager databases.

As shown in Figure 17.30, these stored procedures generate a significant amount of data but may be quite useful in determining the source of any replication issues you may be experiencing.

FIGURE 17.30
Exec SPDiagDRS in
SQL Management
Studio

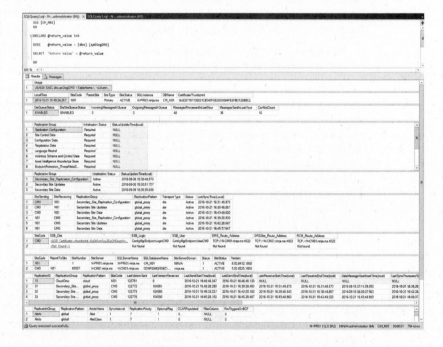

For additional information on resolving database replication issues in Configuration Manager, refer to this troubleshooting guide:

```
https://support.microsoft.com/en-us/help/20033/troubleshoot-database-replication-
service-in-mcm
```

This guide is interactive and will walk you through the resolution process. It also provides additional guidance on the topics discussed in this chapter and on how to analyze the SPDiagDRS data.

Troubleshooting a Client Installation

To troubleshoot a client installation, you will need to understand the three phases of the process. You can troubleshoot each of the phases in real time by reading the correct log files with CMtrace.exe.

The Preinstallation Phase   A useful log file in this phase is ccm.log on the site server.

The Installation Phase   This phase begins when ccmsetup.exe reads the mobileclient.tcf file and starts downloading the required files needed to complete the installation. Useful log files in this phase are ccmsetup.log and client.msi.log, both found in the %windir%\ccmsetup folder on the client.

The Post-installation Phase   This phase is also known as the assignment phase, where the client is being added as a managed client to a primary site. Useful log files in this phase are clientidstartupmanager.log, clientlocation.log, and locationservices.log, all found in the %windir%\ccm\logs folder on the client.

Once you have identified where the problem is, you will be able to select the correct log file for further troubleshooting.

Troubleshooting Inventory

The following sections cover some basic information that will help you troubleshoot specific problems. To troubleshoot and fully understand what's going on behind the scenes, you need to have information about the log files in the process.

Hardware Inventory

When you troubleshoot hardware inventory, you need to know how data travels from the client to the SQL database. Inventory data will be sent from the client to the management point and then to the site server before being added to the database.

Client-Side Processing

All client-side hardware inventory processes are recorded in the InventoryAgent.log file. The log file will contain several lines that are important for you to understand.

The following line tells you what kind of inventory report will be sent from the client to the management point. It can be a full, delta, or resync report.

```
Inventory: Action=Hardware ReportType=Delta
```

The following line queries for data:

```
Collection: Namespace = \\localhost\root\Microsoft\appvirt\client; Query = SELECT
__CLASS, __PATH, __RELPATH, LastLaunchOnSystem, Name, PackageGUID, Version FROM
Application; Timeout = 600 secs
```

The following line gives information about the number of classes that the client is searching for and the number of classes found. The information in this line is worth checking whenever you make changes to the data classes. When you enable an extra data class, the last number should increase by one.

```
Collection: 55/64 inventory data items successfully inventoried.
```

The following line basically informs you that the client-side processing has completed successfully and information has been sent to the management point.

```
Inventory: Successfully sent report. Destination:mp:MP_HinvEndpoint, ID:
{D886D5C8-59E4-4C9C-B9CD-08D7DA40BA20}, Timeout: 80640 minutes MsgMode: Signed,
Not Encrypted
```

Management Point Processing

At the management point, the client data will be converted from an XML file to an MIF file and sent to the site server. You can monitor the process by reading the MP_HINV.log file.

Site Server Processing

At the site server, the client data will be added to the SQL database by the Inventory Data Loader process. In the Dataldr.log file, you will see entries similar to these:

```
Thread: 10368 will use GUID GUID:1E8A9DD4-C572-48F9-BEDB-B33D8E0F07F4
SMS_INVENTORY_DATA_LOADER 8/27/2013 11:34:04 AM 10368 (0x2880)

Processing Inventory for Machine: DC1 Version 1.7 Generated: 08/27/2013 11:33:27
SMS_INVENTORY_DATA_LOADER 8/27/2013 11:34:04 AM 10368 (0x2880)

Begin transaction: Machine=DC1(GUID:1E8A9DD4-C572-48F9-BEDB-B33D8E0F07F4)
SMS_INVENTORY_DATA_LOADER 8/27/2013 11:34:04 AM 10368 (0x2880)

Commit transaction: Machine=DC1(GUID:1E8A9DD4-C572-48F9-BEDB-B33D8E0F07F4)
SMS_INVENTORY_DATA_LOADER 8/27/2013 11:34:04 AM 10368 (0x2880)

Done: Machine=DC1(GUID:1E8A9DD4-C572-48F9-BEDB-B33D8E0F07F4) code=0 (20 stored
procs in XH3JZIA70.MIF) SMS_INVENTORY_DATA_LOADER 8/27/2013 11:34:04 AM  10368
(0x2880)
```

The MIF file is added to the SQL database from

```
<:>\Program Files\Microsoft Configuration Manager\inboxes\auth\dataldr.box\Process
```

If you see a large number of MIF files in one of the dataldr.box folders, it's normally a clear indication of a backlog.

WHEN CLIENTS ARE DELETED FROM THE DATABASE BUT NOT UNINSTALLED

A commonly seen issue occurs when an administrator accidentally deletes all client resource records from a collection, as you can see in Figure 17.31. This will remove client data from the database, but the Configuration Manager Client Agent running on those systems is not aware of that action. In the following sequence, you can see that the client is still sending delta inventory information to the site server, but since the site server does not have any existing records, it will not be able to process that delta data and will ask the client to perform a resync.

FIGURE 17.31
Confirm Deletion of
Resource in Collection

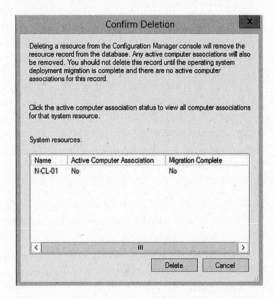

In the InventoryAgent.log file on the client, notice that the first report type is delta.

```
<![LOG[Inventory: Action=Hardware ReportType=Delta]LOG]!><time="12:38:31.453-120"
date="08-27-2013" component="InventoryAgent" context="" type=""1" thread="212"
file="agentstate.cpp:1563">
```

The data loader component receives the delta information and tries to add it to an existing record in the database. The record does not exist in the database, which is why the MIF file is discarded and moved to the Badmifs folder. Furthermore, the data loader component will initiate a resync, which instructs the client to send up a full inventory report.

```
ERROR - attempt to update non-existent row. Invalid command: exec dbo.
pWorkstationStatus_DATA 1,16777222,'08/27/2013 12:49:49',1,'8/27/2013
12:49:42',N'4294967305',1033,120 $$<SMS_INVENTORY_DATA_LOADER><08-27-2013
12:49:49.740-120><thread=2720 (0xAA0)>
```

```
Rollback transaction: Machine=DC1(GUID:1E8A9DD4-C572-48F9-BEDB-B33D8E0F07F4)
$$<SMS_INVENTORY_DATA_LOADER><08-27-2013 12:49:49.744-120><thread=2720 (0xAA0)>
```

```
Remote client hardware inventory resync generated for client GUID:1E8A9DD4-C572-
48F9-BEDB-B33D8E0F07F4; update/insert result = 2 $$<SMS_INVENTORY_DATA_
LOADER><08-27-2013 12:49:49.825-120><thread=2720 (0xAA0)>
```

```
~Send resync command to local site for machine GUID:1E8A9DD4-C572-48F9-BEDB-
B33D8E0F07F4. $$<SMS_INVENTORY_DATA_LOADER><08-27-2013
12:49:49.830-120><thread=2720 (0xAA0)>
```

```
STATMSG: ID=2722 SEV=I LEV=M SOURCE="SMS Server" COMP="SMS_INVENTORY_DATA_LOADER"
SYS=SCCM4.sccmlab.local SITE=RC1 PID=9052 TID=2720 GMTDATE=Sat Aug 27 10:49:49.833
2013 ISTR0="DC1" ISTR1="" ISTR2="" ISTR3="" ISTR4="" ISTR5="" ISTR6="" ISTR7=""
ISTR8="" ISTR9="" NUMATTRS=0 $$<SMS_INVENTORY_DATA_LOADER><08-27-2013
12:49:49.835-120><thread=2720 (0xAA0)>
```

```
~Cannot process MIF XHIJ3F4L2.MIF, moving it to e:\Program Files\Microsoft
Configuration Manager\inboxes\auth\dataldr.box\BADMIFS\44p7g21x.MIF
$$<SMS_INVENTORY_DATA_LOADER><08-27-2013 12:49:49.843-120><thread=2720 (0xAA0)>
```

On the client, the next hardware inventory will send a full hardware report to the management point. Notice the ReportType=Resync notation:

```
![LOG[Inventory: Opening store for action {00000000-0000-0000-0000-000000000001}
...]LOG]!><time="13:03:21.391-120" date="08-27-2013" component="InventoryAgent"
context="" type="1" thread="2668" file="datastore.cpp:176">
```

```
<![LOG[Inventory: Action=Hardware ReportType=ReSync]
LOG]!><time="13:03:37.734-120" date="08-27-2013" component="InventoryAgent"
context="" type="1" thread="2668" file="agentstate.cpp:1563">
```

Once the resync report is processed, the client will be added to the database and will show up in the Configuration Manager administrative console.

When Clients Try to Inventory Data Classes That Don't Exist

As we have already discussed, the Hardware Inventory Client Agent gets information about a computer's hardware from the WMI data classes. Sometimes not all of the WMI data classes that Configuration Manager is set up to inventory are present on a client.

Clients with different operating systems are a good example. The default client settings are configured to inventory certain new WMI classes in Windows 2012 R2 that aren't available on other operating systems. The hardware inventory process will still try to inventory those classes on a Windows 10 or Windows 7 and earlier versions since they also read the settings in the default client settings.

When a client tries to inventory a class that doesn't exist, you will see an entry only in the InventoryAgent.log file, because no status message will be sent to the site server. If you need to figure out whether a client is trying to inventory nonexistent data classes, you will see entries similar to Collection: Class "<Class Name>" does not exist in the InventoryAgent.log file.

Troubleshooting Mobile Devices

The method of troubleshooting problems with mobile devices depends on the management mode chosen. For lite management, troubleshooting will be mostly focused on Exchange Server—both in terms of ensuring that the Exchange ActiveSync connector is running properly and ensuring that the Configuration Manager 2012 Exchange ActiveSync connector is properly configured and operational.

When it comes to depth management, you must check a few more places when you run into problems. Such devices require enrollment before management can begin. The enrollment process is not difficult, but there are a number of moving parts that must be configured properly, not the least of which is certificates. When enrollment fails, it's clear on the device that there was a problem, but it's not always easy to collect diagnostic information from the device to understand why enrollment failed. Fortunately, there is excellent logging for the enrollment process. The EnrollmentService.log and EnrollmentWeb.log files may contain errors that might occur as the enrollment process progresses. These logs are located in the SMS_CCM folder, under the EnrollmentPoint\logs and EnrollmentProxyPoint\logs folders, respectively.

When using the Service Connection Point, you have some log files in the %SMS_LOG_PATH% folder. The log file cloudusersync.log will help you identify issues with synchronizing the users in the collection that holds the users who are allowed to enroll their mobile devices. The log files dmpdownloader.log, dmpuploader.log, dismgr.log, and outboundcontentmanager.log will help you identify issues with uploading and downloading apps, policies, and messages from and to Windows Intune. If you have issues when installing the Service Connection Point, look in the following log files: sitecomp.log, connectorsetup.log, and certmgr.log.

The depth-managed mobile device client has similarities to the computer device client in that client health data is provided. Simply reviewing a device in the collections to ensure client health evaluations are current and successful, along with checking the Client Status data from the Monitoring node, is a good indicator of whether the client is behaving properly.

The Bottom Line

Create a basic maintenance plan. Setting up a basic maintenance plan is a vital step to ensure the proper health of your Configuration Manager (Current Branch) hierarchy.

Master It How do you create a basic maintenance plan?

View log files using CMTrace. Although using CMTrace is not a requirement for viewing log files, it is highly recommended because CMTrace constantly monitors the opened file for updates.

Master It Explain how to use CMTrace to view log files.

Troubleshoot DRS replication. To view the current status of the Configuration Manager DRS replication and to know the latest information about the changes being requested on the site, it's important to be familiar with the log file and the replication process.

Master It To view the latest changes on the replication process, what log file do you need to open?

Chapter 18

Enterprise Mobility and Configuration Manager

Since Configuration Manager 2007, you have been able to manage mobile devices, but real support arrived in Configuration Manager 2012 R2 with the integration of Microsoft Intune. In Configuration Manager Current Branch, the support of Enterprise Mobility Management (EMM) is even better. Configuration Manager Current Branch supports a broad range of mobile device management (MDM) options. These include

- The *lite* version of MDM via the Exchange Connector
- The *depth* mobile device management via the Microsoft Intune subscription and the on-premises MDM capabilities for Windows 10

Also included in the latest version of Configuration Manager is the ability to protect mobile apps and data via mobile application management (MAM) policies. The goal is to ensure that only managed and secured devices are able to access the apps and data via conditional access based on compliance rules. Together with Microsoft Intune, Azure Active Directory, and Configuration Manager, a complete EMM solution can be built.

In this chapter, you will learn to

- Detail the differences between lite and depth management
- Understand how to configure MDM
- Understand the depth-management enrollment process

Mobile Devices in Configuration Manager

Mobile devices are fully supported and manageable in Configuration Manager Current Branch. You can manage mobile devices in one of three ways:

- Lite management via the Exchange Connector
- Depth management via Microsoft Intune
- Depth management via MDM on-premises management options

The three options can be used separately from each other. They can also be combined to gain extra manageability features and to allow you to get the best options for managing mobile devices.

Lite Management via the Exchange Connector   Lite management is the mechanism used to manage Microsoft's Windows Phone platform. It is also the management mode that supports any other device capable of working with an Exchange ActiveSync connection. This includes BlackBerry, iPhone, and Android. Lite management requires Exchange Server 2013 or Exchange Server 2016 on-premises or in Microsoft Office 365 in the cloud.

No client software is installed on the device in a lite-management scenario. The management capabilities available depend on the device and what is offered via the Exchange ActiveSync connector in Configuration Manager.

Depth Management via Microsoft Intune   Depth management via Microsoft Intune is available for devices with operating systems such as Windows Mobile 8, Windows 10 Mobile, iPhone, iPad, Mac OS X, and Android. The support is delivered by connecting Microsoft Intune with Configuration Manager, so that the management is done from the Configuration Manager management console instead of the management portal of Microsoft Intune. This is known as Configuration Manager Hybrid.

Depth Management via On-Premise MDM Options   For Windows 10, a third MDM option is available. Via the device registration point role, Windows 10 can also be enrolled for MDM without being connected with Microsoft Intune. Currently only Windows 10 is supported.

We'll discuss all three options in greater detail later in the chapter.

MDM Is Evolving Quickly

It's also worth mentioning that Configuration Manager together with the Microsoft Intune service is the MDM solution going forward. Microsoft provides choice and flexibility in how you are able to manage your devices: completely on-premises via Configuration Manager; cloud-based via Microsoft Intune; or via a hybrid model, using the Microsoft Intune subscription in Configuration Manager.

In this book we look at the on-premises and hybrid solutions. One way of adding new capabilities to the hybrid solution is done via the Updates and Servicing node, which you can find in the Configuration Manager console.

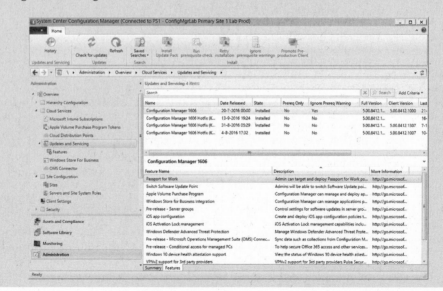

> In the Configuration Manager console, go to the Administration workspace, and select Overview ➤ Cloud Services in the Updates And Servicing node. You can add features or supported platforms via hotfixes or new releases of Configuration Manager. This is a quick and easy way to add new capabilities to your MDM solution. You can select an update and click Install Update Pack or select. The new servicing model is discussed in Chapter 4, "Installation and Site Role Configuration."

The requirements for MDM differ depending on whether devices are being managed using lite-management or depth-management options. For depth management you have two options: depth management via on-premises MDM or depth management via the Microsoft Intune subscription.

Let's first look at the supported operating systems and the options you have in managing them:

Android   Management options:

- Microsoft Intune subscription via Configuration Manager Hybrid
- Exchange Connector

Features:

- Settings management
- Software distribution (Microsoft Intune via Configuration Manager Hybrid only)
- Profile (Wi-Fi, Certificate, VPN, and Email) distribution (Microsoft Intune via Configuration Manager Hybrid only)
- Hardware inventory
- Remote wipe/retire
- Remote lock/reset passcode (Microsoft Intune via Configuration Manager Hybrid only)

Apple iOS   Management options:

- Microsoft Intune subscription via Configuration Manager Hybrid
- Exchange Connector

Features:

- Settings management
- Software distribution (Microsoft Intune via Configuration Manager Hybrid only)
- Profile (Wi-Fi, Certificate, VPN, and Email) distribution (Microsoft Intune via Configuration Manager Hybrid only)
- Hardware inventory
- Remote wipe/retire
- Remote lock/reset passcode (Microsoft Intune via Configuration Manager Hybrid only)

Apple Mac OS X   Management options:

- Microsoft Intune subscription via Configuration Manager Hybrid

Features:

- Settings management
- Profile (Wi-Fi, Certificate, VPN, and Email) distribution (Microsoft Intune via Configuration Manager Hybrid only)
- Hardware inventory
- Remote wipe/retire
- Remote lock/reset passcode (Microsoft Intune via Configuration Manager Hybrid only)

Windows 8.x RT   Management options:

- Microsoft Intune subscription via Configuration Manager Hybrid

Features:

- Settings management
- Software distribution
- Profile (Wi-Fi, Certificate, VPN, and Email) distribution
- Hardware inventory
- Remote wipe/retire
- Remote lock/reset passcode

Windows Phone 8.1   Management options:

- Microsoft Intune subscription via Configuration Manager Hybrid

Features:

- Settings management
- Software distribution (Microsoft Intune via Configuration Manager Hybrid only)
- Remote wipe/retire
- Remote lock/reset passcode (Microsoft Intune via Configuration Manager Hybrid only)

Windows 10 Mobile/Desktop   Management options:

- Microsoft Intune subscription via Configuration Manager Hybrid
- Exchange Connector
- On-premise MDM

Features:

- Settings management
- Software distribution (not via Exchange Connector)

◆ Profile (Wi-Fi, Certificate, VPN, and Email) distribution (not via Exchange Connector)

◆ Hardware inventory

◆ Remote wipe/retire

◆ Remote lock/reset passcode (not via Exchange Connector)

Lite Management

A few components are required for lite management of mobile devices:

◆ A device capable of establishing an ActiveSync connection with an Exchange server

◆ An Exchange Server 2010/2013 or 2016 server providing ActiveSync services, either on-premises or with Office 365 in the cloud

◆ A properly configured ActiveSync connector in Configuration Manager

Configuring Required Components

The first requirement is totally dependent on the capability of the device being used—either a device is able to communicate via an ActiveSync connection or it isn't. Fortunately, most modern devices have this capability. The process of configuring the ActiveSync connection on a device may vary depending on the type of device in use. Thus, the specifics of configuring the ActiveSync connection from a device perspective are beyond the scope of discussion for this chapter.

Configuring an Exchange server to deliver ActiveSync services, the second requirement, is specifically an Exchange Server activity. There are no Configuration Manager requirements to consider when setting up Exchange ActiveSync. Once ActiveSync is configured and working in an Exchange Server environment, Configuration Manager can be configured to use it. The steps for enabling ActiveSync for Exchange Server are beyond the scope of discussion for this chapter. Details on how to configure the Exchange ActiveSync component can be found with a quick Internet search. The following URLs are a good starting point to understand the setup requirements and process:

Exchange 2016: `https://technet.microsoft.com/en-us/library/jj218640(v=exchg.160).aspx`

Exchange 2013: `http://technet.microsoft.com/en-us/library/aa998357.aspx`

Exchange 2010: `http://technet.microsoft.com/en-us/library/bb124234.aspx`

This leaves the third option for discussion—configuring the ActiveSync connector in Configuration Manager. The ActiveSync connector option is configured from the Administration node of the console, as shown in Figure 18.1. In the console the connector is labeled Exchange Server Connectors. Note that the options available in the wizard are the only ones configurable for lite device management in Configuration Manager. There may be other options for ActiveSync management available directly in Exchange Server beyond those listed in the wizard.

FIGURE 18.1
Exchange Server
Connectors location
in the Configuration
Manager console

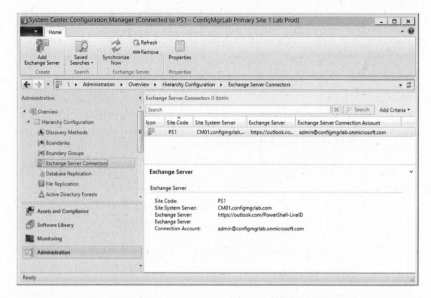

As shown, it's possible to have multiple connectors configured per site, depending on need. You configure a connector by right-clicking Exchange Server Connectors and selecting Add Exchange Server. This will launch the General page of the Add Exchange Server Wizard, as shown in Figure 18.2.

FIGURE 18.2
Add Exchange
Server Wizard—
General page

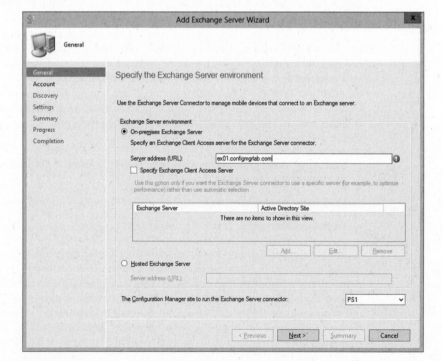

The first choice to make is whether the Exchange server being configured is an on-premises Exchange server or a hosted Exchange server. The connector works fine with both. In either case, you must specify an FQDN for the Exchange server. When you specify On-Premises Exchange Server, you can also specify advanced configuration options. Selecting the Specify Exchange Client Access Server check box allows you to specify a specific client access server (CAS) that should be used by the connector when more than a single CAS is available. If the advanced option is not specified, then Configuration Manager will simply choose a CAS to use based on information published in Active Directory.

The last option on the General page allows you to select which Configuration Manager site the connector should be associated with. Once the configurations on this page are complete, click Next to continue to the Account page, shown in Figure 18.3.

FIGURE 18.3
Add Exchange
Server Wizard—
Account page

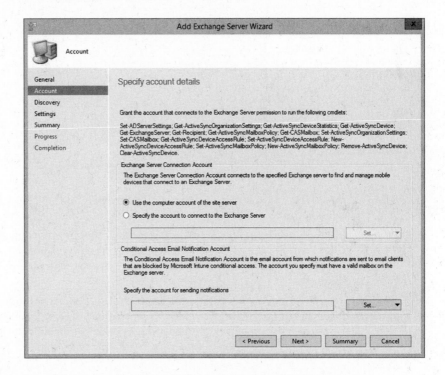

The Account page allows administrators to configure whether the Exchange Server Connection Account should be configured to use the computer account of the site server or a specific account to connect to the Exchange environment. When setting up conditional access in a later stage, you can set up a conditional access email notification account. This account is the email account from which notifications are sent to the users whose email clients are blocked by Microsoft Intune conditional access. The conditional access email notification account needs a valid mailbox on the Exchange server.

Regardless of the configuration you choose here, ensure that the configured account has proper rights to access the Exchange CAS(s) chosen. Once configurations on this page are complete, click Next to continue to the Discovery page, shown in Figure 18.4.

FIGURE 18.4
Add Exchange
Server Wizard—
Discovery page

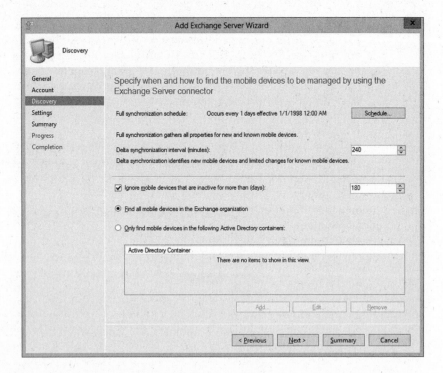

The Discovery page allows administrators to determine how device discovery takes place in the environment.

Full Synchronization Schedule This option configures the schedule and frequency for full synchronization in the environment. Full synchronization gathers all properties for new and existing mobile devices. The default option is for full synchronization to run daily at midnight.

Delta Synchronization Interval (Minutes) This option configures the schedule and frequency for delta synchronization in the environment. Delta synchronization identifies new mobile devices and gathers limited changes for known mobile devices. The default option is for delta synchronization to run every 240 minutes.

FULL VS. DELTA

Full versus delta synchronization is similar in concept to full versus delta discovery or full versus delta collection updates.

Ignore Mobile Devices That Are Inactive For More Than (Days) This option indicates that devices that have been inactive for the configured number of days—by default 180 days—should be ignored from further management attempts.

Find All Mobile Devices In The Exchange Organization/Only Find Mobile Devices In The Following Active Directory Containers The choice you make for the first setting determines whether to attempt management of all mobile devices connecting with Exchange ActiveSync or only those belonging to a specific container. If you select to limit management, individual containers with mobile devices that should be managed must be configured.

Note that if settings are not specifically configured on this page, existing settings configured in Exchange ActiveSync will be persisted as noted by the Status column on the Settings page. If settings are configured through the connector, the Status column will change to indicate Configured By Configuration Manager. Once configurations on this page are complete, click Next to continue to the Settings page, shown in Figure 18.5.

FIGURE 18.5
Add Exchange Server Wizard—Settings page

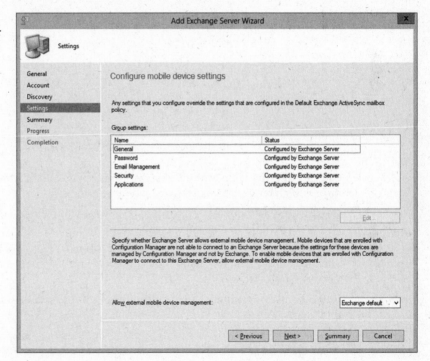

The Settings page is where the action is! This page is the launch point for configuring all options that are available for lite management. The categories for configurable settings are General, Password, Email Management, Security, and Applications. Further discussion on these categories follows. From this page, administrators are also able to choose whether to allow external MDM.

GENERAL SETTINGS

Selecting to edit the General settings will reveal available choices for this category, as shown in Figure 18.6.

FIGURE 18.6
Add Exchange
Server Wizard—
Settings page—
General Settings

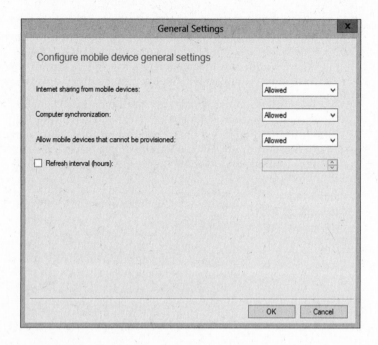

Internet Sharing From Mobile Devices   This option allows administrators to either allow or prohibit Internet sharing on managed mobile devices.

Computer Synchronization   This option allows administers to either allow or prohibit synchronization of the mobile device with computers.

Allow Mobile Devices That Cannot Be Provisioned   This option allows administrators to either allow or prohibit mobile devices that cannot be provisioned from being visible in Configuration Manager.

Refresh Interval (Hours)   This option allows administrators to specify a specific refresh interval, if desired.

PASSWORD SETTINGS

Selecting to edit the Password settings will reveal available choices for this category, as shown in Figure 18.7.

Require Password Settings On Mobile Devices   This option allows administrators to decide whether or not to enforce password settings on the mobile device. If it's set to Optional, additional settings on this page will not be configurable.

Minimum Password Length (Characters)   This option allows administrators to specify a minimum password length for the mobile device. The default length is 4 characters with a maximum length of 16 characters.

Password Expiration In Days   This option allows administrators to configure how frequently the configured password will expire and need to be reset.

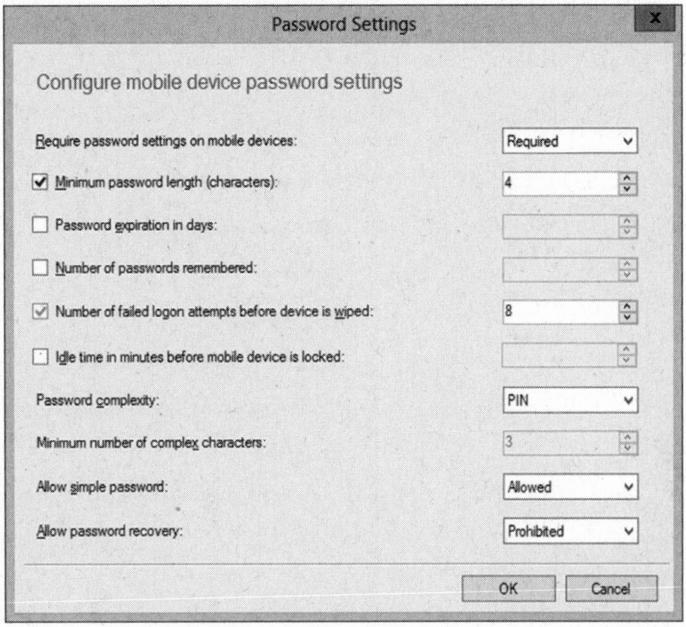

FIGURE 18.7
Add Exchange Server
Wizard—Settings
page—Password
Settings

Number Of Passwords Remembered   This option allows administrators to configure how many passwords are stored, thus preventing reuse of the same password again and again.

Number Of Failed Logon Attempts Before Device Is Wiped   This option allows administrators to specify the number of bad logon attempts before the device is wiped. The default is eight invalid password attempts allowed. After the configured number of failed password attempts, the device is wiped. This is a good option to use for ensuring device security, but with the result being a complete device wipe, you must carefully evaluate the final settings you choose for this option.

Idle Time In Minutes Before Mobile Device Is Locked   This option allows administrators to specify the length of idle time allowed before the device will lock itself, requiring a password to regain access.

Password Complexity   This option allows administrators to specify how complex the device password should be. The default option is to specify a PIN. The other option is to specify a strong password. If a strong password is selected, the option to specify a minimum number of complex characters becomes available. The default number of strong characters is three.

Allow Simple Password   This option specifies whether simple passwords, such as 1234, are allowed on a device. The default option allows a simple password.

Allow Password Recovery   This option allows administrators to configure whether it is possible to recover passwords on a device. The default option prohibits this action.

EMAIL MANAGEMENT SETTINGS

Selecting to edit the Email Management settings reveals available choices for this category, as shown in Figure 18.8.

FIGURE 18.8
Add Exchange Server
Wizard—Settings
page—Email
Management Settings

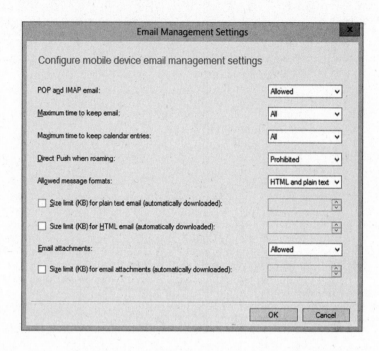

POP And IMAP Email This option allows administrators to specify whether both POP and IMAP email are allowed or prohibited. There is no option to specify that one or the other is available.

Maximum Time To Keep Email This option allows administrators to specify the length of time email will be retained on the device. The default option is All, which indicates that all email should be retained indefinitely. Other available options are One Day, Three Days, One Week, Two Weeks, and One Month.

Maximum Time To Keep Calendar Entries This option allows administrators to specify the length of time calendar entries should be retained on the device. The default option is All, which indicates that all calendar items should be retained indefinitely. Other available options are Two Weeks, One Month, Three Months, and Six Months.

Direct Push When Roaming This option allows administrators to determine whether email can be directly pushed while a device is in roaming status. The default option is Prohibited to help avoid additional expense in such situations.

Allowed Message Formats This option allows administrators to define what email formats are acceptable. The default option is HTML And Plain Text. The only other choice is Plain Text Only.

Size Limit (KB) For Plain Text Email (Automatically Downloaded) If specified, this option allows administrators to specify the maximum size for a plain text email that will be automatically downloaded to devices.

Size Limit (KB) For HTML Email (Automatically Downloaded) This option, not specified by default, allows administrators to specify the maximum size for an HTML-formatted email that will be automatically downloaded to devices.

Email Attachments   This option allows administrators to specify whether email attachments are allowed on connected devices. The default option is Allowed.

Size Limit (KB) For Email Attachments (Automatically Downloaded)   This option, not enabled by default, allows administrators to specify the maximum size for an attachment that will be automatically downloaded to devices.

SECURITY SETTINGS

Selecting to edit the Security settings will reveal available choices for this category, shown in Figure 18.9.

FIGURE 18.9
Add Exchange Server
Wizard—Settings
page—Security
Settings

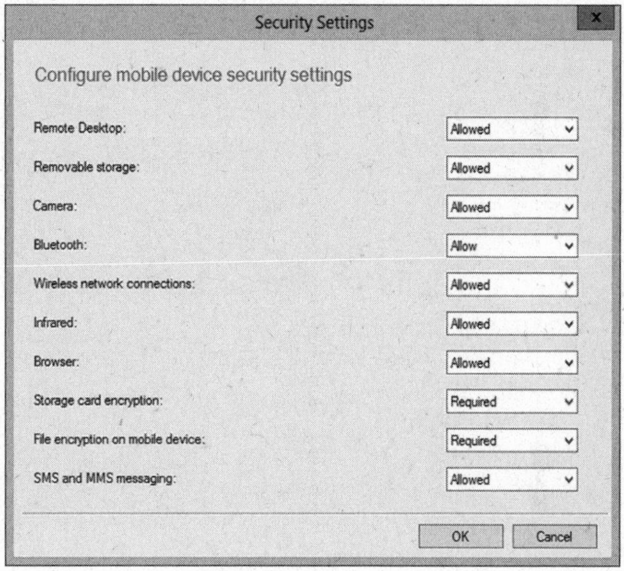

Remote Desktop   This option allows administrators to specify whether Remote Desktop to the device is allowed.

Removable Storage   This option allows administrators to specify whether removable storage is allowed on the device.

Camera   This option allows administrators to specify whether the use of the camera is allowed on the device.

Bluetooth   This option allows administrators to specify whether the use of Bluetooth is allowed on the device. An option is included in this setting to allow configuring hands-free operation only for Bluetooth.

Wireless Network Connections   This option allows administrators to specify whether the use of wireless network connections is allowed on the device.

Infrared   This option allows administrators to specify whether the use of infrared capabilities for a device is allowed.

Browser   This option allows administrators to specify whether the use of a browser is permitted for a device.

Storage Card Encryption   This option allows administrators to configure whether encryption of device storage cards is required or optional.

File Encryption On Mobile Devices   This option allows administrators to configure whether file encryption on mobile devices is required or optional.

SMS And MMS Messaging   This option allows administrators to configure whether messaging is allowed on devices.

APPLICATIONS SETTINGS

Selecting to edit the Applications settings will reveal available choices for this category, shown in Figure 18.10.

FIGURE 18.10
Add Exchange Server
Wizard—Settings
page—Application
Settings

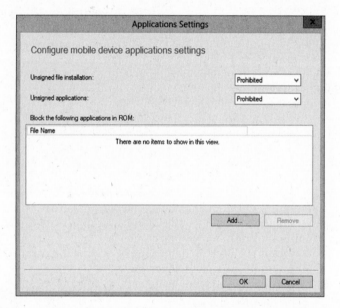

Unsigned File Installation   This option allows administrators to specify whether installation of unsigned files is allowed on devices.

Unsigned Applications   This option allows administrators to specify whether installation of unsigned applications is allowed on devices.

Block The Following Applications In ROM   This option allows administrators to specify a list of applications that should be blocked from being installed on the device.

Results of Lite-Management Configuration

Once all settings are configured as required on these pages, click Next and continue through the wizard, verifying on the Summary page that all options chosen are appropriate. This action implements the settings as required on the Exchange server, and from this point devices connecting to Exchange Server through ActiveSync will receive and implement the configured settings, or at least the ones the device is capable of implementing.

After a few devices have synchronized using the ActiveSync connector, they will be visible and available for management in the Devices node, as shown in Figure 18.11.

FIGURE 18.11
Lite-managed
devices

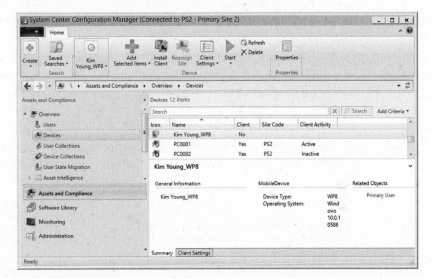

Now that devices are available in Configuration Manager, is it possible to do any management directly at this level? Mostly *no*. Remember, these devices are lite managed, which means almost all management is done through the ActiveSync connector. There are a couple of things that you can do, though. Right-clicking a lite-managed device will show the options available. Specifically, there are options to wipe the device and also to decide whether to block the device. This is also the location to set the primary device user, to open Resource Explorer for the device to view hardware inventory that has been collected, and also to view device properties. These options are shown in Figure 18.12.

FIGURE 18.12
Device context
menu options

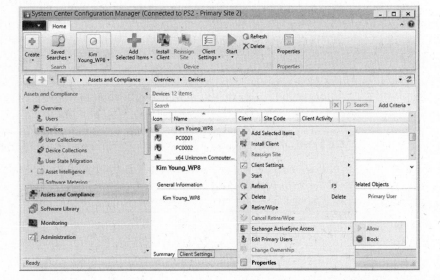

Depth Management via Microsoft Intune

Configuring a hybrid MDM scenario by connecting Configuration Manager with Microsoft Intune allows you to manage the many different mobile devices in your enterprise. Combining the strength of Configuration Manager and Microsoft Intune allows you not only to manage the devices but also to adapt quickly to changes since the new servicing model of Configuration Manager.

A requirement of using the Microsoft Intune subscription is that the site server on which the Service Connection Point is being installed needs to have access to the Internet.

Getting an EMS Subscription

Getting a Microsoft Enterprise Mobility + Security subscription is a good start to getting started with Microsoft Intune, which is part of this suite. Microsoft Enterprise Mobility + Security is a suite of products that allows you to securely manage the devices, the corporate apps that are installed, and the data of the apps or other company-owned data.

Microsoft Enterprise Mobility + Security covers the following main products:

Azure Active Directory Premium   When using Office 365 or Microsoft Intune, the identities need to be available in the Azure Active Directory (Azure AD). Either the identities are synchronized with the password hash with Azure Active Directory Connect (AADConnect) and the users authenticate to Azure AD, or the identities are synchronized via AADConnect and the users authenticate via Active Directory Federation Services (AD FS) at the on-premises Active Directory. The premium edition of Azure AD allows you to get more advanced reports about what is happening with the identities in Azure AD.

Microsoft Advanced Threat Analytics   With Microsoft Advanced Threat Analytics (Microsoft ATA), real-time threads can be identified. ATA allows identification of suspicious activities and advanced threats in near real time.

Microsoft Intune   You can manage mobile devices, the apps, and the data of the apps via Microsoft Intune. This can be either standalone in the cloud or via a hybrid environment where Configuration Manager is connected with Microsoft Intune. This book covers only the hybrid scenario.

Azure Rights Management   The data is critical in this new mobile world! Azure Rights Management allows you to secure the data itself. With Azure Rights Management, identities can be given access to documents for a specific period. While having access, the owner of a document is able to track the access and revoke access to documents. Azure Rights Management is a powerful "tool" to prevent data leakage.

GETTING STARTED WITH A MICROSOFT EMS PROOF OF CONCEPT

If you want to quickly start a standalone or hybrid proof of concept of Microsoft Enterprise Mobility + Security, be sure to take a look at *Microsoft Enterprise Mobility Suite: Planning and Implementation* by Kent Agerlund and Peter Daalmans (Deployment Artist, 2016).

Prerequisites for Microsoft Intune

To be able to use the depth management option via Microsoft Intune, you must meet some prerequisites:

- Acquire a Microsoft Intune subscription.
- Configure your domain name in Windows Intune.
- Add an alternative UPN suffix to your Active Directory domain (optional).
- Synchronize your users with Azure Active Directory.

Let's look at each in more detail.

Acquire a Microsoft Intune subscription.   To acquire access to the Microsoft EMS (or Microsoft Intune) features, you need to obtain a license or create a trail account. A trail is easily created by browsing to `https://ref.ms/ems` and walking through the straightforward process.

Configure your (external) domain name in Microsoft Intune.   When you register for a Microsoft Intune subscription, your organization account that is created looks like `<username>@<domainname>.onmicrosoft.com`. To create a user-friendly way of logging on to the company portal, you want to add your public domain name that is used for your email. Setting up your own domain name is done by following the next steps:

1. Go to your Admin page via `https://portal.office.com/` and log on with your Microsoft Intune administrator username.

2. In the menu, expand Settings and select Domains, as shown in Figure 18.13.

FIGURE 18.13
Domains page Admin center

3. Click Add Domain, supply your domain name, and click Next.

4. Before Microsoft will add your domain name, you need to prove that it is really yours. You can do this by adding a TXT or MX record in your public DNS zone. Add the TXT value (for example, **MS=ms201111197**) to your public DNS zone and click Verify.

5. When verification is done successfully, you will see a message that the domain has been added to your account. Click Save and Close. Your domain is now listed with a status of Verified.

6. To support enterprise enrollment, you need to set up a CNAME DNS record that redirects enterpriseenrollment.<*your domainname*> (for example, enterpriseenrollment.masteringsccm.com) to manage.microsoft.com.

Add an alternative UPN suffix to your Active Directory domain. If you have an Active Directory domain name that is used only internally, such as any .LOCAL or .LAN domain name, and your email domain name differs from Active Directory, you may need to add an alternative Universal Principal Name (UPN) suffix to your Active Directory, as follows:

1. Log on to your domain controller or server with the Active Directory management tools, and from the Start menu or Start screen open the Active Directory Domains And Trusts management console.

2. Right-click Active Directory Domain And Trusts and click Properties.

3. Supply your domain name in the Alternative UPN Suffixes field and click Add, as shown in Figure 18.14.

FIGURE 18.14
Add an alternative
UPN suffix.

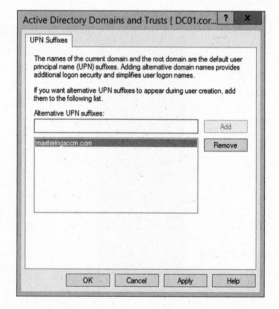

4. Click OK.

5. Be sure to change the UPN of every user that is going to be synchronized to Azure Active Directory

Prepare for synchronizing your users with Azure Active Directory. The next step in preparing your environment for Microsoft Intune is setting up Active Directory synchronization. Synchronize your local Active Directory accounts to the Azure Active Directory so that they can be used with Microsoft Intune. Follow these steps to prepare the Active Directory synchronization:

1. Go to http://portal.office.com and expand Admin centers; then click Azure AD.

2. Go to Active Directory and select the Active Directory that is used by Microsoft Intune.

3. Click Directory Integration and click Activated. Click Save and Yes to activate the Directory Sync.

4. Click Users and click Add User. Create a user that will be used to set up Azure Active Directory Connect, which is used for synchronizing the accounts to Azure AD. Supply a name, as shown in Figure 18.15, and click the arrow to proceed.

FIGURE 18.15
Create a user for
Azure AD Connect.

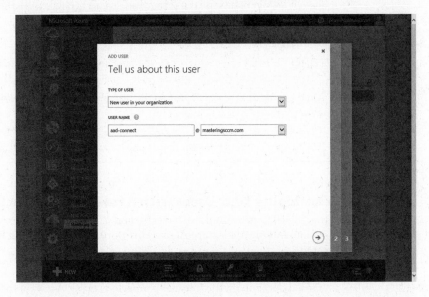

5. Supply the first name, last name, and display name; set the role to Global Admin; and click the right-pointing arrow. Because the account is configured to be a Global Admin, an alternative email address must be configured.

6. Click Create to create a password. After the password has been created, click on the checkmark and log off the Azure Portal. Log on again with the credentials of the AAD Connect user and change the password.

DISABLING THE PASSWORD CHANGE REQUIREMENT OF THE AAD CONNECT ACCOUNT OF MICROSOFT INTUNE

By default a Microsoft Intune account password expires every 90 days. Since Configuration Manager is using your organization account to connect to Microsoft Intune, you might need to reconfigure your Microsoft Intune subscription every 90 days. Follow the next steps to make sure the password of the organization account does not expire. Be sure to set it with a very strong password.

1. Add the Azure Active Directory Module for Windows PowerShell, and load it within Windows PowerShell.

2. Connect to Azure by executing the following command:

   ```
   Connect-MsolService
   ```

3. Supply the username and password of the organizational account, and click OK to connect to Azure Active Directory.

4. To enable the Password Never Expires property of the organizational account in Azure Active Directory, you need to execute the following command. In this example, the organizational account is aad-connect@masteringsccm.onmicrosoft.com; replace this with your own account.

   ```
   Set-MsolUser -UserPrincipalName aad-connect@masteringsccm.onmicrosoft.com
   -PasswordNeverExpires $True
   ```

5. Supply the name of a user account that has the Domain Admins and Enterprise Administrator Active Directory permissions in the User Name field, and click Next.

6. On the Hybrid Deployment page, click Next, and select Enable Password Sync on the Password Synchronization page.

7. Click Next, and after the configuration completes, click Next again. Start the synchronization of the directories by enabling the Synchronize Your Directories Now option. Click Finish.

Synchronizing Your Users with Azure Active Directory

Now that the UPN is configured correctly and the preparation for Azure Active Directory Connect tool is done, the Azure Active Directory Connect tool can be installed and configured.

1. Go to https://ref.ms/Azureconnect, click Download, and save the AzureADConnect.msi file to a location on the Internet-connected server you want to install the tool on.

2. Double-click the AzureADConnect.msi file and click Yes if a User Account Control message is shown.

3. Check "I agree to the license terms and privacy notice" and click Continue on the Welcome screen.

4. Click Customize and click Install.

5. Select Password Synchronization and click Next.

6. To be able to connect to Azure AD, supply the just-created account for the Azure Active Directory Connect tool as shown in Figure 18.16.

FIGURE 18.16
Connecting to
Azure AD

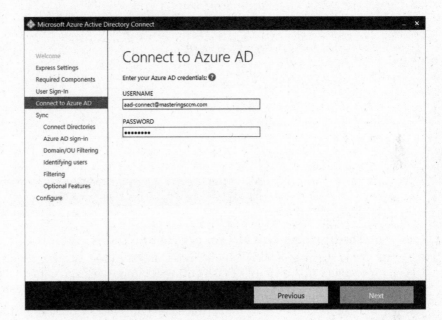

7. After connecting to Azure AD, click Next so that the connection with the local Active Directory can be set up. Use a domain admin account to connect to the local Active Directory and click Add Directory.

8. Click Next to go to the next step. On the Azure AD sign-in configuration page, determine if all Active Directory UPN suffixes are available.

9. To configure the Domain and OU, click Next and select Sync Selected Domains And OUs. Select the top-level domain and deselect all OUs that you do not want to synchronize, as shown in Figure 18.17.

10. Click Next four times and click Install to install and configure the synchronization service on the server.

11. Click Exit to complete setting up the synchronization of the users to Azure Active Directory.

FIGURE 18.17
Selecting domain
and OUs

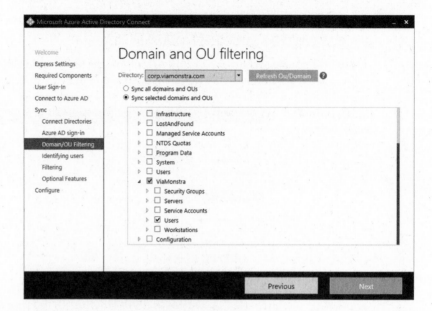

Configuring the Microsoft Intune Subscription

After acquiring a Microsoft Enterprise Mobility + Security license and synchronizing the users to Azure AD, you must add the Microsoft Intune subscription to Configuration Manager. Follow these steps to configure the Microsoft Intune subscription in Configuration Manager:

1. Open the Configuration Manager console, select the Administration workspace, and expand Overview ➢ Cloud Services ➢ Microsoft Intune Subscriptions. Then click Add Microsoft Intune Subscription in the Home ribbon.

2. Click Next in the Create Microsoft Intune Subscription Wizard and click Sign In to sign in to Microsoft Intune with your Microsoft Intune organizational account.

3. Select "I understand that after I complete the sign-in process, the mobile device management authority is permanently set to Configuration Manager and cannot be changed," as shown in Figure 18.18.

FIGURE 18.18
Setting the mobile
device authority

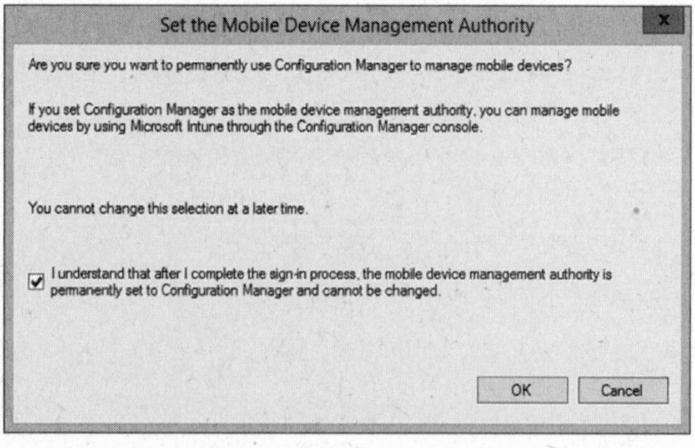

> ### Set the Mobile Device Management Authority
>
> Are you sure you want to permanently use Configuration Manager to manage mobile devices?
>
> If you set Configuration Manager as the mobile device management authority, you can manage mobile devices by using Microsoft Intune through the Configuration Manager console.
>
> You cannot change this selection at a later time.
>
> ☑ I understand that after I complete the sign-in process, the mobile device management authority is permanently set to Configuration Manager and cannot be changed.
>
> OK   Cancel

4. Click OK and supply the Microsoft Intune organizational account and the password; then click Sign In, as shown in Figure 18.19.

FIGURE 18.19
Signing in with your Microsoft Intune organizational account

5. Click Next to go to the General page and configure the options listed here and shown in Figure 18.20:

Collection Click Browse to configure the collection where the users who need access to Microsoft Intune are members. You need to create a special user collection for users who need access to Microsoft Intune. This collection is used to provision the accounts that are members of this collection with a Microsoft Intune license.

Company Name If you want to have your company name shown in the company portal, add it here.

URL To Company Privacy Documentation Managing mobile devices, corporate owned or owned by users, will always raise privacy questions. Be sure to explain what is inventoried and what is not, and what actions you as a Configuration Manager admin can execute so that it is clear for the users what happens if they enroll their device.

MICROSOFT INTUNE PRIVACY EXPLAINED

Microsoft created a PDF that explains exactly how Microsoft handles privacy if you are using Microsoft Intune. Download the PDF here: `https://ref.ms/intuneprivacy/`.

FIGURE 18.20
Create Microsoft
Intune Subscription
Wizard, General
Configuration

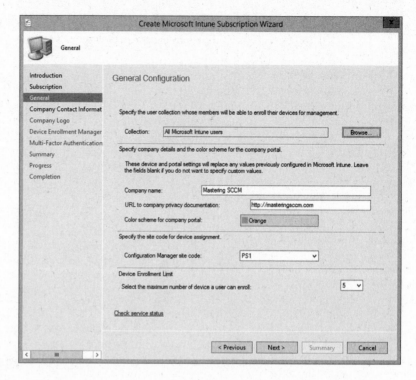

Color Scheme For Company Portal Configure the color scheme for the company portal by selecting one of the preconfigured colors or any other RGB color.

Configuration Manager Site Code Configure the site code of the Configuration Manager site that will be used for site assignment. Only one subscription per site can be configured.

Device Enrollment Limit The Microsoft Intune license allows users to enroll five devices per user. As a Configuration Manager admin you are able to configure how many devices are allowed to be enrolled in your environment.

6. After configuring the General settings, click Next to configure the company contact information. Supply the contact name, phone number, and email address of the IT department. You can also specify a support website, website name, and additional information.

7. Click Next to configure the company logo, check the Include Company Logo check box, and click Browse to be able to navigate to your logo. Your logo must be a PNG or JPG file with a maximum size of 750 KB and a resolution of 400 pixels by 100 pixels. Click Next to continue.

8. The next step is to configure the Device Enrollment Managers. Device Enrollment Managers are used when you want to enroll corporate-owned devices. Currently only Windows 10 or iOS devices can be enrolled by a Device Enrollment Manager.

Device Enrollment Manager A Device Enrollment Manager is able to enroll devices in Intune without needing to configure a user who is going to use the device. The Device Enrollment Manager is able to log on to the company portal and install or uninstall apps and configure access to company data.

Enrolled devices by a Device Enrollment Manager do have some restrictions while using the devices:

◆ The devices are not configured for a user, so the devices cannot have access to email or company data via VPN since you need to have users to gain access.

◆ No conditional access is available since conditional access is based on user access.

◆ Devices cannot be reset via the company portal.

◆ The Apple Volume Purchase Program feature and the Apple Device Enrollment Program for iOS cannot be used.

9. Click Next to enable multifactor authentication. Enabling this option only adds multifactor authentication during enrollment of devices based on Windows 8.1 and Windows Phone 8.1 or later.

10. Click Next to review the summary. After confirming the settings, click Next to create the Microsoft Intune subscription.

11. Click Close.

After the Microsoft Intune subscription is created, a new site server is added automatically. Follow the next steps to view the added site server.

12. Open the Configuration Manager console, select the Administration workspace, and expand Overview ➤ Site Configuration ➤ Servers And Site System Roles. You will see that a site system server named \\manage.microsoft.com is added, as shown in Figure 18.21. This site server is your distribution point within Microsoft Intune.

FIGURE 18.21
A distribution point in Microsoft Intune is added.

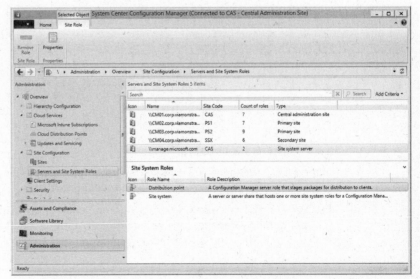

Configuring Mobile Device Platforms

Now that all prerequisites for depth MDM are in place, the supported platforms need to be configured. Without configuring the support of the platforms, users are not able to enroll their device.

ANDROID

To be able to support enrolling Android devices, you don't have to do much more. Follow these steps to configure Android support in Configuration Manager:

1. Open the Configuration Manager console, select the Administration workspace, and expand Overview ➤ Cloud Services ➤ Microsoft Intune Subscriptions. Select the Microsoft Intune subscription, expand Configure Platforms, and click Android.

2. Click Enable Android Enrollment, as shown in Figure 18.22, and click OK.

FIGURE 18.22
Enabling Android support

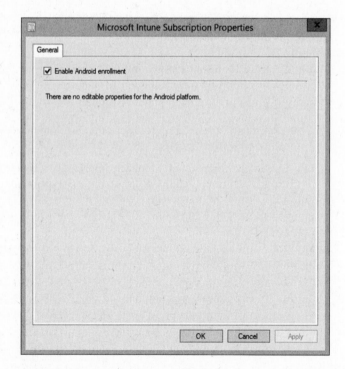

IOS AND MAC OS X (MDM)

To support iOS enrollment, you need to enable platform support and specify the Apple Push Notification service (APNs) certificate. This is done in four steps:

1. Create and download a Certificate Signing Request from Windows Intune. In the Configuration Manager console, navigate to Administration ➤ Overview ➤ Cloud Services ➤ Microsoft Intune Subscriptions and click Create APNs Certificate Request.

Supply a filename and click Download. Log into Microsoft Intune, and the CSR file will be saved at the configured file location. Click Close.

2. Go to the Apple Push Certificate Portal and log on with your Apple ID. Click Create A Certificate, select I Have Read And Agree To These Terms And Conditions, click Accept, click Browse, and click Upload to upload the CSR file you created earlier. Click Download when the certificate is created.

3. Copy the downloaded `MDM_ Microsoft Corporation_Certificate.pem` file to the site server and to the Configuration Manager console by navigating to Administration ➤ Overview ➤ Cloud Services ➤ Microsoft Intune Subscriptions. Select the Microsoft Intune Subscription, expand Configure Platforms, and click iOS.

4. Check Enable iOS And Mac OS X (MDM) Enrollment, as shown in Figure 18.23, and click Browse. Find the downloaded `MDM_ Microsoft Corporation_Certificate.pem` file and select it before clicking Open. Click OK to close the dialog box.

FIGURE 18.23
Enabling iOS and
Mac OS X (MDM)
support

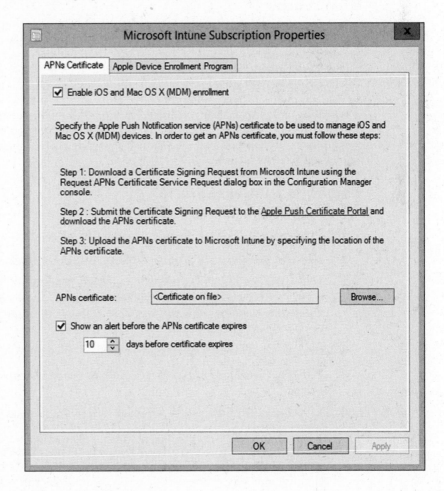

WINDOWS

Follow these steps to enable Windows enrollment support for the Configuration Manager hierarchy:

1. In the Configuration Manager console, navigate to Administration ➤ Overview ➤ Cloud Services ➤ Microsoft Intune Subscriptions. Select the Microsoft Intune Subscription, expand Configure Platforms, and click Windows.

2. Check Enable Windows Enrollment to enable support for Windows enrollment.

3. Optionally you need to add code-signing certificates to allow the installation of corporate-signed certificates. Browse to a code-signing certificate, which you can acquire from Symantec, DigiCert, or any other certification authority you can access.

4. Click OK.

MDM Policies

Settings management options are available for depth devices in addition to the standard client operations. You configure these settings through Compliance Settings. Configuring settings for mobile devices requires creating one or more configuration items and then delivering them to the mobile devices by associating them with configuration baselines, which are then assigned to a given collection. This section will describe the device settings that can be configured through the configuration items per platform.

Also, you can create company resource access profiles and deploy them to your mobile devices. Since the number of configuration items and baselines needed depends on individual configurations, the example will use a unified approach where a single configuration item and baseline are used for all devices.

WINDOWS 8.1 AND WINDOWS 10

First let's look at the Windows 8.1 and Windows 10 settings that can be managed through MDM.

1. Start creating the configuration item by selecting Compliance Settings ➤ Configuration Items.

2. Right-click Configuration Items and select Create Configuration Item.

3. On the General page of the Create Configuration Item Wizard, supply a name and description. Then specify that the configuration item is targeted for a mobile device and choose what platform you want to support, as shown in Figure 18.24. Select Windows 8.1 And Windows 10 for this example.

4. Optionally, select any categories that should be used for this configuration item. Click Next.

5. On the Supported Platforms page, select all the platforms for which the policies apply and click Next.

6. On the Device Settings page, determine which settings should be managed by this configuration item.

   For the example, select all settings groups, except Enterprise Data Protection (this group is covered in the "Mobile Application Management Policies" section), and choose to configure additional settings, as shown in Figure 18.25. This will allow you to review all potential settings that might be enforced on a device.

FIGURE 18.24
Create Configuration
Item Wizard—
General page

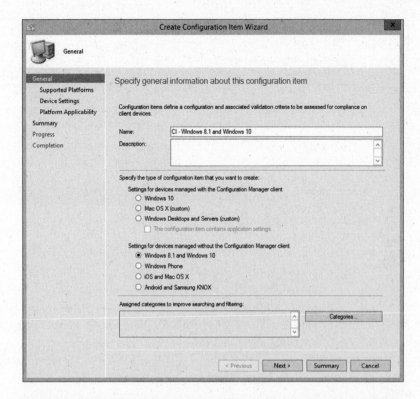

FIGURE 18.25
Create Configuration
Item Wizard—Device
Settings page

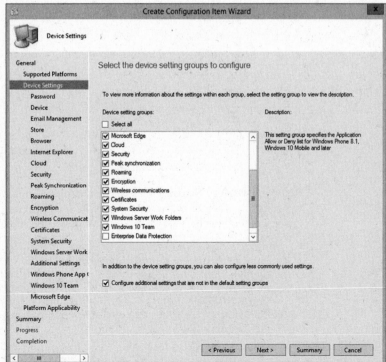

SETTINGS VS. DEVICE CAPABILITY

Not all devices are capable of implementing all settings. It's fine to configure a setting in general, but the settings will be implemented only on capable devices.

7. After selecting the additional settings that will be defined by this configuration item, click Next. Configure the appropriate mobile device password options.

The password settings are shown in Figure 18.26. Password settings are not configured by default.

FIGURE 18.26
Create Configuration Item Wizard— Password page

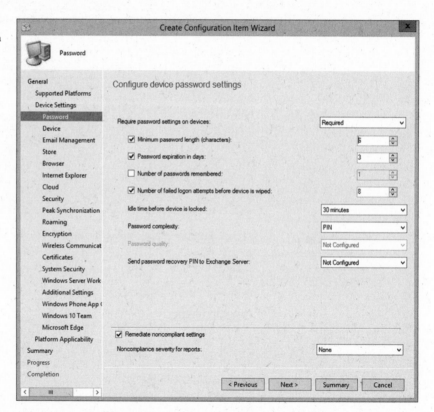

Require Password Settings On Mobile Devices   This option allows administrators to determine whether password settings should be enforced. Assuming this option is enabled, a few specific password configurations are possible:

♦   Minimum Password Length (Characters): This option allows administrators to specify the minimum number of characters that should be supplied as part of the password.

♦   Password Expiration In Days: This option allows administrators to specify the number of days that are allowed to elapse before requiring a password change.

◆ Number Of Passwords Remembered: This option allows administrators to configure how many passwords are retained. This setting is useful to prevent the reuse of passwords.

◆ Number Of Failed Logon Attempts Before Device Is Wiped: This option allows administrators to specify how many incorrect passwords can be supplied before the device is automatically wiped.

Idle Time Before Mobile Device Is Locked   This option, not enabled by default, allows administrators to control how long a device might be left unlocked when idle.

Password Complexity   This option allows administrators to specify the required password complexity level, in this case allowing either a PIN or a strong password.

Password Quality   Not applicable for Windows 8.1 and Windows 10.

Send Password Recovery PIN To Exchange Server   This option allows administrators to configure where the password recovery PIN is stored on the Exchange server.

DEVICE COMPLIANCE REMEDIATION

If a device is not compliant with all required settings, it will be updated to the required state by default as a result of selecting Remediate Noncompliant Settings on the Password page. When device settings are remediated, it is possible to configure that a noncompliance indication will be logged in reports. The option is disabled by default.

---

8. After all password options are configured, click Next.

9. Configure device settings for the device on the Device page, shown in Figure 18.27. Note that not all configuration options may be applicable for the selected platforms; the configuration option will be disabled if it's not supported.

Voice Dialing   Not applicable for Windows 8.1 and Windows 10.

Voice Assistant   Not applicable for Windows 8.1 and Windows 10.

Voice Assistant While Locked   Not applicable for Windows 8.1 and Windows 10.

Screen Capture   This option allows administrators to define whether screen capture is enabled. It can be configured as Enabled or Disabled.

Video Chat Client   Not applicable for Windows 8.1 and Windows 10.

Add Game Center Friends   Not applicable for Windows 8.1 and Windows 10.

Multiplayer Gaming   Not applicable for Windows 8.1 and Windows 10.

Personal Wallet Software While Locked   Not applicable for Windows 8.1 and Windows 10.

Diagnostic Data Submission (Windows 8.1 And Earlier)   This option allows administrators to define whether diagnostic data submission is enabled. It can be configured as Enabled or Disabled.

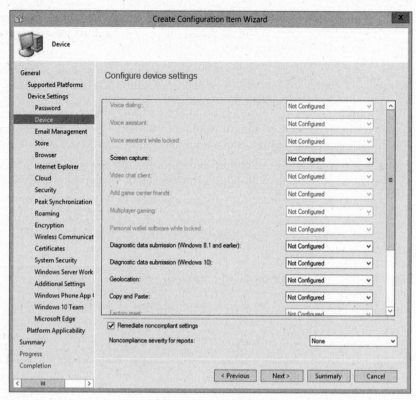

Diagnostic Data Submission (Windows 10) This option allows administrators to define whether diagnostic data submission is enabled. It can be configured as Enabled or Disabled.

Geolocation This option allows administrators to enable or disable the geolocation option on devices. It can be configured as Enabled or Disabled.

Copy and Paste This option allows administrators to specify whether copy and paste of data in and between apps is allowed on devices. It can be configured as Enabled or Disabled.

Factory Reset Not applicable for Windows 8.1 and Windows 10.

Clipboard Share Between Applications Not applicable for Windows 8.1 and Windows 10.

Bluetooth This option allows administrators to allow or prohibit Bluetooth support on a mobile device. It can be configured as Allowed or Prohibited.

Bluetooth Discoverable Mode This option allows administrators to configure whether a device can be discovered via Bluetooth. It can be configured as Allowed or Prohibited.

Bluetooth Advertising This option allows administrators to configure whether a device can advertise itself via Bluetooth. It can be configured as Allowed or Prohibited.

Video Recording This option allows administrators to allow or disable video recording on mobile devices. It can be configured as Allowed or Prohibited.

10. Click Next to configure email options for the device in the Email Management settings, shown in Figure 18.28.

FIGURE 18.28
Create Configuration
Item Wizard—Email
Management page

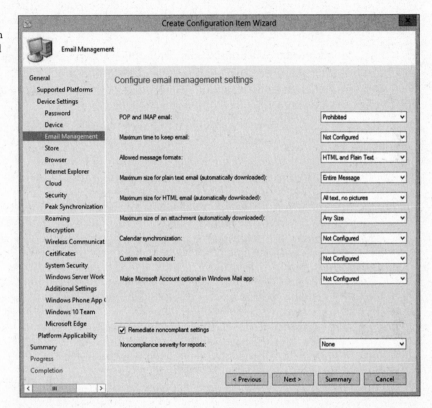

POP And IMAP Email This option allows administrators to define whether POP and IMAP email are allowed. This is not an either/or setting; either both are allowed or both are prohibited.

Maximum Time To Keep Email This option allows administrators to specify how long email should be retained on the device.

Allowed Message Formats This option allows administrators to specify the format allowed for email, either plain text only or both plain text and HTML. If this option is configured, up to two additional options become available for configuration.

Maximum Size For Plain Text Email (Automatically Downloaded) This option lets administrators define the size of a plain-text email that is allowed to be automatically downloaded to the device. Incremental sizes are configurable up to allowing the entire email to be downloaded.

Maximum Size For HTML Email (Automatically Downloaded) This option lets administrators define the size of an HTML email that is allowed to be automatically downloaded to the device. Incremental sizes are configurable up to allowing the entire email to be downloaded.

Maximum Size Of An Attachment (Automatically Downloaded) This option lets administrators define the size of an attachment that is allowed to be automatically downloaded to the device. Incremental sizes are configurable up to allowing the entire attachment to be downloaded.

Calendar Synchronization This option allows administrators to specify whether calendar synchronization to the device is allowed.

Custom Email Account This option lets administrators allow custom email accounts. It can be configured as Allowed or Prohibited.

Make Microsoft Account Optional In Windows Mail App This option allows administrators to make the Microsoft account optional in the Windows Mail app on the device. It can be configured as Yes or No.

11. After all email options are configured, click Next.

12. Configure the store settings, shown in Figure 18.29.

FIGURE 18.29
Create Configuration Item Wizard—Store page

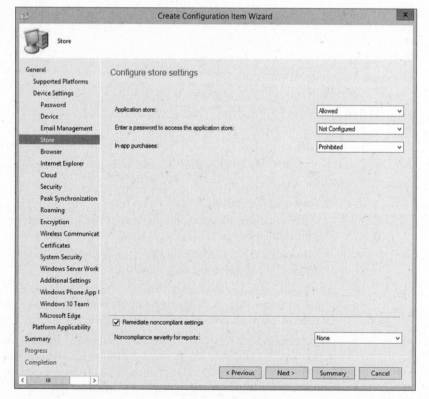

Application Store   This option allows administrators to specify whether accessing and using the application store of the device is allowed.

Enter A Password To Access The Application Store   This option allows administrators to specify whether a user must enter a password when accessing an application store.

In-App Purchases   This option allows administrators to specify whether in-app purchases are allowed.

13. After configuring the application store settings, click Next.

14. Configure the browser settings, shown in Figure 18.30.

FIGURE 18.30
Create Configuration Item Wizard—Browser page

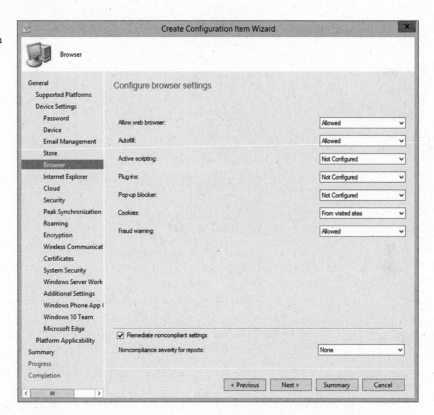

Allow Web Browser   Configure whether a user is allowed to use a web browser.

Autofill   Configure whether the browser is allowed to use autofill.

Active Scripting   Configure whether the browser is allowed to use active scripting.

Plug-ins   Configure whether the browser is allowed to use plug-ins.

Pop-up Blocker   Configure whether the browser is allowed to use the pop-up blocker.

Cookies   Configure whether the browser is allowed to accept cookies from visited sites.

Fraud Warning   Configure whether fraud warnings in the browser are enabled.

15. After configuring the browser settings, click Next.

16. For the Windows-based mobile devices, you can configure Internet Explorer settings, as shown in Figure 18.31.

FIGURE 18.31
Create Configuration
Item Wizard—Internet
Explorer page

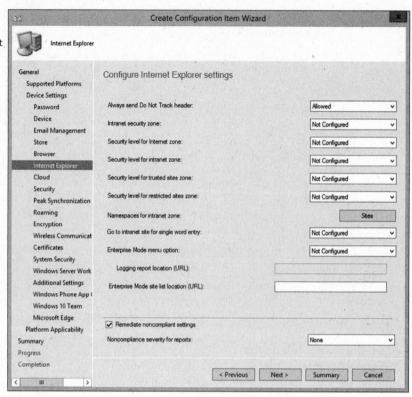

Always Send Do Not Track Header Configure whether the Always Send Do Not Track Header option can be enabled.

Intranet Security Zone Configure whether the Intranet security zone settings can be changed.

Security Level For Internet Zone Configure whether the security level for the Internet zone can be changed.

Security Level For Intranet Zone Configure whether the security level for the intranet zone can be changed.

Security Level For Trusted Sites Zone Configure whether the security level for the trusted sites zone can be changed.

Security Level For Restricted Sites Zone Configure whether the security level for the restricted sites zone can be changed.

Namespaces For Intranet Zone   Preconfigure the namespaces for your intranet zone or enforce that websites be removed from the intranet zone.

Go To Intranet Site For Single Word Entry   Configure whether a user is redirected to an intranet when supplying a single word.

Enterprise Mode Menu Option   Enable or disable the Enterprise Mode menu option in the Internet Explorer browser. After enabling it you are able to configure the Logging Report Location URL.

Enterprise Mode Site List Location   Administrators are able to configure the Enterprise Mode Site List Location URL for this policy.

17. Click Next to configure the cloud settings, as shown in Figure 18.32.

FIGURE 18.32
Create Configuration Item Wizard—Cloud page

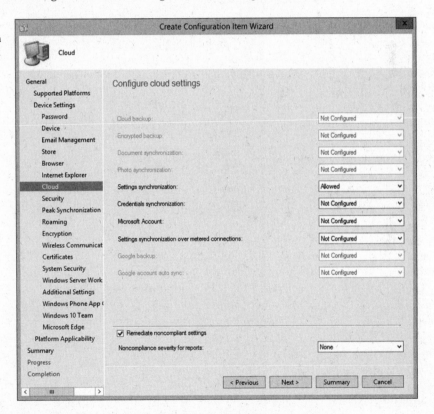

Cloud Backup   Not applicable for Windows 8.1 and Windows 10.

Encrypted Backup   Not applicable for Windows 8.1 and Windows 10.

Document Synchronization   Not applicable for Windows 8.1 and Windows 10.

Photo Synchronization   Not applicable for Windows 8.1 and Windows 10.

Settings Synchronization   Configure whether settings on the mobile devices may be synchronized to a cloud service like SkyDrive or iCloud on the Internet.

Credentials Synchronization Configure whether credentials on the mobile devices may be synchronized to a cloud service like SkyDrive or iCloud on the Internet.

Microsoft Account Administrators are able to allow or disallow the usage of a Microsoft account on the device.

Settings Synchronization Over Metered Connections Configure whether synchronizations over metered connections are allowed.

Google Backup Not applicable for Windows 8.1 and Windows 10.

Google Account Auto Sync Not applicable for Windows 8.1 and Windows 10.

18. Configure the security options for the device. The security management settings are shown in Figure 18.33.

FIGURE 18.33
Create Configuration
Item Wizard—
Security page

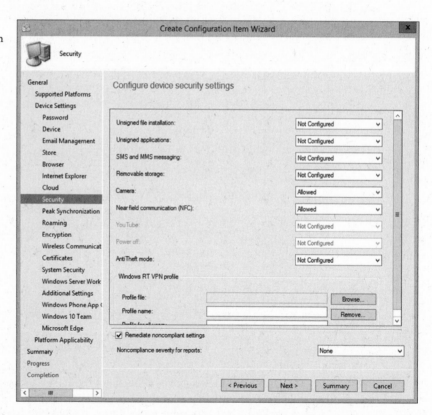

Unsigned File Installation This option allows administrators to specify whether the installation of unsigned files is allowed. If they are allowed, administrators then choose what parties are given this right. Available options are Mobile Operator, Manager, User Authenticated, IT Administrator, User Unauthenticated, and Trusted Provisioning Server.

Unsigned Applications This option lets administrators specify whether the installation of unsigned applications is allowed or prohibited.

SMS And MMS Messaging   This option lets administrators configure whether SMS and MMS messaging are allowed or prohibited on the device.

Removable Storage   This option lets administrators configure whether removable storage is allowed or prohibited on the device.

Camera   This option lets administrators configure whether using the camera is allowed or prohibited on the device.

Near Field Communication (NFC)   This option lets administrators configure whether Bluetooth is allowed or prohibited on the device.

YouTube   Not applicable for Windows 8.1 and Windows 10.

Power Off   Not applicable for Windows 8.1 and Windows 10.

Anti Theft Mode   This option allows administrators to configure whether Windows 10 AntiTheft mode is enabled.

Windows RT VPN Profile   Deploy a VPN profile for a Windows RT device and define whether the profile is available to all users.

19. After all security options are configured, click Next.

20. Configure the synchronization options for the device in the Peak Synchronization settings, shown in Figure 18.34.

FIGURE 18.34
Create Configuration
Item Wizard—Peak
Synchronization
page

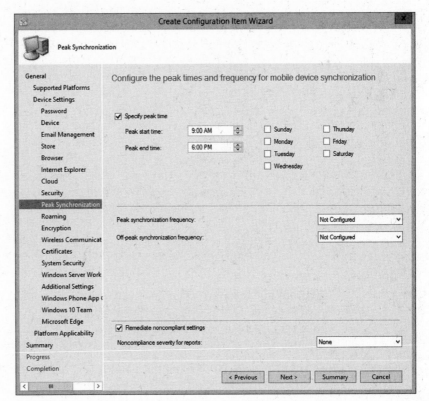

Specify Peak Time   This option allows administrators to define the specific time considered to be peak on devices.

Peak Synchronization Frequency   This option allows administrators to specify how often the device will synchronize during the defined peak time.

Off-Peak Synchronization Frequency   This option allows administrators to specify how often the device will synchronize outside the defined peak time.

21. After all peak synchronization options are configured, click Next.

22. Configure the roaming options for the device in the Roaming settings, shown in Figure 18.35.

FIGURE 18.35
Create Configuration
Item Wizard—
Roaming page

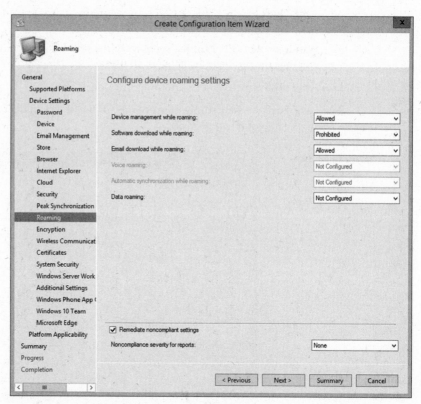

MDM While Roaming   This option allows administrators to configure whether a device should be actively managed when roaming.

Software Download While Roaming   This option allows administrators to specify whether software downloads should be allowed when a device is roaming.

Email Download While Roaming   This option allows administrators to control whether email is downloaded while a device is roaming.

Device Management While Roaming   Allow or disallow the device being managed by your company while roaming in a different country.

Software Download While Roaming   Allow or disallow software download while roaming in a different country.

Email Download While Roaming   Allow or disallow email download while roaming in a different country.

Voice Roaming   Not applicable for Windows 8.1 and Windows 10.

Automatic Synchronization While Roaming   Not applicable for Windows 8.1 and Windows 10.

Data Roaming   This option allows administrators to control whether data usage is allowed while a device is roaming.

23. After all the roaming options are configured, click Next.

24. Configure the encryption options for devices in the Encryption settings, shown in Figure 18.36.

FIGURE 18.36
Create
Configuration
Item Wizard—
Encryption page

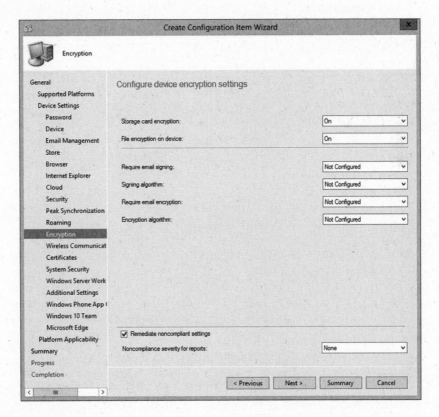

Storage Card Encryption   This option allows administrators to specify whether encryption is on or off for a device's storage card.

File Encryption On Mobile Device   This option allows administrators to configure whether file encryption is on or off for a device.

Require Email Signing/Signing Algorithm   This option allows administrators to specify whether email signing is enabled or disabled. If email signing is enabled, the Signing Algorithm option lets administrators specify whether SHA, MD5, or the default signing algorithm should be used.

Require Email Encryption/Encryption Algorithm   This option allows administrators to configure whether email encryption is on or off for a device. If email encryption is enabled, the Encryption Algorithm option allows administrators to specify which encryption algorithm should be used. Available choices are Triple DES, DES, RC2 128-bit, RC2 64-bit, RC2 40-bit, and the default algorithm.

25. After all encryption options are configured, click Next.

26. Configure the wireless communication options for devices in the Wireless Communication settings, shown in Figure 18.37.

FIGURE 18.37
Create Configuration
Item Wizard—Wireless
Communications page

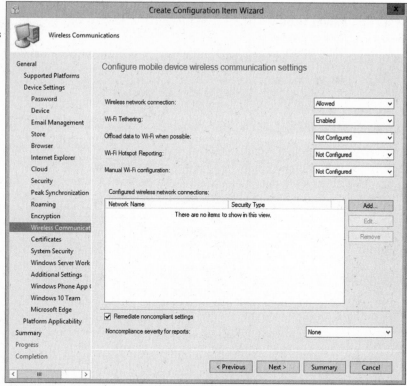

27. Configure whether wireless network connections are allowed or prohibited on the device.

Wireless Network Connection   This option allows administrators to specify whether encryption is on or off for a device's storage card.

Wi-Fi Tethering   This option lets administrators specify whether users can use their device as a mobile hotspot.

Offload Data To Wi-Fi When Possible   This option lets administrators specify whether users can use their Wi-Fi connection on the device when possible.

Wi-Fi Hotspot Reporting   This option allows administrators to control if Wi-Fi hotspots are reported or not.

Manual Wi-Fi Configuration   This option allows administrators to specify whether users are able to configure manual Wi-Fi configuration.

If Wireless Network Connections are allowed, administrators can click the Add button to specify one or more networks and the associated network configuration. Available network configuration options include Proxy, 802.1X, Authentication, Data Encryption, and more. A Wireless Network Connection configuration page is shown in Figure 18.38.

FIGURE 18.38
Wireless Network
Connection page

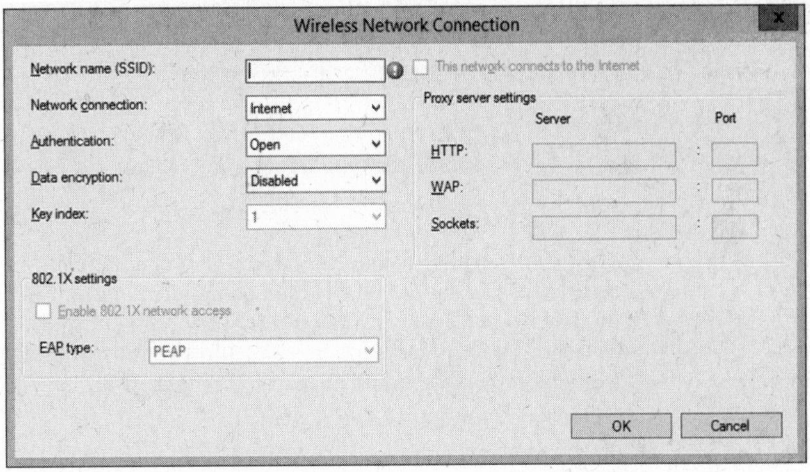

28. After all wireless network connection options are configured, click Next.

29. Configure the certificate options for devices in the Certificates settings, shown in Figure 18.39.

FIGURE 18.39
Create Configuration
Item Wizard—
Certificates page

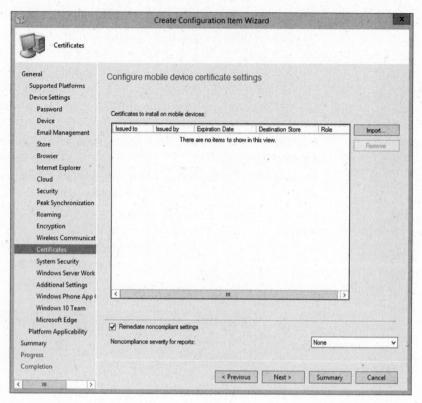

The Certificates To Install On Mobile Devices option allows administrators to specify certificates that should be installed on mobile devices. Clicking the Import button brings up the Import Certificate dialog box, shown in Figure 18.40, which allows certificates to be imported from the filesystem and allows administrators to specify in which certificate store the certificate should be placed on the device.

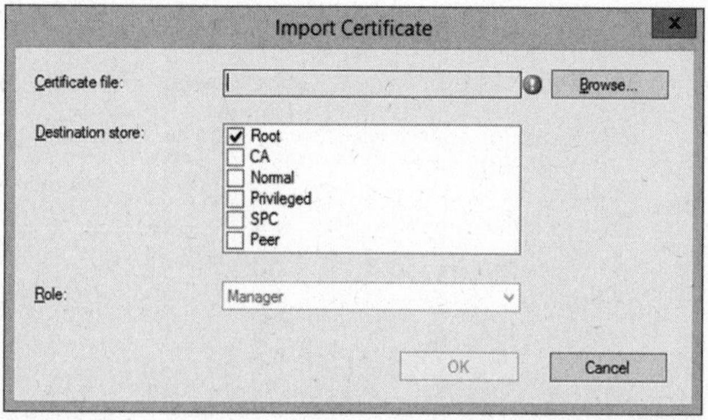

FIGURE 18.40
Import Certificate
dialog box

30. After all certificate options are configured, click Next.

31. Configure extra security settings on the System Security page, shown in Figure 18.41. This system security will apply to Windows-based devices.

FIGURE 18.41

Create Configuration Item Wizard—System Security page

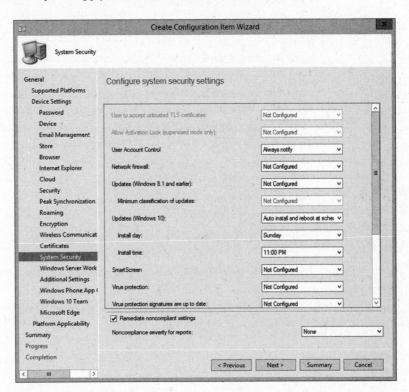

User To Accept Untrusted TLS Certificates This option allows administrators to configure whether a user is allowed to accept untrusted TLS certificates.

User Access Control This option allows administrators to configure how User Access Control is enabled and how it notifies them of changes to the operating system of a device.

Network Firewall This option allows administrators to configure whether the firewall is required.

Updates (Windows 8.1 And Earlier) This option allows administrators to configure whether updates are installed automatically.

Minimum Classification Of Updates Administrators are allowed to configure the minimum classifications of the updates that will be downloaded to Windows computers. Options are None, Important, or Recommended.

Updates (Windows 10) Allow administrators to configure how Windows software updates are downloaded to the devices. Settings that can be configured are Notify Download, Auto Install At Maintenance Time, Auto Install And Reboot At Maintenance Time, and Auto Install And Reboot At Schedule Time. Using the last option will allow administrators to schedule a day and time when the updates need to be installed.

SmartScreen This option allows administrators to configure whether SmartScreen in Internet Explorer is enabled.

Virus Protection This option allows administrators to configure whether virus protection is required for a device.

Virus Protection Signatures Are Up To Date This option allows administrators to configure whether up-to-date virus protection signatures are required.

Lock Screen Control Center This option allows administrators to configure whether the Control Center app can be accessed when a device is locked.

Lock Screen Notification View This option allows administrators to configure whether the notifications can be viewed when a device is locked.

Lock Screen Today Screen This option allows administrators to configure whether the Today Screen app can be accessed when a device is locked.

Fingerprint For Unlocking This option allows administrators to configure whether the fingerprint sensor can be used to unlock the device.

Pre-release Features This option allows administrators to configure whether Microsoft is allowed to deploy pre-release settings and features to the device.

Manual Root Certificate Installation This option allows administrators to allow or block the install of root certificates manually.

32. Click Next to configure the Windows Server Work Folder settings, as shown in Figure 18.42.

FIGURE 18.42
Create Configuration Item Wizard—Windows Server Work Folders page

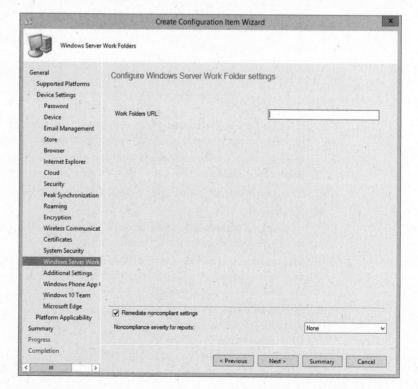

33. Click Next to configure additional settings. You can click Add to include a custom setting. Click Create Setting to create an OMA URI setting, as shown in Figure 18.43.

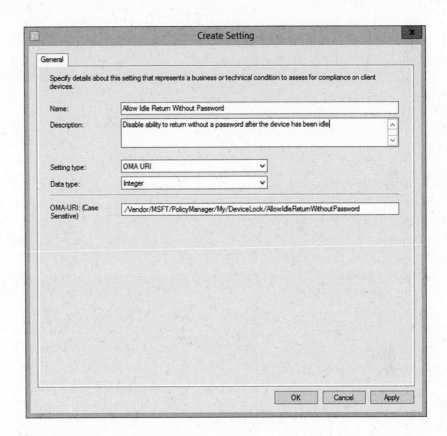

34. Supply a name and change Setting Type to OMA URI, change the data type, and add the OMA URI of the setting that needs to be managed. Click OK.

35. Search for the created custom setting and select it, as shown in Figure 18.44. For a complete list of OMA-URIs, visit

```
https://ref.ms/windows10csp
```

36. In the Create Rule dialog box, review the settings and add a value in the highlighted field in Figure 18.45.

37. Click OK and then Close.

FIGURE 18.44
Select your custom setting in the Browse Settings dialog box.

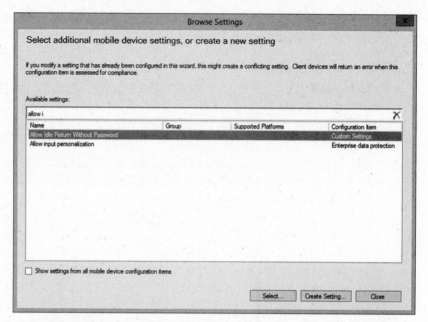

FIGURE 18.45
Create Rule dialog box

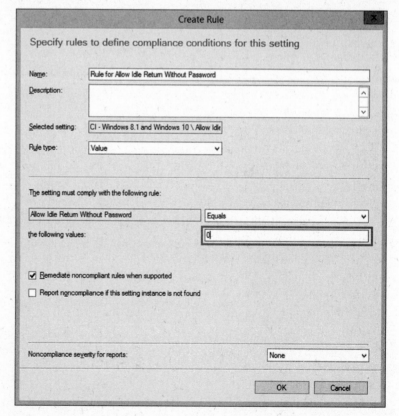

38. Click Next to configure the Windows Phone App Compliance list.

Windows Phone   Add apps by clicking Add and going to the Windows App Store (www.windowsphone.com/en-us/store/overview) in your browser. Search for an app, and then copy its URL and paste it in the Apps URL field of the Add App To The Blocked Apps List dialog box, as shown in Figure 18.46. Look up the name and publisher of the app and fill out the Name and Publisher fields.

FIGURE 18.46

Paste the app's URL from the App Store in the Apps URL field.

39. After adding more apps, click Next to configure the Windows 10 Team options.

40. You can configure Windows 10 Team devices like the Surface Hub, as shown in Figure 18.47.

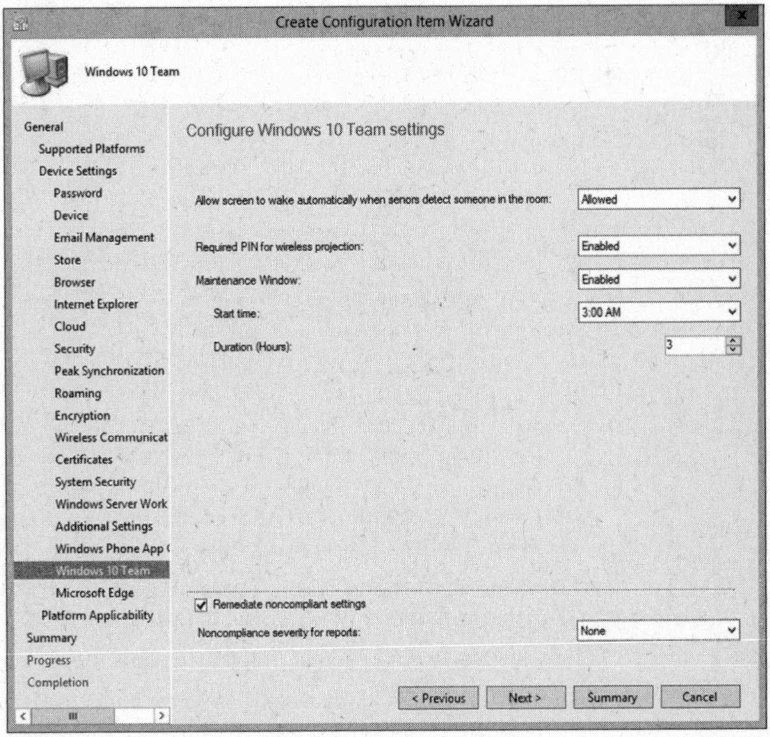

FIGURE 18.47

Create Configuration Item Wizard— Windows 10 Team page

Allow Screen To Wake Automatically When Sensors Detect Someone In The Room A device like a Surface Hub can be configured to wake up automatically when a sensor detects that someone is entering the room.

Require PIN For Wireless Projection When users try to connect to a device like a Surface Hub, you can require that they use a PIN before a wireless projection can be configured.

Maintenance Windows Surface Hub devices are based on Windows 10, so maintenance windows can be configured so that the Windows 10 installation can be kept up to date without disturbing users while presenting via the Surface Hub.

41. After configuring the Windows 10 Team settings, click Next to configure the Microsoft Edge settings shown in Figure 18.48.

FIGURE 18.48
Create Configuration
Item Wizard—
Microsoft Edge page

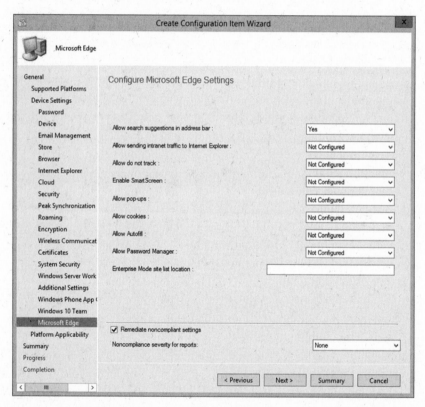

Allow Search Suggestions In Address Bar Allow the search engine to suggest sites while typing in the address bar of Edge.

Allow Sending Intranet Traffic To Internet Explorer Allow users to open Intranet sites in the Internet Explorer of Windows 10 Desktop.

Allow Do Not Track Allow or disallow Edge to track what websites the user visits.

Enable SmartScreen Enable or disable the SmartScreen browser setting on the devices.

Allow Pop-Ups   Enables or disables the pop-up blocker in the Edge browser.

Allow Cookies   Allow or disallow cookies in Edge.

Allow Autofill   Allow or do not allow users to change the autocomplete settings in the Edge browser.

Allow Password Manager   Enable or disable the Password Manager in the Edge browser.

Enterprise Mobile Site List Location   Administrators can configure a location where a list of websites is stored that use the Enterprise mode.

42. Click Next to review the exclusions of platforms for certain settings that are not applicable for the specified platform, as shown in Figure 18.49.

FIGURE 18.49
Create Configuration Item Wizard—Platform Applicability page

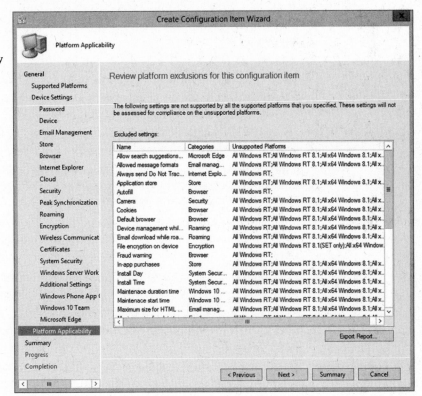

43. From here, complete the wizard to save the configuration item.

Defining the configuration item is not sufficient. Implementing the configuration item requires attaching it to a baseline and assigning that baseline to a collection. This is a general task for compliance setting management and is discussed in Chapter 13, "Compliance Settings."

WINDOWS PHONE

Next we'll look at the Windows Phone settings that can be managed through MDM.

1. Start creating the configuration item by selecting Compliance Settings ➢ Configuration Items.

2. Right-click Configuration Items and select Create Configuration Item.

3. On the General page of the Create Configuration Item Wizard, supply a name and description. Then specify that the configuration item be targeted for a mobile device and choose what platform you want to support, as shown in Figure 18.24 earlier. For this exercise, select Windows Phone.

4. Optionally, select any categories that should be used for this configuration item. Click Next.

5. On the Supported Platforms page, select all the platforms for which the policies apply and click Next.

6. On the Device Settings page, determine which settings should be managed by this configuration item. For the example, select all setting groups, and choose to configure additional settings. This will allow you to review all potential settings that might be enforced on a device. Click Next.

7. Configure the appropriate mobile device password options.The password settings are shown earlier in Figure 18.26. Password settings are not configured by default.

   Require Password Settings On Mobile Devices   This option allows administrators to determine whether password settings should be enforced. Assuming this option is enabled, a few specific password configurations are possible:

   ◆   Minimum Password Length (Characters): This option allows administrators to specify the minimum number of characters that should be supplied as part of the password.

   ◆   Password Expiration In Days: This option allows administrators to specify the number of days that are allowed to elapse before requiring a password change.

   ◆   Number Of Passwords Remembered: This option allows administrators to configure how many passwords are retained. This setting is useful to prevent the reuse of passwords.

   ◆   Number Of Failed Logon Attempts Before Device Is Wiped: This option allows administrators to specify how many incorrect passwords can be supplied before the device is automatically wiped.

   Idle Time Before Mobile Device Is Locked   This option, not enabled by default, allows administrators to control how long a device might be left unlocked when idle.

   Password Complexity   This option allows administrators to specify the required password complexity level, in this case allowing either a PIN or a strong password.

   Password Quality   This option allows you to configure how the password must be built—for instance, if it must be Numeric, Alphabetic, or Alphanumeric. You can also configure it as Required, Low Security Biometric, or Alphanumeric With Symbols.

Send Password Recovery PIN To Exchange Server This option allows administrators to configure where the password recovery PIN is stored on the Exchange server.

8. After all password options are configured, click Next.

9. Configure device settings for the device on the Device page, shown earlier in Figure 18.27. Note that not all configuration options may be applicable for the selected platforms; the configuration option will be disabled if it's not supported.

Voice Dialing Not applicable for Windows Phone.

Voice Assistant Not applicable for Windows Phone.

Voice Assistant While Locked Not applicable for Windows Phone.

Screen Capture This option allows administrators to define whether screen capture is enabled. It can be configured as Enabled or Disabled.

Video Chat Client Not applicable for Windows Phone.

Add Game Center Friends Not applicable for Windows Phone.

Multiplayer Gaming Not applicable for Windows Phone.

Personal Wallet Software While Locked Not applicable for Windows Phone.

Diagnostic Data Submission (Windows 8.1 And Earlier) This option allows administrators to define whether diagnostic data submission is enabled. It can be configured as Enabled or Disabled.

Diagnostic Data Submission (Windows 10) Not applicable for Windows Phone.

Geolocation This option allows administrators to enable or disable the geolocation option on devices. It can be configured as Enabled or Disabled.

Copy and Paste This option allows administrators to specify whether copy and paste of data in and between apps is allowed on devices. It can be configured as Enabled or Disabled.

Factory Reset Not applicable for Windows Phone.

Clipboard Share Between Applications Not applicable for Windows Phone.

Bluetooth This option allows administrators to allow or prohibit Bluetooth support on a mobile device. It can be configured as Allowed or Prohibited.

Bluetooth Discoverable Mode Not applicable for Windows Phone.

Bluetooth Advertising Not applicable for Windows Phone.

Video Recording Not applicable for Windows Phone.

10. Click Next to configure email options for the device in the Email Management settings, shown earlier in Figure 18.28.

POP And IMAP Email This option allows administrators to define whether POP and IMAP email are allowed. This is not an either/or setting; either both are allowed or both are prohibited.

Maximum Time To Keep Email This option allows administrators to specify how long email should be retained on the device.

Allowed Message Formats   This option allows administrators to specify the format allowed for email, either plain text only or both plain text and HTML. If this option is configured, up to two additional options become available for configuration.

Maximum Size For Plain Text Email (Automatically Downloaded)   This option allows administrators to define the size of a plain-text email that is allowed to be automatically downloaded to the device. Incremental sizes are configurable up to allowing the entire email to be downloaded.

Maximum Size For HTML Email (Automatically Downloaded)   This option allows administrators to define the size of an HTML email that is allowed to be automatically downloaded to the device. Incremental sizes are configurable up to allowing the entire email to be downloaded.

Maximum Size Of An Attachment (Automatically Downloaded)   This option allows administrators to define the size of an attachment that is allowed to be automatically downloaded to the device. Incremental sizes are configurable up to allowing the entire attachment to be downloaded.

Calendar Synchronization   This option allows administrators to specify whether calendar synchronization to the device is allowed.

Custom Email Account   This option allows administrators to allow custom email accounts. It can be configured as Allowed or Prohibited.

Make Microsoft Account Optional In Windows Mail App   This option allows administrators to make the Microsoft account optional in the Windows Mail app on the device. It can be configured as Yes or No.

11. After all email options are configured, click Next.

12. Configure the store settings, shown earlier in Figure 18.29.

Application Store   This option allows administrators to specify whether accessing and using the application store of the device is allowed.

Enter A Password To Access The Application Store   This option allows administrators to specify whether a user must enter a password when accessing an application store.

In-App Purchases   This option allows administrators to specify whether in-app purchases are allowed.

13. After configuring the application store settings, click Next.

14. Configure the browser settings, shown earlier in Figure 18.30.

Allow Web Browser   Configure whether a user is allowed to use a web browser.

Autofill   Configure whether the browser is allowed to use autofill.

Active Scripting   Configure whether the browser is allowed to use active scripting.

Plug-ins   Configure whether the browser is allowed to use plug-ins.

Pop-up Blocker   Configure whether the browser is allowed to use the pop-up blocker.

Cookies   Configure whether the browser is allowed to accept cookies from visited sites.

Fraud Warning   Configure whether fraud warnings in the browser are enabled.

15. After configuring the browser settings, click Next.

16. For the Windows-based mobile devices, you can configure Internet Explorer settings, as shown earlier in Figure 18.31.

Always Send Do Not Track Header   Configure whether the Always Send Do Not Track Header option can be enabled.

Intranet Security Zone   Configure whether the intranet security zone settings can be changed.

Security Level For Internet Zone   Configure whether the security level for the Internet zone can be changed.

Security Level For Intranet Zone   Configure whether the security level for the intranet zone can be changed.

Security Level For Trusted Sites Zone   Configure whether the security level for the trusted sites zone can be changed.

Security Level For Restricted Sites Zone   Configure whether the security level for the restricted sites zone can be changed.

Namespaces For Intranet Zone   Preconfigure the namespaces for your intranet zone or enforce that websites be removed from the intranet zone.

Go To Intranet Site For Single Word Entry   Configure whether a user is redirected to an intranet when supplying a single word.

Enterprise Mode Menu Option   Enable or disable the Enterprise Mode menu option in the Internet Explorer browser. After enabling it, you are able to configure the Logging Report Location URL.

Enterprise Mode Site List Location   Administrators are able to configure the Enterprise Mode Site List Location URL for this policy.

17. Click Next to configure the cloud settings, as shown in Figure 18.32 earlier.

Cloud Backup   Not applicable for Windows Phone.

Encrypted Backup   Not applicable for Windows Phone.

Document Synchronization   Not applicable for Windows Phone.

Photo Synchronization   Not applicable for Windows Phone.

Settings Synchronization   Configure whether settings on the mobile devices may be synchronized to a cloud service like SkyDrive or iCloud on the Internet.

Credentials Synchronization   Configure whether credentials on the mobile devices may be synchronized to a cloud service like SkyDrive or iCloud on the Internet.

Microsoft Account   Administrators are able to allow or disallow the usage of a Microsoft account on the device.

Settings Synchronization Over Metered Connections   Configure whether synchronizations over metered connections are allowed.

Google Backup   Not applicable for Windows Phone.

Google Account Auto Sync   Not applicable for Windows Phone.

18. Configure the security options for the device. The security management settings are shown in Figure 18.33 earlier.

Unsigned File Installation   This option lets administrators specify whether the installation of unsigned files is allowed. If they are allowed, administrators then choose what parties are given this right. Available options are Mobile Operator, Manager, User Authenticated, IT Administrator, User Unauthenticated, and Trusted Provisioning Server.

Unsigned Applications   This option lets administrators specify whether the installation of unsigned applications is allowed or prohibited.

SMS And MMS Messaging   This option lets administrators configure whether SMS and MMS messaging are allowed or prohibited on the device.

Removable Storage   This option lets administrators configure whether removable storage is allowed or prohibited on the device.

Camera   This option lets administrators configure whether use of the camera is allowed or prohibited on the device.

Near Field Communication (NFC)   This option lets administrators configure whether Bluetooth is allowed or prohibited on the device.

YouTube   Not applicable for Windows Phone.

Power Off   Not applicable for Windows Phone.

Anti Theft Mode   Not applicable for Windows Phone.

Windows RT VPN Profile   Not applicable for Windows Phone.

19. After all security options are configured, click Next.

20. Configure the synchronization options for the device in the Peak Synchronization settings, shown earlier in Figure 18.34.

Specify Peak Time   This option allows administrators to define the specific time considered to be peak on devices.

Peak Synchronization Frequency   This option allows administrators to specify how often the device will synchronize during the defined peak time.

Off-Peak Synchronization Frequency   This option allows administrators to specify how often the device will synchronize outside the defined peak time.

21. After all peak synchronization options are configured, click Next.

22. Configure the roaming options for the device in the Roaming settings, shown earlier in Figure 18.35.

MDM While Roaming   This option allows administrators to configure whether a device should be actively managed when roaming.

Software Download While Roaming   This option lets administrators specify whether software downloads should be allowed when a device is roaming.

Email Download While Roaming   This option allows administrators to control whether email is downloaded while a device is roaming.

Voice Roaming   Not applicable for Windows Phone.

Automatic Synchronization While Roaming   Not applicable for Windows Phone.

Data Roaming   This option lets administrators control whether data usage is allowed while a device is roaming.

23. After all the roaming options are configured, click Next.

24. Configure the encryption options for devices in the Encryption settings, shown earlier in Figure 18.36.

Storage Card Encryption   This option allows administrators to specify whether encryption is on or off for a device's storage card.

File Encryption On Mobile Device   This option allows administrators to configure whether file encryption is on or off for a device.

Require Email Signing/Signing Algorithm   This option allows administrators to specify whether email signing is enabled or disabled. If email signing is enabled, the Signing Algorithm option allows administrators to specify whether SHA, MD5, or the default signing algorithm should be used.

Require Email Encryption/Encryption Algorithm   This option allows administrators to configure whether email encryption is on or off for a device. If email encryption is enabled, the Encryption Algorithm option allows administrators to specify which encryption algorithm should be used. Available choices are Triple DES, DES, RC2 128-bit, RC2 64-bit, RC2 40-bit, and the default algorithm.

25. After all encryption options are configured, click Next.

26. Configure the wireless communication options for devices in the Wireless Communication settings, shown earlier in Figure 18.37.

27. Configure whether wireless network connections are allowed or prohibited on the device.

Wireless Network Connection   This option allows administrators to specify whether encryption is on or off for a device's storage card.

Wi-Fi Tethering   This option lets administrators specify whether to allow users to use their device as a mobile hotspot.

Offload Data To Wi-Fi When Possible   This option lets administrators allow users to use their Wi-Fi connection on the device when possible.

Wi-Fi Hotspot Reporting   This option allows administrators to control whether Wi-Fi hotspots are reported.

Manual Wi-Fi Configuration   Not applicable for Windows Phone.

If Wireless Network Connections are allowed, administrators can click the Add button to specify one or more networks and the associated network configuration. Available network configuration options include Proxy, 802.1X, Authentication, Data Encryption, and more. A blank Wireless Network Connection configuration page is shown in Figure 18.38 earlier in this chapter.

28. After all wireless network connection options are configured, click Next.

29. Configure the certificate options for devices in the Certificates settings, shown earlier in Figure 18.39.

The Certificates To Install On Mobile Devices option allows administrators to specify certificates that should be installed on mobile devices. Clicking the Import button brings up the Import Certificate dialog box, shown in Figure 18.40 earlier, which allows certificates to be imported from the filesystem and allows administrators to specify in which certificate store the certificate should be placed on the device.

30. After all certificate options are configured, click Next.

31. Configure extra security settings on the System Security page, shown earlier in Figure 18.41.

User To Accept Untrusted TLS Certificates   Not applicable for Windows Phone.

Allow Activation Lock (Supervised Mode Only)   Not applicable for Windows Phone.

User Access Control   This option allows administrators to configure how User Access Control is enabled and how it notifies them of changes to the operating system of a device.

Network Firewall   This option allows administrators to configure whether the firewall is required.

Updates (Windows 8.1 And Earlier)   This option allows administrators to configure whether updates are installed automatically.

Minimum Classification Of Updates   Administrators are allowed to configure the minimum classifications of the updates that will be downloaded to Windows computers. Options are None, Important, or Recommended.

Updates (Windows 10)   Not applicable for Windows Phone.

SmartScreen   This option allows administrators to configure whether SmartScreen in Internet Explorer is enabled.

Virus Protection   This option allows administrators to configure whether virus protection is required for a device.

Virus Protection Signatures Are Up To Date   This option allows administrators to configure whether up-to-date virus protection signatures are required.

Lock Screen Control Center   Not applicable for Windows Phone.

Lock Screen Notification View   Not applicable for Windows Phone.

Lock Screen Today Screen   Not applicable for Windows Phone.

Fingerprint For Unlocking   Not applicable for Windows Phone.

Pre-release Features   Not applicable for Windows Phone.

Manual Root Certificate Installation   Not applicable for Windows Phone.

32. Click Next to configure the Windows Server Work Folder settings, as shown earlier in Figure 18.42 (Windows Phone only).

33. Click Next to configure the Windows Phone, iOS, or Mac OS X App Compliance list.

Windows Phone 8.1   Add apps by clicking Add and going to the Windows App Store (www.windowsphone.com/en-us/store/overview) in your browser. Search for an app, and then copy its URL and paste it in the Apps URL field of the Add App To The Blocked Apps List dialog box, as shown in Figure 18.46 earlier. Look up the name and publisher of the app and fill out the Name and Publisher fields.

34. After adding more apps, click Next to configure the Windows 10 Team options.

> ### UNBLOCK THE COMPANY PORTAL WHEN USING WINDOWS PHONE 8.1
>
> If you define a list of allowed applications for Windows Phone 8.1 devices, the Company Portal app also needs to be added to this list, or else it will be blocked.

35. Click Next to review the exclusions of platforms for certain settings that are not applicable for the specified platform (see Figure 18.49 earlier).

36. From here, complete the wizard to save the configuration item and deploy it via a baseline.

iOS AND MAC OS X

Next we'll look at the iOS and Mac OS X settings that can be managed through MDM.

1. Start creating the configuration item by selecting Compliance Settings ➤ Configuration Items.

2. Right-click Configuration Items and select Create Configuration Item.

3. On the General page of the Create Configuration Item Wizard, supply a name and description and then specify that the configuration item is targeted for a mobile device and choose what platform you want to support (see Figure 18.24 earlier). Select iOS and Mac OS X.

4. Optionally, select any categories that should be used for this configuration item. Click Next.

5. On the Supported Platforms page, select all the platforms for which the policies apply and click Next.

6. On the Device Settings page, determine which settings should be managed by this configuration item.

For the example, select all settings groups and choose to configure additional settings, as shown in Figure 18.25. This will allow you to review all potential settings that might be enforced on a device. Click Next.

7. Configure the appropriate mobile device password options. Password settings (Figure 18.26 earlier) are not configured by default.

Require Password Settings On Mobile Devices   This option allows administrators to determine whether password settings should be enforced. Assuming this option is enabled, a few specific password configurations are possible:

◆ Minimum Password Length (Characters): This option allows administrators to specify the minimum number of characters that should be supplied as part of the password.

◆ Password Expiration In Days: This option lets administrators specify the number of days that are allowed to elapse before requiring a password change.

◆ Number Of Passwords Remembered: This option allows administrators to config-ure how many passwords are retained. This setting is useful to prevent the reuse of passwords.

◆ Number Of Failed Logon Attempts Before Device Is Wiped: This option allows administrators to specify how many incorrect passwords can be supplied before the device is automatically wiped.

Idle Time Before Mobile Device Is Locked   This option, not enabled by default, gives administrators control over how long a device might be left unlocked when idle.

Password Complexity   This option allows administrators to specify the required pass-word complexity level, in this case specifying either a PIN or a strong password.

Password Quality   This option allows you to configure how the password must be built, for instance, if it must be Numeric, Alphabetic, or Alphanumeric. You can also configure it as Required, Low Security Biometric, or Alphanumeric With Symbols.

Send Password Recovery PIN To Exchange Server   This option allows administrators to configure where the password recovery PIN is stored on the Exchange server.

8. After all password options are configured, click Next.

9. Configure device settings for the device on the Device page (Figure 18.27 earlier). Note that not all configuration options may be applicable for the selected platforms; the con-figuration option will be disabled if not supported.

Voice Dialing   This option lets administrators define whether voice dialing is allowed. It can be configured as Allowed or Prohibited.

Voice Assistant   This option lets administrators define whether the Voice Assistant is allowed. It can be configured as Allowed or Prohibited.

Voice Assistant While Locked   This option lets administrators define whether the Voice Assistant is allowed while locked. It can be configured as Allowed or Prohibited.

Screen Capture   This option allows administrators to define whether screen capture is enabled. It can be configured as Enabled or Disabled.

Video Chat Client   This option allows administrators to define whether the video chat client is enabled. It can be configured as Enabled or Disabled.

Add Game Center Friends   This option allows administrators to define whether adding game center friends is allowed. It can be configured as Allowed or Prohibited.

Multiplayer Gaming   This option allows administrators to define whether multiplayer gaming is allowed. It can be configured as Allowed or Prohibited.

Personal Wallet Software While Locked   This option lets administrators define wheth-er personal wallet software is allowed while locked. It can be configured as Allowed or Prohibited.

Diagnostic Data Submission (Windows 8.1 And Earlier)   This option allows adminis-trators to define whether diagnostic data submission is enabled. It can be configured as Enabled or Disabled.

Diagnostic Data Submission (Windows 10)   Not applicable for iOS or Mac OS X.

Geolocation   Not applicable for iOS or Mac OS X.

Copy And Paste   Not applicable for iOS or Mac OS X.

Factory Reset   Not applicable for iOS or Mac OS X.

Clipboard Share Between Applications   Not applicable for iOS or Mac OS X.

Bluetooth   Not applicable for iOS or Mac OS X.

Bluetooth Discoverable Mode   Not applicable for iOS or Mac OS X.

Bluetooth Advertising   Not applicable for iOS or Mac OS X.

Video Recording   Not applicable for iOS or Mac OS X.

10. After configuring the device settings, click Next.

11. Configure the store settings (Figure 18.29 earlier).

Application Store   This option lets administrators specify whether accessing and using the application store of the device is allowed.

Enter A Password To Access The Application Store   This option lets administrators specify whether a user must enter a password when accessing an application store.

In-App Purchases   This option lets administrators specify whether in-app purchases are allowed.

12. After configuring the application store settings, click Next.

13. Configure the browser settings (Figure 18.29 earlier).

Allow Web Browser   Configure if a user is allowed to use a web browser.

Autofill   Configure if the browser is allowed to use autofill.

Active Scripting   Configure if the browser is allowed to use active scripting.

Plug-ins   Configure if the browser is allowed to use plug-ins.

Pop-up Blocker   Configure if the browser is allowed to use the pop-up blocker.

Cookies   Configure if the browser is allowed to accept cookies from visited sites.

Fraud Warning   Configure if fraud warnings in the browser are enabled.

14. After configuring the browser settings, click Next.

15. Click Next to configure the Content Rating settings, as shown in Figure 18.50. Content ratings apply to iOS devices only.

Explicit Content In Media Store   Configure if iOS devices can be restricted to explicit media content in the Apple store.

Ratings Region   Configure from which region the content can be acquired. The following regions can be configured: the United States, Australia, Canada, Germany, France, Ireland, Japan, New Zealand, and the United Kingdom.

Movie Rating   Specify the ratings that movies downloaded from the Apple Store can have. Options are Don't Allow, G, PG, M, MA15+, R18+, and Allow All.

TV Show Rating   Specify the ratings that TV shows downloaded from the Apple Store can have. Options are Don't Allow, P, C, G, PG, M, MA15+, AV15+, and Allow All.

App Rating   Specify the ratings that apps downloaded from the Apple Store can have. Options are Don't Allow, 4+, 9+, 12+, 17+, and Allow All.

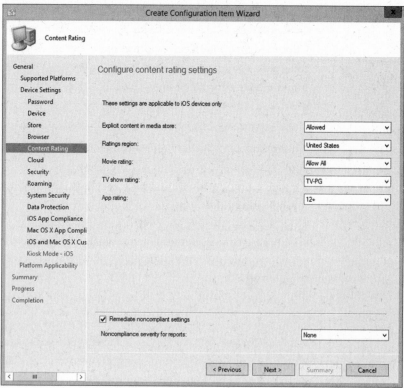

16. Click Next to configure the cloud settings (Figure 18.32 earlier).

Cloud Backup   Configure whether the mobile device can back up the device to a cloud backup service.

Encrypted Backup   Configure whether a backup of device can be encrypted.

Document Synchronization   Configure whether documents on the mobile devices may be synchronized to a cloud service like SkyDrive or iCloud on the Internet.

Photo Synchronization   Configure whether photos on the mobile devices may be synchronized to a cloud service like SkyDrive or iCloud on the Internet.

Settings Synchronization   Not applicable for iOS or Mac OS X.

Credentials Synchronization   Not applicable for iOS or Mac OS X.

Microsoft Account   Not applicable for iOS or Mac OS X.

Settings Synchronization Over Metered Connections   Not applicable for iOS or Mac OS X.

Google Backup   Not applicable for iOS or Mac OS X.

Google Account Auto Sync   Not applicable for iOS or Mac OS X.

17. Configure the security options for the device (Figure 18.33 earlier).

Unsigned File Installation   Not applicable for iOS or Mac OS X.

Unsigned Applications   Not applicable for iOS or Mac OS X.

SMS And MMS Messaging   Not applicable for iOS or Mac OS X.

Removable Storage   Not applicable for iOS or Mac OS X.

Camera   This option allows administrators to configure whether use of the camera is allowed or prohibited on the device.

Near Field Communication (NFC)   Not applicable for iOS or Mac OS X.

YouTube   Not applicable for iOS or Mac OS X.

Power Off   Not applicable for iOS or Mac OS X.

Anti Theft Mode   Not applicable for iOS or Mac OS X.

Windows RT VPN Profile   Not applicable for iOS or Mac OS X.

18. After all security options are configured, click Next.

19. Configure the roaming options for the device in the Roaming settings (Figure 18.35 earlier).

MDM While Roaming   Not applicable for iOS or Mac OS X.

Software Download While Roaming   Not applicable for iOS or Mac OS X.

Email Download While Roaming   Not applicable for iOS or Mac OS X.

Voice Roaming   This option lets administrators control whether voice roaming is allowed.

Automatic Synchronization While Roaming   This option gives administrators control over whether automatic synchronization is allowed while a device is roaming.

Data Roaming   This option allows administrators to control whether data usage is allowed while a device is roaming.

20. After all the roaming options are configured, click Next.

21. Configure extra security settings on the System Security page (Figure 18.41 earlier). This system security will apply to Windows-based devices.

User To Accept Untrusted TLS Certificates   This option allows administrators to configure whether a user is allowed to accept untrusted TLS certificates.

Allow Activation Lock (supervised mode only)   This option allows administrators to configure whether a device can be locked for activation; this way, a device is not bound to a specific or personal Apple ID. When iOS is used for company-owned devices, it can be a painful process when a user leaves the company and does not reset their device. You need to call Apple Support and prove that you are the owner of the device to be able to activate the device again.

User Access Control   Not applicable for iOS or Mac OS X.

Network Firewall   Not applicable for iOS or Mac OS X.

Updates (Windows 8.1 And Earlier)   Not applicable for iOS or Mac OS X.

Minimum Classification Of Updates   Not applicable for iOS or Mac OS X.

Updates (Windows 10)   Not applicable for iOS or Mac OS X.

SmartScreen   Not applicable for iOS or Mac OS X.

Virus Protection   Not applicable for iOS or Mac OS X.

Virus Protection Signatures Are Up To Date   Not applicable for iOS or Mac OS X.

Lock Screen Control Center   This option allows administrators to configure whether the Control Center app can be accessed when a device is locked.

Lock Screen Notification View   This option allows administrators to configure whether the notifications can be viewed when a device is locked.

Lock Screen Today Screen   This option allows administrators to configure whether the Today Screen app can be accessed when a device is locked.

Fingerprint For Unlocking   This option allows administrators to configure whether the fingerprint sensor can be used to unlock the device.

Pre-release Features   Not applicable for iOS or Mac OS X.

Manual Root Certificate Installation   Not applicable for iOS or Mac OS X.

22. Click Next to specify Data Protection settings when configuring a configuration item for iOS and Mac OS X, as shown in Figure 18.51.

FIGURE 18.51
Create Configuration Item Wizard—Data Protection

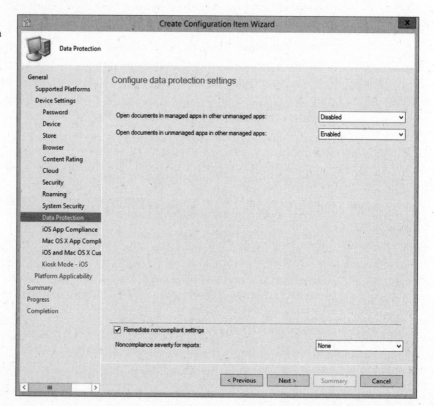

Open Documents In Managed Apps In Other Unmanaged Apps   This option allows administrators to specify whether corporate documents can be viewed in any app, also unmanaged apps.

Open Documents In Unmanaged Apps In Other Managed Apps   This option allows administrators to specify whether documents can be viewed in managed apps.

23. Click Next to configure the iOS or Mac OS X App Compliance list.

iOS   Add apps by clicking Add and going to the iTunes App Store (http://itunes.apple.com). Search for an app, and then copy its URL and paste it in the Add App To The Noncompliant Apps list. Look up the name and publisher of the app and fill out the Name and Publisher fields.

Mac OS X   Add apps by clicking Add to open the dialog box shown in Figure 18.52. Read the following article on Microsoft Docs to learn how to gather the Bundle ID.

https://docs.microsoft.com/en-us/intune/deploy-use/mac-os-x-policy-settings-in-microsoft-intune

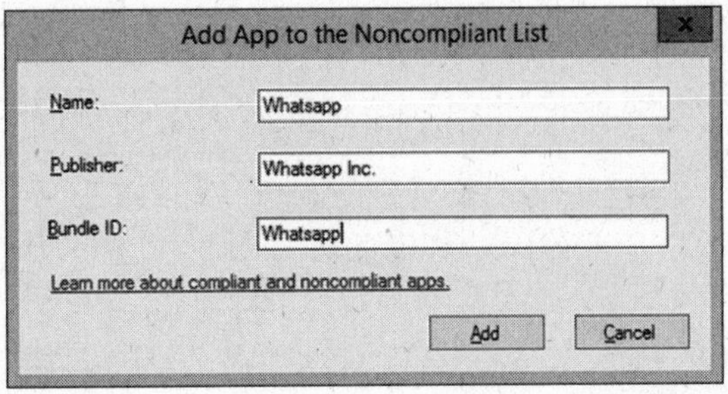

FIGURE 18.52
Add App To The Non-compliant List dialog box

24. Click Next to configure Custom Profiles for iOS and Mac OS X. Supply a name and import a .mobileconfig file (Figure 18.53) and click Next.

Learn how to create a .mobileconfig file with the Apple Configurator here:

www.howtogeek.com/216137/create-a-configuration-profile-to-simplify-vpn-setup-on-iphones-and-ipads/

With the Apple Configurator you are able to configure hundreds of settings that are not exposed in Configuration Manager yet.

25. Click Next to configure the Kiosk mode settings for iOS devices, as shown in Figure 18.54. With Kiosk mode in iOS, you are able to lock down the iOS device in such a way that, for instance, only one application can be used. Click Browse to get the App ID of a managed app located in Configuration Manager or click Get ID to get the App ID from a store app.

Touch   Allow or disallow touch for a device in Kiosk mode.

Screen Rotation   Allow or disallow screen rotation for a device in Kiosk mode.

FIGURE 18.53
Create Configuration
Item Wizard—
Configure iOS And Mac
OS X Custom Profile
Settings page

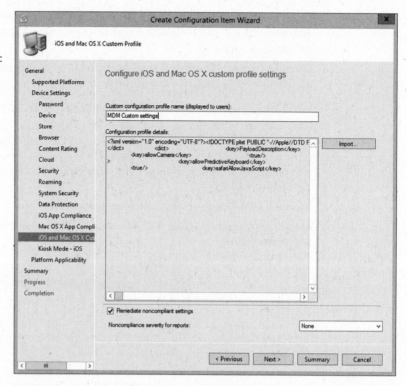

FIGURE 18.54
Create Configuration
Item Wizard—
Configure Kiosk Mode
Settings For iOS
Devices

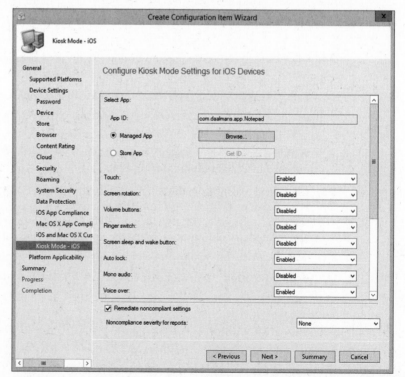

Volume Buttons Allow or disallow the use of the volume buttons for a device in Kiosk mode.

Ringer Switch Allow or disallow the ringer switch for a device in Kiosk mode.

Screen Sleep And Wake Button Allow or disallow the screen sleep and wake button for a device in Kiosk mode.

Auto Lock Allow or disallow auto lock for a device in Kiosk mode.

Mono Audio Allow or disallow mono audio for a device in Kiosk mode.

Voice Over Allow or disallow voiceover and voiceover adjustments for a device in Kiosk mode.

Zoom Allow or disallow zoom and zoom adjustments for a device in Kiosk mode.

Invert Colors Allow or disallow invert colors and invert colors adjustments for a device in Kiosk mode.

Assistive Touch Allow or disallow assistive touch and assistive touch adjustments for a device in Kiosk mode.

Speech Selection Allow or disallow speech selection for a device in Kiosk mode.

26. Click Next to review the exclusions of platforms for certain settings that are not applicable for the specified platform (Figure 18.49) earlier.

27. From here, complete the wizard to save the configuration item and deploy it via a configuration baseline.

ANDROID AND SAMSUNG KNOX

Let's take a look at the Android and Samsung Knox settings that can be managed through MDM.

1. Start creating the configuration item by selecting Compliance Settings ➤ Configuration Items.

2. Right-click Configuration Items and select Create Configuration Item.

3. On the General page of the Create Configuration Item Wizard, supply a name and description. Then specify that the configuration item is targeted for a mobile device and choose what platform you want to support (Figure 18.24 earlier). Select Android and Samsung Knox.

4. Optionally, select any categories that should be used for this configuration item. Click Next.

5. On the Supported Platforms page, select all the platforms for which the policies apply and click Next.

6. On the Device Settings page, determine which settings should be managed by this configuration item.

   For this example, select all settings categories, except Enterprise Data Protection, and choose to configure additional settings (Figure 18.25 earlier). This will allow you to review all potential settings that might be enforced on a device. Click Next.

7. Configure the appropriate mobile device password options (Figure 18.26).

Password settings are not configured by default.

Require Password Settings On Mobile Devices   This option allows administrators to determine whether password settings should be enforced. Assuming this option is enabled, a few specific password configurations are possible:

♦   Minimum Password Length (Characters): This option allows administrators to specify the minimum number of characters that should be supplied as part of the password.

♦   Password Expiration In Days: This option allows administrators to specify the number of days that are allowed to elapse before requiring a password change.

♦   Number Of Passwords Remembered: This option allows administrators to configure how many passwords are retained. This setting is useful to prevent the reuse of passwords.

♦   Number Of Failed Logon Attempts Before Device Is Wiped: This option allows administrators to specify how many incorrect passwords can be supplied before the device is automatically wiped.

Idle Time Before Mobile Device Is Locked   This option, not enabled by default, gives administrators control over how long a device might be left unlocked when idle.

Password Complexity   This option lets administrators specify the required password complexity level, in this case allowing either a PIN or a strong password.

Password Quality   This option allows you to configure how the password must be built, for instance, if it must be Numeric, Alphabetic, or Alphanumeric. You can also configure it as Required, Low Security Biometric, or Alphanumeric With Symbols.

Send Password Recovery PIN To Exchange Server   This option allows administrators to configure where the password recovery PIN is stored on the Exchange server.

8. After all password options are configured, click Next.

9. Configure device settings for the device on the Device page (Figure 18.27 earlier). Note that not all configuration options may be applicable for the selected platforms; the configuration option will be disabled if not supported.

Voice Dialing   Not applicable for Android and Samsung Knox.

Voice Assistant   Not applicable for Android and Samsung Knox.

Voice Assistant While Locked   Not applicable for Android and Samsung Knox.

Screen Capture   Not applicable for Android and Samsung Knox.

Video Chat Client   Not applicable for Android and Samsung Knox.

Add Game Center Friends   Not applicable for Android and Samsung Knox.

Multiplayer Gaming   Not applicable for Android and Samsung Knox.

Personal Wallet Software While Locked   Not applicable for Android and Samsung Knox.

Diagnostic Data Submission (Windows 8.1 And Earlier)   Not applicable for Android and Samsung Knox.

Diagnostic Data Submission (Windows 10)   Not applicable for Android and Samsung Knox.

Geolocation   Not applicable for Android and Samsung Knox.

Copy And Paste   Not applicable for Android and Samsung Knox.

Factory Reset   This option lets administrators allow users to factory-reset their mobile device. It can be configured as Enabled or Disabled.

Clipboard Share Between Applications   This option allows administrators to prohibit or allow clipboard sharing between applications on a mobile device. Normally copied content is shared via the clipboard. It can be configured as Enabled or Disabled.

Bluetooth   Not applicable for Android and Samsung Knox.

Bluetooth Discoverable Mode   Not applicable for Android and Samsung Knox.

Bluetooth Advertising   Not applicable for Android and Samsung Knox.

Video Recording   Not applicable for Android and Samsung Knox.

10. Click Next to configure the cloud settings (Figure 18.32 earlier).

Cloud Backup   Not applicable for Android and Samsung Knox.

Encrypted Backup   Not applicable for Android and Samsung Knox.

Document Synchronization   Not applicable for Android and Samsung Knox.

Photo Synchronization   Not applicable for Android and Samsung Knox.

Settings Synchronization   Not applicable for Android and Samsung Knox.

Credentials Synchronization   Not applicable for Android and Samsung Knox.

Microsoft Account   Not applicable for Android and Samsung Knox.

Settings Synchronization Over Metered Connections   Not applicable for Android and Samsung Knox.

Google Backup   Allow administrators to block or allow Google Backup on Android devices.

Google Account Auto Sync   Allow administrators to block or allow automatic synchronization of Google account settings between devices.

11. Configure the security options for the device (Figure 18.33 earlier).

Unsigned File Installation   Not applicable for Android and Samsung Knox.

Unsigned Applications   Not applicable for Android and Samsung Knox.

SMS And MMS Messaging   Not applicable for Android and Samsung Knox.

Removable Storage   Not applicable for Android and Samsung Knox.

Camera   This option allows administrators to configure whether use of the camera is allowed or prohibited on the device.

Near Field Communication (NFC) Not applicable for Android and Samsung Knox.

YouTube This option allows administrators to configure whether the YouTube app is allowed or prohibited on the device.

Power Off This option allows administrators to configure whether the device can be powered off.

Anti Theft Mode Not applicable for Android and Samsung Knox.

Windows RT VPN Profile Not applicable for Android and Samsung Knox.

12. After all security options are configured, click Next.

13. Configure the encryption options for devices in the Encryption settings (Figure 18.36 earlier).

    Storage Card Encryption Not applicable for Android and Samsung Knox.

    File Encryption On Mobile Device This option allows administrators to configure whether file encryption is on or off for a device.

    Require Email Signing/Signing Algorithm Not applicable for Android and Samsung Knox.

    Require Email Encryption/Encryption Algorithm Not applicable for Android and Samsung Knox.

14. After all encryption options are configured, click Next to configure the Android App Compliance list

    Android Add apps by clicking Add and going to the Google Play Store (https://play.google.com) in your browser. Search for an app, and then copy its URL and paste it in the Add App To The Noncompliant Apps list. Look up the name and publisher of the app and fill out the Name and Publisher fields.

15. After adding more apps, click Next to configure for Android (Samsung Knox) devices the Kiosk mode settings shown in Figure 18.55. With Kiosk mode in Android Knox, you are able to lock down the Android device in such a way that, for instance, only one application can be used. Click Browse to get the App ID of a managed app located in Configuration Manager.

    Volume Buttons Allow or disallow the usage of the volume buttons for a device in Kiosk mode.

    Screen Sleep And Wake Button Allow or disallow the screen sleep and wake button for a device in Kiosk mode.

16. Click Next to review the exclusions of platforms for certain settings that are not applicable for the specified platform (Figure 18.49 earlier).

17. From here, complete the wizard to save the configuration item.

FIGURE 18.55
Create Configuration
Item Wizard—Kiosk
Mode – Samsung Knox
page

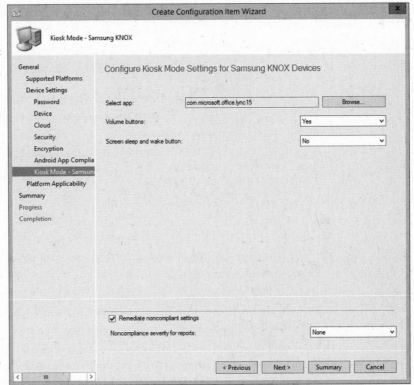

Deploying Resources

Now that we have looked at the configuration settings, let's examine the profiles that can be managed from Configuration Manager Current Branch. You can use Configuration Manager to configure certificate, VPN, and Wi-Fi profiles for devices that are managed via Configuration Manager Current Branch.

1. Start configuring the configuration item by selecting Compliance Settings ➢ Company Resource Access.

2. Click Certificate Profiles ➢ Create Certificate Profile in the Home tab of the ribbon.

3. Supply a name and specify the type of certificate profile that you want to create. This allows you to deploy a trusted CA certificate or use the Simple Certificate Enrollment Protocol (SCEP) settings. Before you can create a profile for a SCEP, you need to first add a Trusted CA certificate. Select the option Trusted CA Certificate and click Next.

4. Select a CA certificate file by clicking Import, and select the destination store before clicking Next, as shown in Figure 18.56. The certificate thumbprint will be imported from the certificate file and displayed.

FIGURE 18.56
Create Certificate
Profile Wizard—
Trusted CA Certificate
page

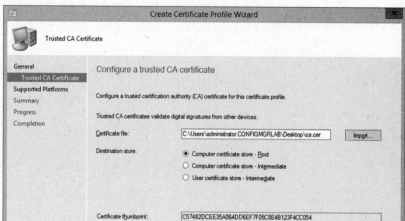

5. Click Next and select the platforms (Windows 8.1, Windows 10, Windows Phone, iPhone, iPad, Mac OS X, and/or Android) that will be provisioned with this new certificate profile. Click Next.

6. Review the Summary page and click Next. Click Close when the certificate profile is created successfully.

7. After the Trusted Root CA certificate profile has been created, you can create a SCEP certificate profile. In a new Create Certificate Profile Wizard, select the option Simple Certificate Enrollment Protocol (SCEP) settings and click Next.

8. Configure the SCEP server URLs or leave the default option Automatically Assign NDES Server URL From Certificate Registration Point Intact and click Next.

9. Configure the SCEP certificate enrollment parameters as shown in Figure 18.57, and click Next.

   Retries/Retry Delay (Minutes)/Renewal Threshold (%)   Configure how often an enrollment retry may take place, with the number of minutes between retries.

   Key Storage Provider (KSP)   This option allows administrators to configure whether to install to Software Key Storage Provider, Passport for Work, Trusted Platform Module (TPM) if present, or fail if TPM is not available.

   Devices For Certificate Enrollment   This option allows administrators to configure whether the certificate is enrolled by the user on any device or only on the user's primary device.

10. The next step is to configure the certificate properties, as shown in Figure 18.58.

Certificate Template Name   Supply a certificate template name by clicking the Browse button. Select the issuing certificate authority (CA) and the certificate template name before clicking OK.

Certificate Type   Define whether the certificate is a User or a Device certificate.

Subject Name Format   Depending on whether the certificate is a User or a Device certificate, you can supply different name formats. If it is a User certificate, you can enable the Include Email Address In Subject Name option.

Subject Alternative Name   Depending on whether the certificate is a User or a Device certificate, you can add subject alternative names to the certificate. Alternative names can be an email address, user principal name (UPN), DNS name, or service principal name (SPN).

Certificate Validity Period   Configure the validity period of the certificate in days, months, or years, depending on the configured certificate template.

Key Usage   If not grayed out (depending on the certificate template), you can enable Key Encipherment and Digital Signature.

Key Size (Bits)   If not grayed out (depending on the certificate template), you can configure the key size of the certificates.

Extended Key Usage   If not grayed out (depending on the certificate template), you can select the extended key usage options. If grayed out, you will see the options available in the certificate template.

Hash Algorithm   Select the SHA-1, SHA-2, or SHA3 hash algorithms that are going to be used.

Root CA Certificate   Select the Trusted Root CA certificate profile you created earlier and click OK.

11. Click Next, and select the platforms that will be provisioned with this new certificate profile. Click Next.

12. Review the Summary page, and click Next. Click Close when the SCEP certificate profile is created successfully.

You can deploy the certificate profiles to your test collections before rolling out the profiles to a broader range of mobile devices. For more information about NDES, visit

```
https://docs.microsoft.com/en-us/sccm/protect/deploy-use/create-certificate-profiles
```

As mentioned earlier, besides certificate profiles, you can use Configuration Manager to create and deploy VPN profiles. To create a VPN profile, follow these steps:

1. Start configuring the configuration item by selecting Compliance Settings ➢ Company Resource Access.

2. Click VPN Profiles and choose Create VPN Profile in the Home tab of the ribbon. Supply a name and click Next, creating a VPN for any supported operating system. You can also import an existing VPN profile from a file or to create a VPN for Windows 10 and mobile devices (MDM only), but in this example we will create a new PPTP profile.

3. As you can see in Figure 18.59, all major VPN brands are supported; the options on the Connection page will differ per brand. In this case, choose PPTP, and then supply a server list (with the VPN server friendly names and IP addresses), decide whether all network traffic must be sent through the VPN connection, and supply the connection-specific DNS suffix.

FIGURE 18.59
Create VPN Profile Wizard—Connection page

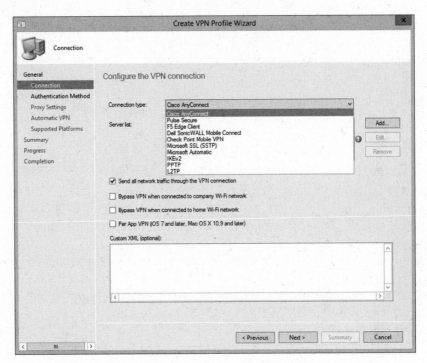

4. After configuring the Connection settings, click Next.

5. On the Authentication Method page, select the authentication method that is supported by the VPN device and click Next.

6. If necessary, configure proxy settings for the VPN profile. Define whether the proxy is automatically set or detected, or configure a proxy server to use. Click Next.

7. Enable VPN on-demand if you want the VPN connection to be started when a native Windows 8.1 or Windows 10 application is started. Supply the DNS suffix, the VPN server that uses that suffix, and when the VPN connection must be initiated, as shown in Figure 18.60.

You can enable the Automatic VPN option while creating the Windows 8 application or on the General page of the Windows 8 Deployment Type while creating the application.

8. Click Next to configure the supported Windows 8.1, Windows 10, Windows Phone, Mac OS X, Android, and iOS platforms, and click Next again to move to the Summary screen.

9. Review the Summary page and click Next. Click Close when the VPN profile is created successfully.

FIGURE 18.60
Create VPN Profile
Wizard—Automatic
VPN page

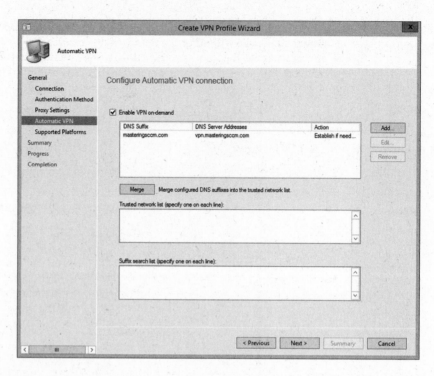

You can deploy the VPN profile to your test collections before rolling out the profiles to a broader range of mobile devices.

In System Center Configuration Manager Current Branch, you can also deploy Email profiles.

1. Start configuring the configuration item by selecting Compliance Settings ➢ Company Resource Access.

2. Click E-Mail Profiles and choose Create Exchange ActiveSync Profile in the Home tab of the ribbon. Supply a name and click Next.

3. Supply an on-premises or online Exchange ActiveSync host, an account name like shown in Figure 18.61.

4. Configure the account username, email address, and authentication method. Click Next to complete the Exchange ActiveSync settings.

5. Configure the synchronization settings, and click Next to configure the supported Windows 10, Windows Phone, Android, and iOS platforms. Click Next again to move to the Summary screen.

6. Review the Summary page and click Next. Click Close when the Exchange ActiveSync profile is created successfully.

FIGURE 18.61
Create Exchange
ActiveSync Email
Profile Wizard—
Exchange ActiveSync
page

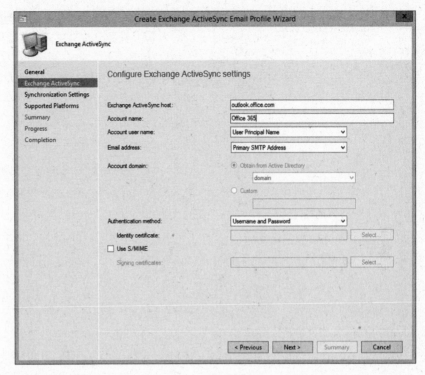

You can deploy the Exchange ActiveSync profile to your test collections before rolling out the profiles to a broader range of mobile devices.

Finally, you can create Wi-Fi profiles to deploy to your corporate mobile devices. To create a Wi-Fi profile, follow these steps:

1. Start configuring the configuration item by selecting Compliance Settings ➢ Company Resource Access.

2. Click Wi-Fi Profiles and choose Create Wi-Fi Profile in the Home tab of the ribbon. Supply a name and click Next. You can also import an existing Wi-Fi profile from a file, but in this example you will create a new Wi-Fi profile.

3. The first step is supplying the general information about the Wi-Fi profile. Supply a network name and the SSID of the Wi-Fi network. You can also enable or disable the following options, as shown in Figure 18.62.

   ◆ Connect Automatically When This Network Is In Range

   ◆ Look For Other Wireless Networks While Connected To This Network

   ◆ Connect When The Network Is Not Broadcasting Its Name (SSID)

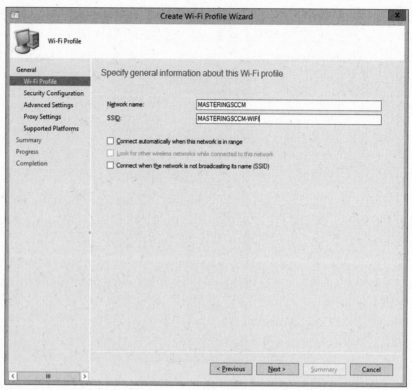

4. The next step is to configure the security configuration. You need to configure a security type with the proper encryption information for your Wi-Fi network, as shown in Figure 18.63. Contact your network administrator for the appropriate information for your Wi-Fi network. Click Next to configure advanced settings. The advanced settings are not available for every security type.

5. If necessary, configure proxy settings for the Wi-Fi profile. Define whether the proxy is automatically set or detected, or configure a proxy server to use.

6. Click Next to configure the supported platforms. Click Next.

7. Review the Summary page and click Next. Click Close when the Wi-Fi profile is created successfully. Again, deploy the Wi-Fi profile first to your test collections before rolling it out in your environment.

FIGURE 18.63
Create Wi-Fi Profile
Wizard—Security
Configuration page

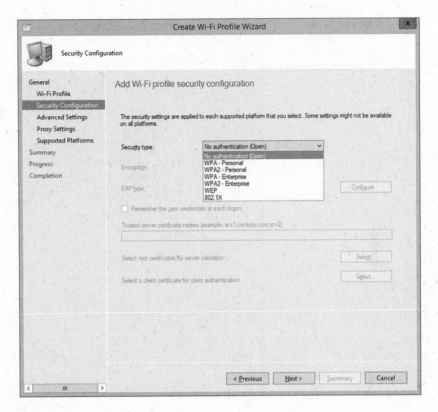

Conditional Access

With conditional access you are able to restrict access to corporate resources based on the compliance state of a device. In this section we will configure conditional access for the various online services of Microsoft.

COMPLIANCE POLICY

The first step in configuring conditional access (in this example, for Exchange Online) is creating a compliance policy.

1. Begin configuring the Compliance Policies by starting the Configuration Manager console. In the Assets And Compliance workspace, expand Overview ➤ Compliance Settings and click Compliance Policies.

2. Click Create Compliance Policy, supply a name, and select Compliance Rules For Devices Managed Without The Configuration Manager Client. Then, select the applicable platform: Windows 8.1 and Windows 10, Windows Phone, Windows 10 Mobile, iOS, Android, or Samsung Knox. For this example, select iOS and click Next.

3. Select the supported platforms, as shown in Figure 18.64.

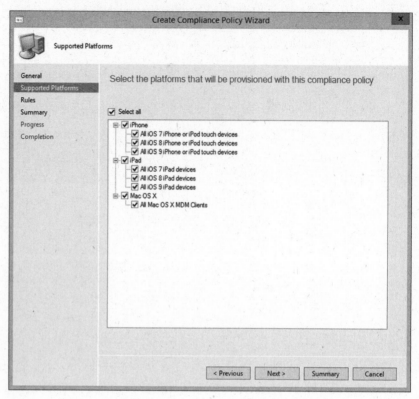

4. After selecting all applicable versions, click Next to configure the rules for a compliant device, as shown in Figure 18.65, and configure the following options:

Require Password Setting On Mobile Device (All Platforms)   Require a user to configure a password (or passcode) on a device to be compliant.

Minutes Of Inactivity Before Password Is Required (All Platforms)   Require to configure an inactivity timeout before the password is required to be compliant.

Minimum Password Length (All Platforms)   Require a user to configure a password/passcode that has the minimum configured length to be compliant.

Allow Simple Passwords (Windows And iOS Only)   Require a user to configure a complex password/passcode if Allow Simple Passwords is disabled.

Device Is Jailbroken Or Rooted (Android And iOS Only)   Require a user to fix a rooted or jailbroken device to be able to have a compliant device again.

Minimum Operating System Version (All Platforms)   Require users to have a minimum operating system; this way, you can block Android 2, 3, or 4.0 devices, for example. Apply your own life-cycle management.

Maximum Operating System Version (All Platforms)   Require users to have a minimum operating system; this way, you can, say, block iOS version 11 devices that you may not support yet. Apply your own life cycle management.

FIGURE 18.65
Create Compliance
Policy Wizard—Rules

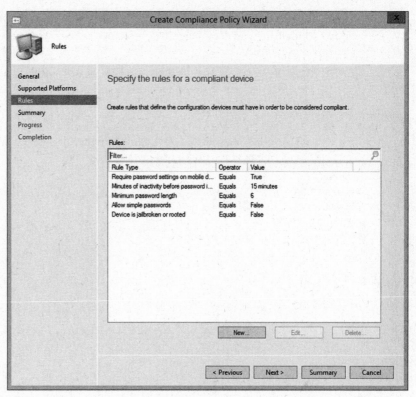

Email Profile Must Be Managed By Intune (iOS Only) When protecting mail, you can create a rule that the email profile must be managed by Intune to have access to your email environment like Office 365.

Minimum Classification Of Required Updates (Windows Only) Require users to configure the minimum classification for the installation of required updates. The value can be None, Recommended, or Important.

Reported As Healthy By Health Attestation Service (Windows 10 Only) Require the device to be reported healthy by the Health Attestation Service to be able to be compliant.

File Encryption On Mobile Device (Windows, Android) Require users to encrypt their device to be compliant.

These rules can be added or deleted from the list.

5. After configuring the rules, click Next to review the summary. Click Next and Close to finish the process of creating a compliance policy.

The next step is deploying the compliance policy to your user collections. You must have enabled the user collections to enroll their device into Intune.

CONDITIONAL ACCESS—EXCHANGE ONLINE

After configuring and deploying the compliance policies, you must configure conditional access. Follow these steps:

1. Start the Configuration Manager console. In the Assets And Compliance workspace, expand Overview ➢ Compliance Settings ➢ Conditional Access and click Exchange Online.

2. Click the Configure Conditional Access Policy In The Intune Console link, as shown in Figure 18.66, or click Configure Conditional Access Policy In The Intune Console in the Home ribbon of the Configuration Manager console.

FIGURE 18.66
Configuring conditional access policy

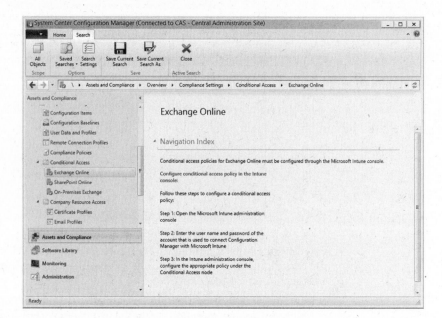

3. Log in with the tenant or global admin of Microsoft Intune and click Enable Conditional Access Policy, as shown in Figure 18.67.

4. Enable the platforms that you would like to support and configure these options:

Block Non-Compliant Devices On Same Platforms As Outlook (OWA)   Block Outlook Web Access for devices that are not managed by Intune and that are not compliant.

Block Non-Compliant Devices On Platforms Supported By Microsoft Intune   Block devices that are not compliant but that are supported by Microsoft Intune. After the device is compliant, access is allowed again.

Block All Other Devices On Platforms Not Supported By Microsoft Intune   If a device is not supported by Microsoft Intune, block it or allow it.

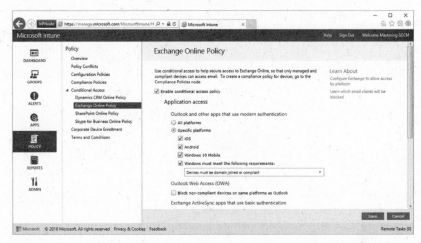

5. Configure the policy deployment by specifying the target groups. The conditional access policy can be targeted to either All Users or one or more security groups.

6. You can configure one or more security groups as exempt groups. The users who are members of the security groups do not need to comply with the conditional access policies.

7. Click Save to save the conditional access policy and close the browser.

CONDITIONAL ACCESS—SHAREPOINT ONLINE

After configuring conditional access for Exchange Online, you have to configure it for SharePoint Online. Follow these steps:

1. Start the Configuration Manager console. In the Assets And Compliance workspace, expand Overview ➤ Compliance Settings ➤ Conditional Access and click SharePoint Online.

2. Click the Configure Conditional Access Policy In The Intune Console link or click Configure Conditional Access Policy In The Intune Console in the Home ribbon of the Configuration Manager console.

3. Log in with the tenant admin of Microsoft Intune and click Enable Conditional Access Policy, as shown in Figure 18.68.

4. Enable the platforms that you would like to support and configure this option:

    Block Non-Compliant Devices On Same Platforms As OneDrive For Business   Block web access to SharePoint Online and access via OneDrive for Business for devices that are not managed by Intune and that are not compliant.

FIGURE 18.68
Enabling conditional
access policy

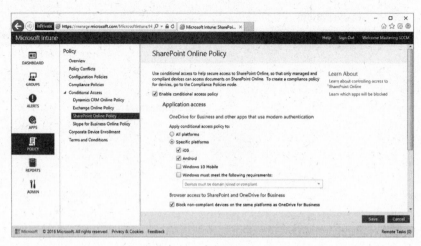

FIGURE 18.68
Enabling conditional
access policy

5. Configure the policy deployment by specifying the target groups. The conditional access policy can be targeted to either All Users or one or more security groups.

6. You can configure one or more security groups as exempt groups. The users who are members of the security groups do not need to comply with the conditional access policies.

7. Click Save to save the conditional access policy and close the browser.

CONDITIONAL ACCESS—ON-PREMISES EXCHANGE

When you have Exchange on-premises, you can also configure conditional access, but you first have to configure the Exchange Server Connector to the Exchange environment. Follow these steps:

1. Start the Configuration Manager console. In the Assets and Compliance workspace, expand Overview ➤ Compliance Settings ➤ Conditional Access, and then click On-Premises Exchange.

2. Click Configure Conditional Access Policy in the Home ribbon of the Configuration Manager console.

3. In the Configure Conditional Access Policy Wizard, enable the Default Rule Override – Always Allow Intune Enrolled And Compliant Devices To Access Exchange option. This option overrides the Exchange ActiveSync access rules of Exchange Server.

4. Click Next to configure the target collections, as shown in Figure 18.69. Click Add and select the user collections you want to target and click OK.

FIGURE 18.69
Configure Conditional
Access Policy Wizard—
Targeted Collections

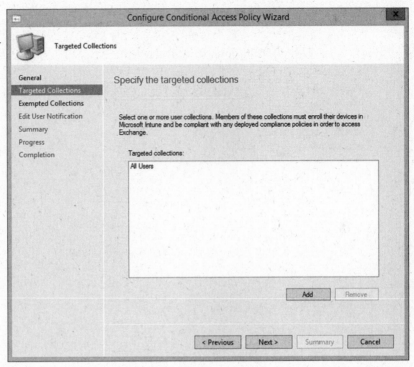

5. Click Next if you want to exempt groups of users of the conditional access policy. Click Add to add the user collection with the users you want to exempt.

6. Click Next to configure the user notification, which is shown if a user is not compliant.

7. Click Next to review the summary. Click Next and Close to finish creating the conditional access policy for the on-premises Exchange.

Mobile Application Management Policies

Securing devices and the services via conditional access is one part of the Enterprise Mobility + Security solution of Microsoft. Securing the apps and its data is the second part. Mobile Application Management (MAM) policies are used to manage the Intune enlightened apps. Intune *enlightened* apps, also called managed apps, are applications that support the MAM policies of Intune. See a complete list here: https://ref.ms/mamlist.

Four different MAM policies can be configured: the general MAM iOS policy, the general MAM Android policy, and the managed browser policies for both iOS and Android. Follow these steps:

1. Start the Configuration Manager console. In the Software Library workspace, expand Overview ➤ Application Management and click Application Management Policies.

2. Click Create Application Management Policy, supply a name and description, and click Next to configure the policy type.

3. Select the platform you want to support and leave Policy Type set to General. Click Next.

4. Configure the application management policy for your needs, as shown in Figure 18.70. The following options are available:

FIGURE 18.70
Create Application
Management Policy
Wizard—application
management policy
for iOS

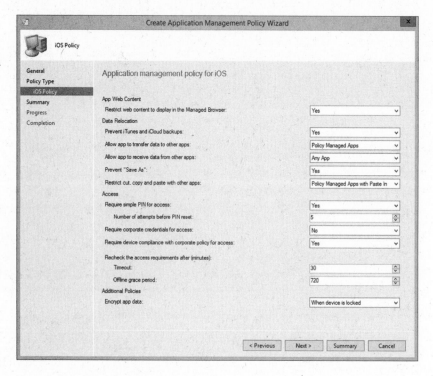

Restrict Web Content To Display In The Managed Browser Force a URL to be opened in the managed browser when the URL in a managed app is being clicked. When this option is not selected, URLs will be opened in the default browser of the device.

Prevent iTunes And iCloud Backups Restrict the data of the managed app to be backed up to iTunes or the iCloud.

Restrict Android Backups Restrict the data of the managed app to back up to Google.

Allow App To Transfer Data To Other Apps Allow users to transfer data to other apps; this can be set to None, Policy Managed Apps, or Any App.

Allow App To Receive Data From Other Apps Allow users to receive data from other apps; this can be set to None, Policy Managed Apps, or Any App.

Prevent "Save As" Prevent or allow users to save documents via Save As in apps like Microsoft Word and Microsoft Excel.

Restrict Cut, Copy And Paste With Other Apps   Restrict or allow cutting, copying, and pasting data from managed apps to non-managed apps.

Require Simple PIN Access   Require a PIN before accessing the policy managed apps.

Require Corporate Credentials For Access   Require that users authenticate with their corporate credentials to get access to the managed application.

Require Device Compliance With Corporate Policy For Access   Require that the device be compliant with corporate access to be able to access a managed application.

Recheck The Access Requirements After (Minutes)   Recheck if the access requirements are still met after the specified number of minutes. Also configure a grace period for devices that are not always online.

Encrypt App Data   Encrypt app data can be enabled for Android. For iOS, you can configure when data is encrypted: When A Device Is Locked, When A Device Is Locked (Except Open Files), After Device Restart, or Using The Device Settings.

Block Screen Capture (Android Only)   Disable the ability to capture the screen of an app that is managed via the application management policies.

5.   Click Next to review the summary.

6.   After reviewing the summary, click Next and Close to end the wizard.

Next you need to add an app that is enabled for mobile application management, as discussed in Chapter 4, "Installation and Site Role Configuration," and deploy it to a collection with users. The wizard lets you add the mobile application policy you want to deploy with the application.

If you have a line-of-business (LOB) app that has been developed by a software vendor or you are developing one yourself, you can either wrap the iOS or Android app or you can integrate the Microsoft Intune Software Developer Kit (SDK). Read more about the wrapper and Microsoft Intune SDK here:

```
https://docs.microsoft.com/en-us/intune/deploy-use/decide-how-to-prepare-apps-
for-mobile-application-management-with-microsoft-intune
```

On-Premises MDM

The third MDM option is currently only available for Windows 10 devices. Currently only MDM via hybrid (as described earlier) and on-premises MDM cannot be mixed. To be able to support Windows 10 devices to use MDM management via Configuration Manager, some changes to the Configuration Manager infrastructure must be in place:

◆   HTTPS enabled Distribution Point site role

◆   HTTPS enabled Management Point site role

◆   Enrollment Point site role

◆   Enrollment Proxy Point site role

Chapter 4 shows how to configure Configuration Manager to support HTTPS and how to configure the site roles that are required. Besides the necessary site roles, you must configure the following components:

- Microsoft Intune Subscription
- Client Settings
- Allow Windows Platform Support

Microsoft Intune Subscription

You configure the Microsoft subscription as described in the "Configuring the Microsoft Intune Subscription" section earlier in this chapter. The Microsoft Intune Subscription is used for licensing purpose; no data will be shared with Microsoft Intune, and the Windows 10 devices will not communicate with Microsoft Intune.

1. Open the Configuration Manager console, select the Administration workspace, expand Overview ➤ Cloud Services ➤ Microsoft Intune Subscriptions, and select Microsoft Intune Subscription.

2. Click Properties in the home ribbon of the console. Enable the Only Manage Devices On Premises option in the Microsoft Intune Subscription Properties dialog box, as shown in Figure 18.71.

FIGURE 18.71
Microsoft Intune
Subscription
Properties dialog box

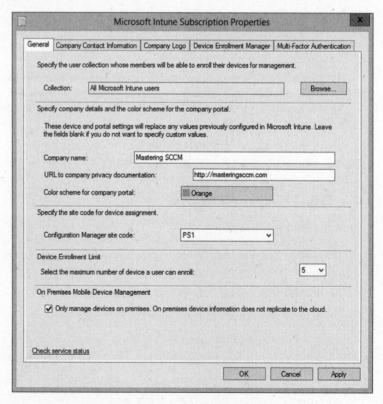

3. Click OK to finish the configuration to support on-premises MDM.

Client Settings

In the client settings, you must use configure enrollment support using the enrollment point in Configuration Manager. Be sure that the profile with the certificate of your CA is created, as described earlier in the "Deploying Resources" section. With the certificate profile in place, the client settings need to be configured as follows:

1. Open the Configuration Manager console, select the Administration workspace, expand Overview ➢ Client Settings, and select Default Client Settings.

2. Click Properties in the home ribbon of the console and click the Enrollment section of Default Settings.

3. Set Allow Users To Enroll Modern Devices to Yes and click Set Profile.

4. Click Create and supply a name and description for the enrollment profile. Be sure that the certificate of the CA is listed, as shown in Figure 18.72.

FIGURE 18.72
Creating the
enrollment profile

Create Enrollment Profile

Specify the settings to create a new enrollment profile for modern devices.

Name: `Windows10`

Description:

Select a management site that contains a management point that is enabled for modern devices.

Management site code: `PS1`

Certification Configuration

Filter...

Name
ConfigMgrLab CA

OK   Cancel

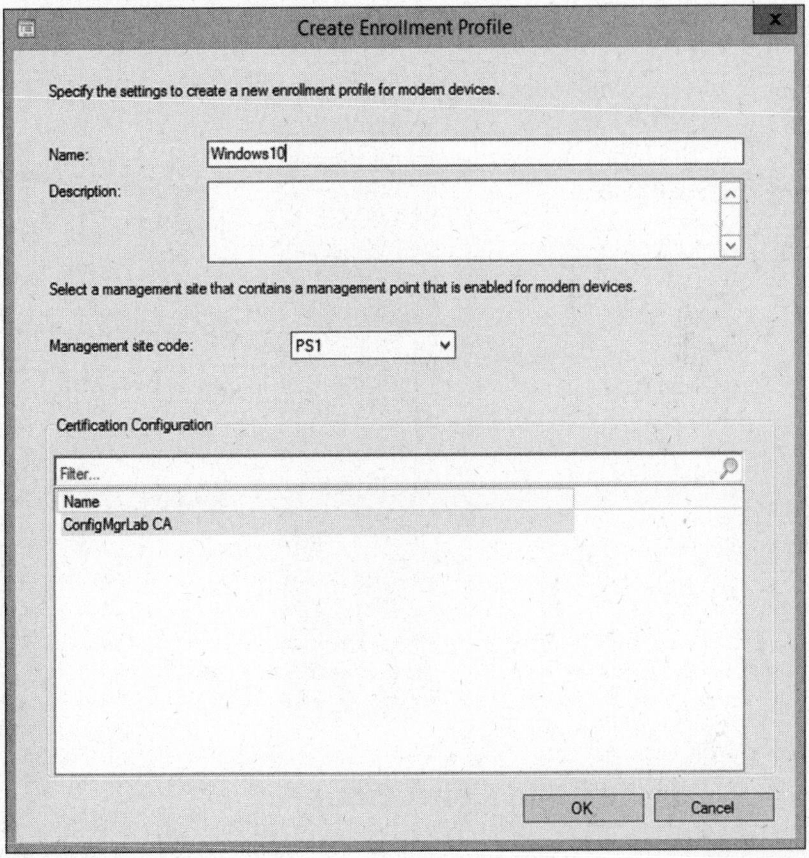

5. Click OK to create the enrollment profile and click OK to set the enrollment profile.

6. Click OK to save the client settings.

Allow Windows Platform Support

Finally, you must enable support for enrolling the Windows 10 devices via on-premises MDM.

1. Open the Configuration Manager console, select the Administration workspace, expand Overview ➢ Cloud Services ➢ Microsoft Intune Subscriptions, and select Microsoft Intune Subscription.

2. Click Configure Platforms and select Windows.

3. Enable the option Enable Windows Enrollment in the General tab of the Microsoft Intune Subscription Properties dialog box and click OK.

Once all components are configured on a Windows 10 device, it can be enrolled and managed via on-premises MDM. While enrolling the device you will see that the logon page is not referring to Microsoft Intune but to System Center Configuration Manager, as shown in Figure 18.73.

FIGURE 18.73
System Center Configuration Manager logon page

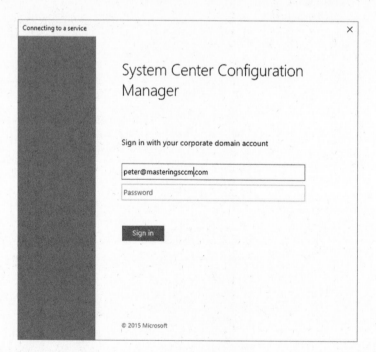

Terms and Conditions

When allowing users to access corporate data on their mobile devices, typically company terms and conditions apply. In Configuration Manager Current Branch, terms and conditions can be configured and deployed to users so that they need to accept the terms and conditions while enrolling their device in Configuration Manager. If a user does not accept the terms and conditions, the device will not be enrolled. Terms and conditions can be configured as follows:

1. Start the Configuration Manager console. In the Assets And Compliance workspace, expand Overview ➤ Compliance Settings and click Terms And Conditions.

2. Click Create Terms And Conditions in the home ribbon of the console and supply a name for the terms and conditions.

3. Click Next to supply a title, text for the terms, and an explanation of what it means if the user accepts the terms and conditions.

4. Click Next to review the terms and conditions in the summary.

5. Click Next and Close.

6. Select the newly created terms and conditions in the console and click Deploy in the Home ribbon.

7. Click Browse, as shown in Figure 18.74; select the collection you want to deploy the terms and conditions to; and click OK.

FIGURE 18.74
Deploy Terms And Conditions

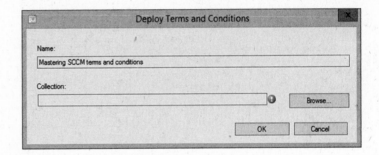

8. Click OK to deploy the terms and conditions.

Corporate-Owned iOS Devices

When using Apple iOS devices in your environment with the Apple Device Enrollment Program (DEP), while enrolling the device Configuration Manager Current Branch is able to deploy profiles created by the Apple Configurator. Configuring DEP support for Configuration Manager is done by uploading a DEP token via the Microsoft Intune Subscription Properties while configuring iOS support.

After configuring DEP support, you can create enrollment profiles to simplify the enrollment process and to lock down the devices via, for instance, supervised mode.

Read more about Apple DEP here:

www.apple.com/business/dep

and

https://ref.ms/appledep

Corporate-Owned Windows Devices

When using on-premises MDM via Configuration Manager Current Branch, you can create enrollment profiles to automate the enrollment process of Windows 10 devices. Create a Windows 10 enrollment profile as follows:

1. Start the Configuration Manager console. In the Assets And Compliance workspace, expand Overview ➤ All Corporate-owned Devices ➤ Windows And Enrollment Profile.

2. Click Create Enrollment Profile in the Home ribbon of the Configuration Manager console and supply a name. Supply a description and from the Management Authority dropdown, select On-Premises, as shown in Figure 18.75. Selecting the Cloud option will allow you to enroll devices using Configuration Manager with Microsoft Intune (hybrid) instead of Configuration Manager on-premises.

FIGURE 18.75
Setting the management authority

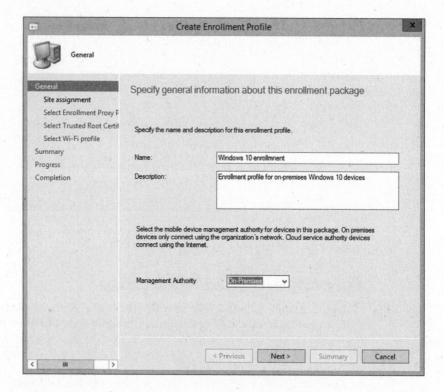

3. Click Next to configure the site assignment, select the management site code, and click Next.

4. Select the option Intranet Only and select the enrollment points that are listed in the Endpoints field. Click Next.

5. Select Trusted Root Certificate and click Next.

6. Optionally select the available Wi-Fi profile, configure the proxy settings, and click Next.

7. Review the details, confirm the settings, and click Next.

8. Click close to finish the creation of the enrollment profile.

   To be able to use the enrollment profile, you must export the profile from Configuration Manager.

9. Select the enrollment profile you created and click Export in the Home ribbon of the Configuration Manager console.

10. Configure the validity period during which the profile can be used for enrolling devices. By default, after 14 days the enrollment expires and cannot be used anymore.

11. Supply a package name and location where the enrollment profile package should be exported (such as c:\temp\enroll-win.ppkg) and select Encrypt Package if you want to encrypt the package.

12. Click Export. Copy the files (such as enroll-win.ppkg and enroll-win.cat) to a USB stick or similar and click the PPKG file to automatically enroll a device into Configuration Manager On-Premises MDM.

   If the package needs to be encrypted, an encryption password is supplied to decrypt the package.

Enrolling Devices

Once the prerequisites for the Microsoft Intune subscription are in place and the Microsoft Intune subscription and the supported platforms are configured, you need to enroll your devices. Enrolling devices is done by the users themselves. Each operating system requires different steps.

Android

To enroll an Android device, users need to follow these steps:

1. Go to the Google Play App Store, and search for the Microsoft Intune Company Portal app.

2. Select the app and click the Install button. Click Accept to acknowledge that the Microsoft Intune company portal is able to access your storage, information about the identity, available files, device ID, phone number information, and Wi-Fi communication.

3. After the installation is finished, click Open, as shown in Figure 18.76. Next, you need to add your device to Microsoft Intune and Configuration Manager before you can use the company portal to install company-owned apps. Click Add This Device.

FIGURE 18.76
Open the Microsoft
Intune company portal.

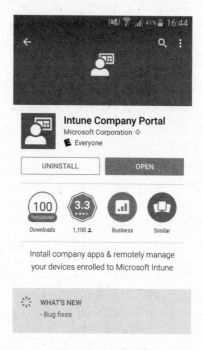

4. Log on with your Microsoft Intune account that is allowed to enroll mobile devices. Click Sign In after supplying your Microsoft Intune credentials.

5. The enrollment process is divided into two parts: the enrollment itself and a check if the device is compliant with the policies that have been configured earlier. Click Begin and Enroll to start the enrollment process. As part of the enrollment process, the user is told why enrollment is necessary and what can be done and what cannot be done by the administrator. You will be asked to activate the device administrator. This means that the company portal will be getting the device administrator permissions to perform the following actions:

◆ Erase all data (when executing a remote device wipe)

◆ Change the screen-unlock password

◆ Set password rules

◆ Monitor screen-unlock attempts

◆ Lock the screen

◆ Set lock-screen password expiration

◆ Set storage encryption

◆ Disable cameras

◆ Disable features in the keyguard

Click Activate.

6. After activation, the mobile device will be added to the Microsoft Intune company portal, and you will be able to use the portal to install your applications if the device is compliant.

iOS

Enrolling an iOS device can be done via the Microsoft Intune company portal. Users need to follow these steps:

1. Search in the Apple App Store for the Microsoft Intune Company Portal app, and install the app.

2. Click Open to open the app, and log on with your Microsoft Intune user account.

3. You will be prompted that company access must be set up, as shown in Figure 18.77. Click Begin to start the enrollment process. As with Android, the user is told what is being done and what is possible with their device. Click Continue twice before starting the process by clicking Begin.

FIGURE 18.77
Beginning the
company access setup

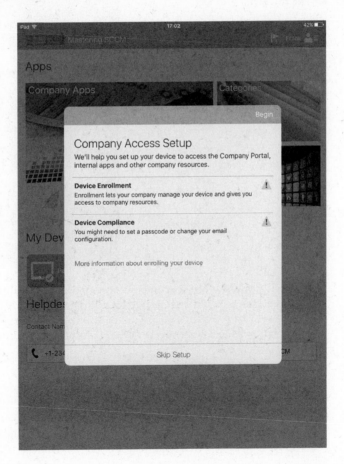

4. In the Install Profile dialog box, click Install and Install.

5. In the MDM dialog box, click Install and Trust in the Remote Management pop-up.

6. Click Done once the enrollment process is finished.

7. Click Open to go back to the company portal. The final step is to validate if the device is compliant. If it is compliant, you can continue accessing the applications; if the device is not compliant, be sure to fix any compliancy issues.

Windows Phone 8.x

In Windows Phone 8.x, you can enroll your device without installing an app or browsing to a Microsoft Intune website. To enroll your Windows Phone 8.x device, users need to follow these steps:

1. Choose Settings ➤ Workplace and click Add Account.

2. Supply your email address and password; then click Sign In, as shown in Figure 18.78.

FIGURE 18.78
Enroll Windows
Phone device

3. Click Done when the company account is successfully added; leave Install Company App Or Hub selected if using Windows Phone 8. After clicking Done, you may receive a message that company policies can be applied. Your company can offer policies, certificates, and apps that help you connect to your business or secure your mobile device.

Windows RT and Windows 8.1

Windows RT and Windows 8.1 devices can also be managed without joining them to your domain. An option called Workplace Join allows you to enroll your device in Configuration Manager Current Branch. After enrolling your device, you can receive apps and settings from Configuration Manager Current Branch. Joining your Windows RT or Windows 8.1 device can be done as follows:

1. In Windows, choose PC Settings ➤ Network ➤ Workplace.

2. Click Join, supply your user ID, and click Turn On, as shown in Figure 18.79.

FIGURE 18.79
Turning on
Workplace Join

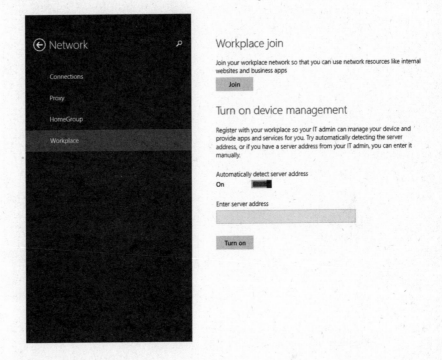

3. Select I Agree and click Turn On.

Windows 10

Both Windows 10 PCs and Windows 10 mobile devices can be managed via MDM. The way this works is almost the same as the earlier supported Windows versions. Enrolling Windows 10 devices can be done as follows:

1. In Windows, choose Settings ➢ Accounts ➢ Work Access and click Enroll In To Device Management.

2. Supply the email address of the user who wants to enroll the device and click Connect. Supply the password and click Sign In.

3. Click Done after the account is set up correctly, and the enrolled organization will show as connected, as in Figure 18.80.

FIGURE 18.80
Device enrolled in
device management

FIGURE 18.80
Device enrolled in
device management

After all devices are enrolled, they will show up in the Configuration Manager Current Branch console, as shown in Figure 18.81.

FIGURE 18.81
Enrolled devices
in Configuration
Manager

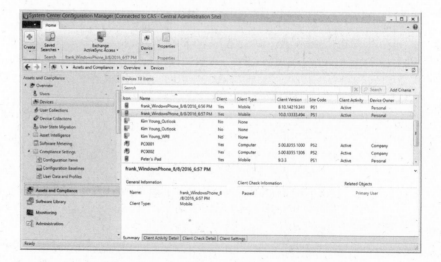

Troubleshooting

The method of troubleshooting problems with mobile devices depends on the management mode chosen. For lite management, troubleshooting will be mostly focused on Exchange Server—both in terms of ensuring that the Exchange ActiveSync Connector is running properly and ensuring that the Configuration Manager Exchange ActiveSync Connector is properly configured and operational.

When it comes to depth management, there are a few more places to check when you run into problems. Depth-managed devices require enrollment before management can begin. The enrollment process is not difficult, but there are a number of moving parts that must be configured properly, not the least of which is certificates. When enrollment fails, it's clear on the device that there was a problem, but it's not always easy to collect diagnostic information from the device to understand why enrollment failed. Fortunately, there is excellent logging for the enrollment process. The EnrollmentService.log and EnrollmentWeb.log may contain errors that might occur as the enrollment process progresses. These logs are located in the SMS_CCM folder, under the EnrollmentPoint\logs and EnrollmentProxyPoint\logs folders, respectively.

When using the Service Connection Point, you have some different log files in the %SMS_LOG_PATH% folder. The log file cloudusersync.log will help you identify issues with synchronizing the users in the collection that holds the users who are allowed to enroll their mobile devices. The log files dmpdownloader.log, dmpuploader.log, dismgr.log, and outboundcontentmanager.log will help you identify issues with uploading and downloading apps, policies, and messages from and to Windows Intune. If you have issues when installing the Windows Intune Connector, look in the following log files: sitecomp.log, connectorsetup.log, and certmgr.log.

The depth-managed mobile device client has similarities to the computer device client in that client health data is provided. Simply reviewing a device in the collections to ensure client health evaluations are current and successful, along with checking the Client Status data from the Monitoring node, is a good indicator of whether the client is behaving properly.

If you need to troubleshoot enrollment issues when using a hybrid environment, try the System Center Configuration Manager Hybrid Diagnostics tool, which can be downloaded here: https://ref.ms/hybridtroubleshooter/.

The Bottom Line

Detail the differences between lite and depth management. The management options and settings available for mobile devices will vary depending on whether lite- or depth-management options are in place.

Master It List MDM capabilities for lite versus depth management.

Understand how to configure MDM. Properly configuring MDM requires addressing several potential scenarios. From a Configuration Manager perspective, though, the choice is simple: lite or depth management.

Master It List the items that need to be configured for both lite and depth management.

Understand the depth-management enrollment process. From the user perspective, the enrollment process for depth management is straightforward. Behind the scenes, there are a number of moving parts. Each of these components is critical to the enrollment process.

Master It List the components required to enroll depth-managed devices.

Appendix

The Bottom Line Answers

Each "Bottom Line" section in the chapters suggests exercises to deepen skills and understanding. Sometimes there is only one possible solution, but often you are encouraged to use your skills to create something that builds on what you know and lets you explore one of many possible solutions.

Chapter 2: Planning a Configuration Manager Infrastructure

Plan and design a Central Administration Site.   One of the first questions you will ask yourself while starting to design and plan a new Configuration Manager hierarchy is "Do I need a Central Administration Site?" The answer to this question is essential for your final design.

Master It   Determine when a CAS is needed.

Solution   When there is a need for more than one primary site in your Configuration Manager infrastructure, you also need a CAS. If not, you can extend a primary site into a CAS only once.

Plan and design an effective Configuration Manager infrastructure.   When planning and designing a new Configuration Manager infrastructure, it is important to plan your site placement appropriately. The design rules for primary sites have changed from how they were in Configuration Manager 2007.

Master It   Understand the reasons for not needing an additional primary site implementation.

Solution   You don't need to implement an additional primary site for the following reasons:

◆   Decentralized administration

◆   Logical data segmentation

◆   Discrete client settings

◆   Languages

◆   Content routing for deep hierarchies

Identify the enhancements to the distribution point site system role. Distribution points in older versions were used to provide local points for accessing content and later also for App-V streaming. In Configuration Manager distribution points do a lot more.

Master It Distribution points have been enhanced. What roles and components are merged with the new distribution point, and what's new?

Solution Tricky question; not only are the PXE-enabled distribution points and the multicast-enabled distribution points merged with the new distribution point, but also the old branch distribution point and the distribution share are merged. The distribution point can be installed on Windows versions for servers and computers. Some new features of the distribution point are

◆ Bandwidth control

◆ Scheduling and throttling data synchronization

◆ Ability to specify drives for content

◆ Content validation on the distribution point

◆ Support for content prestaging

Prepare your current Configuration Manager 2007 environment for migration to Configuration Manager. An in-place upgrade of Configuration Manager 2007 to Configuration Manager is not supported. Configuration Manager has a migration feature within the feature set to enable side-by-side migration.

Master It How can you as a Configuration Manager administrator or consultant prepare a current Configuration Manager 2007 environment for migration to Configuration Manager?

Solution Steps you can take to prepare for the migration to Configuration Manager include the following:

◆ Flatten your hierarchy where possible.

◆ Plan for Windows Server OS Upgrade and SQL Server Upgrade.

◆ Use the UNC path in your packages instead of local paths.

Chapter 3: Migrating to Configuration Manager

Determine what you are able to migrate with the migration feature. The migration feature in Configuration Manager allows you to migrate the old Configuration Manager investments to a new Configuration Manager hierarchy side by side.

Master It With the migration feature, you cannot migrate objects like the following:

◆ Queries

◆ Security rights for the site and objects

◆ Configuration Manager reports from SQL Server Reporting Services

- Configuration Manager 2007 web reports
- Client inventory and history data
- AMT client-provisioning information
- Files in the client cache

Identify what objects you *can* migrate.

Solution   You are able to migrate to a new Configuration Manager environment nearly every investment you made in earlier versions. The following list includes all the objects that can be migrated:

- Collections
- Advertisements and deployments
- Boundaries
- Boundary groups
- Global conditions
- Software distribution packages
- Applications
- Virtual application packages
- App-V virtual environments
- Software updates
  - Deployments
  - Deployment packages
  - Deployment templates
  - Software update lists
  - Software update groups
  - Automatic deployment rules
- Operating system deployment
  - Boot images
  - Driver packages
  - Drivers
  - Images
  - Installer
  - Task sequences

- ◆ Settings management

  - ◆ Configuration baselines

  - ◆ Configuration items

- ◆ Asset intelligence

  - ◆ Catalog

  - ◆ Hardware requirements

  - ◆ User-defined categorization list

- ◆ Software metering rules

- ◆ Saved searches

Discover which migration approach is supported. Configuration Manager provides migration features that can be used for your migration of Configuration Manager 2007 to the current version.

Master It With the earlier upgrades or migrations of Configuration Manager in your mind, what migration approaches are supported when migrating from previous versions of Configuration Manager?

Solution Configuration Manager officially supports only one migration approach, the side-by-side migration approach, when using the migration feature. The wipe-and-load approach is used only if you do not need to migrate anything from your old Configuration Manager environment.

Ascertain what kind of interoperability is supported during the migration. Interoperability like that supported in earlier versions is no longer supported; nevertheless, the migration feature of Configuration Manager supports some interoperability during the migration process. Depending on the size of your Configuration Manager source hierarchy, the migration can take some time.

Master It Interoperability like you were used to in SMS 2003 and Configuration Manager 2007 is no longer supported. Give two examples of interoperability features in the current version of Configuration Manager.

Solution For interoperability purposes you are able to use shared distribution points in the process of migrating objects from a source hierarchy to the new one. Another interoperability feature is the ability to re-migrate update objects. In other words, you can re-migrate objects that have been updated in the source Configuration Manager hierarchy while migrating other objects.

Chapter 4: Installation and Site Role Configuration

Understand Configuration Manager sites and the new approach to hierarchy design. Configuration Manager has three types of sites: the central administration site, which is new, and the primary and secondary sites, which should be familiar to you. Although two of the three site types are familiar, their use and approach to hierarchy design—or whether a hierarchy is needed at all—are quite different now.

Master It Describe the purpose of each site type and map each to specific management needs.

Solution

◆ Central Administration Site: Only present if a hierarchy is being configured. Provides centralized administration for the hierarchy but no direct client management.

◆ Primary site: Clients are assigned to primary sites, and this is where they receive management instruction, regardless of where in the hierarchy the client might be located.

◆ Secondary site: This type of site is of use only in situations where bandwidth conditions are so slow or unstable as to require a site server to throttle even small traffic, such as discovery and inventory information.

Construct a Configuration Manager hierarchy. The site hierarchy in Configuration Manager consists of the site types just described. The approach to design is very different from the previous version, with the number of primary sites being limited to a single tier. The chapter walked through configuring a hierarchy with all three site types.

Master It Describe a Configuration Manager site hierarchy. Detail components needed for site-to-site communication and security settings.

Solution

◆ Hierarchies always consist of a CAS and at least one primary child site. Additional primary child sites might be in place as well. Secondary sites should rarely be used but may be added if needed.

◆ Site-to-site communication requires site servers to have proper addresses and senders to be configured and correct credentials to be assigned where applicable.

◆ Configuration Manager installations create several local security groups that are used to grant access to site resources and facilitate site-to-site communication.

Determine when to expand a hierarchy and when to simply add a site system role for additional service. A major design goal of Configuration Manager is simplified hierarchy design. Administrators familiar with previous versions may be tempted to retain old hierarchy approaches when designing Configuration Manager. Taking such an approach will often lead to inefficient designs and additional server cost and in some cases simply won't work.

Master It Understand the changes in sites and site components that lend themselves to hierarchy simplification and enable parity management with fewer site servers.

Solution

◆ Distribution point modifications include the ability to throttle content directly to remote distribution points. In addition, it is now possible to install distribution points on workstation systems directly where needed.

◆ Boundary groups simplify hierarchy configurations by allowing administrators to strictly define which distribution points are used to service specific client content requests.

- The updated security model in Configuration Manager allows administrators to scale out a single site while still maintaining logical separation of user role and function. There is no longer a technical need to have separate primary sites for servers and workstations. When managed properly, a single primary site is able to manage both seamlessly while protecting resources from access by unauthorized users.

Deploy and configure the various site system roles available per site.   There are many roles available to enable management at a site. Understanding each role and the service it delivers is critical to getting the most out of your investment in Configuration Manager.

Master It   Review critical system roles and understand the services that are enabled through each.

Solution

- Critical site system roles are those that are required for basic Configuration Manager functionality at most sites. These include the management point and distribution point roles.

- Management points facilitate client-to-site server communication.

- Distribution points store content that may be needed by clients of the site.

Chapter 5: Client Installation

Configure boundaries and boundary groups.   Before starting any client installation, verify that you have configured a boundary group for site assignment.

Master It   Let Configuration Manager Forest Discovery automatically create the boundaries and add them to the correct boundary groups.

Solution   Once you have configured Forest Discovery, add the automatically created IP subnets to a new or existing discovery group.

Select the relevant discovery methods.   You configure discovery methods in the Configuration Manager console. The Active Directory discovery methods all require a schedule and an LDAP path. There are schedules for delta and full discovery. In Configuration Manager, delta discovery will also find changes to existing objects; this eliminates the need to run a full discovery more than once a week.

Master It   Always know what you want to discover and where. Based on that knowledge, configure the needed discovery methods.

Solution   The correct discovery method depends on how you want to deploy clients and work with features like application deployment. For a client push installation to work, it is a good idea to configure Active Directory Computer Discovery. On the other hand, if you want to deploy applications to end users, you also need to configure Active Directory User Discovery.

Employ the correct client installation methods.   When configuring the client installation methods, make sure you know the pros and cons for each method. Some require firewall settings; others require local administrative permissions. You need to make sure that all the required settings are in place. Do not start any installation until you have the needed site systems, boundary groups, and command lines specified.

Master It   Configure the correct command-line properties and ensure they will work for all environments (local forest, workgroup, and DMZ). Create multiple client push installation accounts, and ensure that you have a good understanding of the three phases (preinstallation, installation, and post-installation).

Solution   Configure the command-line properties in the properties for the client push installation method. That way, you ensure that the properties are always replicated to Active Directory and can be read during the client installation.

Furthermore, you should add the command-line properties that will also work in another forest and workgroup in the client push properties.

Manage Unix/Linux and Mac devices.   Configuration Manager provides support for managing Unix/Linux and Mac computers as devices. You are now able to manage your entire computer infrastructure from a single management console.

Master It   Understand the installation methods available for deploying the Configuration Manager client to the Unix/Linux computers and Mac computers. Remember that client push cannot be used for these devices.

Solution   The client installation process for Unix/Linux devices has several required parameters, such as the site code, the management point, and the installation package to use. Use the optional parameters to define other client configuration features, such as the fallback status point to use or the folder that will be used for the client installation.

Ensure client health.   Client status might not be the first task you think about when implementing a system like Configuration Manager. But it is crucial to the daily administration that you can trust the numbers you see in the reports and in the console. One way to ensure that is by making certain that all clients are healthy and are providing the server with up-to-date status messages and discovery information.

Master It   Discuss the different environments that exist in your organization, and use that information when configuring client health alerts. Make sure that you know the client activity during a normal period and that you have a set of defined SLAs for each of the environments (laptops, road warriors, servers, call center, and so forth).

Solution   Create unique collections corresponding to each computer role type that you have. In the properties for every collection, configure the unique client status values.

Chapter 6: Client Health

Detail client health evaluations in Configuration Manager Current Branch.   Health evaluations and remediations take place daily on every Configuration Manager client in the hierarchy. This information is updated at the site and is available for review on every client and also summarized for every client across the hierarchy.

Master It   List the health evaluations and remediations that take place on Configuration Manager clients.

Solution

- Review the CCMEval.log file to see all evaluations and remediations that are taking place on clients.
- Review the CCMEval.xml file to understand the details behind each evaluation.

Review client health results in the Configuration Manager console. Client health data is available in several locations of the console to allow access to health for individual devices and summarized data for all clients in the hierarchy.

Master It List the locations in the console where individual client health and summarized client health data are accessible.

Solution

♦ Individual client health data is available by viewing devices individually in collections.

♦ Summarized client health data is available in the Monitoring workspace of the Configuration Manager console by choosing the Client Status node and then the Client Activity and Client Check nodes.

♦ Configuration Manager reports also offer a view into client health data.

Chapter 7: Application Deployment

Explain the options available for Application Deployment. The new Application Deployment model is a significant and welcome change for deploying software in the enterprise. There are many new components including a rules-based Requirements engine, the ability to detect whether the application is already installed, the option to configure application dependencies and relationships, and more.

Master It List several configuration options available for applications and deployment types.

Solution

♦ Applications: The ability to publish in the Application Catalog, define supersedence, and reference information.

♦ Deployment types: The ability to set dependency information, specify criteria defining whether an application is already installed, configure requirements, and set return codes.

Detail the various components required for Application Deployment. Success with Application Deployment requires that several other Configuration Manager components be available and properly configured. The list includes management point(s), distribution point(s), IIS, BITS, the client itself, and possibly more.

Master It List the components required for configuring an application deployment.

Solution The application and at least one deployment type and deployment content must be staged on at least one available distribution point. Clients must receive the deployment and pass any configured requirements, allowing the deployment to be initiated.

Understand the role of and manage distribution points. The role of distribution points has not changed significantly in that this is the role that makes content available to

Configuration Manager devices and users. The options available for implementing the role have changed significantly with the inclusion of throttling control content flow from site server to remote distribution points, the single-instance storage approach for placing content on distribution points, the ability to detect content corruption, and the requirement that all distribution points be BITS enabled.

Master It   Discuss the differences between implementing a distribution point role on the site server locally and remotely.

Solution

◆ Local distribution point: Content is transferred by local file copy; there is no ability to throttle a local distribution point.

◆ Remote distribution point: Content is transferred by network file copy without compression. The ability to throttle content is available, but content is not compressed.

Chapter 8: Software Updates

Plan to use Software Updates.   You can use the same method of deployment intelligence that was used in Chapter 2 to gather information for planning to implement Software Updates. This will be very helpful in making sure that you get the most out of the Software Updates feature for your organization.

Master It   What is the first step in gathering deployment intelligence when you are planning to implement Software Updates?

Solution   The first step is to determine what needs to be accomplished with Software Updates.

Configure Software Updates.   Before you can use Software Updates in your environment, you must set up and configure the various components of this feature.

Master It   What is the first thing you have to install before you can use Software Updates?

Solution   You must install Windows Server Update Services (WSUS). You can use either the full install or the WSUS administrative console, depending on what you are setting up.

Use the Software Updates feature to manage software updates.   The hardest thing to do in SMS 2003 relating to patch management was to programmatically prioritize software updates that are critical so they can be deployed with a higher priority than other updates.

Master It   What does Configuration Manager provide that can help with prioritizing software updates?

Solution   Configuration Manager now includes the severity of all the updates that are synchronized into the Configuration Manager database. With that data, you can sort updates by that category and create search criteria and update groups based on their severity level. You can then use them as a source for your software update components.

Use automatic update deployment to deploy software updates. When you deployed software in Configuration Manager 2007, you deployed software updates through a procedure that consumed a lot of time.

Master It Configuration Manager Current Branch has a new feature called Automatic Deployment Rules. What kinds of updates are suitable to deploy via the automatic deployment rules?

Solution Patch Tuesday software updates and definition files for Forefront Endpoint Protection can be deployed via the automatic deployment rules. Be sure to always test the updates to see if they have any impact on your environment.

Chapter 9: Operating System Deployment

Specify a Network Access account. The Network Access account is the account Configuration Manager will use to access the system while running WinPE.

Master It How do you specify the Network Access account?

Solution Open the Configuration Manager Console, and do the following:

1. Choose the Administration workspace and expand Overview ➤ Site Configuration ➤ Sites.

2. Select one of the sites for which you want to configure the Network Access account, and click Configure Site Components on the Home tab of the ribbon.

3. Select Software Distribution.

4. Select the Network Access Account tab, set the Network Access account to the account created earlier, and click OK.

Enable PXE support. PXE support in Configuration Manager is used to begin the operating system deployment process. The PXE feature responds to Configuration Manager clients making PXE boot requests.

Master It How do you set up PXE support?

Solution Open the Configuration Manager console, and do the following:

1. Choose the Administration workspace and expand Overview ➤ Distribution Points.

2. Select the site server on which the distribution point resides, and click Properties on the Site Role area of the ribbon.

3. Select the PXE tab and click Enable PXE Service Point.

Update the driver catalog package. The driver catalog allows you to add drivers to the already created packages and images you have within your organization so you are not constantly re-creating your images when you get a new machine in your environment.

Master It How do you update the driver catalog package?

Solution From within the Configuration Manager console, do the following:

1. Choose the Software Library workspace, expand Overview ➤ Operating Systems, and select Drivers.

2. Click Import Driver on the Home tab of the ribbon of the Configuration Manager console.

3. Browse to the network location of the drivers you want to import.

4. Specify which package and boot images you want to import the specific drivers into.

Update an image from the console.   In the past it was a big issue to keep your images up to date; no easy procedure existed. Configuration Manager now includes a feature called Schedule Updates that updates your Windows images.

Master It   How do you easily update your Windows images?

Solution   From within the Configuration Manager console, do the following:

1. Choose the Software Library workspace, expand Overview ➢ Operating Systems, and select Operating System Images.

2. From there select a Windows image and click Schedule Updates in the Home tab of the ribbon of the Configuration Manager console.

The process of updating the images is scheduled; after finishing, the wizard and the update will start automatically.

Support Windows 10.   You can support Windows 10 by using the traditional way of OSD or by using the new Windows 10 Servicing features.

Master It   How can you support Windows 10?

Solution

1. Choose the Software Library workspace, expand Overview ➢ Windows 10 Servicing, and select Service Plans.

2. From there, create a Servicing Plan to support the servicing of the Windows 10 machines.

Chapter 10: Inventory and Software Metering

Configure and manage software inventory.   Configuring software inventory has changed in Configuration Manager, although the client-processing part is almost the same as in earlier versions of Configuration Manager.

Master It   By default, Configuration Manager does not inventory for any file types. Where would you go to do that?

Solution   Take the following steps:

1. Navigate to the Administration workspace; under Overview, select Client Settings, and then open the Default Client Settings properties.

2. Select Software Inventory.

3. Click Set Types.

4. Click the New button, and configure the files or file types you want to include in the software-scanning process.

Configure and manage hardware inventory. Hardware inventory provides a wealth of information on the hardware resources in your organization. That information is vital when planning for things such as updating standard business software or upgrading the standard operating system your organization uses. If the standard hardware inventory collected is not enough for your needs, then you have many options to extend the hardware inventory to get that vital information.

Master It Where do you enable or disable data classes in hardware inventory?

Solution You need to open the default client agent settings or create a custom client setting. Custom client settings can only be used when you want to enable data classes that already exist in Configuration Manager. For custom classes (or to delete classes), you must modify the default client settings.

Configure and manage software metering. Keeping track of software that is installed and actually being used is a large part of being able to manage software licenses effectively. By pairing software metering in Configuration Manager with software inventory, you can get detailed information on just what software is out there and who is or is not using it. This goes a long way to help keep your software licensing in compliance.

Master It How long do you have to wait, at the very least, after you configure software metering before you can expect to see any data returned?

Solution You must wait at least 12 hours. Software Metering Data Summarization runs daily by default and will run only against data that is at least 12 hours old. This wait period is required for all software metering reports to produce any meaningful data.

Chapter 11: Asset Intelligence

Enable Asset Intelligence. If you installed Configuration Manager from scratch, you will find that Asset Intelligence is not enabled by default. Depending on the data that you want information on, you will have to select the Configuration Manager Asset Intelligence reporting classes and make sure that client agents are enabled.

Master It Which classes in the Asset Intelligence Edit Inventory Classes dialog do you have to enable to use Asset Intelligence?

Solution You need to enable the following classes in the Asset Intelligence Edit Inventory Classes dialog to use Asset Intelligence:

SMS_SystemConsoleUsage

SMS_SystemConsoleUser

SMS_InstalledSoftware

SMS_AutoStartSoftware

SMS_BrowserHelperObject

SoftwareLicensingService

SoftwareLicensingProduct

```
Win32_USBDevice

SMS_SoftwareTag
```

Configure the Asset Intelligence synchronization point. The Asset Intelligence synchronization point is used to connect to System Center Online to synchronize Asset Intelligence Catalog information and get periodic updates.

Master It What do you need to do in order to configure the Asset Intelligence synchronization point?

Solution

♦ You need to configure it on only the CAS or stand-alone primary site.

♦ You may want to obtain an optional System Center Online authentication certificate.

♦ If no valid certificate is issued, you can install the Asset Intelligence synchronization point without a certificate.

Import the Microsoft Volume License Statement. In Configuration Manager you can import the Microsoft Volume License Statement and the General License Statement so that the software inventory and Asset Intelligence can count the number of licenses currently in use in the environment.

Master It What file types does Configuration Manager support for the license statements?

Solution It will be a CSV file if the file to be imported is a General License Statement. If you are going to import a Microsoft Volume License Statement, it will be an XML or CSV file. You can obtain this file by logging into the following website: `http://licensing.microsoft.com`. Or you can request this file from your Microsoft Technical Account Manager or Account Manager.

Chapter 12: Reporting

Install the Reporting Services point. Installing a Reporting Services site system within Configuration Manager allows not only administrators but everyone to view reports in some fashion via either different file formats or a direct link within the Report Manager Website.

Master It What is the procedure to enable Reporting with Configuration Manager?

Solution Open the Configuration Manager console, and do the following:

1. Navigate to the Administration workspace.

2. Expand Overview ➤ Site Configuration ➤ Servers And Site System Roles.

3. Right-click the server and select Add Site System Roles.

4. Select Reporting Point Role and follow the rest of the wizard.

Manage reporting security. Reporting security is an integrated part of the built-in security. You provide users with access to reports by adding them to a predefined security role or by creating a custom role with permissions to run or modify reports.

Master It   Add users to a security role that is able to view reports.

Solution   Open the Configuration Manager console, and do the following:

1. Navigate to the Administration workspace ➤ Overview ➤ Security ➤ Administrative Users.

2. Click Add User Or Group from the ribbon.

3. Then select Read Only Access.

Create and manage report subscriptions.   Creating subscriptions can be very helpful in many scenarios. You can configure subscriptions from Report Manager or in the Configuration Manager console.

Master It   Create an email-based subscription.

Solution   Open the Configuration Manager console, and do the following:

1. Navigate to the Monitoring workspace.

2. Expand Overview ➤ Reports.

3. Select the report, and click Create Subscription from the ribbon.

Create custom reports.   You may find some scenarios where the included reports in Configuration Manager may not meet your reporting needs and you need to create a custom report.

Master It   Create a custom report. Determine whether the query in the report should use table functions or views.

Solution   Open the Configuration Manager console, and do the following:

1. Navigate to the Monitoring workspace.

2. Expand Overview ➤ Reports, and select the appropriate folder.

3. Click Create Report from the ribbon to start the process in Report Builder.

Chapter 13: Compliance Settings

Enable the client settings.   Until the client settings are enabled for your Configuration Manager clients, your clients will not evaluate any of the configuration baselines. This is the first step in using Compliance Settings to validate client settings.

Master It   Enable Compliance Settings for the Configuration Manager clients.

Solution   In the Compliance Settings section of the client settings, set Enable Compliance Evaluation On Clients to True.

Create configuration items.   Configuration items are the pieces that make up a configuration baseline. There are a number of different configuration item types in Configuration Manager, and depending on the type you choose to create, you are presented with certain options when creating your configuration item. The steps to create configuration items were covered in the first part of this chapter, and they included several examples of how to create the different types of configuration items.

Master It   Create a configuration item for an application that checks a registry string value.

Solution   Start the wizard from the Assets And Compliance workspace, Compliance Settings node; make sure you have Configuration Items selected, and right-click it. Choose Create Configuration Item. In the wizard, complete the following settings:

1. On the General tab, enter appropriate information for these fields:

   Name: Application name and value description

   Description: Configuration item for …

   Categories: Add categories

2. On the Settings tab, choose New Settings Registry Key from the menu and enter the information for the Configuration Item.

Define a configuration baseline.   This is where you take one or more of the CIs and put them into a package that the Configuration Manager client downloads and at the scheduled time validates by checking the CIs against the computer. The Configuration Manager client then reports the outcome of those checks back to Configuration Manager, where you can then run reports to see if your clients are within the specified configuration. These steps were covered in the last section of the chapter.

Master It   Assemble a configuration baseline with one or more configuration items you have created.

Solution   Follow these steps:

1. In the Assets And Compliance workspace, expand Compliance Settings, and then choose Configuration Baselines.

2. Right-click and choose Create Configuration Baseline.

3. Enter an appropriate name and description for this baseline, and select or create any categories necessary.

   The Configuration Data list displays all the configuration items or configuration baselines that are included in the configuration baseline.

4. Click Add to add a new configuration item, and choose the configuration items you have created.

5. Click OK and Apply, and your baseline will be created.

6. Deploy the configuration baseline to a collection.

Chapter 14: Endpoint Protection

Deploy and configure the Endpoint Protection site system and client.   The three main components of enabling Endpoint Protection are as follows:

- Install and configure the Endpoint Protection site system.

- Enable and configure the Endpoint Protection client.

- Configure the antimalware policies.

Master It Do you need to create a package or application to deploy the Endpoint Protection client? Do Windows 10 computers use the Endpoint Protection agent?

Solution No. The installation media for the System Center Endpoint Protection client (SCEPInstall.exe) is distributed to the managed devices as part of the Configuration Manager client install media. Remember that the SCEP client won't actually be installed on managed devices until the Endpoint Protection client is enabled and configured in an assigned client settings policy. Also remember that the Endpoint Protection client cannot be enabled until the Endpoint Protection site system role is enabled.

Create and assign an Endpoint Protection policy. Endpoint Protection has two types of policy:

♦ Antimalware

♦ Windows Firewall

The antimalware policy is used to define the antimalware settings, whereas the Windows Firewall policy can be used to control the configuration of Windows Firewall on managed computers. Both types of Endpoint Protection policies are created and modified in the Configuration Manager console.

Master It If you modify the default client antimalware policy and also create a custom antimalware policy with different values for the settings and apply it to a collection, which settings will be applied?

Solution Changes made to the default policy will be applied to all managed computers in the environment. However, the custom policy will override any settings that are in conflict with the default policy.

Chapter 15: Role-Based Administration

Understand the role-based administration model in Configuration Manager. SMS and Configuration Manager 2007 used a class and instance security model, which could be confusing at times. Configuration Manager now adopts the RBAC model, thereby making the administration of security in Configuration Manager a less-daunting task.

Master It What does RBAC stand for? And what does role-based administration mean?

Solution RBAC is an acronym for Role-Based Access Control and is the security model used in many products in the System Center suite, including Configuration Manager.

Role-based administration means that the Configuration Manager administrator can use a combination of security roles, security scopes, and collections to define what the administrative users can view and manage. Configuration Manager has the ability to apply role-based administration to reports as well, greatly simplifying the process of securing access to report data.

Distinguish security roles from security scopes. Security roles and security scopes are important components of the role-based security model in Configuration Manager.

Master It Can you identify the key differences between a security role and a security scope?

Solution   The primary difference between the two is that a security role is used to organize tasks or functions, whereas a security scope is used to define access to objects. The security role is the action (or lack thereof if trying to block access), whereas the security scope is what is acted upon (or lack thereof if trying to block access).

Understand which objects in Configuration Manager define an administrative user.   The administrative user consists of the security role, the security scope, and collections. In this chapter you learned the differences between a security role and a security scope, and you know that collections can be used to control the objects that an administrative user can access.

Master It   As the Configuration Manager administrator, do you need to create a custom Configuration Manager console so that the administrative user can see only what you want them to see?

Solution   No. The beauty of the role-based administration model is that users will see only what they have access to in the Configuration Manager console. You do not need to provide a modified console for them. They simply log on to the environment with their administrative user account and open the Configuration Manager console, and they will see only the objects they have access to. Objects that they do not have access to will be hidden.

Understand how to simulate permissions in the Configuration Manager console.   The RBAC model in Configuration Manager greatly simplifies the process for creating administrative users and defining what objects in Configuration Manager they can access.

Master It   Besides the Configuration Manager console itself, what other tool can you use to simulate Configuration Manager user security and verify that the security model will provide the desired level of access?

Solution   Use the RBA Viewer application from the Configuration Manager Toolkit. It will allow you to easily define new security roles, simulate the access the new role will have in the Configuration Manager console, and provide the ability to simulate the console experience under a specific user account.

Chapter 16: Disaster Recovery

Configure backups for Configuration Manager sites.   Backing up Configuration Manager sites can be automated by scheduling the Backup Site Server maintenance task. When the Configuration Manager backup service (SMS_SITE_BACKUP) starts, it uses instructions in the backup control file, located at

`[ConfigMgr Install Location]Microsoft Configuration Manager\Inboxes\smsbkup.box\ smsbkup.ctl`

Master It   Recovering a complete Configuration Manager site is only supported with site backups from what source?

Solution   The backups must be created by the Backup Configuration Manager Site Server maintenance task.

Archive backup snapshots to another location.   The Backup Site Server task creates a backup snapshot and can be used to recover a Configuration Manager site system if it fails. The next time the backup task runs, it makes a new backup snapshot that will overwrite the one that was made during the last snapshot. This could be a problem if the current backup snapshot becomes corrupted for some reason, because there is no other backup to restore from.

Master It What process could you use to copy backup snapshots from the site server to a new location?

Solution You can use `AfterBackup.bat`.

Reinstall the site components and reset file and registry permissions to their default settings. It's possible that at some point the site will have issues or become corrupted. Or maybe the Configuration Manager folder permissions were modified and are impacting the functionality of the site.

Master It How can you restore the file and registry permissions without performing a complete restore?

Solution Run `setup.exe` from the Start menu or from the `<Configuration Manager installation directory>\Microsoft Configuration Manager\bin\x64` folder. Select Perform Site Maintenance Or Reset This Site and click Next. On the Site Maintenance page, select Reset Site With No Configuration Changes and finish the wizard.

Chapter 17: Troubleshooting

Create a basic maintenance plan. Setting up a basic maintenance plan is a vital step to ensure the proper health of your Configuration Manager (Current Branch) hierarchy.

Master It How do you create a basic maintenance plan?

Solution Develop a plan, similar to the guidelines discussed in the section "Creating the Maintenance Plan" in Chapter 17. Review and modify the plan on a biannual basis, and update it throughout the year to ensure nothing gets overlooked and the documentation is up to date with the current design of the Configuration Manager site.

View log files using CMTrace. Although using CMTrace is not a requirement for viewing log files, it is highly recommended because CMTrace constantly monitors the opened file for updates.

Master It Explain how to use CMTrace to view log files.

Solution Configuration Manager CMTrace is located on your installation media in `SMSSETUP\Tools\cmtrace.exe`. Click File, browse to the log file you want to review, and open it.

Troubleshoot DRS replication. To view the current status of the Configuration Manager DRS replication and to know the latest information about the changes being requested on the site, it's important to be familiar with the log file and the replication process.

Master It To view the latest changes on the replication process, what log file do you need to open?

Solution Locate the `RCMCtrl.log` file and open it using CMTrace. Locate the DRS initiation and RCM changes.

Other solutions might include executing the `spDiagDRS` stored procedure to view the current replication status and details about the data that is being replicated. You can find more details about the `RCMCtrl.log` at the beginning of Chapter 17.

Chapter 18: Enterprise Mobility and Configuration Manager

Detail the differences between lite and depth management. The management options and settings available for mobile devices will vary depending on whether lite- or depth-management options are in place.

Master It List MDM capabilities for lite versus depth management.

Solution Lite management of devices allows for limited device inventory, settings management, and remote wipe.

Depth management of devices allows for over-the-air enrollment, full inventory, more complete settings management, software distribution, and remote (selective) wipe. Also, on-premises MDM is considered to be depth management.

Understand how to configure MDM. Properly configuring MDM requires addressing several potential scenarios. From a Configuration Manager perspective, though, the choice is simple: lite or depth management.

Master It List the items that need to be configured for both lite and depth management.

Solution Lite management requires a properly configured ActiveSync connection between the Exchange server and managed devices as well as proper configuration of the Configuration Manager Exchange ActiveSync connector.

Depth management requires configuring the Service Connection Point and using Microsoft Intune as a middle tier between your Configuration Manager environment and your mobile devices.

The second option involves the proper configuration of an enterprise certification authority, Active Directory, and several different site system roles. The site system roles include the enrollment point, enrollment proxy point, device management point, and distribution point to be able to support the on-premises management of Windows 10 and later versions via the MDM channel.

Understand the depth-management enrollment process. From the user perspective, the enrollment process for depth management is straightforward. Behind the scenes, there are a number of moving parts. Each of these components is critical to the enrollment process.

Master It List the components required to enroll depth-managed devices.

Solution

- Enrollment Web Proxy site system role
- Enrollment Service Point site system role
- Management point enabled to support mobile devices via HTTPS
- Distribution point enabled to support mobile devices via HTTPS
- Enterprise Microsoft certification authority
- Active Directory services
- Microsoft Intune subscription
- Service Connection Point

Index